π_0	hypothetical populatic
π_1, π_2	hypothetical proportic
P( )	probability of
p	sample proportion; pr
p_1, p_2	sample proportions foi . . . . . . ,
Q	semi-interquartile range
Q_1	first quartile
Q_3	third quartile
q_r	statistic for Newman-Keuls multiple range test
ρ	population coefficient of correlation
ρ^2	population coefficient of determination
R	Spearman correlation coefficient; coefficient of multiple correlation
r	sample correlation coefficient
r^2	sample coefficient of determination
σ	population standard deviation; standard deviation of a probability distribution
σ^2	population variance; variance of a probability distribution
σ_d	standard error of the difference
σ_p	standard error of proportion
σ_s	standard error of standard deviation
$\sigma_{\bar{x}}$	standard error of the mean
s	sample standard deviation
s^2	sample variance
$\hat{s}^2$	pooled variance
s_a	standard error of the regression constant (A)
s_b	standard error of the regression coefficient (B)
s_d	standard error of the difference estimated from sample standard deviations
s_{dp}	standard error of the difference for proportion estimated from sample proportions
s_e	standard error of estimate for sample regression line
$s_{E(y|x)}$	standard error of the estimated mean
s_f	standard error of forecast
s_p	standard error of proportion estimated from sample proportion
$s_{\bar{x}}$	standard error of the mean estimated from sample standard deviation
T	trend; Wilcoxon T statistic
TSS	total sum of squares
t	Student's t
t_a	value of t for which a is the proportion of the area under the curve to its right
U	Mann-Whitney U statistic
χ^2	Chi-square
χ^2_a	value of Chi-square for which a is the proportion of the area under the curve to its right
x	data point of a random variable
$\bar{x}$	sample mean
$\bar{x}_d$	mean difference of two samples
$\hat{y}$	estimated value of y from sample regression equation
z	standard score
z_a	value of z for which a is the proportion of the area under the normal curve to its right
$\doteq$	is approximately equal to
$<$	is less than
$\leq$	is less than or equal to
$>$	is greater than
$\geq$	is greater than or equal to
$\binom{n}{r}$	combination of n objects taken r at a time
!	factorial
$\square$	decision point
$\circ$	probability point

ELEMENTARY BUSINESS STATISTICS

Donald R. Byrkit
The University of West Florida

D. VAN NOSTRAND COMPANY
New York   Cincinnati   Toronto   London   Melbourne

TO MY WIFE MARNETTE—
whose patience and encouragement
helped make this book possible.

D. Van Nostrand Company Regional Offices:
New York   Cincinnati

D. Van Nostrand Company International Offices:
London   Toronto   Melbourne

Library of Congress Catalog Card Number: 78-62491
ISBN: 0-442-21408-1

Published by D. Van Nostrand Company
135 West 50th Street, New York, N.Y. 10020

10 9 8 7 6 5 4 3 2 1

Preface

This text is the outgrowth of the author's experience in teaching a beginning course in statistics to students whose primary area of study is business management. Mathematical exposition, therefore, is kept to a minimum and the major emphasis is on reasonable demonstration by example.

The material included in the text consists of all the basic material normally expected in an introductory course and a selection of supplementary material as well. The approach to probability is simplified, consisting solely of the minimum amount necessary to facilitate understanding of the subsequent material in inferential statistics. It has been the author's experience that probability is the primary stumbling block for business students, and most texts present more material than is strictly needed for the work that follows. Since probability is a valuable and interesting topic on its own merits, a more complete exposition has been included in Appendix B.

In addition to basic material, several sections have been designated as optional and may be omitted without disturbing continuity. Technical notes are inserted occasionally to add supplementary material where logical; these may also be omitted. Special features of the text include confidence intervals for differences and for standard deviation, analysis of variance in greater depth than is usual for a first course, an introduction to decision theory, and an early exposure to hypothesis testing.

Chapters 1–3 cover descriptive statistics and probability distributions and are an essential introduction to the remainder of the text. Chapters 4 and 5 cover the binomial, hypergeometric, and Poisson (discrete) distributions and the normal distribution. Hypothesis testing is introduced for the first time in Sections 4.4 and 5.4, but it may be omitted here, if desired, and discussed briefly in connection with Section 7.1, where the topic is discussed in detail. Chapters 6 and 7 cover sampling distributions and some applications to confidence intervals and hypothesis testing for means and proportions. Additional topics in statistical inference include the Chi-Square distribution (Chapter 8) and a detailed study of analysis of variance (Chapter 9), which includes the Hartley test for homogeneity of variance and the Newman-Keuls *post hoc* testing technique as well as the randomized complete-block and the two factor design. Some inference is also included in Chapter 10, which treats linear regression in detail, including analysis of variance, with an introductory look at curvilinear and multiple regression. This leads naturally into time series analysis in Chapter 11, which concludes with an introduction to index numbers. Chapter 12 presents several of the most widely used nonparametric tests, and the text closes with elementary decision theory in Chapter 13. A review of mathematics needed to understand the text is included as Appendix A.

Each chapter section is followed by a set of problems that provide practice in the statistical techniques presented in the section and examples of the application of these techniques to practical business problems. A brief summary, glossary of terms and symbols, and additional problems conclude each chapter. Answers to approximately half the problems are provided. Answers to the remainder of the problems as well as detailed solutions to most of the problems are given in the accompanying instructor's manual.

Widespread use of hand calculators has eliminated the need for concession to human frailty insofar as tedious arithmetic is concerned, and raw data formulas are emphasized. (Coding, no longer important even in time series analysis, is not discussed here.)

The text is designed to be used in its entirety in a year-long course of 5–6 semester hours or 8–10 quarter hours with students of average mathematical ability and no preparation beyond a course in algebra. For a one-term course some selection of topics is necessary. Chapters 1–3 are essential, but Sections 4.4, 5.4, and possibly 4.3 could be eliminated from Chapters 4 and 5. After that, personal preference is the guide. Chapter 7 follows from Chapter 6, Section 11.1 needs Section 10.1, and the various parts of Chapter 12 are linked directly to the parametric tests which they replace. A one-term course preparing for additional statistics courses could consist of Chapters 1–8, while a one-term terminal course for business majors might consist of Chapters 1–3, Sections 4.1–4.3, 5.1, 5.2, 6.1–6.3, 7.1–7.3, 8.1, 8.2, 10.1–10.3, Chapter 11, and possibly Chapter 13 or other topics as desired.

Many sources helped in the writing of this book. The author is especially grateful to Dr. Jean Namias, Phil Desper, Jeanne Libby, and to the following reviewers: Dr. Louis F. Bush of San Diego City College, Dr. James R. McGuigan of Wayne State University, Dr. Jerry L. Hintze of the University of Denver, Dr. Anne B. Koehler of Miami University, Dr. J. Elaine Lockley of Mountain View College, Dr. Roy Mazzagatti of Miami-Dade Junior College, Dr. Buddy L. Myers of Kent State University, Dr. Jean Namias of Montclair State College, Dr. Wayne Stevenson of the University of Utah, and Dr. Michael Umble of Baylor University.

I am indebted to the Biometrika Trustees for permission to use Tables 8, 12, 18, and 31 from *Biometrika Tables for Statisticians*, Volume 1, Third Edition, by Pearson and Hartley; to Lederle Laboratories for permission to reprint data from *Some Rapid Approximate Statistical Procedures*, by Wilcoxon and Wilcox; to the authors and publishers of *Probability: A First Course*, Second Edition, 1970, by Mosteller, Rourke and Thomas (Addison-Wesley), for permission to reprint Table IV, Part B; to the authors and publishers of *Statistical Tables*, by R. R. Sokal and F. J. Rohlf (W. H. Freeman and Company), for permission to reprint part of Table O; to the author and publishers of *Introduction to Statistical Inference* by E. S. Keeping (Van Nostrand Reinhold) for permission to reprint Table B.2; and to the author and publishers of *The Analysis of Variance* by Henry Scheffe (John Wiley & Sons, Inc.) for permission to reprint pp. 434–436.

Donald R. Byrkit

Contents

CHAPTER 1

Organization and Presentation of Data

1.1 FREQUENCY DISTRIBUTIONS

Statistics can be described as the science of classifying and organizing data in order to draw inferences. An important aspect of classifying data is the efficient and effective organization and presentation of data. An unorganized mass of figures is more often confusing than clarifying. This chapter is concerned with the methods of deriving meaning from numerical data.

The term **data**, as used in the preceding paragraph, refers to the set of observations, values, elements, or objects under consideration. The complete set of all possible elements is called a **population** while anything less than the complete set is called a **sample**. Each of the elements is called a **data point**, or **piece of data**. The amount of money spent by a customer in a store on a particular day, for example, is a piece of data, while the collection of all expenditures by all customers on that day would comprise a complete set of data. This latter, in turn, could be considered a sample of the population of all expenditures of all customers on all days in that store.

Data are of two types, quantitative and qualitative. **Qualitative data**, or **attributes** (sometimes called **categorical data**), result from information which has been sorted into categories. Each piece of data clearly belongs to one classification or category. Automobiles on a parking lot classified by make give one example of attribute data. **Quantitative**, or **variable data**, is data which is a result of counting or measuring. We might count the number of nicks and scratches in the paint of each car, then give the number of cars with 0 scratches, 1 scratch, 2 scratches, and so forth. A car has a whole number of scratches (it cannot have 3.7 scratches, for instance), so there are clear divisions between the values. This type of data is called **discrete**. If we weighed the cars, we could get the weight to the nearest pound, but it would be possible for a car to weigh slightly more or less than we reported. A reported weight of 3,456 pounds, for example, would probably indicate a weight somewhere between 3,455.5 and 3,456.5 pounds. This is an example of a **continuous** variable. Generally, data arising from measurement are continuous, while data arising from counting or arbitrary classification are discrete. An example of the latter is the familiar grading system where the grades are 4.0, 3.5, 3.0, 2.5, 2.0, 1.5, 1.0, and 0 (A, B+, B, C+, C, D+, D, F system). Often there exists an option as to what type of system to use. In the example of the customer in the store, we could classify each customer as to whether he or she bought anything, which would be a qualitative classification; by the number of items bought, which would be variable, but discrete; by the amount of time spent in the store, which would be continuous; or by any of several other methods. A most likely classification would be the amount of money spent. While technically discrete, since the customer does not spend fractional parts of a penny, it is a common practice to consider as "practically" continuous a variable whose unit is quite small in relation to the amounts involved. If we were talking about the different amounts of pennies several children had, the variable would obviously be discrete. In terms of the national debt, the variable could be considered, for all practical purposes, continuous. A matter of judgment is involved.

Suppose you asked someone for data on the height of adult males in a city of some 25,000 population, and the person responded by giving you a list of 8,968 heights. Unless the data were organized in some fashion, this list in its raw form would not be too usable. One of the means employed to organize data is known as the **frequency distribution**. In its simplest form, the frequency distribution consists of listing each possible value the data could have and enumerating the total number, called the **frequency**, for each value. In the height example, if height is measured to the nearest inch, such a frequency distribution might appear as follows:

Height (Inches)	Frequency
83	11
82	44
81	116
80	132
79	157
78	284
77	316
76	388
75	547
74	731
73	783
72	808
71	817
70	931
69	848
68	712
67	604
66	411

Height (Inches)	Frequency
65	206
64	94
63	28
Total	8,968

Such a table tells you at a glance that most of the data points have values from 67 to 75, inclusive, that the number above 78 and below 65 is relatively quite small, and, in short, gives you a very good and accurate profile of this set of data.

It is often useful to determine the **proportion** of cases for each value of the variable. This is also called the **relative frequency**, which is the number of cases (frequency) for a given value divided by the total number of cases (total frequency). Actually, relative frequency can be interpreted as a percent. In the preceding example 931 men were 70 inches tall out of the total of 8,968, so the relative frequency for 70 inches was 931/8,968 or about 0.104, or 10.4%.

It is helpful to have a procedure to follow when constructing a frequency table. For small amounts of data, we can rewrite the data given into ascending (or descending) order. We then have the data placed in order and the construction of the table is relatively simple. Another plan, more useful in cases where a great deal of data is involved, is to find the highest and lowest values, then list these values and all cases between them. In a second column we *tally* the cases by putting a slash (tally) mark for each one as we come to it, usually crossing out the number in the original list, then summarize the results in a frequency table. The relative frequency can be included, if desired. As we shall see in the next chapter, the relative frequency can be highly important if the set of data is a representative sample of some population. The table should be complete, including the title, with enough information to make the table completely self-explanatory if not accompanied with explanatory material.

EXAMPLE 1   As a part of preliminary cost study, the amount of weekly sales at each of a department store chain's 25 outlets was obtained. The data given below represent the average weekly sales per store for the last three months given to the nearest thousand dollars. Construct a table showing frequency and relative frequency for each sales figure.

7	9	8	11	6
13	7	19	9	9
7	13	22	9	12
10	9	13	9	15
7	11	8	9	13

SOLUTION   There are just a few pieces of data here, so rewriting these in order would be logical. An example of the tally method might be helpful at this point, however, so it is presented here.

Sales ($000's)	Tally
22	/
21	
20	
19	/
18	
17	
16	
15	/
14	
13	////
12	/
11	//
10	/
9	////// //
8	//
7	/////
6	/

Using the tally chart we can construct the following table.

Average Weekly Sales, Le Chateau Stores[a]		
Sales ($000's)	No. of Stores	Relative Frequency
22	1	.04
21	0	0.
20	0	0.
19	1	.04
18	0	0.
17	0	0.
16	0	0.
15	1	.04
14	0	0.
13	4	.16
12	1	.04
11	2	.08
10	1	.04
9	7	.28
8	2	.08
7	4	.16
6	1	.04
Total	25	1.00

[a]Survey covering June-August, 1977

COMMENT   When several values of the variable contain no entries or relatively few entries, it is often convenient to combine them into one class. This is often done when these classes fall at one end of the distribution. Here we could write

$$14-22 \qquad 3 \qquad .12$$

This does not significantly impair our understanding of the table, but may make it difficult to perform arithmetic on the data. It should never be done, for example, if any further analysis is contemplated. It is useful *only* for presentation, and never for interpretation.

DISCUSSION   It generally does not matter whether tables are arranged in ascending or descending order. The guiding principles should be ease and clarity of presentation.

For some purposes a **cumulative frequency table** is useful. Although it does not matter whether the accumulation is done in ascending or descending order, the most frequent uses for such a table are found when the data are arranged in descending order with the cumulative frequency listed. The cumulative frequency is the sum of all frequencies equal to or less than the listed value. The **relative cumulative frequency** is the proportion of all frequencies *equal to or less than* the listed value. It can also be called the **cumulative relative frequency**. A table for the sales data follows.

Sales ($000's)	Number of Stores	Cumulative Frequency	Relative Cumulative Frequency
6	1	1	.04
7	4	5	.20
8	2	7	.28
9	7	14	.56
10	1	15	.60
11	2	17	.68
12	1	18	.72
13	4	22	.88
14–22	3	25	1.00

In general, only those columns which are needed would be listed. In the above table, we would probably have at most three columns, listing the data we wished to present.

A frequency table may also be used to classify attributes. As mentioned before, attributes are a type of data that cannot be measured, but can only be described. For example, a table may classify the automobiles in a parking lot by make.

Make	Number of Cars
Chevrolet	33
Ford	28
Pontiac	11
Volkswagen	9
Plymouth	7
Other makes	4
Total	92

Another example of attributes is the division of data into **strata**, such as low, middle, and high income groups. The difference between the two types of data is that data which is categorical only, without any ordering, is called a **nominal** classification (from the Latin for name), while categorical data in which an ordering is implicit is called an **ordinal** classification (from order). Data which is ranked is also an ordinal classification; for example, the finish of runners in a race is ordinal.

The other two classifications of data are interval and ratio. **Interval** data is data in which the differences between values are meaningful; that is, a difference of ten units means the same thing wherever it occurs. An example is temperature. A rise of twenty degrees means the same whether it is an increase from 80° to 100° or from $-8°$ to $+12°$. **Ratio** data is data which has a natural zero, so that ratios of values are meaningful. Weight and distance are examples of ratio data. A weight of 50 pounds is 5 times as heavy as a weight of 10 pounds and a distance of 65 miles is 13 times as far as a distance of 5 miles. This is not true of all interval data. A temperature of 50° is not 5 times as hot as a temperature of 10°. Such a statement has no meaning whatsoever.

Now suppose that a set of data gives the incomes of families in a city. Such a listing of *all* the values is called a census. It is obvious that a listing of all possible incomes (even to the nearest dollar) would involve a listing of hundreds, even thousands of numbers. One way out of such a difficulty is the method of **grouping data**. Thus we may consider all incomes from, say 4,000 to 7,999 dollars as constituting one **class**.

A few general observations govern the grouping of data into classes. First, we do not want too many or too few classes, since this might result in a distortion of the picture we want to convey. Second, the classes should be of the same width (although this rule may be bent in certain circumstances). Third, the classes should be convenient to handle. To achieve these aims, it has been found that eight to fifteen classes are a reasonable number. To determine class width, the range is divided by the approximate number of classes decided upon, then the number is rounded out to the nearest convenient division. The **range** of a set of data is defined as being the highest value minus the lowest value and is thus the distance between the two extremes. If the data are discrete, however, we add one to this value since both endpoints are included.

The height data presented earlier is an example of **continuous** data which has been grouped into separate or distinct classes. In this kind of arrangement, a height of 72 inches represents all heights from 71.5 to 72.5 inches. It is convenient and useful to accept this representation since otherwise we may run into difficulties when we classify the data into larger classes. For example, if we decide to combine our data into classes covering 4 inches and we start with 63 inches, our classes become 63–67, 67–71, 71–75, 75–79, and 79–83 inches. The problems this poses are obvious. Into which class does a height of 71 inches fall? Furthermore, if 71 inches represents 70.5 to 71.5 inches, two different people, each of whose height would be 71 inches, to the nearest inch, might fall in different classes; the one slightly less than 71 inches into 67–71, while the one just over 71 inches into 71–75. To avoid this problem with the endpoints we let the endpoints of each class fall *between* the integral values of the class. Each integer becomes the midpoint of an interval extending one-half unit in each direction. Thus the lowest height represented may be 62.5 inches while the highest may be 83.5 inches. The range, then, is 21 inches, 83.5—62.5. This is the same result obtained by taking 83 minus 63 and adding 1 since the data are given as discrete. If we wished to have ten classes, the above procedure would give 2.1 inches, while eight classes produce a class width of 2.63 inches. Generally we wish the class width to be an integer. There are some advantages to having an odd number for the class interval. This is because the center of each class, called the **class mark**, is then an integer. Suppose in this example we let the class interval be 3 inches. Since the lowest represented height is 63 inches, we can start there, if we wish, and the lowest class would be 63 to 65 inches. Since 63 can represent a height as low as 62.5 inches and 65 a height as high as 65.5 inches, the class could also be considered to be 62.5 to 65.5 inches. The next class could be considered to be 66 to 68 inches or 65.5 to 68.5 inches. Generally, the lowest and highest values specified for each class, called the **class limits**, conform to the data as given. If the data are given to the nearest inch, the class limits are given to the nearest inch. The actual dividing lines between the classes are called the **class boundaries**, and extend one-half unit of measurement in either direction. In the example given, the class limits are 63–65 and 66–68, while the class boundaries are 62.5–65.5 and 65.5–68.5. The **class mark** is the center of each interval and can be found by adding the class limits or class boundaries and dividing by two. For example, $(63+65)/2=64$ and $(62.5+65.5)/2=64$, so the class mark for this class is 64. To check our work, note that the difference between successive lower class limits, between successive upper class limits, and between class marks, all equal the class width. Many experts prefer to present a table in terms of the boundaries for each class, but it seems more natural to list the classes in terms of the units of the data presented, and many other experts adhere to this view. This procedure will be followed in this text.

Using these general guidelines, the frequency table given below could be constructed for the height data. We present all the data described in the preceding paragraphs, although it is unlikely that any table will actually give all this information.

| | Height (inches) | | | | | Relative |
Class Limits	Class Boundaries	Class Mark	Frequency	Relative Frequency	Cumulative Frequency	Cumulative Frequency
63–65	62.5–65.5	64	328	0.037	328	0.037
66–68	65.5–68.5	67	1,727	0.193	2,055	0.229
69–71	68.5–71.5	70	2,596	0.289	4,651	0.519
72–74	71.5–74.5	73	2,322	0.259	6,973	0.777
75–77	74.5–77.5	76	1,251	0.139	8,224	0.917
78–80	77.5–80.5	79	573	0.064	8,797	0.981
81–83	80.5–83.5	82	171	0.019	8,968	1.000
	Total		8,968	1.000		

EXAMPLE 2   Suppose that income data for another city shows the lowest income to be $343 per year, and the highest $43,764. Construct a frequency distribution with approximately fifteen classes for these data.

SOLUTION   The range is $43,764—$343, or $43,421. Dividing this by 15, we obtain $2,895. A convenient class interval is $3,000. We could start with $343, but it is usual to start with some "nice" number; in this case zero or $1,000 would be a good place to start except that since 343 is less than 1,000, zero would be better. We might arrange the data like this.

Income (dollars)	Number of Families
42,000–44,999	3
39,000–41,999	7
36,000–38,999	12
33,000–35,999	17
30,000–32,999	28
27,000–29,999	60
24,000–26,999	216
21,000–23,999	268
18,000–20,999	448
15,000–17,999	621
12,000–14,999	949
9,000–11,999	1,421
6,000– 8,999	2,844
3,000– 5,999	2,123
0– 2,999	294
Total	9,311

DISCUSSION   A value such as $29,999.37 does not fit into this table, but the limits given are to the nearest dollar. Class boundaries are considered to extend down one-half dollar from the lower class limit and up one-half dollar from the higher class limit. Thus the class given by 27,000 to 29,999 is actually the interval 26,999.50 to 29,999.50, while 30,000 to 32,999 would actually represent 29,999.50 to 32,999.50. A value actually on the class boundary, such as 29,999.50 is, by convention, put in the higher class; thus an income of *exactly* $29,999.50 would go into the class 30,000 to 32,999. Note that the class marks are rather nasty numbers to work with; the class 30,000 to 32,999 would have the class mark 31,499.50. Since the error (of .50) is small in relation to the magnitude of the numbers involved, we would be justified in using 31,500 as the class mark here and round other class marks accordingly.

It is tempting, and sometimes convenient, to represent attenuated cases such as this one by lumping everything higher than, say, $30,000 into one class, such as

30,000 and above

This does not hinder our understanding of the table, but it may make it impossible to perform arithmetic on the data since an open class, one which lacks either an upper or lower class limit, has *no* class mark.

•Problems

1. Efficiency ratings of several thousand salesmen for a large corporation were found to fall between a high of 168 and a low of 72.
   (a) What is the range of the scores?
   (b) What class width should be selected to divide the data into approximately twelve classes?
   (c) Make two lists of classes, one using the value from (b), one using ten as class width. (Note: answers may vary, depending on the lower limit of the first class selected.)

2. Consider the following classes given for a frequency distribution: 20–26, 27–33, 34–40, 41–47, 48–54.
   (a) What are the class boundaries?
   (b) The class width is the difference between upper and lower boundaries. What is the class width?
   (c) The apparent class width is the difference between the class limits. What is the apparent class width?
   (d) What are the class marks?

3. Given the 8 class intervals: 50–59, 60–69, 70–79, 80–89, 90–99, 100–109, 110–119, 120–129
   (a) What is the class width for these intervals?
   (b) What is the class mark for the interval 50–59?
   (c) In which class does the number 79.4 belong?
   (d) In which class does the number 99.5 belong?

4. The following are the weekly sales, in dollars, of Rogers' Cat Food at each of 80 retail outlets.

14	27	81	36	92	60	17	34	83	54
37	40	27	30	26	36	29	71	23	37
31	37	12	36	61	17	70	36	35	77
83	13	39	61	48	54	23	37	35	23
61	97	31	46	13	24	30	19	26	73
70	17	23	10	38	11	65	67	14	45
70	55	24	27	45	64	24	86	28	16
27	25	11	15	53	65	12	58	62	53

(a) Group these numbers into a frequency table with eight classes.
(b) Use the results of (a) to make a relative frequency table.
(c) Use the results of (a) to make a cumulative frequency table.
(d) Use the results of (b) or (c) to make a cumulative relative frequency table.

5. The following are items produced by a machine, per day, over the last 12 work weeks (6 days per week).

31	29	35	37	39	35	40	32	37	35	36	41
42	33	39	35	41	36	37	37	34	41	37	31
38	43	37	38	37	34	36	35	36	32	39	37
34	36	37	35	37	35	33	36	30	34	33	37
38	36	37	36	36	33	40	39	38	37	37	37
35	37	40	33	37	38	38	36	37	35	33	36

(a) Determine the proper class width if we wish to divide the data into seven to twelve classes.
(b) Make frequency, relative frequency, and cumulative frequency tables for the data.

6. Pollution indices for a city for 120 consecutive days are given below.

47	70	84	46	29	64	43	61	46	40	41	59
58	72	88	57	39	60	47	62	58	38	33	54
67	59	81	63	44	57	54	54	60	47	42	63
72	54	77	69	57	51	59	57	52	62	48	60
88	61	54	61	61	61	67	30	54	70	52	69
74	50	70	72	60	58	62	44	48	54	41	66
67	73	42	52	53	59	68	33	58	83	48	58
73	68	41	44	50	54	70	41	54	88	44	42
64	79	43	37	44	60	74	49	67	69	42	47
61	82	37	33	58	48	66	52	49	57	45	48

(a) Group the numbers into a frequency table with a class width of 5.
(b) Make a relative cumulative frequency table for this set of data.

7. The following are prices of regular gasoline observed at each of 30 different gasoline stations during a given week.

56.1	54.4	47.6	58.1	49.9	54.9
52.9	56.9	54.9	48.4	57.4	54.9
60.9	51.9	52.9	55.9	52.9	58.5
49.9	54.9	56.9	59.9	53.9	62.4
50.9	51.0	58.1	55.9	50.4	52.9

(a) What is the range of these prices?

(b) What class width will yield eight classes? Make a list of these eight classes beginning with 47.0. Note that the numbers are given to the nearest tenth, not in integers.

(c) What are the boundaries for the first class?

(d) Make a frequency table for the raw data.

(e) Make a frequency table for the data using the classes obtained in (b) above.

1.2 GRAPHICAL METHODS

One disadvantage of frequency distribution tables is that their presentation lacks visual appeal. They do not call attention to the outstanding or important features of the distribution as a **graphical presentation** does. Graphs appear in many forms, only a few of the more important of which will be discussed here. Certain types of data lend themselves well to certain types of graphs.

Data which are classified naturally into distinct groups are usually represented well by means of **bar graphs**. The type of data arising from a nominal classification is of this type. An example of this type is the following.

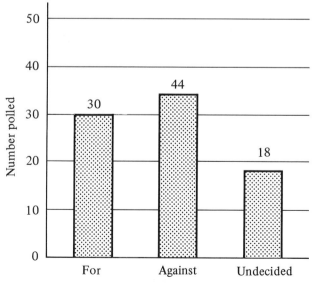

Results of a Poll of Voters on an
Upcoming Bond Election

It is not necessary to list the number of cases at the top of the bar, but it sometimes is an aid in the presentation.

Another example which may fit is that of age groups. Although age is a function of time, therefore a continuous variable, our usual method of reporting age is at variance with the usual concepts of rounding. Where we speak of the time between events rounded to the nearest year, so that eighteen years would represent anywhere from 17.5 to 18.5 years, an *age* of eighteen years means age as of last birthday. Thus an age of 18 means anywhere from 18.0 to 19.0. Under these circumstances a bar graph is a reasonable way of graphing ages. Such an example is given here.

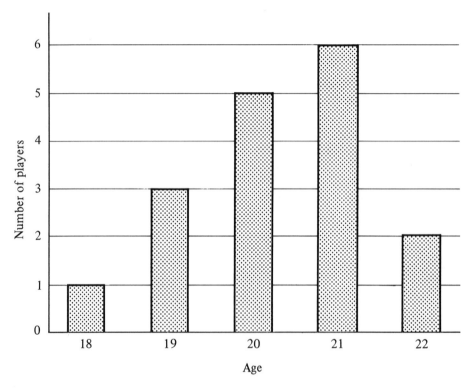

Distribution of Ages of Players on the
Meridian College Basketball Team

The width of the bar has *no significance* on a bar graph. In fact a single line will work as well. It can be seen that a bar graph is particularly suitable for attribute data. Note that it is conventional to separate the bars in a bar graph. The amount of separation also has no significance, but it is usual to make the width of the bars uniform as well as to make the separation between the bars uniform.

A bar graph can be used for any nominal data or for data reported in distinct groups, but for data which is on an interval scale it is more usual to use a graph called a **histogram**. Exceptions exist, as in the basketball team data, but in general, data in classes in numerical order are best presented in a histogram. In a histogram the class intervals are generally equal since the *areas*, not simply the heights, of the rectangles represent the frequencies. The assumption in a histogram is that the scale is continuous and the data are spread evenly throughout the class. Histograms are discussed further in section 3.2. An example of a histogram is given here.

In this example one can see that most of the shipments were about 30, 40, or 60 pounds. The classes are 10 pounds with multiples of 10 falling at or near the center of the classes at the class mark. Close examination reveals that it is likely the classes begin at about 4.5, with class widths of 10, hence class marks of 9.5, 19.5, 29.5, etc.

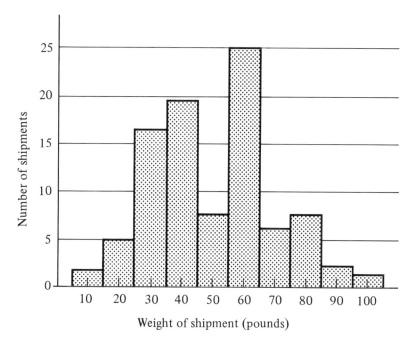

Distribution of Diamond Shipment
Weight from the Abercrombie Mine
for 1977

If the vertical scale represents *relative frequency*, the histogram is called a **relative frequency histogram**. The only difference is the vertical scale, as shown below.

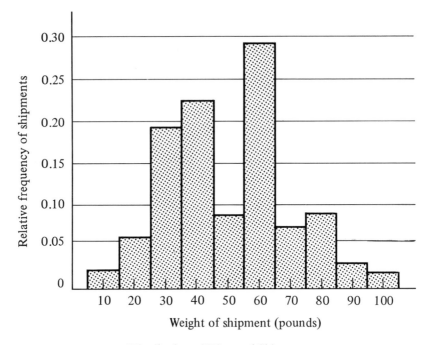

Distribution of Diamond Shipment
Weight from the Abercrombie Mine
for 1977

There are a number of important items to remember about a histogram. First, all classes should have the same width. Minor exceptions are permitted, but need to be handled with care. This will be discussed in section 3.2. Second, if a class has no entries—that is, a frequency of zero, a gap will appear in the histogram. If, for example, the diamond shipment example included no shipments at about 110 pounds, that portion of the histogram would look like this.

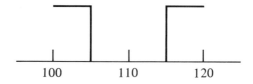

The **frequency polygon**, or **line graph**, is often used as a substitute for a histogram. It seems to have more visual appeal, but we lose the comparative power of the histogram since areas are no longer totally representative. For a frequency polygon, the class mark is used to represent the class, and a dot is placed above the class mark opposite the proper frequency. This is equivalent to placing a dot in the center of the uppermost edge of the rectangle in a histogram. Remember, if a class has no entries, the dot should be placed on the base line (representing zero). The height of the dot corresponds to the frequency of the class. A general practice is to add a class with zero frequency at each end to complete the polygon and give the graph a "finished" look. An example of a frequency polygon based on the diamond shipment data follows:

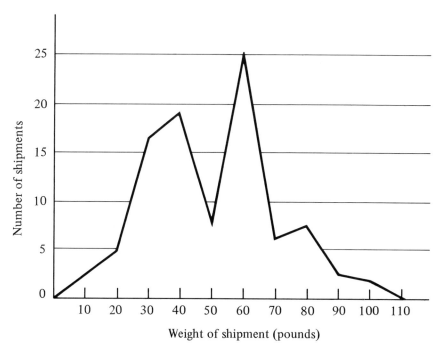

Distribution of Diamond Shipment
Weight from the Abercrombie Mine
for 1977

Another type of graphical representation, widely used in business is a time series chart. Such a chart is analogous to a histogram in that the horizontal axis usually represents continuous data—time periods. However, the primary difference is that, usually, the histogram's vertical axis generally represents frequency of occurrence of the variable whereas in a time series chart the variable is usually plotted on the vertical axis. An example of monthly and

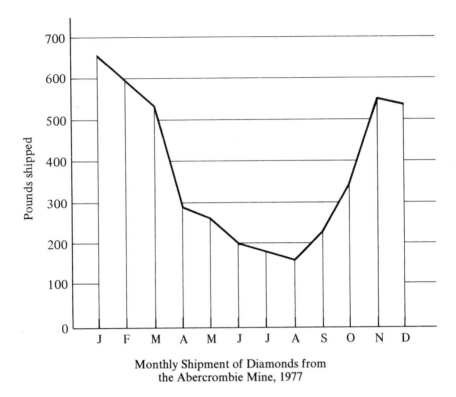

Monthly Shipment of Diamonds from
the Abercrombie Mine, 1977

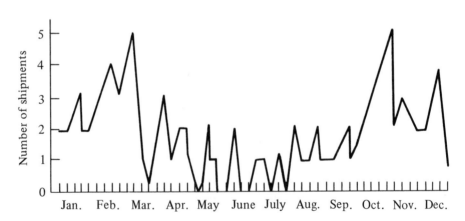

Weekly Shipments of Diamonds from
the Abercrombie Mine, 1977

weekly time series charts is given here. Note however that these charts are not polygons in the sense of those in the foregoing material.

Notice that these two graphs differ in their emphasis as well as the time period involved.

Sometimes we wish to show cumulative data; that is, we want to represent the number of cases, or proportion of cases, which fall at or below or at or above a certain value of the variable. The graph used for this purpose is called an **ogive**. It may be ascending or descending. It may show cumulative frequency or cumulative relative frequency. Here we show an example of construction of an ascending cumulative relative frequency ogive. To construct such an ogive we use the upper class boundaries, since we have not accumulated all the data from a class until we reach the upper class boundary. Such an ogive is also useful for determining percentiles. (See section 2.3.)

EXAMPLE 1   Suppose we collect heights of 50 incoming freshmen men and arrange the data as given below. Construct an ogive of the ascending relative frequency type. (Note that the term cumulative is not needed since an ogive, by its very nature, is a cumulative graph.)

Height (In.)	Frequency	Relative Frequency	Cumulative Relative Frequency
63–65	3	0.06	0.06
66–68	5	0.10	0.16
69–71	12	0.24	0.40
72–74	15	0.30	0.70
75–77	9	0.18	0.88
78–80	4	0.08	0.96
81–83	2	0.04	1.00
Total	50	1.00	

SOLUTION   We must begin by using the class boundaries to construct the table. The table begins at the lowest class boundary, 62.5, and we have accumulated 0.06 of the total by the time we reach 65.5. Each cumulative relative frequency is plotted at the upper boundary of each class and the dots joined. Intermediate relative frequencies can be estimated from the graph.

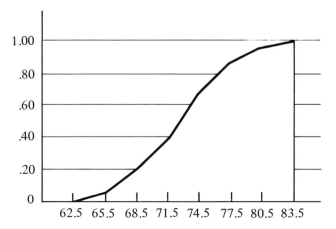

A "reverse" ogive, showing cumulative relative frequencies at or above a given value may also be plotted from the same data. Such an ogive is shown below.

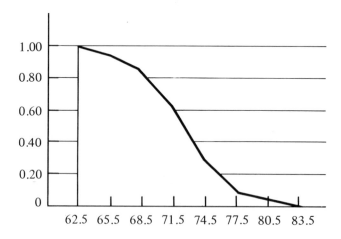

Methods of graphical representation are limited only by the imagination. Other particularly useful methods include **pictograms** and **pie charts**. Both are particularly susceptible to distortion, however, so great care should be taken. Pie charts are particularly useful in presenting percentages or proportions and are familiar to many because of their widespread use in showing sources of dollar income and expenditure in the national government. Distortion is possible if the chart is shown at an angle, as below.

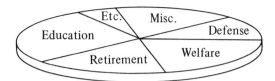

The following drawing illustrates the only correct method of presenting a pie chart.

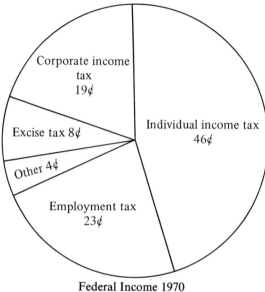

Federal Income 1970

A hazard of pictograms is the possibility of conveying a false impression.

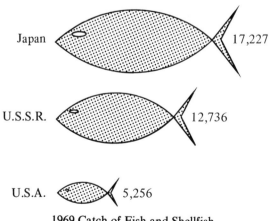

1969 Catch of Fish and Shellfish
(Millions of Pounds)

Although the fish on top is just about three times as long as the one on the bottom, its area is about ten times as great, and this is the impression the eye receives. A similar impression is given by adding the illusion of depth.

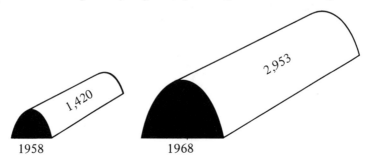

1,420   1958

2,953   1968

The graph which follows conveys a fairer impression.

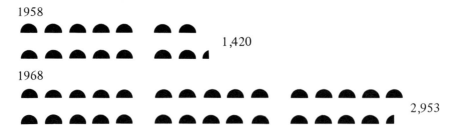

1958

1,420

1968

2,953

U.S.A. Aluminum Production
(Thousands of Tons)
Each ingot represents 10,000 tons.

The problem of creating a false impression is not restricted to pictograms. The vertical scale can cause problems if it does not start at zero. Unions asking for a wage increase could use the following graph to support their claim that the company is "reaping in profits."

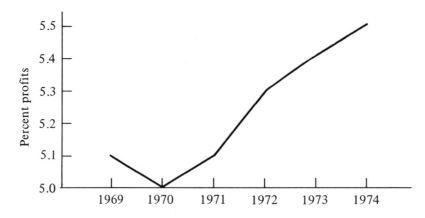

In proper perspective, the graph should look like this.

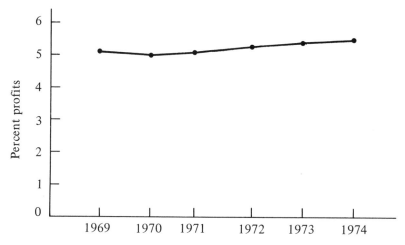

In the first graph we get a picture of sharply increasing profits. In the second we see that profits were approximately stable throughout this period. A similarly misleading graph could probably be used by the company to show increases in worker income.

Occasionally it may be that we would prefer not to start the scale (either vertical or horizontal) at zero because of the fact that the data are compressed onto a fairly small segment of values. To avoid giving the impression that we are doing so deliberately to distort perspective, it is usual to indicate this by means of a broken line or other such "flag" to draw attention to the fact that the scale does not start at zero. Such an example is the following:

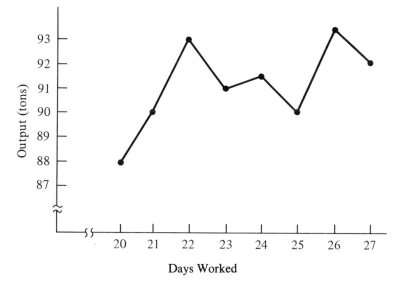

•Problems

1. Construct a bar graph for the sales data of example 1, section 1.1.
2. Construct a histogram for the height data of section 1.1.
3. Construct a histogram and relative frequency polygon for the data of problem 4, section 1.1.
4. Construct an ogive for the diamond shipment data of this section.
5. Draw a relative frequency histogram and a relative frequency polygon for the data of problem 6, section 1.1.
6. Draw a histogram and an ogive for the data of problem 5, section 1.1.
7. Draw a pictogram for the basketball team data of this section.
8. Construct a pie chart, using proportions or percentages, of the results of the voter poll.
9. Using the income data of example 2, section 1.1, draw
   (a) a histogram;
   (b) a relative frequency histogram;
   (c) a frequency polygon;
   (d) a relative frequency polygon;
   (e) an ogive—ascending, relative.
10. Make a histogram and a relative frequency polygon for the data of problem 7, section 1.1.

1.3   SUMMARY

The organization and presentation of data is one of the primary purposes of descriptive statistics. Large amounts of data must be well organized in order to be understandable, and smaller amounts of data as well may also be more meaningful after organization.

One of the best ways to organize data is to use a frequency distribution. To organize the data into a frequency distribution, we first determine the desired number of classes which will cover the entire set of data. Each piece of data is then placed into exactly one class and the results are presented in a table. In general, each class is of the same width, although attenuated distributions may have data from one or both ends combined into a single, larger class. Related data distributions are the relative frequency, cumulative frequency, and cumulative relative frequency distributions.

Bar graphs, histograms, frequency polygons, time series charts, ogives, pictograms, and pie charts are used to present data in a visually appealing manner. From a statistical viewpoint, histograms are the most important because classes in a histogram can be compared by areas. Great care must be exercised when using graphs to avoid conveying a false impression.

•Problems

1. A set of data has a high of 363 and a low of 107. Construct a table with 11 classes which contain the data. Give the class limits, class boundaries, and class marks. (Answers may vary somewhat.)

2. Suppose that weights of shipments to the nearest pound are grouped into classes 0–75, 76–150, 151–225, 226–300, 301–375, 376–450, 451–525, 526–600, 601–675, 676–750, 751–825, 826–900, and 901 or more. Is it possible to determine the number of shipments
    (a) weighing 300 pounds or less?
    (b) weighing less than 300 pounds?
    (c) weighing more than 750 pounds?
    (d) weighing 750 pounds or more?
    (e) weighing more than 1,000 pounds?
    (f) weighing less than 700 pounds?

3. The class marks of a distribution of sales (in dollars) are 125.5, 175.5, 225.5, 275.5, 325.5, 375.5, 425.5, 475.5, 525.5, and 575.5. What are the class limits? The class boundaries?

4. In a contest to see which dealership could sell the most cars, among several hundred dealerships the fewest cars sold was 180, the most sold was 320.
    (a) What is the range of these scores?
    (b) Make a list of classes for the data using 20 as class width.
    (c) What class width will yield approximately ten classes?

5. The following frequency table shows the heights of 100 randomly selected students:

Heights		Frequency	Cumulative Frequency
5 ft.,	4 in.	1	1
5 ft.,	5 in.	6	7
5 ft.,	6 in.	10	
5 ft.,	7 in.	22	
5 ft.,	8 in.	21	
5 ft.,	9 in.	17	
5 ft.,	10 in.	14	
5 ft.,	11 in.	5	
6 ft.,	0 in.	3	
6 ft.,	1 in.	1	
Total		100	

   (a) Complete the cumulative frequency column in the above table.

(b) If a student's height were 5 ft., $6\frac{1}{2}$ in., to what class would his height belong?

(c) If a student were in the class 5 ft., 8 in., at least what proportion of these students would he exceed in height?

6. A frequency distribution is given below.

Class	Frequency
11.00–12.99	2
13.00–14.99	7
15.00–16.99	13
17.00–18.99	24
19.00–20.99	11
21.00–22.99	4

(a) What are the boundaries for the class 17.00–18.99?

(b) What is the unit of measurement?

(c) What is the class mark for the class 13.00–14.99?

(d) What is the class width?

(e) What is the range if the highest score was 22.68 and the lowest 11.74?

7. Sales of a certain type of candy bar over a period of sixty days are listed here.

```
48  34  36  40  26  29  25  30  22  32  34  41
47  24  42  37  37  30  26  37  42  41  41  23
31  22  34  41  24  42  35  41  40  29  32  32
22  31  28  41  27  34  37  24  33  33  24  28
29  43  46  32  32  28  34  34  28  27  43  34
```

Set up a frequency distribution and draw a bar graph for the data. Recall that these values are discrete.

8. The following data represent the cost of books for the current quarter for a random sample of 50 students at a southern university.

```
41  25  35  57  40  34  62  27  45  36
38  47  41  33  42  37  52  39  43  37
47  37  52  60  38  58  28  31  41  47
50  46  40  34  56  41  60  43  54  42
37  48  35  41  44  30  46  42  28  38
```

(a) What is the range of the data?

(b) Group the data into classes, starting at 25 and using a class width of 5.

(c) Construct a table showing frequency and cumulative frequency for these classes.

(d) Draw a frequency polygon for the data.

9. The following are I.Q. scores of 110 randomly selected high school students.

154	131	122	100	113	119	121	128	128	112
133	119	115	117	110	104	125	85	120	135
93	103	103	121	109	147	103	113	107	98
128	93	90	105	118	134	89	143	108	142
85	108	108	136	151	117	110	80	111	127
100	100	114	123	126	119	123	132	97	110
105	111	127	108	106	91	122	102	111	106
150	130	87	98	108	137	124	96	100	101
118	104	127	94	115	101	125	129	131	110
97	135	108	139	133	107	115	83	109	116
110	113	112	82	114	112	113	142	145	123

(a) Make a (raw data) frequency distribution for the above scores.
(b) Group the data into 15 classes and make a frequency and relative frequency table.
(c) Draw a histogram and a relative frequency polygon.
(d) Make an ascending cumulative relative frequency table and draw an ogive.

10. A family's monthly expenses were listed as follows: housing $380; utilities $140; medical expenses $15; food $130; transportation $135; clothing $25; savings $25; miscellaneous $50. Draw a pie chart showing this information in terms of percentages or proportions.

CHAPTER 1.

Glossary of Terms

attributes	interval
bar graph	nominal
class	ogive
class boundary	ordinal
class limit	pictogram
class mark	pie chart
class width	population
continuous	qualitative
cumulative frequency	quantitative
data	range
data point	ratio
discrete	relative frequency
frequency	sample
frequency distribution	strata
frequency polygon	tally
histogram	

Chapter 2

Measures of Location and Dispersion

2.1 MEASURES OF CENTRAL TENDENCY

Although organized data is more meaningful in presentation form than un-organized data, there are still many other things which can be learned by a closer examination. In this chapter we will learn a few of the ways to *describe* a set of data which can aid in our understanding.

When we deal with a set of data, we generally assume that the data all come from the same source; that is, we assume we have a representative sample of some population. A **population** is a set of data which consists of all possible or hypothetically possible observations of a certain phenomenon. A **sample** is a limited set of data drawn from the complete set of values, the population. There are many kinds of samples, some of which are not representative of the population from which the sample is drawn. Types of samples will be discussed in Chapter 6.

Since the characteristics of a complete population are rarely known, except, perhaps, theoretically, most information which a statistician or businessman uses comes from samples. We cannot know, for example, the actual distribution of weights of all the people in the world.

Quite often it is desirable to describe a set of data by using one number which is felt to be most representative of the set. The numbers most used are measures of central tendency or averages. There are three such numbers and each has its uses. Consider the following episode.

A campaigner knocks on a door, asking for contributions to the County Fund. He stresses that he expects a lot, since the average income in the neighborhood is $26,000. A few days later, a campaigner asks for contributions for the poor of the neighborhood. After all, he says, the average income in the neighborhood is only $5,000. Confused, the object of this attention asks a nearby university sociologist, who tells him that the average income in the neighborhood is $12,000! Who is correct, and who is lying, if anyone?

To sort out the truth, look at the actual yearly salaries of the thirteen families in the neighborhood.

Income (dollars)	Frequency
$200,000	1
34,000	1
18,000	1
14,000	1
12,000	3
8,000	2
5,000	4

A picture begins to unfold here. If we add up all 13 salaries and divide by 13, we obtain $26,000, which is known as the **mean**. If we count down from the top (or up from the bottom) until we reach the middle (seventh) income, we obtain $12,000, which is known as the **median**. If we look at the most frequently occurring income we obtain $5,000, which is known as the **mode**. Each can be called the average.

The mode is the least stable and the least frequently used of these values. For instance, a raise of $3,000 to two of the lowest paid people would change the mode from $5,000 to $8,000; this change would increase the mean from $26,000 to about $26,242 and leave the median unchanged. Use of the mode is generally restricted to those cases in which it is desired to represent a set of data by its most *typical* value. The mode is sometimes symbolized *Mo*.

If more than one value appears with the same frequency, there is no mode. A set of data with two values having the same frequency is called **bimodal**; if more than two values have the same frequency, it is **multimodal**. In the foregoing income data, a raise of $3,000 to one of the individuals making $5,000 would give a frequency of 3 at $5,000, $8,000, and $12,000. In this case, no mode would be of any value. Although strictly speaking, a distribution is bimodal only if two values of the variable have exactly the same frequency, it is often useful to relax the use of the term when dealing with grouped data. If there are two classes containing the most frequently occurring values (even though they may not be *exactly* the same) and these classes are separated by other classes containing fewer frequencies (rather like two mountain peaks separated by a valley), the term bimodal is sometimes applied as a descriptive term to such a distribution. A histogram of such a bimodal distribution follows.

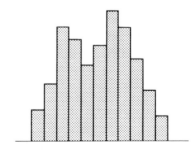

In cases of this sort, it may be that we have collected data from two or more different sources. A height distribution of the general adult population might be bimodal with peaks at 5′ 5″ (the modal female height) and 5′ 10″ (the modal male height). When such bimodality occurs, it is a signal for us to examine the possibility that the data are drawn from distinct populations.

The median, or central value of the data sample is most useful when there are extremes which might influence the mean unduly. In the neighborhood case, the $200,000 value is quite extreme, far and away above the rest of the values, so the median is certain to be a more representative central point than the mean.

To find out which number is at the median, we observe that, by definition, the median is the number at the central position. If we were to list all the numbers in the distribution in increasing or decreasing value and count until we found the middle number, we would have the median. Thus the median of three values is the one in the middle. The median of four numbers is between the second and third one; for convenience, we say halfway between them. As a general rule, if there are n cases (total frequency), we simply take $(\frac{1}{2})(n+1)$. If n is odd, as in the previous case, it will give us a specific location of a number. If n is even, it may not. For example, if $n = 30$, $(\frac{1}{2})(30+1) = 15.5$. The median, then, lies between the fifteenth and sixteenth numbers; if different, take the average of the two numbers (i.e., one-half their sum). It is usually helpful, in the case of small samples, to arrange the numbers in order first, then simply count from the top or bottom.

> **EXAMPLE 1** Determine the median of the following numbers:
> 47, 44, 41, 40, 39, 38, 37, 36, 33, 32, 28, 28, 22, 20, 14, 6, 3.

SOLUTION The total frequency is eighteen, so the median lies at $(\frac{1}{2})(18+1)$ or 9.5. The data are already arranged in order and the ninth and tenth numbers are 36 and 33, so the median (symbol Md) is $(\frac{1}{2})(36+33)$ or $Md = 34.5$.

COMMENT Note that the data must be arranged in numerical order for the counting process to take place. For example, if we have four numbers, 65, 11, 3, 23, the median is at 2.5, but is *not* equal to 7. We must arrange the numbers in order, as 3, 11, 23, 65, to find that the median is 17.

The most stable, most frequently used measure of central tendency is the mean. The mean is the value usually referred to by the term **average**; it is also called the **arithmetic average**. It is particularly effective with large amounts of data, especially if the data tend to mass near the center with frequencies decreasing about equally in both directions. If exact figures are known, the mean can be found by the following formula.

**Mean of
a Sample**

The mean of a sample containing n pieces of data is given by

$$\bar{x} = \frac{\sum x}{n}$$

Here $\bar{x}$ represents the mean; $\sum$ means "the sum of"; x is each value; n is the total number in the sample. The mean of a sample is referred to in the literature by m, M, $\overline{X}$, and other symbols as well. The $\bar{x}$ symbolism is obtained from physics where it is used to symbolize the first moment of inertia and has become entrenched in traditional literature. The use of m or M (the first letter of the word "mean") is gaining acceptance in the social sciences, but has a disadvantage when used with more than one variable, requiring subscripts as m_x and m_y, rather than the more convenient $\bar{x}$ and $\bar{y}$.

EXAMPLE 2   A random sample of five accounts in a department store showed the following balances at the end of the month: $67.32; $108.97; $17.64; $412.11; $81.96. Compute the mean balance.

SOLUTION   Since the sum of the five amounts is $688.00, the mean is given by $\bar{x} = \$688/5 = \$137.60$.

EXAMPLE 3   The ages of 25 people in a certain income bracket are distributed as follows:

Age	29	33	37	38	39	40	42	43	45	47	50	59	66
Frequency	1	1	3	4	2	3	2	2	3	1	1	1	1

What is the mean age in this sample?

SOLUTION   We can use the defining formula and take the sum of the ages as $29 + 33 + 37 + 37 + 37 + 38 + 38 + 38 + 38 + 39 + 39 + \cdots$ and so forth, but it is much more efficient to simply multiply each value by its frequency to find the sum rather than adding it in the required number of times. Thus we have the sum given by

$$29 + 33 + 3(37) + 4(38) + 2(39) + 3(40) + 2(42) + 2(43) + 3(45)$$
$$+ 47 + 50 + 59 + 66 = 29 + 33 + 111 + 152 + 78 + 120 + 84 + 86 + 135$$
$$+ 47 + 50 + 59 + 66 = 1050,$$

so
$$\bar{x}=(1050)/25=42.$$
Here we have used an alternate formula for the mean
$$\bar{x}=\frac{\Sigma x \cdot f}{n}$$
where $\bar{x}$ represents the mean, Σ means "the sum of," f is the frequency per class, $x \cdot f$ is each value times its frequency, and n is the total number of data points, equal to Σf, the sum of all the frequencies.

COMMENT   A common error in finding the mean of data with more than one frequency for some values is overlooking the frequencies in either finding the total to divide or the total frequencies. Each value should be counted each time it occurs, both as a value of x, and as one value toward the total of n.

EXAMPLE 4 Find the mean of the thirteen incomes discussed at the beginning of the section.

SOLUTION

$$\bar{x}=\frac{(200,000)(1)+(34,000)(1)+(18,000)(1)+(14,000)(1)+(12,000)(3)+(8,000)(2)+(5,000)(4)}{13}$$

$$=\frac{338,000}{13}$$

$$=26,000$$

DISCUSSION   Note that the mean of the twelve salaries excluding $200,000 is $11,500. The median of these is $10,000 (midway between $8,000 and $12,000) while the mode is still $5,000. In many cases involving small sets of data, the median is the best representative measure of the information because the mean is unduly influenced by extremes.

If the data are grouped, some accuracy is lost because we do not know exactly what each value represents. The ease of presentation of grouped data may compensate for the loss of accuracy. The *mode* is still easy to find with grouped data. The modal class is the class with the greatest frequency. It is probably most accurate simply to find the modal class although, if desired, the mode can be considered to be the class mark of the modal class, although this may not be strictly accurate.

To determine the *median* from grouped data, it is assumed that the data points are distributed evenly over each interval. If an interval has four data points (i.e., the class has a frequency of four), they divide the class into *five* subintervals. If a class has only one data point, it divides the class into two subintervals. Once we have located the class containing the median (using the location given by $\frac{1}{2}(n+1)$), then if L is the lower limit of the class containing the median, j represents the number of pieces of data in the class (class frequency), k represents the location of the mean in the class; that is, $k = \left[\frac{1}{2}(n+1)\text{minus the cumulative frequency at the next lower class}\right]$, and w is the class width, then

$$Md = L + \frac{k}{j+1}(w)$$

Suppose, for instance, the median is the 43rd number from the bottom ($n=85$) and is located in the class 102–107 which has four data points in it, and that there are 40 data points below this class. Then $L=101.5$, $k=3$, $j=4$, and $w=6$ (that is, 107.5 minus 101.5) so that

$$Md = 101.5 + \frac{3}{4+1}(6) = 101.5 + 3.6 = 105.1$$

In practice the median is often rounded off and given as an approximation. In this case, the median would be 105.

In calculating the *mean* from grouped data it is assumed that each piece of data in the class falls at the class mark (center) of each interval. The results would be the same if the data in each class were considered to be spread out over the interval because of the way in which the mean is calculated. In the income data the class interval 27,000 to 29,999 would be represented by 28,500. NOTE   The class mark is actually 28,499.50, but minor discrepancies of this sort are generally ignored since they are such a small fraction of the numbers involved.

EXAMPLE 5   Find the median and mean of the data represented by the following frequency distribution.

Class	Frequency
171–175	4
166–170	8
161–165	14
156–160	22
151–155	27
146–150	19
141–145	17
136–140	11
131–135	3

SOLUTION   There are 125 pieces of data in the distribution so the median is located at number $\frac{1}{2}(125+1)$ or number 63. The cumulative frequency through class 146–150 is 50, so the median lies in class 151–155. We need 13 of the 27 data points in that class, the lower limit of the class is 150.5, and the class width is 5, so

$$Md = 150.5 + \frac{13}{28}(5) \doteq 152.8$$

Note that the symbol "$\doteq$" means "is approximately equal to" and should be used whenever the values are not precisely equal.

To determine the mean of the grouped data it is convenient to construct a table which summarizes the whole procedure. Letting x represent the class mark and f the frequency in the class, we have

x	f	$x \cdot f$	
173	4	692	
168	8	1344	
163	14	2282	
158	22	3476	
153	27	4131	$\bar{x} = 19{,}085/125$
148	19	2812	
143	17	2431	$= 152.68 \doteq 152.7$
138	11	1518	
133	3	399	
Total	125	19,085	

TECHNICAL NOTE   If the numbers are large, a calculator is nearly indispensible. Some calculators give the mean automatically, but the majority of low-priced calculators do not. For statistical use, a calculator should have at least one storage register, preferably more, and at least one into which data can be accumulated. In this way intermediate answers can be stored and recalled when needed. Elaborate procedures called *coding* were used prior to the advent of the minicalculator, most of which are not needed today, but there are still times when a form of coding can be useful, such as when the numbers are so large as to overflow the calculator, particularly when squaring, as in the next section. In such cases it is helpful to use an **assumed mean**, usually an integer x' (read x prime) in the vicinity of the true mean. The mean difference between x' and each value of x is calculated and added to x' to obtain the true mean. The formula is as follows:

Mean of a Sample from an Assumed Mean

$$\bar{x} = \frac{\Sigma(x - x')}{n} + x'$$

EXAMPLE 6 Use an assumed mean to find the mean of the data of example 5.

SOLUTION   For grouped data it is convenient to use a class mark near the center, preferably one with a large number in the class; in this case we will use 153. The following table summarizes the work.

x	f	$x - 153$	$(x - 153) \cdot f$
173	4	20	80
168	8	15	120
163	14	10	140
158	22	5	110
153	27	0	0
148	19	-5	-95
143	17	-10	-170
138	11	-15	-165
133	3	-20	-60
Total	125		-40

Then $\bar{x} = -40/125 + 153 = -0.32 + 153 = 152.68 \doteq 152.7$.

NOTE   In the remainder of the text, most problems assume that a calculator is available to readers, although one may not be necessary. In the event that one is not available, the reader may wish to check the examples by using an alternate procedure. Problems marked **c** are recommended only if a calculator is available.

•Problems

Using the best technique, determine the mean, median, and mode of each of the samples in problems 1–4.

1. 20, 22, 23, 26, 29, 30
2. 28, 25, 20, 33, 27, 29, 23, 21, 24, 18, 30, 25
3. 1.34, 1.69, 1.78, 1.89, 2.03, 2.27, 2.39, 2.88, 3.16, 3.34, 4.92, 5.57, 6.83, 7.44, 9.63, 11.82
4.

x	Frequency	x	Frequency
134	1	171	12
137	1	173	10
143	1	174	13
150	2	178	8
152	3	181	6

x	Frequency	x	Frequency
153	1	186	3
161	3	193	2
164	2	201	1
166	8	217	1
169	7	234	1
170	13	246	1

Determine the mean, median, and mode of each of the following sets of data.

5. The sales data of example 1, section 1.1.
6. The data of problem 6, section 1.3. Use the actual class marks, then round upward to two decimal places, calculating both ways to see if the difference to two decimal places is worth the extra arithmetic.
c7. The height data of section 1.1. Use the raw data, then the data as given in the grouped frequency table and compare the results.
c8. The cat food data of problem 4, section 1.1.
c9. The machine production data of problem 5, section 1.1.
c10. The pollution indices of problem 6, section 1.1.
c11. The candy bar sales of problem 7, section 1.3.
c12. The I. Q. scores of problem 9, section 1.3.
c13. The income data given below. To avoid overloading the calculator, use class marks to the nearest dollar, in thousands, e.g., the class mark of the highest class would be 43.5 thousand.

Income (dollars)	Number of Families
42,000–44,999	3
39,000–41,999	7
36,000–38,999	12
33,000–35,999	17
30,000–32,999	28
27,000–29,999	60
24,000–26,999	216
21,000–23,999	268
18,000–20,999	448
15,000–17,999	621
12,000–14,999	949
9,000–11,999	1,421
6,000–8,999	2,844
3,000–5,999	2,123
0–2,999	294

2.2   MEASURES OF DISPERSION

When we determine the approximate center of a distribution, we obtain one description of it. We can describe it even better by obtaining a measure which tells us something about the spread of the distribution. This kind of measure tells us whether the values in the distribution cluster closely about the mean or are somewhat dispersed, or are widely dispersed. A measure of dispersion which is large compared to the mean indicates that the distribution is spread out, while a small number for this measure shows that the data points cluster closely about the mean.

The simplest measure of dispersion, which was discussed in Chapter 1, is the range, which gives the distance between the highest and lowest values in the data set. The range is obtained by subtracting the lowest value in the data set from the highest value. If the set contains a few, or even one, extreme scores, the range will give a misleading picture of the dispersion, so its use is limited.

The range has definite uses, however, in circumstances in which the data set does not contain extreme values. It is a quick, easy measure of dispersion, although it may not be very representative. A position-vacant advertisement may give a salary range of $600–$765 per month, depending upon qualifications. The use of the term "range" is rather loose in this case, however, since a statistical range would be $165. In addition to this sort of use, the range can be used to estimate the standard deviation, another measure of distribution dispersion, which is discussed in this section. For very large samples, one hundred or over, the standard deviation is approximately one-fifth of the range, by rule of thumb. For smaller samples, the rule will be given later.

For distributions which are relatively symmetrical about the mean and taper off in both directions, the best measure of dispersion about the mean is the *standard deviation*, which will be used extensively throughout the rest of the book. Such distributions include the "normal" or "bell-shaped" distribution, pictured here.

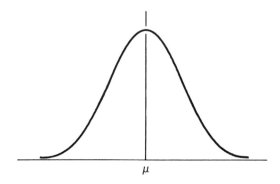

μ

Before we discuss the standard deviation, it may be worthwhile to look at another measure of dispersion, the *mean deviation*. The difference between the value of each data point in the distribution and the mean of the distribution is the *deviation* of that data point. We might think that the mean of all the deviations would be a good indicator of the dispersion or spread of the distribution. The deviations above the mean, however, balance those below the mean, so the sum of all the deviations is always zero, no matter what the distribution looks like. If we take the absolute values of the deviations, which ignore the plus and minus signs, we obtain a measure of dispersion called the **mean absolute deviation** (*MAD*) or simply the **mean deviation**. A formula for the mean deviation is this one.

Mean Deviation of a Sample	$$MAD = \frac{\Sigma|x - \bar{x}|}{n}$$

The mean deviation of a sample containing the data points 1, 3, 4, 7, 9, 12, is found easily. The mean is $(1+3+4+7+9+12)/6$ or 6. The absolute values of the differences between the mean and each data point are found and added.

x	$x - \bar{x}$	$|x - \bar{x}|$
1	−5	5
3	−3	3
4	−2	2
7	1	1
9	3	3
12	6	6
Total 36	0	20

Then the mean deviation is $20/6 \doteq 3.33$. Note in the above table that the sum of all $x - \bar{x}$ terms is zero. This is always true and may be used to check your arithmetic.

The mean deviation is a valid measure of dispersion, but its applicability is limited. The cancelling effect of adding the $x - \bar{x}$ terms can also be eliminated by squaring the terms before adding. Thus the sum is positive but the units are squared. We get back to the original units by taking the square root. This principle is utilized to find the **standard deviation**.

Standard Deviation of a Sample

The standard deviation of a sample with mean $\bar{x}$ and containing n pieces of data is given by

$$s = \sqrt{\frac{\Sigma(x - \bar{x})^2}{n-1}}$$

Here s is used to indicate that it is the standard deviation of a sample, $\bar{x}$ is the mean of the sample, and n is the number of data points in the sample. The square of the standard deviation is also a measure of dispersion. It is called the **variance**, s^2, which is defined as

$$s^2 = \frac{\Sigma(x - \bar{x})^2}{n-1}$$

It might be more natural to divide by n, but statisticians have found that division by n yields a value which is, on the average, too small to provide what is technically known as an "unbiased" estimate of the variance of the population. The term "unbiased" as applied to an estimator means that if we take a great number of samples of the same size from a population, the mean of the variances of these samples will be a better estimate of the population variance than the variance of each sample by itself. The *expected value* (defined in the next chapter) of the sample variances is equal to the population variance. We arrive at an unbiased estimate of the population variance if we divide by $n-1$ rather than n when calculating the sample variance. All other uses for s^2 are basically unaffected by this change. Division by n rather than $n-1$ gives a "descriptive" measure of the dispersion of the sample; frequently this is denoted by s'.

Since errors in arithmetic are possible, it is useful to have an amazingly accurate rule-of-thumb to estimate the sample variance. If the sample has been drawn from an approximately normal (bell-shaped) distribution, the calculated value of s should not differ substantially from a fraction of the range, depending on the size of the sample. For a sample of 5, the standard deviation should be about $2/5$ of the range; for a sample of 10, about $1/3$ of the range; for a sample of 25, about $1/4$ of the range, and for a sample of 100 or more, about $1/5$ of the range. Intermediate sample sizes can have the fraction estimated from this information.

One reason for using the standard deviation as our primary measure of dispersion is that it has been investigated extensively. One investigation, which produced *Chebyshev's rule*, found that for *any* set of data, 3/4 of all pieces of data lie within two standard deviations of the mean, 8/9 lie within three standard deviations of the mean, and, in general, $1-1/k^2$ of the values lie within k standard deviations of the mean. If a distribution has a mean of 75 and a standard deviation of 10, then 3/4 of all data lie between 55 and 95, and 8/9 of the data lie between 45 and 105. For distributions which more closely approximate the normal distribution, which is bell-shaped, symmetrical about the mean, and trails off sharply in both directions, about 2/3 of the data lie within one standard deviation of the mean, 95% within two, and more than 99% within three standard deviations of the mean. Features of the normal distribution will be discussed at greater length in Chapter 5 and later in the text.

EXAMPLE 1   Find the standard deviation of 1, 3, 4, 7, 9, 12.

SOLUTION   We set up a table as given below.

x	$x-\bar{x}$	$(x-\bar{x})^2$
1	-5	25
3	-3	9
4	-2	4
7	1	1
9	3	9
12	6	36
36	0	84

Then $s = \sqrt{84/5} = \sqrt{16.8} \doteq 4.1$. A table of square roots is given in Table 1 in the Tables section at the end of the book. Instructions for the use of Table 1 are given in Appendix A.

EXAMPLE 2   A sample of five accounts in a department store showed the following balances at the end of the month: $67.32; $108.97; $17.64; $412.11; $81.96. The mean, from example 2, section 2.1, is $137.60; determine the standard deviation of the sample.

SOLUTION   Again a table is helpful.

	x	$x-\bar{x}$	$(x-\bar{x})^2$	
	67.32	-70.28	4,939.2784	
	108.97	-28.63	819.6769	$s^2 = 98,600.9066/4$
	17.64	-119.96	14,390.4016	$s^2 = 24,650.2665$
	412.11	274.51	75,355.7401	$s \doteq 157.00$
	81.96	-55.64	3,095.8096	
Total	688.00	0	98,600.9066	

The extreme tedium of working with numbers so cumbersome, even if a calculator is used, points out the desirability of using an alternate formula which does not require the calculation of the deviations from the mean for each entry. The numerator of the formula for the variance, $\Sigma(x-\bar{x})^2$, is called the *sum of squares of deviations from the sample mean* or simply the **sum of squares** for x. This is denoted SSX. It is an easy algebraic exercise to show that the sum of squares is also equal to $\Sigma x^2 - n(\bar{x})^2$, and also is equal to $\Sigma x^2 - (\Sigma x)^2/n$. In the previous example, the squares of the numbers involved were 4531.9824, 11,874.4609, 311.1696, 169,834.6521, 6717.4416, and the total of these five squares is 193,269.7066. Since the mean is 137.60, the SSX is equal to $193,269.7066 - 5(137.60)^2 = 98,600.9066$; SSX is also equal to $193,269.7066 - (688)^2/5 = 98,600.9066$. In either case the variance is equal to $98,600.9066/4 = 24,650.2665$ and $s \doteq 157.00$, as before.

The foregoing discussion gives two additional, and very useful formulas for finding the standard deviation. They are presented here without their derivation from the original formula.

Alternate Formulas for the Standard Deviation

$$s = \sqrt{\frac{\Sigma x - n(\bar{x})^2}{n-1}}.$$

$$s = \sqrt{\frac{\Sigma x^2 - \dfrac{(\Sigma x)^2}{n}}{n-1}} = \sqrt{\frac{n\Sigma x^2 - (\Sigma x)^2}{n(n-1)}}$$

The first of these is most useful if the mean is already known while the other use raw data. The first form of the second is called the *machine formula* for the standard deviation. If working from raw data and using a calculator with only one storage register, the following procedure will be useful in finding the standard deviation: square each value of x, accumulating in the storage register as you go along. When you are finished, the memory will have Σx^2 stored in it. Then add the values of x in the usual way, so that Σx will be displayed. If the mean is desired, divide by n to obtain $\bar{x}$, square the result, multiply by n, change the sign, then add the value recalled from memory, dividing then by $n-1$. If the mean is not needed, simply take the display (Σx), square it, divide by n, change the sign, add the number stored in memory, divide the result by $n-1$. In either case, the number resulting is the variance. If the standard deviation is needed, take the square root. To illustrate, take the standard deviation of the set of data: 1, 3, 4, 7, 9. $(1)^2+(3)^2+(4)^2+(7)^2+(9)^2=1+9+16+49+81=156$. $1+3+4+7+9=24$. Then using the first formula, if $\bar{x}=24/5=4.8$, then $SSX=156-5(4.8)^2=156-115.20=40.8$, $s^2=40.8/4=10.2$, so $s\doteq3.19$. Using the second formula, $SSX=156-(24)^2/5=156-(576)/5=156-115.20=40.8$, so $s\doteq3.19$, as before.

The second alternate formula is slightly preferable to the first if the value of the mean is approximate, since it avoids some rounding error.

EXAMPLE 3 Estimate the mean and standard deviation of the following sample of Nielsen ratings: 20.6, 11.3, 13.7, 9.2, 18.1, 7.2.

SOLUTION Using the machine formula we have

	x	x^2
	20.6	424.36
	11.3	127.69
	13.7	187.69
	9.2	84.64
	18.1	327.61
	7.2	51.84
Total	80.1	1,203.83

Then, $\bar{x}=80.1/6=13.35$, and

$$s^2=\frac{1,203.83-\dfrac{(80.1)^2}{6}}{5}=\frac{1,203.83-\dfrac{6,416.01}{6}}{5}$$

$$=\frac{1,203.83-1,069.335}{5}=\frac{134.495}{5}\doteq26.90$$

and

$$s\doteq\sqrt{26.90}\doteq5.2.$$

If the data are grouped into classes by means of a frequency distribution, both the mean and standard deviation are found by using the class marks—the centers of the classes.

The introduction of the frequencies entails a slight modification of the formula for the standard deviation. Using the raw data formulas, we have the following formulas for finding the standard deviation from grouped data.

$$s = \sqrt{\frac{\Sigma(x^2 \cdot f) - \frac{(\Sigma x \cdot f)^2}{n}}{n-1}} = \sqrt{\frac{n\Sigma(x^2 \cdot f) - (\Sigma x \cdot f)^2}{n(n-1)}}$$

EXAMPLE 4   Using the age data of example 3, section 2.1, calculate the standard deviation of the ages.

SOLUTION   The standard deviation can be calculated in the same way as in the preceding example. Note, however, that the introduction of frequencies necessitates three additional columns if the calculations are done the long way. If a calculator is used, each number may be entered the appropriate number of times.

	x	f	$x \cdot f$	x^2	$x^2 \cdot f$
	29	1	29	841	841
	33	1	33	1,089	1,089
	37	3	111	1,369	4,107
	38	4	152	1,444	5,776
	39	2	78	1,521	3,042
	40	3	120	1,600	4,800
	42	2	84	1,764	3,528
	43	2	86	1,849	3,698
	45	3	135	2,025	6,075
	47	1	47	2,209	2,209
	50	1	50	2,500	2,500
	59	1	59	3,481	3,481
	66	1	66	4,356	4,356
Total		25	1,050		45,502

Then

$$s = \sqrt{\frac{45,502 - \frac{(1,050)^2}{25}}{24}} = \sqrt{\frac{1,402}{24}} = \sqrt{58.4167} \doteq 7.64$$

TECHNICAL NOTE   If a calculator is not available or the numbers are so large that they do not fit well in your calculator, we can use the assumed mean mentioned in connection with *coding*, which was described in the previous section. As mentioned there, an assumed mean, x', can be subtracted from each number. In calculating the standard deviation, the calculations are done as usual, using x' in place of $\bar{x}$, then *before* dividing by $n-1$ a correction factor,

$(\bar{x} - x')^2$ is subtracted from the total to compensate for the fact that x' is not the true mean. The formulas used are the following:

Mean and Standard Deviation From an Assumed Mean	$\bar{x} = \dfrac{\Sigma(x - x')^2}{n} + x'$ $s = \sqrt{\dfrac{\Sigma(x - x')^2 - nc^2}{n - 1}}$ where $c = (\bar{x} - x')$

EXAMPLE 6 Given the following frequency distribution, estimate the mean and the standard deviation.

Class	Frequency
171–175	4
166–170	8
161–165	14
156–160	22
151–155	27
146–150	19
141–145	17
136–140	11
131–135	3

SOLUTION Using the class marks and an assumed mean of 153 (since this is close to the median of the distribution and is a class mark), we have the following table.

x	f	$x - 153$	$(x - 153) \cdot f$	$(x - 153)^2$	$(x - 153)^2 \cdot f$
173	4	20	80	400	1,600
168	8	15	120	225	1,800
163	14	10	140	100	1,400
158	22	5	110	25	550
153	27	0	0	0	0
148	19	−5	−95	25	475
143	17	−10	−170	100	1,700
138	11	−15	−165	225	2,475
133	3	−20	−60	400	1,200
	125		−40		11,200

Then $\bar{x} = -40/125 + 153 = -0.32 + 152.68 \doteq 152.7$; and

$$s^2 = \frac{11,200 - 125(-0.32)^2}{124} = \frac{11,200 - 12.8}{124} \doteq 90.22$$

and

$$s \doteq \sqrt{90.22} \doteq 9.50$$

Use of the standard deviation as the best measure of spread for a distribution is predicated on the assumption that the distribution is reasonably symmetric, or at least without a marked amount of **skewedness**. A distribution is said to be skewed if it is highly asymetric—if most of the values of the variable are bunched at one end of the distribution and trail off at the other end. A distribution is said to be **positively skewed** if the trailing end is off to the right and **negatively skewed** if it is off to the left. Drawings of skewed distributions are given below. The mean and median are marked.

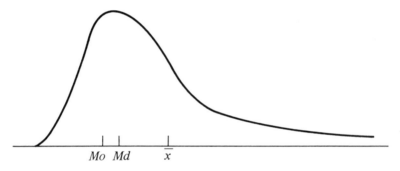

Mo Md $\bar{x}$

A positively skewed distribution

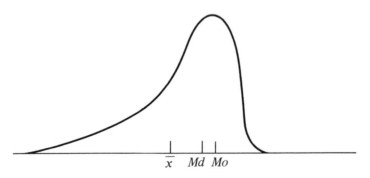

$\bar{x}$ Md Mo

A negatively skewed distribution

Distributions which are bounded at one end and unbounded or practically unbounded at the other end are usually skewed. An example is income; income is bounded below at zero, but generally has a very high upper end, far above the median of the distribution.

Even with a skewed distribution, however, the mean and standard deviation are still a good measure of central tendency and dispersion unless the amount of skewedness is highly marked. Pearson has introduced an index of skewedness given by

---

Pearson's Index of Skewedness

$$\text{Index} = \frac{3(\bar{x} - Md)}{s}$$

---

which gives the difference between the mean and median as a proportion of one-third the standard deviation. *If this index falls between* -1 *and* $+1$, *the skewedness is not too marked.* For values over $+1$, the distribution is definitely positively skewed; for values less than -1, the distribution is definitely negatively skewed.

If a distribution is markedly skewed, or if the variable is not measured on an interval or ratio scale, the mean and standard deviation should not be used. In such cases the best measure of central tendency is the median. The best measure of dispersion is called the *semi-interquartile range*. To find this measure we must first determine some measures of *location*. Measures of location are discussed in general in the next section, but it is appropriate to discuss the **quartiles** at this time. The first quartile, Q_1, is the value which exceeds one-fourth of the data, the second quartile, Q_2, is the value which exceeds one-half the data, and the third quartile, Q_3, is the value which exceeds three-fourths the data; all assuming the set of observations is ranked from smallest to largest. It can be seen that Q_2 is the median; thus we are concerned basically only with Q_1 and Q_3 as quartiles.

To locate Q_1 and Q_3, we proceed as with the median: Q_1 is at $\frac{1}{4}(n+1)$ and Q_3 is at $\frac{3}{4}(n+1)$ from the bottom of the distribution.

The quartiles are not themselves measures of dispersion, but their placement says something about the dispersion of the distribution. The distance between Q_3 and Q_1 is called the **interquartile range**. A more widely used measure is the **semi-interquartile range,** Q, given by $Q = \frac{1}{2}(Q_3 - Q_1)$. This gives roughly the distance on either side of the median which will encompass about half the scores. As with the standard deviation, large values of Q in comparison to the median indicate a wide spread, small values indicate little spread.

EXAMPLE 7 Find Q for the data of example 7.

SOLUTION   There are 125 pieces of data in the distribution, so Q_1 is located at $\frac{1}{4}(126) = 31.5$ and Q_3 is located at $\frac{3}{4}(126) = 93.5$. Q_1 is located in the interval 146–150 with a cumulative frequency of 31 below it, so using the formula $L + \{k/(j+1)\}(w)$ as before, we find that $Q_1 = 145.5 + (0.5/20)(5) = 145.625$ or about 145.6. Q_3 lies in the interval 156–160 with a cumulative frequency of 77 below it, so $Q_3 = 155.5 + (16.5/23)(5) \doteq 159.1$. Then $Q \doteq \frac{1}{2}(159.1 - 145.6) = 5.25$.

For the data of the above example, the mean is about 152.7, the median is 152.8, $s \doteq 9.50$, so Pearson's index of skewedness is 0.3/9.5 or about 0.03. This very small number indicates a symmetric distribution.

•Problems

Using the best technique, determine the variance and standard deviation of the samples in problems 1–3.

1.   20, 22, 23, 26, 29, 30.

2.   28, 25, 20, 33, 27, 29, 23, 21, 24, 18, 30, 25.

3.   1.34, 1.69, 1.78, 1.89, 2.03, 2.27, 2.39, 2.88, 3.16, 3.34, 4.92, 5.57, 6.83, 7.44, 9.63, 11.82.

4.   Given the following frequency distribution of scores made by soldiers on an officer qualification test, deteermine the median and the semi-interquartile range.

Class	Frequency
51–65	12
66–80	21
81–95	33
96–110	42
111–125	19
126–140	14
141–155	6

5.   Determine the standard deviation and the semi-interquartile range for the frequency distribution of problem 4 of section 2.1.

In problems 6–14 determine the standard deviation of each set of data.

6.   The sales data of example 1, section 1.1.

7.   The data of problem 6, section 1.3. Use the actual class marks, then round upward to two decimal places, calculating both ways to see if the difference to two decimal places is worth the extra arithmetic.

8.   The height data of section 1.1. Use the raw data, then the data as given in the grouped frequency table and compare the results.

c9. The cat food data of problem 4, section 1.1.

c10. The machine production data of problem 5, section 1.1.

c11. The pollution indices of problem 6, section 1.1.

c12. The candy bar sales of problem 7, section 1.3.

c13. The I.Q. scores of problem 9, section 1.3.

c14. The income data of problem 13, section 2.1. Also compute the semi-inter-quartile range. Calculate Pearson's Index of Skewedness for the data since there is obviously some skewing. Is the standard deviation an appropriate measure of dispersion for this set of data?

2.3 *OTHER MEASURES OF LOCATION AND COMPARISON*

Pieces of data have values which are generally called "raw scores." Raw scores are basically meaningless in and of themselves. A man's blood test shows a cholesterol count of 320. Is that good or bad? Average is said to be 200. He is above the average, but how much above? Suppose we also know that the standard deviation of such data is about 60. He is then two standard deviations above the mean. According to Chebyshev's rule, no less than 75% of the data of such a distribution lies within two standard deviations of the mean. It is likely, therefore that less than 10% of all men have a cholesterol count this high. According to Chebyshev's rule, 75% of all cholesterol counts, or more, will lie between 80 and 320. Thus we can estimate that no more than $12\frac{1}{2}\%$ will lie below 80 and no more than $12\frac{1}{2}\%$ will lie above 320. Chebyshev's rule says nothing about splitting the other 25%, but splitting about half at each end is not highly unlikely. Thus we estimate that at least $87\frac{1}{2}\%$ of cholesterol counts will lie below 320. Actually, if cholesterol counts are approximately normal, about $97\frac{1}{2}\%$ will lie below 320. A guess that at least 90% lie below 320 is probably reasonable, and we can conclude that his cholesterol count is too high. Judicious application of Chebyshev's rule and use of the normal distribution which will be covered extensively in Chapter 5 allow interpretation of raw scores converted to *standard scores*. The number of standard deviations a given value is above or below the mean is called the **standard score** or **z-score** and is determined by the following formula:

Standard Score of a Sample

$$z = \frac{x - \bar{x}}{s}$$

where x is the value under consideration, $\bar{x}$ is the mean of the sample, and s is the standard deviation. The value of z locates the approximate place of the value in the distribution in relation to the spread of the set of data. For normally distributed data, a later chapter will give methods for determining the percent (or proportion) of the entire distribution which lies between any two values. The z-score also gives us a way to compare scores measuring similar quantities or attributes which were obtained on different instruments or from different samples. If two students take different IQ tests, for example, their scores are not directly comparable. Suppose John scores 112 on IQ test A while Fred scores 118 on IQ test B. Which was really the better score? If IQ test A had a mean of 98 and a standard deviation of 16, John's standard score was $(112-98)/16 = 14/16 \doteq 0.88$. If IQ test B had a mean of 104 and a standard deviation of 18, Fred's standard score was $(118-104)/18 = 14/18 \doteq 0.78$. John did better than Fred in this comparison. This does not mean, however, that John's IQ (whatever that may be) is higher than Fred's. On a retest it is possible that the results would be reversed since there is likely to be considerable variation, even in the same person taking the same test at a later time. The difference in scores might have been due simply to chance or to error in measurement. All we can do at this point is to compare their scores on the tests taken.

Another measure of location is the **percentile**. In this case the data must be arranged in order, preferably from low to high. The pth percentile is the value which exceeds p percent of the scores. In case there were exactly 100 pieces of data, the lowest score would be at the zero percentile because it exceeds none of the scores, while the highest score would be at the ninety-ninth percentile because it exceeds 99% of the scores. There is of course no hundredth percentile since this would indicate that a score exceeded all of the scores, including itself.

The use of percentiles is generally limited to large numbers of scores; its use with small distributions is probably not as useful as the actual distribution itself. To determine the percentile rank of a particular score, count the scores below it and divide by the total number of scores, then multiply by one hundred. Thus if r is the rank of a score (counted from the bottom—same as the cumulative frequency), its percentile would be given by

$$p = \frac{r-1}{n} \cdot (100)$$

where n is the number of the scores. To determine the score having a particular percentile rank, two different methods are used, one for raw data, one for data grouped into classes. For raw data we determine the upper limit of p percent of the scores, then the pth percentile is the score which just exceeds this. To obtain the 34th percentile of a set of 173 scores, for example, we take $(0.34) \cdot (173) = 58.82$. The lowest score above the score number 58.82, then, is the 59th score from the bottom. This score, whatever its value, would be the 34th percentile. There can never be a precisely accurate correspondence between percentile ranks and the data themselves unless $n = 100$, and this should be borne in mind when working with percentiles. In a set of 50 scores, for example, the fifty-sixth percentile would be the score above $(0.56)(50)=28$, or the twenty-ninth score from the bottom. The fifty-seventh percentile would be the score above $(0.57)(50)=28.5$ or again, the twenty-ninth score from the bottom. By definition, the twenty-ninth score in a set of fifty would be at the 56th percentile. Thus, for distributions with fewer than 100 entries, some scores would serve as more than one percentile value, while for distributions with more than 100 entries, sometimes more than one score would have the same percentile rank (to two digits, at any rate).

For grouped data, the location of the percentile is found as with the median and the quartile; the score at percentile p is defined to be the value of the score at rank $(p/100)(n+1)$ from the bottom of a distribution with n values. This definition is also consistent with the accepted definition of Q_1, Md, and Q_3 as, respectively, the twenty-fifth, fiftieth, and seventy-fifth percentiles.

Once having found the location we determine which class the score is in, then compute its value using the formula $L+\{k/(j+1)\}(w)$ as before.

EXAMPLE 1 Determine the fifth, ninetieth, and ninety-ninth percentiles for the following frequency distribution.

Class	Frequency
171–175	4
166–170	8
161–165	14
156–160	22
151–155	27
146–150	19
141–145	17
136–140	11
131–135	3
Total	125

SOLUTION Using the definition, the fifth percentile is number $(5/100)(126)$ or number 6.3 from the bottom. We note that this is in the interval 136–140. Since the cumulative frequency below this interval is 3, we need 3.3 in this interval; using the formula, $L=135.5$, $k=3.3$, $j=11$, and $w=5$. Thus $x=135.5+(3.3/12)(5) \doteq 136.9$ or about 137. The ninetieth percentile is at $(90/100)(126)$ or 113.4 from the bottom. The cumulative frequency below class 161–165 is 99, below class 166–170 is 113, so the ninetieth percentile is the top score in class 161–165. Using the formula, $L=165.5$, $k=14.4$, $j=15$, $w=5$, so $x=160.5+(14.4/15)(5)=165.3$ or about 165. Finally, the ninety-ninth percentile is located at $(99/100)(126)$ or 124.74 from the bottom or nearly at the top (125th) value. Here $L=170.5$, $k=3.74$, $j=4$, $w=5$, so $x=170.5+(3.74/5)(5)=174.24$ or about 174.

NOTE   Since the results are only approximate anyway, some users of percentiles will not use the fractions in 6.3, 113.4, 124.74, rather rounding off to 6,
113, 125, respectively. The values obtained using these numbers are $136.75 \doteq 137$
for the fifth percentile, 165.17 or about 165 for the ninetieth percentile, and
$174.5 \doteq 174$ for the ninety-ninth percentile.

Comparisons using percentiles are quite simple. If two raw scores are
converted into percentiles, the score with the higher percentile is better than the
other score in relation to the sample from which each is taken.

To make score comparison easy, it is a quite usual practice to **standardize**
an evaluation instrument. This is done by applying it to a large group; perhaps
giving a new IQ test to a, hopefully, representative sample of people around the
country. Standard scores and percentiles are then computed based on this
sample, and anyone subsequently taking the test can be compared to the
reference sample.

There is an interesting and helpful way of using an ogive to determine
percentiles, or to find the score located at a particular percentile. Consider the
ogive of example 1, section 1.2. This ogive is reproduced below, with the vertical
axis, representing percentiles (cumulative relative frequency), somewhat finer
than there.

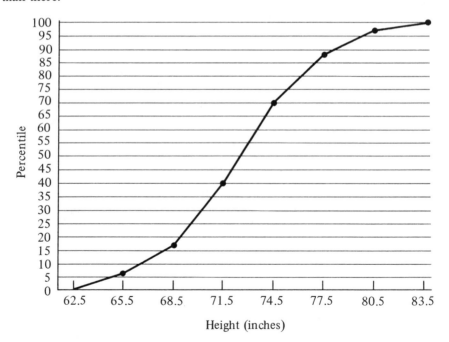

Height (inches)

If the ogive is reasonably smooth, the relationship between any value of the
variable and its corresponding percentile may be obtained by drawing vertical

and horizontal lines from a point on the graph to the axes. In the drawing which follows, a point was selected at random and vertical and horizontal lines drawn to the axes. The height corresponding to that point is 73.8 inches and the percentile is 63. Thus the 63rd percentile can be said to be 73.8 inches, and approximately 63 percent of freshmen are 73.8 or fewer inches tall.

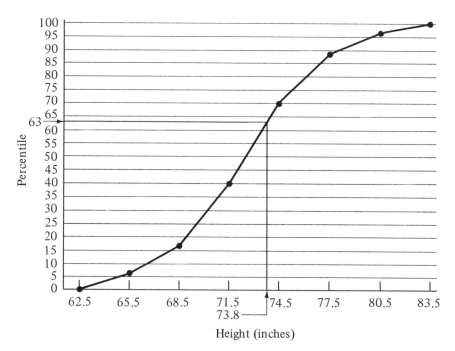

Height (inches)

A few cautions are in order in this use of the ogive. The graph assumes that the variable (number of men) is continuous, but 63 percent of 50 men is 31.5 men. However, the percentile of a piece of data is defined as the percent of pieces of data which the particular piece of data exceeds. The percent of the total number of pieces of data, *up to and including* a particular piece of data, may be read directly from the ogive. Careful interpretation is required, however, depending upon whether the variable is continuous or discrete and upon the size of the sample. If the score 176 exceeds or equals 80 percent of all scores plotted on an ogive for a sample of 100, then 176 exceeds 79 scores and 176 is at the 79th percentile. If the sample includes 1,000 scores, however, and 176 equals or exceeds 80 percent of the scores, it would exceed 799 and would therefore be at the 79.9th percentile, or about the 80th percentile. Also, discrete data requires us to assume that a score is represented by a range—a score of 176 would be represented by 175.5 to 176.5. Thus to determine the percentile value of 176, we would use 175.5 as the lower limit, and the actual point of intersection will be the percentile rank of a score of 176.

In general, to determine the percentile rank of a discrete score, use the lower limit of the unit interval representing the score, draw a vertical line to intersect the ogive, then a horizontal line from the point of intersection to the vertical axis, then read off the percentile rank. For a continuous score, (i.e., a score from a continuous distribution) we look at the size of the sample; we draw the vertical line from the score, obtain the percentile rank from the vertical scale, then, if the sample is small, say less than 200, we subtract one to obtain the percentile.

To obtain a score from a given percentile, the procedure is reversed.

EXAMPLE 2 Using the ogive for the height data, determine the 21st percentile and the percentile rank of 75 inches.

SOLUTION Although the data given are discrete, we will first solve the problem as if it were continuous, to illustrate the procedure, then solve it correctly as a discrete variable.

As a continuous variable from a small sample, we note that the 21st percentile would exceed 21 percent of the scores, and would thus have a cumulative frequency itself of 22 percent. Locating 22 percent, we draw a horizontal line until it intersects the graph, then a vertical line which intersects the horizontal axis at about 69.5 inches. Thus, if the variable were continuous, the 21st percentile would be 69.5 inches. To determine the percentile rank of 75 inches, we locate 75 on the horizontal axis, as shown in the drawing, draw a vertical line until it intersects the graph, then draw a horizontal line from that point on the graph until it intersects the vertical axis. In this case the vertical axis is intersected at about 75 so the cumulative frequency is 75 and, for a small

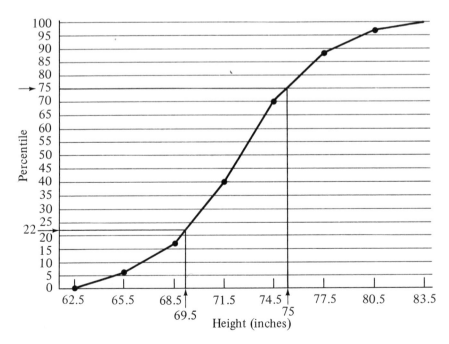

sample, it thus exceeds 74 percent of the scores, so 75 inches has a percentile rank of 74.

For a discrete distribution, the procedure is just slightly different, taking into account the fact that the scores are represented on a continuous graph, such as this one, by *ranges* of values. To determine the 21st percentile, we draw the horizontal line from 21, estimating the point at which the vertical line crosses the horizontal axis to be about 69.3. Thus a value of 69 (i.e., 68.5 to 69.5) has a cumulative frequency of 21 percent, so the 21st percentile is the score which just exceeds that, or 70 inches. To determine the percentile rank of 75, we note that 75 just exceeds 74.5 (in a discrete distribution) so we draw the vertical line from 74.5, obtaining a percentile value of 70; thus 75 inches has a percentile rank of 70. See the following drawing.

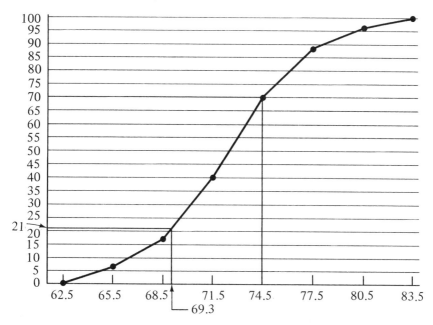

It can be seen from the foregoing that a certain amount of latitude must be given in determining percentiles; this is mitigated by the fact that the results, from grouped data, are estimates at best. In spite of limitations, percentiles remain one of the best ways to determine location in large masses of data.

•Problems

1. A distribution has a mean of 47 and a standard deviation of 12. Determine standard scores for data points 17, 24, 33, 44, 53, 67, and 81.

2. For the frequency distribution of problem 4, section 2.1, determine the

tenth, twenty-second, forty-third, seventy-first, ninety-third, and ninety-sixth percentiles.

3. A distribution has a mean of 156 with a standard deviation of 34. What is the value with a standard score of -1.63? -0.44? 0.76? 2.38?

4. For the data of problem 3, section 2.2, determine the percentile ranks of 2.03, 3.16, 4.92, and 9.63.

5. A subject was given three tests for potential leadership ability. The means and standard deviations of scores for each test, determined by the reference sample, were as follows: Test A, $\bar{x}=4.20, s=0.40$; Test B, $\bar{x}=160, s=20$; Test C, $\bar{x}=36.2, s=5.6$. The subject's scores for the three tests were as follows: Test A, 4.38; Test B, 168; Test C, 37.6. Comparing his results to the reference samples, on which test did he do the best? the worst?

6. Referring to the income data given in problem 13, section 2.1, determine the fifth, twenty-seventh, forty-fourth, sixty-third, eighty-second, and ninety-fourth percentiles.

7. Refer to problem 9, section 1.3; use the ogive to determine the tenth, twenty-fifth, and sixty-fifth percentiles, and to determine the percentile rank of scores of 90, 100, and 125.

2.4 SUMMARY

In order to characterize a distribution we obtain a **measure of central tendency**— a value which is approximately at the center of the distribution—and a **measure of dispersion**—a number which tells us something about the spread of the distribution. One useful measure of central tendency is called the mode. The **mode** is the value or class with the greatest number of data points. If two or more values or classes have the greatest number of data points and are separated by other values or classes, the distribution is bi- or multimodal and may represent more than one population.

The **median** of a set of data is the value which separates the data into two equal sets; one with values greater than the median, the other with values less than the median. The median is most useful to describe data which are scattered, data which are ranked, or data which are bunched at one end, or skewed, or data which contain a few extreme scores.

For most sets of data the primary measure of central tendency is the **mean**.

Mean of a Sample	The mean of a sample containing n pieces of data is given by $$\bar{x}=\frac{\Sigma x}{n} \text{ or } \bar{x}=\frac{\Sigma x \cdot f}{n} \text{ (for grouped data)}$$

For sets of data for which the mean is appropriate, the best measure of dispersion is the **standard deviation**. The most important formulas for finding the standard deviation are given here.

Formulas for the Standard Deviation of a Sample

$$s = \sqrt{\frac{\Sigma(x-\bar{x})^2}{n-1}} = \sqrt{\frac{\Sigma x^2 - n(\bar{x})^2}{n-1}}$$

$$s = \sqrt{\frac{\Sigma x^2 - \frac{(\Sigma x)^2}{n}}{n-1}} = \sqrt{\frac{n\Sigma x^2 - (\Sigma x)^2}{n(n-1)}}$$

$$s = \sqrt{\frac{\Sigma x^2 \cdot f - \frac{(\Sigma x \cdot f)^2}{n}}{n-1}} = \sqrt{\frac{n\Sigma x^2 \cdot f - (\Sigma x \cdot f)^2}{n(n-1)}}$$

The third set of formulas above is for grouped data.

By the empirical rule, if a set of data is normally distributed (bell-shaped, with the data trailing off symmetrically in both directions), about 2/3 of the data lie within one standard deviation of the mean and about 95% lie within two standard deviations of the mean. By **Chebyshev's rule**, no matter what shape the distribution has, at least $1 - 1/k^2$ of the data lie within k standard deviations of the mean.

One way of determining whether the mean or the median is more appropriate to use for a set of data is to calculate Pearson's index of skewedness. If the value of this index is greater than $+1$, the distribution is positively skewed; if it is less than -1, the distribution is negatively skewed. The mean and standard deviation are not appropriate measures for a skewed distribution.

Pearson's Index of Skewedness

$$\text{Index} = \frac{3(\bar{x} - Md)}{s}$$

The relationship between the standard deviation and the size of a sample is set forth in the following table. If a set of data is approximately normally distributed, the standard deviation should not differ appreciably from the fraction of the range listed for the appropriate sample size.

Sample size	5	10	25	100
Fraction	2/5	1/3	1/4	1/5

For data for which the median is appropriate, the best measure of dispersion is the **semi-interquartile range, Q,** which is equal to one-half the difference between the first and third quartiles. **Quartiles, percentiles,** and the median, are all measures of location and comparison for this type of data.

Measures of location and comparison for data for which the mean. is appropriate include **standard scores (z-scores).** Measures of location are useful for comparing scores obtained from different evaluative instruments which evaluate the same thing.

•Problems

1. Twenty-five different stores are rated by an impartial team as to cost-effectiveness ratio, with the following ratings.

87	71	83	67	78
77	69	76	68	85
84	85	70	68	80
74	79	66	85	73
81	78	81	77	75

   (a) Find the mean, median, and mode for the data.
   (b) Determine the standard deviation. Compare with the rule of thumb.
   (c) What is Q?
   (d) Determine the standard score of the highest and lowest values.
   (e) Find the fortieth and fifty-ninth percentiles.

2. A store manager wishes to determine if a product sells well enough to warrant carrying it on the shelves. The number of units sold in each of the last twelve weeks is as follows:

   61 44 51 32 76 44 38 52 43 56 18 67

   (a) Determine the mean and median of the data.
   (b) Determine the standard deviation. Compare with the rule of thumb.
   (c) Find the standard score for the highest and lowest values.
   (d) What is Q?

3. The number of defectives per lot of one thousand parts put out by each of one hundred different machines in a large plant for the most recent shipment is given here.

15	7	11	17	9	23	13	6	9	15
11	6	18	5	14	11	22	9	15	8
3	11	14	18	17	21	19	2	17	3
17	8	14	8	18	9	17	24	13	9
19	15	11	17	20	7	11	14	18	12
8	16	8	10	31	11	17	13	7	13
27	19	9	2	5	12	7	11	9	10
8	14	8	11	6	3	19	22	7	11
11	5	3	18	22	16	8	14	7	17
4	10	7	11	8	17	13	9	11	4

(a) Determine the mean, median, and mode for this set of data.
(b) Calculate the standard deviation.
(c) Find Q.
(d) Determine the fifth, twenty-eighth, fifty-seventh, and seventy-eighth percentiles.
(e) Determine the percentile rank of scores of 8, 14, 19, and 24.

4. A restaurant serves chicken and seafood dinners. The number of seafood dinners served each day for 60 days is given here.

43	44	58	39	41	54	61	39	36	56
48	41	47	51	57	46	31	48	39	48
52	63	51	28	48	33	44	48	57	37
40	45	38	44	58	54	37	41	51	36
47	44	53	37	33	44	37	46	48	66
44	38	44	39	52	55	38	40	46	46

(a) Find the mean, median, and mode of the data.
(b) Determine the standard deviation.
(c) Calculate the value of Q.
(d) Determine the fifteenth, forty-fourth, fifty-eighth, and eighty-third percentiles.

5. A machine has been set to bore holes in aluminum extrusions; the holes will have a mean diameter of 0.15 mm with a standard deviation of 0.005 mm. Extrusions with holes smaller than 0.14 mm or those with holes greater than 0.16 mm are unusable. What proportion would you expect to be unusable
(a) if the distribution of hole sizes is normal?
(b) if nothing is known about the distribution?

6. Bids for a project at site A (in thousands of dollars) were 150, 175, 150, 200, 175. Bids for a similar project at site B were 250, 200, 175, 225, 200, 250, 200, 220. The bids of the XYZ Corporation were 175 at site A, 200 at site B. Which bid was highest *relative* to its group? (Hint: find the standard score for each value.)

7. Mr. Jones belonged to a group for which the systolic blood pressure should be 130, with a standard deviation of 10; for Mr. Adams' group, the systolic blood pressure should be 140 with a standard deviation of 12. If Mr. Jones' blood pressure is 142 and Mr. Adams' blood pressure is 152, which is higher compared to its group?

CHAPTER 2.

Glossary of Terms

assumed mean	percentile
bimodal	population
central tendency	quartiles
Chebyshev's rule	sample
deviation	semi-interquartile range
dispersion	skewed
mean	standard deviation
mean absolute deviation	standard score
median	sum of squares
mode	symmetric
normal distribution	variance

Glossary of Symbols

f	frequency
Md	median
Mo	mode
Q	semi-interquartile range
Q_1	first quartile
Q_3	third quartile
s_2	sample standard deviation
s	sample variance
Σ	sum of
SS	sum of squares
$\bar{x}$	sample mean
z	standard score
$\doteq$	is approximately equal to

Chapter 3

Probability Distributions

3.1 PROBABILITY

Although the primary emphasis of this text is statistics and the use of statistical tools, a knowledge of basic probability is necessary to be able to make proper use of appropriate statistical techniques and to understand the results of their use. Probability deals with the determination of the chances that a particular outcome will occur in a known population of outcomes. For instance, if a lot of eighty parts contains five which are defective, we can determine the chance that a sample of six parts drawn from this lot will contain exactly one defective.

Statistics, on the other hand, deals with the attempt to determine the makeup of a population by using results taken from samples belonging to the population. If a lot of eighty parts contains an unknown number of defectives, and a sample of six parts had exactly one defective, this information coupled with statistical techniques will enable us to make educated guesses as to the number of defectives in the entire lot. Thus probability and statistics are complementary. Probability helps one to understand the relationship between the population and the sample taken from it. Using probability we can infer something about a sample taken from a known population, and we can infer something about a population from the characteristics of a known sample taken from it.

In this chapter we present a bare outline of some of the concepts of probability which are necessary for an understanding of the material which follows. After completing this chapter, the reader is invited to study Appendix B, in which the basic rules of probability are presented and discussed at somewhat greater length.

Let us first try to determine what is meant by the term *probability*. Some years ago, in Monte Carlo, a certain roulette wheel paid off on red for more than twenty consecutive times. Each time during the streak, players made their bets on red or black. Some reasoned that since red and black each appear eighteen times on the wheel they are equally likely and each should come up an equal number of times. Thus, they reasoned, each time red came up made black more likely on the next turn of the wheel. This, they said, is what is meant by the *law of averages*. They also lost a lot of money.

The **law of averages** is a name given to what may be the most widely misinterpreted mathematical statement in existence. In point of fact, there is no such thing as a law of averages. The popular conception is a misunderstood interpretation of a mathematical statement known as the **law of large numbers**. Simply stated, this law says that if an act is repeated a large number of times, the proportion of those times a particular thing happens tends to a fixed number. For instance, if you tossed a coin several million times, you would expect the coin to fall heads up approximately one-half of the tosses. This means that if a coin is tossed a large number of times, the proportion of heads tends to one-half of the total number of tosses. The number one-half is called the **probability** that a head will occur on one toss of the coin.

If four cards—an ace, a king, a queen, and a jack—are thoroughly shuffled and the top card turned over, you would expect it to be the ace about one-fourth of the time. Thus the probability that the ace will be the top card in this case is one-fourth.

Now suppose that you performed the experiment twenty times and no ace appeared. What then of the probability that the ace will appear on the twenty-first drawing? The cards have no memory—each repetition of the experiment has no effect on any other repetition—nor do they have a conscience. The repetitions are **independent**. The cards are no more—and no less—likely to produce an ace on the next repetition than on any other.

In the case of the roulette wheel, there was no connection between any two of the repetitions and no greater likelihood of black on the *next* roll than on any other. The law of large numbers *guarantees* that after an extensive number of trials it is very likely that the proportions of red and black will be approximately equal on an honest roulette wheel; heads and tails will each turn up approximately half the time in coin flipping; and a six will occur on approximately one-sixth of the rolls of a fair die. It says nothing, however about any particular set of occurrences, much less about a particular instance. The law of large numbers does not work by compensation; instead, any unusual deviation is simply buried over the long haul. If a fair coin turns up heads ten times in a row, this occurrence will have little effect upon the proportion of heads after one hundred tosses, appreciably none after one thousand.

The law of large numbers is not necessary, of course, to determine all probabilities. It is not even usable in many cases, such as the determination of the probability of rain on a given day. The principle, however, can be abstracted in many cases. If we wish to determine the probability that a coin will fall head up when tossed, we can toss it a few million times, determine the proportion of heads, and use this to estimate the probability of a head on a single toss. A more practical method is to observe that there are exactly two possibilities, a head and a tail, and they are equally likely. The probability is therefore one-half (1/2 or

0.50) that a head will appear on one toss. In one throw of a die, there are six possibilities, each equally likely, so that the probability that a particular number, say six, will appear on top on a single throw is one-sixth. If one person is to be selected by lot from among five—say two men and three women—the probability that the person selected will be a man is 2/5 since two of the five possibilities are men and the possibilities are equally likely.

The above are examples of **theoretical probability**; that is, probabilities which have been determined on the basis of some expected or theoretical outcomes. Another example of a theoretical probability is the replacement problem. A small boy knocks five books off a shelf. These books are volumes 1–5 of an encyclopedia. The books are scrambled and he replaces them randomly and hurriedly on the shelf. What is the probability that they are in the correct order? Since there are five possible volumes to put in the first place, four volumes to put in the second place after the first place is filled, three subsequent choices for the third place, two for the fourth, and only one for the fifth and last place, there are exactly $5 \cdot 4 \cdot 3 \cdot 2 \cdot 1$ or 120 different ways to place the books back on the shelf, only one of which is correct. If it is assumed that all possibilities are equally likely, the probability that the books have been replaced in the correct order is 1/120.

It is apparent that in order to determine probability it is often necessary to be able to count the number of ways something might occur. If, for instance, three roads lead from town A to town B, and two roads lead from town B to town C, the number of different paths from town A to town C, using these paths, is six. For each of the three roads from A to B, the traveler has a choice of two roads from B to C, so there are $3 \cdot 2$ or 6 different choices. If the number of roads from C to D is four, our traveler has a choice of four roads for each of the six from A to C, so that the number of paths he may travel from A to D, using these roads, is $3 \cdot 2 \cdot 4$ or 24. This example illustrates a basic principle; if an act is performed in several steps and each step can be performed in several different ways, the total number of ways the act can be performed is the product of the individual numbers of ways each step can be performed. This can be stated concisely as follows:

Multiplication Rule	Suppose that an act requires n steps to complete. If these steps can be performed successively in $m_1, m_2, m_3, \ldots, m_n$ ways, then the act can be performed in the order stated in $m_1 \cdot m_2 \cdot m_3 \cdots m_n$ different ways.

If the act requires two steps, the first step can be done in m_1 different ways and the second in m_2 different ways, then the act can be performed in $m_1 \cdot m_2$ different ways. As an extension of this, note that successive probabilities may also be multiplied. If one of two boxes contains a nickel and four pennies, while the other contains a penny and nine nickels, and the box is chosen at random and the coin selected at random, the probability that the first box will be selected is $1/2$ or 0.5. If the first box is selected, the probability that the nickel will be selected is $1/5$ or 0.2. Thus the probability of first selecting the first box and *then* selecting the nickel would be $(0.5) \cdot (0.2)$ or 0.10. The probability of selecting the first box and then selecting a penny would be $(0.5) \cdot (0.8) = 0.40$. The probability of selecting the second box, then selecting a nickel would be $(0.5) \cdot (0.9) = 0.45$, and the probability of selecting the second box and then selecting a penny would be $(0.5) \cdot (0.1) = 0.05$. On the average, then, if we repeated the experiment a large number of times, we would get a nickel $0.10 + 0.45 = 0.55$ of the time, so the probability of getting a nickel would be 0.55 and the probability of getting a penny would be 0.45.

Since a great many cases involving probability deal with equally likely outcomes, in such cases the classical probability rule is applicable. Intuitively, we can see that if an act can be performed in s equally likely ways, of which r of these ways constitute an *event*, the probability of that event occurring on one trial or repetition of the act, or experiment, is r/s.

> *Classical Probability*
>
> If an experiment has s equally likely outcomes, r of which constitute an event, then the probability of the event is r/s.

EXAMPLE 1 What is the probability of obtaining two heads on two tosses of a fair coin?

SOLUTION This experiment consists of two steps, each of which can be performed in two ways, so there are $2 \cdot 2$ or four equally likely outcomes. One of these outcomes, head followed by head, makes up the desired event. The probability of this event is $1/4$ or 0.25.

In addition to theoretical probability, there are two other types of probability. **Subjective probability** is basically determined by an observer's evaluation of all possibilities and assignment of relative chances to each of them on the basis of this assessment. A familiar example of subjective probability is the weatherman's probability of rain tomorrow. **Empirical probability** is probability based on past events. On the assumption that such past events are reasonably representative of future events, the relative frequency of past events is used to represent the probabilities of future events.

EXAMPLE 2 Over the past two hundred working days, the number of defective parts produced by a machine is given by the table which follows. Determine the probability that tomorrow's output will have none defective, at least one defective, an odd number of defectives, no more than 5 defective, and more than 13 defective.

Number defective	Days	Relative frequency
0	50	0.25
1	32	0.16
2	22	0.11
3	18	0.09
4	12	0.06
5	12	0.06
6	10	0.05
7	10	0.05
8	10	0.05
9	8	0.04
10	6	0.03
11	6	0.03
12	2	0.01
13	2	0.01

SOLUTION Using the relative frequency as the empirical probability of the number of defectives, and letting $P(x)$ represent the probability of x defectives in tomorrow's output, then $P(0)=0.25$, $P(\text{at least one})=P(x>0)=0.75$ since the sum of the relative frequencies (i.e., probabilities) of all numbers greater than zero is 0.75. $P(x \text{ is an odd number})=P(x=1, 3, 5, 7, 9, 11, \text{ or } 13)=0.16+0.09+0.06+0.05+0.04+0.03+0.01=0.44$. $P(x \text{ is no more than } 5)=P(x \text{ is } 5 \text{ or less})=P(0, 1, 2, 3, 4, \text{ or } 5)=0.25+0.16+0.11+0.09+0.06+0.06=0.73$. Finally, $P(x>13)=0$ since there are no points corresponding to that event.

•Problems

1. Toss a coin twenty times and record the number of heads. Perform the experiment twenty times and add the totals. Do you notice a leveling effect? If you do not obtain a ratio of approximately 1/2 heads, repeat an additional ten times. The probability of obtaining fewer than 268 or more than 332 heads in the 30 experiments is only 0.01!

2. Select a page from your telephone book and record the frequency of occurrence of last digits of telephone numbers. Combine your results in class and determine the proportions for each digit. The proportions should be approximately equal.

3. Shuffle a deck of cards and deal them out, one at a time, until the first heart appears. Record the number of cards dealt, including the heart. Perform the experiment one hundred times or combine results of five to ten experiments of each student in the class. Compare your average number of cards dealt with the theoretical number, approximately 3.79 per deal. (See solution for explanation.)

4. Joe's Pizza Parlor is offering a special. For a given price one can purchase a large pizza and a drink or else a small pizza, a burger, and a drink. Pizzas come plain or with a choice of either of two toppings. Joe serves hamburgers, cheeseburgers, garlic burgers, and onion burgers. For drinks, the choices are cola, root beer, orange, grape, and cherry. How many different dinners can be purchased on the special?

5. A firm is surveying a community's buying habits preparatory to opening a new store. The survey directions are to choose one family from each floor of an apartment building. The worker enters a building with eight families on the first floor, four on the second, and three on the third. In how many ways can he choose his sample of three? What is the probability that Mr. White's family, which lives on the first floor, is chosen as one of the three?

6. One of a group of twelve students is to be chosen class president. If eight are men and four are women, and all are equally likely to be chosen, what is the probability that the one chosen is a man? What is the probability that Fred Jones, one of the men, will be chosen? Note that the assumption of equally likely outcomes may not be justified.

7. A family is considering buying a dog. If the probability that they will buy a small dog is 0.1, that they will buy a medium-sized dog is 0.3, that they will buy a large dog is 0.2, and that they will buy a very large dog is 0.1, what is the probability that they will buy a dog?

8. An urn contains 3 white, 2 red, 1 blue, and 4 black balls. If one ball is drawn at random, what is the probability that it is
    (a) black?
    (b) either black or white?
    (c) not white?
    (d) both red and blue?

3.2 RANDOM VARIABLES AND PROBABILITY DISTRIBUTIONS

One of the central ideas in probability, and in statistics, is that of a **probability distribution**. A probability distribution describes how probabilities are distributed in a *sample space*. A **sample space** is the set of all possible outcomes for a given "experiment." We can best understand the concept of a probability distribution by first understanding the concept of a *random variable*.

A **random variable** is defined in relation to a sample space simply by assigning numbers to all the possible outcomes or events in the sample space generated by a particular probability experiment. In the preceding section, in example two, a frequency distribution of the number of defective parts produced by a machine was given. In this case the number of defective parts was the random variable and the possible values of this random variable were all integers from zero to thirteen. The assignment of probabilities was made on the basis of the relative frequencies of the various outcomes and the result was a probability distribution. Another example might be the relative frequency of unemployment percentages. The random variable would be the percent of unemployment and the implied possible values of the variable would include all real numbers from zero to one hundred. In practical terms, it would range from the lowest percent of unemployment to the highest.

These two random variables illustrate two different types, namely discrete random variables—those which can take on only a countable number of values —and continuous random variables—those which can be indefinitely subdivided. In the defective parts example, we could not have a fractional number of defective parts, while in the unemployment case, the actual percent of unemployment could be as finely stated as we wished; perhaps 7.134567921 percent unemployment. Discrete random variables are much easier to work with than continuous ones, so we will begin our discussion of probability distributions by investigating the general discrete probability distribution.

Let us look at a particularly simple example of a discrete random variable. If two dice are rolled and the number of dots which come up are observed, the sample space generated by the experiment can be examined. To do this, list an array of ordered pairs which gives all possible outcomes as points of the sample space. Since there are six outcomes on one die and six on the second, by the multiplication rule there are 6·6 or 36 points in all. To understand that the ordered pairs (1, 2) and (2, 1) represent different points, suppose that one of the dice is red, the other green. You can then look at the number of dots on the red die first and then at the number of dots on the green die. The first number in each ordered pair represents the number of dots on the red die; the second number is the number of dots on the green die. The complete set of all points in the sample space is given below.

(1, 1)	(2, 1)	(3, 1)	(4, 1)	(5, 1)	(6, 1)
(1, 2)	(2, 2)	(3, 2)	(4, 2)	(5, 2)	(6, 2)
(1, 3)	(2, 3)	(3, 3)	(4, 3)	(5, 3)	(6, 3)
(1, 4)	(2, 4)	(3, 4)	(4, 4)	(5, 4)	(6, 4)
(1, 5)	(2, 5)	(3, 5)	(4, 5)	(5, 5)	(6, 5)
(1, 6)	(2, 6)	(3, 6)	(4, 6)	(5, 6)	(6, 6)

A random variable can be defined on this sample space by letting x, the variable, represent the number of dots showing on the two dice. Then x can take on all integral values from 2 through 12.

If a coin is tossed four times and we let the random variable be the number of heads that come up, the variable can take on all integral values from 0 through 4.

It can thus be seen that a random variable can be used to assign numbers to the disjoint events which make up a sample space. The entire collection of values the random variable can take on, together with the associated probabilities for each of these values, define a probability distribution.

More than one random variable can be defined on a sample space. For example, if we toss a coin until a tail appears, or three times, whichever comes first, there are four points in the sample space. They can be listed as follows: {T, HT, HHT, HHH}. One method at arriving at this sample space is the use of a tree diagram as illustrated below.

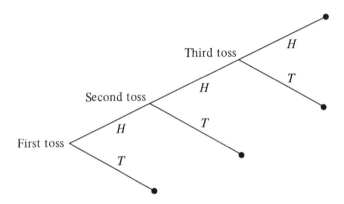

The various points of this sample space are not equally likely. The probability of getting a tail on the first toss is $1/2$, while the probability of getting a head on the first toss and then a tail is $(1/2)\cdot(1/2)$ or $1/4$; that is, we will get a head on the first toss half the time, and each time we get a head on the first toss, we would expect to get a tail on the second toss half the time. We may assign numbers to the various outcomes according to several different schemes. We may be interested only in the number of *tosses* in this experiment. This random variable has the possible values 1, 2, 3. We may be interested in the number of *heads*; this variable has the values 0, 1, 2, or 3. Finally, we may be interested in the number of *tails*; this variable has the values 0 and 1.

EXAMPLE 1   A coin is tossed until a tail appears, or three times, whichever comes first. Let x represent the number of tosses on one experiment, y represent the number of heads on one experiment, and z represent the number of tails on one experiment. Determine the probability distributions for x, y, and z.

SOLUTION   The sample space consists of four possible outcomes. We list these together with the value of each random variable which is associated with each point.

Point	Probability	Value of		
		x	y	z
T	1/2	1	0	1
H, T	1/4	2	1	1
H, H, T	1/8	3	2	1
H, H, H	1/8	3	3	0

If we let $P(x)$ represent the probability of x, $P(y)$ the probability of y, and so forth, we can make up a table of all possibilities. The values of x are 1,2,3; the probabilities associated with these values are 1/2, 1/4, and 1/4 (since two points both have three tosses), so the probability distribution can be represented by a table such as the following:

x	1	2	3
P(x)	1/2	1/4	1/4

Probability distribution tables can be listed either horizontally (as above) or vertically. By examining the table above, we can obtain the following probability distributions for y and z.

y	P(y)
0	1/2
1	1/4
2	1/8
3	1/8

z	P(z)
0	1/8
1	7/8

Thus the probability that a tail will be obtained on one repetition of the experiment is 7/8.

   If you have difficulty obtaining the probabilities for the various points of the sample space, note that each toss of the coin has two outcomes, each equally likely, so with a probability of 1/2. A second toss will occur only if a head appears on the first, so the probability of obtaining a head and a tail is the probability of getting a head on the first toss times the probability of getting a tail on the second toss. The probability of obtaining a head on the first toss and a head on the second toss is also 1/4, but by the nature of the experiment as defined, a third toss would be necessary, with the probability of obtaining a head equal to 1/2 and the probability of obtaining a tail equal to 1/2. Thus the probability of obtaining a head on all three tosses would be 1/8 and the probability of obtaining two heads, then a tail would also be 1/8.

EXAMPLE 2 Two dice are tossed. If x represents the total number of dots on the two faces, determine a probability distribution for this random variable.

SOLUTION   Referring to the sample space given previously, we find that the sample points group themselves into distinct events as shown below.

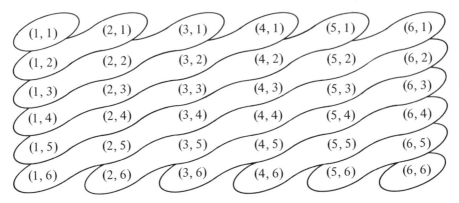

We see that there are 36 points in total, each equally likely, so the probability corresponding to each event is the number of points in the event divided by 36. As can be seen from this illustration, the number of points which correspond to the value $x=2$ is one, so $P(2)=1/36$. We can summarize the results with a table such as the following.

x	P(x)
2	1/36
3	2/36
4	3/36
5	4/36
6	5/36
7	6/36
8	5/36
9	4/36
10	3/36
11	2/36
12	1/36

An examination of the foregoing examples yields the rather unsurprising result that the sum of the probabilities is always equal to one. If we examine the probability distribution of any random variable, and if we exclude as a possible value of the variable any value with zero probability, we have the following characterization of a discrete probability distribution.

Discrete Probability Distribution	For any discrete random variable x, the probability $P(x)$ is positive for each value of x, and the sum of the probabilities is one.

Discrete probability distributions can be graphed by various techinques, one of the most important of which is the histogram, previously discussed in section 1.2. In the histogram, each value of the variable is represented by a unit of length on the base and a rectangle drawn above it to indicate its probability. If we had a probability distribution defined by $P(x) = x/15$ for $x = 1, 2, 3, 4, 5$, the histogram for this distribution would be represented as follows.

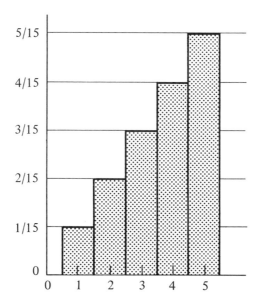

Note that the numbers $1, 2, 3, 4, 5$ lie in the *center* of the rectangles. That is, we represent "1" by the interval from 0.5 to 1.5, "2" by the interval 1.5 to 2.5, and so forth. By doing this, the probability of an event is equal to the area of the rectangle representing it. For example, the probability of obtaining a "2" in this experiment is $1 \cdot (2/15)$. Note also that the scales on the bottom and on the side are different. This is allowable since the relations between the probabilities remain clear. As another example, let us construct a histogram for the two dice experiment.

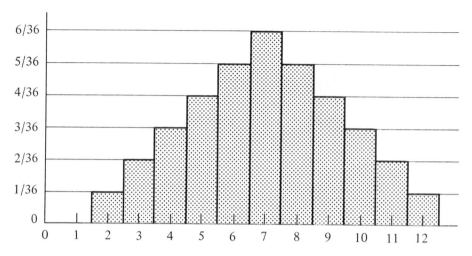

Again, each probability is represented by the area of the rectangle and each discrete value of the variable is represented by an interval; for example "8" is represented by 7.5 to 8.5, so the rectangle has a base equal to one, height equal to 5/36, and an area equal to 5/36 square units (the probability). The sum of the area of all the rectangles representing the distribution adds up to one.

It can be seen that a probability distribution is related quite closely to a frequency distribution. In each case there is a variable which takes on different possible values; in the one case we have the frequency of occurrence of each value, in the other we have the probability of occurrence of each value. Descriptive measures of probability distributions are quite valuable for a variety of reasons. The most important ones are the mean, variance, and standard deviation. The formulas applicable to samples cannot be used in probability distributions. In order to understand the formulas required, it is first necessary to examine the concept of *expected value*.

The **expected value** of a random variable is the sum of each value of the variable multiplied by its probability. In more precise terms we have the following definition:

Expected Value

If a variable x has values $x_1, x_2, x_3, \ldots, x_n$ and probabilities $P(x_1), P(x_2), P(x_3), \ldots, P(x_n)$ respectively, then the expected value of the variable, x, is given by
$$E(x) = x_1 \cdot P(x_1) + x_2 \cdot P(x_2) + \cdots + x_n \cdot P(x_n).$$

Thus for any random variable, $x, E(x) = \Sigma x \cdot P(x)$ for each value of the random variable x.

EXAMPLE 3 An ordinary die is rolled once. What is the expected value of the number of dots on the uppermost face?

SOLUTION The random variable, x, has possible values 1, 2, 3, 4, 5, and 6, each with probability $1/6$. The expected value is thus

$$E(x) = 1 \cdot (1/6) + 2 \cdot (1/6) + 3 \cdot (1/6) + 4 \cdot (1/6) + 5 \cdot (1/6) + 6 \cdot (1/6)$$

$$= 3.5$$

DISCUSSION The number obtained, 3.5, is impossible to obtain on one roll of the die and is not, in fact, a possible value of the random variable. The term "expected value" (sometimes called "mathematical expectation" or simply "expectation") is not something we expected, but rather a weighted average—each of the possible outcomes weighted by its own probability. It is a long term average. If we repeated the experiment of tossing a die a large number of times, we would "expect" the overall mean of the variable to be 3.5.

EXAMPLE 4 A promotor has scheduled an outdoor event which will be cancelled in case of rain. He estimates the probability of rain to be 0.04. If the event is cancelled, he will lose the $1,000 he has invested in publicity and supplies. If it is a success, however, he expects 500 people to come, each spending an average of $5.00. If he will need to spend an additional $1.50 in supplies for each person who comes (on the average), what is his expected return?

SOLUTION If it does not rain, he expects a return of 500($3.50)−$1,000 or $750; the probability that this will happen is 0.96. If it rains, he will have a loss of $1,000 (a return of −$1,000); the probability of this happening is 0.04. Thus his expected return is $750(0.96)+(−$1,000)(0.04)=$680.

EXAMPLE 5 A man wishes to take out accident insurance for $100,000 covering his first parachute jump. The insurance company does a little research and finds that, out of 243,117 recorded jumps of the same type as this one, only 84 have resulted in accidents. If they wish to charge $14 administrative fee, what should the premium be in order to make it "fair" to both parties? The term "fair" means that expected value for both parties is zero; that is, expected profit must equal expected loss, exclusive of any handling charges which are reasonable and applicable.

SOLUTION   The probability that the insurance company will have to pay off is 84/243,117, so the expected value of the policy is ($100,000)(84/243,117) or about $34.55. Thus the company should charge $48.55. To check, note that the probability that the company will make $34.55 is $1-(84/243,117)$ or 243,033/243,117; 84/243,117 is the probability that the company will lose $99,965.45. The expected value of the policy to the company, then, is

$$(\$34.55)(243,033/243,117)+(-\$99,965.45)(84/243,117) \doteq -0.001$$

which is zero for all practical purposes. The reason it is not exactly zero is because $34.55 is rounded off slightly from $34.55126544.

The concept of expected value can be applied directly to a probability distribution. The mean of a probability distribution is simply the expected value of the variable. The mean of the distribution is symbolized by the Greek letter μ (mu).

Mean of a Probability Distribution   For any discrete probability distribution, $\mu = E(x)$; that is, $\mu = \Sigma x \cdot P(x)$ for each value of the random variable x.

EXAMPLE 6   Determine the mean of the probability distribution for the number of defective parts given in example 2, section 3.1.

SOLUTION   The distribution is reproduced below. Let x represent the number of defective parts and $P(x)$ the probability of occurrence of each value of the variable.

x	P(x)
0	0.25
1	0.16
2	0.11
3	0.09
4	0.06
5	0.06
6	0.05
7	0.05

x	P(x)
8	0.05
9	0.04
10	0.03
11	0.03
12	0.01
13	0.01

Then $\mu = 0(0.25) + 1(0.16) + 2(0.11) + 3(0.09) + \cdots + 12(0.01) + 13(0.01)$
  $= 3.48$

This can be interpreted to mean that the expected number of defective parts, *on the average*, for the next *n* lots will be 3.48. Obviously no one lot will have exactly 3.48 defective parts. If, however, defective parts meant returns, and returns cost, say $5.00 per part in replacement, this would mean that we should set aside, or expect to pay, an average of $17.40 per shipment in replacement of defective parts.

EXAMPLE 7 Find the mean of the following probability distributions:

x	P(x)		y	P(y)
1	1/6		1	1/9
2	1/6		2	1/18
3	1/6		3	1/3
4	1/6		4	5/18
5	1/6		5	1/6
6	1/6		6	1/18

SOLUTION $E(x) = 1(1/6) + 2(1/6) + 3(1/6) + 4(1/6) + 5(1/6) + 6(1/6)$

  $\mu_x = 3.5$

  $E(y) = 1(1/9) + 2(1/18) + 3(1/3) + 4(5/18) + 5(1/6) + 6(1/18)$

  $\mu_y = 3.5$

Each probability distribution has the mean 3.5. Subscripts are used to differentiate the means.

Both of the distributions in example 7 had integral values from 1 through 6 and means of 3.5. Yet these distributions are quite different. Histograms for the two distributions show this:

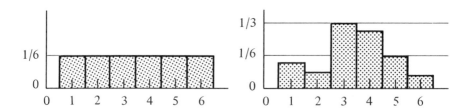

The second of these distributions is "heavier" in the vicinity of the mean. In fact, 11/18 of this distribution lies within one unit of the mean in contrast to only 1/3 (or 6/18) of the first distribution. This cannot be seen from the mean, however, or from the values of the random variable. A number of different measures have been used to record the actual dispersion of a distribution, but the most effective are two related measures, the **variance** and **standard deviation**, both of which were encountered in relation to samples in the last chapter. Since a probability distribution is not a sample, a different approach to these measures must be used. The variance is the expected value of the squared deviations from the mean, $E(x-\mu)^2$. For a probability distribution, the variance is symbolized by σ^2, where σ is the Greek letter sigma (lower case). For a discrete probability distribution, the special rule is given here.

Variance of a Probability Distribution

For any discrete probability distribution, $\sigma^2 = E(x-\mu)^2$; that is, $\sigma^2 = \Sigma(x-\mu)^2 \cdot P(x)$ for each value of the random variable x.

EXAMPLE 8   Find the variances of the probability distributions given in example 7 above.

SOLUTION   A table with appropriate headings is often useful. First, of course, we must find the mean, then find $(x-\mu)$ for each x and square it, multiply by the probability, then take the sum.

x	$P(x)$	$x \cdot P(x)$	$x - \mu$	$(x-\mu)^2$	$(x-\mu)^2 \cdot P(x)$
1	1/6	1/6	$-5/2$	25/4	25/24
2	1/6	2/6	$-3/2$	9/4	9/24
3	1/6	3/6	$-1/2$	1/4	1/24
4	1/6	4/6	1/2	1/4	1/24
5	1/6	5/6	3/2	9/4	9/24
6	1/6	6/6	5/2	25/4	25/24
		$\mu = 3.5$ (or 7/2)			$\sigma^2 = 70/24 \doteq 2.92$

In general, the above procedure is not the most efficient one to use in finding the variance of a probability distribution. Instead it can be shown that $E(x-\mu)^2 = E(x^2) - \mu^2$. For discrete probability distributions the formula becomes

$$\sigma^2 = (\Sigma x^2 P(x)) - \mu^2$$

This says to square each value, multiply by its probability, then sum. This sum must be corrected by subtracting the square of the mean.

We use this method to find the variance of the second probability distribution of example 7.

y	$P(y)$	$y \cdot P(y)$	y^2	$y^2 \cdot P(y)$
1	1/9	1/9	1	1/9
2	1/18	1/9	4	2/9
3	1/3	1	9	3
4	5/18	10/9	16	40/9
5	1/6	5/6	25	25/6
6	1/18	1/3	36	2
		$\mu = 3.5$ (or 7/2)		251/18

Then

$$\sigma^2 = \frac{251}{18} - \left(\frac{7}{2}\right)^2 = \frac{502}{36} - \frac{441}{36} = \frac{61}{36} \doteq 1.69.$$

Note that the variances are consistent with the fact that *more* of the area in the first histogram is away from the mean than in the second. Thus if two distributions with similar valued random variables have different variances, a smaller variance indicates that more of the distribution tends toward the center (or mean) of the distribution.

Useful as the variance is, it has one major drawback—it is not in the same units as the random variable. Its units are the *square* of the value units. Thus it cannot be plotted on the graph (or histogram) of the distribution. The simple procedure of taking the square root of the variance gives a number which can be plotted. This measure is called the standard deviation and is symbolized by σ. In terms of the distribution itself, it is the square root of the mean squared deviation.

Standard Deviation of a Probability Distribution

For any discrete probability distribution,

$$\sigma = \sqrt{\Sigma(x-\mu)^2 P(x)} = \sqrt{x^2 P(x) - \mu^2}$$

for each value of the random variable x.

EXAMPLE 9   Find the standard deviation of the probability distribution of example 6.

SOLUTION   The table is reproduced below, with appropriate calculations.

x	$P(x)$	x^2	$x^2 \cdot P(x)$
0	0.25	0	0
1	0.16	1	0.16
2	0.11	4	0.44
3	0.09	9	0.81
4	0.06	16	0.96
5	0.06	25	1.50
6	0.05	36	1.80
7	0.05	49	2.45
8	0.05	64	3.20
9	0.04	81	3.24
10	0.03	100	3.00
11	0.03	121	3.63
12	0.01	144	1.44
13	0.01	169	1.69
			24.32

Then $\sigma^2 = 24.32 - (3.48)^2 = 12.2096$, so $\sigma = \sqrt{12.2096} \doteq 3.49$.

•Problems

1. Find the mean and standard deviation of the probability distribution defined by the following table:

x	$P(x)$
1	3/80
3	27/80
7	11/80
9	17/80
14	13/80
16	9/80

2. A probability distribution is defined by the following table:

Class	Probability
4–6	0.08
7–9	0.17
10–12	0.31
13–15	0.19
16–18	0.12
19–21	0.06
22–24	0.04
25–27	0.02
28–30	0.01

   (a) Draw a histogram for the distribution.
   (b) Draw a smooth curve approximating the histogram.
   (c) Using class marks, calculate the mean and standard deviation for the distribution.

3. Suppose the probabilities that a world series will last 4, 5, 6, or 7 games are, respectively, 0.1, 0.2, 0.4, and 0.3. Determine the mean, variance, and standard deviation of the distribution.

4. The probabilities that 0, 1, 2, 3, or 4 accidents will occur in the Holland Tunnel between 7:30 and 10:30 on a Monday morning are, respectively, 0.92, 0.04, 0.02, 0.01, and 0.01. How many accidents would be expected during this period on a particular Monday morning? During 100 such periods?

5. Mr. Jones is selling his business. A realtor promises that the probability he will make $20,000 is 0.20, that he will make $12,000 is 0.35, that he will make $4,000 is 0.10, and that he will break even is 0.15. The realtor concedes, however, that the probability that Mr. Jones will lose $6,000 is

0.15, and that there is even a possibility that Mr. Jones will lose $12,000. He claims, however, that there are no other possibilities. If he is correct on all counts, what is Mr. Jones' expected return on this sale?

6. Two dice are tossed and the sum of the dots on the top faces recorded. Calculate the mean and variance of this probability distribution.

7. If one team is approximately twice as strong as the other in a World Series, the probabilities that the series will end in 4, 5, 6, or 7 games are, respectively, 0.21, 0.30, 0.27, and 0.22. What is the expected number of games in such a series? If Mrs. Black has tickets only to the fourth and fifth games, what is the expected number of games she will see?

8. A coin is tossed four times, or until a head appears, whichever comes first. Calculate the expected number of tosses on one experiment; calculate the expected number of tails.

9. A man wishes to buy a one-year term insurance policy on his life for $50,000. The insurance company calculates that the probability he will die during this period to be 0.0042. If the premium includes $30 administrative costs, what should be the premium for the policy?

10. On a roulette wheel, there are 38 slots, equally spaced, numbered $00, 0, 1, 2, 3, \ldots, 36$. For a $1.00 bet, if your number wins you receive $35.00 (in addition to your $1.00 being returned); otherwise you lose your $1.00. Determine the expected value, on one bet, of a gambler who bets on a number.

11. On the roulette wheel described in problem 10, 18 slots are red, 18 are black, 00 and 0 are green. A person can, if he desires, place a bet on red or black, or on odd or even (00 and 0 are considered to be neither). For a $1.00 bet, if he wins, he receives an additional $1.00; if he loses, he is out $1.00. Calculate the expected value, on one bet, of a gambler who bets one color, or on odd, or on even.

3.3   SUMMARY

In this chapter we have presented some of the basic notions of probability and probability distributions.

Theoretical probability is determined on the basis of an examination of all possible outcomes and a theoretical exact determination of relative likelihood of each. Subjective probability is determined by an observer's evaluation of all possibilities and assignment of relative chances to each of them on the basis of this assessment. Empirical probability is probability based on the relative frequency of past events.

Two concepts used to help us determine probabilities are the multiplication rule and the definition of classical probability.

Multiplication Rule	Suppose that an act requires n steps to complete. If these steps can be performed successively in m_1, $m_2, m_3, \ldots, m_n$ ways, then the act can be performed in the order stated in $m_1 \cdot m_2 \cdot m_3 \cdots m_n$ different ways.

Classical Probability	If an experiment has s equally likely outcomes, r of which constitute an event, then the probability of the event is r/s.

In this chapter we have also studied probability distributions, with emphasis on discrete probability distributions. For a discrete probability distribution the probability, $P(x)$, is positive for each value of x, and the sum of the probabilities is one.

In order to study characteristics of a probability distribution, we discussed expected value. The expected value of a variable is given by $E(x) = \sum x \cdot P(x)$, the sum of each value of the variable times its probability. The most important characteristics of a probability distribution are the mean and standard deviation. These special formulas are given here again.

Mean and Standard Deviation of a Probability Distribution	$\mu = E(x) = \sum x \cdot P(x)$ $\sigma = \sqrt{E(x-\mu)^2} = \sqrt{(\sum x^2 \cdot P(x)) - \mu^2}$

•Problems

1. From experience, the toll taker feels that the probability that an automobile paying toll on the Sunshine Skyway is a Chevrolet is 0.21, that it is a Ford is 0.17, that it is a Pontiac is 0.11. Assuming that he is correct, if an automobile pulls up to pay a toll, what is the probability that it is
   (a) a Chevrolet or a Ford?
   (b) a Ford or a Pontiac?
   (c) neither a Chevrolet nor a Pontiac?
   (d) none of these three makes?

2. A retired teacher is considering purchasing a fast food franchise. Franchise A requires an investment of $50,000, of which $35,000 can be borrowed and repaid from the profits at the rate of $1122.11 per month for three years. Franchise B requires an investment of $40,000 of which $25,000 can be borrowed and repaid from the profits at the rate of $801.50 per month for three years. The teacher has the needed $15,000, and she examines the records of both franchises and estimates the approximate net weekly income for the two franchises to have the following probability distributions:

| | Probability | |
Weekly income	Franchise A	Franchise B
$200	0.10	0.05
300	0.20	0.30
400	0.25	0.40
500	0.25	0.20
600	0.20	0.05

   (a) Which franchise has the higher expected weekly income?
   (b) Which franchise has the more variable income? (Hint: determine the standard deviation for both distributions.)
   (c) Which franchise has the greater expected monthly excess of income over the franchise fee payment? (Use one month $=4\frac{1}{3}$ weeks.)
   (d) What factors can you think of which may influence the teacher's decision as to which franchise to purchase?

3. For the past six months the unemployment rate has been over 10 percent eight percent of the time; at least 8 percent, but less than 10 percent, forty percent of the time, at least 6 percent, but less than 8 percent, fifty percent of the time, and less than 6 percent the remainder of the time. Using these relative frequencies as estimates of future probability what is the probability that the unemployment rate during the next week will be
   (a) less than 8 percent?
   (b) at least 6 percent, but less than 10 percent?
   (c) at least 8 percent?

4. A probability distribution is defined by $P(x)=(x^2+1)/n$ for $x=1, 2, 3, 4$. Determine the value of n. Make a histogram for the distribution.

5. Calculate the mean and standard deviation of each

    (a)

x	13	17	21	24	25
$P(x)$	0.2	0.4	0.2	0.1	0.1

    (b)

x	107	114	121	128	135
$P(x)$	0.22	0.27	0.16	0.21	0.14

    (c)

x	5	11	13	18	22	27	33	34	39
$P(x)$	0.20	0.14	0.23	0.11	0.13	0.09	0.05	0.04	0.01

    (d)

x	1,000	1,100	1,200	1,300
$P(x)$	0.1	0.2	0.3	0.4

6. Eight pints of blood are stored in the hospital laboratory. It is known that exactly three of these are Type O, but it is not known which three. Two pints of Type O blood are needed. One pint at a time is removed from storage and typed. If it is Type O it is used; if not it is labelled as to type and the next pint tested.

    (a) Make a probability distribution for the number of pints it will be necessary to type in order to obtain a pint of Type O.

    (b) Determine the mean and standard deviation for this distribution.

CHAPTER 3

Glossary of Terms

classical probability
empirical probability
expected value
independent
law of large numbers
probability
probability distribution

random variable
sample space
statistics
subjective probability
theoretical probability
tree diagram

Glossary of Symbols

$E(\ )$ expected value of

μ mean of a probability distribution

$P(\ )$ probability of

σ standard deviation of a probability distribution

σ^2 variance of a probability distribution

Binomial Probability

4.1 THE BINOMIAL DISTRIBUTION

Many business decisions are made in an atmosphere of an either-or situation. A contract is signed, or it isn't. A product is defective or it isn't. A purchase is made or it isn't. In all cases in which there are only two outcomes, the situation is said to have a **binomial** result. Many cases involve sampling from a population which has only two outcomes; in such a case the population is called a **binomial population**. The term "binomial" comes from the Latin and means, literally, "two names."

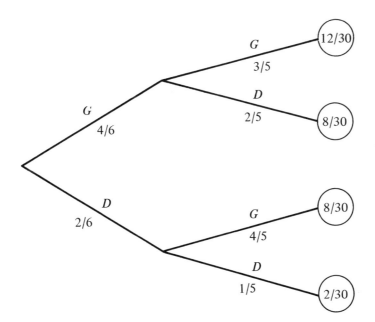

Two particular types of binomial sampling arise naturally. If a coin is tossed, the outcome on the first toss has no effect on the outcome of the second toss; these outcomes are independent. If we have six light bulbs, four of which are good, and two of which are defective, and we select two, the outcome of the second draw very much depends upon the outcome of the first draw, unless we replace the first one after it is drawn. The probability that the first bulb drawn is a good one is 4/6 (or 2/3). If the first one is good, the probability that the second one is good is now 3/5, since we have only five bulbs left, of which three are good. If the first one is defective, the probability that the second one is good is 4/5. The different outcomes, with their probabilities are shown on the tree diagram on page 83.

The numbers which are circled are the probabilities of the particular event occurring. The probability that the first one is good, and the second one is good is (4/6)(3/5) or 12/30; the probability that the first one is good and the second one is bad is (4/6)(2/5) or 8/30; the probability that the first one is bad and the second one good is (2/6)(4/5) or 8/30, and the probability that the first one is bad and the second one is bad is (2/6)(1/5) or 2/30. If we consider the random variable to be the number of good bulbs on one draw of two bulbs (or on two draws of one bulb without replacement) from our set of four good and two defective bulbs, we have $P(2) = 12/30 = 2/5$, $P(1) = 16/30 = 8/15$, and $P(0) = 2/30 = 1/15$. The procedure of sampling without replacement is of great use when we are presented with a finite, usually relatively small, set of items, from which we wish to draw a sample to infer characteristics. For example, perhaps we know that a lot of 500 ball bearings comes from a shipment in which 200 are unusable because they are too large, or else from a shipment from which only 50 are unusable for the same reason. We wish to draw a sample, say, of 25, and decide on the basis of this sample which shipment the lot comes from. The probability that all 25 are good, if it comes from the first shipment is given by the product

$$\frac{300}{500} \cdot \frac{299}{499} \cdot \frac{298}{498} \cdot \frac{297}{497} \cdots \frac{276}{476}.$$

If it comes from the second shipment the probability that all 25 are good is

$$\frac{450}{500} \cdot \frac{449}{499} \cdot \frac{448}{498} \cdots \frac{426}{476}.$$

Probabilities for 24, 23, 22, 21, etc., can be calculated similarly, but it is obviously tedious to do it this way. Fortunately, a simpler method exists.

To use the simpler method it first is necessary for us to learn about *permutations* and *combinations*. Consider a set of three letters, A, B, C. In how many ways can these three letters be arranged as a set of three? This question can be answered by listing the arrangements as follows: {ABC, ACB, BAC, BCA, CAB, CBA}. Counting these arrangements, we find that there are six different ones. Instead of writing down these combinations, we could have applied our basic multiplication rule. There are three choices for the first place, two for the second one, and one for the third, so by the multiplication rule we have $3 \cdot 2 \cdot 1$ different choices, or 6. If we wished to consider any three different letters of the alphabet instead of restricting ourselves to A, B, and C, we would have $26 \cdot 25 \cdot 24$ or 15,600 different arrangements or **permutations**. This principle can be formulated as follows:

Permutation Rule	If r objects are to be selected from a set of n different objects in such a way that the order of selection is important, the number of permutations is given by $$n \cdot (n-1) \cdot (n-2) \cdots (n-r+1).$$

This rule follows directly from the multiplication rule where $m_1 = n, m_2 = n-1, m_3 = n-2, \ldots, m_r = [n-(r-1)] = n-r+1$. In particular, the number of permutations of n objects taken all together is $n(n-1)(n-2) \cdots 3 \cdot 2 \cdot 1$. This expression is generally written $n!$ (read "n factorial") to facilitate writing it down.

It follows than that the number given in the permutation rule can be written as $n!/(n-r)!$ since

$$\frac{n!}{(n-r)!} = \frac{n(n-1)(n-2)\cdots(n-r+1)(n-r)(n-r-1)\cdots 3\cdot 2\cdot 1}{(n-r)(n-r-1)\cdots 3\cdot 2\cdot 1}$$

$$= n(n-1)(n-2)\cdots(n-r+1)\frac{(n-r)!}{(n-r)!}$$

$$= n(n-1)(n-2)\cdots(n-r+1).$$

Note that for this to be valid in all cases, we must define $0! = 1$. For example, the number of permutations of n objects taken n (all) at a time is $n!$ By the formula, when $r = n$, $n!/(n-n)! = n!/0! = n!$ only when $0! = 1$.

If the order is not significant, as when sampling is interested only in the outcome taken as a whole, not in a particular order, the formula for permutations does not apply. For instance, if three letters are to be selected from the set $\{a, e, i, o, u\}$, the number of permutations is given by $5 \cdot 4 \cdot 3$ or 60. If the order is not important, and the selection {a, e, o} and the selection {e, o, a} are considered to be the same, we must derive a new formula. Sets of this type are called **combinations**. We list all the 60 permutations of three letters selected from {a, e, i, o, u} below.

aei	aie	eai	eia	iae	iea
aeo	aoe	eao	eoa	oae	oea
aeu	aue	eau	eua	uae	uea
aio	aoi	iao	ioa	oai	oia
aiu	aui	iau	iua	uai	uia
aou	auo	oau	oua	uao	uoa
eio	eoi	ieo	ioe	oei	oie
eiu	eui	ieu	iue	uei	uie
eou	euo	oeu	oue	ueo	uoe
iou	iuo	oiu	oui	uio	uoi

These sixty permutations are here grouped into ten sets of six each; each set of six consists of the permutations of the same three letters. There are, then, exactly 60/6 or 10 different sets of three letters, if order is disregarded. Thus to determine the number of combinations of three letters selected from a set of five, we determine the total number of permutations, $5 \cdot 4 \cdot 3$, and divide by the number of permutations of each distinct group of three letters. If we were to select four different letters from the alphabet, without regard to order, we note that there are $26 \cdot 25 \cdot 24 \cdot 23$ different permutations of four letters, and each different set of four letters can be arranged in $4 \cdot 3 \cdot 2 \cdot 1$ different orders, so the total number of combinations is

$$\frac{26 \cdot 25 \cdot 24 \cdot 23}{4 \cdot 3 \cdot 2 \cdot 1}$$

or 14,950. This generalizes to the following rule:

Combination Rule

The number of combinations of n objects taken r at a time is given by

$$\frac{n(n-1)(n-2)\cdots(n-r+1)}{r(r-1)(r-2)\cdots 3 \cdot 2 \cdot 1} \text{ or } \frac{n!}{r!(n-r)!}$$

This number is most commonly symbolized as $\binom{n}{r}$. Note that this is a symbol for a positive integer and not a fraction such as n/r.

> **EXAMPLE 1** How many committees of six can be chosen from an organization with thirty members?

SOLUTION Using the combination rule,

$$\binom{30}{6} = \frac{30 \cdot 29 \cdot 28 \cdot 27 \cdot 26 \cdot 25}{6 \cdot 5 \cdot 4 \cdot 3 \cdot 2 \cdot 1} = 593,775.$$

COMMENT In using a calculator to calculate combinations, it is possible that multiplication of the numbers in the numerator may yield an overflow. To avoid this, start out by taking 30 divided by 6, multiply by 29, divide by 5, multiply by 27, divide by 4, and so on. Without a calculator, of course, it is better to simplify first. See Appendix A for an illustration.

One other detail is of interest. If r is more than half of n, we may observe that, for every combination of r elements selected, there is a corresponding combination of $(n-r)$ elements left out. It follows then that

$$\binom{n}{r} = \binom{n}{n-r}.$$

Thus if we were to select 10 birthday cards from a group of 15, this is equivalent to selecting a group of 5 from the 15, so instead of writing

$$\frac{15 \cdot 14 \cdot 13 \cdot 12 \cdot 11 \cdot 10 \cdot 9 \cdot 8 \cdot 7 \cdot 6}{10 \cdot 9 \cdot 8 \cdot 7 \cdot 6 \cdot 5 \cdot 4 \cdot 3 \cdot 2 \cdot 1}$$

we could just write

$$\frac{15 \cdot 14 \cdot 13 \cdot 12 \cdot 11}{5 \cdot 4 \cdot 3 \cdot 2 \cdot 1}.$$

Notice that 10, 9, 8, 7, 6 would cancel out in the former.

Now suppose that the group in example 1 consisted of 20 men and 10 women. How many different ways can we select a committee composed of 4 men and 2 women? There are $\binom{20}{4}$ or 4,845 ways to select 4 men from 20, and, for each of these, there are $\binom{10}{2}$ or 45 ways to select 2 women from 10. There are then $\binom{20}{4} \cdot \binom{10}{2} = 218,025$ ways of selecting exactly 4 men and 2 women from this group. Since there are $\binom{30}{6}$ or 593,775 ways of selecting a committee of 6, the probability that a committee of six persons selected from a group of 20 men and 10 women will have exactly 4 men and 2 women is equal to

218,025/593,775 or about 0.367. This generalizes easily to the so-called **hypergeometric distribution**.

<table>
<tr>
<td>*Hyper-
Geometric
Distribution*</td>
<td>If a population consists of A objects of one kind and B objects of a second kind, the probability of selecting (at random, without replacement) x objects of type A and $n-x$ objects of type B is given by

$$P(x) = \frac{\binom{A}{x}\binom{B}{n-x}}{\binom{A+B}{n}}$$</td>
</tr>
</table>

EXAMPLE 2   Use the definition of the hypergeometric distribution to determine the probability distribution of the number of good bulbs in a set of three bulbs selected at random from a set of ten bulbs, of which eight are good and two are bad.

SOLUTION   The variable takes on the values 1, 2, 3, since if $x=0$, there would have to be 3 bad ones. Then, using the formula, we have

$$P(1) = \frac{\binom{8}{1}\binom{2}{2}}{\binom{10}{3}} = \frac{8 \cdot 1}{120} = \frac{1}{15}, \text{ since } \binom{10}{3} = \frac{10 \cdot 9 \cdot 8}{3 \cdot 2 \cdot 1} = 120,$$

$$P(2) = \frac{\binom{8}{2}\binom{2}{1}}{\binom{10}{3}} = \frac{\frac{8 \cdot 7}{2 \cdot 1} 2}{120} = \frac{28 \cdot 2}{120} = \frac{7}{15},$$

$$P(3) = \frac{\binom{8}{3}\binom{2}{0}}{\binom{10}{3}} = \frac{\frac{8 \cdot 7 \cdot 6}{3 \cdot 2 \cdot 1}}{120} = \frac{56}{120} = \frac{7}{15}.$$

It should be noted that there are often short cuts in computation when working with a hypergeometric probability distribution.

The hypergeometric distribution is important particularly in cases in which A and B are relatively small, particularly if n is not less than, say 10% of the total $A + B$. For large values of A and B, however, the calculations get progressively more difficult. For example, if we are selecting a sample of 25 from the lot of 500 mentioned before, of which 200 are defective, the probability of, say, 10 defective is given by

$$P(10) = \frac{\binom{200}{10}\binom{300}{15}}{\binom{500}{25}}$$

which can be calculated (and is equal to about 0.165), but there are other distributions which can be used to approximate this quite closely. One of these is the binomial distribution, which is useful in many cases in which it is directly applicable, and useful in many others in which it is used to approximate the hypergeometric.

If we were to replace each light bulb drawn before drawing the next in example 2 above, the probability of a good bulb would not change from draw to draw. This is called *sampling with replacement*. If we know that a machine produces defective parts 25% of the time and if the production of one part has no effect on the next, the probability of the next part produced is 0.25 at any time. If we know that each of five boxes contains 25 parts, exactly one of which is defective, and we select one part from each box at random, what is the probability that none of the parts is defective, or that all the parts will be defective, or that two of the parts will be defective?

These are examples of a **binomial experiment.**

Binomial Experiment

A binomial experiment is an experiment consisting of a fixed number of trials for which

1. there are exactly two possible outcomes for each trial;
2. outcomes and probabilities remain constant from trial to trial; and
3. successive trials are independent.

The probability of success is usually symbolized by p in a binomial experiment, and the probability of failure is symbolized by $1-p$ (or sometimes by q, with the understanding that $p+q=1$.) In the five boxes, if "success" is defined as selecting a defective part, then $p=1/25$ or 0.04. The probability of "failure" is 24/25 or 0.96. Note that the words "success" and "failure" do not necessarily carry the usual connotation; if we were examining the results of operating table errors in which the patient suffered serious consequences, the term "success" might refer to the patient dying, which would hardly be a success in any usual use of the word. The probability of all five parts being defective is $(0.04)(0.04)(0.04)(0.04)(0.04)=(0.04)^5$. The probability of selecting no defective parts is $(0.96)^5$. How do we calculate the probability of exactly two defective parts? If there are two defective parts there are three good ones, and the probability that the first two are defective and the last three are good is $(0.04)^2(0.96)^3$. In fact, no matter in what order the two bad and three good parts occur, the probability remains the same. All we need to do, then, is to determine how many orders there are. What we are doing is selecting two bad parts from five boxes, and the number of different combinations of two boxes selected from five is $\binom{5}{2}$ or ten. Each particular combination has the same probability as that mentioned before: $(0.04)^2(0.96)^3$. Since there are two of these combinations, the probability of two successes is $10(0.04)^2(0.96)^3$ or about 0.014.

In general, if a binomial experiment is repeated n times, the probability that x successes will occur in a particular order is $p^x(1-p)^{n-x}$, while there are $\binom{n}{x}$ possible orders. This leads to the following rule.

Binomial Probability	If a binomial experiment has n trials and the probability of "success" on one trial is p, the probability of exactly x successes is given by $$P(x)=\binom{n}{x}p^x(1-p)^{n-x}$$

If x represents a random variable, the set of all values which the variable can take, namely 0 through n, together with the associated probabilities, is called a **binomial distribution**. Note that the essential difference between the binomial and hypergeometric distributions is whether the sampling is done with or without replacement.

EXAMPLE 3   A company opens five branch outlets. From experience they know that approximately one-fifth of new outlets experience difficulty in penetrating the sales region and fail. Using this estimate determine the probability distribution for the number of these outlets which will fail.

SOLUTION The number of outlets which can fail is 0, 1, 2, 3, 4, or 5. The outcome is binomial since an outlet either fails or it doesn't; we assume that the probability is 1/5 for any particular store and that the success or failure of any outlet does not affect that of any other outlet. Under these assumptions, we have a binomial distribution and the results may be tabulated as follows:

$$n=5, \quad p=0.2, \quad 1-p=0.8$$

x	$P(x)$
0	$\binom{5}{0}(0.2)^0 \cdot (0.8)^5 = 0.32768 \doteq 0.328$
1	$\binom{5}{1}(0.2)^1 \cdot (0.8)^4 = 0.40960 \doteq 0.410$
2	$\binom{5}{2}(0.2)^2 \cdot (0.8)^3 = 0.20480 \doteq 0.205$
3	$\binom{5}{3}(0.2)^3 \cdot (0.8)^2 = 0.05120 \doteq 0.051$
4	$\binom{5}{4}(0.2)^4 \cdot (0.8)^1 = 0.00640 \doteq 0.006$
5	$\binom{5}{5}(0.2)^5 \cdot (0.8)^0 = 0.00032 \doteq 0+$

The symbol $0+$ above means that, since all other decimals were rounded off to three places, that number when rounded off to three places would be zero, but the number is not zero; that is, it is less than 0.0005 but greater than zero.

DISCUSSION Note that since five outlets are opened and one-fifth of all newly opened outlets fail, it is tempting to conclude that exactly one $(5 \cdot (1/5))$ will fail. Reasoning such as this is similar to misapplications of the law of large numbers. This is the expected value—the expected number of failures.

The mean and variance of both the binomial and hypergeometric distributions can be calculated as with any probability distribution. There are, however, special formulas for both distributions. For the binomial distribution, if n is the number of trials, p is the probability of success, then $\mu = np$, $\sigma^2 = np(1-p)$ and $\sigma = \sqrt{np(1-p)}$. For the hypergeometric distribution, if there are A objects of one kind, B objects of a second kind, and n is the number of objects drawn, then the distribution of type A objects drawn has mean

$$\mu = \frac{nA}{A+B}, \quad \sigma^2 = \frac{nAB(A+B-n)}{(A+B)^2(A+B-1)}.$$

EXAMPLE 4 Determine the mean and standard deviation of the data of example 3 by using the usual methods, and by using the special formula.

SOLUTION   Using the usual method, we have the following table:

x	$P(x)$	$x \cdot P(x)$	x^2	$x^2 P(x)$	
0	0.32768	0	0	0	
1	0.40960	0.40960	1	0.40960	
2	0.20480	0.40960	4	0.81920	
3	0.05120	0.15360	9	0.46080	
4	0.00640	0.02560	16	0.10240	$\sigma^2 = 1.8 - (1)^2 = 0.8$
5	0.00032	0.00160	25	0.00800	
		$\mu = 1.00000$		1.80000	

Using the short cut formulas, $\mu = np = 5(0.2) = 1$, $\sigma^2 = np(1-p) = 5(0.2)(0.8) = 0.8$.

> **EXAMPLE 5**   A shipment contains 1,000 phonograph cartridges, 950 of Type M91, 50 of Type M95. Unfortunately the various cartridges became jumbled during the shipment and it cannot be determined which is which without breaking the seals and opening the boxes. A customer wants 5 Type M95 and 15 Type M91. The exasperated clerk simply takes 20 at random from the shipment and gives them to the customer. What is the probability that the customer actually receives what was ordered? What is the mean and variance of the distribution?

SOLUTION   Since this involves sampling without replacement, the hypergeometric distribution is the appropriate model. The probability of obtaining exactly 5 Type M95 is given by

$$P(5) = \frac{\binom{50}{5}\binom{950}{15}}{\binom{1000}{20}} \doteq .001978 \doteq 0.002$$

and

$$\mu = \frac{20(50)}{1000} = 1, \text{ and } \sigma^2 = \frac{20(50)(950)(980)}{(1000)^2(999)} \doteq 0.932.$$

Since calculation of the above is tedious, we observe that a sample of 20 is a small portion of the shipment of 1,000, and decide that the binomial model is close enough. To do this, we ignore that the sampling is without replacement and act as though the assumptions for the binomial are met. Under these assumptions, we have $n = 20$, $p = 0.05$, so

$$P(5) = \binom{20}{5}(0.05)^5(0.95)^{15} \doteq 0.00224 \doteq 0.002$$

and $\mu = 20(0.05) = 1$, $\sigma^2 = 20(0.05)(0.95) = 0.95$, which is very close indeed. There are even simplifications for the binomial, as we shall see, to make it even easier for us.

To justify even further the use of the binomial as an approximation to the hypergeometric distribution, consider a group of people, of which $1/5$ own Chevrolets. If one person is selected from the group, the probability that that person will own a Chevrolet is $1/5$ or 0.200. If we replace that person and select a second person at random (it may or may not be the same person), the probability that that person will own a Chevrolet is also 0.200. If, as is usually the case, the second selection is made without replacing the first one, the acts are not independent, but *conditional*; that is, the condition of the first selection affects the second, so the binomial model is not appropriate, rather the hypergeometric model should be used. Let us examine, however, the effect of group size on the probability of the second selection. In a group of ten people, if the first one selected owns a Chevrolet, the probability that the second will own a Chevrolet is reduced to $1/9$; if the person selected first does not own a Chevrolet, the probability that the second person does is $2/9$. Obviously the probabilities are quite different. As the group gets larger, however, the gap between the probabilities lessens considerably. The following chart gives the probability that the second person selected owns a Chevrolet if the first person selected (1) owns a Chevrolet or (2) does not own a Chevrolet.

	P(Second person owns a Chevrolet if	
N = group size	first person does)	first person doesn't)
10	0.1111	0.2222
50	0.1837	0.2041
100	0.1919	0.2020
500	0.1984	0.2004
1,000	0.1992	0.2002
5,000	0.1998	0.20004
10,000	0.1999	0.20002

We can see that, for a sufficiently large population size, the probabilities do not differ appreciably from 0.2. For a group (population) of 10,000, for example, the probability that the last person selected owns a Chevrolet, if the first 99 did not is raised to 0.202, which is not much of a change. For complete precision the hypergeometric should be used, but if the sample is relatively small, the population large, and p not much over 0.25 (or $1 - p$ not much over 0.25), minor discrepancies are usually ignored and the binomial model used.

•Problems

1. A box contains four good light bulbs, two defective ones. A bulb is selected at random and put in the socket. If it works, it is left there; if defective, it is discarded and another bulb selected. The process is continued until a good bulb is found. Give the probability distribution for the number of bulbs which will be tried. Give the mean and variance of the distribution.

2. A box contains four good light bulbs, two defective ones, as in problem 1, but this time there are two sockets to fill. The same process is used as in problem 1. Give the probability distribution for the number of bulbs which will be tried. Give the mean and the variance of the distribution.

3. In a study of oxygen deprivation effects, four guinea pigs are born to a litter which had been subjected to a 15% reduction in the amount of oxygen to the placenta. Theoretically, one-third of the group would show effects of this treatment. Let x represent the number of guinea pigs in a litter of four showing the effects of this treatment. Determine the probability distribution for x, its mean and standard deviation.

4. Two baseball teams play a three game series. The probability that the home team will win any particular game is 0.55. Assume that the outcomes are independent. Give the probability distribution for the number of games won by the home team.

5. Two dice are thrown. A success is a 7 or 11. The experiment is repeated four times. What is the mean and variance of the distribution of successes?

6. What is the probability that a five card poker hand contains exactly two aces? One ace? No aces?

c7. The sex ratio of humans at birth is 100 females to 105 males. What are the theoretical proportions of 3, 2, and 1 males in a sample of 5 newborns? What is the mean number of males for the distribution?

8. Four students on campus are selected at random and asked if they qualify for the work study program. If 1/10 of all students on campus qualify for work study, give the probability distribution for x, the number of students in the sample qualifying for work study. Determine the mean and standard deviation for x. Assume the student body is very large.

9. A random sample of five persons is selected from a group of 300 persons, in which 100 favor capital punishment and 200 are opposed. Determine the probability that exactly two of those selected favor capital punishment. Use the hypergeometric distribution. If we use the binomial model, what would the probability be? Complete both distributions and compare the results.

10. Repeat problem 9 if 100 favor capital punishment and 400 are opposed.

11. Repeat problem 9 if 1,000 favor capital punishment and 4,000 are opposed.

4.2 USING BINOMIAL TABLES

Even the relatively small numbers of the previous section make the task of computing the probabilities of a range of values quite tedious. Extensive tables for the probabilities in the binomial distribution are available. These tables generally come in two parts. One part gives individual probabilities: the probability of obtaining exactly x successes in n trials of a binomial experiment. The other part gives cumulative probabilities: the probability of obtaining r *or more* successes in n trials of a binomial experiment. Since the entries for individual probabilities can be found easily from the cumulative tables, but the converse is not true, we shall restrict our attention solely to the cumulative tables.

A short table of cumulative probabilities is given in Table 2. Values are given for $n = 2, 3, 4, \ldots, 25$, and for $p = 0.01, 0.05, 0.10, 0.20, 0.30, 0.40, 0.50, 0.60,$ 0.70, 0.80, 0.90, 0.95, and 0.99. Each three-digit entry in the table should be read as a decimal; that is, an entry of 983 means a probability of 0.983. The symbol $1-$ means that the probability is less than 1, but larger than 0.9995, while the symbol $0+$ means a positive probability less than 0.0005. There are actually twenty-four such tables which are presented consecutively since the column headings do not change.

Now suppose we wish to compute the probability of five or more successes in eight trials when $p = 0.4$. We have $n = 8, r = 5, p = 0.4$, so we go to the corresponding entry in the table and find the entry 174. This tells us that $P(x \geq 5) \doteq 0.174$. We can check by finding the individual probabilities and adding them together as follows:

$$P(x \geq 5) = P(5) + P(6) + P(7) + P(8)$$

$$= \binom{8}{5}(0.4)^5(0.6)^3 + \binom{8}{6}(0.4)^6(0.6)^2$$

$$+ \binom{8}{7}(0.4)^7(0.6) + (0.4)^8$$

$$= 56(0.01024)(0.216) + 28(0.004096)(0.36)$$

$$+ 8(0.0016384)(0.6) + (0.00065536)$$

$$= 0.12386304 + 0.04128768 + 0.00786432 + 0.00065536$$

$$= 0.1736704$$

$$\doteq 0.174$$

Notice how much simpler it is to look in the tables.

To find the probability of fewer than r successes, note that $P(x<r)=1-P(x\geq r)$. Thus the probability of fewer than five successes in eight trials with $p=0.4$ is about $1-0.174$ or 0.826.

We could also look for probabilities of failure. Fewer than five successes is equivalent to four or more failures. The probability of failure is 0.6, so we can look in the table for $n=8$, $r=4$, $p=0.6$, and directly read 0.826, so that $P(x<5)\doteq 0.826$.

Finally, to find the probability of exactly five successes in eight trials for $p=0.4$, we can find $P(x\geq 5)$ and $P(x\geq 6)$ and subtract to get $P(5)$, since $P(x\geq 5)=P(5)+P(6)+P(7)+P(8)$, and $P(x\geq 6)=P(6)+P(7)+P(8)$ so that $P(x\geq 5)-P(x\geq 6)=P(5)$. We already have $P(x\geq 5)\doteq 0.174$; from Table 2, with $n=8$, $r=6$, $p=0.4$, we find $P(x\geq 6)\doteq 0.050$. Thus $P(5)\doteq 0.174-0.050\doteq 0.124$. Direct calculation (from above) gives $P(5)=0.12386304\doteq 0.124$.

For illustrative purposes a small portion of Table 2 is reproduced here.

				p	
n	r	0.05	0.30	0.60	0.70
10	0	1	1	1	1
	1	401	972	1 $-$	1 $-$
	2	086	851	998	1 $-$
	3	012	617	988	998
	4	001	350	945	989
	5	0+	150	834	953
	6	0+	047	633	850
	7	0+	011	382	650
	8	0+	002	167	383
	9	0+	0+	046	149
	10	0+	0+	006	028

Each entry in the table refers to a binomial experiment for which n, the number of trials, is equal to ten. The letter r stands for r or more successes. Thus if the probability of success on one trial is 0.30 and there are ten trials, then the probability of four or more successes is 0.350. The term $r=4$ is used to imply that x is 4, 5, 6, 7, 8, 9, or 10. Thus $P(x\geq 4)\doteq 0.350$ for the case where $n=10$ and $p=0.30$. Similarly, if $n=10$, $p=0.60$, then $P(x\geq 7)\doteq 0.382$, and $P(x\geq 8)\doteq 0.167$. Then, for $n=10$, $p=0.60$, $P(7)\doteq 0.382-0.167=0.215$.

EXAMPLE 1   Use the binomial tables to calculate $P(x\geq 6)$ and $P(6)$ for $n=10$, $p=0.6$.

SOLUTION $P(x\geq 6)\doteq 0.633$; $P(x\geq 7)\doteq 0.382$, so $P(6)\doteq 0.633-0.382=0.251$. Direct calculation yields $P(6)\doteq 0.2508\doteq 0.251$.

EXAMPLE 2   If $n=10$, $p=0.7$, use two methods to calculate $P(x<5)$.

SOLUTION   Method 1: $P(x<5)=1-P(x\geq5)\doteq1-0.953=0.047$.
    Method 2: $P(x<5)$ using $p=0.70$ is identical to $P(x\geq6)$ if $p=0.30$
$P(x\geq6)\doteq0.047$.

EXAMPLE 3   A medical study showed that, in a survey of 15,000 men
who had a heart attack and recovered, then subsequently died, 60% died of
a second heart attack, while 40% died of other causes. The case histories of
20 men who have had a heart attack are under study. Using the empirically
determined probability and the assumption that the binomial model may be
used here (even though the hypergeometric is appropriate), determine the
probability that ten or fewer of these men will die of a second heart attack.
(Note that the assumption means that the result will be an approximation,
but the fact that the sample is quite small compared with the population—
that of all living men who have had a heart attack—makes the approximation quite a good one.)

SOLUTION   Here we have $p=0.60$, $n=20$, $r=11$ so, from Table 2, $P(x\geq11)$
$\doteq0.755$. Then $P(x\leq10)\doteq0.245$.

Probabilities of ranges of values can be calculated from the tables quite
easily as well. In example 3, for instance, suppose we want the probability that
at least eight, but no more than 15 of the men will die from a second heart
attack. We can determine $P(x\geq8)=0.979$; this, however, includes the probabilities of 16, 17, 18, 19, and 20 as well. $P(x\geq16)=0.051$, so $P(8\leq x\leq15)=0.979-$
$0.051=0.928$. This would, of course, be the sum of $P(8)$ through $P(15)$.

EXAMPLE 4   From experience a salesman knows that 65% of the
potential customers who spend more than fifteen minutes examining a
particular display will buy something. What is the probability that at least
seven of the first ten customers entering the store and spending more than
fifteen minutes examining the display will buy something?

SOLUTION   With the proper tables, one would look for $n=10$, $r=7$, $p=0.65$.
Our limited tables, however, do not have $p=0.65$. To find the value we can use
interpolation. Since $P(x\geq7)=0.382$ for $p=0.60$, $n=10$, and $P(x\geq7)=0.650$ for
$p=0.70$, $n=10$, it is reasonable to assume that, since 0.65 is midway between
0.60 and 0.70, the desired probability will be approximately midway between
0.382 and 0.650. If we take half the difference between the two and add it to the
smaller value, we obtain 0.516. We then estimate $P(x\geq7)\doteq0.516$ for $p=0.65$,
$n=10$.

Interpolation in this way is based on the assumption that if we plot the graph of the probabilities, the graph drawn between any two points on the graph is a straight line. This is not always true. In fact, it is possible to have $P(x)$ for $p = \frac{1}{2}(p_1 + p_2)$ to be greater than either $P(x)$ for p_1 or $P(x)$ for p_2. In such a case, linear interpolation would yield the wrong answer. However, it is correct in many, if not most cases, and increased familiarity with the tables and their uses can lead to an awareness of when the approximation is valid and when it is not.

> **EXAMPLE 5** From past experience a golfer knows that he will hit his drive into a sandtrap from the green about 1/3 of the time. Using this assumption what is the probability that he will hit the ball into a sand trap on exactly five of the first nine holes?

SOLUTION The probability 1/3 is not on Table 2, so we must use interpolation. We can determine either $P(5)$ for $p = 0.3$, $P(5)$ for $p = 0.4$, and interpolate, or determine $P(x \geq 5)$ and $P(x \geq 6)$ for $p = 1/3$ by interpolation, and subtract. Both methods should yield the correct answer which, by direct calculation, is about 0.102.

Method 1: For $p = 0.30$, $P(x \geq 5) \doteq 0.099$, $P(x \geq 6) \doteq 0.025$, so $P(5) \doteq 0.074$; for $p = 0.40$, $P(x \geq 5) \doteq 0.267$, $P(x \geq 6) \doteq 0.099$, so $P(5) \doteq 0.168$. Since 1/3 is 0.333..., is 1/3 of the way from 0.30 to 0.40, we take 1/3 of the difference between 0.074 and 0.168. The difference is 0.094, so we add 1/3 of this, about 0.031, to 0.074, obtaining $P(5) \doteq 0.105$.

Method 2: For $p = 0.30$, $P(x \geq 5) \doteq 0.099$; for $p = 0.40$, $P(x \geq 5) \doteq 0.267$; interpolating, we obtain, $P(x \geq 5) \doteq 0.099 + (1/3)(0.267 - 0.99) = 0.155$ for $p = 1/3$. To determine $P(x \geq 6)$ for $p = 1/3$, we take $0.025 + (1/3)(0.099 - 0.025) \doteq 0.50$. Then, for $p = 1/3$, $n = 9$, $P(5) \doteq 0.155 - 0.050 = 0.105$.

•Problems

In problems 1–10, x is the number of successes in n trials of a binomial experiment with probability of success equal to p. Determine the probabilities in problems 1–6.

1. $P(x \geq 11)$ and $P(11)$ for $n = 20$, $p = 0.7$.
2. $P(x \leq 5)$ and $P(5)$ for $n = 12$, $p = 0.2$.
3. $P(x > 18)$ and $P(20)$ for $n = 22$, $p = 0.8$.
4. $P(x > 14)$ and $P(x < 14)$ for $n = 25$, $p = 0.4$.
5. $P(x \geq 7)$ and $P(7)$ for $n = 15$, $p = 0.45$.

6. $P(x < 12)$ and $P(12)$ for $n = 25$, $p = 0.75$.

7. For $n = 20$, find the value of p for which $P(x \geq 14) = 0.250$.

8. For $n = 15$, $p = 0.6$, find the value of r for which $P(x \geq r) < 0.05$.

9. For $n = 25$, $p = 0.4$, find the value of r for which $P(x \geq r) < 0.10$.

10. For $n = 18$, $p = 0.35$, find the value of r for which $P(x \geq r) < 0.05$.

11. A gas station has been grossing over \$1,000 a day on the average of 8 days in ten over the past several months. Assuming this to be an accurate measure, what is the probability that the station will gross over \$1,000 at least five times in the next six days? Fewer than ten times in the next 14 days?

12. A coin is tossed 16 times. What is the probability that there will be more than 4 heads, but less than 12 heads?

13. A soft drink company claims that their cola tastes "unique." Four different brands of cola are set before a taster who is to choose the one which is "different" (supposedly, of course, the company's brand). Now suppose that there really is no difference in the way that they taste to the tasters, but each of three tasters picks one of the drinks anyway, not knowing which is which since they are in identical containers, distinguished only by letters on the side. What is the probability that at least two of the tasters will select the "correct" drink by chance alone?

14. Of every 1,000 parts produced by a machine, on the average, ten are defective. What is the probability that some, but not all, of a sample of three of these parts are defective?

c15. The sex ratio of humans at birth is 100 females to 105 males. What is the probability that, in six single births, at least half the babies born are females. Compare this with the result which would be obtained if we used a sex ratio of 1 to 1.

16. A random sample is drawn from a group of Spanish-American people in a large city. If the group is large enough to use the binomial model, and if one-fifth of the group are unable to speak English, what is the probability that at least half the sample will be able to speak English in a sample of 6? 7? 8? 15? 20? 25?

17. If 30% of the viewers in a town watch a particular television show, what is the probability that a majority of 25 persons sampled will not watch the show?

18. A salesman has made sales on about 15% of his calls. What is the probability that he will make sales on exactly five of his next 20 calls? On at least five of his next 20 calls?

19. A basketball player makes about 75% of his free throws. What is the probability that he will make exactly four of his next eight attempts? At least four of his next eight attempts?

20. A multiple choice quiz has 20 questions with four responses on each

question. To pass, you must get at least 12 correct. If you guess on every question, what is the probability that you will pass?

4.3   THE POISSON DISTRIBUTION (OPTIONAL)

The last discrete distribution to be investigated in detail is the **Poisson distribution,** named for the early nineteenth century French mathematician S. D. Poisson. Unlike the hypergeometric and binomial distributions, the Poisson distribution is focussed on the mean number of occurrences per unit time, distance, or area, when that mean number is small. Assumptions include independence of occurrences, uniform distribution of occurrences over the interval, and independence of starting point. Uniform distribution of occurrences means that, if we would expect 0.5 occurrences in one time period, we would expect 1.5 occurrences in three time periods. Independence of the starting point means that it does not matter when or where we begin examining the outcomes.

   Examples of distributions having a Poisson model include the number of telephone calls passing through a switchboard, the number of electron tubes requiring replacement in an assembly per period of time, breakage of parts per job, number of blemishes per square foot in the enamel finish of an automobile, number of fish caught per person in a unit of time. One formula for the distribution is this one:

Poisson Distribution

$$P(x) = \frac{e^{-m} \cdot m^x}{x!} \text{ for } x = 0, 1, 2, 3, \cdots$$

where m is the mean or expected number of occurrences of x, the random variable, per unit.

   As an example, suppose that an office is considering reducing the number of telephone lines in the office as an economy measure. Keeping careful records, they find that the average number of telephone calls during the busiest period, 10 AM to Noon and 1 PM to 4 PM (a period of 5 hours) was 75, and the average length of a call was 6 minutes. The minimum number of lines needed would be a number which would make the probability that all the lines are busy as small as possible. Since the average call lasts 6 minutes, we want to determine the probable number of calls in any given 6 minute period. There are 50 six-minute periods in five hours, so that there are an average of $75/50 = 1.5$ calls per six-minute period. We conclude that the distribution of calls in a six-minute period is Poisson with a mean of 1.5. Table 3 lists cumulative Poisson probabilities for a selected set of values of m. Let us look at the portion of the table relevant to this example.

r	$m = 1.5$
0	1
1	777
2	442
3	191
4	066
5	019
6	005
7	001
8	

The blank opposite the 8 means that the probability of 8 or more occurrences is very close to zero. Note that, by its very nature, the Poisson distribution does not have a finite limit, but probabilities quickly approach 0.

According to this table, the probability of five or more phone calls in a six-minute period is about 0.019, less than one chance in 50, while the probability of four or more is 0.066. To be on the safe side, the office manager would probably have five lines, so that they will probably all be busy only about 2% of the time. If he or she decided to have only four lines, they would probably be all busy about 7% of the time. If that is acceptable, the four lines would be enough.

Individual probabilities can also be calculated as with the binomial. For example, if $m = 1.5$, we can subtract successive probabilities to obtain $P(0) \doteq 0.223$, $P(1) \doteq 0.335$, $P(2) \doteq 0.251$, etc. Poisson distributions occur quite often in business settings, particularly in queuing situations, as lines at the tellers' windows in a bank, or at the checkout stand at a supermarket (how many should be open?).

EXAMPLE 1 The number of tropical storms in a given area is approximated by a Poisson distribution in which m is the mean number of storms per period of time. The tropical storm period lasts approximately five months and, assuming that the storms are just as likely to occur at any part of this period as at any other, calculate the probability that a tropical storm will occur during the period a tourist will be staying in an area of Florida in which there have been an average of four tropical storms per year. He will be staying there from September 1 to the 15th.

SOLUTION Since this is half a month, the mean number for that period would be 0.4. From Table 3, the probability of one or more storms during that period is 0.330.

EXAMPLE 2   An oil company is planning on drilling three wells in an estuarine area in Central America. One part used in the drilling has a breakage rate of once per five wells drilled. In order to avoid having to send back for additional parts, they wish to take along replacements as needed. On the other hand, any parts not used will be discarded, and they are expensive. How many extra parts should be taken so that the probability of having to send back for more parts is less than 0.05?

SOLUTION   Since the part breaks on the average of once every five wells, the mean number breaking per well is 0.2; for three wells—the unit we are concerned with—the breakage rate is 0.6. From Table 3, with $m = 0.6$, the probability of two or more breakages is 0.122, while the probability of three or more breakages is 0.023. Thus we should take two extra parts.

One of the particularly good uses for the Poisson distribution is as an approximation to the binomial when p is small. As a rule of thumb, if p is less than 0.10 and n is at least $1000p$, the binomial can be approximated by a Poisson with $m = np$. Note also that this applies as well if $1 - p$ is less than 0.10. The reason that this is quite useful is that the Poisson distribution depends only upon m, while the binomial depends upon both. For example, if a sample of 20 is drawn from a set of TV picture tubes of which 1% are defective, the cumulative binomial distribution and cumulative Poisson (for $m = 0.2$) are given below:

Binomial		Poisson	
r	(Table 2)	r	(Table 3)
0	1	0	1
1	182	1	181
2	017	2	018
3	001	3	001
4	0+	4	

The agreement is almost perfect. *Of even more importance is the fact that the Poisson can be used to fill in gaps on the binomial tables*, say for values of p such as 0.005, 0.02, 0.03, etc.

EXAMPLE 3   Determine the probability distribution for the number of new car buyers in a sample of college students taken from a population in which approximately 2% are new car buyers.

SOLUTION   The Poisson approximation to the binomial can be used here with $m = 25(0.02) = 0.5$. From Table 3, the cumulative probability distribution can be converted to an individual probability distribution by subtracting successive terms. We then have the following:

x	$P(x)$
0	0.607
1	0.303
2	0.076
3	0.012
4	0.002
over 4	0+

We can calculate probabilities directly, if desired, as a check. If so, we obtain the following:

x	$P(x)$
0	0.603
1	0.308
2	0.075
3	0.012
4	0.001
5	0+

Again, the agreement is quite good. As n increases, while p remains the same, the approximation gets even closer.

As a final comment, the mean and variance of the Poisson distribution are both equal to m. This is also in quite close agreement with the mean and variance of a binomial distribution if p is small. For instance, in example 3, the Poisson distribution has $m = 0.5$ and variance equal to 0.5; the binomial distribution with $n = 25$, $p = 0.02$, has mean equal to $25(0.02) = 0.5$ and variance equal to $25(0.02)(0.98) = 0.49$.

•Problems

1. Customers arrive randomly at a bank on Friday at an average rate of 60 during the period from 11:30 to 1:00. What is the probability that more than ten customers will arrive during a given twelve-minutes?

2. The number of typographical errors on a page follows a Poisson distribution. A typist has made an average of 2.5 typographical errors per page

over the past few weeks. He finds that, if he makes more than four errors on a page, it is faster to retype the page than to go back and change the mistakes. What is the probability that he will retype a given page? What is the expected number of pages he will retype in a manuscript of 150 pages?

3. The number of orders received for a certain item was found to be Poisson with a mean of ten per day. The items are manufactured and delivered to the shipping room twice per day. How many should be kept on hand in order to keep the probability of running out of the item during any particular half-day period less than 0.05? Assume that five are delivered to the shipping room twice per day. What is the probability that there will be no orders for the item on a particular day? During a particular half-day?

4. An appliance is sold with or without a service contract. Service contracts cost $30 per year. The mean number of calls for service on this appliance have been determined to be 1.5 per year. The cost of a service call is $15. Both service contracts and service calls cover labor only and parts are additional. If Mr. Jones buys an appliance, what is the probability that he would be better off buying a service contract than paying for the calls as they occur? What is the probability that he would be better off not buying the service contract? What is the probability that it would not make any difference?

5. A group of 200 college students has 20 which are graduating *cum laude*. A random sample of ten students is to be selected from the group for a discussion with the president. Determine the probability that at least two of the ten will be *cum laude* graduates

   (a) using the hypergeometric distribution. (Hint: determine $P(0)$ and $P(1)$, then subtract from 1.00.)
   (b) using the binomial approximation to the hypergeometric.
   (c) using the Poisson approximation to the binomial.

6. Repeat problem 5, finding the probability that exactly four of the ten will be *cum laude* graduates.

7. Repeat problem 5 if the group is 1,000 college students with 20 *cum laude* graduates.

8. Repeat problem 7, finding the probability that exactly four of the ten will be *cum laude* graduates. Compare the results of problems 5–8.

9. Approximately 1% of television tubes manufactured by XWP Corp. are defective. A shipment of 100 is sent to ArKay Corp. for their use. Give the probability distribution for the number of defectives in the shipment. XWP must pay a penalty if more than 4% of any shipment is defective. What is the probability they will have to pay ArKay a penalty?

10. Accidents in the XWP plant occur at the rate of approximately one every two months and appear to be randomly occurring. Each accident costs the company about $1,500 in work stoppage and slowdown. If more than two accidents occur in a month, the company suffers additional costs in

employee discontent and slowdown estimated at about $5,000. The company decides to take out insurance to pay $5,000 in any month in which more than two accidents occur. Disregarding administrative costs, what would a reasonable monthly premium be for this protection?

4.4 INTRODUCTION TO HYPOTHESIS TESTING

A great many decisions can be handled using hypothesis testing techniques. Such a situation occurs when we decide whether to accept or reject a hypothesis. Is television set A better than set B? Which should we buy? Is a new advertising technique better than the one in use? Such questions can often be handled effectively using the binomial distribution. Generally our samples are sufficiently small so that ignoring the lack of replacement does not materially affect the validity of using the binomial model.

Suppose, for example, that records indicate that, using the billing system presently in use, errors have been made on $2/5$ of all bills. We interpret this to mean that, if a processed bill is selected at random, the probability that it will contain an error is $2/5$ (or 0.4). A new procedure has been developed by the office manager, and is to be tested by using it on a sample of bills, then rechecking the bills carefully to determine which have errors, and drawing conclusions about the effectiveness of the new procedure based on the probability that the number of errors observed would actually occur if there was no difference between the old and new procedures.

Suppose, for example, that the sample consisted of 15 bills which had been processed by the new method. Using the old method, the expected number of errors is $(2/5)(15) = 6$, so if fewer than six have errors, this may be considered to be some evidence that the new method is better. The fewer bills with errors, the stronger is the evidence that the new method is better. At some point we must be able to say, "Yes, the evidence is sufficient to indicate that the new method is better." But even if all 15 bills were correct, there is still the possibility that the new method really is not better and that the outcome is due to chance. If all 15 bills are correct, the probability of this being due to chance (if the probability of one bill being correct is $3/5$) is $(3/5)^{15}$ or about 0.00047. This probability is quite small—about one chance in two thousand—but it could happen. Thus we can *never* be *certain* about the effectiveness of the new method. We must always take some chances. *Determining when to take these chances and controlling the risk involved is the essence of statistical hypothesis testing.*

In the bill processing experiment, we wanted to test the effectiveness of the new method. Our **research hypothesis** was that the new method of processing bills is more effective than the old method. That means that we would expect *fewer* than $2/5$ of the bills to contain errors. (Conversely, we would expect *more* than $3/5$ of the bills to be correct. Either approach is correct.) But how many fewer? We have no way of guessing what to look for, so we approach the problem another way. We suppose that there is no difference between the new method and the old one; that is, we assume that the probability of a particular bill having an error is 2/5. This is called the **null hypothesis** (the hypothesis of no difference.) We then base our conclusions about the outcome of the experiment on the assumption that the null hypothesis is true. After performing our experiment, we use the null hypothesis to determine the probability of the actual outcome; that is, we determine the probability that *no more* than that many bills would have errors. The probability, designated α (alpha), *is the probability that we would make an error by concluding that the new method is better.*

If we find that r bills have errors, we can calculate α for $n = 15$, $p = 0.4$, either directly or from Table 2. We have the following table of probabilities for $r \leq 6$.

r	α
0	0+
1	0.005
2	0.027
3	0.091
4	0.217
5	0.403
6	0.610

If as few as four bills have errors, there is about one chance in five that the results are due to chance. This may be, and usually is, considered to be too great a chance and the results are not considered conclusive. If two or fewer bills, however, have errors, the probabilities that the results are due to chance are much smaller; only one chance in about 37 exists that the outcome would occur if the new method were not better. At this level of α, we would probably conclude that the new method is better.

In most cases an acceptable α is selected beforehand and the possible outcomes are divided into two groups. One group makes up the **rejection region**, while the other forms the **acceptance region**. Suppose that we decide that a suitable α is 0.05. This means that we are willing to take one chance in twenty of incorrectly concluding that the new method is better. We would then say that the rejection region is composed of all r values of two or less since $P(x \leq 2) < 0.05$, while any value of r more than two is in the acceptance region.

The names of these regions are derived from the fact that if we get a value in the rejection region we are justified in rejecting the hypothesis that there is no difference between the two methods and concluding that the new one is better (with a probability of 0.05 or less of being wrong). If the obtained value falls in the acceptance region, we may be justified in accepting the hypothesis of no difference. If we do conclude this, however, we run a different risk. We may *incorrectly* conclude that the new method is not better. This is possible because the new method may be better, even though our results failed to show it. The probability of this happening is designated β (beta) and is dependent upon the actual probability of an error in a bill using the new method. Since this probability is not known, β cannot be calculated directly, but it is known that β is inversely dependent (proportional) on α for a given sample size. Thus, decreasing α, to be more certain that we do not conclude the new method is better when it is not, will increase β, the likelihood of making the opposite error. Conversely, if we wish to decrease β, α must be increased. If α is fixed by preselection, the only way to decrease β is to increase the sample size. This is a reason for using samples which are relatively large. Further discussion of hypothesis testing can be found in section 5.4 and in Chapter 7.

EXAMPLE 1 A businessman carries two products, A and B, which are identical except for brand name. His inventory has grown to the point where he wishes to discontinue one of the brands. Brand A does a great deal of advertising, so he is tempted to carry that brand only. Past records show that about equal amounts of the two brands are sold, but he feels that his customers have been showing a preference for brand B in recent weeks. Describe an experiment to help him make his decision based on the next 25 sales of the product.

SOLUTION He will order brand A unless he is convinced brand B is preferred by more of his customers. Suppose we let p represent the probability that brand B is preferred by his customers. This is numerically equal to the proportion of customers preferring brand B. If more than half his customers prefer brand B, he will order brand B. If fewer than half prefer B, he will order brand A. If exactly half prefer each brand, he will stock brand A. Thus the crucial value of p is 0.5. He wishes to order brand A unless he feels sure that $p > 0.5$. He tests the hypothesis that $p = 0.5$ by examining the consequences of this hypothesis with respect to his sample of 25. Suppose that he is willing to accept one chance in ten of being wrong in rejecting brand B. This is equivalent to setting $\alpha = 0.10$. (This is a bit higher than usual, but acceptable.) He uses the binomial probability table and finds that if $n = 25$, $p = 0.5$, then $P(x \geq 17) \doteq 0.054$ and $P(x \geq 16) \doteq 0.115$. He then concludes that if 17 or more customers buy brand B, he will stock brand B, but if 16 or fewer buy brand B, he will stock brand A. Since the random variable can take on the values $0, 1, 2,\ldots,25$ this means that the rejection region is $17, 18, 19,\ldots,25$, while the acceptance region is $0, 1, 2,\ldots,16$.

DISCUSSION Suppose that the true probability is 0.6. If this is the case, $P(x \geq 17) \doteq 0.274$, so the probability that he will make a mistake by stocking brand A is $\beta = 0.726$, the probability that fewer than 17 customers will buy brand B, even though brand B is preferred by about 60% of the customers. If $p = 0.8$, however, $\beta \doteq 0.047$ since then $P(x \geq 17) \doteq 0.953$. The quantity $1 - \beta$ is called the power of a test, the probability of being able to detect a statistical difference for a particular value of p. A danger of relatively small samples, then, is that the tests may not be powerful enough to detect relatively small deviations from the tested hypothesis. It might be better in this case to use a larger number of customers spread out over a period of several days. In addition the option of reserving judgment may be used; this option is described in Chapter 7.

•Problems

1. A manufacturer claims that, on the average, no more than 1 out of 20 flashbulbs he makes will fail to fire. A photographer buys 20 bulbs and finds that three of them fail to fire. Using a value of 0.05 for α, can the photographer refute the manufacturer's claim?

2. Suppose, in problem 1, the photographer had bought 25 bulbs and found that four of them failed to fire. Determine acceptance and rejection regions for the hypothesis that the manufacturer's claim is correct as against one that he is incorrect and draw a conclusion.

3. A psychologist has developed what he calls an "irresistible advertising display" which he claims will entice customers who buy a product to buy the one displayed at least 60% of the time. A dog food manufacturer decides to give the display a try and sets it up in the local supermarket. How many of the first 23 customers for dog food must buy his brand in order for it to be considered that the psychologist has proved his point, allowing a chance of 0.20 of being in error?

4. An electronic typesetter is in use, but is error prone, with about 30% of all pages set having errors on it. An R&D team has developed an attachment which they claim will reduce the errors. They are now ready to test the device and attach it to a typesetter which has an error rate of 30%, and set 25 pages in the usual way. The number of pages containing at least one error is given by x.
   (a) If $\alpha = 0.05$, what values of x will lead to the conclusion that the attachment is effective?
   (b) If $\alpha = 0.10$, what values of x will lead to the conclusion that the attachment is effective.
   (c) Suppose it is discovered that three of the pages were fed into the typesetter incorrectly. Using the remaining pages, for what values of x with $\alpha = 0.05$, can it be concluded that the attachment is effective?
   (d) Suppose there are errors on four of the 25 pages. What conclusion will be reached if $\alpha = 0.05$? What is the value of β in this case if the probability of error had actually decreased to 0.20?

5. A manufacturer samples his daily output for acceptability. He is willing to accept 5% defectives for the total output. He tests a sample of 20 units daily and records the number of defectives. Letting $\alpha = 0.10$, he will accept the daily output unless this sample leads him to believe that the day's output contains more than 5% defectives. What is his rejection region? His acceptance region?

4.5 SUMMARY

In this chapter we have examined some of the basic aspects of binomial probability and three distributions of probability in binomial populations. Some of the more important formulas presented in the chapter are given below.

Combination Rule

The number of combinations of n objects taken r at a time is given by

$$\binom{n}{r} = \frac{n!}{r!(n-r)!} \quad \text{or}$$

$$= \frac{n(n-1)(n-2)\cdots(n-r+1)}{r(r-1)(r-2)\cdots 3\cdot 2\cdot 1}$$

Hyper-Geometric Distribution

If a population consists of A objects of one kind and B objects of a second kind, the probability of selecting x objects of type A and $n-x$ objects of type B in a drawing of n objects is given by

$$P(x) = \frac{\binom{A}{x}\binom{B}{n-x}}{\binom{A+B}{n}}$$

If the conditions of a binomial experiment are met, the binomial distribution may be calculated by use of the binomial formula.

Binomial Formula

$$P(x) = \binom{n}{x}p^x(1-p)^{n-x} \quad \text{for } x = 1, 2, 3, \ldots, n$$

The binomial may also be used as an approximation to the hypergeometric if the population $(A + B)$ is sufficiently large.

For events which occur uniformly over a given period of time of given unit interval of any type, the appropriate distribution may be the Poisson, which is most often calculated from the tables (Table 3). A binomial distribution with small p can often be approximated by the Poisson.

Any probability distribution has a mean and a variance. They can be calculated as follows:

	Distribution	Mean	Variance
Mean and Variance of a Probability Distribution	Discrete	$\sum x P(x)$	$\sum x^2 P(x) - \mu^2$
	Hypergeometric	$\dfrac{nA}{A+B}$	$\dfrac{nAB(A+B-n)}{(A+B)^2(A+B-1)}$
	Binomial	np	$np(1-p)$
	Poisson	m	m

An additional concept is that of hypothesis testing. This concept was introduced using the binomial distribution. For a sample of size n, we wished to show, with some reasonable assurance, that the probability of some outcome differs from a certain value p. To do this we selected α, the acceptable probability of concluding incorrectly that the desired outcome had occurred. Then we divided the possible outcomes into acceptance and rejection regions. For the hypothesis that the probability is greater than p, we did this by finding a number r such that, for a given n and p, $P(x \geq r) < \alpha$ and $P(x \geq r-1) > \alpha$, if the probability is actually p. Then if our sample contained at least r favorable outcomes, we rejected the hypothesis that the probability of the outcome is p and concluded that it is greater than p, with the probability of α or less of being wrong. If our sample had fewer than r favorable outcomes, we concluded that the true probability is not greater than p (or is equal to p), subject to a finite probability (β) of being wrong.

•Problems

1. Four aces are tossed into a hat, one ace from each suit. A card is drawn, observed, and returned to the hat. Assuming consecutive trials are independent, how many drawings must be made so that the probability of drawing the ace of spades at least once is greater than four-fifths?

2. It is known that the mortality rate for a certain disease is 60%. At a particular hospital nine of the last ten patients admitted with the disease have been cured. What is the probability of at least this many having been cured if the known mortality rate applies? Does this indicate that the results are possibly due to chance, or should an investigation be made to see if some new treatment is in use at this hospital?

3. Over the past one hundred working days, the number of orders for a particular item per day has been as follows:

Items ordered	0	1	2	3	4	5	6
Number of days	11	16	21	24	15	9	4

   (a) Let x represent the number of orders on a day. If $P(x)$ is given by the relative frequencies above, determine the mean and variance of the probability distribution for x.
   (b) What is the probability of more than four items being ordered in a particular day?
   (c) The office manager hypothesizes that the distribution of orders is probably approximately Poisson with $m=2.5$. Determine the distribution of items ordered under this assumption and compare it with the empirical distribution given above. Given these results and the results in (a), do you think he might be correct? (A procedure to test this hypothesis will be given later in a discussion of *goodness of fit*.)

4. A public opinion poll is being taken on the issue of free housing for indigent laborers. If actually 70% of the population favors the issue, what is the probability that, of 15 persons interviewed, 9, 10, 11, or 12 favor the free housing
   c(a) calculating the probabilities directly;
   (b) using the probability tables.

5. Repeat problem 4 if 65% of the population favors the issue.

6. A store manager wished to test whether or not a new weekly newspaper would reach the market he wished. He knew that about one-tenth of the market saw his advertisement in the competing weekly newspaper. He took an ad in the new weekly, then interviewed 25 persons selected at random to determine whether or not they saw the ad. If one-tenth of the market saw this ad, he would be willing to place it in either paper. The ad manager

claims, however, that more than one-tenth of the market will see the ad. How many people, of the sample of 25, would have to have seen the ad for the store manager to conclude that the probability of that many or more seeing it by chance if the proportion is actually one-tenth is less than 0.05?

7. A large number of applicants for a position included one-tenth minority race applicants. Seven persons were asked for an interview. Assuming that the number of applicants was sufficiently large to justify the use of the binomial distribution, and that the qualifications of all individuals were about the same, what is the probability that at least one of the minority applicants would be called for an interview? Suppose that actually two minority members were called for an interview. What is the probability that more than one minority member would be interviewed by chance? If three or more minority members were called, do you think the employer would be open to charges of reverse discrimination?

8. Among persons contracting leukemia, spontaneous remission occurs in about 1% of the cases. Among 50 persons given a new treatment at a local hospital, three experience complete remission. If we do not believe the remissions are caused by the new treatment and instead are due to chance, what is the probability that more than two would have spontaneous remission if it is indeed due to chance?

9. On the average a man will catch two fish per hour in Perdido Bay. What is the probability that he will catch at least three fish in the next hour?

10. The hypergeometric distribution can be easily extended by analogy to more than a two characteristic population. A mother goes to the grocery store and takes six cans of baby food at random off a shelf containing six cans of applesauce, four of peaches, and three of pears. What is the probability she took two of each kind? At least one of each kind?

11. Psychological testing devices are frequently used to test the presence of "extrasensory perception (ESP)." In one test, for mind-reading ability, subject *A* and subject *B* are in different rooms. Subject *A* has 4 cards: a triangle, a square, a cross, and a circle. Subject *A* randomly selects one of the cards and concentrates on it while subject *B* writes down what she thinks subject *A* has selected. After 20 trials, the lists are compared. A test for clairvoyance involves keeping the cards face down. Subject *B* writes down what she thinks the card is after it is selected, but before subject *A* looks at it. The cards are scrambled after each selection. Binomial probability tables are used to compute the degree of subject *B*'s ESP ability by calculating the probability of guessing *at least* as many correctly by chance alone. The level of significance determined in this way would be used to classify the person's ESP ability. Classifications vary, but one way would be to call 0.25 or less "some degree of ESP," 0.10 or less "a marked degree of ESP," 0.05 or less "a high degree of ESP," 0.01 or less "a very high degree of ESP." Significance levels of 0.001 or less would be rare enough to be called "a remarkable degree of ESP." Suppose that a subject called 12 of

20 cards correctly on the mind-reading test and 7 of 20 on the clairvoyance test. Classify the subject according to ESP ability.

12. An efficiency expert believes that additional incentive offered to workers on an assembly line will lead to increased efficiency in production. He randomly selected 15 assembly lines in various plants and offered the workers on those lines additional coffee breaks without referring to the fact that he hoped to increase their production. He then compared the production of those lines with their former production to see which, if any, did exhibit increased production. If he is willing to accept one chance in 20 of being wrong in concluding that the incentive did increase production, give his null and alternate hypotheses and acceptance and rejection regions. Repeat the problem if he is willing only to accept one chance in 100 of making such an error.

CHAPTER 4

Glossary of Terms

acceptance region	hypergeometric distribution
alternate hypothesis	hypothesis testing
binomial experiment	null hypothesis
binomial distribution	permutation
binomial population	Poisson distribution
binomial probability	rejection region
combination	research hypothesis
conditional probability	sampling with replacement
factorial	sampling without replacement

Glossary of Symbols

α	probability of erroneously rejecting null hypothesis
β	probability of erroneously accepting null hypothesis
m	mean number of occurrences, in a Poisson distribution
p	probability of success, on one binomial trial
$<$	is less than
$\leq$	is less than or equal to
$>$	is more than
$\geq$	is more than or equal to
$\binom{n}{r}$	combinations of n objects taken r at a time
$!$	factorial

Chapter 5

The Normal Distribution

5.1 CONTINUOUS AND DISCRETE VARIABLES

The random variables studied in the previous chapters were discrete; that is, they could take on only a unique and countable number of values. Another important type of random variable is the **continuous random variable**. This is not a good place to discuss the mathematical notions of the varieties of infinities or the precise definitions of "continuous." Intuitively, if a variable is continuous, it can be subdivided infinitely. There is no "smallest" measure such as a toss, a cent, a sale, or another discrete quantity. Examples of truly continuous variables are time, weight, and temperature. These variables are continuous, although they can be made discrete artificially by measuring them to the nearest unit—say to the nearest pound. A probability distribution based on a continuous variable is called a **probability density**. One of the major drawbacks to studying probability densities at an elementary level is that this study requires more than a nodding acquaintance with calculus. In view of this fact, we shall study only the basic properties of a few probability densities.

In the case of probability distributions, we could construct histograms to portray the distribution. For instance, the distribution of bowling scores among 10,000 randomly selected games might be given by the following table.

Score (Pins)	Number of Games	Probability
Under 126	812	0.0812
126–150	1,764	0.1764
151–175	2,433	0.2433
176–200	1,911	0.1911
201–225	1,646	0.1646
226–250	1,037	0.1037
251–275	294	0.0294
276–300	103	0.0103

A histogram representing these data is given here. One unit on the horizontal scale represents 25 pins. Each interval extends 0.5 in each direction. The second bar from the left, for example, extends over the interval from 125.5 to 150.5 pins.

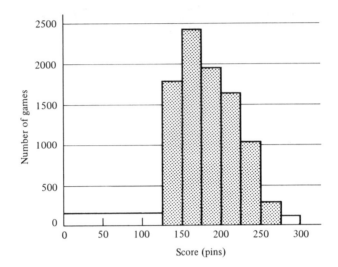

Since the first interval (0 to 125) is five times the size of the other intervals, its height is 162.4, or one-fifth of 812. This is because the proportion of scores is represented by the *area* of the rectangle. Now since the unit of difference in scores (one pin) is relatively small in relation to the range of the distribution (300 pins), the histogram may be approximated by a smooth curve. A curve derived from this histogram is given here.

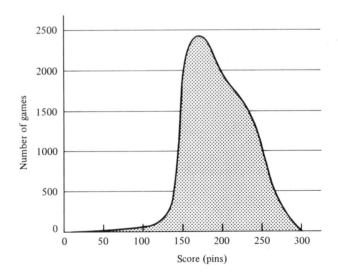

In many ways, this curve may well be a better representation of the original raw data than the histogram since a histogram derived from the raw data would have each rectangle one unit wide. This example illustrates one of the important uses of continuous probability densities—the approximation to a discrete probability distribution. Such an approximation will be most useful if it gives an accurate impression of the data. It should have approximately the same area in the intervals as the histogram; that is, 0 to 125 should contain 0.0812 of the data, 126 to 150 should contain 0.1764 of the data, and so on. Note one essential difference—in the raw data, there is nothing between 125 and 126, nothing between 200 and 201, and so on. In making a histogram, we extend each interval up 0.5 and down 0.5 from the endpoints. With the continuous approximation a similar plan is followed, called a **correction for continuity**. Each number in the original (discrete) distribution is represented in the continuous approximation by an interval from one-half unit below the number to one-half unit above the number. Thus 50 would be represented by the interval 49.5 to 50.5 and the area under the curve from 49.5 to 50.5 would be equal to the proportion of cases (see the following figure).

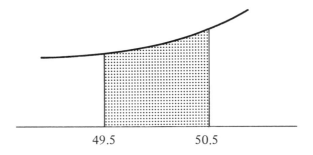

49.5   50.5

Thus, if three of the original 10,000 games bowled were scores of 50, the area under the curve between 49.5 and 50.5 would be 0.0003 of the area under the entire curve. It would be too much, of course, to expect an approximation to agree in such fine detail. In the bowling data given, 125 would be represented by the interval 124.5 to 125.5. Since 125 belongs in the first interval, but 126 in the second, all scores 125 and under would belong to the interval 0 to 125.5. Then the areas would be given by the following continuous approximation:

Interval	Area (probability)
0–125.5	0.0812
125.5–150.5	0.1764
150.5–175.5	0.2433
175.5–200.5	0.1911
200.5–225.5	0.1646
225.5–250.5	0.1037
250.5–275.5	0.0294
275.5–300.5	0.0103

The most striking feature of a probability density (i.e., a probability function over a continuous variable) is that the area under the curve is always equal to one. Probabilities of values of the random variable are always given in ranges of values; the probability that a value of the random variable will be between two possible limits is the area of the curve between those limits. Thus if we have a probability density represented by the curve below, the probability that the value of the random variable will be between x_1 and x_2 is the area under the curve between those limits. That is, $P(x_1 < x < x_2) = $ shaded area.

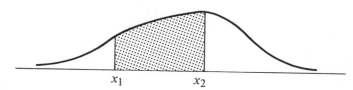

There is no difference between $P(x_1 < x < x_2)$ and $P(x_1 \leq x \leq x_2)$, because, in a continuous distribution, the area under the curve above x_1 (and x_2 also) is technically zero; this is the area of a line segment.

5.2   THE NORMAL DISTRIBUTION

One of the most important and useful sets of continuous distributions in statistics is the set of **normal distributions**. Reference is often made to *the* normal distribution. This means the *standard* normal distribution, which will be discussed later in this section.

This curve was first developed to deal with errors in experimental work and was then found to have many other applications as we shall see. A graph of a normal distribution is given below.

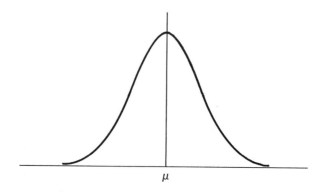

A normal distribution is symmetrical about the mean, trailing off abruptly in both directions. It is also often called the *bell-shaped curve* for obvious reasons. A normal distribution is determined completely by its mean and standard deviation. Because of this, graphs of normal distributions with the same mean, but different standard deviations, differ only in amount of dispersion, and height, as shown in the following figure.

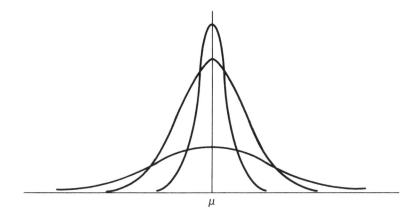

These curves are similar because they reach their highest point about the same mean, and taper off equally in both directions.

Normal distributions with the same standard deviation, but different means, look identical in shape and differ only in their placement on the x-axis as shown here:

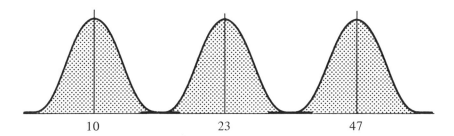

Theoretically, although it may not be apparent from these small drawings, the curve never touches the x-axis. However, it approaches it so closely when the value of x is about four standard deviations from the mean that any area lying further from the mean than that is, for practical purposes, negligible.

The above observations were based on the assumption that the normal distributions considered were probability densities. One of the properties of a probability density function is that the total area under its curve is equal to one. Thus the normal distribution which is a probability density function has a total area of one. A normal distribution with $\mu = 0$, $\sigma = 1$ is called the **standard normal**

distribution. Any normal distribution can be scaled as follows:

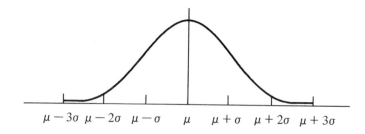

$$\mu - 3\sigma \quad \mu - 2\sigma \quad \mu - \sigma \qquad \mu \qquad \mu + \sigma \quad \mu + 2\sigma \quad \mu + 3\sigma$$

The relationship of any value of x to μ can be expressed in terms of the number of standard deviations distant from the mean. For example, if $\mu = 32$, $\sigma = 9$, a score of 45.5 is exactly 13.5 units abvove the mean, or $(13.5)/9$, that is, 1.5 standard deviations above the mean. A score of 18.5 is 13.5 units below the mean, or 1.5 standard deviations below the mean. This can be symbolized as -1.5 as opposed to $+1.5$ for 45.5. As mentioned in Chapter 2, these scores are called **standard scores**, also referred to as **z-values** or **z-scores**. The name comes from the fact that such scores are standard deviations of the standard normal distribution whose random variable is always called z. Thus if $z = 1.37$, this value would be 1.37 standard deviations above the mean. It follows that values of x for any normal distribution can be related to standard scores by the

*Standard
Score Formula*
$$z = \frac{x - \mu}{\sigma}$$

EXAMPLE 1   Determine standard scores for $x = 18.3, 27.9, 34.4, 39.3$ in the normal distribution for which $\mu = 30.1$ and $\sigma = 2.4$.

SOLUTION   If

$$x = 18.3, \; z = \frac{18.3 - 30.1}{2.4} = \frac{-11.8}{2.4} \doteq -4.92$$

if

$$x = 27.9, \; z = \frac{27.9 - 30.1}{2.4} = \frac{-2.2}{2.4} \doteq -0.92$$

if

$$x = 34.4, z = \frac{34.4 - 30.1}{2.4} = \frac{4.3}{2.4} \doteq 1.79$$

if

$$x = 39.3, z = \frac{39.3 - 30.1}{2.4} = \frac{9.2}{2.4} \doteq 3.83$$

EXAMPLE 2 Determine values of x in the distribution of example 1 for which the standard scores are $z = -3.07, -1.04, 0.73, 2.44$.

SOLUTION If $z = (x - \mu)/\sigma$, then $z\sigma = x - \mu$ or $z\sigma + \mu = x$; if you prefer, $x = z\sigma + \mu$. Thus if

$$z = -3.07, x = (-3.07)(2.4) + 30.1 \doteq -7.4 + 30.1 = 22.7$$

if

$$z = -1.04, x = (-1.04)(2.4) + 30.1 \doteq -2.5 + 30.1 = 27.6$$

if

$$z = 0.73, x = (0.73)(2.4) + 30.1 \doteq 1.8 + 30.1 = 31.9$$

if

$$z = 2.44, x = (2.44)(2.4) + 30.1 \doteq 5.9 + 30.1 = 36.0$$

EXAMPLE 3 In a normal distribution, a value of 42.1 is 1.3 standard deviations above the mean of 31.7. What is the standard deviation of the distribution?

SOLUTION In this case, we know x, z, μ, but not σ. Since $z = (x - \mu)/\sigma$, $\sigma = (x - \mu)/z$, so if $x = 42.1$, $z = 1.3$, and $\mu = 31.7$,

$$\sigma = \frac{42.1 - 31.7}{1.3} = \frac{10.4}{1.3} = 8.0$$

EXAMPLE 4 A normal distribution has a standard deviation of 11.7. If a value of 11.3 lies 2.1 standard deviations above the mean, determine the mean of the distribution.

SOLUTION   Here we know x, z, σ, but not μ. Since $z = (x - \mu)/\sigma$, $z\sigma = x - \mu$. Therefore, $z\sigma + \mu = x$, or $\mu = x - z\sigma$. Then if $x = 11.3$, $\sigma = 11.7$, $z = 2.1$, $\mu = 11.3 - (2.1)(11.7) \doteq 11.3 - 24.6 = -13.3$.

The fact that any normal distribution can be related to the standard normal distribution is very important. Because of this, the standard normal distribution has been studied in detail and the results can be transferred to any normal distribution. The table of areas found in Table 4 is used to work with the standard normal distribution. Most tables of this sort are arranged like this, so if the student becomes proficient with this table, he will also be able to use similar tables.

In Table 4, the entries on the left and top correspond to values of z given to two decimal places. The integer value and the first decimal value are given in the column at the left, and the second decimal value in the top row. The entries in the body of the table are the areas under the normal curve between the mean, 0, and the given value of z correct to four decimal places. Remember that the standard normal curve is also a probability density, so that the area under the curve is also the probability that the random variable has a value between the mean and the given z. Of course most of the applications of the normal curve involve approximations so that results obtained by using Table 4 should also be viewed as approximations, probably not correct to more than two decimals.

For instance, if $z = 1.62$, to find the corresponding area look down the left column to find 1.6; look along the top row to find 0.02. The entry which is in both the row of 1.6 and the column 0.02 is 0.4474. This means that the area under the standard normal curve between 0 and 1.62 is 0.4474 as illustrated:

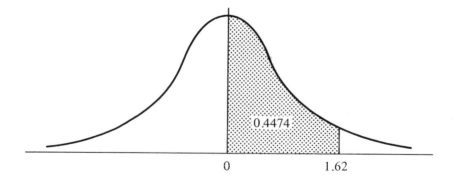

Several other pieces of information can be derived from this observation. Since the normal curve is symmetric, each side contains exactly 1/2 of the area of the curve. Thus, the area under the curve to the right of 1.62 is $0.5000 - 0.4474$ or 0.0526. This is also illustrated here.

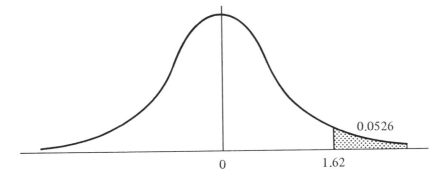

In addition, since the normal curve is symmetric, the area between $-z$ and 0 is equal to the area between 0 and z. Therefore, in this case the area between -1.62 and 0 is also 0.4474 and the area to the left of -1.62 is 0.0526 as shown:

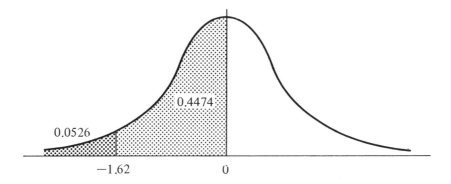

Finally, the area between -1.62 and 1.62 is therefore twice the area between 0 and 1.62 or 0.8948. The probability that the variable in a standard normal distribution has a value between -1.62 and 1.62 is equal to 0.8948. This is illustrated by the following:

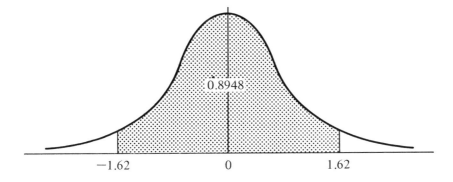

Various combinations can be obtained with these mathematical tools which apply to the standard normal curve.

EXAMPLE 5   Find the area under the standard normal curve between 0 and z if $z = 0.07, 0.83, 1.70, 2.56, -0.24, -1.12, -3.01$.

SOLUTION   From the table we read the following values:

z	Area between 0 and z
0.07	0.0279
0.83	0.2967
1.70	0.4554
2.56	0.4948
-0.24	0.0948
-1.12	0.3686
-3.01	0.4987

DISCUSSION   Remember that the area under the curve must always be positive. Remember also that the entries on the edge of the table (left and top) represent standard deviations distant from the mean (standard scores) while the entries in the body of the table represent areas under the standard normal curve between the mean and the given standard score (z-value). The student should verify example 5 and the remainder of the examples in this section, and keep at it until proficiency is achieved in the use of Table 4.

EXAMPLE 6   Find the standard score for which the area under the standard normal curve between it and the mean is 0.2109, $0.3621, 0.4345, 0.4599, 0.4908$.

SOLUTION   From the table we have

Area	z
0.2019	0.53
0.3621	1.09
0.4345	1.51
0.4599	1.75
0.4908	2.36

DISCUSSION   For 0.4908, note that no entry in the table is precisely 0.4908. The two entries closest to it are 0.4906 and 0.4909. Since 0.4908 is closer to 0.4909 than 0.4906 we use the value of 0.4909. An approximation method known as linear interpolation can be used if desired, but this is not necessary since two decimal accuracy is sufficient for most of our purposes in using standard scores.

In cases where the given area is midway between two table entries, such as 0.3953, in the absence of other information (such as more complete tables) we shall follow the rule of using the closest value of z for which the second decimal is even, that is, 0, 2, 4, 6, or 8. For an area of 0.3953, then, $z = 1.26$ to two decimal places.

EXAMPLE 7   Determine the value of z for which 0.3300 of the area under the standard normal curve is to its left.

SOLUTION   In solving problems such as this, sketching the curve is always useful, though, perhaps, not necessary. Here we know that *less* than half the area under the curve is to the left of the desired z-score so that z must be negative, since exactly half the area under the curve is to the left of zero. Furthermore, the table gives areas between z and the mean.

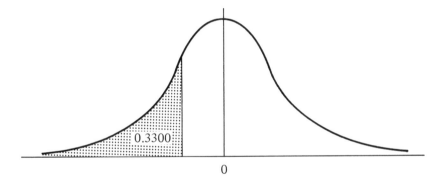

The area we will look up is the complement of the area between z and the mean; that is, $0.5000 - 0.3300$ or 0.1700 of the area between z and the mean. The corresponding z-score in the table is 0.44. Since we know z must be negative, it follows that $z = -0.44$ as illustrated by the following figure.

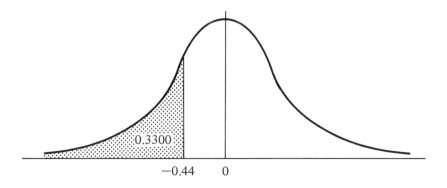

EXAMPLE 8 Find the area under the normal curve between $z = -1.34$ and $z = 0.57$; between $z = 0.59$ and $z = 1.27$.

SOLUTION For $z = -1.34$ and $z = 0.57$, the values of the areas from the table are, respectively, 0.4099 and 0.2157. Since these are on the *opposite* sides of the mean, they must be added together.

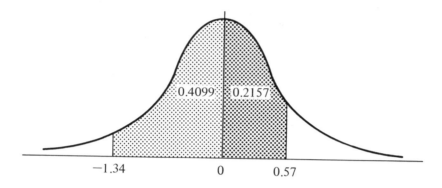

Thus, the area under the normal curve between $z = -1.34$ and $z = 0.57$ is 0.6256.

For $z = 0.59$ and $z = 1.27$ the corresponding areas are 0.2224 and 0.3980. Since the z-scores are both positive, the corresponding areas overlap and their *difference* is the desired area.

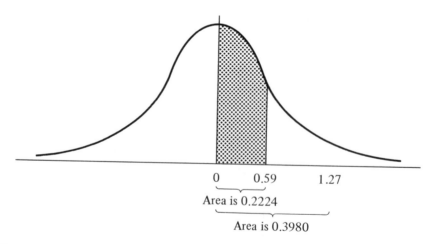

Thus, the area under the normal curve between $z = 0.59$ and $z = 1.27$ is 0.1756.

EXAMPLE 9 For a normal distribution with a mean 38.7, standard deviation 10.2, estimate the probability that a value will fall between 29.6 and 44.8.

SOLUTION   Each score must be converted to a standard score. For 29.6,

$$z = \frac{29.6 - 38.7}{10.2} = \frac{-9.1}{10.2} \doteq -0.89;$$

for 44.8,

$$z = \frac{44.8 - 38.7}{10.2} = \frac{6.1}{10.2} \doteq 0.60.$$

The corresponding areas under the standard normal curve are 0.3133 and 0.2257. Since the z-scores are on opposite sides of the mean (as are the original values) the areas must be added to determine the area between the scores. Adding, we obtain $P(29.6 < x < 44.8) = 0.5390$, where x is the variable of the given distribution.

EXAMPLE 10   A normal distribution has a mean of 133 with a standard deviation of 21. Determine a number such that 80% of all scores will fall within that number of the mean.

SOLUTION   If 80% of the scores fall within the desired number of the mean, then 40% fall between the mean, 133, and $133 + n$, where n is the number. This is because the normal curve is symmetric. The z-score corresponding to 0.4000 is 1.28, to two decimals. Then we have $1.28 = (x - 133)/21$, so that $x = 1.28(21) + 133 \doteq 160$. Thus 40% of all scores fall between 133 and 160, so that $n = 27$, and 80% of all scores fall within 27 units of the mean; that is, 80% of all scores lie between 106 and 160.

TECHNICAL NOTE   One bit of notation which often is useful is the use of a subscript to indicate the area under the normal distribution *to the right* of a particular value of z. The notation $z_{.05}$, for example, indicates the value of z for which 0.05 (or 5%) of the area under the standard normal distribution is to its right. This value can be estimated from the table to be almost exactly 1.645, or, using the rule stated before, 1.64. Similarly, $z_{.15} \doteq 1.04$. Since the subscript indicates areas to the *right* of the z (that is, $P(z > z_\alpha) = \alpha$), if the subscript is greater than 0.50, the value of z will be negative. For example $z_{.85} = -1.04$ since 85% of the area in a standard normal distribution lies to the right of -1.04. It follows, then, that for any value of α, $z_\alpha = -z_{1-\alpha}$; for instance, $z_{.10} \doteq 1.28$ and $z_{.90} \doteq -1.28$. These statements mean that $P(z > 1.28) \doteq 0.10$, while $P(z > -1.28) \doteq 0.90$.

•Problems

1. Estimate standard scores for the following values of x in a normal distribution with mean 284.7 and standard deviation 14.6.

    (a) $x = 261.4$ (d) $x = 280.4$
    (b) $x = 303.7$ (e) $x = 293.9$
    (c) $x = 259.3$ (f) $x = 321.2$

2. Give values of x for the following standard scores in a normal distribution with $\mu = 10.4$, $\sigma = 11.8$.

    (a) $z = 1.64$ (d) $z = 0.50$
    (b) $z = 2.07$ (e) $z = -0.13$
    (c) $z = -2.16$ (f) $z = 1.14$

3. Find the area under the standard normal curve between

    (a) $z = 0$ and $z = 2.18$ (d) $z = -0.49$ and $z = -0.12$
    (b) $z = -1.04$ and $z = 1.54$ (e) $z = -3.04$ and $z = 1.63$
    (c) $z = 1.56$ and $z = 2.93$ (f) $z = -0.43$ and $z = 2.09$

4. Find the area under the standard normal curve

    (a)   to the right of $z = 1.43$ (c)   to the right of $z = -0.77$
    (b)   to the left of $z = -1.03$ (d)   to the left of $z = 2.01$

5. Find the area under the standard normal curve between z and $-z$ if

    (a) $z = 1$ (e) $z = 1.64$
    (b) $z = 2$ (f) $z = 1.96$
    (c) $z = 3$ (g) $z = 2.33$
    (d) $z = 1.28$ (h) $z = 2.58$

6. Determine $z_{.1230}$.

7. If a normal distribution has mean 193.4 and standard deviation 13.7, calculate the probability that a particular value of the variable lies

    (a)   above 210.4   (e)   between 173.4 and 186.8
    (b)   below 186.5   (f)   between 166.1 and 207.9
    (c)   above 179.9   (g)   between 200.0 and 210.0
    (d)   below 200.0   (h)   above 200.0 or below 180.0

8. The mean of a normal distribution is 100.0. If the probability that the variable assumes a value greater than 121.0 is 0.1446, what is the standard deviation of the distribution?

9. A normal distribution has a standard deviation of 134. The probability that the variable takes a value less than 1,072 is 0.7734. What is the mean of the distribution?

10. Find to three decimal places, if possible, the value of z such that exactly 50% of the area under the standard normal curve lies between $-z$ and z. This value, once more widely used, is called the **probable error** of z for the standard normal distribution. Using the obtained value, estimate the probable error of x in a normal distribution with $\mu = 2,750$, $\sigma = 40$.

11. Determine the value of the standard scores given below.

(a) $z_{.01}$

(b) $z_{.005}$

(c) $z_{.025}$

(d) $z_{.05}$

(e) $z_{.10}$

(f) $z_{.99}$

(g) $z_{.995}$

(h) $z_{.975}$

(i) $z_{.95}$

(j) $z_{.90}$

5.3 APPLICATIONS OF THE NORMAL DISTRIBUTION

Many sets of data have distributions which are approximately normal. For these sets, the methods of section 5.2 are applicable.

> **EXAMPLE 1** A certain brand of spaghetti sauce is packed in cans which are supposed to have a net weight of 15.5 ounces. Since the packing is done by machine and weight will vary from can to can, the machine will usually be set to average a little more than the stated net weight. Suppose the machine is set to fill the cans with a mean of 15.7 ounces and the distribution of fills has a standard deviation of 0.12 ounces. How many of a lot of 10,000 cans would you expect to find with less than the stated net weight of 15.5 ounces?

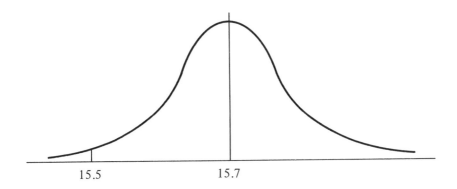

15.5   15.7

SOLUTION   The standard score value is obtained by the formula

$$z = \frac{15.5 - 15.7}{0.12} = \frac{-0.2}{0.12} \doteq -1.67$$

so that this is about 1.67 standard deviations below the mean. According to Table 4, 0.4525 of the area under the curve lies between 15.5 and 15.7, so 0.0475 of the area lies to the left of 15.5. Since the area under the curve represents (in this example) 10,000 cans, you would expect about 475 of the 10,000 cans to weigh less than 15.5 ounces. On the other hand, about 475 cans would weigh more than 15.9 ounces. This is a practical problem and, since standard deviation is relatively difficult to adjust on such a machine, any changes to be made would be made on the mean.

EXAMPLE 2   Workers in an industrial plant assemble a delicate instrument in a part of the plant. The time required for a skilled worker to assemble the instrument ranges from 35 to 55 minutes with a mean of 45 minutes. The times are normally distributed with a standard deviation of 4 minutes. One worker is observed as he assembles the instrument. What is the probability that he will take between 48 and 50 minutes to assemble the instrument?

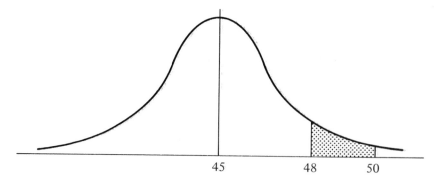

45   48   50

SOLUTION   If z_1 denotes the standard score for 48 and z_2 the standard score for 50, we have

$$z_1 = \frac{48-45}{4} = 0.75, \ z_2 = \frac{50-45}{4} = 1.25$$

The areas under the normal curve associated with each (from Table 4) are, respectively, 0.2734 and 0.3944. The area between 48 and 50, then, is $0.3944 - 0.2734$ or 0.1210. Thus, $P(48 < x < 50) = 0.1210$ where x is the time required to assemble one instrument.

The preceding two examples have dealt with continuous variables. Time, weight, distance, volume, etc. are examples of variables which are continuous. If variables are discrete, or are continuous variables measured to the nearest unit (such as to the nearest minute) a continuity correction should be used. For instance, in example 2 if the time had been measured to the nearest minute "*between* 48 and 50" would be 49 only and would be represented by 48.5 to 49.5 which would change the result considerably. The use of such terms as "between" and "inclusive" is much more critical with a discrete variable than a continuous one. The question of when to and when not to use the continuity correction has not yet been satisfactorily resolved. The recommendation in this text will be to use it whenever the data are truly discrete (without an underlying continuous variable as in example 2) and are measured in integers. Thus data measured in dollars should be corrected for, but data measured in dollars and cents should not. The prime consideration is whether lack of the continuity correction will or will not seriously distort the results. This interpretation will not satisfy all statisticians, or even authors of elementary statistics texts, but it is sufficient for our purposes and does at least standardize our responses.

EXAMPLE 3 A machine produces light bulbs. They are shipped in lots of 1,000. On the average, a lot will have 10 defective bulbs; the distribution of defective bulbs is approximately normal with a standard deviation of 3.15. What is the probability that a particular lot will have at least three but not more than six defective bulbs? What is the probability that it will have more than 15 defective bulbs?

SOLUTION Since the data (number of defective bulbs) are discrete and measured in integers, a continuity correction must be applied. Since the interval representing three is 2.5 to 3.5 and the interval representing six is 5.5 to 6.5, the interval representing at least three, but not more than six, is 2.5 to 6.5 since both three and six are included.

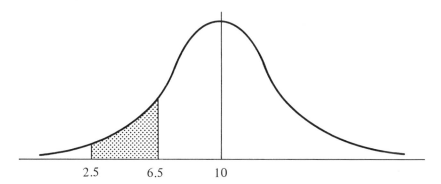

Then, if z_1 and z_2 represent the standard scores for 2.5 and 6.5, respectively, we have

$$z_1 = \frac{2.5 - 10}{3.15} = \frac{-7.5}{3.15} \doteq -2.38 \text{ and } z_2 = \frac{6.5 - 10}{3.15} = \frac{-3.5}{3.15} \doteq -1.11$$

The associated areas (from Table 4) are 0.4913 and 0.3665. The area between 2.5 and 6.5, then, is $0.4913 - 0.3665$ or 0.1248. Thus we say that

$P(2.5 < x < 6.5) \doteq 0.1248$. In terms of the original, discrete data, $P(3 \leq x \leq 6) \doteq 0.1248$.

To determine $P(x > 15)$, note that 15 is represented by the interval 14.5 to 15.5. To be greater than 15 means, after application of the continuity correction, greater than 15.5, since 15 is not to be included.

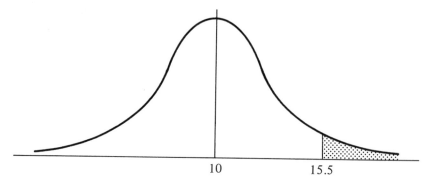

Here

$$z = \frac{15.5 - 10}{3.15} = \frac{5.5}{3.15} \doteq 1.75,$$

The associated area is 0.4599, so

$$P(x > 15) \doteq 0.0401$$

EXAMPLE 4 In a certain apartment district, the monthly rental for apartments is approximately normally distributed with a mean of $384.22 and a standard deviation of $126.40. Above what value is the highest 30% of the monthly rentals in this district?

SOLUTION Although the variable is discrete, its values are not given in integers, so we do not apply the continuity correction. According to Table 4, 20% of the values are between the mean and z for $z \doteq 0.52$. At that point, 30% of the values are above it.

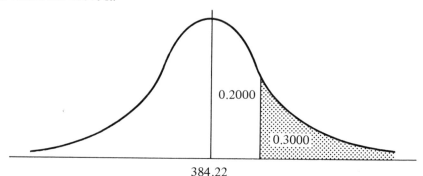

Thus we have $0.52 = (x - 384.22)/126.40$, so $(0.52)(126.40) = x - 384.2$ or $x = (0.52)(126.40) + 384.22$ or about 449.95. Thus about 30% of the rentals are above $449.95. Since 0.52 is only an approximation, we are probably not accurate to more than the nearest dollar. A slightly more accurate figure could be obtained using linear interpolation or more accurate tables.

In example 3, the light bulbs were either defective or not. If we note that ten defective out of 1,000 is a probability of 0.01, we can calculate the probability of 3, 4, 5, 6 defective directly by using the binomial formulas. It was noted in Chapter 4 that the Poisson distribution can be used to approximate the binomial for small values of p. As the value of p increases, however, the approximation becomes less accurate. On the other hand, it is even worse to contemplate the amount of calculation needed to determine the probability, say, of 30 or more heads in 50 tosses of a coin. This would require 21 separate calculations making the project laborious and cumbersome. Fortunately, as n (the number of trials) increases, if the probability of success is about 0.50, the normal distribution is satisfactory as a continuous approximation to the binomial. Below is a graph of a binomial distribution for $n = 10$, $p = 0.5$, with a continuous distribution superimposed upon it.

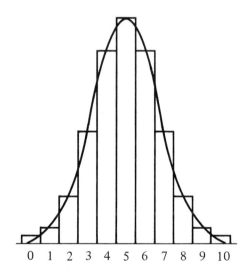

As the number of trials becomes greater and greater, the binomial distribution becomes closer and closer to being a normal distribution and for very large numbers of trials, the probability of success can differ substantially from 0.50. The accuracy of the approximation depends, of course, on the number of trials and the actual probabilities involved. As a rule of thumb, the continuous approximation should not be used unless both np (number of successes) and $n(1-p)$ (number of failures) are greater than five where n is the number of trials and p is the probability of success. If the Poisson approximation can be used, it is generally more accurate than the normal approximation.

In the event these conditions are satisfied, a binomial distribution can be approximated by a normal distribution with the same mean and standard deviation. The mean and standard deviation of a binomial distribution are given by np and $\sqrt{np(1-p)}$ respectively, so this information is always readily available and, since the values of the variable $(0,1,2,\ldots,n)$ are always discrete and measured in integers, a continuity correction must always be applied.

Thus, in example 3, we have a binomial distribution with $p=0.01$ and $n=1,000$. The histogram for the data from three to six would appear as the following graph.

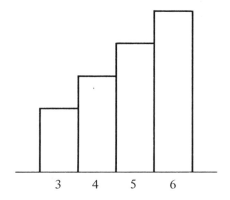

The normal curve, superimposed on the binomial distribution, would then appear this way, with the class boundaries indicated.

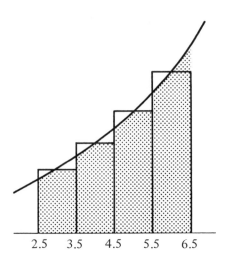

The shaded area on the graph is as close an approximation as possible to the area in the rectangles—the areas associated with 3, 4, 5, and 6 defective bulbs. Hence the proportion of the area under the curve which is shaded is approximately $P(3 \leq x \leq 6)$ which was calculated to be about 0.1248. Direct calculation using the binomial formula yields a value of 0.1262 which agrees relatively well since the probability is far removed from 0.5. Actually, since 1,000/0.01 is far greater than 1,000, the Poisson approximation is indicated with a mean of ten. Using Table 3, we obtain a value of 0.127, which is somewhat better than 0.1248.

EXAMPLE 4 Determine the probability of obtaining from 6 to 10 "sevens," inclusive, in 45 rolls of a pair of dice. Estimate the probability of obtaining exactly 3 "sevens."

SOLUTION The probability of obtaining a seven on one roll is 1/6, so $\mu = 45(1/6) = 7.5$, and $\sigma = \sqrt{45(1/6)(5/6)} = 2.5$. Since both six and ten are to be included, we wish to determine the probability of the interval 5.5 to 10.5. The standard scores are

$$z_1 = \frac{5.5 - 7.5}{2.5} = \frac{-2}{2.5} = -0.80 \text{ and } z_2 = \frac{10.5 - 7.5}{2.5} = \frac{3}{2.5} = 1.20$$

The corresponding areas are 0.2881 and 0.3849. Since they are on opposite sides of the mean, we have $P(6 \leq x \leq 10) = 0.6730$. Direct calculation yields a value of 0.666.

To determine the probability of exactly 3 "sevens," note that 3 is represented by the interval 2.5 to 3.5. Thus, we have

$$z_1 = \frac{2.5 - 7.5}{2.5} = \frac{-5}{2.5} = -2.00 \text{ and } z_2 = \frac{3.5 - 7.5}{2.5} = \frac{-4}{2.5} = -1.60$$

The corresponding areas are 0.4772 and 0.4452. Since the z-scores are on the same side of the mean (both negative), we must subtract to obtain $P(3) = 0.0320$. Direct calculation yields a value of 0.031 which is very good agreement for an approximation.

•Problems

1. Number 10 cans of peaches are supposed to hold 72 ounces. The canner sets the machine to fill the can with, on the average, 72.3 ounces. The distribution of fill weights is approximately normal with a standard deviation of 0.2 ounces. (a) How many of 100,000 cans will have less than 72 ounces? (b) The manufacturer feels that this is too many. Assuming the standard deviation remains unchanged, what mean should the manufacturer set if he wants no more than 300 of the cans to contain less than 72 ounces?

2. Light bulbs have lives that are normally distributed except for those that don't work at all. If a shipment of good light bulbs is known to have a mean life of 916 hours with a standard deviation of 32 hours, what is the probability that a light bulb selected at random will last more than 1,000 hours?

3. Two brands of dog food cost the same amount and it is estimated that they are equally likely to be purchased by a consumer. If this is so, find the probability that, of the next 12 purchases of these two kinds of dog food, 3 will be of brand A. Use the normal approximation and check by using the binomial formula. Is the basic assumption for using the normal approximation to the binomial satisfied?

4. A basket of peaches in a certain fruit stand will have about 84 peaches. This varies a bit, however, and is normally distributed with the mean number of peaches per basket at 84 and a standard deviation of 2 peaches. What is the probability that the basket will contain between 80 and 90 peaches? (NOTE: "Between" does not include the end points.) What is the probability that it will contain exactly 86 peaches? How many of 10,000 such baskets would you expect to contain exactly 86 peaches?

5. A test has 225 multiple choice questions, each with 1 correct and 4 incorrect answers. Each question is answered randomly, without regard to the true state of things. If a passing grade is more than 60 correct answers, what is the probability of obtaining a passing grade on the 225 question test?

6. If it is known that 25% of statistics students study for a test, what is the probability that less than one-third of a random sample of 48 students will study for tomorrow's test?

7. Dowel rods for a certain product must have a diameter of 4.000 mm with a tolerance of 0.020 mm. Rods with diameters greater than 4.020 mm or less than 3.980 mm are not usable. Company A guarantees that the standard deviation on a lot with mean 4.000 mm will be 0.015 mm and will charge $400 per lot of 10,000. Company B guarantees that the standard deviation on a lot with mean 4.000 mm will be 0.012 mm and will charge $460 per lot of 10,000. Which company should be selected for the order if the main criterion is cost per usable dowel rod?

8. A thumbtack is tossed 84 times. It falls point up, on the average, about 30% of the time. What is the probability that it will fall point up at least 10 times, but no more than 25 times?

9. To test whether a process is in control, a reading is taken on a machine. If the reading is greater than 860.0, the machine is retooled. If the process is in control, the daily readings will have a mean of 832.4 with a standard deviation of 10.2. What is the probability of retooling a machine by mistake? That is, what is the probability of getting a reading above 860.0 when the process is actually in control?

10. A survey organization regularly sends out questionnaires. The number of replies on a mailing of 1,000 is approximately normally distributed with a mean of 785 and a standard deviation of 41. If a mailing of 1,000 questionnaires is made, what is the probability, on the basis of past experience, of receiving more than 850 replies?

11. In a certain area of a large city, incomes classified as below minimum subsistence level are said to be possessed by 45% of the families. A random sample of 300 families is interviewed. If we use the binomial model, what is the probability that more than half the families in the sample will have incomes so classified if the claim is true?

12. Weights of male students in a large university are approximately normally distributed. Estimate the mean and standard deviation of the distribution if 6.68% of the students weigh less than 125 pounds and 15.87% weigh more than 170 pounds.

5.4 MORE ON HYPOTHESIS TESTING

In section 4.4 we investigated an experiment concerning errors in billing. The use of the normal approximation to the binomial allows us to extend the number in the sample without extensive binomial tables.

Remember that in this experiment we had a new method for processing bills whose effectiveness we wished to assess. With the old method we expected about 2/5 of the bills to contain errors. Thus our *null hypothesis* was that $p=2/5$ where p is the probability of a particular bill containing an error. We can use the normal approximation to the binomial for sample sizes greater than 25 which meet the criteria; that is, both np and $n(1-p)$ must be greater than 5. Relatively large samples with p small (or with $1-p$ small) may meet the criteria for using the Poisson approximation to the binomial.

Now suppose we wish to decide if the new method is effective, but we wish to take a chance of only 0.05 of being mistaken concluding it is effective. Since 0.05 is the proportion in the upper tail for $z=1.64$ (actually 1.645), then 0.05 is in the lower tail for $z=-1.64$, and we let

$$-1.64 = \frac{x-\mu}{\sigma} = \frac{x-np}{\sqrt{np(1-p)}}$$

for $p=2/5$ and our sample size. If the sample is, say, 84, then $np=33.6$, $\sqrt{np(1-p)} = \sqrt{20.16} \doteq 4.49$, so

$$-1.64 = \frac{x-33.6}{4.49}, \text{ or } x=(-1.64)(4.49)+33.6 \doteq 26.24.$$

Thus our *rejection region* is for $x<26.24$. If 26 or fewer bills in the sample of 84 have an error, we can say that the new method has an error rate less than 2/5, so it is more effective than the old method with a probability of only 0.05 (or less) of being mistaken.

In the example of section 4.4, a businessman carries two products identical except for brand names, brand A and brand B. His inventory requires that he carry only one of the brands. Brand A does a great deal of advertising, so he is tempted to carry this brand only. On the other hand, if more of his customers prefer brand B he would rather carry that brand. He sets up an experiment based on the next 25 sales of the product. His null hypothesis is $p = 0.50$ where p is the probability that brand B is preferred. He is willing to accept a probability of 0.10 of being wrong in rejecting brand B and finds that he will stock brand B only if 17 or more of the next 25 customers buy brand B; otherwise, he will stock brand A. One problem is that, if the true probability is, say, 0.6, he will run a chance of 0.726 of stocking brand A mistakenly. One way to improve this situation is to increase the sample size. Suppose he takes into account all sales of the product for the next two weeks. The formal method of testing this hypothesis is set forth in Chapter 7, and the particular technique is given in section 7.3. In the formal methods the rejection region is given in terms of z values rather than x values. Nonetheless, if the sample size is known, the rejection region can be determined for x values. In this case, if the sample is, say, 163, then for $p = 0.5$, $np = 81.5$, $\sqrt{np(1-p)} \doteq 6.38$, and 0.10 of the area is in the upper tail for $z = 1.28$, so we have

$$1.28 = \frac{x - 81.5}{6.38}$$

or $x = (1.28)(6.38) + 81.5 \doteq 89.67$. Thus if 90 or more customers buy brand B, he would stock it; otherwise he would stock brand A. Now, if the true probability is 0.6, β, the probability of landing in the acceptance region (89 or less), can be determined. That is, for $p = 0.6$, $np = 97.8$, $\sqrt{np(1-p)} \doteq 6.25$, and we can determine the probability that x is less than 90. We determine the appropriate z-value for $x = 89.5$ (since the continuity correction must be used) is

$$z = \frac{89.5 - 97.8}{6.25} \doteq -1.33$$

Only 0.0918 of the area under the normal curve is to the left of -1.33, so the probability of fewer than 90 customers buying brand B if actually 60% of the customers prefer brand B is about 0.09. Thus, increasing the number of customers from 25 to 163 has reduced the likelihood of stocking brand A in error if 60% of the customers prefer brand B from 0.73 to 0.09. The *power* of a test for detecting differences of a given size is $1 - \beta$, so the power of the z-test for detecting a difference of 0.10 $(0.60 - 0.50)$ has risen from 0.27 (for the sample of 25) to 0.91 (for the sample of 163). For even larger samples, the power increases to approach 1.

•Problems

1. Determine β for the example of this section for $p=0.7$ if $n=25$; if $n=163$.
2. A wax company has developed a new floor wax which is similar to that of a competitor. They wish to determine the durability of the wax under common conditions. The competitor's wax has a shine duration of six weeks. They coat 100 kitchen floors with the wax and observe the duration of the shine. They are hypothesizing that their wax is more durable than the competitor's wax, so they are testing the null hypothesis that the shine will last six weeks. One way this can be approached is to obtain the mean duration of the shine of the 100 floors and compare with six weeks. This method will be discussed in section 7.2. A second way would be to observe the proportion of floors in which the shine lasted longer than six weeks. Then the null hypothesis would be $p=0.5$, where p is the proportion of floors with shine lasting six weeks. What is the rejection region for $\alpha=0.05$? That is, how many of the floors would have to have the shine last longer than six weeks to be able to conclude that their wax is more durable, with a probability of 0.05 or less of being wrong? What is the rejection region for $\alpha=0.02$?
3. A television network is offering a new show and expects at least 40% of the viewers to watch the premiere performance. A poll is taken by telephone of 400 viewers and it is found that 189 are watching the new show. Set up null and alternate hypotheses for this experiment, determine the rejection region for $\alpha=0.05$, and draw conclusions based on the results.
4. Patients who contract a certain rare disease have only 0.01 probability of survival with old methods of treatment. A new technique is being tried in limited locations in the country. A total of 400 patients have been treated with this technique and ten have survived. Using the Poisson approximation to the binomial with $\alpha=0.05$, test whether or not we can say the new method is more successful than previous methods and thus merits consideration for an expensive research program.

5.5 *SUMMARY*

In this chapter we discussed continuous probability distributions with special emphasis on the normal distribution.

A normal distribution is related to the standard normal distribution ($\mu=0$, $\sigma=1$) by the formula

Standard Score Formula

$$z = \frac{x - \mu}{\sigma}$$

The values of z are used to enter Table 4 to obtain the area under the standard normal curve between $|z|$ and 0. The probability that a value of the random variable (x) lies between two values x_1 and x_2 is equal to the area under the normal curve between z_1 and z_2 where z_1 corresponds to x_1 and z_2 corresponds to x_2.

Any binomial distribution may be approximated by a normal distribution if both the expected number of successes (np) and failures $(n(1-p))$ are at least 5. If so, the distribution will have $\mu = np$, $\sigma = \sqrt{np(1-p)}$.

In the normal approximation to the binomial and all other continuous approximations to discrete data distributions, a continuity correction must be applied if the variable is truly discrete and measured in integers. In these cases each integer, x, is represented by the interval from $x - 0.5$ to $x + 0.5$.

It is also possible to extend the hypothesis testing technique discussed in section 4.4 by using the normal approximation to the binomial.

•Problems

1. On a certain IQ test, scores are approximately normally distributed with a mean of 100 and a standard deviation of 16. Assuming an underlying continuous distribution determine the following:
    (a) the proportion of scores falling between 80 and 110
    (b) the proportion of scores falling above 130
    (c) the proportion of scores falling below 85
    (d) the score above which lie 25% of the scores
    (e) the score corresponding to a standard score of 1.12
    (f) the score corresponding to a standard score of -0.87
    (g) the probability that a score selected at random will lie between 100 and 120
    (h) the probability that a score selected at random will be less than 110

2. A test for manual dexterity is found to have approximately a normal distribution. The mean is found to be 37.6 and the probability that a score is below 30.0 is 0.0918. Calculate the standard deviation.

3. A memorization test has a standard deviation of 11.62. If 69.5% of the scores exceed 70.34, what is the mean score for the test?

4. A machine which fills fruit juice cans can be set to fill the cans with a mean of anywhere from 44.80 ounces to 48.20 ounces. The standard deviation of the fills will be 0.08 ounces regardless of the mean. If the manufacturer, in order to comply with federal regulations, wishes no more than 100 cans of every 10,000 to contain less than 46 ounces, what should he set as the mean fill? If he wants no more than 100 of every 100,000 cans to fall below 46 ounces, at what value should the mean fill be set?

5. A true–false test is answered by tossing a coin for each question. The test consists of 100 questions. A passing grade is 60. What is the probability of passing the test using this method?

6. In a large community only 45% of the registered voters are in favor of a bond issue. If only 600 voters go to the polls, what is the probability that the issue will pass? A tie counts as a defeat. (Assume that 600 is a random sample of a fairly large population.)

7. A die is rolled 180 times.
   (a) What is the probability of obtaining exactly 20 sixes?
   (b) What is the probability of getting more than 40 threes?
   (c) What is the probability of getting at least 50 numbers divisible by 3?

8. On the average, 60% of the graduates of a certain high school go on to college. This year's graduating class has 150 students in it. Using past records as a criterion, what is the probability that fewer than 75 of the graduates will attend college? One hundred or more? Exactly one hundred?

9. To test the hypothesis that fewer than 30% of all consumers will choose a higher priced but more attractively packaged version of a product, both versions are displayed prominently in a store and a careful record is kept of the sales of each type. The experiment will be based on the results of the first 200 sales. What rejection region leads to the conclusion that actually fewer than 30% of all consumers will buy the higher priced version, for $\alpha = 0.05$? What conclusion will be drawn if actually 53 persons buy the higher priced type? If the actual probability is 0.25, what is β for this experiment?

10. An amateur gardener decides to put in a border of petunias along his driveway. He buys a package of mixed petunia seeds. One-fifth of the seeds should grow into pink petunias and four-fifths into red and white variegated petunias. Assume that the seeds were selected at random from a population mixed to this proportion and that the binomial model applies. If there are 200 seeds in the package, what is the probability that there will be at least 30 but not more than 50 pink petunias if all the seeds germinate?

11. A biologist needs a minimum of 10 specimens of a species of annelid with an abnormal alimentary dysfunction. On the average, about 20% of all members of this species possess this characteristic. If she goes on an expedition to collect specimens, it is fairly costly to bring back more than needed, but impractical to test each for the dysfunction in the field. Further, it is even more costly to mount an additional expedition to collect more if an insufficient number are brought back the first time. She brings back a sufficient number of specimens to give her a high probability of having at least ten of the needed specimens. Since 10 is 20% of 50, the inexperienced researcher might feel that it is sufficient to bring back a sample of 50. Using the normal approximation, what is the probability that a sample of 50 would contain at least ten with the specified characteristic?

If she wants to be 99% confident of having enough, how many specimens should she bring back? (This part is difficult.)

12. In an experiment concerning sex bias, 50 personnel managers were given the same five files each and asked to select a person for a job from these five. Although the same files were given, the names which indicated sex were varied among the files. The qualifications werc approximatcly cqual so that the applicants should have had equal chances of being selected and randomization of the names was done to further equalize the chances. Three of the names were male and two were female. Seventeen of the respondents chose a female name, 33 chose a male name. Using a 0.05 level of significance, do you feel that this shows sex bias on the part of the personnel managers?

CHAPTER 5

Glossary of Terms

continuous random variable
correction for continuity
histogram
normal approximation to the
  binomial

normal distribution
probability density
standard normal distribution
standard score

Glossary of Symbols

z standard score

Statistical Inference: Estimation

6.1 SAMPLES AND SAMPLING DISTRIBUTIONS

For the past several chapters we have been dealing with the characteristics of a complete statistical population. In Chapter 2 we defined a population as a set of data which consists of all possible or hypothetically possible observations of a certain phenomenon.

Probability, in a broad sense, deals with using known population characteristics to obtain information about a *sample*, or subset of the population. More often, perhaps most often, our data are incomplete. We know the characteristics of a sample but not the population from which it was drawn. The extent to which we can apply our knowledge of this sample to estimate the characteristics of the population constitutes, in a broad sense, the field of **statistical inference**.

To learn about a population—workers of a certain type, students in a certain school, customers of a particular store, fertilizers, buying habits of a group of people—it is quite often expedient to select a sample and generalize the results to the population from which the sample was taken. Two sources of error may affect the results of our sample and the extent to which it represents the population from which it is drawn. The first is called **systematic error**, sometimes **measurement error**. This type of error is the result of incorrectly obtaining data. Examples include weighing with a scale which weighs incorrectly—measuring with a rule which is not accurate, or, on a questionnaire, asking ill-defined or misleading questions. It also may be the result of asking the wrong question. Asking a person "Are you a Republican or a Democrat?" when we wish to know whether a person is a political liberal or conservative will yield quite misleading answers, particularly in localities where practically everyone belongs to one party, at least for the purpose of local elections. Systematic error can be avoided, but one must be aware of the possibility.

The other source of error is called **sampling error**. Sampling error is simply the difference in the characteristic under study between the sample and the population. Regardless of the way in which the sample is chosen, the possibility of sampling error is inherent. If a sample is chosen in such a way as to be a **random sample**, however, the probability of the size of the error can be determined by use of statistical techniques. A sample of a population is a random sample if *every sample of a given size is equally likely*. Thus, if the population contains N pieces of data, there are $\binom{N}{n}$ samples of size n, and if the sample is selected in such a way that each sample has probability $1/\binom{N}{n}$ of being selected, then the sample is a random sample.

Methods of sampling are quite important, and only a small amount of space will be devoted to it here. Entire texts have been devoted to the problem of obtaining a sample, such as W. G. Cochran, *Sampling Techniques*, 2nd Edition, (Wiley, 1963). One sample to be avoided is a ready-made sample, such as the set of students in a class, which is called an **incidental sample**. Since the value of a sample depends on the degree to which it represents the original population, an incidental sample should not be used except in cases in which no other sample is available. In such cases, the extent of the sampling error cannot be estimated.

Common notions of the term, "random," need to be examined if we are to understand what is truly meant by the term. For example, if someone were asked to open a book at random, chances are the page selected would be somewhere in the middle third of the book. There is almost no chance that such a person would open the book near the front or the back. Yet such systematic exclusion means that the resulting "sample" is not truly random.

Suppose we were asked to poll 10% of the student body. We may not be able to obtain a random sample by asking questions of every tenth student. Consider the students standing in line to register. If we chose students 10, 20, 30, 40, and so on, we would have 10% of the students, but the sample would not have been chosen at random because the sample which contains students 6 and 7 would have had no chance of being chosen, no matter which student we began with. On the other hand, if the students were grouped in the line at random, without system or pattern, such a sample could be considered, for all practical purposes, to have been randomly obtained. It is unlikely that they would have been, however, for students often register by alphabetical classification. They could also be grouped together by major, or simply in friendship groups. Some *bias* may have been introduced into the method of selection. A random sample could be obtained by using a spinner with numbers one through ten on it, which are equally likely to show up, selecting a "lucky" number, say "one," and spinning the spinner each time a student appears. If a "one" shows up, we would poll the student, otherwise, we would not. Other methods involve the use of tables of random numbers which may be found in many statistics texts or in specially prepared books (see Table 12). In reality, of course, although one of these methods may be used beforehand, we would probably preselect which students would be picked. If we wanted to ask, on the average, every twelfth student in the cafeteria line if he or she was satisfied with the service, we could use a pair of dice and call "10" a success, since $P(10) = 1/12$. Then we could toss the dice, counting the tosses, and record the number of tosses on which "10" occurred. Such a list might look like this:

$$11, 17, 24, 42, 44, 50, 57, 78, 103, 104, 119, 143, \cdots$$

We would continue until we had enough. Then, when the students were in the line, we would simply count and ask students 11, 17, 24, 42, 44, and so on, and be assured that our sample was a randomly selected sample of the students in the line that day. If we could be absolutely sure that the students were randomly arranged in the line, it would be all right to choose every twelfth one. As a general rule, a random sample can be obtained from any population by a random selection procedure, and from a randomly arranged population by a systematic selection procedure. If a sample is obtained from a biased population in a systematic way, however, it cannot be considered random, and the statistical methods applicable to random samples will not be valid. If one were to poll the faculty of a university by stopping in at every tenth office, the result would probably not be random. If the mathematics faculty were arranged in nine consecutive offices, it might be that they had *no* chance of inclusion.

A good procedure in selecting a sample is to use a table of random numbers, a sample of which is given in Table 12. If we do, we are assured of the randomness of our selection procedure. In such a table the digits 0, 1, 2, 3, 4, 5, 6, 7, 8, and 9, are arranged in sequence completely at random. The sequence is often generated by a computer. In this way the probability of a particular digit being in a particular place is the same for each digit. The numbers can be used singly $(0, 1, \ldots, 9)$, as two-digit numbers $(00, 01, \ldots, 99)$, or however needed. To use the table to select a sample, we determine the size of the population to be sampled. We then use the number of digits necessary to assign every member of the population a number. For example, if we are to select a sample of 50 from a population of 5,054 students, we must use four-digit numbers. The numbers 0001 to 5054 will represent the numbers. The numbers 5055 through 9999 and 0000 are ignored. (If there were less than 5,000 students, say 4,500, we could let the numbers do double duty—0001 to 4500 and 5001 to 9500 representing students with, say 3123 and 8123 representing the same student.) There are often specific procedures for entering the table, but these are usually given in the book of tables itself. One way to do it is to open the book anywhere and put our finger anywhere in the table. Rather than starting at this point (because the place selected is not really at random) this will give us the place to start as follows. Suppose the book contains more than 99, but less than 1,000 pages. Then the first three digits will specify the page on which we are to begin. The next two digits identify the line and the final two digits the column. Since there are usually 50 lines and 50 columns on the pages, we may agree beforehand to let two-digit numbers above 50 to be reduced by 50, or to ignore them altogether. Now suppose the numbers obtained were 1092778. We would then turn to page 109, line 27, column 28 (since $78 - 50 = 28$). Then suppose the entries at that point are $309660050861926 70496\cdots$. We use these digits four at a time to obtain 3096, 6005, 0861, 9267, 0496. Numbers for which there are no students are ignored. Thus, if we have numbered the students from 1 to 5,054, we would select the students numbered 3,086, 861, and 496 as our first selections. When we run out of numbers in the line at which we entered the table, we go on to the next line. We would stop when 50 different students had been selected.

A table of random numbers can also be used to simulate experiments. A toss of twenty-five coins can be simulated by entering the table and calling odd digits "heads" and even digits "tails." These are equally likely. If, in another case, we want to make the probability of success 5/12, for example, we can let 01, 02, 03, 04, 05 represent success; 06, 07, 08, 09, 10, 11, 12 represent failure, and all other two-digit representations are ignored. This would be quite time consuming, however, so it would be better to look at the greatest multiple of twelve less than 100, which is 96. Since 5/12 of 96 is 40, we could let any 40 two-digit numbers represent success, 56 represent failure, and ignore 4. It would be simplest to let 01 through 40 represent success, 41 through 96 failure, and ignore 97 through 00. The table may be used for any such assignment of numbers or experiment. All that is necessary is to be absolutely certain that such use preserves probabilities.

Many other methods of sample selection exist, such as selecting matched pairs or stratified samples, but for our purposes we shall assume that our samples are obtained by random sampling.

The paramount importance of random sampling is that, if a population is normally distributed with a known standard deviation, the exact nature of sampling errors can be determined. Although the standard deviation is not generally known, nor is it always known whether a population is normally distributed, certain assumptions and/or modifications can make the methods applicable in all but a small minority of cases. These methods allow us to determine how accurately sample characteristics or measures, such as the mean and standard deviation, called **statistics**, estimate those same characteristics or measures of the population, called **parameters**.

A basic problem in statistical inference is to infer population parameters from sample statistics with a stated degree of accuracy. For instance, suppose we want to determine the mean number of automobiles which pass a certain corner between 7 A.M. and 11 P.M. for the purpose of deciding whether or not to build a service station on the corner. With the permission of the highway department, we install traffic counters and take daily readings for ten weekdays with the following results.

Days	1	2	3	4	5	6	7	8	9	10
Number of Cars	284	386	273	308	317	281	309	290	278	271

These numbers have a mean of 299.7. We may then use this number as an estimate of the number of cars which pass the corner each weekday. However, there are a number of hazards attached to such a use. Although we do not have information to the contrary, it is obvious that if we used another sample (if the experiment were repeated), we would probably obtain some other mean. Statistical inference provides us with a method of estimating the true mean to a desired degree of accuracy. In order to employ this method, we must study the theoretical sampling distribution.

The sampling distribution of a statistic is the probability distribution of that statistic for all samples of a given size. Whether the sampling is done with or without replacement makes a difference, as we shall see. Sampling with replacement is analogous to sampling from a very large population. For example, suppose that we have a "population" consisting of six daily sales reports and the number of sales in the reports are 2, 3, 4, 5, 6, and 7. To estimate the mean of the population, suppose we took a sample of two reports and determined the mean of each sample. Further, suppose this is done with replacement. There are $6 \cdot 6$ or 36 different possibilities, with means ranging from 2 to 7. The probability distributions for these means are given below:

$\bar{x}$	$P(\bar{x})$	$\bar{x}$	$P(\bar{x})$
2.0	1/36	5.0	5/36
2.5	2/36	5.5	4/36
3.0	3/36	6.0	3/36
3.5	4/36	6.5	2/36
4.0	5/36	7.0	1/36
4.5	6/36		

To show how these values were obtained, we present the chart below. The total number of samples possible is 36, and these 36 possibilities are listed here, together with the mean of each.

All Possible Samples, with Replacement, of Size 2, from the Given Population of Size 6					
Sample Selected			Sample Selected		
First	Second	Mean	First	Second	Mean
2	2	2.0	5	2	3.5
2	3	2.5	5	3	4.0
2	4	3.0	5	4	4.5
2	5	3.5	5	5	5.0
2	6	4.0	5	6	5.5
2	7	4.5	5	7	6.0
3	2	2.5	6	2	4.0
3	3	3.0	6	3	4.5
3	4	3.5	6	4	5.0
3	5	4.0	6	5	5.5
3	6	4.5	6	6	6.0
3	7	5.0	6	7	6.5
4	2	3.0	7	2	4.5
4	3	3.5	7	3	5.0
4	4	4.0	7	4	5.5
4	5	4.5	7	5	6.0
4	6	5.0	7	6	6.5
4	7	5.5	7	7	7.0

A simple count of the number at each mean will yield the probability distribution for $\bar{x}$ given before.

If a sample of 3 is taken, sample means range from 2.0 to 7.0, as before. These can be done as above, but there are now 216 different samples. A simpler, more convenient way to obtain the probabilities is to note that the totals on the first two draws range from 4 to 14 (double the means), with probabilities as given. Then the next draw will be one of the numbers from 2 through 7, each with probability 1/6, and totals can be calculated as follows.

Sum of first two draws	Prob.	Third draw 2	3	4	5	6	7	Probability of each entry in row
4	1/36	6	7	8	9	10	11	1/216
5	2/36	7	8	9	10	11	12	2/216
6	3/36	8	9	10	11	12	13	3/216
7	4/36	9	10	11	12	13	14	4/216
8	5/36	10	11	12	13	14	15	5/216
9	6/36	11	12	13	14	15	16	6/216
10	5/36	12	13	14	15	16	17	5/216
11	4/36	13	14	15	16	17	18	4/216
12	3/36	14	15	16	17	18	19	3/216
13	2/36	15	16	17	18	19	20	2/216
14	1/36	16	17	18	19	20	21	1/216

Then the probability of each sum can be calculated. For example, $P(9) = 1/216 + 2/216 + 3/216 + 4/216 = 10/216$. The sample mean can be calculated by dividing totals by three. We then have the distribution of sample means of samples of size three.

$\bar{x}$	$P(\bar{x})$
2.00	1/216
2.33	3/216
2.67	6/216
3.00	10/216
3.33	15/216
3.67	21/216
4.00	25/216
4.33	27/216
4.67	27/216
5.00	25/216
5.33	21/216
5.67	15/216
6.00	10/216
6.33	6/216
6.67	3/216
7.00	1/216

Finally, suppose we take a sample of size four, again with replacement. Sample means again range from 2.0 to 7.0, with a distribution as follows.

$\bar{x}$	$P(\bar{x})$
2.00	1/1296
2.25	4/1296
2.50	10/1296
2.75	20/1296
3.00	35/1296
3.25	56/1296
3.50	80/1296
3.75	104/1296
4.00	125/1296
4.25	140/1296
4.50	146/1296
4.75	140/1296
5.00	125/1296
5.25	104/1296
5.50	80/1296
5.75	56/1296
6.00	35/1296
6.25	20/1296
6.50	10/1296
6.75	4/1296
7.00	1/1296

For comparison, we give a relative frequency polygon for each distribution, together with the mean and standard deviation of each. For reference the population is given here.

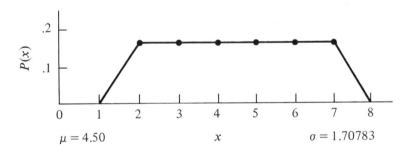

$\mu = 4.50$ x $\sigma = 1.70783$

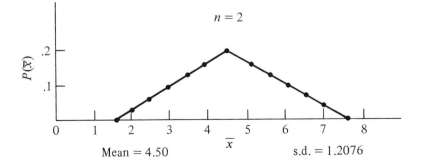

$n = 2$

Mean = 4.50 $\bar{x}$ s.d. = 1.2076

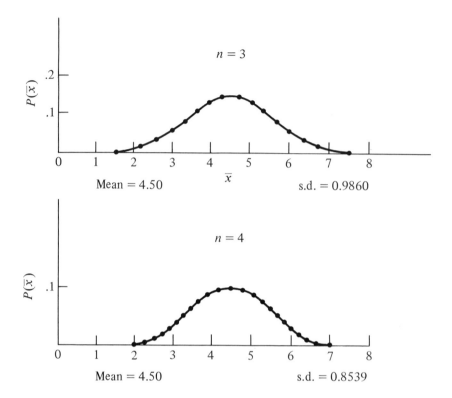

Each of the above is an example of a **theoretical sampling distribution of the mean**, for samples of the given size. For sampling distributions of means, the mean is denoted by $\mu_{\bar{x}}$, and in each of the above cases is 4.50, and the standard deviation of each distribution is denoted by $\sigma_{\bar{x}}$. The standard deviation of any sampling distribution is called the **standard error** of the distribution. For the sampling distribution of the mean, $\sigma_{\bar{x}}$ is called the **standard error of the mean**. Note that, as n increases, the standard error decreases. The standard deviation for the "population" of 2, 3, 4, 5, 6, 7 can be calculated to be 1.70783. Standard errors of the sampling distributions can be calculated from the distributions with these results: for $n=2$, $\sigma_{\bar{x}}=1.2076$, for $n=3$, $\sigma_{\bar{x}}=0.9860$, for $n=4$, $\sigma_{\bar{x}}=0.8539$. Now for any sampling distribution of means of samples of size n, drawn with replacement, $\sigma_{\bar{x}}=\sigma/\sqrt{n}$. This checks here as $1.2076 \doteq 1.70783/\sqrt{2}$, $0.9860 \doteq 1.70783/\sqrt{3}$, and $0.8539 \doteq 1.70783/\sqrt{4}$. Note also that each distribution is more and more like a normal in appearance. No matter what shape the distribution from which the samples are taken, as n gets larger and larger, each successive sampling distribution approaches closer and closer to a normal in appearance. If the original distribution is nearly normal, of course, the sampling distributions will appear normal even for small values of n; if the original distribution *is* normal, *all* sampling distributions for the mean will also be normal, no matter *what* size n is.

As an extreme example, suppose a sample of eight chips is drawn from a large number of poker chips of which half are red and half are blue. If we assign red chips the value "5" and blue chips the value "10," then the theoretical probability distribution is based on a random variable which has the values 5 and 10, each with probability 0.5. The mean of this distribution is 7.5, the standard deviation is 2.5. The sampling distribution for the mean of samples of size eight is given below, rounded off to four decimal places.

$\bar{x}$	$P(\bar{x})$
5.000	0.0039
5.625	0.0312
6.250	0.1094
6.875	0.2188
7.500	0.2734
8.125	0.2188
8.750	0.1094
9.375	0.0312
10.000	0.0039

A graph of the distribution is given below. Note that $\mu_{\bar{x}} = 7.5$ and $\sigma_{\bar{x}} = 2.5/\sqrt{8} \doteq 0.884$.

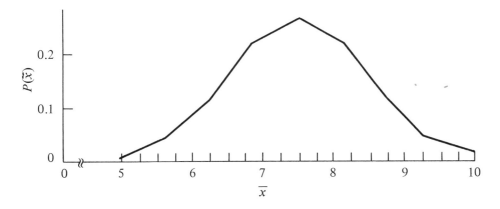

As the sample sizes get larger and larger, no matter what the shape of the original distribution, the sampling distribution of the mean gets closer and closer to a normal distribution with mean equal to the mean of the original distribution. The standard deviation of that distribution depends on the standard deviation of the original distribution, the size of the sample, and the manner in which the sample was taken. For samples with replacement (or for an infinite population), we have seen where $\sigma_{\bar{x}} = \sigma/\sqrt{n}$. For samples drawn without replacement, a **finite population correction factor** must be used. All of the above are examples of one of the most powerful and remarkable results of statistical theory, the **Central Limit Theorem** which states that the theoretical sampling distribution of the means of all samples of size n approaches a normal distribution for n sufficiently large, with mean $\mu_{\bar{x}} = \mu$ and standard deviation $\sigma_{\bar{x}}$, the standard error of the mean defined as follows:

Standard Error Of The Mean

The set of all samples of size n drawn from a population of size N with mean μ and standard deviation σ has the mean $\mu_{\bar{x}} = \mu$ and standard deviation $\sigma_{\bar{x}}$ (for n sufficiently large) given by

$$\sigma_{\bar{x}} = \frac{\sigma}{\sqrt{n}} \sqrt{\frac{N-n}{N-1}}$$

Note that if N is very large, or infinite, the term $\sqrt{(N-n)/(N-1)}$ approaches one. If sampling is done from an infinite population or with replacement, this *finite population correction factor* is omitted. In addition, if the sample constitutes less than 5% of the population, this factor may be omitted because it is very close to one, and we have $\sigma_{\bar{x}} = \sigma/\sqrt{n}$ as in the preceding examples. An example in which the need for the correction factor is apparent is given below.

Consider again the population of daily reports with sales of 2,3,4,5,6,7, and suppose we again take a sample of four from the population. Suppose, however, that this time the sampling is done without replacement. There are then $\binom{6}{4}$ or 15 different possible samples. We determine the mean of each sample of four and list the means as a distribution with the sample means as the random variable.

Sample	Number of sales	$\bar{x}$
1	2,3,4,5	3.50
2	2,3,4,6	3.75
3	2,3,4,7	4.00
4	2,3,5,6	4.00
5	2,3,5,7	4.25
6	2,3,6,7	4.50
7	2,4,5,6	4.25
8	2,4,5,7	4.50
9	2,4,6,7	4.75
10	2,5,6,7	5.00
11	3,4,5,6	4.50

Sample	Number of sales	$\bar{x}$
12	3,4,5,7	4.75
13	3,4,6,7	5.00
14	3,5,6,7	5.25
15	4,5,6,7	5.50

The distribution of sample means can be treated as a probability distribution with the results listed below.

$\bar{x}$	$P(\bar{x})$
3.50	1/15
3.75	1/15
4.00	2/15
4.25	2/15
4.50	3/15
4.75	2/15
5.00	2/15
5.25	1/15
5.50	1/15

The mean of this distribution is 4.50, again equal to the population mean and the standard deviation is about 0.54. The population standard deviation was about 1.7083, and $1.7083/\sqrt{4}$ is about 0.8539, which was the standard error of the distribution for $n=4$ when the sampling was done with replacement. Here the sampling is done without replacement, and 4 is certainly more than 5% of 6, so we must use the correction factor, in this case $\sqrt{2/5}$. Then we have $(1.7083/\sqrt{4})(\sqrt{2/5}) \doteq 0.540$, which checks out.

The Central Limit Theorem, then, allows us to relate samples of size n, for n sufficiently large, to a normal distribution. We can then use

$$z = \frac{\bar{x} - \mu}{\sigma_{\bar{x}}} \quad \text{where} \quad \sigma_{\bar{x}} = \frac{\sigma}{\sqrt{n}} \quad \text{or} \quad \sigma_{\bar{x}} = \frac{\sigma}{\sqrt{n}}\sqrt{\frac{N-n}{N-1}}$$

as appropriate, to relate to the *standard* normal distribution. The term "n sufficiently large" may mean different things to different people, but if the population is normally distributed and the population standard deviation is known, n can be any size; if the population is not normal, or has an unknown shape, the theorem still will apply for n of at least 20. For larger values of n, the approximation is increasingly accurate. In practice, the correction factor is rarely used, since the size of the population is either unknown, but large, or else is large compared to the sample.

EXAMPLE 1 A large population is normally distributed with a mean of 50 and a standard deviation of 12. A random sample of 36 is selected from the population. What is the probability that the mean of the sample is greater than 52?

SOLUTION   Assuming that the population is larger than 720 (so that 36 is less than 5%), according to the Central Limit Theorem, the sample mean will be normally distributed with mean 50 and standard error $12/\sqrt{36}$ or 2. The corresponding standard score is then given by

$$z = \frac{52-50}{2} = 1.00$$

so that the area under the normal curve to the right of $z = 1.00$ is equal (from Table 4) to $0.5000 - 0.3413$ or 0.1587. Thus, the probability that the sample mean will be greater than 52 is about 0.16.

EXAMPLE 2   A sample of 100 pieces of copper tubing is examined for defects. If the process is in control, there will be a mean of 3.000 defects per tube, with a standard deviation of 0.400. If the sample contains a mean of 3.100 defects or more, the entire shipment of 1,000 pieces will be refused on the assumption that the process is out of control. Assuming that the process is in control and the shipment is representative, what is the probability that a shipment will be refused by error?

SOLUTION   The shipment will be refused if the mean number of defects in the sample is greater than 3.100. If the mean of the shipment is actually 3.000 with a standard deviation of 0.400, the probability can be found with the aid of the standard score,

$$z = \frac{3.100 - 3.000}{\sigma_{\bar{x}}}$$

Since 100 is 10% of 1,000, it will be necessary to use the correction factor,

$$\sigma_{\bar{x}} = \frac{0.400}{\sqrt{100}} \sqrt{\frac{1,000 - 100}{1,000 - 1}} = \frac{0.400}{10} \sqrt{\frac{900}{999}}$$

$$\sigma_{\bar{x}} = \frac{(0.400)(30)}{(10)(31.61)} \doteq 0.038$$

Thus $z = 0.100/0.038 \doteq 2.63$, and from Table 4 we see that the probability is $0.500 - 0.4957 = 0.0043$. Thus, the sampling procedure seems to be a good one.

•Problems

1. Suppose that a population is infinite, or sampling is done with replacement, and has a standard deviation of 100. Calculate the standard error of the mean for random samples of size $n=$

    (a) 100
    (b) 1,000
    (c) 10,000
    (d) 36

    (e) 144
    (f) 64
    (g) 128
    (h) 1,024

2. A population of 10,000 has a mean of 187 with a standard deviation of 31. A random sample of 100 is taken. What is the probability that the mean of the sample is greater than 190 if

    (a) no correction for finite population is made?
    (b) a correction for finite population is made?

3. Repeat problem 2 if the population is 2,000 and the sample is 200.

4. A researcher reports that he has a sample of persons for whom the mean number of jobs held in the past five years is 7.6. He reports that the standard error of the mean for the sample is 0.925 based on a standard deviation of 3.7. He neglects to report the sample size, however. From the information given, can you reconstruct his sample size? If so, how large was his sample?

5. An elevator bears a plate which states that the load limit is 2,640 pounds and that no more than 16 persons may occupy the elevator at any one time. Assume that the (large) population which rides the elevator is composed of men and women, but that the men weigh, on the average, more than the women, and the weight of the men have a normal distribution with a mean of 156 pounds and a standard deviation of 12 pounds. What is the probability of overloading the elevator with exactly 16 male passengers?

6. A random sample of 100 is taken from an extremely large population with mean 72.0 and standard deviation 8.0. What is the probability that the difference between the sample mean and the population mean is less than 0.50; that is, what is the probability that the sample mean will be more than 71.5 but less than 72.5?

7. Ten years ago, students at Hay University had a mean score of 18.3 on a manual dexterity test, with a standard deviation of 2.4. Assume these are parameters representative of the entire population at that time. A researcher wishes to discover whether there has been any change during the past ten years. He tests 64 students (of the University's 3,752) and obtains a mean score of 19.1 with a standard deviation of 2.2. What is the probability of obtaining a mean at least this high by chance, if the true situation remains as it was ten years ago?

8. A random sample of 40 aluminum stampings is checked each day to insure that the process is in control. If it is, a day's output of 6,000 stampings can be expected to have a mean index of 80.32 with a standard deviation of 3.16. If the process is out of control, retooling must be accomplished. To this end, if the sample mean is greater than 81.62 or less than 79.02, retooling will begin. What is the probability of retooling by mistake?

9. Some students in a particular college favor coed dorms, while others do not. Suppose the dean of the college decided to conduct a survey to determine the proportion of students favoring coed dorms. The dean sends out two assistants to interview students at random. One assistant goes to the campus coffee shop and finds that 75 of 125 students favor coed dorms. The other assistant goes to the college gym and finds that 65 of 150 students favor coed dorms. If the results obtained by each interviewer are combined, would the results be a better representation of campus views, or should just one or the other of the samples be used? Do you feel that any of the results can be used, or should another poll be taken? If so, what procedure would you suggest?

6.2   ESTIMATING THE POPULATION MEAN

In many cases it is impossible to calculate the population mean or other population parameter directly and it must be estimated. One of the simplest ways to do this is to take a random sample, calculate the statistics for the sample which corresponds to the population parameter we are interested in, and then use the sample statistic as an estimate of the population parameter. This kind of estimate is called a **point estimate**.

For example, suppose that we wish to gauge the average take-home pay of New York secretaries. If we take a random sample of 100, we may find that this sample has a mean of $190.40 and a standard deviation of $43.60. In the absence of better information we may infer that these values approximate those of the corresponding population parameters. We also know, however, that we would be likely to obtain different values for both $\bar{x}$ and s if we were to take a different sample. The Central Limit Theorem tells us that the sample means of all samples of the same size drawn from the same population are approximately normally distributed with mean μ and standard deviation $\sigma_{\bar{x}}$ (the standard error of the mean), where μ is the population mean and $\sigma_{\bar{x}}$ depends upon the standard deviation of the population and the size of the sample (and the population). For a sample of one, the standard error is σ. This is sometimes symbolized by σ_x, the standard error of x.

In section 5.2 we investigated the properties of the standard normal distribution. Table 4 gives the area under this curve between the mean (0) and the given value of z. Using the Central Limit Theorem we can relate the distribution of the sample means to the standard normal distribution by using the formula

$$z = \frac{\bar{x} - \mu}{\sigma_{\bar{x}}}$$

where $\bar{x}$ is the mean of a particular sample.

If we obtain a point estimate, $\bar{x}$, for μ, the difference between $\bar{x}$ and μ is called the **error of estimation**, incurred by using $\bar{x}$ in place of the unknown μ. The difference between $\bar{x}$ and μ is written $|\bar{x} - \mu|$ and it is the absolute value of $(\bar{x} - \mu)$, which is the positive difference between these two values. This is equal to $(\bar{x} - \mu)$ if $\bar{x}$ is greater than μ, and equal to $(\mu - \bar{x})$ if $\bar{x}$ is less than μ.

Suppose we wish to know the probability that we will miss estimating correctly the population mean by, say, 3 or less, if we use the mean of a sample of 100 drawn from a population of 100,000 with a known standard deviation of 15. Here $\sigma_{\bar{x}} = 15/\sqrt{100} = 1.50$, so we have the following sampling curve.

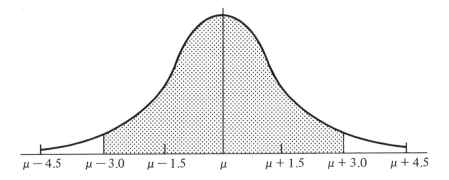

$\mu - 4.5 \qquad \mu - 3.0 \qquad \mu - 1.5 \qquad \mu \qquad \mu + 1.5 \qquad \mu + 3.0 \qquad \mu + 4.5$

Since $3 = 2\sigma_{\bar{x}}$, it follows that we are looking for the probability that the sample mean will fall between $\mu - 2\sigma_{\bar{x}}$ and $\mu + 2\sigma_{\bar{x}}$, that is, between $z = -2$ and $z = +2$. From Table 4, we have 0.4772 of the area under the curve between 0 and 2.00, so the area under the curve between $z = -2.00$ and $z = 2.00$ is 0.9544. The probability that the error is 3 or less is 0.9544. This means that the probability is 0.9544 that a sample of 100 drawn from this population will have a mean which differs from the true population mean by no more than 3. Thus the maximum error with a probability 0.9544 is 3. If the population mean turned out to be 51.4, say, then the probability would be 0.9544 that the mean of any particular sample would be between 48.4 and 54.4. This could be written as $P(48.4 < \bar{x} < 51.4) = 0.9544$.

Now since we probably don't know the population mean (that is why we are taking a sample), if we obtain a sample mean of, say 52.3, since we know that the probability is 0.9544 that the difference between the sample mean and the true mean is less than 3, adding and subtracting 3 to the sample mean of 52.3 yields a **confidence interval** for the population mean.

The idea of a confidence interval is simple enough. Suppose that we take a sample, construct its mean, then add and subtract two standard errors. If the sample mean is within two standard errors of the population mean, then the interval so constructed will contain the population mean; if not, it will not contain the population mean, as shown below.

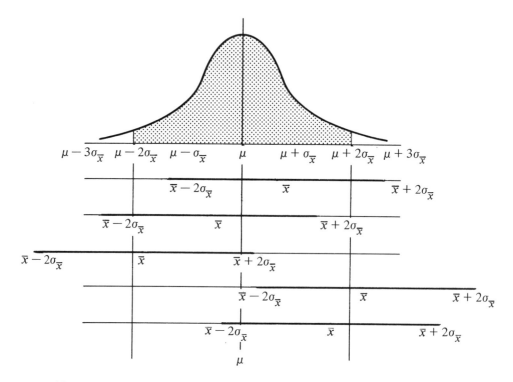

Since 95.44% of all sample means will lie within two standard errors of the population mean, it follows that 95.44% of all the confidence intervals constructed in this way from the same size samples taken from the same population will contain the population mean.

Generally, something other than 95.44% is used; something a little less unwieldy, such as 95%. A look at Table 4 will reveal that, for $z = 1.96$, 0.025 of the area under the curve lies to the right of z, and so, for $z = -1.96$, 0.025 of the area under the curve lies to the left, so that 95% of the area under the curve lies between 1.96 and -1.96. Using the notation introduced in section 5.2, we have $z_{.025} = 1.96$. In fact, for any size confidence interval, if α is the amount in the two tails, then $1 - \alpha$ is the amount between the tails, and $z_{\alpha/2}$ is the number of standard deviations to use.

A few observations are in order. First, the Central Limit Theorem guarantees that such confidence intervals can be constructed from samples of any size if the parent population is normal and the population standard deviation is known. If the population is not normal, we may still apply the Central Limit Theorem for samples of size at least 20 if the population standard deviation is known. (For small samples, if the population standard deviation is known, an alternate approach, using Chebyshev's Rule will be given in section 6.5.) If the standard deviation of the population is unknown, and it usually is, we may still apply the Central Limit Theorem, if the sample is sufficiently large, replacing the unknown population standard deviation with the best estimate we have for it, the sample standard deviation. The difference is quite small and may be neglected if the sample size is at least 50. If the parent population is known to be approximately normal, samples as small as 30 may be used. (For samples less than 30, an alternate approach is available for normal populations, and will be given in section 6.5.) An example will serve to illustrate the method used, as well as the terminology.

A metallurgist wishes to determine the melting point of a new alloy. He takes 36 pieces of the alloy and records the melting point of each piece. The mean of the 36 numbers is found to be 2,356.0° C, and the standard deviation is 3.6°. What can he say about the melting point of the alloy? He may use 2,356° as a point estimate, but he is also aware that a different sample of pieces may have a mean which differs from the mean of this sample. He can use the Central Limit Theorem to obtain a confidence interval. It is reasonable to suppose that the melting points of individual pieces of the alloy will be at least approximately normally distributed about the true mean, so we can use 3.6 to estimate the standard deviation of the population—in this case the set of all melting points of all individual pieces of the alloy. To obtain a 95% confidence interval, he uses $3.6/\sqrt{36}$ as standard error of the mean, 1.96 as the appropriate value of z, and obtains $1.96(0.6) = 1.176 \doteq 1.2$. Thus the probability is 0.95 (or 95%) that the sample mean is, within 1.2° of the true mean. If we add and subtract this number to (and from) the sample mean, we obtain the **confidence limits**. Thus 2,354.8° and 2,357.2° are the confidence limits, and the interval from 2,354.8 to 2,357.2 is a 95% confidence interval for the population mean; i.e., the true melting point of the alloy. The 95% is called the **degree of confidence**.

The term *confidence* may be somewhat misleading. It is difficult to think about the concept of being 95% confident. A popular way of looking at such intervals is to consider the degree of confidence to be the probability that the population mean is in the confidence interval, i.e., $P(a < \mu < b)$, where a and b are the confidence limits. This is misleading since it treats the population mean as a random variable, which it is not. The population mean is fixed, not a variable. What is accurate is to say that 95% (or $(1 - \alpha)\%$) of all confidence intervals constructed from large samples will contain—or cover—the population mean. The probability that a particular confidence interval will be one of those, then, is 95% (or $(1 - \alpha)\%$).

The most common values for a confidence interval are 90, 95, 98, and 99%, or 0.90, 0.95, 0.98, and 0.99. In any case, the confidence interval is determined by its end points, $\bar{x} - z_{\alpha/2}s_{\bar{x}}$ and $\bar{x} + z_{\alpha/2}s_{\bar{x}}$, where $\bar{x}$ is the sample mean, s is the sample standard deviation, $s_{\bar{x}}$ is the estimate for the standard error of the mean obtained by replacing σ with s, and $z_{\alpha/2}$ is determined by the value of α; that is, the population mean lies in $1 - \alpha$ of the confidence intervals where

$$z_{.05} = 1.645 \text{ (if the degree of confidence is 0.90)}$$

$$z_{.025} = 1.96 \text{ (if the degree of confidence is 0.95)}$$

$$z_{.01} = 2.33 \text{ (if the degree of confidence is 0.98)}$$

$$z_{.005} = 2.58 \text{ (if the degree of confidence is 0.99)}$$

Thus, if we wish to be "more confident" and have a greater percentage of confidence intervals covering the mean, we must accept a greater error of estimate. Conversely, if we wish a narrower interval, we must accept a lower confidence level and consequently a higher likelihood of the population mean lying outside the interval.

EXAMPLE 1   A sample of 40 loaves of bread is weighed and found to have a mean weight of 20.24 ounces with a standard deviation of 0.34 ounce. If the sample is a small portion of the daily output, determine 0.95 and 0.99 confidence intervals for the mean weight of the entire daily output.

SOLUTION   Here $s_{\bar{x}} = 0.34/\sqrt{40} \doteq 0.054$, so the error of estimation for a 95% confidence interval would be $1.96(0.054) \doteq 0.106 \doteq 0.11$. The end points (confidence limits) are $20.24 - 0.11 = 20.13$ and $20.24 + 0.11 = 20.35$, so the 0.95 confidence interval for μ is 20.13 to 20.35. For a 99% confidence interval, the error of estimation would be $2.58(0.054) \doteq 0.14$; the end points are $20.24 - 0.14 = 20.10$ and $20.24 + 0.14 = 20.38$. Thus the 0.99 confidence interval for μ is 20.10 to 20.38.

DISCUSSION   The foregoing shows that the more confident we wish to be, the wider the latitude that must be allowed. Thus, we are 95% sure that the true mean is between 20.13 and 20.35 and 99% sure that the true mean is between 20.10 and 20.38. Note that the terms 0.95 and 95% (etc.) are interchangeable. Note also the assumption of normality. Assuming that all loaves are nominally the same size and weight, a normal distribution of the weights would be reasonable.

EXAMPLE 2   A sample of 64 "30 ampere" fuses is found to have a mean peak load of 30.840 amperes with a standard deviation of 0.420 amperes. Estimate 0.90 and 0.98 confidence intervals for the mean peak load for the entire shipment of 1,000 fuses.

SOLUTION   Since 64 is greater than 5% of 1,000, the finite population correction factor must be used so

$$s_{\bar{x}} = \frac{0.420}{\sqrt{64}} \sqrt{\frac{1,000-64}{1,000-1}} = \frac{0.420}{8} \sqrt{\frac{936}{999}}$$

$$\doteq 0.0525(0.9680) \doteq 0.051$$

Thus, the error of estimate with a probability of 0.90 is 1.645(0.051) or 0.084; with a probability of 0.98 is 2.33(0.051) or 0.119. Thus the 90% confidence interval is 30.756 to 30.924, and the 98% confidence interval is 30.721 to 30.959.

EXAMPLE 3   A researcher wishes to poll a sample in order to get public opinion on a certain issue. He will ask the people in his sample to rate their confidence in the administration on a scale of 0 to 100. Assuming an underlying continuous distribution, and assuming that measures of this type can be safely assumed to have standard deviations no greater than 20, how many people should he poll in order to estimate the population mean within 5 units, with a probability of 0.90 of being correct?

SOLUTION   Let E represent the maximum allowable error of estimate. Then, since $E = |\bar{x} - \mu|$, we have $E = z_{\alpha/2}\sigma_{\bar{x}}$. If the population is large or sampling is to be done with replacement, we have $E = z_{\alpha/2}(\sigma/\sqrt{n})$. Upon solving for n, we find that

$$n = \left[\frac{z_{\alpha/2}\cdot\sigma}{E} \right]^2$$

Here $E = 5$, $\sigma = 20$ is a safe estimate, and $z \doteq 1.645$, so we have

$$n = \left[\frac{(1.645)(20)}{5} \right]^2 = [(1.645)(4)]^2$$

$$= (6.58)^2 \doteq 43.30$$

Since we cannot poll a fractional number of persons, and 43 is too few, we must poll 44. Note that, since we will have to use s in the computation of the confidence interval, the Central Limit Theorem will not apply for a sample under 50 unless the population is normal, so that if we cannot meet that assumption we should use a sample of at least 50.

In some cases, the use of the formula will give a sample size less than 30. If we must use s in the computation of the confidence interval, as is usually the case, we cannot use the Central Limit Theorem at all. In such a case two courses of action are possible. We can either go to a sample of 50, which is always satisfactory if the formula gives us less than 50, or, if the normality of the population is likely, we can use 30 or, even better, modify the formula using an appropriate value of t (see section 6.5).

One of the problems in using the above formula is that a reasonable estimate for the standard deviation is sometimes hard to find. A pilot or earlier study is often useful or, if the range of the variable is known, a reasonable estimate can be made using the rule of thumb given in section 2.2 (for a normal population). In no case could the standard deviation ever exceed the range.

TECHNICAL NOTE 1   If the size of the population is known (N), a slight modification of the formula will yield a slightly more accurate result. For simplicity, assume the correction factor to be $\sqrt{(N-n)/N}$. (The difference is negligible.) Then the formula becomes

$$n = \frac{(z_{\alpha/2} \cdot \sigma)^2}{E^2 + (z_{\alpha/2} \cdot \sigma)^2 / N}$$

TECHNICAL NOTE 2   The sampling distribution for the standard deviation of all samples of size n taken from a large population can be closely approximated by a normal curve (for large n) with mean $\mu_s = \sigma$ and standard deviation $\sigma_s = \sigma / \sqrt{2n}$, where σ is the population standard deviation. This version of the Central Limit Theorem can be applied for $n \geq 30$. For small samples, see section 6.6.

Use of the above leads to the fact that confidence intervals for the standard deviation σ of a population, as estimated from the standard deviation s of a sample of size n, are given by

$$\frac{s}{1 + z_{\alpha/2}/\sqrt{2n}} < \sigma < \frac{s}{1 - z_{\alpha/2}/\sqrt{2n}}$$

for a $1 - \alpha$ degree of confidence if $n > 30$ and does not constitute more than 5% of the population. Note that this may be useful in estimating the maximum value of σ when calculating a needed sample size.

•Problems

1. A random sample of 81 copper tubes is drawn from a shipment of 500 tubes, and the tubes are found to have a mean interior diameter of 2.080 cm with a standard deviation of 0.030 cm. Estimate 0.95 and 0.99 confidence intervals for the mean interior diameter of the shipment.

2. A sample of 100 "ten pound" sacks of sugar from a large shipment is found to have a mean weight of 9.93 pounds with a standard deviation of 0.18 pounds. Calculate 0.90 and 0.98 confidence intervals for the mean weight of the sacks in the shipment.

3. A sociologist wishes to sample a population to estimate the validity of a test given several years ago. The standard deviation of that test, 14.8, is used to estimate the current standard deviation and she wants to arrive at the current mean within 2.0 units. What sample size should she use to be sure she is correct with a probability of

   (a) 0.90?
   (b) 0.95?
   (c) 0.98?
   (d) 0.99?

4. A load of 2,500 sacks of grain is inspected by weighing a random sample of 50 sacks and determining a 0.95 confidence interval for the mean weight of the entire load. If the mean of the sample is less than 150 pounds and the confidence interval does not contain 150 pounds, the shipment will be rejected. On a particular day, the mean is 149.0 pounds with a standard deviation of 5.2 pounds. Will the load be rejected?

5. A random sample of 50 grapefruit from a grove has weights as follows (in ounces): 10.7; 13.8; 9.7; 10.2; 9.6; 11.4; 11.9; 13.2; 10.8; 12.3; 10.3; 12.8; 9.1; 8.6; 13.1; 10.6; 11.4; 10.8; 9.1; 11.2; 7.6; 11.6; 13.2; 10.4; 9.9; 11.3; 10.6; 10.3; 10.9; 11.0; 9.3; 9.9; 13.0; 8.8; 10.6; 10.7; 12.4; 12.0; 13.1; 10.5; 9.8; 12.1; 11.8; 10.8; 11.2; 9.4; 8.9; 12.2; 10.7; 11.3. The mean is 10.92 and $s \doteq 1.38$ (Verify these values if a calculator is available.) Estimate the 0.95 and 0.99 confidence intervals for the mean weight of tall grapefruit in the grove.

6. A water company wishes to discover the mean water consumption for the month of July in all homes in a certain area. If there are 618 homes in the area and a random sample of 30 homes shows a mean of 11,644 gallons with a standard deviation of 1,206 gallons, estimate the 0.95 confidence interval for the population mean (a) without the correction factor and (b) with the correction factor. Compare the results. What assumption is made if we use the Central Limit Theorem? Is this assumption reasonable?

7. A total of 400 castings is selected at random from a very large shipment and examined for flaws. The mean number of flaws is found to be 13.40, with a standard deviation of 3.60. What can be said about the possible size of the error, with a probability of 0.98, if 13.40 is used to estimate the mean number of errors in the shipment?

8. A sample of 36 drawn from a normally distributed population of 1500 has values as follows: 86; 113; 94; 63; 80; 97; 108; 94; 122; 54; 76; 103; 94; 77; 96; 69; 93; 68; 91; 114; 88; 93; 124; 102; 105; 87; 94; 83; 91; 95; 104;

72; 131; 88; 67; 111. Calculate the error of estimate if the mean is used to estimate the mean of the population. The desired probability level is 0.90. Determine the probability that the error of estimate will be less than 8.0.

9. Using the data of problem 8, determine the size of sample necessary if the error of estimate is to be 2.5 with a probability of 0.90; 0.95; 0.99.

10. Income data for a set of 100 incomes, chosen at random from a large population, showed a mean family income of $16,443 with a standard deviation of $3,762. Construct a 95% confidence interval for the population mean. Suppose it is known that the standard deviation of the population is actually quite close to $3,000. What would be the 95% confidence interval in that case? If you were to use one of these, which would be more accurate? How large a sample would be necessary to construct a 95% confidence interval with a width (upper limit minus lower limit) of $1,000?

11. Using the information given in Technical Note 2, calculate the probability that for a sample of size n drawn from a large population with standard deviation σ, s will differ from σ by less than E if

   (a) $n = 32$, $\sigma = 10.4$, $E = 2.4$
   (b) $n = 128$, $\sigma = 1.08$, $E = 0.12$
   (c) $n = 100$, $\sigma = 134.2$, $E = 15.0$
   (d) $n = 50$, $\sigma = 1089$, $E = 200$

12. Using the information given in Technical Note 2, determine 95% and 99% confidence intervals for σ if

   (a) $s = 11.4$, $n = 32$
   (b) $s = 137.6$, $n = 50$
   (c) $s = 0.012$, $n = 120$
   (d) $s = 10.030$, $n = 68$

13. Suppose that a sample of 40 drawn from a shipment of 5,000 similar sales orders shows an average order of $154.87 with a standard deviation of $88.30.

   (a) Determine a 95% confidence interval for the population mean.
   (b) Using the standard deviation of the sample as an estimate of the population standard deviation, determine the necessary sample size to be 95% sure your estimate is off by no more than $10.00 (i.e., the width of the confidence interval is $20.00).
   (c) Construct a 95% confidence interval for the population standard deviation.
   (d) Use the upper confidence limit for the population standard deviation as determined in (c) to estimate the sample size as in (b). Is this estimate more likely to be accurate than the one in (b)?

(e) Suppose the orders ranged from $15 to $722. Would the use of 1/5 of the range as an estimate for the standard deviation be too far off the mark? What sample size would be needed in this case? Which of the three values obtained ((b), (d), (e)) would be the most workable and most likely to be acceptable in obtaining the desired result? Why?

6.3 ESTIMATING POPULATION PROPORTION

Most of the variables we have been dealing with up to this point have been measurable. A very important class of variables, called **attributes**, cannot be measured, but can only be described. These things are such things as sex or marital status of individuals, occupation, preferences, vacant, or occupied status of an apartment, and so on. It is usual to describe attributes in terms of a *proportion* of a sample or a population.

In a manner similar to that described in the preceding section, population proportions can be estimated from sample proportions.

If π represents the probability that a member of a population possesses an attribute, π also represents the proportion of the population with that attribute. This usage of the Greek letter "pi" for population proportion is consistent with the use of μ and σ for other population parameters.

As an example, if the probability of drawing a red marble from an urn is 0.20, we conclude that 20% of the marbles in the urn are red. Conversely, if we know that 3/5 of the apartments in a building are vacant, we know that the probability of a randomly selected apartment being vacant is 3/5.

Because of this fact, proportions constitute a binomial population and, in most cases, the binomial distribution can be used. If sampling is done without replacement, of course, the hypergeometric distribution is the appropriate model. In either case, it is more usual to use the normal approximation to the binomial (see section 5.3). Thus if the actual population proportion is π, the number of "successes" calculated from the set of all samples of size n, it will be approximately normally distributed with mean $n\pi$ and standard deviation $\sqrt{n\pi(1-\pi)}$, if both $n\pi$ (number of successes) and $n(1-\pi)$ (number of failures) are at least 5. Then if we let x represent the number of "successes" in a sample of size n with the attribute, the statistic

$$z = \frac{x - n\pi}{\sqrt{n\pi(1-\pi)}}$$

will relate our sampling distribution to the normal distribution. If we let p represent the sample proportion (some authors use p_s), then $x/n = p$, or $x = np$, so that, by dividing both numerator and denominator by n, we have

$$z = \frac{np - n\pi}{\sqrt{n\pi(1-\pi)}} = \frac{p - \pi}{\sqrt{\pi(1-\pi)/n}} = \frac{p - \pi}{\sigma_p}$$

The quantity σ_p is called the **standard error of proportion** and is given by

Standard Error Of Proportion	$\sigma_p = \sqrt{\dfrac{\pi(1-\pi)}{n}}$

As in the sampling distribution of the mean, discussed in the previous section, an analogue of the Central Limit Theorem applies; for sampling done from a finite population without replacement, the finite population correction factor should be used if n is at least 5% of N, the population size. This finite population correction factor (*FPCF*) is the same, namely $\sqrt{(N-n)/(N-1)}$.

Again, the difference between the actual population proportion, π, and the sample proportion, p, is the error of estimate, given by $z_{\alpha/2} \cdot \sigma_p$ for a $1-\alpha$ confidence level, with σ_p again replaced by s_p where

$$s_p = \sqrt{\frac{p(1-p)}{n}}$$

(multiplied by the *FPCF*, if appropriate).

The safeguards for sample size, n being greater than 20, 30, or 50, as the case may be, do not apply here, since the applicability of the normal approximation assures that the normality assumption is met. The assumption of randomness of the sample is, of course, quite important. The values for $z_{\alpha/2}$ remain the same as discussed in section 6.2, so the confidence interval for a population proportion π, as obtained from the sample proportion p, has endpoints $p - z_{\alpha/2} \cdot s_p$ and $p + z_{\alpha/2} \cdot s_p$. That is, $1-\alpha$ of all confidence intervals obtained from random samples of the same size satisfy

$$p - z_{\alpha/2} \cdot s_p < \pi < p + z_{\alpha/2} \cdot s_p$$

where

$$z_{.05} = 1.645 \qquad \text{(if the degree of confidence is 0.90)}$$

$$z_{.025} = 1.96 \qquad \text{(if the degree of confidence is 0.95)}$$

$$z_{.01} = 2.33 \qquad \text{(if the degree of confidence is 0.98)}$$

$$z_{.005} = 2.58 \qquad \text{(if the degree of confidence is 0.99)}$$

EXAMPLE 1   A sample of 100 fuses from a large shipment is found to have 10 which are defective. Construct 95% and 99% confidence intervals for the proportion of defective fuses in the shipment.

SOLUTION   We have $n = 100$, $p = 0.10$, so we approximate σ_p by

$$s_p = \sqrt{\frac{(0.1)(0.9)}{100}} = \sqrt{\frac{0.09}{100}} = \sqrt{0.0009} = 0.03$$

For a 95% confidence interval, $z_{.025} = 1.96$, $1.96(0.03) \doteq 0.06$, so we have confidence limits of 0.04 and 0.16 and a 95% confidence interval of 0.04 to 0.16. For a 99% confidence interval, $z_{.005} = 2.58$, $2.58(0.03) \doteq 0.08$, so the confidence limits are 0.02 and 0.18, and the 99% confidence interval is 0.02 to 0.18.

DISCUSSION   Confidence limits for proportions are fixed from 0 to 1.00, so if by chance one of the confidence limits is either negative or greater than 1.00, common sense dictates that it be replaced by the 0 or 1. If we had a proportion of 0.35, and the error of the estimate were, say, 0.40, the upper limit would be 0.75, but the lower limit would be 0.

A very common error made by students is to obtain the confidence limits by adding and subtracting the error of estimate to and from x, rather than p. In the above case, it would have yielded 9.94 to 10.06 as confidence interval for π. Although this is obviously incorrect, it nonetheless is an error that is frequently made, and should be guarded against.

As in section 6.2, the number needed in a sample for some specified allowable error, E, confidence interval width, $2E$, with specified probability $1 - \alpha$ can be determined. The allowable error, E, is equal to $z_{\alpha/2} \cdot \sigma_p$. If we do not use the *FPCF*,

$$E = z_{\alpha/2} \sqrt{\frac{\pi(1 - \pi)}{n}}$$

can be solved for n to obtain

$$n = \frac{(z_{\alpha/2})^2 (\pi)(1 - \pi)}{E^2}$$

If the population size, N, is known, and we use $\sqrt{(N - n)/N}$, we obtain

$$n = \frac{(z_{\alpha/2})^2 (\pi)(1 - \pi)}{E^2 + (z_{\alpha/2})^2 (\pi)(1 - \pi)/N}$$

If we can estimate the population proportion, we can arrive at some estimate of the sample size needed. One way is to use a sample proportion from a pilot study; even better would be to construct a confidence interval for π. If both confidence limits are greater than 0.5, or less than 0.5, use the one closer to 0.5; if 0.5 is included in the interval, 0.5 should be used. If no estimate is made, 0.5 should be used. The reason for this is that, if $\pi = 0.5$, $\pi(1 - \pi) = 0.25$. For any other value of π, $\pi(1 - \pi)$ is less than 0.25. Note that $(0.3)(0.7) = 0.21$, $(0.4)(0.6) = 0.24$, etc. Thus, if we know absolutely nothing about π, we can still obtain the maximum needed sample size by using $\pi = 0.5$. For any other value of π, the needed sample size would be less. For example, if $z^2/E^2 = 10,000$, and if we could estimate $\pi = 0.3$, then $(0.3)(0.7) = 0.21$ and we would have $n = 2,100$. For $\pi = 0.4$, we would have $n = 2,400$; for $\pi = 0.5$, $n = 2,500$; for $\pi = 0.6$, $n = 2,400$, and so on. Thus $\pi = 0.5$ yields the largest needed sample size and we would know that if we took a sample of that size, no matter what the true value of π, our sample would be adequate.

EXAMPLE 2   A sample of a certain hybrid strain of corn will be examined to see what proportion exhibits a certain genetic characteristic. What sample size should be examined to justify generalizing the result to the entire population accurate to within 0.01 with a probability of 0.95? Assume (a) it is reasonable to use a figure of 0.20 as an estimate for π and (b) nothing is known about π.

SOLUTION   If $E = 0.01$, $z_{.025} = 1.96$ (for a 95% degree of confidence), we have

$$n = \frac{(1.96)^2(\pi)(1 - \pi)}{(0.01)^2}$$

(a)   Assuming $\pi = 0.20$, we have

$$n = \frac{(1.96)^2(0.20)(0.80)}{(0.01)^2} \doteq 6,146.6$$

so we need a sample of 6,147.

(b)   Knowing nothing about π, we let $\pi = 0.50$ since then n is a maximum, and we have

$$n = \frac{(1.96)^2(0.50)(0.50)}{(0.01)^2} \doteq 9,604$$

so we need a sample of 9,604.

•Problems

1. To obtain data for a paper, an MBA major plans to interview people to determine if their reaction to a certain advertising stimulus is positive or negative. She wants to estimate the true proportion to within 0.02 with a probability of 0.95. If a pilot study showed 60 of 100 people with positive reactions, how many should she interview?

2. After a certain amount of training, 48 of 58 rats tested managed to negotiate a maze successfully without error. Give a 95% confidence interval for the proportion of rats, in general, given the same amount of training, who would be able to traverse the maze successfully, without error.

3. A small businessman interviewed 120 of 650 families in an apartment complex which supplies most of his customers, and found that 48 of them preferred a particular brand of instant coffee to any other brand. Give 95% and 99% confidence intervals for the proportion of families in the complex preferring that brand of instant coffee.

4. In a shipment of 1,000 phonograph records, 1 of the first 10 inspected showed defects. Using this as an estimate for the proportion of defectives in the shipment, how many should be inspected as a random sample to estimate the true proportion of defectives correct to within 0.05? Use a 95% degree of confidence.

5. Of 164 persons interviewed, 52 preferred black coffee, 78 preferred cream in their coffee, while the remainder did not drink coffee. Assuming the sample was random, calculate 0.95 and 0.99 confidence intervals for the proportion of coffee drinkers who like cream in their coffee.

6. A total of 363 people are interviewed in a city, the interviews randomly spaced over the city and randomly spaced in time as well. Of those interviewed, 244 saw the new adult comedy "Suds" on television. Of these, 57 said they were offended by the show. Determine a 90% confidence interval for the proportion of the population who saw "Suds," and a 90% confidence interval for the proportion of viewers who were offended by the show.

7. Referring to the data in exercise 6, with what probability can we assert that the point estimate for the proportion of people who viewed "Suds" differed from the true proportion by no more than 0.03? With what probability can we conclude that the point estimate for the proportion of viewers who were offended by "Suds" differs from the true proportion by no more than 0.03?

8. Again referring to the data in exercise 6, how large a sample would be necessary to be able to obtain a 95% confidence interval for the proportion of people who watched "Suds" that is no more than 0.08 wide? How do you think you would determine a sample size if we wanted the proportion of

viewers who were offended by "Suds" correct to within 0.04 with a 95% degree of confidence? Remember that you can control the size of the sample, but not the number of people in the sample who watched "Suds."

6.4   ESTIMATING DIFFERENCES (OPTIONAL)

Quite often it is important to compare samples representing different populations. One may wish to determine which advertising display will sell more merchandise, which neighborhood has a higher mean income, whether men and women engineers make the same or different incomes, and other such questions. Whether or not the samples taken represent populations which are equal is more properly a question for the next chapter, but a question which immediately follows an answer that, yes, two samples do indeed represent populations which differ, is "how much do they differ?"

Suppose that two different types of displays of a razor blade are set up in various stores over town in such a way as to have each display type in about the same kinds and locations of stores; in other words, so that the only relevant variable is the type of display. Suppose that the average weekly sales, in units, are 22.4, with a standard deviation of 6.7, in 54 stores for type I display, and 26.5 with a standard deviation of 9.1, in 49 stores, for type II display. Now the difference in the mean, $\bar{x}_d$, is -4.1 (that is, $\bar{x}_1 - \bar{x}_2 = 22.4 - 26.5 = -4.1$), but this difference is only based on this sample of 54 and 49 stores. If different stores, or different weeks were taken, chances are that the difference would be some other value. To estimate this difference, and obtain a confidence interval for the mean difference, a **sampling distribution for the differences between means** can be constructed as in section 6.2.

If μ_1 and μ_2 represent the true population means for two populations, $\bar{x}_1$ and $\bar{x}_2$ represent the means of any two samples of size n drawn from, respectively, populations 1 and 2, then $\bar{x}_d$ (the difference between the sample means, $\bar{x}_1 - \bar{x}_2 = \bar{x}_d$) will be normally distributed with mean $\mu_1 - \mu_2 = \mu_d$ and standard deviation σ_d (the *standard error of the difference*), provided that the samples are independent and randomly obtained and the parent populations are normal. Only the first assumption is absolutely essential. As with the use of the simple form of the Central Limit Theorem in section 6.2, if the samples are sufficiently large, the assumption of normality may be relaxed. Conditions for the relaxation will be discussed shortly. If both assumptions are met, we have a sampling distribution for $\bar{x}_d$ with mean μ_d and standard deviation σ_d. The variance of the distribution σ_d^2 is simply the sum of the variances for the sampling distributions of the means for the individual populations; that is,

$$\sigma_d^2 = \sigma_{\bar{x}_1}^2 + \sigma_{\bar{x}_2}^2$$

Thus, for samples of size n_1 and n_2 from populations with variances σ_1^2 and σ_2^2, the **standard error of the difference** is given by

Standard Error Of The Difference	$$\sigma_d = \sqrt{\frac{\sigma_1^2}{n_1} + \frac{\sigma_2^2}{n_2}}$$

Then we will have

$$z = \frac{\bar{x}_d - \mu_d}{\sigma_d} = \frac{(\bar{x}_1 - \bar{x}_2) - (\mu_1 - \mu_2)}{\sigma_d}$$

In the same way as in section 6.2, a $(1 - \alpha)$ confidence interval for the differences between the population means can be constructed with the limits $\bar{x}_d - z_{\alpha/2}\sigma_d$ and $\bar{x}_d + z_{\alpha/2}\sigma_d$.

The foregoing all apply, provided the two population variances are known and the populations are known to be normal. If the populations are not known to be normal, we may still use this method if the samples each contain at least 20.

Unfortunately, as is usual, it is unlikely that the population standard deviations will be known. In such cases it is customary to use the sample variances, s_1^2 and s_2^2 to estimate the corresponding population variances, provided the samples are large enough. Again "large enough" is open to interpretation, but we again use the values as in section 6.2. If the populations are approximately normal and each sample is at least 30, or if the population shapes are unknown and each sample is at least 50, we replace σ_d by s_d (standard error of the difference estimated from sample standard deviations) where

$$s_d = \sqrt{\frac{s_1^2}{n_1} + \frac{s_2^2}{n_2}}$$

In summary, then, in most cases a $1 - \alpha$ confidence interval for the difference between the mean of two populations, μ_d, can be constructed from the sample means and standard deviations if the samples are sufficiently large as defined before. The lower confidence limit will be $\bar{x}_d - z_{\alpha/2}s_d$ and the lower confidence limit will be $\bar{x}_d + z_{\alpha/2}s_d$.

COMMENT   In some articles and books, the subscripts for the mean difference and standard error of the difference are given as $\bar{x}_1 - \bar{x}_2$ or some variant thereof. Thus $\mu_d = \mu_{\bar{x}_1 - \bar{x}_2} = \mu_1 - \mu_2$ and $\sigma_d = \sigma_{\bar{x}_1 - \bar{x}_2}$ and $s_d = s_{\bar{x}_1 - \bar{x}_2}$.

EXAMPLE 1   Two different types of displays of a razor blade are set up in various stores over town, randomly chosen, with the type of display randomly decided (by flipping a coin). The razor blades sold in type I displays averaged weekly sales of 22.4 with a standard deviation of 6.7, in 54 stores; the razor blades sold in type II displays averaged weekly sales of 26.5 with a standard deviation of 9.1, in 49 stores. Determine a 95% confidence interval for the true difference in mean weekly sales (that is, the difference expected of all sales of the blade from type I displays versus all sales from type II displays).

SOLUTION   Here $\bar{x}_d = 22.4 - 26.5 = -4.1$. The standard error is estimated by

$$s_d = \sqrt{\frac{(6.7)^2}{54} + \frac{(9.1)^2}{49}} \doteq 1.62$$

For a 95% confidence interval, $z_{.025} = 1.96$, so the error term is approximately $(1.96)(1.62) \doteq 3.2$. Finally, the confidence limits are $-4.1 - 3.2 = -7.3$ and $-4.1 + 3.2 = -0.9$. Thus the confidence interval for $\mu_1 - \mu_2$ is -7.3 to -0.9. We can thus be 95% sure that display type II will sell an average of from 0.9 to 7.3 more units per week per store than display type I.

A similar analysis can be applied to proportions in two samples. Suppose that 317 of 548 persons surveyed considered themselves liberals politically and the remainder moderates or conservatives. Suppose also that 113 of the liberals and 63 of the conservative/moderates said that they felt the administration is doing a good job. We have about 36% of the liberals and 27% of the conservatives feeling that the administration is doing a good job. We can get a confidence interval for the difference in proportion of liberals and proportion of conservatives who feel that the administration is doing a good job. Let π_1 and π_2 represent the true proportions of two populations who possess a particular attribute. Then p_1 and p_2 can represent the proportions of samples of size n_1 and n_2 from the respective populations possessing the attribute. For sufficiently large samples, the differences $p_1 - p_2$ (or p_d) will be normally distributed with mean $p_1 - p_2$ (or p_d) and standard error σ_{dp} (standard error of the difference for proportions), sometimes written $\sigma_{p_1 - p_2}$. The standard error of the difference for proportions depends upon p_1 and p_2, which are not known, and is usually estimated by s_{dp}. Since $\sigma_{dp}^2 = \sigma_{p_1}^2 + \sigma_{p_2}^2$, the estimate for s_{dp} is

Standard Error Of The Difference For Proportions

$$s_{dp} = \sqrt{\frac{p_1(1-p_1)}{n_1} + \frac{p_2(1-p_2)}{n_2}}$$

The term "sufficiently large samples" is here interpreted to mean that all categories possess at least five observations; that is, $n_1 p_1$, $n_1(1-p_1)$, $n_2 p_2$, and $n_2(1-p_2)$ are all at least five.

An alternative method for estimating s_{dp} is by means of "pooling" the data, based on the assumption that π_1 and π_2 are equal, to obtain a pooled sample proportion, $\hat{p}$, obtained simply by combining the two samples together. Then we have

$$s_{dp} = \sqrt{\hat{p}(1-\hat{p})\left(\frac{1}{n_1} + \frac{1}{n_2}\right)}$$

In most cases where we are estimating differences in proportions, we cannot justify the assumption that $\pi_1 = \pi_2$, so pooling is not usually done.

We then have

$$z = \frac{(p_1 - p_2) - (\pi_1 - \pi_2)}{s_{dp}}$$

so that a $1 - \alpha$ confidence interval for the difference between two population proportions can be estimated from sample proportions p_1 and p_2 where the confidence limits are $p_1 - p_2 - z_{\alpha/2} s_{dp}$ and $p_1 - p_2 + z_{\alpha/2} s_{dp}$.

EXAMPLE 2 Of 548 persons randomly selected and questioned, 317 identified themselves as political liberals, of whom 113 felt that the administration is doing a good job, and 231 identified themselves as moderates or conservatives, of whom 63 felt that the administration is doing a good job. Determine a 99% confidence interval for the difference in proportion of liberals and conservative/moderates who feel that the administration is doing a good job.

SOLUTION The sample proportions p_L and p_C are about 0.36 and 0.27, respectively. (Note that the use of descriptive subscripts can be helpful since it is obvious which group they represent.) The standard error, s_{dp}, is given by $\sqrt{(0.36)(0.64)/317 + (0.27)(0.73)/231} \doteq 0.04$; $z_{.005} = 2.58$ and $(2.58)(0.04) \doteq 0.10$. Thus the confidence limits are $0.09 - 0.10 = -0.01$ and $0.09 + 0.10 = 0.19$ and the confidence interval is -0.01 to 0.19. Note that the limits are of opposite sign, so that the interval crosses zero. We are thus 99% confident that the difference in proportion of liberals and moderate/conservatives who think the administration is doing a good job lies between 0.01 greater conservatives and 0.19 greater liberals. Great care must be taken to interpret any confidence interval for differences if the upper and lower confidence limits are opposite in sign. If the true population parameters are fairly close, this is likely to happen more often than not.

•Problems

1. A building contractor needs to buy circuit breakers for installation in his houses. As he wishes to buy the best he can for the money, he obtains two samples of 50 circuit breakers each from each of two manufacturers. The breakers should be able to withstand very brief overloads (say, up to 9/10 of a second) but should not withstand an overload for more than one second. His sample of circuit breakers from manufacturer A had a mean blowing time of 0.78 seconds, with a standard deviation of 0.066 seconds, while the sample from manufacturer B had a mean blowing time of 0.87 seconds with a standard deviation of 0.072 seconds. Determine 90% and 95% confidence intervals for the difference in blowing time between the two manufacturers.

2. In order to determine the best site for a service station, two likely locations are surveyed and counts kept for a month of the number of cars passing the location. At location T, the mean daily traffic was 116.3 with a standard deviation of 22.8 for 31 days. At location S, the mean daily traffic for 30 days (one day's results were lost) was 138.2 with a standard deviation of 38.8. Determine a 99% confidence interval for the difference in mean daily traffic at the two locations.

3. Because of production cutbacks, it has become necessary for a firm to shut down one of its plants. To aid in its decision, the board of directors is examining randomly selected orders to the two plants over the past six months. The mean of 44 orders at the Mariposa plant is $11,544 with a standard deviation of $1,944, while the mean of 36 orders at the Santa Luna plant is $14,114 with a standard deviation of $3,916. Determine a 95% confidence interval for the mean difference in orders at the two plants.

4. Two cities of approximately the same size and type, South Fidelia and Punta Grassa, are interested in the proportion of city employees who actually live

within the city limits. A survey of 132 randomly selected employees of the city of South Fidelia discloses that 91 of them live within the city limits, while only 65 of 104 of a random sample of Punta Grassa employees live within the city limits. Use this set of data to determine a 90% confidence interval for the difference in the proportions of city employees living within the city limits of the two cities.

5. Two sites are being considered for the building of a shopping center. The major store in the shopping center will be J. Sawbuck and Company. Sawbuck hired a firm to survey shoppers in the two areas to see if they would patronize the new store. The sample of 350 residents of East Wadling-ton Heights showed that 154 said they would patronize the new Sawbuck store if it were built in their area, while 233 of 400 residents of Clearwater Park said they would patronize the new Sawbuck store if it were built in their area. Determine a 95% confidence interval for the difference between the two population proportions.

6. A company has heard from a small but vocal minority that its already liberal fringe benefit plan is not liberal enough. Since the majority of the complaining workers work the night shift, the company decided to compare the opinions of night shift workers and day shift workers as to degree of satisfaction with the fringe benefits. Two independently selected random samples were given questionnaires concerning the fringe benefit policy, asking them to rate various aspects and return them. No identification was given on the forms, except for which shift they worked, so the answers could be frank. A score of 80 would be perfect, couldn't be better, while the result of rating the fringe benefits unacceptable in every respect would result in a rating of 8. A total of 37 day-shift workers rated the fringe benefit package an average of 61.3 with a standard deviation of 11.5, while 52 night-shift workers rated the package an average of 47.7 with a standard deviation of 24.6. Use this information to estimate a 90% confidence interval for the difference in ratings between the two shifts.

7. An apartment owner had two buildings, identical except that one of them was painted yellow, the other one was painted brown. He wondered whether there was any difference between occupancy rates in the two buildings (rents were the same for identical apartments), so he looked over the records for the past four years, since the buildings were painted. If any apartment was vacant for more than six months, total, he rated it "poor occupancy rate." Each building contained 26 apartments. In the yellow building, seven apartments were thus rated "poor," while 11 of the apartments in the brown building were so rated. Determine a 95% confidence interval for the difference in proportion of "poor occupancy rate" apartments in any two such buildings. The implication here is that such a difference may be due to the difference in color, and the "populations" would be yellow apartment buildings and brown apartment buildings.

8. Two machines are being examined for possible replacement. Machine *A* produced 27 defectives of the last run of 200, while machine *B* produced 18 defectives of the last 200. Estimate the difference in proportion of defectives in the two machines, using a 98% interval.

6.5 CONFIDENCE INTERVALS FOR SMALL SAMPLES

The preceding sections have all assumed either that the assumptions underlying the construction of the sampling distributions have been met or that the sample sizes have been large enough to relax the assumptions. In the case of proportions, the normal approximation to the binomial is used for large enough sample sizes. For smaller samples, the binomial itself must be used, and, although the procedure is relatively straightforward, it is sticky enough for the best advice to be "consult a mathematical statistician" (*CAMS*).

In the estimation procedure for population means or differences between population means, in addition to independent random sampling, the Central Limit Theorem assumes that the population standard deviations are known. If this is so, and the populations are normal, confidence intervals can be calculated for samples of any size. If the population standard deviations are known, even if normality of the population distributions is in doubt, if the samples are at least 20, the Central Limit Theorem still applies. If the sample or samples are smaller than 20, one possible recourse is *Chebyshev's rule*, introduced in section 2.2. Chebyshev's rule states that, for any distribution, $1 - 1/k^2$ of all pieces of data lie within k standard deviations of the mean. Thus if we want a $1 - \alpha$ confidence interval, we want $1 - \alpha$ of all pieces of data to lie within k standard deviations of the mean, so it follows that, if we set $\alpha = 1/k^2$, this will be satisfied. Solving for k, we find that $k = 1/\sqrt{\alpha}$; thus a $1 - \alpha$ confidence interval for a population mean will be given by the interval $\bar{x} - \sigma_{\bar{x}}/\sqrt{\alpha}$ to $\bar{x} + \sigma_{\bar{x}}/\sqrt{\alpha}$, and a $1 - \alpha$ confidence interval for the difference between two population means will be given by the interval $(\bar{x}_1 - \bar{x}_2) - \sigma_d/\sqrt{\alpha}$ to $(\bar{x}_1 - \bar{x}_2) - \sigma_d/\sqrt{\alpha}$.

EXAMPLE 1   In a manufacturing process, a hole is bored out in the interior of a metal part by a cutter attached to the end of a rod which is inserted into a depression drilled into the metal. The cutter is set initially to bore holes 11.45 cm in diameter, but unfortunately the cutter always slips after it has been set, although usually only a small fraction of a centimeter. This slippage always occurs during the processing of the first part, and the amount is unpredictable. It has been found that it is better to finish the run (usually 10,000), than to attempt to readjust since determination of the actual diameter of the hole bored requires destruction of the part, and a readjustment is subject to slippage which does not always result in an improvement. The standard procedure is to take a random sample after the production run and obtain a confidence interval for the true mean from this. The distribution of diameters is not normal since the cutting head wears uniformly, decreasing in size by about 0.023 cm during the course of the run. Hole diameters are distributed approximately normally except for this deviation, however. Thus diameters are not normally distributed, or the Central Limit Theorem could be applied, nor uniformly distributed, in which case we would only have to examine the first or second part of the run. Additionally, the only way to determine the diameter of the hole is to break open the part. Since the cutting head does wear uniformly, however, the standard deviation of the diameters does not vary from run to run, remaining approximately 0.0066. If a sample of ten parts is taken and the mean diameter is found to be 11.447 cm, determine 80%, 90%, and 95% confidence intervals for the population mean diameter.

SOLUTION   The standard error of the mean is $0.0066/\sqrt{10}$ or about 0.0021. For an 80% confidence interval, $1 - 1/k^2 = 0.80$, so $1/k^2 = 0.20$, $k^2 = 5$, and $k = \sqrt{5}$, or about 2.236; thus the error term is $(2.236)(0.0021)$ or about 0.005. Alternatively, since $1 - \alpha = 0.80$, $\alpha = 0.20$, so the error term is $(0.0021)/(\sqrt{0.20})$ $\doteq 0.005$. Thus an 80% confidence interval is 11.442 to 11.452 cm. For a 90% confidence interval, the error term is $(0.0021)/\sqrt{0.10}$ or about 0.007, so a 90% confidence interval is 11.440 to 11.454. For a 95% confidence interval the error term is $(0.0021)/\sqrt{0.05} \doteq 0.009$ so a 95% confidence interval is 11.438 to 11.456.

If the population standard deviation is not known, but the shape of the population is known to be approximately normal, the Central Limit Theorem can be applied, using s as an approximation to σ if the sample contains at least 30. For samples less than 30, the sampling distribution of the mean is not accurately approximated by a normal distribution. The sampling distribution is

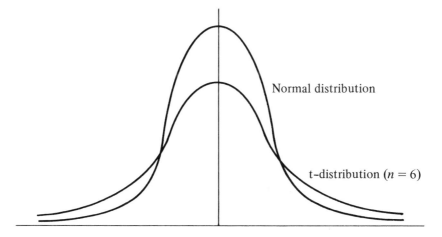

Normal distribution

t-distribution ($n = 6$)

approximately bell shaped, but the proportion of the areas under the curve is greater in the tails than that of a normal curve and the curve is consequently flatter. In fact, the smaller the sample size, the flatter the curve. This sampling distribution is called the **t-distribution** (or *Student t-distribution*, since it was first introduced by W.S. Gosset under the pseudonym "Student"), and it may be used for samples drawn from populations which are approximately normal.

The preceding figure shows a *t*-distribution for a sample of 6 compared to a normal distribution with the same mean and standard deviation. Each *n*, where *n* corresponds to the size of the sample, generates a different *t*-distribution; that is, *t*-distributions with the same mean and standard deviation, but based on different sized samples, will all be different. As *n* increases to infinity, the *t*-distribution approaches the normal distribution and for practical purposes can be considered as such for $n \geq 30$.

For each sample of size $n < 30$ drawn from a normally distributed population we can use the statistic

$$t = \frac{\bar{x} - \mu}{s / \sqrt{n}}$$

for the sampling distribution. Each sample of size *n* would generate a *t*-distribution which could have its areas tabulated as the normal curve does in Table 4. Such tables are available, but for our purposes we need only those values which correspond to 0.90, 0.95, 0.98, and 0.99 confidence intervals. As with Table 4, only the positive points for *t* are given since the *t*-distribution is symmetric.

In cases in which the sample size is less than 30, then, the error of estimation is equal to $t_{\alpha/2} s / \sqrt{n}$, and the confidence interval would be $\bar{x} - t_{\alpha/2} s / \sqrt{n}$ to $\bar{x} + t_{\alpha/2} s / \sqrt{n}$ for appropriate *t* depending on the degree of confidence selected. Note that, in cases when *s* is used in place of σ, the *t*-distribution is actually the most appropriate, but the use of *z* for $n \geq 30$ is almost universally accepted.

In Table 5, the numbers at the top give the area under the curve to the right of the given *t*, while the numbers at the side give the **degrees of freedom**. For a single sample of size *n*, the number of degrees of freedom is $n - 1$. Generally speaking, degrees of freedom can be considered to be the number of independent observations used to make an estimate. If we know $n - 1$ of *n* observations with a known mean, the *n*th is automatically determined. So if we know 9 of 10 numbers whose sum is 100, the tenth is also known. Here $n - 1$ is 9, the number of degrees of freedom we have. The numbers in the body of the table are the values of t_k, where *k* is the column heading, for the number of degrees of freedom at the side of the table. For a sample of 17, for instance, there are 16 degrees of freedom. For a 95% confidence interval we would need $t_{.025}$, so from Table 5 we read $t_{.025} = 2.120$ rather than 1.96 (which is $z_{.025}$). Note that $t_k = z_k$ for infinite degrees of freedom.

EXAMPLE 2   A sample of 25 numbers randomly selected from a normally distributed population is found to have a mean of 32.60 and a standard deviation of 1.30. Derive 95% and 99% confidence intervals for the population mean.

SOLUTION   As in section 6.2, the confidence interval is determined by the confidence limits; here we substitute $t_{\alpha/2}$ for $z_{\alpha/2}$ and use $s/\sqrt{n}$ for the standard error term. Since $t_{.025}$ for 24 degrees of freedom is 2.064, the error term is $(2.064)(1.30)/\sqrt{25} \doteq 0.54$. Thus the 95% confidence limits are $32.60 - 0.54 = 32.06$ and $32.60 + 0.54 = 33.14$ and the 95% confidence interval is 32.06 to 33.14. For a 99% confidence interval, $t_{.005} = 2.797$ for 24 degrees of freedom. The error term is then equal to $(2.797)(1.30)/\sqrt{25} \doteq 0.73$, so the 99% confidence interval is 31.87 to 33.33.

In the final case, in which the population standard deviation is not known, the shape of the population is not known; we still can use the Central Limit Theorem if the sample is sufficiently large. For populations which are not too badly skewed, a sample size of 50 or more is usually sufficient, although if there is a great deal of skew (as in income data), it might be better to get samples of 100 or more. In such cases, large sample methods for a normal population apply. There is no general rule applicable to small samples if absolutely nothing is known about the population. If the shape of the population distribution is not known, but derivable, a sampling distribution can be determined. In other cases, a reasonable upper bound for the population standard deviation can be determined—it is never greater than the range, for example—so that Chebyshev's rule can be used. In such cases *CAMS* (consult a mathematical statistician).

Similar remarks apply to finding a confidence interval for the difference between two population means. We have already mentioned the case in which the standard deviations of the populations are known and Chebyshev's rule applies. If the population standard deviations are not known and the normality of the populations is questionable, the remarks of the preceding paragraph apply. If, however, we can reasonably infer that the populations are approximately normal, the *t*-distribution can be applied to determine the confidence interval if one or both of the samples is less than 30. To do so it is necessary to have one additional assumption in order to find a method which is not too messy. We assume that both populations have the same standard deviation. This would mean that the standard error of the difference would be

$$\sigma_d = \sigma\sqrt{\frac{1}{n_1} + \frac{1}{n_2}}$$

If we assume that both populations have the same variance, we can use the sample variances of both samples to estimate the common population variance obtaining the *pooled variance* $\hat{s}^2$. This is obtained by pooling the sums of squares in the two samples and dividing the result by the total number of degrees of freedom in the two samples. Thus

$$\hat{s}^2 = \frac{\Sigma(x_1 - \bar{x}_1)^2 + \Sigma(x_2 - \bar{x}_2)^2}{n_1 + n_2 - 2}$$

If the variances of the two samples are known, the pooled variance is

$$\hat{s}^2 = \frac{(n_1 - 1)s_1^2 + (n_2 - 1)s_2^2}{n_1 + n_2 - 2}$$

Then a $1 - \alpha$ confidence interval for the difference between the mean has the limits $(\bar{x}_1 - \bar{x}_2) - t_{\alpha/2}\hat{s}\sqrt{(1/n_1) + (1/n_2)}$ and $(\bar{x}_1 - \bar{x}_2) + t_{\alpha/2}\hat{s}\sqrt{(1/n_1) + (1/n_2)}$

A method for determining whether or not the assumption that the population variances are equal is reasonable will be given in the next section. If they are not equal, some approximate methods exist, but will not be discussed here. One such discussion appears in Smith and Williams, *Statistical Analysis for Business: A Conceptual Approach* (Wadsworth, 1976), 445–451.

Note that if $n_1 = n_2 = n$ (both samples are the same size), $\hat{s}^2$ becomes $(s_1^2 + s_2^2)/2$, so that $\hat{s}\sqrt{(1/n_1) + (1/n_2)}$ simply reduces to $\sqrt{(s_1^2 + s_2^2)/n}$.

EXAMPLE 3 A chemical company wants to build a new plant in either East Quincy or New South Hampton. One of the criteria is the index of methane in the air since the plant will put some methane into the atmosphere. Readings of methane proportions are taken at randomly spaced intervals in the two cities. Eight readings in East Quincy showed an average of 0.23 parts per million with a standard deviation of 0.07 ppm while eleven readings in New South Hampton showed an average of 0.32 parts per million with a standard deviation of 0.12 ppm. Determine a 95% confidence interval for the difference in actual mean methane levels for the two cities.

SOLUTION Using the assumption that it is reasonable to assume that the variances are equal (and we will see in the next section that it is), we first calculate $\hat{s}$. We have

$$\hat{s} = \sqrt{\frac{7(0.07)^2 + 10(0.12)^2}{17}} \doteq 0.1024$$

Since the samples have a total of 17 degrees of freedom, $t_{.025} = 2.110$, so the error term is $(2.110)(0.1024)\sqrt{(1/8 + 1/11)} \doteq 0.100$. Since $(0.23 - 0.32) = -0.09$, the confidence interval is -0.19 to $+0.01$, indicating that, although it is likely that East Quincy has a lower mean methane index than New South Hampton, there is still some chance that it will be slightly higher. Looked at in another light, there is a 0.025 chance (1 in 40) that the difference will be less than -0.19, but also one chance in 40 that it will be greater than 0.01.

•Problems

1. A new alloy is subjected to 9 determinations of hardness, with the result that the mean value on Moh's scale is 0.630 with a standard deviation of 0.081. Estimate 0.95 and 0.99 confidence intervals for the true hardness of the alloy.

2. Referring to problem 1, a second measuring instrument is used on the same alloy. Nine determinations with the second instrument yield a mean value of 0.572 with a standard deviation of 0.074. Determine a 90% confidence interval for the difference in mean hardness as measured by the two different instruments (as applied to this alloy).

3. A super ball is dropped and the height of the bounce is measured. The proportion of the original height to which the ball returns is called the **coefficient of restitution** for the substance. Four determinations of the coefficient of restitution for this super ball yield values of 0.84, 0.78, 0.86, and 0.81. Estimate the 95% and 99% confidence intervals for the coefficient of restitution of this ball.

4. On 15 tests, the reaction time of a volunteer to a given stimulus has the following values in seconds: 0.12, 0.14, 0.09, 0.13, 0.11, 0.12, 0.11, 0.11, 0.09, 0.13, 0.14, 0.10, 0.11, 0.10, 0.12. Assuming that the tests were performed under similar conditions, and that the assumptions underlying the t-distribution apply, estimate a 99% confidence interval for the mean reaction time of this individual to the stimulus.

5. A study of telephone calls at a business office was made. Incoming calls were timed and outgoing calls were timed for one day. Assuming that the day's calls made up a random sample of calls (which may be open to argument) determine 95% confidence intervals for the length of incoming calls, for the length of outgoing calls, and for the mean difference in length of the two types of calls. Seventeen incoming calls lasted an average of 5.16 minutes with a standard deviation of 1.12 minutes, while twelve outgoing calls lasted an average of 4.13 minutes with a standard deviation of 2.36 minutes.

6. Suppose that a sample of eleven is drawn from a normally distributed population with a known standard deviation of 11.62. If the sample mean is 38.44, derive a 95% confidence interval for the population mean. If the sample standard deviation is 11.04, compute a 95% confidence interval using *t* and compare it to the one obtained earlier. Thus if σ is known, we can estimate more closely than if *s* must be used, even if *s* is less than σ.

6.6   SOME OTHER SAMPLING DISTRIBUTIONS (OPTIONAL)

The previous sections have all used the normal or *t*-distributions as sampling distributions. There are a large number of other sampling distributions, of varying degrees of importance. Two of the other sampling distributions with wide applicability are the *Chi-Square distribution* and the *F-distribution*. There are other applications, but both of these distributions arise in connection with a study of sample variances.

The sampling distribution of sample standard deviations was mentioned in Technical Note 2 of section 6.2. It was observed that, for sufficiently large samples, sample standard deviations taken from a population with standard deviation σ will be normally distributed with mean σ and standard deviation $\sigma/\sqrt{2n}$. For small samples, $n < 30$, if we take all possible sample variances from a sample of size *n*, the statistic $\Sigma(x - \bar{x})^2/\sigma^2$ has a sampling distribution known as Chi-Square (χ^2). Since this distribution has also been studied extensively, for any sample, a value of Chi-Square can be computed from

$$\chi^2 = \frac{\Sigma(x - \bar{x})^2}{\sigma^2} = \frac{(n-1)s^2}{\sigma^2}$$

and compared to a table of values to determine the probability of s^2 being

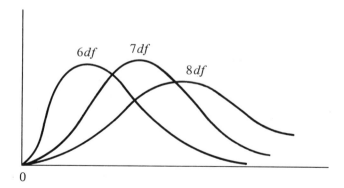

greater than a particular value. The particular shape of a Chi-Square distribution depends on the value of n, in this case, and, more generally, on the number of degrees of freedom. As with the t-distribution, the shape of the distribution varies with degrees of freedom; in the case of Chi-Square, however, the distribution can never be negative, so it is bounded below, and, of course, may be skewed to the right. As the number of degrees of freedom increases without bound, the mean increases as well, and the distribution approaches symmetry. The graph of Chi-Square for 6, 7, and 8 degrees of freedom is illustrated below.

The Chi-Square distributions have been extensively studied and tables prepared for each number of degrees of freedom, as with the normal and t-distributions. Since they are not symmetric, however, the two tails cannot be considered to be mirror images. With the normal distribution, we use $z_{.025}$ for both ends of the confidence interval for the population mean; the lower limit is $\bar{x} - z_{.025}s_{\bar{x}}$ and the upper limit is $\bar{x} + z_{.025}s_{\bar{x}}$. This is merely a convenience however, as we want the lower to be $\bar{x} + z_{.975}s_{\bar{x}}$. It just so happens that $z_{.975} = -z_{.025}$. For the Chi-Square, no such luck is in store for us. To get a 95% confidence interval for a population standard deviation or variance, we want 2.5% to lie in each tail.

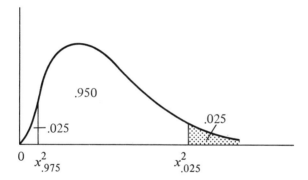

The value of χ^2 for which 0.025 is in the right hand tail would be designated $\chi^2_{.025}$; the value with 0.025 in the *left* tail would be designated $\chi^2_{.975}$, since 0.975 is to the right of it. Thus for a $1 - \alpha$ confidence interval, we need both the values of $\chi^2_{\alpha/2}$ and $\chi^2_{1-\alpha/2}$.

Thus, for 95% of the sample variances calculated from a sample of size n

$$\chi^2_{.975} < \frac{(n-1)s^2}{\sigma^2} < \chi^2_{.025}$$

By solving this inequality for σ^2, we get a 95% confidence interval for the population variance; that is, for all samples, size n, the statement

$$\frac{(n-1)s^2}{\chi^2_{.025}} < \sigma^2 < \frac{(n-1)s^2}{\chi^2_{.975}}$$

is true 95% of the time. Similarly, for any $1-\alpha$ confidence interval, the lower and upper limits are given by $(n-1)s^2/\chi^2_{\alpha/2}$ and $(n-1)s^2/\chi^2_{1-\alpha/2}$. The values of χ^2 are given in Table 6.

EXAMPLE 1 A sample of twelve castings is taken from a daily production run. In many cases, the standard deviation is a good indication of quality control—an indication of variability. If the standard deviation of the mean number of flaws per casting for the sample is 6.34, determine a 95% confidence interval for the population variance (that is, the variance of the run) and a 90% confidence interval for the population standard deviation.

SOLUTION   From Table 6, with 11 degrees of freedom, $\chi^2_{.025}$ is 21.92, while $\chi^2_{.975}$ is 3.82. The confidence limits, then, are $(11)(6.34)^2/21.92 = 20.17$ and $(11)(6.34)^2/3.82 = 115.75$, so the 95% confidence interval for the population variance is 20.17 to 115.75. For a 90% confidence interval, we use $\chi^2_{.05} = 19.68$ and $\chi^2_{.95} = 4.57$. The confidence limits are $(11)(6.34)^2/19.68 = 22.47$ and $(11)(6.34)^2/4.57 \doteq 96.75$. For the population *standard deviation*, the limits will be the square roots of those, so the confidence interval for the population standard deviation is 4.74 to 9.84.

Another sampling distribution of great value is the **F-distribution**, named after Sir Ronald Fisher. The F-distribution is the ratio of two Chi-Squares, and arises in many cases, particularly where variances are concerned. A derivation of the F-distribution may be found in Smith and Williams, *Statistical Analysis for Business: A Conceptual Approach* (Wadsworth, 1976), pp. 468 ff.

One particular instance of an F-distribution is the case in which all possible samples of sizes n_1 and n_2 are taken from the same population, or from populations with equal variances. If the ratio of all possible variances s_1^2/s_2^2, is formed, the result is an F-distribution. Each F-distribution depends upon *two* sets of degrees of freedom, one for the numerator of the ratio, the other for the denominator of the ratio. In the case at hand, if all possible ratios of s_1^2/s_2^2 are formed, with samples of size n_1 and n_2, where all the numerators are variances of the samples of size n_1 and all the denominators are variances of samples of size n_2, the numbers of degrees of freedom are $n_1 - 1$, and $n_2 - 1$. Tables 7 and 8 give the values of F for which 5% and 1%, respectively, of all values of F exceed those values; that is, for each of the possible pairs of degrees of freedom, Tables 7 and 8 give the values of $F_{.05}$ and $F_{.01}$, respectively. The F-ratio thus obtained forms a valuable check on the equality of variances, so necessary for the use of the t-distribution in the case of the difference between means estimated from two independent samples. Suppose our two samples are those of example 3 of the previous section. There we have variances of $(0.07)^2 = 0.0049$ for the sample from East Quincy, size 8, while eleven readings in New South Hampton had a variance of $(0.12)^2 = 0.0144$. Note in Table 7 that only the values of $F_{.05}$ are given. The F-distribution has a shape somewhat like that of a Chi-Square distribution, so it is not symmetric.

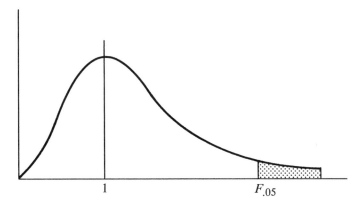

We could consider the ratio of $0.0049/0.0144$ in an F-distribution with 7 and 10 degrees of freedom, *or* the ratio of $0.0144/0.0049$ in an F-distribution with 10 and 7 degrees of freedom. Because of this duality, it is usual to consider only the ratio

$$F = \frac{s_1^2}{s_2^2}$$

where s_1^2 is the larger of the two variances. If necessary, the 1 and 2 can be interchanged. In this case, then, we would be interested in an F-distribution with 10 and 7 degrees of freedom. From Table 7, in such a distribution, only 5% of all values of F would be greater than 3.64. The convention, then, in deciding whether or not the sample variances are representative of equal population variances, is to compute the F-ratio, larger variance over smaller variance, comparing with the critical value $F_{.05}$ (or $F_{.01}$ if you want to be less conservative), concluding that there is reason to believe that the population variances are not equal only if the obtained F-ratio is greater than the value of $F_{.05}$ for the appropriate number of degrees of freedom. In this instance, since $0.0144/0.0049 = 2.94$ which is less than 3.64, we conclude that the variation in sample variances is within chance limits and that the assumption of equality of variances is reasonable.

EXAMPLE 2   Two samples of production line workers are asked to try new procedures designed to perform the same task. The first sample, of 25 workers, required a mean of 4.11 minutes with a standard deviation of 1.85 minutes to perform the task. The second sample, with 24 workers (one had become ill) took a mean of 3.35 minutes to do the task with a standard deviation of 1.17 minutes. Assuming that the samples were independent random samples, and it is reasonable to assume normality, test whether or not the assumption of equality of variance is satisfied in order to use a t-distribution to estimate the mean difference between the two procedures.

SOLUTION   The F ratio of these samples is $(1.85)^2/(1.17)^2 \doteq 2.50$. From Table 7, with 24 and 23 degrees of freedom, we find that the critical value of F (that is, $F_{.05}$) is 2.01. This means that, if the population variances are indeed equal, the probability of obtaining a sample F greater than 2.01 is 0.05. We can conclude that the difference in sample variances is probably not due to chance, and that the use of the t-distribution would be inappropriate.

•Problems

1. Variance is an important aspect of quality control, in that variability of output is a measure of consistency. If a machine putting out ball bearings is too variable in its output, too many of the production run will be unacceptable—either too large or too small in diameter. Suppose that the first 25 ball bearings produced by a machine have a mean diameter of 6.003 mm with a standard deviation of 0.017 mm. Determine 90%, 95%, 98%, and 99% confidence intervals for the standard deviation of the run.

2. Using the methods of technical note 2, section 6.2, repeat problem 1 above if the sample is of size 50.

3. Use the methods of this section to determine whether or not the t-distribution is actually appropriate in problems 1 and 2 of section 6.4.

6.7   SUMMARY

Estimating parameters from sample statistics is possible if certain assumptions are made and the necessary conditions met. Estimation of population parameters generally involves an interval called a **confidence interval**. We state that there is a certain **degree of confidence**, usually 0.90, 0.95, or 0.99 (90%, 95%, 99%) that the confidence interval contains the parameter. The end points of the interval are called the **confidence limits**. The specific procedure used depends on the shape of the distribution, whether the population standard deviation is known or unknown, and the size of the sample.

The table below summarizes the different possibilities. In each case it is assumed that the sample is a random sample selected from the population. The symbols used are explained in the text and in the glossary.

Shape of Distribution	Population Standard Deviation	Sample Size	Confidence Limits
Normal	Known	Any n	$\bar{x} \pm z_{\alpha/2} \cdot \sigma_{\bar{x}}$
	Unknown	$n \geq 30$	$\bar{x} \pm z_{\alpha/2} \cdot s_{\bar{x}}$
		$n < 30$	$\bar{x} \pm t_{\alpha/2} \cdot s / \sqrt{n}$
Not normal	Known	$n \geq 20$	$\bar{x} \pm z_{\alpha/2} \cdot \sigma_{\bar{x}}$
		$n < 20$	$\bar{x} \pm \sigma_{\bar{x}} / \sqrt{\alpha}$
	Unknown	$n \geq 50$	$\bar{x} \pm z_{\alpha/2} \cdot s_{\bar{x}}$
		$n < 50$	$CAMS^*$

*Consult a mathematical statistician.

A confidence interval for the population proportion π can be obtained from a sample, provided that the number of observations in each of the categories is at least 5. In such a case a $1 - \alpha$ confidence interval for p has the limits $p \pm z_{\alpha/2} s_p$. As in the case of the confidence interval for the mean, a finite population correction factor must be applied if the sample is obtained without replacement from a finite population and constitutes more than 5% of the population.

A confidence interval for the population standard deviation can be obtained from a sample; if the sample is at least 30, the confidence limits for σ will be

$$\frac{s}{1 + z_{\alpha/2}/\sqrt{2n}} \quad \text{and} \quad \frac{s}{1 - (z_{\alpha/2})/\sqrt{2n}}$$

For small samples, $n < 30$, the confidence limits for σ are given by

$$\sqrt{\frac{(n-1)s^2}{\chi^2_{.025}}} \quad \text{and} \quad \sqrt{\frac{(n-1)s^2}{\chi^2_{.975}}}$$

In order to estimate the mean of a population within E units with a $1 - \alpha$ degree of confidence, the sample should be at least n where

$$n = \left[z_{\alpha/2} \frac{\sigma}{E} \right]^2$$

where σ is the best upper bound estimate for the population standard deviation.

If sampling is from a finite population, we must modify the formula to include the finite population correction factor (*FPCF*).

For estimating the proportion of a population within E units with a $1 - \alpha$ degree of confidence, the sample should be at least n where

$$n = \frac{z_{\alpha/2}^2 \pi (1 - \pi)}{E^2}$$

and where π represents a reasonable estimate of the population proportion. If no estimate is available, using $\pi = 0.5$ will give the largest sample size necessary for the stated degree of accuracy. Again, if sampling is done from a finite population, a formula incorporating the *FPCF* will give a slightly better (and smaller) estimate for the necessary n.

In order to obtain confidence intervals for the difference between two population means, a similar procedure can be used. Again, the specific procedure used depends upon the shape of both parent populations, and whether or not the population standard deviations are known, as well as the size of the samples. The table below summarizes the different possibilities. The symbols used are explained in the text and the glossary.

Shape of Distributions	Population Standard Deviations	Sample Size	Confidence Limits
Both normal	Both known	Any size	$(\bar{x}_1 - \bar{x}_2) \pm z_{\alpha/2}\sigma_d$
	Unknown[a]	$n_1 \geq 30$ $n_2 \geq 30$	$(\bar{x}_1 - \bar{x}_2) \pm z_{\alpha/2}s_d$
		$n_1 < 30$ or $n_2 < 30$	$(\bar{x}_1 - \bar{x}_2) \pm t_{\alpha/2}\hat{s}\sqrt{(1/n_1) + (1/n_2)}$
One or both not normal	Both known	$n_1 \geq 20$ $n_2 \geq 20$	$(\bar{x}_1 - \bar{x}_2) \pm z_{\alpha/2}\sigma_d$
		$n_1 < 20$ or $n_2 < 20$	$(\bar{x}_1 - \bar{x}_2) \pm \sigma_d/\sqrt{\alpha}$
	Unknown[a]	$n_1 \geq 50$ $n_2 \geq 50$	$(\bar{x}_1 - \bar{x}_2) \pm z_{\alpha/2}s_d$
		$n < 50$ or $n < 50$	*CAMS*

[a]If one population standard deviation is known, substitute for the sample standard deviation in s_d. $\hat{s}$ depends upon sample s only.

One additional assumption is required in the above table. In order to calculate $\hat{s}$ and use the t-distribution, it is necessary that the variances of the two populations be equal. To determine whether or not this assumption is reasonable, the larger sample variance is divided by the smaller sample variance to obtain an F-ratio. If the obtained F-ratio is greater than F_α, we conclude that the assumption of equality of population variances is not warranted, and the t-statistic cannot be used. If the obtained F is less than F_α, we conclude that the difference is due to chance and that the assumption of equality of variance is satisfied.

A similar procedure can be used to find a confidence interval for the difference between population proportions. A $1-\alpha$ confidence interval for $\pi_1 - \pi_2$ has the limits $p_1 - p_2 \pm z_{\alpha/2} s_{dp}$ provided that the number of observations in each category is at least 5.

•Problems

1. A random sample of 120 Graduate Record Examination scores is taken from those of a university's graduating class of 4,182. If the mean of the sample was 1,082 with a standard deviation of 108, estimate 95% and 99% confidence intervals for (a) the population mean, and (b) the population standard deviation.

2. A newspaper believes that 75% of retired couples prefer apartment living to house living. It wishes to sample retired couples and obtain a 0.99 confidence interval for the true proportion correct to within 0.05. What sample size should be taken (a) if the newspaper estimate is used as a basis, and (b) if no estimate is used?

3. A test run of 25 tires showed a mean mileage of 28,642 miles with a standard deviation of 1,246 miles. Determine 95% and 99% confidence intervals for the true mean mileage of that brand and type of tire.

4. Two samples of potential customers were each shown an advertising presentation and asked to rate the presentation on a scale of 1 to 10 in terms of whether or not it would make them more likely to buy the product. A total of 23 people rated presentation A a mean of 5.6 with a standard deviation of 1.9, while presentation B had a mean rating of 6.3 with a standard deviation of 1.6 for its sample of 27. Is the t-distribution appropriate to estimate the difference between the two presentations? If so, determine a 90% confidence interval for the difference between the mean ratings of the two presentations.

5. Four subjects were randomly selected from a population and asked to make subjective judgments on a situation involving interpersonal relationships. These judgments took the form of a rating sheet with the ratings

weighted and an overall score obtained. These 4 subjects obtained scores of 173, 217, 143, and 166. Assuming the necessary conditions are met, estimate the 0.95 confidence interval for the population mean.

6. If a corporation wishes to obtain the mean income of a certain area, correct to within $100 with a probability of 0.95, what size random sample should be taken if $500 is a reasonable estimate for the standard deviation?

7. A random sample of 16 coffee cans is taken from a day's large output. The weights of the contents are known to be normally distributed with a standard deviation of 0.15 ounce and means which vary slightly from day to day. The sample is found to have a mean weight of 16.02 ounces with a standard deviation of 0.21 ounce. Calculate 0.95 and 0.98 confidence intervals for the mean weight of the day's output.

8. A random sample of 200 families out of 750 in a certain apartment complex is interviewed, and the mean number of children per family is found to be 3.2 with a standard deviation of 0.8. Calculate the 95% confidence interval for the mean number of children per family in the apartment complex.

9. A random sample of 80 insurance salesmen working for Inequitable Life showed 56 in opposition to proposed revisions in the pension plan which Inequitable currently has for its insurance salesmen. Construct 95% and 99% confidence intervals for the proportion of the salesmen working for Inequitable who oppose the revisions.

10. Efficiency ratings of 12 identical machines chosen at random from among those produced by a company over the past five years (several thousand) were used to estimate the mean efficiency rating of all machines produced by the company over the past five years. The ratings of the twelve were 0.820, 0.913, 0.764, 0.881, 0.902, 0.893, 0.663, 0.862, 0.812, 0.778, 0.932, 0.824. If the mean of the sample is used to estimate the population mean, what can be said with a probability of 0.95 about the possible size of the error?

11. In reference to problem 9, a random sample of 75 insurance salesmen who work for Providential Insurance were given the Inequitable pension plan as if it were being proposed for Providential salesmen. A total of 44 were opposed to it. Determine a 90% confidence interval for the difference between the proportions of insurance salesmen opposed to the plan in the two companies.

12. A new method of processing bills is introduced into the accounting department of a large chain. Of a random sample of 84 bills, 36 are processed more efficiently, while the remainder are not. Give 0.95 and 0.99 confidence intervals for the proportion of all bills which can be expected to be processed more efficiently by the new method.

13. A sample of 200 light bulbs from a large number showed exactly 24 to be defective. Construct 95% and 99% confidence intervals for the proportion of defectives in the total number.

14. A machine must maintain a certain level of quality control in its output or it will have to be shut down for repairs. A machine produces 20 IC components during a particular day's run. The mean impedance for the components is 154 ohms with a standard deviation of 8.3 ohms. Determine 90% and 95% confidence intervals for the mean impedance of the machine's output if the variation is not normally distributed. Calculate 90% and 95% confidence intervals for the variance of the output. Assume that the day's run is a random sample of the machine's current output.

15. The light bulbs in problem 13 were manufactured by Company *G*. A sample of 180 light bulbs from Company *S* showed 27 to be defective. Construct a 95% confidence interval for the actual difference in proportion of defectives manufactured by the two companies.

CHAPTER 6

Glossary of Terms

attributes	population parameter
bias	proportion
Central Limit Theorem	random numbers
Chebyshev's rule	random sample
Chi-square	sample statistics
confidence interval	sampling
confidence limits	sampling distribution
degree of confidence	sampling error
degrees of freedom	standard error
error of estimation	standard error of difference
estimation	standard error of difference
finite population correction	for proportions
factor	standard error of the mean
incidental sample	standard error of proportion
interval estimate	statistical inference
measurement error	Student's *t*-distribution
point estimate	*t*-distribution

Glossary of Symbols

E	maximum allowable error with a given probability
F	F-ratio
μ	population mean
μ_d	mean difference
μ_s	mean, sampling distribution of the standard deviation
$\mu_{\bar{x}}$	mean, sampling distribution of the mean
N	population size
n	sample size
π	population proportion

p	sample proportion
σ	population standard deviation
σ_d	standard error of the difference
σ_p	standard error of proportion
σ_s	standard error of standard deviation
$\sigma_{\bar{x}}$	standard error of the mean
s_2	sample standard deviation
$\hat{s}$	pooled variance
s_d	standard error of the difference estimated from sample standard deviations
s_{dp}	standard error of the difference for proportions estimated from sample proportions
s_p	standard error of proportion estimated from sample proportion
$s_{\bar{x}}$	standard error of the mean estimated from sample standard deviation
t	Student's t
t_a	value of t for which a is the proportion of the area under the curve to its right
$\bar{x}$	sample mean
$\bar{x}_d$	difference between sample means
z_a	value of z for which a is the proportion of the area under the normal curve to its right
χ^2	Chi-square
χ_a^2	value of Chi-square for which a is the proportion of the area under the curve to its right

Chapter 7

Statistical Inference: Hypothesis Testing

7.1 *HYPOTHESIS TESTING TECHNIQUES*

In addition to estimation, one of the primary purposes of statistical inference is to test conjectures or hypotheses. Hypothesis testing was introduced in section 4.4 and discussed again in section 5.4. The techniques used there were specifically focused on binomial testing. In this chapter we investigate the general method of hypothesis testing with specific applications using the sampling distributions introduced in Chapter 6.

Let us recall the businessman's problem introduced in section 4.4. He wanted to decide whether or not a new method of processing bills should be used in order to reduce errors. Errors have been made on 2/5 (40%) of all bills processed with the system currently in use. He wanted to decide whether to switch to the new system developed by the office manager. The *null hypothesis* was that there would be no difference between the new and old methods in proportion of errors. The *alternate hypothesis* was that there would be fewer errors with the new method.

The basic idea of hypothesis testing rests on the null hypothesis technique. We know what shape and characteristics the sampling distribution will have if the null hypothesis is true, so we can base our conclusions on a comparison of the sample results we actually obtain with that sampling distribution, and decide whether or not the results were consistent with the assumption that the null hypothesis is true.

If the sample statistic we obtain is out of line with what we would expect if the null hypothesis were true, we may conclude that it is likely the null hypothesis is not true and, if the results are consistent with our alternate hypothesis, we may decide that it is likely that the alternate hypothesis is true. There are some variations from this, of course, but the basic idea holds true for all hypothesis testing.

The businessman would use the null hypothesis that the proportion of errors using the new method is 2/5. His alternate hypothesis would be that the proportion of errors is less than 2/5. The choice of these would be dictated by the fact that 2/5 is his point of comparison, and that if the new method has errors in fewer than 2/5 of the bills, he would want to use the new method, which corresponds to the alternate hypothesis, while if this were not so, he would want to continue with the old method. Thus, in business decisions, we are generally not so much concerned with proving either the null or alternate hypothesis as with the actions which correspond to them.

Now since a sample does not constitute all the cases, it is entirely possible to make an error in the conclusion. Either one can reject a true null hypothesis, or else one can accept a false null hypothesis. These two types of error are called type I and type II errors, respectively. These types are presented in the following table.

Null	Action	
Hypothesis is	Accept null Hypothesis	Reject null Hypothesis
true	no error	type I error
false	type II error	no error

The probability of error is implicit in any hypothesis test. These probabilities are designated α, the probability of type I error, and β, the probability of type II error. Although the types of errors were not discussed in section 4.4, their probabilities were discussed, and it was noted that there is a complex relationship between α, β, and sample size. The value of α is preselected, since it can be controlled, and it is called the *level of significance* for the test. Usual levels of significance are 0.10, 0.05, or 0.01, depending on how sure we wish to be that we are not rejecting a true null hypothesis by chance. Levels of 0.01, sometimes 0.001, are usually reserved for scientific investigations, although a business decision involving large amounts of risk, or of money, as in quality control problems, may sometimes be set at 0.01.

Selection of α gives a specific rejection and acceptance region for the assumption that H_0 is true, and also gives us a way of looking at β. For instance, if we use a null hypothesis that a population mean is some specific value μ_0, and it is actually some other value μ_1, we have the following curves for the sampling distribution of the mean.

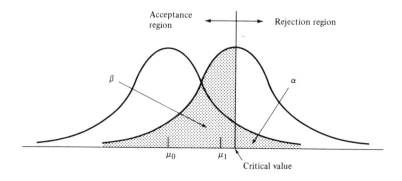

The curve on the left is the sampling distribution which would result if H_0 were true, and the area under that curve in the rejection region is the value of α. On the other hand, if the population mean is actually μ_1, the curve on the right is the true sampling distribution, and the area under that curve in the acceptance region is the value of β. Note that calculation of β depends on knowing the true state of things, which we cannot ever know, or we would not be doing any testing.

For a given sample size, decreasing the value of α (moving the critical value to the right in the above drawing) will increase the value of β. If α is kept constant, the only way to reduce β is to increase the sample size, as that will decrease the standard error and make both curves narrower.

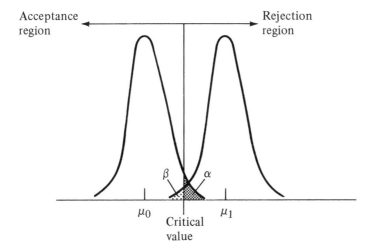

One of the problems with extremely large sample sizes, however, is the possibility of rejecting H_0 when actually the differences, as between μ_0 and μ_1, while real, are so small as to be of no practical significance. Some specific procedures for attempting to control for type II error exist, but are beyond the scope of this text.

One of the ways of allowing for type II error is called "reserving judgment." If we cannot reject the null hypothesis, we may not wish to accept it either because we feel that there is a high probability of making a type II error. In such a case we reserve judgment, if possible, failing to make a decision one way or the other.

Hypothesis testing techniques are generally applied to what is loosely termed an "experiment." The applicability of the techniques and the validity of the results depends directly upon the extent to which the assumptions underlying the use of the statistical techniques are met. In any experiment, there are sources of error which may affect the result and render any conclusion meaningless. A true experiment manipulates one variable at a time, and examines the results. Design of the study is essential if conclusions are to be valid, and any study should be designed before any data is collected in order to determine which, if any statistical tests will be appropriate. Many sources of error can be controlled or eliminated if the sample or samples to be used in the study are selected randomly from the population. In cases where random selection is impossible, specific techniques involving pretesting are usually necessary. One of the best discussions of experimental error types and control, as well as designs and methods of analysis, can be found in the booklet, *Experimental and Quasi-Experimental Designs for Research*, by Donald T. Campbell and Julian C. Stanley (Rand McNally College Publishing Company, 1963). Although initially designed as a guide to educational research, the principles are universal and transcend disciplines.

The first step in hypothesis testing, after identifying the general problem and the research hypothesis or conjecture to be tested, is the identification of the null hypothesis. The null hypothesis must be specific so that the assumption that it is true will lead to the possibility of using one of the standard sampling distributions.

Before any experiment is performed, a research hypothesis should be formulated. The research hypothesis sums up what the experimenter expects to find out from the experiment and forms the basis for the null and alternate hypotheses which are used in the statistical hypothesis testing.

If a research hypothesis is an investigation into whether a population parameter is a particular value or not, or whether two methods are equally valuable or not, the selection of the null and alternate hypotheses is easy. The null hypothesis is simply a statement of equality, while the alternate is its denial. We may be testing a hypothesis, for example, that the mean sales for the month for all salespersons on the staff was the same as last month, versus that it was not. If the mean sales last month was 156 units, then we would have $\mu = 156$ for the null hypothesis, and $\mu \neq 156$ for the alternate hypothesis. In such a case the alternate hypothesis is said to be two-sided, since if our sample showed significantly less than 156 or significantly more than 156, we would reject H_0 and conclude that the alternate is true. The term "significantly," here, means that our sample statistic fell in the rejection region of the sampling distribution determined by H_0, the rejection region consisting of $\alpha/2$ of the area under the curve in each tail.

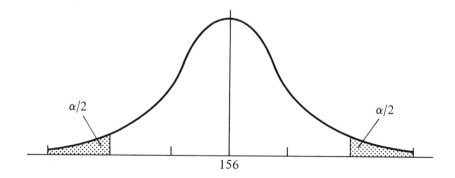

Quite often, however, our research hypothesis is such that we are interested only in investigating a rejection region in one tail of the sampling distribution. The businessman's problem, mentioned at the beginning of this section, is an example of what is termed a one-sided alternative. In his case, he was interested in replacing the old system with the new one *only* if it could be shown that the new system was better; that is, that the proportion of bills with errors would be less than 2/5. If it were equal to 2/5, or more than 2/5, he would retain the old system. He was testing the null hypothesis that $\pi = 2/5$, where π represented the proportion of bills with errors under the new system, against the alternate hypothesis that $\pi < 2/5$. His alternate hypothesis was one-sided, and his rejection region one-tailed. He would reject H_0 in favor of the alternative (and thus use the new system) only if his sample showed significantly less than 2/5 of the bills with errors. The term "significantly" again means that the sample statistic fell in the rejection region of the sampling distribution determined by H_0, the rejection region consisting of α of the area under the curve in *one* tail; in this case the lower tail.

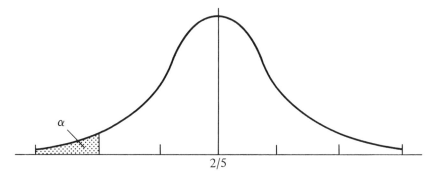

The selection of a one-sided alternate hypothesis requires a bit more care than that of a two-sided alternative. Because of the nature of hypothesis testing, the burden of proof is on the alternate hypothesis. If we wish to "prove" that the alternate hypothesis is "true," our sample must be in the rejection region, which requires that the difference must be one which is large enough to show up. Note that the use of the word "prove" should be used with caution. We cannot use statistics to actually prove statements, but only to demonstrate a high degree of likelihood that the statements are true.

In the one-sided case, selection of an alternate hypothesis requires examination of the consequences of the outcomes. In the businessman's problem, he would need to decide what he would do if the new method and the old method were equivalent. That is, if $\pi = 2/5$ for the new method, would he keep the old method or change to the new one? We assumed, in formulating the alternate $\pi < 2/5$, that he would keep the old method if they were equal. This would put the burden of proof on the new method to show that it was better. Suppose, however, that there were some other plusses with the new method; perhaps it is less expensive. Thus if they were equivalent, and if $\pi = 2/5$, he might wish to switch to the new method. Thus his alternate hypothesis in that case would be $\pi > 2/5$. If he could conclude the alternate hypothesis, that the new method was not as effective as the old, he would retain the old method. In that case, the burden of proof would be on the old method.

The major thrust in hypothesis testing is whether or not the alternate hypothesis has been substantiated at the desired *level of significance*. The **level of significance** is the probability of making a type I error, α, and corresponds to the experimenter's willingness to take a chance of being wrong in rejecting the null hypothesis. The criteria for setting α may include such considerations as the time factor, the number of alternatives, the cost of making an error and, in general, the consequences of such an error. A 0.10 level of significance is sometimes used in cases where the consequences are minimal.

Controlling for type II error is much more difficult. We cannot calculate β exactly unless the actual population parameter is known. As mentioned before, we can eliminate the possibility of type II error by reserving judgment in cases where a decision does not have to be reached. This procedure is useful in cases when consequences of a type II error are great, or its likelihood appears to be high.

Values of β can be calculated, of course, if we assume that the parameter has a particular value. By determining values of β for possible values of the parameter, we can plot a distribution approximating all possible values of β called the **operating-characteristic** curve (or O-C curve). Examples of calculations for β are given in sections 4.4 and 5.4. As was stated there, the only way to decrease β is to increase the sample size or to allow α to increase. One use of the O-C curve is that it allows us to weigh the probability of a type II error. In the case of large samples, β is usually relatively small, so reserving judgment is done more often with a small sample than a large one.

Another use of β is in calculating the *power* of a test. The **power** of a statistical test is defined as the probability of rejecting H_0 for a specific value of the parameter. Thus, for a particular value of a parameter, the power of the test being used is $1 - \beta$. A power curve can also be calculated for a particular problem, and is the complement of the O-C curve.

EXAMPLE 1 A farmer takes a sample of grapefruit and weighs them. His standard requires a mean weight of 12.5 ounces for his crop. The crop will not be marketed if the mean weight is less than 12.5 ounces. Give suitable null and alternate hypotheses if (a) he has high standards and will not market the crop unless it averages more than 12.5 ounces, (b) he is anxious to market the crop unless it is demonstrably substandard.

SOLUTION   In either case we have $H_0: \mu = 12.5$, where μ is the mean weight of the crop. In case (a) however, if H_0 is true, he will not market the crop; he will market it only if $\mu > 12.5$, so we have for (a),

$$H_0 : \mu = 12.5$$

$$H_1 : \mu > 12.5$$

In case (b), if H_0 is true, the crop is not substandard, so he will market it. He will not market it only if $\mu < 12.5$, so we have, for (b),

$$H_0 : \mu = 12.5$$

$$H_1 : \mu < 12.5$$

EXAMPLE 2 Two applicants for a job agree to a competition in which each will perform the operation required for the job a number of times in order to have a sample of each applicant's performance on the job. The applicant whose performance is significantly better will be given the job. Set up suitable null and alternate hypotheses for the experiment.

SOLUTION The key word here is *significantly*. Differences may be slight and may not show up as true differences until after a number of trials. Hence we are searching for true differences in their long-term performance. If P_1 and P_2 represent the two individuals' *true* performance on the job, we have

$$H_0 : P_1 = P_2$$

$$H_1 : P_1 \neq P_2$$

The alternate hypothesis is two-sided, since we are only interested in there being some difference in the two performances. We do not address ourselves here to the problem of what to do if we cannot reject H_0; perhaps they will both be hired, or some other criteria will be devised.

With the foregoing as background, let us return to the businessman's dilemma of example 1 of sections 4.4 and 5.4. On his store shelves he has two products, identical except for brand name. Since his space is limited, he has decided to eliminate one brand from his inventory. Brand A and brand B have had approximately equal sales over the past several months, but he feels that recently his customers have shown a preference for brand B. On the other hand, brand A is advertised more extensively than brand B. He would like to stock the brand preferred by his customers, but if there is no real preference he wants to take advantage of the advertising offered by brand A. He therefore decided to perform a experiment by observing the buying habits of a sample of customers buying the product. He is thus testing a hypothesis.

What hypothesis is he testing? He feels that brand *B* is actually preferred by his customers; this is his **research hypothesis**, the hypothesis he wishes to prove. To control for type I error he sets up his **null hypothesis** that the customers prefer the two brands equally. Thus he bases his assumptions on the hypothesis that the proportion of customers preferring brand *A* is equal to the proportion of customers preferring brand *B*. This is symbolized $P_B = P_A$ (or some other appropriate designation). His **alternate hypothesis** corresponds to the research hypothesis and is determined by the research hypothesis. In this case it would be $P_B > P_A$. That is, if $P_B > P_A$ he will stock brand *B* only, otherwise he will stock brand *A* only. Note that the two hypotheses being tested will result in different outcomes. The very real possibility that $P_B < P_A$ will result in stocking brand *A* only, as will acceptance of the null hypothesis, so it need not be considered separately.

After deciding on the null and alternate hypotheses, he must set the **level of significance**, which is his willingness to accept a chance of making a type I error. This is α, and we generally set $\alpha = 0.05$, allowing one chance in twenty of being wrong if we reject H_0. As mentioned before, $\alpha = 0.01$ is also used sometimes, as well as other values, less frequently.

Before undertaking the experiment, it is usual to set up a research design, which takes into account the type of sample, controls on the variables, and appropriate test statistics available. The **test statistic** is the basis for decision. The test statistic is the variable which is used to accept or reject the null hypothesis (or to reserve judgment). In the businessman's case, when the problem was considered before, the test statistic was the number of customers choosing brand *B*. It is more usual to relate the data to one of the standard sampling distributions, such as were examined in Chapter 6, and to calculate a value of *z* or some other test statistic that is compared to **acceptance** and **rejection regions**. The points which divide these regions are called the **critical values** and are set forth in the **criteria**. In the businessman's example of section 5.4, the criteria, based on a sample size of 163, were to reject the hypothesis if 90 or more customers bought brand *B*, and accept it otherwise. More typically we would relate our sample immediately to the normal distribution and reject the null hypothesis if, in this case, $z > 1.28$. Referring to section 5.4, you will see that this value of *z* was used to obtain the figure of 90 customers. In practice, we use the standard score formula to determine the value of *z* which our sample yields and compare it to the critical value. In this case the critical value is 1.28. The general procedure is to set up the criteria independently of the precise size of the sample (although it is generally necessary to know if the sample is large or small) and state them prior to actual performance of the experiment. Further discussion of acceptance and rejection regions is given in the next section.

After the preliminary work is completed, the experiment is performed and the results tabulated. These results are used to calculate the value of the test statistic for the sample(s) which is compared to the criteria. A **decision** is then made whether to accept or reject the null hypothesis, or to reserve judgment. Based upon this decision, a conclusion will be reached which agrees with the actual meaning of the hypothesis; which tells what will be *done*, if anything, as a result of the decision. This five-step format is known as the **hypothesis-testing procedure** and may be summarized as follows:

1. **Statement of hypotheses**

   H_0: Statement of the null hypothesis
   H_1: Statement of the alternate hypothesis to be accepted if H_0 is rejected.

2. **Level of significance**

   α: The acceptable probability of making a type I error; that is, of rejecting H_0 erroneously. This is usually 0.05 or 0.01, by common usage. Significance level is always set before the experiment is conducted.

3. **Criteria**

   These criteria are the basis for decisions, and are determined entirely by three conditions: the appropriate sampling distribution, the alternate hypothesis (one- or two-sided), and the level of significance. They generally give a statement of a rejection region, such as the following: reject H_0 if $z > 1.96$ or if $z < -1.96$. This particular case, as will be seen later, is used when the test statistic is z, from the normal distribution, the alternate hypothesis is two-sided, and $\alpha = 0.05$.

4. **Results**

   In performing the experiment, the researcher must actually apply the procedures indicated in the criteria and obtain a result.

5. **Conclusions**

   The conclusions of the experiment consist of the decision reached, whether to reject H_0 or not, and the consequences of that decision. The decision will always be to reject H_0 or to fail to reject H_0, and will be completely determined by comparing the results with the criteria. The conclusions also include the consequences of the decision, such as: The firm will open a branch office, will not open a branch office, or will reserve judgment, perhaps pending the results of further tests. It should be noted that reserving judgment in any but an academic setting, in which there are no overt consequences, should be followed by any further testing or sampling which may be useful to bring the experiment to a final conclusion. Note further that reserving judgment is done *only* when we fail to reject H_0; *if the decision is to reject H_0 we cannot reserve judgment*.

This five-step procedure is applicable to most statistical tests and, if followed, it will provide a safeguard against improper uses or conclusions.

Selection of the criteria, as noted before, is dictated entirely by the selection of α, by the nature of H_1, and the sampling distribution used. In general, this distribution will, in turn, be indicated by the problem itself, and the design. Care should be taken to meet the assumptions which are made in order to use the test. These will be discussed as each test is presented and used.

In the businessman's problem, suppose that 101 of 163 customers buy brand B. In the proper format, the presentation of the experiment would appear as follows.

1. $H_0: P_B = P_A$
   $H_1: P_B > P_A$
2. $\alpha = 0.10$
3. Criteria: Reject H_0 if $x \geq 90$
4. Results: $x = 101$
5. Conclusions: reject H_0; the proportion of customers preferring brand B is greater than the proportion preferring brand A. Stock only brand B.

In any experiment, the most important aspect is that of *prior planning*. The **design of an experiment** should precede the actual experimentation itself. Every statistician is familiar with cases in which an experimenter submits a mass of data and asks for an interpretation of the data only to be told that the data is useless because it has not been properly collected or does not test what the experimenter wants to find out, or does not meet the assumptions needed to run any sort of analysis, etc. Of course, statistical tests can be done on any data; if the necessary assumptions are not met, however, the results may not *mean* anything.

It is very important, then, to determine *in advance* what hypothesis is being tested, and then to design an experiment using appropriate techniques and meeting the necessary assumptions which will make it possible to use statistical inference to answer the experimental questions. It is helpful when looking at an experiment to be able to evaluate the design and tell whether or not the results actually say what we are told they say. For example, were the samples chosen in such a way that we can be reasonably certain they were random? If not, was this compensated for by use of pretesting and proper analysis? Are the samples independent (if appropriate)? Were the proper tests used? These questions are very important and must be answered if the results are to be interpreted correctly.

For further information the reader should consult any of the available books on design and analysis of experiments, particularly Campbell and Stanley, *op cit*, and B.J. Winer, *Statistical Principles in Experimental Design* (McGraw-Hill); or C.R. Hicks: *Fundamental Concepts in the Design of Experiments* (Holt, Rinehart, and Winston), or R.R. Sokal and F.J. Rohlf, *Biometry* (Freeman). The latter named book is specialized for use for biologists, but still contains useful general principles.

•Problems

1. A firm decides to open a branch office if the volume of business justifies it. It samples its daily orders to estimate the proportion of orders going into that area. The crucial amount is 5%. Formulate suitable null and alternate hypotheses for this experiment if (a) the firm is cautious and does not wish to open a new office unless it must, and (b) the firm is experiencing a period of expansion and wishes to open a branch office on the slightest justification.

2. A storekeeper is testing a new method of advertising Wilde's Cherry Cough Drops. He knows that expected sales would be approximately 32 cases per month using his old advertising method, but wishes to retain the new methods, if at all possible. (a) Give suitable null and alternate hypotheses for his methods. (b) The merchant across the street is watching the experiment with interest, and will use the new methods if definitely superior to the old. Give suitable null and alternate hypotheses for this version of the experiment.

3. A recent (1977–8) advertisement states that "aspirin substitutes have not been shown to be safer than aspirin." How might this assertion have been obtained? Can you conclude that aspirin is just as safe as aspirin substitutes? Can you conclude that aspirin substitutes are not safer than aspirin? Can you conclude that aspirin is not safer than aspirin substitutes? Is it important to know who is making the statement? Why? What conclusions can you draw from the statement?

4. A businessman claims that his business is going to be better than last month and examines a sample of orders to verify or disprove his contention. What null and alternate hypotheses would be appropriate to his "experiment"?

5. An oil firm is testing a gasoline additive which may or may not increase gasoline mileage. In order to discover the additive's properties, they test the gasoline with the additive in a large sample of automobiles against the same gasoline without the additive in the same sample. As a result of the sample they draw conclusions. Three different sets of null and alternate hypotheses are possible. List each one and discuss the probable motivation for each.

6. A researcher tests samples of two models of sewing machines, A and B, and wants to draw conclusions as to which model actually does the better job. As a result of her sample she finds that the sample of model A has a better job performance than the sample of model B. As a result of her tests, she decides that the probability of type II error precludes acceptance of the results as conclusive. (a) What were her hypotheses? (b) Was the sample of model A significantly better than that of model B? (c) What were her conclusions?

7. The quality control procedure in a canning plant is to select a random sample of 40 cans and take the mean weight. If the procedure is in control, the population mean weight will be 16.42 ounces. The level of significance

used is 0.05, and the shipment will be passed unless the sample is significantly below standard. Monday's sample is weighed and its mean tested against the norm. It is found to be below 16.42, such that only 1 sample in 15 would fall so low by chance if the mean of the population is actually 16.42. Will the shipment be passed? Will the shipment be passed if the mean of only 1 sample in 25 would fall so low by chance? Suppose the sample mean is greatly in excess of 16.42. In terms of the criteria stated, would the sample be passed if only 1 sample in 25 would weigh so much by chance, if the population mean is actually 16.42?

7.2   TESTS FOR THE MEAN OF A POPULATION

In Chapter 6, the purpose of obtaining a sample was to estimate a population parameter. In many cases, the purpose is to test a hypothesis instead. The two procedures are related, however, as we shall see. In this section we shall study methods of testing the hypothesis that the mean of a population is equal to some given value.

Now suppose, for some reason, we have a research hypothesis which leads us to believe that a population has a mean which is different from some value μ_0. By the procedures outlined in section 7.1, we have

$$H_0: \quad \mu = \mu_0$$

$$H_1: \quad \mu \neq \mu_0$$

where μ is the actual population mean and μ_0 is the hypothetical value, the value assumed for the purposes of testing.

If the mean actually is μ_0, if the sample is random, and if the population is normally distributed, according to the Central Limit Theorem, a distribution of all means of samples of the same size (sampling distribution of the mean) will be normally distributed with mean μ_0 and standard error $\sigma_{\bar{x}}$. (Note that the term *standard error* is routinely used to indicate the standard deviation of some sampling distribution.) Here $\sigma_{\bar{x}}$ is the standard deviation of the theoretical sampling distribution of the mean ($\bar{x}$). It tells how much sample means can be expected to vary from sample to sample of the same size from the same population. The level of significance, α, is the chance we are willing to take of making a type I error. If μ_0 is the actual population mean, α is the probability of rejecting H_0 by error.

As noted in Chapter 6, the assumption of normality of the parent population may be relaxed for a sufficiently large sample size so that, in most cases, the sampling distribution of the mean is approximately normally distributed with mean μ_0 and standard error $\sigma_{\bar{x}}$ as illustrated.

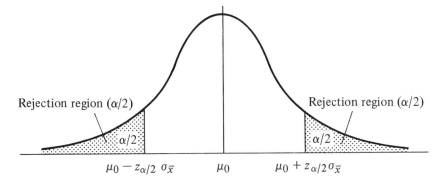

This curve can be related to the standard normal curve by the formula

$$z = \frac{\bar{x} - \mu_0}{\sigma_{\bar{x}}}$$

where $\bar{x}$ is a particular sample mean. There is some value of z, namely $z_{\alpha/2}$, such that $\alpha/2$ of the area under the curve is to the right of $z_{\alpha/2}$ and $\alpha/2$ of the area under the curve is to the left of $-z_{\alpha/2}$. These areas constitute the **rejection region**. If, for example, $\alpha = 0.05$, we know that $z_{.025} = 1.96$, so that 0.025 of the area under a standard normal curve is to the right of 1.96, and 0.025 of the area under the curve is to the left of -1.96. If the true population mean is actually μ_0, one of twenty (i.e., 0.05) of the sample means will fall in the tails *by chance alone*. Thus, if we reject the null hypothesis at a significance level of 0.05, we are still admitting that there is one chance in twenty that the null hypothesis is true and that it was pure luck (bad) that gave us a sample which led us to reject it. If we had specified a significance level of 0.01, we would be admitting only one chance in one hundred of making the same mistake. (Of course, this would also increase our chances of making a type II error.) In the latter case the critical value of z would be 2.58 rather than 1.96. That is, if the mean is actually μ_0, the mean of one sample in one hundred on the average will fall more than 2.58 standard errors either above or below μ_0 by chance alone.

The critical value is dependent on the nature of the alternate hypothesis as well as α. If the alternate hypothesis is one-sided, it is (in this case) either $\mu > \mu_0$ or $\mu < \mu_0$. If we had

$$H_0: \quad \mu = \mu_0$$

$$H_1: \quad \mu > \mu_0$$

we would not reject H_0 if our sample mean were below μ_0, even far below, since we are interested only in the case in which μ is greater than the hypothetical population mean. In this case we would reject H_0 only if our sample mean, $\bar{x}$, were so far above μ_0 that it would occur only α of the time, by chance.

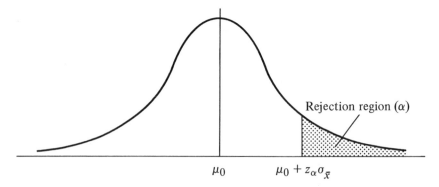

This type of test is called a **one-tailed** or directional test as contrasted to the **two-tailed** or nondirectional test described previously. For $\alpha = 0.05$, note that $z_{.05} = 1.645$; then 5% of the cases would fall above $z = 1.645$. Another 5% of the cases would fall below $z = -1.645$; this latter would be used in the cases where we had $H_1: \mu < \mu_0$. If $\alpha = 0.01$, the corresponding critical values would be 2.33 or -2.33. The critical values will be incorporated into the criterion portion of the experimental format as appears later.

The foregoing discussion was based on the assumptions that the sample is an independent random sample of a normal population and the standard deviation of the population is known. As in Chapter 6, modifications must be made for deviations from these assumptions. In any case, the sample must be an independent random sample from the population. If the standard deviation of the population is not known, as is generally the case, we use $s_{\bar{x}}$ in place of $\sigma_{\bar{x}}$ if the sample contains at least 50. For samples drawn from populations which we may reasonably assume are normal, the substitution may be done for samples as small as 30.

EXAMPLE 1   A firm wants to decide whether or not to purchase a new letter sorter for its office. Since it is too expensive to buy the sorter if it will not be used, the firm arranges to try the sorter for six weeks to make a decision. Since the firm works on Saturday, this means 36 working days. The office manager decides that she will order the machine if she can be 95% sure that it will sort more than 4,000 letters per day. Thus she performs an experiment, taking what she hopes to be a random sample of 36 days' performance of the machine and a significance level of 0.05. What will her decision be if this sample has a mean of 4,132 letters sorted per day with a standard deviation of 324?

SOLUTION   Following the procedures outlined in section 7.1, we have H_0: $\mu = 4,000$. Since the firm will buy the sorter if, and only if it will sort more than 4,000, then $\mu > 4,000$ becomes the alternate hypothesis. This makes the test one-tailed, and $z_{.05}$ is 1.645. Using the transformation formula, we determine the actual value of z in this case if $\mu=4{,}000$, apply the criteria, make the decision, and arrive at the conclusion. The entire procedure is summarized here. Use of a continuity correction is unnecessary since the *means* of the set can be rational values and so are not measured in integers only.

1. H_0: $\mu=4{,}000$
   H_1: $\mu>4{,}000$
2. $\alpha=0.05$
3. Criteria: Reject H_0 if $z>1.645$
4. Results: Here $\bar{x}=4{,}132$, $\mu_0=4{,}000$, and $s_{\bar{x}}=324/\sqrt{36}=54$ hence $z=\dfrac{\bar{x}-\mu_0}{s_{\bar{x}}}$

$$=\frac{4{,}132-4{,}000}{54}=\frac{132}{54}\doteq2.44$$

5. Conclusions: Since $2.44>1.645$, we reject H_0 in favor of H_1. Thus the mean probably is actually greater than 4,000, and the firm will purchase the sorter.

DISCUSSION   Two points are in order here. The sample actually was not random, and must be interpreted in this light, namely that it may have simply been a run of heavy days. Also, if the firm had made its criteria whether the sorter had been able to sort 4,000 or more letters per day (rather than more than 4,000), thus including 4,000 in the rejection region, so to speak, the experiment would nonetheless have been handled exactly as it was. The null hypothesis is always a positive statement which is used as the basis for constructing the test statistic. Judgment must always be used and the burden of proof placed in the right area.

If the sample is too small to use the preceding method, Chebyshev's rule can be used if the standard deviation of the population is known and the sample is at least 20. The test statistic would be

$$k=\frac{\bar{x}-\mu_0}{\sigma_{\bar{x}}}$$

For $\alpha=0.05$, a two-sided test would require $k>1/\sqrt{0.05}\doteq4.472$ or $k<-4.472$; a one-sided test would have the critical value of 3.162.

If, as in most cases, the population standard deviation is not known, and if the parent population is normal, the t-distribution described in section 6.5 may be used. We still use the same hypothesis-testing procedure, but base the criteria instead on the statistic

$$t=\frac{\bar{x}-\mu_0}{s/\sqrt{n}}$$

As discussed in section 6.5, we use $n-1$ degrees of freedom for a single sample of size n. The critical values are t_α for a one-sided alternative and $t_{\alpha/2}$ for a two-sided alternative, as with the normal. Table 5 is used to find the critical values for t. If you can determine what the critical value for z would be, if the normal distribution were appropriate, the value can be found in the bottom of each column on Table 5. The critical value for the corresponding t, then, is in the same column, opposite the correct number of degrees of freedom.

The relationship between z and t can be clarified by noting that the normal distribution is the limiting distribution for Student's t. That is, for larger degrees of freedom, the critical values of t get closer to those for z. Ideally, the t-distribution should be used, and is appropriate, in all cases where the sample standard deviation is used, but in the past this has not been practical because of the difficulty of providing tables of the t-distribution for each number of degrees of freedom. Some medium and relatively low-priced calculators now available can determine critical values of t and other test statistics for large numbers of degrees of freedom.

We can summarize the procedures for large and small samples as follows. In each case the null hypothesis is $\mu = \mu_0$.

Population Standard Deviation	Shape of Distribution		Sample Size	Alternate Hypothesis	Criteria: Reject H_0 if
Known (use $\sigma_{\bar{x}}$)	Normal		Any n	$H_1: \mu \neq \mu_0$	$z > z_{\alpha/2}$ or if $z < -z_{\alpha/2}$
		OR		$H_1: \mu > \mu_0$	$z > z_\alpha$
	Not normal		$n \geq 20$	$H_1: \mu < \mu_0$	$z < -z_\alpha$
	Not normal		$n \leq 20$	$H_1: \mu \neq \mu_0$	$k > 1/\sqrt{\alpha}$ or if $k < -1/\sqrt{\alpha}$
				$H_1: \mu > \mu_0$	$k > 1/\sqrt{2\alpha}$
				$H_1: \mu < \mu_0$	$k < -1/\sqrt{2\alpha}$
Unknown	Normal		$n \geq 30$	$H_1: \mu \neq \mu_0$	$z > z_{\alpha/2}$ or if $z < -z_{\alpha/2}$
		OR		$H_1: \mu > \mu_0$	$z > z_\alpha$
	Not normal (use $s_{\bar{x}}$)		$n \geq 50$	$H_1: \mu < \mu_0$	$z < -z_\alpha$
	Normal (use $s/\sqrt{n}$ and $n-1$ df)		$n < 30$	$H_1: \mu \neq \mu_0$	$t > t_{\alpha/2}$ or if $t < -t_{\alpha/2}$
				$H_1: \mu > \mu_0$	$t > t_\alpha$
				$H_1: \mu < \mu_0$	$t < -t_\alpha$
	Not normal		$n < 50$	No specific general method	

EXAMPLE 2   A chemist is testing the hypothesis that the boiling point of a certain substance is 846° C. He makes four determinations and obtains values of 844°, 847°, 845°, 844°. What conclusions can be drawn at a significance level of 0.05?

SOLUTION   A reasonable assumption is that such determinations are at least approximately normally distributed, so the following procedure may be used.

1. H_0: $\mu = 846$
   H_1: $\mu \neq 846$
2. $\alpha = 0.05$
3. Criteria: Reject H_0 if $t > 3.182$ or if $t < -3.182$. This is a two-tailed test with three degrees of freedom.
4. Results: Using the data, we have $\bar{x} = 845$, $s \doteq 1.4$, so

$$t = \frac{845 - 846}{1.4/\sqrt{4}} = \frac{-1}{0.7} \doteq -1.43$$

5. Conclusions: Since -1.43 is not greater than 3.182 nor less than -3.182, we fail to reject H_0. Thus he cannot say that the boiling point is not 846°. The value of -1.43 falls in the acceptance region on the curve and he may wish to accept H_0 and conclude that the boiling point is 846°. However such a decision depends on many other things, such as other characteristics of the substance as compared to those of the substance he suspects it is, plus his willingness to make a type II error. This particular case does more to substantiate H_0 than deny it.

EXAMPLE 3   A drug manufacturer claims that their new drug causes faster red cell build up in anemic persons than the drug currently used. A team of doctors tested the drug on 6 persons and compared the results with the current build-up factor of 8.3. The six subjects had factors of 6.3, 7.8, 8.1, 8.3, 8.7, and 9.4. Test the manufacturer's claim at a 0.01 level of significance.

SOLUTION   Assuming the factors to be normally distributed in the population (a reasonable assumption), the t-test is appropriate. We have

1. H_0: $\mu = 8.3$
   H_1: $\mu > 8.3$ (since this is the claim)
2. $\alpha = 0.01$
3. Criteria: Reject H_0 if $t > 3.365$

4. Results: We have $\bar{x}=8.1$, $s \doteq 1.04$, so

$$t = \frac{8.1-8.3}{1.04/\sqrt{6}} \doteq -0.47$$

5. Conclusions: Since $-0.47 \not> 3.365$, we fail to reject H_0. Since t is negative, the results not only fail to support the contention, they deny it, and we can conclude that the new drug is no better than the old.

•Problems

1. In nine tests under prescribed conditions, an automobile averaged 17 miles per gallon with a standard deviation of 1.7 miles. Test the hypothesis (at $x=0.05$) that the true mean is above 16 miles per gallon.

2. A type of new tires is run through an endurance test to see whether or not they can average 20,000 miles under the worst conditions. A sample of 100 sets is tested and lasts an average of 20,226 miles, with a standard deviation of 863 miles. If the company does not wish to market the tires unless they have been shown to wear significantly more than 20,000 miles under these conditions, will they be marketed? A significance level of 0.05 is used.

3. A shipment of 10,000 copper rods must be accepted or rejected on the basis of a sample of 100. The shipment will be accepted unless there are significantly more than an average of 13.7 blemishes per bar. The sample of 100 showed an average of 13.9 blemishes with a standard deviation of 1.4. Using a significance level of 0.01, will the shipment be accepted or rejected? You cannot reserve judgment.

4. Coffee cans are filled to a "net weight" of 16 ounces, but there is considerable variability. In fact, a random sample of 8 cans of a particular brand showed net weights of 15.4, 16.1, 15.8, 16.1, 16.2, 15.5, 16.0, 15.1 ounces. Test (at $x=0.05$) the hypothesis that the net weight of this brand of coffee is actually 16 ounces.

5. A new drug is hailed by its manufacturer as an excellent treatment for a disease. Using standard treatment, patients take an average of 9.2 days to recover. Using the new drug, 50 patients take an average of 9.3 days with a standard deviation of 1.1 days. The manufacturer claims that this shows that the old treatment is not significantly better than the new, so they will market it. Can their claim be substantiated at a 0.05 level of significance?

6. A disgruntled golfer claims that a new set of golf clubs has upset his game. He points to the fact that he used to average 93.4 strokes per round, but in the 36 rounds he has played since obtaining the new clubs, his average has

jumped to 96.2 with a standard deviation of 8.1. Test his claim with $\alpha = 0.05$. Remember that low scores are desired in golf.

7. A government testing agency routinely tests food products to see if they fail to meet government requirements at 0.01 level of significance. In order to be labelled "ice cream," the product must maintain at least 10% butterfat content. What conclusions would they draw if a random sample of ten half-gallons of a certain brand had butterfat percents of 9.6, 10.1, 9.9, 9.7, 10.0, 9.9, 9.8, 10.1, 9.9 and 9.7?

8. Injections of a drug must be properly maintained. A certain firm manufactures ampoules labelled 400 units, and takes quality control samples using a 0.05 level of significance to reject lots which may not be maintaining the level of quality. Daily, a sample of 10 ampoules from each of 6 lots is analyzed for content, and each lot is accepted or rejected on the basis of the sample. Which samples will be accepted and which rejected if the following are the results for a particular day?

$$\text{Lot } A: \bar{x} = 400.7, \quad s = 3.4$$

$$\text{Lot } B: \bar{x} = 401.1, \quad s = 1.8$$

$$\text{Lot } C: \bar{x} = 398.7, \quad s = 3.2$$

$$\text{Lot } D: \bar{x} = 401.3, \quad s = 0.6$$

$$\text{Lot } E: \bar{x} = 401.7, \quad s = 2.4$$

$$\text{Lot } F: \bar{x} = 399.2, \quad s = 0.8$$

9. A cigarette manufacturer claims that one of their brands contains no more than 18 mg of "tar." Five cigarettes are smoked and found to contain, respectively, 21, 17, 19, 18, and 21 mg of "tar." Can the manufacturer's claim be rejected at a significance level of 0.05?

10. Suppose that a second set of 8 coffee cans showed the same mean and standard deviation as the set given in problem 4. Combine the two samples and test the same hypothesis. What conclusions do you reach this time? Note the effect of sample size on results and conclusions.

11. A County Farm Agent wishes to determine the effect of a new fertilizer on the yield of corn per acre, as compared to that of the most popular brand. The popular brand is known to yield an average of 2.12 tons per acre. He persuades 64 farmers to each plant an acre of corn and treat it with the new fertilizer. These 64 acres had an average yield of 2.18 tons per acre with a standard deviation of 0.30 tons. Assuming the yield is attributed solely to the fertilizer and that the sample is random or representative, what can be said about the new fertilizer at a significance level of 0.05?

12. Specifications for a candy bar machine call for it to make bars weighing a mean of 2.30 ounces with a standard deviation of 0.12 ounces. A daily

sample of 100 bars is weighed *in toto* to decide if the machine is in control. If the bars are significantly above or below the preset amount, the machine should be retooled. If a significance level of 0.05 is used, above and below what 100 bar weights should the machine be retooled?

7.3　TESTS FOR POPULATION PROPORTION

The methods of the preceding sections can be extended to hypotheses concerning attributes if we focus on the proportion of a population possessing the attribute under question. In section 6.3 confidence intervals for population proportion were obtained from sample proportions. In the very same manner, hypotheses concerning proportions can be tested using the normal distribution, provided the sample is sufficiently large. If π_0 is the hypothetical population proportion and p is the sample proportion, we can use the statistic

$$z = \frac{p - \pi_0}{\sigma_p}$$

One fundamental difference between hypothesis testing for population proportion and confidence intervals is that, for confidence intervals, the population proportion is not known and we must use s_p. In testing a hypothesis, we *assume* that $\pi = \pi_0$ and we may use σ_p based on this assumption. The appropriateness of using the normal distribution is also based on $n\pi_0$ and $n(1 - \pi_0)$ being at least 5; that is, we would *expect* at least 5 observations in each category. It would not matter if the actual number in the sample were less than 5.

EXAMPLE 1　A real estate promoter claims that at least 75% of the retired couples in an apartment village of over 2,200 couples prefer apartment living to single-unit living. Try to disprove this assertion at the 0.05 level of significance if a random sample of 100 couples interviewed showed that 63 of them did, in fact, prefer apartment living.

SOLUTION　The experimental procedure outlined in section 7.1 applies. The correction factor need not be used since 100 is less than 5% of 2,200.

1. H_0: $\pi = 0.75$
   H_1: $\pi < 0.75$
2. $\alpha = 0.05$
3. Criteria: Reject H_0 if $z < -1.645$
4. Results:

$$\sigma_p = \sqrt{\frac{(0.75)(0.25)}{100}} \doteq 0.043, \text{ so}$$

$$z = \frac{0.63 - 0.75}{0.043} = \frac{-0.12}{0.043} \doteq -2.79$$

5. Conclusions: $-2.79 < -1.645$, so H_0 is rejected. The promoter's claim is exaggerated.

EXAMPLE 2 Of 400 samples of hybrid corn studied, 79 were found to have the recessive characteristic under study. By the Mendelian Law of Inheritance, 0.25 of the variety of corn the stock was taken from would exhibit the characteristic. A researcher hypothesized that the new hybrid is different from the parent stock variety. Test the hypothesis at a 0.05 level of significance.

SOLUTION If this were the parent variety, we would expect 0.25 to have the characteristic, so any deviation might indicate that there was a difference. Thus we have

1. H_0: $\pi = 0.25$
   H_1: $\pi \neq 0.25$
2. $\alpha = 0.05$
3. Criteria: Reject H_0 if $z > 1.96$ or if $z < -1.96$.
4. Results:

$$\sigma_p = \sqrt{\frac{(0.25)(0.75)}{400}} \doteq 0.022, \text{ and } p = \frac{79}{400} \doteq 0.198$$

so

$$z = \frac{0.198 - 0.250}{0.022} = \frac{-0.052}{0.022} \doteq -2.36$$

5. Conclusions: Since $-2.36 < -1.96$, we reject H_0 and conclude that there is evidence at the 0.05 level that the sample comes from a strain different from the parent stock. Note, however, that if we had set $\alpha = 0.01$, we could have concluded the opposite, though probably reserved judgment.

•Problems

1. The businessman's problem, discussed at length in sections 4.4, 5.4, and 7.1, was given in terms of number of customers buying brand B. Restate the problem in the terms of this section (in proportions) if 101 of 163 customers bought brand B.

2. A television manufacturer claims that at least 80% of its color picture tubes last at least two years. A random sample of 200 tubes sold over two years ago showed that 144 of them lasted at least two years. Test the manufacturer's claim at the 0.05 significance level.

3. A supply house has ordered a large shipment of dingbats and is willing to accept no more than 3% defectives. If a sample of 200 contains 8 defectives, should the shipment be rejected at 0.05 level of significance?

4. The Canter Poll claims that 0.60 of the electorate supports a certain proposition to be placed on the ballot. The Stringer Poll decided to test this contention at the 0.05 level. What are their conclusions if a random sample of 1,563 people revealed 884 who supported the proposition?

5. To test a hypothesis that, on the average, more than 4 out of 10 persons buying soft drinks still prefer bottles, a soft drink firm uses one day's sales of drinks to test the hypothesis at $\alpha = 0.05$. Stretching the assumptions of a representative sample quite a bit, what conclusions can they draw if the day's sales showed 687 bottle sales and 876 can sales?

6. In repeated tests with a pair of dice, seven was rolled 138 times in 540 tries. Does this support or deny (at the 0.05 significance level) a contention that the dice are loaded?

7. In a study relating student seating (proximity to the teacher) to grades, three classes with a total of 97 students were randomly rearranged with respect to seating arrangement. If a student moved closer to the teacher and grades increased, or the student moved further from the teacher and grades decreased, this was considered a success. A random relationship between proximity to the teacher and grades would lead to a probability of success of 0.5. Sixty-four students were considered to be successes. Can we conclude that the hypothesis $\pi > 0.5$ is substantiated at the 0.05 level of significance? This would show that proximity to the teacher is a factor in success in school as indicated by grades.

8. Use the data of problem 9, section 6.1 to test the hypothesis that at least one-third of the students on campus favor co-ed dorms. Combine the two samples and use the 0.05 level of significance.

7.4   DIFFERENCES BETWEEN MEANS

One important application of statistical inference is answering questions posed by research hypotheses which ask which of two methods yields the best result, or whether two samples belong to the same or different populations.

The important question to answer is whether the two samples are dependent or independent. If we take two measures on the same sample, such as before and after, the samples are dependent. If the two samples can be paired using some criterion, they may also be considered to be dependent. The analysis for dependent samples is much more sensitive than for independent samples. On the other hand, pairing should not be done indiscriminantly to increase sensitivity, because then the results will be made meaningless.

If samples are paired, the simplest procedure is simply to take the difference between them, and treat it as one sample. An example will clarify this procedure. Suppose that ten people took part in a diet experiment. Their weights were measured at the beginning and at the end of the experiment. The results are presented in the following Table.

Subject	Starting Weight	Ending Weight	Net Difference
A	183	177	+6
B	144	145	−1
C	151	145	+6
D	163	162	+1
E	155	151	+4
F	159	163	−4
G	178	173	+5
H	184	185	−1
I	142	139	+3
J	137	138	−1

EXAMPLE 1 Using the data given previously, discover whether or not the diet is effective. Use a 0.05 level of significance.

SOLUTION Letting $\bar{x}_1$ represent the mean weight of the sample before the diet, $\bar{x}_2$ the weight after, μ_1 the mean weight of the population before the diet, and μ_2 the mean weight after the diet, we are testing the hypothesis that $\mu_1 = \mu_2$ (or that $\mu_1 - \mu_2 = 0$) against $\mu_1 > \mu_2$ (because otherwise the diet is not effective.) We are really not interested in $\bar{x}_1$ or $\bar{x}_2$, merely their difference. We let SE represent the standard error for the difference values, so the following procedure is appropriate.

1. H_0: $\mu_1 = \mu_2$
   H_1: $\mu_1 > \mu_2$
2. $\alpha = 0.05$
3. Criteria: Reject H_0 if $t > 1.833$ (since there are ten difference values, hence 9 degrees of freedom)
4. Results: The mean of the difference scores, $\bar{x}_1 - \bar{x}_2 = 1.8$, the standard deviation is about 3.49, so $SE = 3.49/\sqrt{10}$. Then $t = 1.8/1.10 \doteq 1.64$.
5. Conclusions: We do not reject H_0; we reserve judgment in this case. Either get a larger sample, or try another week of the diet.

If more than 30 pieces of data are involved, the appropriate z-score rather than the t-score would be used.

It would also be possible to test against some specific hypothetical difference. In such a case the appropriate statistic would be

$$\frac{\bar{x}_1 - \bar{x}_2 - (\mu_1 - \mu_2)}{SE}$$

and would equal either t, or z, as appropriate.

A somewhat more complicated case occurs when the two samples are *independent*. The procedure for finding confidence intervals for the difference between population means from sample means was set forth in section 6.4 and, for small samples, in section 6.5. A variation of the same procedure yields hypothesis testing procedures for the differences between means. For large samples we use the statistic

$$z = \frac{\bar{x}_1 - \bar{x}_2 - (\mu_1 - \mu_2)}{s_d}$$

where $s_d = \sqrt{s_1^2/n_1 + s_2^2/n_2}$ and the populations are both normal with n_1 and n_2 both at least 30, or, for any populations, n_1 and n_2 are both at least 50. If we can use σ_d, the samples can be of any size if distributions are normal, and both n_1 and n_2 must be at least 20, if not normal; for samples less than 20, Chebyshev's rule can be used.

For small samples, if the populations are not normal, and n_1 and n_2 are less than 50, no generalization is possible. For normal populations, however, if we can assume that both populations have the same variance, and if either $n_1 < 30$ or $n_2 < 30$, we use

$$t = \frac{\bar{x}_1 - \bar{x}_2 - (\mu_1 - \mu_2)}{\hat{s}\sqrt{1/n_1 + 1/n_2}}$$

where $\hat{s}$ is the square root of the pooled variance; that is,

$$\hat{s} = \sqrt{\frac{(n_1 - 1)s_1^2 + (n_2 - 1)s_2^2}{n_1 + n_2 - 2}}$$

and the number of degrees of freedom is $n_1 + n_2 - 2$; that is, the sum of the degrees of freedom in the two samples. A procedure to validate the assumption that the population variances are equal is given in section 6.6.

EXAMPLE 2 Two samples of accounts receivable are drawn from two departments of a company. The 37 accounts from one department had a mean of $116 with a standard deviation of $13; the 52 from the other department had a mean of $121 with a standard deviation of $21. Test the hypothesis that there is no differrence between the two departments in mean dollar amounts of accounts receivable. Use the 0.05 level of significance.

SOLUTION   The standard procedure is as follows:

1. H_0: $\mu_1 = \mu_2$
   H_1: $\mu_1 \neq \mu_2$
2. $\alpha = 0.05$
3. Criteria: Reject H_0 if $z > 1.96$ or if $z < -1.96$.
4. Results: The given data are summarized here.

$$n_1 = 37 \qquad n_2 = 52,$$

$$\bar{x}_1 = 116 \qquad \bar{x}_2 = 121,$$

$$s_1 = 13 \qquad s_2 = 21,$$

Then

$$s_d = \sqrt{\frac{(13)^2}{37} + \frac{(21)^2}{52}} \doteq \sqrt{13.05} \doteq 3.6$$

and

$$z = \frac{116 - 121}{3.6} = \frac{-5}{3.6} \doteq -1.39$$

5. Conclusions: Since -1.39 is not greater than 1.96 nor less than -1.96, we fail to reject H_0. In this case z is relatively large, making us hesitant to accept H_0, and it would be quite easy to take another sample.

EXAMPLE 3   An attitude survey toward management was administered as a pilot study to four blue collar workers and five white collar workers for the Hoos' Tool Company to see if there is any difference (at the 0.05 level) between the scores as representing the two groups. The blue collar workers scored 23, 18, 22, 21, and the white collar workers made scores of 23, 28, 25, 24, 26. What conclusions can be drawn from this study if it is hypothesized that white collar workers will score higher than blue?

SOLUTION

1. H_0: $\mu_1 = \mu_2$
   H_1: $\mu_1 > \mu_2$
   (where μ_1 and μ_2 represent the mean scores of white and blue collar workers, respectively)
2. $\alpha = 0.05$
3. Criteria: Reject H_0 if $t > 1.895$

4. Results: We compute mean and variance of each sample. For the white collar workers, $\Sigma x = 126$, so $\bar{x}_1 = 25.2$; $\Sigma x^2 = 3,190$, so $s_1^2 = 14.8/4 = 3.7$. For the blue collar workers, $\Sigma x = 84$, so $\bar{x}_2 = 21.0$; $\Sigma x^2 = 1,778$, so $s_2^2 = 14.0/3 \doteq 4.67$. Then

$$\hat{s} = \sqrt{\frac{(4)(3.7) + (3)(4.67)}{7}} = \sqrt{\frac{28.8}{7}} \doteq 2.03$$

so

$$t = \frac{25.2 - 21.0}{2.03\sqrt{\dfrac{1}{5} + \dfrac{1}{4}}} \doteq \frac{4.20}{1.36} \doteq 3.09.$$

5. Conclusions: Since 3.09 is greater than 1.895, the null hypothesis is rejected and we conclude that the white collar workers do have a higher mean score on this survey.

COMMENT   To test whether the assumption that the population variances are equal is reasonable, we note that $4.67/3.7 \doteq 1.26$. With 3 and 4 degrees of freedom, the critical value of F is 6.59, so we conclude the sample variances are **homogeneous**; that is, that they may have come from populations with equal variance. Note also that in the calculation for $\hat{s}$, the variances, 3.7 and 4.67, were multiplied, respectively, by 4 and 3, to obtain 14.8 and 14, which were the numerators in calculating the values of s_1^2 and s_2^2. (These values are called *sums of squares*.)

    If, as in this case, the t-test shows that the difference between the scores is significant, it can be helpful to calculate confidence intervals for the difference. In this case 95% confidence limits would have $t_{.025} = 2.365$, so we would add and subtract $(2.365)(1.36)$ or about 3.2 to the obtained difference of $25.2 - 21.0 = 4.2$, obtaining a 95% confidence interval showing the white collar workers would score 4.2 ± 3.2, or from 1.0 to 7.4 points, on the average, above blue collar workers.

•Problems

1. The department of Institutional Research at The University of West Florida wishes to determine how seniors there do on the Graduate Record Examination compared to seniors at Florida State University. A random sample of 50 UWF seniors was found to have a mean of 1,183 on the GRE with a standard deviation of 137. The FSU sample of 100 had a mean of 1,168 with a standard deviation of 146. Test (at $\alpha = 0.05$) the hypothesis that there is no difference in the population.

2. A group of 10 subjects was given tests before and after being subjected to a hypothetical learning situation. If the table to follow shows the results of the experiment, test the hypothesis that learning actually took place at a

significance level of 0.05. Assume that an increase in score indicates that learning actually took place.

Subject	Before	After
1	27	29
2	21	32
3	34	29
4	24	27
5	30	31
6	27	26
7	33	35
8	31	30
9	22	29
10	27	28

3. To determine which of two brands of golf balls is better for his long game, a professional golfer drives two samples of 50 balls from the tee, using the same club for each shot, alternating brands at random. For brand 1 the mean yardage is 231 yards with a standard deviation of 24 yards. For brand 2 the mean yardage is 226 yards with a standard deviation of 20 yards. Can he conclude that there is a difference in the balls? Use $\alpha = 0.01$.

4. An amateur chemist discovered some residue left in a test tube and hypothesizes that it is the same as the residue left in a different tube last week. He subjects it to four determinations of a melting point, arriving at 1,543 C, 1,540 C, 1,542 C and 1,543 C. The residue last week was tested three times for its melting point, getting 1,545 C, 1,544 C, and 1,544 C. Do these results tend to substantiate or deny the hypothesis that the residues are the same substance? Use a 0.05 level of significance.

5. To test the effect of two different fertilizers on corn yield, 6 one-acre plots of corn are fertilized with fertilizer 1 and 6 one-acre plots of corn are fertilized with fertilizer 2. The plots fertilized with fertilizer 1 showed a mean yield of 1.32 tons per plot with a standard deviation of 0.22 tons; those fertilized with fertilizer 2 showed a mean yield of 1.41 tons per plot with a standard deviation of 0.31 tons. Do these results support the manufacturer's claim that fertilizer 2 is superior to fertilizer 1? Use a 0.01 level of significance.

6. A hospital is considering two suppliers for ampoules of a wonder drug. Both suppliers deliver ampoules which are supposed to contain 500,000 units of the drug. An analysis was made of a sample of 6 ampoules from each company. Brand A had a mean of 510,000 units with a standard deviation of 20,000, while brand B had a mean of 490,000 units with a standard deviation of 15,000. Can you conclude there is probably no difference between the brands? Use a 0.05 level of significance.

7. Two varieties of corn are planted in paired plots to see if there is a difference in the yield. Calculate whether or not there is a significant difference at a 0.05 level of significance. Yields are given in tons per plot. Paired plots are of the same size, though different pairs are not necessarily of a similar size.

Pair	Variety A	Variety B
1	123	108
2	91	76
3	102	103
4	64	60
5	144	135

8. A survey was made which tested the hypothesis that college graduates read at least two books per year *more* than non-college graduates. As a result the null hypothesis was H_0: $\mu_1 = \mu_2 + 2$, against a suitable alternate hypothesis, where μ_1 is the number of books per year read by college graduates and μ_2 is the corresponding value for non-college graduates. What were their conclusions at a 0.05 level of significance if their results are given as follows?

$$\text{College graduates:} \quad n_1 = 66, \bar{x}_1 = 4.3, s_1 = 4.6$$

$$\text{Non-college grads:} \quad n_2 = 78, \bar{x}_2 = 1.9, s_2 = 3.1$$

9. To test the efficiency of a procedure designed to increase the daily output of a machine, five machines are tested with and without the procedure, with the following results:

Machine	With	Without
A	15.6	14.4
B	18.2	16.7
C	14.3	13.1
D	14.9	14.4
E	16.7	14.7

Test the hypothesis that the procedure is effective. Use $\alpha = 0.05$.

10. Repeat problem 9 assuming that the data were obtained from two independent random samples.

7.5   DIFFERENCES BETWEEN PROPORTIONS

A final type of simple hypothesis testing is deciding whether or not the difference between proportions obtained from two independent samples is significant. Confidence intervals for differences between proportions were discussed in section 6.4. Using the same assumptions, we can compare proportions in two independent samples using the statistic

$$z = \frac{p_1 - p_2 - (\pi_1 - \pi_2)}{s_{dp}}$$

where s_{dp} is the standard error of the difference for proportions estimated by

$$s_{dp} = \sqrt{\frac{p_1(1-p_1)}{n_1} + \frac{p_2(1-p_2)}{n_2}}$$

and p_1 and p_2 are sample proportions, π_1 and π_2 are population proportions, and n_1 and n_2 are the sample sizes. We still need sufficiently large samples so that $n_1 p_1$, $n_1(1-p_1)$, $n_2 p_2$ and $n_2(1-p_2)$ are all at least 5; that is, each of the four categories contains at least 5 observations.

EXAMPLE 1 A certain grocery chain is considering opening its newest branch at one of two locations. A poll of 60 people in Bloomsbury Heights showed 45 who said they would shop at the store if located in Bloomsbury Heights, while 48 of 80 people polled in East Westfield said they would shop at the store if it opened in East Westfield. Does this result support the contention (at a significance level of 0.05) that a greater percentage of people in Bloomsbury Heights would patronize a store than in East Westfield?

SOLUTION Since our research hypothesis is that the proportion for Bloomsbury Heights (π_1) is greater than that for East Westfield (π_2), our test is one-tailed. We have

1. H_0: $\pi_1 = \pi_2$
   H_1: $\pi_1 > \pi_2$
2. $\alpha = 0.05$
3. Criteria: Reject H_0 if $z > 1.645$.
4. Results: $n_1 = 60$, $p_1 = 0.75$, $n_2 = 80$, $p_2 = 0.60$, so we have

$$s_{dp} = \sqrt{\frac{(0.75)(0.25)}{60} + \frac{(0.60)(0.40)}{80}}$$

$$= \sqrt{\frac{0.1875}{60} + \frac{0.2400}{80}}$$

$$= \sqrt{0.003125 + 0.003}$$

$$= \sqrt{0.006125}$$

$$\doteq 0.078$$

Then

$$z = \frac{0.75 - 0.60}{0.078} = \frac{0.15}{0.078} \doteq 1.92$$

5. Conclusions: $1.92 > 1.645$, so reject H_0; a greater proportion of Bloomsbury Heights than East Westfield residents would patronize a new store in their community.

DISCUSSION   The apparently great difference (0.15) between the two sample proportions is barely significant. In fact, it would not be significant at the 0.01 level. In proportions it is important to obtain a fairly large sample size to be sure of getting good results.

NOTE: If the hypothesis is $\pi_1 = \pi_2$, it is reasonable to use a pooled sample proportion $\hat{p}$, obtained simply by combining the two samples together, provided they are not too different in size. Then we have

$$s_{dp} = \sqrt{\hat{p}(1 - \hat{p})\left(\frac{1}{n_1} + \frac{1}{n_2}\right)}$$

In this example $p = (45 + 48)/(60 + 80) = 93/140 \doteq 0.66$, so we would have

$$s_{dp} = \sqrt{(0.66)(0.34)\left(\frac{1}{60} + \frac{1}{80}\right)}$$

$$= \sqrt{0.006545}$$

$$\doteq 0.081$$

Then we have $z = 0.15/0.081 \doteq 1.85$. The use of this estimate tends to be a bit conservative. As a general rule, particularly with modern calculators, it is probably best to just use the basic formula for s_{dp}. If there *are* significant differences, that is, $\pi_1 \neq \pi_2$, then the pooling is not justified. Further, if a confidence interval is obtained after the fact, the unpooled standard error should be used.

•Problems

1. Two companies submit bids and a sample of ball bearings to gain a contract. Firm *A* has 82 acceptable ball bearings out of 90 while firm *B* has

96 acceptable out of 110. Firm *B*'s price is slightly lower than firm *A*'s, so that unless it can be shown that firm *A* has a higher percentage of acceptable bearings (with $\alpha = 0.05$), firm *B* will get the contract. Who should get the contract?

2. Two moving companies are applying for the job of moving a major concern across country. The office manager views completion of the move within the promised time as the major criteria. She feels that she can flip a coin and decide which to use on the basis of evidence that company *A* has completed 344 out of 388 moves on time during the last year while company *B* has completed 217 of 232 on time. Test her hypothesis at the 0.05 level of significance.

3. A psychologist tests men and women for mental dexterity, grading each subject pass or fail on a task requiring such activity. If 83 of 124 men and 72 of 103 women passed the test, can she conclude that men and women differ significantly ($\alpha = 0.01$) on mental dexterity as measured by this test?

4. A class is randomly divided into two sections of 18 each, and one section is given instruction in assembling a puzzle. Then each subject is tested to see if he can assemble the puzzle within one minute. The results in the test group (given instructions) showed that 11 of the students could do the task, while the results in the control group (given no instructions) showed that only 9 of the students could do the task. Do these results bear out at the 0.05 significance level the contention that instruction in assembling a puzzle aids in actually assembling the puzzle?

5. Use the data of problem 9, section 6.1 to test the hypothesis that the samples represent different populations; that is, that the differences between the proportions are real. Use the 0.05 level of significance. How does this affect a decision to pool the data?

6. A biologist wishes to determine whether two insect populations found in different locations in a forest are actually two different species. The prime morphological characteristic which differentiates the two populations appears to be the incidence of white eyes. The biologist observes that 32 of 100 from one population and 23 of 100 from the other population have white eyes. Can he conclude that the two populations are different species? Use the 0.05 level of significance.

7. A recent campus poll showed 40% of students living on campus opposed to pets on campus. Feeling that there are perhaps differences depending upon where the students live, the campus newspaper polls students living in dormitories and students living in fraternity and sorority houses separately. The newspaper claims on the basis of the poll that more students living in fraternity and sorority houses are opposed to pets on campus than those living in dormitories. If the poll showed that 21 of 39 fraternity/sorority house residents were opposed to pets on campus, but 37 of 94 dorm residents, test the newspaper's claim at the 0.05 level of significance.

7.6   SUMMARY

Hypothesis testing and decision making are important aspects of statistical inference. Most statistics involving samples require that the sample(s) be representative. The most frequently used method of assuring representative samples is by means of random selection. Additional assumptions are often required for specific tests. Two types of experimental error are encountered: type I error occurs when a true hypothesis is rejected; type II error occurs when a false hypothesis is accepted.

Since it is difficult to control for type II error (other than by obtaining as large a sample as possible), hypotheses to be tested are formulated positively, in such a way that the probability of a type I error, α, can be controlled. The hypothesis to be tested is called the null hypothesis, and is the basis for the formulation of the test statistic. The hypothesis which will be accepted if the null hypothesis is rejected is called the alternate hypothesis. The acceptable probability of type I error, α, is called the level of significance.

The use of the following five step procedure will insure that hypothesis testing has been properly carried out.

1. **Statement of hypotheses**:
   H_0: Null hypothesis.
   H_1: Alternate hypothesis.
2. **Level of significance**:
   $\alpha =$ some number, usually 0.05 or 0.01.
3. **Criteria**:
   Determined by H_1, and the actual nature of population and size of the sample.
4. **Results**:
   Actual values obtained by applying the appropriate tests.
5. **Conclusions**:
   Either reject H_0 or fail to reject H_0, followed by the consequences of this decision.

This chapter dealt with various hypotheses about sample means and proportions. The techniques outlined above were used. Criteria are based upon specific hypotheses and sampling distributions depending upon the parameter in question. The most generally used criteria are summarized below. Some special cases are summarized in the chart on page 208 for testing hypotheses involving the mean of one sample, and can be extended to two samples.

Tests concerning means

1. Mean of one sample

$$H_0: \quad \mu = \mu_0$$

$$H_1: \quad \mu > \mu_0, \qquad \mu \neq \mu_0, \qquad \mu < \mu_0$$

Sampling statistic—criteria based upon the value of

$$z = \frac{\bar{x} - \mu_0}{s_{\bar{x}}} \quad \text{(for large samples)}$$

or

$$t = \frac{\bar{x} - \mu_0}{s/\sqrt{n}} \quad \text{(for small samples—} df = n-1\text{)}$$

2. Two sample means

Case I. Two means from one sample (such as before and after) or paired observations from two samples.

$$H_0: \quad \mu_1 = \mu_2$$

$$H_1: \quad \mu_1 > \mu_2, \quad \mu_1 \neq \mu_2, \quad \mu_1 < \mu_2$$

Sampling statistic—criteria based upon the value of

$$z = \frac{\bar{x}_1 - \bar{x}_2 - (\mu_1 - \mu_2)}{SE} \quad \text{(for large samples)}$$

or

$$t = \frac{\bar{x}_1 - \bar{x}_2 - (\mu_1 - \mu_2)}{SE} \quad \text{(for small samples—} df = n-1\text{)}$$

where SE is the standard error for the differences scores, calculated as in test 1.

Case II. Means from two independent samples.

$$H_0 \text{ and } H_1 \text{ as in case I.}$$

Sampling statistic—criteria based upon the value of

$$z = \frac{\bar{x}_1 - \bar{x}_2 - (\mu_1 - \mu_2)}{s_d} \quad \text{(for large samples)}$$

or

$$t = \frac{\bar{x}_1 - \bar{x}_2 - (\mu_1 - \mu_2)}{\hat{s}\sqrt{1/n_1 + 1/n_2}} \quad \text{(for small samples—} df = n_1 + n_2 - 2\text{)}$$

If $n_1 = n_2 = n$, the denominator for t may be written simply as $\sqrt{(s_1^2 + s_2^2)/n}$.

Tests concerning proportions

1. Proportion of one sample

$$H_0: \quad \pi = \pi_0$$

$$H_1: \quad \pi > \pi_0, \quad \pi \neq \pi_0, \quad \pi < \pi_0$$

Sampling statistic—criteria based upon the value of

$$z = \frac{p - \pi_0}{\sigma_p}$$

provided both $n\pi_0$ and $n(1 - \pi_0)$ are at least 5.

2. Proportions in two samples

$$H_0: \quad \pi_1 = \pi_2$$

$$H_1: \quad \pi_1 > \pi_2, \quad \pi_1 \neq \pi_2, \quad \pi_1 < \pi_2$$

Sampling statistic—criteria based upon the value of

$$z = \frac{p_1 - p_2 - (\pi_1 - \pi_2)}{s_{dp}}$$

provided that $n_1 p_1$, $n_1(1 - p_1)$, $n_2 p_2$, $n_2(1 - p_2)$ are all at least 5.

Relation between confidence interval and rejection region

1. Two-tailed tests

Using the appropriate z or t value for the significance level α, the rejection region can be found. But if the probability is α that a sample falls in the rejection region by chance, the probability is $1 - \alpha$ that it does not. Therefore, the complement of the rejection region is the $1 - \alpha$ confidence interval for the parameter. Hence the rule

> A null hypothesis concerning means or proportions will be rejected in favor of a two-sided alternative hypothesis at a significance level α if and only if the hypothetical parameter (μ_0, π_0) is *not* included in the $1 - \alpha$ confidence interval obtained from the sample.

2. One-tailed tests

In this case we have α in one tail so that the appropriate confidence interval is for $1 - 2\alpha$. Thus the rule

> A null hypothesis concerning means or proportions will be rejected in favor of a one-sided alternative hypothesis if and only if the hypothetical parameter is *not* included in the $1 - 2\alpha$ confidence

interval obtained from the sample, and the sample does not contradict the alternate hypothesis.

The purpose of the latter clause is to rule out one tail.

TECHNICAL NOTE Additional hypothesis tests can be obtained by extension from section 6.6 and Technical Note 2 in section 6.2.

Tests concerning variances

1. Variance in one sample

$$H_0: \quad \sigma^2 = \sigma_0^2$$

$$H_1: \quad \sigma^2 > \sigma_0^2, \qquad \sigma^2 \neq \sigma_0^2, \qquad \sigma^2 < \sigma_0^2$$

Sampling statistic—criteria based on the value of

$$z = \frac{s - \sigma_0}{\sigma_0/\sqrt{2n}} \qquad \text{(for large samples)}$$

$$\chi^2 = \frac{(n-1)s^2}{\sigma_0^2} \qquad \text{(for small samples—} df = n-1)$$

2. Variances in two samples

$$H_0: \quad \sigma_1^2 = \sigma_2^2$$

$$H_1: \quad \sigma_1^2 \neq \sigma_2^2$$

Sampling statistic—criteria based on the value of

$$F = \frac{s_1^2}{s_2^2}$$

or

$$F = \frac{s_2^2}{s_1^2}$$

whichever is greater. $Df = (n_1 - 1, n_2 - 1)$ or $(n_2 - 1, n_1 - 1)$, with the first of each pair corresponding to the numerator.

•Problems

1. A firm wishes to examine whether or not it should expand its offerings and is considering increasing the output of type 7 widgets if necessary. It decides to increase the output if the daily demand volume exceeds 27,500

on the average. A sample of 40 days during the past 6 months is examined and it is found that the mean daily demand is 27,654 with a standard deviation of 384. If the level of significance chosen is 0.05, does this sample tend to indicate that the mean daily demand volume exceeds 27,500?

2. In a study of 100 patients admitted to a hospital suffering from appendicitis, the mean stay was found to be 9.33 days with a standard deviation of 2.83 days. Does this support the contention of the hospital administrator that this is significantly less than the national average of 10.17 days? Use the 0.05 level of significance.

3. In a high school, students are interviewed regarding the desirability of having a prom this year. Of 317 girls interviewed, 208 wanted a prom; 107 of 203 boys wanted a prom. Does this sample show (at $\alpha = 0.01$) that there is a difference in the proportion of boys wanting a prom as opposed to the proportion of girls?

4. A traffic engineer tries two different settings for traffic signals in an attempt to find the most efficient setting, using number of traffic delays per week as his criterion. Using setting 1, he obtained a mean of 26.1 traffic delays per week, for 11 weeks, with a standard deviation of 5.6 delays. Using setting B, he obtained a mean of 22.4 traffic delays per week for 13 weeks, with a standard deviation of 6.3 delays. What can he conclude (at $\alpha = 0.05$) about the two settings?

5. Under the usual treatment, a certain disease produces undesirable side effects in 25% of the victims. A new drug has been developed which is claimed to be effective in reducing the side effects with this disease. A sample of 225 patients with the disease is treated with the new drug. Test the hypothesis that the drug is effective in reducing the proportion of patients developing side effects at the 0.05 level of significance if 43 patients develop the side effects.

6. Testing for tensile strength of a new alloy, a metallurgist obtains readings on separate tests of 117.6, 122.4, 119.8, 118.8, 121.6, and 123.4. The theoretical tensile strength is 120.0. Do these tests tend to confirm or deny the theory? Use $\alpha = 0.05$.

7. Forty percent of the geldings racing at a certain track ran in the money, while only thirty-two percent of the fillies did so. If the sample is based on the performance of 105 geldings and 75 fillies, test the jockey's hypothesis (at the 0.05 significance level) that geldings run better than fillies.

8. A hospital administrator introduces a new accounting system designed to reduce the average amount of unpaid bills. Under the old system, the average unpaid bill was $217.00 with a standard deviation of $34.00. Under the new system, the first 50 unpaid bills showed an average of $203.00 with a standard deviation of $47.00. Is this good enough evidence to assert that the new system has reduced the amount of the average unpaid bill? Use the 0.01 level of significance.

9. Two companies submit samples of light bulbs for bids. On the average, each of company A's sample of 300 bulbs has a mean life of 1,065 hours with a standard deviation of 133 hours. Company B's sample of 300 exhibits a mean life of 1,047 hours with a standard deviation of 56 hours. If mean bulb life is the prime criterion for awarding the contract, does the sample yield sufficient information to decide, using $\alpha = 0.05$, which company should get the contract? If so, which one?

10. Use the data of problem 9, but the criterion is that the company which will produce the greatest proportion of bulbs lasting at least 1,000 hours will get the contract.

11. A medical researcher studies the effect of two drugs on guinea pigs infected with pneumococcus bacillus. One group of 44 animals has a mortality of 17 while the second group of 52 animals has a mortaility of 24. Can he conclude, at the 0.01 level of significance, that there is a difference in the effectiveness of the two drugs?

12. A random sample of a day's output of a chemical revealed that the ester level for 20 vials was 11.6% with a standard deviation of 0.8%. Specifications require a minimum of 12%, but allow the output to pass if a sample is not significantly lower with $\alpha = 0.05$. Will the output be passed?

13. An antipyretic is being tested as a replacement for aspirin. A total of nine experimental animals are artificially given high temperatures and the drug administered. Given the before and after temperatures, test whether or not the drug can be considered effective at the 0.05 level of significance.

Before	107.2	111.4	109.3	106.5	113.7	108.4	107.7	111.9	109.3
After	106.1	111.7	105.4	107.2	109.8	108.8	106.9	109.6	110.5

14. A traffic survey claims that the mean length of time required to go through a tunnel at rush hour is 3.5 minutes. A skeptical motorist decides to test this hypothesis. He times his trips through the tunnel for a total of 22 trips during rush hour. He finds that his mean time was 4.4 minutes with a standard deviation of 0.8 minutes. Can he conclude that the traffic survey claim was too low? Use the results of his trips and a 0.05 level of significance.

15. Sixteen tests were made of the effervescing time of a certain combination of ingredients. The purpose of the tests was to discover if this combination was the same as that of a rival product which has a mean effervescing time of 16.2 seconds. The sample mean was 14.8 seconds with a standard deviation of 1.6 seconds. What was the conclusion at a 0.01 level of significance?

16. In a study of attitudes of personnel managers toward women the Attitude Toward Women Scale (ATWS) was used to assess general attitude. The questionnaire was administered to 172 personnel managers, of which 48

were managers in large businesses (employing at least 50 employees) and 124 were managers in small businesses. In the large businesses, the mean score was 86.4, with a standard deviation of 18.50 and in the small businesses, the mean was 99.7 with a standard deviation of 18.32. Use the 0.01 level of significance to test the hypothesis that attitudes toward women differ among personnel managers depending upon size of business.

17. A study of a group of twelve unsuccessful salesmen and twelve successful salesmen with similar training and experience was conducted to assess differences in self-concept. The following results were obtained on the Osgood Semantic Differential Test. The successful salesmen had a mean of 96.4 with standard deviation 8.1; the unsuccessful salesmen had a mean of 98.5 with standard deviation 10.8. Are the obtained differences significant at the 0.05 level of significance? (Are the variances homogeneous?)

CHAPTER 7

Glossary of Terms

acceptance region
alternate hypothesis
criteria
critical values
decision
design of an experiment
homogeneous variances
hypothesis testing procedure
level of significance
null hypothesis
one-sided alternative

one-sided rejection region
operating-characteristic curve
power of a test
rejection region
reserve judgment
test statistic
two-sided alternative
two-sided rejection region
type I error
type II error

Glossary of Symbols

α	probability of type I error
β	probability of type II error
H_0	null hypothesis
H_1	alternate hypothesis
μ	population mean
μ_0	hypothetical population mean
μ_1, μ_2	hypothetical means for two populations
π	population proportion
π_0	hypothetical population proportion
π_1, π_2	hypothetical proportions for two populations
p	sample proportion
p_1, p_2	proportions for two samples
SE	standard error for paired sample differences
$\bar{x}$	sample mean

The Chi-Square Distribution

8.1 PROPORTIONS IN SEVERAL SAMPLES

The Chi-Square distribution, first mentioned in section 6.6, is another sampling distribution which has applications to hypothesis testing. This distribution is most useful whenever it is desirable to compare expected outcomes with observed ones in order to decide whether or not some hypothesis is true. It is quite often used in cases where the outcomes consist of count data. The first application of Chi-Square will be as a method of comparing proportions in several samples.

The methods of Chapter 7 apply when the null hypothesis is a statement that a population parameter is equal to a particular value or that two population parameters are equal. In cases where more than two samples are involved, these methods cannot be used. If it is desired to test the hypothesis that proportions in three or more samples are equal, the Chi-Square distribution can be used. Perhaps a simple example will illustrate the use.

Suppose, for instance, that we have taken a poll on a campus to determine if students should sit on the University Council and have a voice in the administration of the University. The results have been classified by level of the respondent with the following results:

	Freshmen	Sophomores	Juniors	Seniors	Totals
Should have a voice	121	112	92	83	408
Should not have a voice	99	98	98	97	392
Totals	220	210	190	180	800

We would like to decide if the proportion which approves the proposition is the same for each class. If the table is a listing of all students, no hypothesis testing is necessary; we have all the information. If, however, the table lists random samples of each class, we must decide whether the observed differences between the classes are due to chance or to the samples having been drawn from populations with different proportions of opinion. To test this idea, we hypothesize that all the samples were drawn from populations with the same proportion and that any differences in proportions are due to chance. If this is true, then we should be able to predict the proportion of students in each class who hold each opinion by pooling the proportions in the samples to obtain an estimate for the overall proportion (of students of all classes) who hold each opinion.

In this case, 392 of 800 students, or 0.49, feel that students should not have a voice in student government, while 408 of 800, 0.51, feel that they should have. If these proportions are reasonable estimates of the population proportion of students in each class who hold these opinions, then we can obtain an *expected* value for the number of students in each sample who hold this opinion. In the freshman class, for example, 0.51 of 220 is 112.2. This is based on the assumption that 0.51 is the proportion of all students in the school who hold this opinion, and that it is also the proportion of students in each class who hold the opinion.

We now use the **Chi-Square** statistic (χ^2) to evaluate the differences between the expected and observed values for each class. This statistic is calculated by taking the difference between the observed value and expected value, squaring it, and dividing it by the expected value. This is done for each cell (observed value) and the sum of these calculations is called the sample value of Chi-Square. Thus we have

Chi-Square
$$\chi^2 = \sum \frac{(\text{observed} - \text{expected})^2}{\text{expected}}$$

If the proportions in each class were equal and the samples reflected this, then the observed and expected values would be in close agreement and χ^2 would be very small. However, even if the proportions in each class were, in fact, equal, we would expect to find some variation in the samples just by chance. The Chi-Square statistic allows us to decide whether the variation is likely due to chance or to true differences in proportions.

The Chi-Square distribution, like the t-distribution, is determined by the number of degrees of freedom. Each number of degrees of freedom gives rise to a different Chi-Square curve.

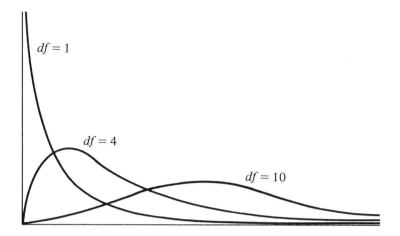

Note that the amount of skewing decreases as the degrees of freedom increase and, in fact, the Chi-Square curve approaches a normal curve for large values of degrees of freedom. In the example we have been discussing, there are four samples, so there are three degrees of freedom. For a Chi-Square test involving k samples with two proportions per sample, there are $k-1$ degrees of freedom. This can be justified intuitively by the fact that if we calculate $k-1$ of the expected frequencies in either row, all other expected frequencies can be obtained by subtraction from the totals in each row and sample.

Table 6 gives critical values of Chi-Square, χ_a^2, where a is the proportion of the area under the curve to the right of χ_a^2. For six degrees of freedom, for instance, the values of $\chi_{.05}^2$ and $\chi_{.01}^2$ are, respectively, 12.592 and 16.812.

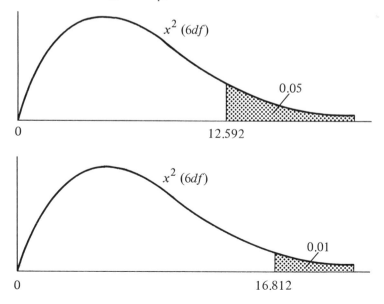

Thus, if a hypothesis of equal proportions is true about a sample with six degrees of freedom, we would expect a sample χ^2 greater than 12.592 no more than one time in twenty by chance, and greater than 16.812 no more than one time in a hundred by chance.

This type of a Chi-Square test, by its nature, is one-tailed, since $\chi^2 = 0$ indicates that all observed outcomes are exactly as expected and we would be able to accept the null hypothesis in this case.

A few cautions are necessary in the use of the Chi-Square statistical procedure. One necessary assumption is that the samples are independently obtained so that bias is avoided. Another is that each observation falls into *exactly one* cell. A third is that the samples are relatively large so that a small difference between expected and observed values is not magnified by a small expected value. Although some disagreement exists on this point, and there is some variation, an expected value of at least five per cell is considered sufficient.

One additional problem arises because of the fact that the Chi-Square distribution is defined over a continuous variable, but the values observed are of necessity integers, therefore discrete. Yates suggested that this could be compensated for by reducing the difference between each expected and observed value by 0.5, thus using a continuity correction. This means that, if the observed value is greater than the expected value, it should be decreased by 0.5; if the observed value is less than the expected value, it should be increased by 0.5; in this way, row and column totals will remain constant. If the difference between the observed and expected value is 0.5 or less, it is counted as zero. Although not all statisticians accept Yates' analysis, its use would tend to render the test slightly conservative, which is usually desirable. For large expected values the consequences of not using Yates' correction factor is slight, but it should probably be used in any cell in which the expected value is less than ten.

The assumptions concerning independence and falling into exactly one cell are necessary to fulfill. However, if there are less than five expected in some cells it may be possible to combine cells in some reasonable manner, or to eliminate cells if necessary. For instance, if we had not had a sufficient sample size of juniors to meet this assumption, juniors and seniors could have been combined into a category of "upperclassmen." Note that combining should not be done haphazardly. Combining freshmen and seniors, for example, would have no logical basis. It would be better in such a case to eliminate a sample and concentrate on the remainder. Note that if two cells are combined into one, the number of degrees of freedom is reduced accordingly.

EXAMPLE 1   Using the data given, test the hypothesis that responses do not differ according to class; that is, that the proportion in each category is the same, regardless of class, in the total population of students. Use a 0.05 level of significance.

SOLUTION Since we found that 0.51 of the total sample belonged to the "should" category, we can determine the expected number in each cell and calculate the sample value of χ^2, comparing it with the critical value, $\chi^2_{.05}$. The appropriate procedure is outlined as follows:

1. H_0: $\pi_1 = \pi_2 = \pi_3 = \pi_4$ (The true proportions are all equal.)
   H_1: The proportions are not all equal.
2. $\alpha = 0.05$
3. Criteria: There are three degrees of freedom. From Table 6, $\chi^2_{.05} = 7.815$ for three degrees of freedom. Thus we will reject H_0 if $\chi^2 > 7.815$.
4. Results: The table is summarized here with the expected number in each cell in parentheses below the observed number. The expected numbers are found, as explained, by taking the pooled proportion as an esitmate of each sample proportion. Expected numbers are calculated to one decimal. If a calculator is used, expected values may be determined to as many places as desired, but the differences in results are negligible.

	Freshmen	Sophomores	Juniors	Seniors	Total
Should have a voice	121	112	92	83	408
	(112.2)	(107.1)	(96.9)	(91.8)	
Should not have a voice	99	98	98	97	392
	(107.8)	(102.9)	(93.1)	(88.2)	
Totals	220	210	190	180	800

The expected outcomes may be calculated separately if desired, but, as an illustration of the fact that there are only three independent quantities, we shall show that only three expected outcomes need to be determined. Earlier we found the expected number of freshmen in the first row by taking $(408/800)(220)$; that is $(0.51)(220) = 112.2$. The expected number in the second row, then, would be $220 - 112.2 = 107.8$. The expected number of sophomores in the *second* row would be $(392/800)(210)$; that is, $(0.49)(210) = 102.9$. The expected number in the *first* row, then, would be $210 - 102.9 = 107.1$. We need only one more expected outcome to determine all the others. The expected number of juniors in the first row is $(0.51)(190) = 96.9$, so the expected number in the second row is $190 - 96.9 = 93.1$. Since the expected number of freshmen, sophomores, and juniors, combined, in the first row is $112.2 + 107.1 + 96.9 = 316.2$, the expected number of seniors in the first row is $408 - 316.2 = 91.8$, and the expected number in the second row is $190 - 91.8 = 88.2$.

With modern pocket calculators, however, with constant multipliers, memory registers, and so on, it is probably easier to just use 0.51 (then 0.49) as a constant multiplier and obtain each expected frequency in that way.

Then

$$\chi^2 = \frac{(121-112.2)^2}{112.2} + \frac{(112-107.1)^2}{107.1} + \frac{(92-96.9)^2}{96.9} + \frac{(83-91.8)^2}{91.8}$$

$$+ \frac{(99-107.8)^2}{107.8} + \frac{(98-102.9)^2}{102.9} + \frac{(98-93.1)^2}{93.1} + \frac{(97-88.2)^2}{88.2}$$

$$\doteq 4.093$$

5. Conclusions: Since 4.093 is not greater than 7.815, we cannot reject H_0 and we conclude that our sample does not show a significant difference among the proportions of the classes.

NOTE: A formula which is somewhat more adapted to use of the hand-held electronic calculator is the following, where N represents the total number of observations:

$$\chi^2 = \sum \frac{(\text{observed})^2}{\text{expected}} - N$$

In the above problem, the calculations would be as follows:

$$\chi^2 = \frac{(121)^2}{112.2} + \frac{(112)^2}{107.1} + \frac{(92)^2}{96.9} + \frac{(83)^2}{91.8} + \frac{(99)^2}{107.8} + \frac{(98)^2}{102.9} + \frac{(98)^2}{93.1} + \frac{(97)^2}{88.2} - 800$$

$$\doteq 804.093 - 800 = 4.093$$

The above formula cannot be used if Yates' correction factor is needed.

EXAMPLE 2   In order to get an idea of brand loyalty or return buying, a merchant asks the customers buying deodorant whether or not they have bought "Certain" before. He also notes whether or not they are now buying "Certain" or some other brand. At the end of the day he has the following information:

Deodorant bought Today	Deodorant Customers Prior Experience	
	Have bought "Certain"	Have not bought "Certain"
"Certain"	8	6
"Other brand"	4	12

Assuming that we may accept the randomness of the sample, and that no customer bought more than one brand of deodorant, determine whether or not there is a difference in the proportion of customers who have previously bought "Certain" and are buying "Certain" today, and of customers who have not previously bought "Certain" and are buying "Certain" today. Use the 0.05 level.

SOLUTION   Of the 30 customers, 14 bought "Certain" today; the proportion of customers buying "Certain" in the sample, then, is $14/30 \doteq 0.4667$. The expected values in each cell may be computed by the same procedure as above. In the sample of size 12, the expected value is $(0.4667)(12) \doteq 5.6$. All other expected values may be found by subtraction, or we note that in the sample of size 18, the expected value is $(0.4667)(18) \doteq 8.4$. Other expected values are $(0.5333)(12) \doteq 6.4$ and $(0.5333)(18) \doteq 9.6$. These values are shown in parentheses below.

Brand bought Today	Have bought "Certain"	Have not bought "Certain"	Total
"Certain"	8 (5.6)	6 (8.4)	14
Other	4 (6.4)	12 (9.6)	16
Total	12	18	30

Since the smallest expected value is 5.6, Chi-Square is appropriate because it is at least 5. On the other hand, because it is less than 10, Yates' correction factor should be used. The calculations are as follows:

$$\chi^2 = \frac{(7.5-5.6)^2}{5.6} + \frac{(6.5-8.4)^2}{8.4} + \frac{(4.5-6.4)^2}{6.4} + \frac{(11.5-9.6)^2}{9.6}$$

$$\doteq 2.015$$

The critical value for $\alpha = 0.05$ with one degree of freedom is 3.841, so we cannot conclude that any differences are due to chance. What appears to be a real difference may be due to the small size of the sample.

•Problems

1. A survey of business failures during the past year showed that 44 of 110 small businesses failing had been in business for less than a year. The same survey showed that 24 of 75 medium size businesses and 14 of 50 large

businesses failing had been in business for less than a year. Estimate (at $\alpha = 0.05$) if the difference in observed proportions is due to chance.

2. A poll was conducted to discover whether citizens were more concerned with the problem of inflation or corruption in government. The questions asked were: which of the two issues they considered more pressing and their party affiliation or preference. Using the results given here, test the hypothesis that party preference does not affect the proportion of people concerned with inflation (or corruption) as the primary issue. Use $\alpha = 0.05$.

	Republican	Democrat	Independent
Inflation	187	316	191
Corruption	154	187	97

3. In a recent poll, 1,000 residents in a particular city were asked their opinion about a proposed zoning ordinance. The individuals were classified according to educational level and the responses were recorded within each educational level. Use the 0.05 level of significance to test the hypothesis that the proportions of residents agreeing, disagreeing, and with no opinion about the proposed zoning ordinance do not differ by educational level.

	Educational Level		
	Less than High School	High School but No College	Attended College
Agree	77	159	164
Disagree	131	157	112
No Opinion	42	134	24

4. Suppose that five samples of fish roe were taken from different species to determine if the proportion of viable roe was the same for each species. The number of viable and nonviable roe for each species is given below:

	Species				
	I	II	III	IV	V
Viable roe	134	78	104	89	95
Nonviable roe	16	22	46	11	5

Use the 0.05 level of significance to test whether the proportion is the same for each species.

5. A researcher wishes to determine if there is a relationship between age and opinion on the Equal Rights Amendment. She conducts a poll and obtains the results given below. Test the hypothesis that the proportion of those

having each opinion does not vary significantly by age. Use the 0.05 level of significance.

Opinion			Age			
	15–24	25–34	35–44	45–54	55–64	**Over 64**
Agree	23	26	36	20	12	8
Disagree	9	16	38	31	23	18
No Opinion	8	8	6	9	5	4

8.2   *CONTINGENCY TABLES*

The Chi-Square distribution is also used to work with a hypothesis that count data are in two independent classifications. For instance, in a year's statistics classes at a university, grades were distributed as follows by category of prior course work.

	Prior Course Work In	*A*	*B*	*C*	*D*	*F*	*Total*
				Grade			
1.	College algebra, but not logic	15	20	40	5	0	80
2.	Logic, but not college algebra	10	15	70	20	5	120
3.	Both college algebra and logic	10	20	25	5	0	60
4.	Neither college algebra nor logic	15	15	75	30	55	190
	Totals	50	70	210	60	60	450

We want to analyze the data to discover whether there is a relation between prior course work and grade in the course, or whether these factors are independent.

In category 1, 80/450 (about 0.178) of the students had prior course work in college algebra, but not logic, so if a student were to be chosen at random from among the 450, the probability would be 80/450 that the student had had prior course work in college algebra but not logic. Since 50/450 (about 0.111) of the students received a grade of "*A*" in the course, the probability would be 50/450 that a randomly chosen student would have received an "*A*." If the classifications are statistically independent, the joint probability that a student chosen at random will belong to *both* categories is the product of these probabilities, (80/450)(50/450) or about (0.01975). The *expected number* of students, of the 450, who will fit in both classifications, then, is that probability times 450. Since $(80/450)(50/450)(450) = (80)(50)/(450)$, it can be observed that the expected number in the cell is equal to the product of the number in the row containing the cell and the column containing the cell, divided by the total number in the sample. This can be graphically illustrated as follows.

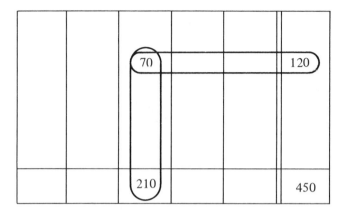

Calculating the expected number in each cell allows us to compute a value of Chi-Square for the sample and compare it to the critical value. The number of degrees of freedom is equal to $(r-1)(k-1)$, where r is the number of rows and k is the number of columns. In this case there are $(4-1)(5-1)$ or 12 degrees of freedom. The justification here is that if we calculate expected frequencies in $k-1$ cells of $r-1$ rows, all the other expected frequencies can be obtained by subtraction from the row and column totals. Thus there are $(r-1)(k-1)$ independent quantities.

A table which sets forth count data in this fashion, classifying observations from a sample into two categories, is called a contingency table. The use of Chi-Square in this case has assumptions similar to those with proportions.

Note that if the observed data happen to be tabulated in terms of percent, these data should be converted back to absolute magnitudes before the test is calculated.

EXAMPLE 1   Test the hypothesis that the grade achieved in the course is independent of prior course work in college algebra or logic in the table given. Use the 0.01 level of significance.

SOLUTION   Considering the data as an independently obtained random sample of all students ever having had the course and using the experimental procedure we have

1. H_0: Grade achievement in statistics and prior course work in college algebra and logic are independent.
   H_1: They are not independent.
2. $\alpha = 0.01$
3. Criteria: Since $df = (4-1)(5-1) = 12$, reject H_0 if $\chi^2 > 26.217$.

4. Results: If it were necessary, some columns could be combined, but it would be more difficult to combine rows. Each expected frequency is calculated (e.g., the first cell is found to be $(80)(50)/(450) \doteq 8.9$), and the data follows with the expected frequency in parentheses.

	Grade				
Category	A	B	C	D	F
1.	15	20	40	5	0
	(8.9)	(12.4)	(37.3)	(10.7)	(10.7)
2.	10	15	70	20	5
	(13.3)	(18.7)	(56.0)	(16.0)	(16.0)
3.	10	20	25	5	0
	(6.7)	(9.3)	(28.0)	(8.0)	(8.0)
4.	15	15	75	30	55
	(21.1)	(29.6)	(88.7)	(25.3)	(25.3)

Then

$$\chi^2 = \frac{(15-8.9)^2}{8.9} + \frac{(20-12.4)^2}{12.4} + \frac{(40-37.3)^2}{37.3} + \frac{(5-10.7)^2}{10.7}$$

$$+ \frac{(0-10.7)^2}{10.7} + \frac{(10-13.3)^2}{13.3} + \frac{(15-18.7)^2}{18.7} + \frac{(70-56)^2}{56}$$

$$+ \frac{(20-16)^2}{16} + \frac{(5-16)^2}{16} + \frac{(10-6.7)^2}{6.7} + \frac{(20-9.3)^2}{9.3} + \frac{(25-28)^2}{28}$$

$$+ \frac{(5-8)^2}{8} + \frac{(0-8)^2}{8} + \frac{(15-21.1)^2}{21.1} + \frac{(15-29.6)^2}{29.6}$$

$$+ \frac{(75-88.7)^2}{88.7} + \frac{(30-25.3)^2}{25.3} + \frac{(55-25.3)^2}{25.3}$$

$$\doteq 106.59$$

5. Conclusions: Since $106.59 > 26.217$, we reject H_0 and conclude that there is some relationship between taking one or another of the two courses, or both, and subsequent success in statistics.

Again, the calculator formula could be used. This formula is particularly useful if the calculator has modified algebraic logic; that is, $3 + 4 \cdot 5$ can be entered in exactly that fashion to obtain 23 without using parentheses. If you enter $3+4\cdot5=$ and obtain 35, your calculator has simple algebraic logic and the individual terms should be summed in the memory. Using the calculator form we have

$$\chi^2 = \frac{15^2}{8.9} + \frac{20^2}{12.4} + \frac{40^2}{37.3} + \frac{5^2}{10.7} + \frac{0}{10.7} + \frac{10^2}{13.3} + \frac{15^2}{18.7} + \frac{70^2}{56}$$

$$+ \frac{20^2}{16} + \frac{5^2}{16} + \frac{10^2}{6.7} + \frac{20^2}{9.3} + \frac{25^2}{28} + \frac{5^2}{8} + \frac{0}{8} + \frac{15^2}{21.1} + \frac{15^2}{29.6}$$

$$+ \frac{75^2}{88.7} + \frac{30^2}{25.3} + \frac{55^2}{25.3} - 450$$

$$= 556.59 - 450 = 106.59.$$

NOTE   Since several of the expected values were less than ten, it would seem that Yates' correction factor should be used and, in fact, it should. There are two cases, however, in which Yates' correction factor need not be used since its use tends to be conservative, to reduce the sample value of Chi-Square somewhat. One is the case where the sample Chi-Square is considerably greater than the critical value, so that a small reduction would not have much effect; the other case is the one in which the sample value of Chi-Square is below the critical value. Reducing it further would add no significant information.

EXAMPLE 2   A college follows up its graduating class and collects income data for students five years after graduation. Excluding students still in school, the data on income level as compared with grade-point average (GPA) follows. Test a hypothesis that there is no relationship between income level five years after graduation and undergraduate GPA, that is, that the two variables are independent. Use $\alpha=0.05$.

GPA	Income Level (Dollars Per Year)				
	1 *Under 5,000*	*2* *5,000–9,999*	*3* *10,000–14,999*	*4* *15000–19,999*	*5* *20,000* *and up*
3.50–4.00	1	18	22	9	2
3.00–3.49	5	63	39	16	11
2.50–2.99	10	152	77	38	14
2.00–2.49	11	84	46	34	2

SOLUTION   Since we are able to calculate expected frequencies in each cell and can meet the other assumptions, the Chi-Square test is appropriate. Using the experimental procedure, we have

1. H_0: Undergraduate grade achievement and income level five years after graduation are independent.

   H_1: They are not independent.

2. $\alpha = 0.05$

3. Criteria: Since $df = (4-1)(5-1) = 12$, reject H_0 if $\chi^2 > 21.026$.

4. Results: Calculating the expected frequencies (in parentheses) we obtain the following table.

GPA	Income Level Category					
	1	2	3	4	5	Total
3.50–4.00	1	18	22	9	2	52
	(2.1)	(25.2)	(14.6)	(7.7)	(2.3)	
3.00–3.49	5	63	39	16	11	134
	(5.5)	(65.0)	(37.7)	(19.9)	(5.9)	
2.50–2.99	10	152	77	38	14	291
	(12.0)	(141.1)	(81.9)	(43.2)	(12.9)	
2.00–2.49	11	84	46	34	2	177
	(7.3)	(85.8)	(49.8)	(26.3)	(7.8)	
Totals	27	317	184	97	29	654

Since two of the expected frequencies are below 5, Chi-Square should not be used with this arrangement of data. However we could combine the columns on each end, or combine the top two rows. The latter course involves the least loss of data sensitivity, so we can combine "3.00–3.49" and "3.50–4.00" to obtain the following table.

GPA	1	2	3	4	5
3.00–4.00	6	81	61	25	13
	(7.7)	(90.2)	(52.3)	(27.6)	(8.2)
2.50–2.99	10	152	77	38	14
	(12.0)	(141.1)	(81.9)	(43.2)	(12.9)
2.00–2.49	11	84	46	34	2
	(7.3)	(85.8)	(49.8)	(26.3)	(7.8)

Expected frequencies should be recalculated because of the possibility of a rounding error.

Note that this changes the number of degrees of freedom since the number of rows is changed from four to three. Degrees of freedom are then changed from 12 to 8 and the critical value is reduced to 15.507. Finally, since several of the cells have expected values less than ten, Yates' correction factor is appropriate. We then have

$$\chi^2 = \frac{(6.5-7.7)^2}{7.7} + \frac{(81.5-90.2)^2}{90.2} + \frac{(60.5-52.3)^2}{52.3} + \frac{(25.5-27.6)^2}{27.6}$$

$$+ \frac{(12.5-8.2)^2}{8.2} + \frac{(10.5-12.0)^2}{12.0} + \frac{(151.5-141.1)^2}{141.1}$$

$$+ \frac{(77.5-81.9)^2}{81.9} + \frac{(38.5-43.2)^2}{43.2} + \frac{(13.5-12.9)^2}{12.9}$$

$$+ \frac{(10.5-7.3)^2}{7.3} + \frac{(84.5-85.8)^2}{85.8} + \frac{(46.5-49.8)^2}{49.8}$$

$$+ \frac{(33.5-26.3)^2}{26.3} + \frac{(2.5-7.8)^2}{7.8}$$

$$\doteq 13.67$$

5. Conclusions: Since $13.67 \not> 15.507$, we fail to reject H_0 and conclude that the evidence is not strong enough to warrant a decision that the variables are not independent. Note however that this is fairly close to the critical value; further, failure to use Yates' correction factor would yield a sample Chi-Square value of 16.774. Thus it is probably better to reserve judgment in this case.

EXAMPLE 3 An instructor wishes to determine whether the two attributes "fear of math" and "sex" are independent. An attitude inventory test is administered to 200 students to determine their anxiety level toward mathematics. They are then classified into the groups "fears math" and "does not fear math." The results are given in the table.

	Attitude	
	Fears Math	**Does Not Fear Math**
Male	36	52
Female	26	86

Use the Chi-Square test to determine, at the 0.05 level, whether attitude toward math and sex are independent.

SOLUTION We can calculate the expected outcomes easily by filling in the peripheral figures.

36	52	88
26	86	112
62	138	200

Then the expected number for the first cell in the first row (c_{11}) is $(62)(88)/200$ or 27.28. The other cells are calculated and found to be as follows:

27.28	60.72
34.72	77.28

Then

$$\chi^2 = \frac{(36-27.28)^2}{27.28} + \frac{(52-60.72)^2}{60.72} + \frac{(26-34.72)^2}{34.72}$$

$$\chi^2 \doteq 2.79 + 1.25 + 2.19 + 0.98 = 7.21$$

Summarizing the experiment, we have the following:

1. H_0: Sex and fear of math are independent
   H_1: Sex and fear of math are not independent
2. $\alpha = 0.05$
3. Criteria: Reject H_0 if $\chi^2 > 3.84$ (for 1 degree of freedom)
4. Results: $\chi^2 = 7.21$
5. Conclusions: Reject H_0; the variables are not independent. In this group, males appear to have more fear of math than females.

NOTE   Two remarks are in order at this time. First, note that regardless of the research hypothesis, use of Chi-Square for a contingency table requires a hypothesis that the variables *are* independent. It is not possible to obtain the test statistic in any other way.

Second, a special formula is available for a 2×2 contingency table. If the entries in the cells are a, b, c, d, as shown below,

a	b
c	d

and the total of all cells is N, then

$$\chi^2 = \frac{N(ad-bc)^2}{(a+b)(c+d)(a+c)(b+d)}$$

Applied to the data of the previous exercise, we have

$$\chi^2 = \frac{200[(36 \cdot 86)-(25 \cdot 52)]^2}{(88)(112)(62)(138)} = \frac{200(1744)^2}{84,327,936} \doteq 7.21$$

If Yates' correction factor is needed, a slight variation allows a similar formula to be used.

$$\chi^2 = \frac{N(|ad - bc| - N/2)^2}{(a+b)(c+d)(a+c)(b+d)}$$

•Problems

1. Using the data of example 2, test the hypothesis by combining columns rather than rows. Note that loss of degrees of freedom (sensitivity of data) caused a marked difference.

2. A survey of 450 randomly selected persons was made and two pieces of information—education level and income level—were collected. The results are as follows:

Education	Income		
	High	Medium	Low
Less than high school	30	50	70
High school graduate	80	100	120

Are income level and education level independent?

3. A sociologist contends that requirements for mortgage approval by lending institutions tend to keep lower income people from buying houses even if the houses are actually in their price range. To back up this contention he cites the following data:

	Income Level (Dollars Per Year)			
	Less than 5,000	5,000–9,999	10,000–14,999	15,000 over
Home owners	38	64	31	12
Renters	55	58	15	8

Assuming his sample was random, does this actually support his contention at a 0.05 level of significance?

4. A marriage counsellor kept records of the reasons given by husband and wife for marriage difficulty. NOTE: The stated reasons may not necessarily be the true reasons. He classified each couple into two categories—by husband's reason and by wife's reason—with the results which follow. Test the hypothesis at a 0.05 level of significance that husbands' and wives' reasons are independent.

Wife's Reason	Husband's Reason For Marital Discord			
	Money	Children	Consideration*	All Other
Money	86	31	132	19
Children	17	64	43	13
Consideration*	54	39	132	33
All other	30	17	37	54

*Including "doesn't love me any more."

5. In a study of technological complexity of societies and the relative punitiveness of legal sanctions in twenty West and North African societies, the following results were obtained.

Technological Complexity	Punitiveness	
	Low	High
Low	8	2
High	2	8

Use Chi-Square analysis to determine whether punitiveness of legal sanctions and technological complexity in these societies are independent. Use the 0.05 level of significance.

6. A study was conducted to study the relationship between religious affiliation and attitude toward artificial birth control. Use the data given below to test whether the variables are independent. Use $\alpha = 0.01$.

	Protestant	Catholic	Jewish
For Birth Control	123	64	43
Against Birth Control	77	86	57

7. An auto dealer wishes to know the particular reason why customers buy the model car that they buy. He collects the following information. Appearance and performance were separately named the most important reason by the following numbers of men and women buyers.

	Appearance	Performance
Men	23	57
Women	27	38

Use χ^2 and the 0.01 level of significance to determine whether sex and reason are independent.

8. A study relating anxiety to success in Naval Aviation training was conducted using 258 Aviation Officer Candidates who were randomly selected from beginning aviation training classes. Each was given a test of anxiety and classified as very high, high, medium, or low. At the conclusion of the program, 189 students had passed while 69 had dropped out. The number in each anxiety level is given below:

Anxiety Level	Pass	Drop
Very high	8	11
high	54	25
medium	87	29
low	40	4

Test whether the tendency to drop out was independent of anxiety level. Use the 0.05 level of significance.

9. A study comparing dream recall vs. need for achievement as measured on a standard test gave the following results.

Need To Achieve	Dream Recall Categories		
	Non-Recallers	Moderate Recallers	Frequent Recallers
Low	4	9	3
Medium	19	17	22
High	7	4	5

Use Chi-Square analysis to determine if any association exists between frequency of dream recall and need for achievement as measured on this test. Use the 0.05 level of significance.

8.3   TESTING GOODNESS OF FIT

The Chi-Square distribution can also be used to test hypotheses that the outcomes of an experiment conform to some specified distribution. In such a case, the expected values can be computed for each possible outcome and a value of Chi-Square calculated. If the sample value of Chi-Square is greater than the predetermined critical value, it can be concluded (unless the probability of type II error appears to be too great) that the outcomes do so conform. Degrees of freedom used to determine the critical value are generally given by $k-1$, where k is the number of categories into which the data is divided. Under certain circumstances, the number of degrees of freedom is reduced further; this occurs when additional population parameters are estimated from the sample. We shall see, in example 3, that we must estimate the mean and variance (standard deviation) in order to obtain the expected values. In such a case the number of degrees of freedom is $k - 1 - m$, where m is the number of parameters estimated.

EXAMPLE 1   A firm wishes to estimate the economic composition of a community where they are considering opening a branch office. They have examined data concerning this and similar communities and have obtained a hypothetical distribution of income which they feel to be approximately accurate. To check this accuracy, they take a random sample of 500 families and obtain the family incomes. They have hypothesized the following distribution of income levels:

Category	Income Level	Proportion
I	over $25,000	0.40
II	$20,000–$24,999	0.20
III	$15,000–$19,999	0.20
IV	$10,000–$14,999	0.10
V	under $10,000	0.10

The sample had the following results.

Category	I	II	III	IV	V	Total
Number	166	97	134	61	42	800

Do these results substantiate the hypothesized distribution at the 0.05 level of significance?

SOLUTION   The five-step formal experimental procedure used in the preceding chapter may still be used, particularly if it is wished to be sure and do all the necessary work; however, by this time a little sophistication should have crept in, and we may dispense with the *formal* procedure, bearing in mind that the same steps are still being followed.

Here we have $k - 1 = 4$ degrees of freedom, so the critical value of $\chi^2_{.05}$ is 9.488 and we will conclude that the sample conforms satisfactorily to the expectation (i.e., that it could very possibly have come from such a population) if the sample Chi-Square is less than 9.488, and reject this conclusion if the sample value is greater than 9.488. The expected values can be calculated simply by taking the hypothesized proportion of 500 for each category and χ^2 can be calculated as follows:

Category	I	II	III	IV	V	Total
Number	166	97	134	61	42	500
Expected	200	100	100	50	50	500

Then

$$\chi^2 = \frac{166^2}{200} + \frac{97^2}{100} + \frac{134^2}{100} + \frac{61^2}{50} + \frac{42^2}{50} - 500$$

$$= 21.13$$

Since $21.13 > 9.488$, reject the hypothesis and conclude that the population income levels are not described well by the hypothetical distribution.

EXAMPLE 2   A poll asks shoppers to name their favorite one of four soft drinks. The results are as follows:

Brand	A	B	C	D	Total
No. preferring	190	198	187	225	800

Test the hypothesis that difference in preference is due to chance.

SOLUTION   We would expect 200 people to choose each brand if there were only chance differences (since this would imply $\pi = 1/4$ in each case), so we would have

$$\chi^2 = \frac{190^2}{200} + \frac{198^2}{200} + \frac{187^2}{200} + \frac{225^2}{200} - 800$$

$$= 4.49$$

The critical value of $\chi^2_{.05}$ with three degrees of freedom is 7.815. Since 4.49 does not exceed 7.815, we can conclude that the differences are due to chance.

One of the widely repeated assumptions in most of the tests of the last two chapters was that the distribution from which the sample was taken was normal (or what to do if it were not). Chi-Square analysis gives a method for testing this assumption. An example will suffice to show the method, but one comment is in order before beginning. We assume throughout this chapter that expected values must be at least five observations per cell. This assumption can be relaxed in some cases. The primary reason for this restriction is that small differences between expected and observed outcomes can be magnified if the expected value (which is the denominator of the fraction) is small and the difference is fairly large. If the two values are in fact fairly close, and Yates' correction factor is used, it is satisfactory to have small expected values. The judgment of the person making the calculations is important. As a rule of thumb, if small values are expected, but the overall sample Chi-Square is not significant, the procedure is all right. If the sample Chi-Square is significant, but the cells with small expected values were not major contributors to the total, the procedure is still probably all right. If those cells are a major contributing factor, however, the results are probably invalid, and some combinations should take place.

The procedure can be outlined as follows. To determine whether it is reasonable to conclude that a set of sample data could probably have come from a normal distribution, first use the mean and standard deviation of the sample to estimate the mean and/or standard deviation of the population if not known or assumed. Then group the sample data into convenient classes, calculate z-values for the class boundaries, determine the proportion of the area under a normal curve which would lie between these boundaries, multiply by the sample size to obtain the expected values, calculate the sample Chi-Square in the usual way, comparing with a critical value with $k - 1 - m$ degrees of freedom, where k is the number of classes and m is the number of parameters estimated. If the sample value of Chi-Square is less than the appropriate critical value (usually with $\alpha = 0.05$), we conclude that the sample could have come from a normal distribution; that is, such a hypothesis is not inconsistent with the observed facts.

EXAMPLE 3 Problem 4 of section 2.1 lists 100 pieces of data ranging from 134 to 246. Use Chi-Square to determine whether it is reasonable to conclude that the population from which the sample was taken is a normal population. Use $\alpha = 0.05$.

SOLUTION First we take the mean and standard deviation of the sample. Here $\bar{x} \doteq 172.5$ and $s \doteq 14.7$. If the sample is from a normal population, we would probably not have a need for classes more than three standard deviations above or below the mean, so we would not have any classes beginning below about 128 or above about 217. A class size of about ten would be convenient, although other numbers are reasonable. We thus have the following grouped frequency table.

Class	Frequency
130–139	2
140–149	1
150–159	6
160–169	20
170–179	56
180–189	9
190–199	2
200–209	1
210–above	3

We now consider the class boundaries and determine the z-values and associated areas for each class boundary. In each case we use a mean of 172.5 and standard deviation 14.7. For instance, for the boundary of 139.5, $z = (x - \mu)/\sigma = (139.5 - 172.5)/14.7 = -2.24$. From Table 4, this corresponds to an area of 0.4875. For the boundary of 149.5, $z = (149.5 - 172.5)/14.7 = -1.56$. This corresponds to an area of 0.4406. The area under a normal curve between these boundaries, then, would be $0.4875 - 0.4406 = 0.0469$. Other areas can be found accordingly.

Class Boundary	z	Area
139.5	−2.24	0.4875
149.5	−1.56	0.4406
159.5	−0.88	0.3106
169.5	−0.20	0.0793
179.5	0.48	0.1844
189.5	1.16	0.3770
199.5	1.84	0.4671
209.5	2.52	0.4941

The probabilities for each class, then, can be obtained by taking the differences in the areas for the class boundaries (the sum, for the class containing the mean).

Class	Probability	Expected Value
Below 140	$0.5000 - 0.4875 = 0.0125$	1.25
140–149	$0.4875 - 0.4406 = 0.0469$	4.69
150–159	$0.4406 - 0.3106 = 0.1300$	13.00
160–169	$0.3106 - 0.0793 = 0.2313$	23.13
170–179	$0.0793 + 0.1844 = 0.2637$	26.37
180–189	$0.3770 - 0.1844 = 0.1926$	19.26
190–199	$0.4671 - 0.3770 = 0.0901$	9.01
200–209	$0.4941 - 0.4671 = 0.0270$	2.70
210 or over	$0.5000 - 0.4941 = 0.0059$	0.59

Since several expected values are less than 5, they should be examined closely. An expected value of 1.25 for the lowest class, compared with an observed value of 2 (which will be corrected to 1.5) is not perturbing, but an expected value of 0.59 compared to 3 (even corrected to 2.5) gives a cell component of 6.18, which is very high. Combining the last two classes gives an expected value of 3.29 compared with an observed value of 4 (corrected to 3.5), which is quite close. We then combine the first two and last two classes, and take expected values to one decimal place, since the mean and standard deviation were each computed to one decimal place, and compare the expected values with the observed values to obtain the sample value of Chi-Square. The results of the partitioning of the normal distribution can be shown graphically (p. 253).

Class	Observed	Expected
Below 150	3	5.9
150–159	6	13.0
160–169	20	23.1
170–179	56	26.4
180–189	9	19.3
190–199	2	9.0
200 or above	4	3.3

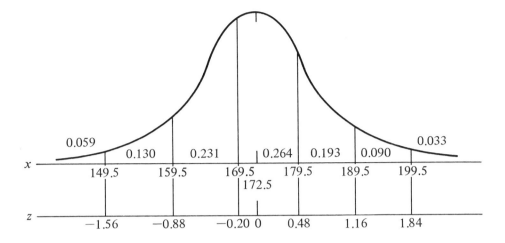

Then

$$\chi^2 = \frac{3^2}{5.9} + \frac{6^2}{13.0} + \frac{20^2}{23.1} + \frac{56^2}{26.4} + \frac{9^2}{19.3} + \frac{2^2}{9.0} + \frac{4^2}{3.3} - 100$$

$$\doteq 49.89$$

Even using Yates' correction factor reduces the obtained χ^2 only to 46.28 (and this would not be necessary since the 49.89 is highly significant). There are $7-1-2=4$ degrees of freedom, so the critical value of $\chi^2_{.05}$ is 9.488; $\chi^2_{.01} = 13.277$, so we can safely conclude that the sample is not from a normal distribution. This might be contrary to your first impression, since the distribution is rather bell shaped, but it turned out to be too centrally oriented for its dispersion.

•Problems

1. We want to test a die to see if it is fair. We roll it 60 times with the following results. Test the fairness of the die, using $\alpha = 0.05$.

Number	1	2	3	4	5	6
Frequency	8	13	10	8	12	9

2. Four balls are drawn from an urn, with replacement, and the number of white balls in each set of four recorded. The experiment is repeated 100

times with the following results:

Number of White Balls	Number of Occurrences
0	11
1	16
2	38
3	33
4	2

Test the hypothesis (at $\alpha = 0.01$) that exactly 40% of the balls in the urn are white.

3. A student poll obtained data on the relative popularity of 3 statistics instructors. Of 150 students who had a preference, 62 preferred instructor A, 47 instructor B, and 41 preferred instructor C. Accepting this as a random sample of statistics students, test the hypothesis that the 3 instructors are equally popular. Use $\alpha = 0.05$.

4. Using the data of example 1, section 8.2, test the hypothesis that prior course work in college algebra and logic have equal effects on success in statistics as measured by the proportion of students with each background that each grade category contains.

c5. Chi-square tests for curve fitting are particularly useful in genetics to test whether a set of offspring has bred true-to-type or is mutant. Suppose, for example, that we examine the result of several litters of guinea pigs with respect to color of coat and length of hair. We have the following results.

	Expected	Observed
long hair brown-white	53.1	61
long hair black-white	26.5	33
long hair brown-black	17.7	23
long hair white	8.8	12
short hair brown-white	79.6	72
short hair black-white	53.1	49
short hair brown-black	26.5	21
short hair white	17.7	12
Total		283

Expected frequencies were calculated using genetic probabilities and a ratio of 12:6:4:2:18:12:6:4 was hypothetically determined for this situation. Use the 0.05 level of significance to test the hypothesis that observed frequencies conform satisfactorily to the prediction. Rejection of that hypothesis would lead us to a speculation that we have a mutation.

6. Prior to an election a public opinion poll claimed that 38% of the voters were for candidate A, 33% for candidate B, 12% for candidate C, and the remainder undecided. Candidate A received 5,132 votes, candidate B 4,376 votes, and candidate C 2,034 votes. Assuming that the undecided voters voted in the same proportion as the rest of the voters, would we say ($\alpha = 0.05$) that the poll reasonably predicted the outcome of the election?

7. When a bridge mix (candy) is boxed, the manufacturer claims that the pieces include chocolate covered peanuts, chocolate covered raisins, nougat centers, and fudge centers in the ratio 3:3:2:2. A sample of 200 pieces contains 43 peanuts, 51 raisins, 54 nougat centers, and 52 fudge centers. Can this be used to refute the manufacturer's claim at the 0.05 level of significance?

8. Use the method of example 3 to test whether or not each of the following samples could reasonably have come from a normal distribution.

(a) The height data of example 1, section 1.2.
(b) The income data of problem 13, section 2.1.
(c) The bowling example of section 5.1.
(d) The data of problem 4, section 6.5.
(e) The data of problem 10, section 6.7.

8.4 SUMMARY

The Chi-Square (χ^2) distribution is often useful when comparing expected outcomes to observed outcomes. This distribution is particularly useful in assessing if proportions among several samples differ significantly, if two classifications of a sample are independent, and if results of a sample conform to a hypothetical distribution.

The basic formula for calculating the sample value of Chi-Square is the following

$$\chi^2 = \Sigma \frac{(\text{expected} - \text{observed})^2}{\text{expected}}$$

Some alternate formulas will be given below.

The obtained sample value of χ^2 is then compared to the critical value χ^2_α obtained from table 6 with appropriate degrees of freedom—$(k-1)$ in the case of k sample proportions, $(r-1)(k-1)$ in the case of an $r \times k$ contingency table, $k-1-m$ in the case of a goodness-of-fit test with k classes and m parameters estimated.

If the obtained sample χ^2 exceeds the critical value, it follows that the proportions are significantly different, or that the classifications are not independent, or that the fit to the predicted distribution is not good.

The Chi-Square distribution does not, of itself, assume that the data are normally distributed, and does not generally depend on population parameters. For this reason it is called a nonparametric statistic. Other such statistics are discussed in Chapter 12.

The use of Chi-Square assumes that each observation fits in exactly one cell, that the data are independently obtained, and that each cell has an expected value of at least five (although some exceptions are possible). If expected values in any cell fall below ten, Yates' correction factor is appropriate, reducing the difference between expected and observed values by 0.5 before squaring.

Some special formulas for Chi-Square computation are the following:

If Yates' correction factor is not used, the following formula may be used and is particularly well adapted to use in a hand-held calculator.

$$\chi^2 = \Sigma \frac{(\text{observed})^2}{\text{expected}} - N$$

For a two-by-two contingency table with entries arranged as below

a	b
c	d

the following formula is appropriate without Yates' correction

$$\chi^2 = \frac{N(ad - bc)^2}{(a+b)(c+d)(a+c)(b+d)}$$

and the following formula incorporates Yates' correction

$$\chi^2 = \frac{N(|ad - bc| - N/2)^2}{(a+b)(c+d)(a+c)(b+d)}$$

TECHNICAL NOTE   Chi-Square is also used to test hypotheses concerning the variance of a population. Confidence intervals for the population variance based on the sample variance were discussed in Technical Note 2, section 6.2 (for large samples) and in section 6.6 (for small samples). To test the hypothesis that $\sigma^2 = \sigma_0^2$, if $n \geq 30$, we use the test statistic

$$z = \frac{s - \sigma_0}{\sigma_0 / \sqrt{2n}}$$

For small samples, $n < 30$, we obtain the ratio $(n-1)s^2/\sigma_0^2$. This is a value of Chi-Square. If the alternate hypothesis is $\sigma^2 \neq \sigma_0^2$, reject H_0 if the sample

Chi-Square, χ^2, is greater than $\chi^2_{\alpha/2}$ or less than $\chi^2_{1-\alpha/2}$ for $n-1$ degrees of freedom. If the alternate hypothesis is $\sigma^2 > \sigma_0^2$, reject H_0 if $\chi^2 > \chi^2_\alpha$ for $n-1$ degrees of freedom; if the alternate hypothesis is $\sigma^2 < \sigma_0^2$, reject H_0 if $\chi^2 < \chi^2_{1-\alpha}$ with $n-1$ degrees of freedom.

•Problems

1. In an apartment complex, a sociologist asked a sample of workers if they were satisfied with their work. He then classified the work into three categories. His results were as follows.

	White Collar	Blue Collar	Menial
Satisfied	81	124	44
Unsatisfied	49	76	56

Test the hypothesis, at $\alpha = 0.05$, that job satisfaction is not related to type of job or that the proportion of satisfied workers is the same in each category.

2. In a large firm, sales people were classified as aggressive, nonaggressive, and shy. Their sales for the month were classified as high, average, or low. Given the data which follows, test the hypothesis that relative aggressiveness and sales are independent. Use $\alpha = 0.01$.

	Sales		
	High	*Average*	*Low*
Aggressive	64	28	38
Nonaggressive	45	22	29
Shy	28	29	27

3. A coin is tossed 3 times and the number of heads recorded. The experiment is repeated 80 times, with the results given here.

Number of Heads	Frequency of Occurrence
0	7
1	24
2	35
3	14

Test the hypothesis that the coin is biased. Use $\alpha=0.05$. If it is biased, in what direction is the bias?

4. Polls were taken in various locations with regard to the opinion of citizens on a proposed bond issue. Results were as follows:

	Avon Park	Wilson Center	Bayview	Dodd Park
Favoring	58	115	64	81
Opposing	103	139	88	92
No Opinion	137	104	90	58

(a) Test the hypothesis that, of those with an opinion, proportions favoring the bond issue are the same from area to area (assuming the samples are random).

(b) Test the hypothesis that the proportion of those with no opinion are the same from area to area.

(c) Test the hypothesis that the proportions of each category are the same from area to area. (Degrees of freedom are equal to $(r-1)(k-1)$ for this type of analysis.) Use the 0.05 level of significance for each part.

5. A store manufacturer hypothesized that the number of customers who entered his store during the first ten minutes after he returned from lunch (i.e., from 1:00 to 1:10) followed a Poisson distribution. He observed the occurrences over a period of 20 weeks (120 days) and found that the distribution of customers was as follows:

No. of customers	0	1	2	3	4	5	6	7	8
No. of occurrences	10	25	32	22	17	9	4	0	1

Calculate the sample mean and use this to estimate the mean of the distribution. Then determine the expected number of each value of the variable (no. of customers) using the table, then use Chi-Square to test the hypothesis at the 0.05 level. Don't forget to reduce *df* by one more since we estimated the mean.

6. To increase sales, a hardware store chain decided to try giving incentive bonuses to managers of stores if sales increased a minimum of a certain percent over the preceding week. To determine the worth of such a program, only one-fourth of the stores were included in the experiment, while the managers of the remaining stores did not know of the experiment. The results of the first week showed that, of 34 stores in which the managers were offered bonuses, 18 had sales increasing at least 5% over the preceding week, while 8 had sales decreasing at least 5% from the preceding week. Of the remaining 101 stores, 45 had sales up at least 5%, and 17 had sales down 5%. From this information, can you conclude that the incentive program seems likely to work? Use a 0.05 level of significance.

7. A medical researcher is testing the hypothesis that there is a relationship between blood type and susceptibility to a certain liver condition. Now about 40% of the population has blood type O, 30% has type A, 20% has type B, and 10% has type AB. He obtains data on all patients admitted to the hospitals in his area during the past ten years who have had this condition and finds that there were 1,043 who had blood type O, 801 with blood type A, 861 with blood type B, and 745 with blood type AB. Can he safely conclude, at a significance level of 0.01, that there is a relationship?

8. A biologist exposes some culture plates to each of five different, but related, strains of bacillus. She wishes to test the hypothesis that strain makes no difference in the number of plates which will attain propagation level in 36 hours. Given the data below, decide whether or not the hypothesis is substantiated at the 0.05 level of significance.

	Strain				
	A	B	C	D	E
Number reaching propagation level	32	23	28	36	31
Number not reaching propagation level	68	77	72	64	69

9. To test whether susceptibility to disease A and prior contracting of disease B are related, a sample of 1,000 persons is randomly selected during an epidemic of disease A. The severity of each case of disease A in the sample and the prior severity of any case of disease B are recorded. The results are given in the table below. Test, at the 0.01 level of significance, to see if theere is any relationship between disease A and prior experience with disease B.

	Disease A		
Disease B	Did not contract	Light case	Severe case
Did not contract	302	267	31
Light case	86	156	8
Severe case	12	77	61

Problems 10 and 11 are based on the Technical Note in this section.

10. An industrial process requires a tight quality control and each day's output is sampled for mean and variance. To be in control, the day's output should have a variance no greater than 0.17 mm. If a random sample of 25

pieces showed a variance of 0.19 mm, would this be sufficient evidence that the machine should be retooled? If not, for what value of sample variance should retooling begin?

11. A processor accepts a shipment as representative on the basis of a test on the mean of a sample which showed that a sample of nine items had a mean of 11.47 defects, compared with a standard of 9.00. The sample standard deviation was 4.21, yielding $t = 1.76$, less than the 0.05 critical value of 1.86. He notes that the standard deviation of the standard is 2.56, and he is not even sure that the t-distribution applies (that is, that the population is normal) so he wishes to test whether the sample variance is significantly ($\alpha = 0.05$) different from the standard (hypothetical) variance. Use the Chi-Square test to see if this difference is significant.

CHAPTER 8

Glossary of Terms

category	goodness of fit
cell	independent
Chi-Square	observed value
contingency tables	Yates' correction factor
expected value	

Glossary of Symbols

χ^2	Chi-Square
χ_a^2	value of Chi-Square for which a is the proportion under the curve to its right
N	total number of observations
$\pi_1, \pi_2, \pi_3, \pi_4$, etc.	hypothetical proportions for several populations

CONTROLE DES PASSEPORTS

GB

LKU
55

Chapter 9

Analysis of Variance

9.1 INTRODUCTION

In Chapter 8, we discussed a method useful in testing the hypothesis that differences among several sample proportions are due to chance. It is also useful to have a method to test the hypothesis that differences among several sample *means* are due to chance or, alternatively, that the samples are drawn from the same population.

The procedure used for this is called **analysis of variance**. The basic idea is that, where several samples are used in an experiment, two or more estimates for the population variance are made, each assuming that all samples came from the same population, and these are compared. If they are close, the hypothesis that the samples come from the same population is justified. The F-sampling distribution, first mentioned in section 6.6, is used to determine how close is "close enough." If the differences are found to be significant, further procedures are then used to determine the actual source of the differences. In this sense, the primary use for the analysis of variance technique is to determine whether or not further procedures are justified.

In most essential details, analysis of variance is an extension of the two-sample t-test (section 7.4) to k samples. As such, it has the same assumptions—that the population (or populations) from which the samples are drawn are normally distributed, that the samples are random and independently obtained, and that the samples are drawn from the same population or from populations with equal variances. The latter requirement is for *homoscedacity*, or *homogeneity of sample variances*. If it appears to be possible that the equality of population variance assumption is satisfied, the sample variances are said to be **homogeneous**.

The analysis of variance procedures are rather robust with respect to normality and homogeneity, that is, they can stand up to some bending, but the hypothesis of independence (and randomness) must be met. For the normality assumption, experience indicates that some deviation is acceptable, and if the samples are reasonably small, normality cannot be shown very easily to be satisfied or not satisfied. Larger samples can be tested by Chi-Square (section 8.3) to see if they could have come from a normal population.

To test for homogeneity of sample variances, Hartley devised a procedure which is an extension of the simple F-test for equality of two sample variances. If the sample variances are known, then F-ratios can be constructed from them in pairs. The largest of these values is called F_{max}, and is the ratio of the largest sample variance to the smallest sample variance. If this is greater than the critical value listed in Table 9, the variances are not homogeneous at the desired level of significance, and analysis of variance is not appropriate. The appropriate critical value is determined by the number of samples, k, the significance level, α, and the number of degrees of freedom, $n-1$, of the largest sample (not necessarily the largest sample used to obtain F_{max}, but the largest sample in the experiment).

EXAMPLE 1   Forty salesmen were randomly divided into four groups of ten and each group was given a course of training by a different method. The number of sales for the salesmen in each group were tabulated and are given below. The period covered is six weeks. Of the original forty, some had dropped out and some, for one reason or another did not have available records. Assuming that the normality and independence assumptions are met, use F_{max} to determine whether or not analysis of variance is appropriate to analyze the data.

I: 13, 11, 6, 18, 7, 15, 14
II: 9, 13, 15, 11, 10, 6, 7, 9
III: 6, 9, 13, 10, 9, 7
IV: 16, 10, 14, 17, 9, 11, 14

SOLUTION: For each group the variances can be computed. We have the following data:

$$\Sigma x_1 = 84 \qquad \Sigma x_2 = 80 \qquad \Sigma x_3 = 54 \qquad \Sigma x_4 = 91$$
$$\Sigma x_1^2 = 1{,}120 \qquad \Sigma x_2^2 = 862 \qquad \Sigma x_3^2 = 516 \qquad \Sigma x_4^2 = 1{,}239$$
$$n_1 = 7 \qquad n_2 = 8 \qquad n_3 = 6 \qquad n_4 = 7$$

Then

$$s_1^2 = \frac{1{,}120 - (84^2/7)}{6} \qquad s_2^2 = \frac{862 - (80^2/8)}{7}$$

$$s_3^2 = \frac{516 - (54^2/6)}{5} \qquad s_4^2 = \frac{1{,}239 - (91^2/7)}{6}$$

so

$$s_1^2 \doteq 18.667; \qquad s_2^2 \doteq 8.857: \qquad s_3^2 = 6; \qquad s_4^2 \doteq 9.333.$$

Thus

$$F_{\max} = \frac{18.667}{6} \doteq 3.111.$$

From Table 9, the critical value of $F_{\max}$ for four samples and seven degrees of freedom is 8.44 for $\alpha = 0.05$. This is symbolized $F_{\max_{.05}}(4, 7) = 8.44$. Thus we can conclude that the variances are homogeneous.

The remainder of this chapter will be devoted to simple one-way analysis of variance, the Scheffé and Newman–Keuls *Post Hoc* tests, and two-way analysis of variance both without and with interaction effects. An exhaustive treatment of analysis of variance, including other tests for homogeneity of variance, other *post hoc* tests, analysis of variance with repeated measures on one or more variables, two-way analysis of variance with unequal cell sizes, analysis of covariance and much more is in B. J. Winer, *Statistical Principles in Experimental Design* (McGraw-Hill, 1971). Frequent reference will be made to this book for special cases or further reading.

If the normality assumption is violated, or if the variances are not homogeneous, the Kruskal–Wallis *H*-test, described in Chapter 12, may often be used. This is not as powerful as the techniques described here. If normality is not violated, but the variances are not homogeneous, it may be possible to stabilize them by using a transformation. Some such transformations are given in Winer, pages 399–400.

If the assumptions are satisfied, analysis of variance may be performed.

9.2 ESTIMATING POPULATION VARIANCE

Suppose we have several samples, each containing n pieces of data. Each sample variance, $s_1^2, s_2^2, s_3^2, \ldots, s_k^2$ for k samples is an estimate of the population variance if all samples are drawn from the same (or equivalent) populations.

Since each is an unbiased estimate of the population variance, an even better estimate can be made by taking the mean of all these variances. This is often called the **mean square within samples**. Since each differs from the true population variance by an amount of sampling error, this is often called the **mean square due to error**. For purposes of extension to two-way analysis, we shall use the latter term. Another term often used is **residual mean square**.

> **Mean Square Due to Error**
>
> $$MSE = \frac{s_1^2 + s_2^2 + s_3^2 + \cdots + s_k^2}{k}$$
>
> if the k samples are equal in size.

If we knew the actual population variance, σ^2, we would be able to obtain the standard error of the mean by the formula $\sigma_{\bar{x}} = \sigma / \sqrt{n}$; that is, $\sigma_{\bar{x}}^2 = \sigma^2 / n$ so that $\sigma^2 = n\sigma_{\bar{x}}^2$. If we had all samples of size n, the variance of the sample means would be $\sigma_{\bar{x}}^2$. Since we have k samples of size n, the variance of those sample means is an estimate of $\sigma_{\bar{x}}^2$. Thus we can estimate σ^2 a second way. The value obtained is called the mean square between samples or mean square due to treatments (assuming a difference in treatment among the several samples).

> **Mean Square Due to Treatments**
>
> $$MST = \frac{n}{k-1} \left[(\bar{x}_1 - \bar{x})^2 + (\bar{x}_2 - \bar{x})^2 + \cdots + (\bar{x}_k - \bar{x})^2 \right]$$
>
> where each of the k samples is of size n with means $\bar{x}_1, \bar{x}_2, \ldots, \bar{x}_k$, and $\bar{x}$ is the overall mean.

From these two estimates for the population variance, we obtain the ratio $F = MST/MSE$. If both estimates for the population variance are reasonably close, F will be close to one; if there is no difference between the sample means, MST will be zero, so $F = 0$. If MST is appreciably larger than MSE, then we can attribute the differences between the samples to the treatments more than to chance, and conclude that there are real (nonchance) variations among the sample means for the preselected level of significance. If the differences are due to chance, the set of all possible samples from the population generates an F-distribution based on the null hypothesis of equality of means. The distribution depends upon two parameters, the degrees of freedom between samples, $k-1$, for the numerator, and the sum of the degrees of freedom in the samples, for the denominator. This latter number is equal to $N-k$, where N is the total number of observations in all samples or cells; one degree of freedom is lost for each sample. Tables 7 and 8 give the critical values for F for the 0.05 and 0.01 levels of significance. If the obtained sample F is greater than the value of F_α, we reject the hypothesis that the sample means are equal and conclude that the differences among the samples are not due to chance so that further tests are appropriate.

EXAMPLE 1 Suppose that three dice are rolled four times and the results are recorded as four different samples:

$$\begin{array}{llll} \text{I:} & 2 & 4 & 3 \\ \text{II:} & 3 & 6 & 3 \\ \text{III:} & 4 & 6 & 5 \\ \text{IV:} & 4 & 5 & 3 \end{array}$$

Use analysis of variance to test the hypothesis that the samples come from equal populations.

SOLUTION The means of the samples are, respectively, 3, 4, 5, 4 and the overall mean is 4. Thus

$$MST = \frac{3}{4-1}\left[(3-4)^2 + (4-4)^2 + (5-4)^2 + (4-4)^2\right] = 2$$

Also

$$s_1^2 = \frac{29 - (9^2/3)}{2} = 1$$

$$s_2^2 = \frac{54 - (12^2/3)}{2} = 3$$

$$s_3^2 = \frac{77 - (15^2/3)}{2} = 1$$

$$s_4^2 = \frac{50 - (12^2/3)}{2} = 1$$

so

$$MSE = \frac{1+3+1+1}{4} = 1.5$$

and

$$F = 2/1.5 \doteq 1.333$$

Now suppose we add two units to each number in sample II, four units to each number in sample III, and ten units to each number in sample IV. The new sample means are 3, 6, 9, 14, and the overall mean is 8, so

$$MST = \frac{3}{4-1}\left[(3-8)^2 + (6-8)^2 + (9-8)^2 + (14-8)^2\right] = 66$$

The variances within each sample remain the same, since shifting an entire sample any number of units does not change its dispersion. Thus $F = 66/1.5 = 44$. From Table 8, the critical value of $F_{.01}$ for 3 and 8 degrees of freedom is 7.59, so we can conclude that the differences among the samples are significant at the 0.01 level.

> **EXAMPLE 2**   A supermarket chain consents to participate in an advertising test for a product. Thirty stores of approximately equal size and volume of sales are selected and randomly divided into three groups of ten each. In the first group, nothing is done other than the usual. In the other two groups, an advertising display is erected utilizing two different posters. One type of poster is used in the second group, and a second type of poster is used in the third group. The number of sales of the product, in units, was recorded for one week. The results follow. Test the hypothesis that there are no differences among the groups. Use the 0.05 level of significance.
>
> I: 38, 54, 39, 52, 63, 54, 47, 52, 46, 25
> II: 58, 44, 63, 94, 72, 42, 89, 68, 53, 47
> III: 76, 51, 83, 84, 51, 67, 40, 89, 76, 53

SOLUTION: The best way to analyze the data is by use of analysis of variance. Since $k = 3, N = 30$, there are 2 and 27 degrees of freedom, for which $F_{.05}(2, 27) = 3.35$. The null hypothesis is that the means are equal for the three groups. Arranging the data in tabular form we have

x_1	x_1^2	x_2	x_2^2	x_3	x_3^2
38	1444	58	3364	76	5776
54	2916	44	1936	51	2601
39	1521	63	3969	83	6889
52	2704	94	8836	84	7056
63	3969	72	5184	51	2601
54	2916	42	1764	67	4489
47	2209	89	7921	40	1600
52	2704	68	4624	89	7921
46	2116	53	2809	76	5776
25	625	47	2209	53	2809
470	23,124	630	42,616	670	47,518

$\bar{x}_1 = 47.0$

$s_1^2 = \dfrac{23,124 - (470^2/10)}{9}$
$= 1,034/9 \doteq 114.89$

$\bar{x}_2 = 63.0$

$s_2^2 = \dfrac{42,616 - (630^2/10)}{9}$
$= 2,926/9 \doteq 325.11$

$\bar{x}_3 = 67.0$

$s_3^2 = \dfrac{47,518 - (670^2/10)}{9}$
$= 2,628/9 = 292.00$

$$\bar{x} = \frac{470 + 630 + 670}{30} = 59.0$$

Then

$$MST = \frac{10}{3-1}\left[(47-59)^2 + (63-59)^2 + (67-59)^2\right]$$

$$= 1,120$$

and

$$MSE = \frac{114.89 + 325.11 + 292}{3} = 244$$

Since $F_{max} = 325.11/114.89 \doteq 2.83 \not> 5.34$ ($F_{max_{.05}}(3,9) = 5.34$) and normality does not appear to be violated, analysis of variance is appropriate. Then $F = 1,120/244 \doteq 4.59$.

Since $4.59 > 3.35$, reject H_0 and conclude that there are differences among the three groups. Testing further differences between pairs of groups will be covered in section 9.4.

COMMENT   The method given above is rarely used in practice. In most cases, raw data formulas are used, particularly as they are applicable to both equal and unequal sample sizes. These formulas and procedures will be given in the next section.

•Problems

1. Students are assigned randomly to 4 different groups and 4 different methods are used to teach the same material to the groups, one method per group. Use analysis of variance to unearth any significant difference between the groups, given means and standard deviations of each of the samples. Each group contained 21 students. Use the 0.05 level of significance. Note the effect of different groupings and of the size of the standard deviations.

    (a) $\bar{x}_1 = 78.4$, $\bar{x}_2 = 88.4$, $\bar{x}_3 = 71.6$, $\bar{x}_4 = 70.4$
    $s_1 = 14.7$, $s_2 = 14.4$, $s_3 = 21.6$, $s_4 = 19.8$

    (b) $\bar{x}_1 = 78.4$, $\bar{x}_2 = 88.4$, $\bar{x}_3 = 71.6$, $\bar{x}_4 = 70.4$
    $s_1 = 19.7$, $s_2 = 18.4$, $s_3 = 24.6$, $s_4 = 29.8$

    (c) $\bar{x}_1 = 78.4$, $\bar{x}_2 = 88.4$, $\bar{x}_3 = 81.6$, $\bar{x}_4 = 80.4$
    $s_1 = 14.7$, $s_2 = 14.4$, $s_3 = 21.6$, $s_4 = 19.8$

2. Anthropologists uncovered three burial mounds some distance apart. They found 4 adult skulls in each mound. The skulls measured as follows in each

mound (in cm):

$$I:48.4,46.2,47.1,46.3$$
$$II:52.8,49.6,50.5,48.7$$
$$III:44.2,44.7,46.1,45.4$$

Try to estimate at the 0.05 level of significance if the skulls are representative of the same population.

3. Sociologists studying 6 different cultures did some research into the "waiting time" of an interview—that is, the time spent in amenities before getting down to business. Eleven interviews were timed in each culture. Waiting times are given in minutes. Use analysis of variance to decide whether there are differences among the cultures in regard to this aspect. Use the 0.01 level of significance.

Culture	Waiting Times
A	11, 7, 8, 4, 6, 9, 8, 5, 7, 9, 10
B	6, 4, 8, 2, 7, 6, 3, 5, 7, 6, 3
C	5, 9, 8, 7, 6, 10, 9, 11, 9, 8, 7
D	6, 6, 5, 4, 5, 7, 6, 3, 5, 4, 8
E	13, 14, 16, 12, 17, 11, 14, 16, 13, 11, 12
F	7, 6, 5, 9, 11, 3, 8, 14, 3, 7, 5

9.3 ONE-WAY ANALYSIS OF VARIANCE

The methods described in the previous section can be used only if all samples have an equal number of data points. These methods do not utilize, except indirectly, the raw scores.

If we take the formula for *MST* given in the previous section, replace each mean by its raw score value (i.e., $\bar{x}_i = (\Sigma x_i)/n$, expand the parentheses, collect terms and apply a little algebra, we obtain

$$MST = \frac{n}{k-1}\left[\frac{(\Sigma x_1)^2 + (\Sigma x_2)^2 + (\Sigma x_3)^2 + \cdots + (\Sigma x_k)^2}{n^2} - \frac{k(\Sigma x)^2}{N^2}\right]$$

Noting that $k-1$ is the number of degrees of freedom associated with *MST*, we define the sum of squares for treatments to be equal to $(k-1)MST$, so that $MST = SST/(k-1)$. We note that $nk = N$, so that

$$SST = \frac{(\Sigma x_1)^2 + (\Sigma x_2)^2 + \cdots + (\Sigma x_k)^2}{n} - \frac{(\Sigma x)^2}{N}$$

If the samples are not equal in size, we break apart the first fraction, dividing each $(\Sigma x_i)^2$ by its own sample size to obtain

Sum of Squares Due to Treatments

$$SST = \left[\frac{(\Sigma x_1)^2}{n_1} + \frac{(\Sigma x_2)^2}{n_2} + \cdots + \frac{(\Sigma x_k)^2}{n_k} \right] - \frac{(\Sigma x)^2}{N}$$

For a similar raw data formula for the error term, we multiply the *MSE* formula by $(n-1)$ top and bottom to obtain

$$MSE = \frac{(n-1)s_1^2 + (n-1)s_2^2 + \cdots + (n-1)s_k^2}{N-k}$$

since $k(n-1) = kn - k = N - k$. Since $(n-1)s_i^2 = \Sigma x_i^2 - (\Sigma x_i)^2/n$, the numerator of this fraction, the sum of squares due to error (*SSE*) is

$$SSE = \Sigma x_1^2 - (\Sigma x_1)^2/n + \Sigma x_2^2 - (\Sigma x_2)^2/n + \cdots + \Sigma x_k^2 - (\Sigma x_k)^2/n$$

$$= \Sigma x_1^2 + \Sigma x_2^2 + \cdots + \Sigma x_k^2 - \frac{(\Sigma x_1)^2 + (\Sigma x_2)^2 + \cdots + (\Sigma x_k)^2}{n}$$

Noting that $\Sigma x_1^2 + \Sigma x_2^2 + \cdots + \Sigma x_k^2 = \Sigma x^2$ and again breaking apart the fraction into individual terms if the samples are not equal in size, we have

Sum of Squares Due to Error

$$SSE = (\Sigma x^2) - \left[\frac{(\Sigma x_1)^2}{n_1} + \frac{(\Sigma x_2)^2}{n_2} + \cdots + \frac{(\Sigma x_k)^2}{n_k} \right]$$

The overall or total sum of squares for the entire set of data is equal to $N-1$ times the variance of the total, or

Total Sum of Squares	$$TSS = \Sigma x^2 - \frac{(\Sigma x)^2}{N}$$

Note that $TSS = SST + SSE$. A good check for internal consistency is to determine all three independently and make sure that $TSS = SST + SSE$.

EXAMPLE 1   Use the data of example 1, section 9.1 and determine if the differences among the groups can be attributed to chance. Use the 0.05 level of significance.

SOLUTION   The tabular form is again used to obtain the needed values. For 3 and 24 degrees of freedom, the critical value is $F_{.05}(3,24) = 3.01$.

I		II		III		IV	
x	x^2	x	x^2	x	x^2	x	x^2
13	169	9	81	6	36	16	256
11	121	13	169	9	81	10	100
6	36	15	225	13	169	14	196
18	324	11	121	10	100	17	289
7	49	10	100	9	81	9	81
15	225	6	36	7	49	11	121
14	196	7	49			14	196
		9	81				

$$\Sigma x_1 = 84 \qquad \Sigma x_2 = 80 \qquad \Sigma x_3 = 54 \qquad \Sigma x_4 = 91$$
$$\Sigma x_1^2 = 1{,}120 \qquad \Sigma x_2^2 = 862 \qquad \Sigma x_3^2 = 516 \qquad \Sigma x_4^2 = 1{,}239$$
$$n_1 = 7 \qquad n_2 = 8 \qquad n_3 = 6 \qquad n_4 = 7$$
$$\bar{x}_1 = 12 \qquad \bar{x}_2 = 10 \qquad \bar{x}_3 = 9 \qquad \bar{x}_4 = 13$$

Then

$$\Sigma x = 84 + 80 + 54 + 91 = 309$$

$$\Sigma x^2 = 1{,}120 + 862 + 516 + 1{,}239 = 3{,}737$$

$$N = 28$$

$$k = 4$$

Thus, we have

$$SST = \frac{(84)^2}{7} + \frac{(80)^2}{8} + \frac{(54)^2}{6} + \frac{(91)^2}{7} - \frac{(309)^2}{28}$$

$$= 3,477 - 3,410.04$$

$$= 66.96$$

$$SSE = 3,737 - 3,477$$

$$= 260$$

$$TSS = 3,737 - 3,410.04 = 326.96$$

$$MST = \frac{66.96}{4-1} = \frac{66.96}{3} = 22.32$$

$$MSE = \frac{260}{28-4} = \frac{260}{24} \doteq 10.83$$

$$F = \frac{22.32}{10.83} \doteq 2.06$$

Generally, these are summarized in a table such as the one that follows.

Source of Variation	df	SS	MS	F
Treatments	3	66.96	22.32	2.06
Error	24	260.00	10.83	
Total	27	326.96		

Critical value of F for $\alpha = 0.05$ is $F = 3.01$. The differences are not significant.

EXAMPLE 2   Twenty-four employees were hired and, at that time, given a test designed to predict success on the job. Higher scores theoretically indicated greater likelihood of success. After 6 months, their progress was evaluated. They were classified as successful, moderately successful, barely adequate, and inadequate. Although three of the 24 were no longer with the company, they had been employed long enough to have been classified (two as inadequate, one as moderately successful). The scores made are given below. Use analysis of variance to test if there are differences among the groups in test scores and draw conclusions. Use a 0.05 level of significance.

Group	Test scores
Successful	64, 49, 61, 57, 54, 44, 49
Moderately Successful	55, 60, 38, 44, 41, 45, 41
Barely Adequate	33, 19, 64, 38, 37, 31
Inadequate	33, 22, 48, 16

SOLUTION   We summarize the pertinent totals below.

	Group				
	S	M	B	I	Total
Σx	378.	324.	222.	119.	1,043.
Σx^2	20,720.	15,392.	9,320.	4,133.	49,565.
n	7.	7.	6.	4.	24.
$\bar{x}$	54.00	46.29	37.00	29.75	
s^2	51.33	65.90	221.20	197.58	

$F_{max} = 221.20/51.33 \doteq 4.31 \not> 10.4$ ($F_{max_{.05}}(4,6) = 10.4$) so analysis of variance is appropriate. Then

$$\frac{(378)^2}{7} + \frac{(324)^2}{7} + \frac{(222)^2}{6} + \frac{(119)^2}{4} \doteq 47,162.82$$

so we have

$$SST = 47,162.82 - (1043)^2/24 \doteq 1835.78$$

$$SSE = 49,565 - 47,162.82 = 2402.18$$

$$TSS = 49,565 - (1043)^2/24 \doteq 4237.96$$

The following table summarizes the analysis of variance.

Source of Variation	df	SS	MS	F
Treatments	3	1835.78	611.93	5.10*
Error	20	2402.18	120.11	
Total	23	4237.96		
$F_{.05}(3,20) = 3.10$				
*Significant at the 0.05 level				

We can thus conclude that there are real differences between the groups. Which groups actually scored significantly higher than which other groups, however, can only be decided by further analysis. This will be discussed in the next section.

•Problems

1. Stenographers trained in three different systems of stenography are given tests to measure their maximum dictation rate in words per minute. Assum-

ing the stenographers are sampled at random, test the hypothesis that the systems are equally effective at the 0.05 level of significance.

System	Maximum Dictation Rates
A	147, 188, 162, 144, 157, 179, 165, 180
B	143, 161, 167, 145, 173, 160, 154
C	173, 152, 194, 186, 166, 194, 178, 192, 186

2. Five companies submit samples of paint to a company which is considering the purchase of a large quantity. Six samples of each paint are tested for drying time. Drying times are given as follows. Determine whether the differences are significant at a 0.05 level.

Company	Drying Times (Minutes)
I	34, 36, 29, 38, 35, 32
II	30, 34, 30, 32, 31, 28
III	27, 32, 31, 30, 34, 30
IV	28, 35, 29, 29, 37, 33
V	34, 31, 36, 38, 40, 37

3. Four samples of thirty soldiers taken from different companies are given marksmanship tests. The mean number of points per ten shots per man are given as follows. Do the data substantiate, at a 0.01 level, the contention that the companies are equal in marksmanship?

Company	Results (mean scored)	Standard Deviation
A	$\bar{x}_A = 57.8$	$s_A = 14.3$
B	$\bar{x}_B = 62.3$	$s_B = 17.4$
C	$\bar{x}_C = 58.4$	$s_C = 16.5$
D	$\bar{x}_D = 48.9$	$s_D = 22.6$

4. A medical researcher is testing the effect of a drug in inhibiting the release of adrenalin. She wishes to use the 0.05 level of significance. She selects five samples each composed of ten male individuals and injects the members of the samples with 0 cc, 10 cc, 20 cc, 30 cc, and 40 cc, respectively. She then subjects each man to a stress situation and measures the stress level at which adrenalin is released by each individual. Given the data below, test the hypothesis that there are nonchance variations among the groups which may be caused by the effect of the drug.

cc of drug injected	Stress Level at Which Adrenalin Is Released
0	14, 21, 16, 18, 23, 15, 19, 22, 26, 17
10	13, 17, 19, 18, 21, 16, 25, 18, 22, 23
20	16, 22, 18, 23, 22, 25, 19, 17, 21, 25
30	21, 19, 24, 22, 28, 23, 22, 28, 24, 20
40	26, 22, 23, 25, 27, 29, 22, 24, 27, 26

9.4 POST HOC TESTS (OPTIONAL)

Up to this point, analysis of variance has been used to test whether or not differences exist among several samples. If such differences do exist, analysis of variance does not tell which ones are meaningful. In example 1, section 9.2, group 3 had a mean of 67, group 2 a mean of 63, and group 1 a mean of 47. From examination of the results, it would appear that both group 3 and group 2 were significantly higher than group 1, and it is probable, in this case, that group 3 was certainly better than group 1. It is possible, however, that group 3 was significantly better than *both* of the other groups, and group 2 better than group 1. It is also possible that none of the differences was significant. Unfortunately, it is possible, on occasion, to obtain a significant F by chance. One might be tempted to run t-tests between the various pairs of sample means. It is highly possible, however, that significant differences might be obtained by chance, even where there are none. The more samples there are, the greater would this likelihood be. Dealing with this problem is the subject of *post hoc* analysis.

Tests following analysis of variance are called **post hoc tests**, from the Latin words meaning "after that." A number of methods of *post hoc* analysis have been proposed, each with its rationale. Two such tests will be given here.

One very simple post hoc test is due to Scheffé. It uses the test statistic

$$F = \frac{(\bar{x}_i - \bar{x}_j)^2}{2(k-1)(MSE)/\tilde{n}}$$

Here $\bar{x}_i$ and $\bar{x}_j$ are means of any two samples, k is the number of samples, and $\tilde{n}$ is the geometric mean of the sample sizes; that is,

$$\tilde{n} = \frac{1}{(1/n_1 + 1/n_2 + \cdots + 1/n_k)/k} = \frac{1}{(\Sigma 1/n_i)/k}$$

Although this latter formula may look formidable, it is easy to evaluate with a hand-held calculator. For a simple calculator with a memory, simply enter the value of n_1, punch $1/x$, store in memory; enter n_2, punch $1/x$, add to memory;

continue until all sample sizes have been entered. Then recall memory, divide by k, punch $1/x$ again, and read $\tilde{n}$. For a calculator with algebraic logic, the procedure is even easier. Enter n_1, punch $1/x$, $+$, then enter n_2, punch $1/x$, $+$, enter n_3, punch $1/x$, $+$, and so forth, until you have entered n_k, and punched $1/x$. Then press $=$, $\div k$, $=$, $1/x$, and the result is $\tilde{n}$. *If all samples are equal in size, all of size n, then* $\tilde{n} = n$.

This procedure can be used for each pair of means, and often is done this way. The results are usually displayed in a table, and the value of F obtained is compared with the critical value used in the analysis of variance. For the data of example 1, section 9.2, we had $k = 3$, $MSE = 244$, $n = 10$, $F_{.05} = 3.35$. The test statistic, then, is

$$F = \frac{(\bar{x}_i - \bar{x}_j)^2}{2(2)(244)/10}$$

$$= \frac{(\bar{x}_i - \bar{x}_i)^2}{97.6}$$

Since $\bar{x}_1 = 47$, $\bar{x}_2 = 63$, $\bar{x}_3 = 67$, we have three comparisons: for group 1 vs. group 2, $F = (47 - 63)^2/97.6 \doteq 2.62$, for group 1 vs. group 3, $F = (47 - 67)^2/97.6 \doteq 4.10$, and group 2 vs. group 3 has $F = (63 - 67)^2/97.6 \doteq 0.16$. Of these, only the second is significant, indicating that group 3 did significantly better than group 1, and that no other inference can be drawn. This information is usually summarized in a table as the following:

Comparison	F
1 vs. 2	2.62
1 vs. 3	4.10*
2 vs. 3	0.16

*significant at the 0.05 level

Although this method is fine for small k, for more than three samples it can become cumbersome to calculate a separate value of F for each pair of samples. For five samples, for instance, ten separate computations are required. A simpler, more direct way is to calculate the difference which would yield the critical value for F. That is,

$$(\bar{x}_i - \bar{x}_j)^2 = 2(k-1)(MSE)F/\tilde{n}$$

Now if F^* represents the critical value of F, then substitution of F^* for F in the right side of the above equation will give a value such that, if $(\bar{x}_i - \bar{x}_j)^2$ exceeds this value, the difference between the sample means is significant. This value is called the **critical value for differences between samples** and symbolized by CV_d.

We then have

$$CV_d = \sqrt{2(k-1)(MSE)F^*/\bar{n}}$$

In the preceding example, $CV_d = \sqrt{2(2)(244)(3.35)/10} \doteq 18.08$. The differences between the groups were 16, 20, and 4. Only the difference of 20 was significant. One way in which this particular approach is utilized is to construct a table of differences as follows. Arrange the sample means from highest to lowest, here 67, 63, 47 were the means of groups 3, 2, 1, respectively. The table is constructed by putting these groups and the means on the top and the left of a table.

	3	2	1
	67	63	47
3–67			
2–63			
1–47			

The differences are then entered in the boxes corresponding to the two groups. Only once, of course, since the difference between group 1 and group 3 is the same as that between group 3 and group 1. Often the means are omitted and only the group or sample designations are given. Here the table of differences would be as follows:

Table of Differences

	Group		
	3	2	1
2	—		
2	4	—	
1	20*	16	

Significant differences, if any, are starred.

EXAMPLE 1   Use Scheffé's method to test the differences between the sample means of example 2, section 9.3.

SOLUTION   The MSE was 120.11, $k=4$, $F^*=3.10$, so

$$CV_d = \sqrt{2(3)(120.11)(3.10)/5.69}$$

$$\doteq 19.81$$

where $\bar{n} = 1/[(1/7 + 1/7 + 1/6 + 1/4)/4] \doteq 5.69$. The means are: successful (S), 54.00, moderately successful (M), 46.29, barely adequate (B), 37.00, Inadequate

(*I*), 29.75. The differences are as follows:

	S	M	B	I
S	—			
M	7.71	—		
B	17.00	9.29	—	
I	24.25*	16.54	7.25	—

Only the successful group made test scores significantly higher than any other group, in this case, the inadequate group.

One of the virtues of Scheffé's test is its simplicity. One critical value is all that needs to be computed, and this can then be compared to the differences between sample means and significant differences easily found. One of the failings of Scheffé's test is that it is quite conservative. This is perhaps a consequence of its simplicity. There are a large number of other *post hoc* tests, each usually bearing the name of its originator, such as Tukey, Duncan, and Newman–Keuls. Of these, the Tukey is most conservative (though not as conservative as the Scheffé), while the Duncan is least conservative. The Duncan and Newman–Keuls tests use the same statistic, q_r, and differ only in the critical values. The Newman–Keuls critical values will be used here, but the Duncan values are available in various places, such as *Biometrics*, **13**, 164–176. A test developed by Dunnett tests only a control variable against each of the others. See Winer, *op cit.*, 201–204.

The **Newman–Keuls statistic, q,** is determined by the following formula:

$$q = \frac{|\bar{x}_i - \bar{x}_j|}{\sqrt{MSE/\tilde{n}}}$$

Critical values for q, however, depend on how far apart the sample means are. Those closest together will require a smaller value of q to be significant than those further apart. Again, as in the Scheffé test, it is usually simpler to determine critical values for differences and compare them to the table of differences. The critical values are determined by the formula

$$CV_r = q_r \sqrt{MSE/\tilde{n}}$$

The r here refers to the number of steps between the sample or group means and can be obtained as follows. Arrange the means from highest to lowest as in determining a table of values. For this purpose we use the data from example 1. Here $CV_r = q_r \sqrt{(120.11)/5.69} \doteq 4.59 q_r$. Arranging the groups from high mean to low mean, we have

	S	M	B	I
S	1			
M	2	1		
B	3	2	1	
I	4	3	2	1

The numbers in the body of the table refer to the number of *steps* between the means. It might seem logical to have these numbers be one less than they are, but this is the way that is accepted, and this is the way that will be used here. The r, incidentally, stands for *range*. *Post-hoc* tests such as these are called multiple-range tests since they test differences among several sample means.

We then refer to Table 10, Critical Values of q_r, to obtain these values. The degrees of freedom used are those for the *MSE* term; in this case (see example 2, section 9.3) $df = 20$. Referring to Table 10, we have the following:

r	q_r	CV_r
4	3.96	18.18
3	3.58	16.43
2	2.95	13.54

Preparing a table of differences, we compare the differences corresponding to a particular value of r with CV_r for that r. In order to avoid anomalies, the comparisons must be made in a certain way. First examine the difference with the largest r; if the difference is not significant, no further comparisons may be made. If it is significant, examine the differences with the next smaller r; if neither is significant, no further comparisons may be made. If either one is significant, differences above and to the right of significant differences may be examined, but others may not. As an example, suppose a table has the following differences:

	I	II	III	IV	V
I	—				
II	a	—			
III	b	e*	—		
IV	c*	f*	h	—	
V	d*	g	i	j	—

Significant differences are marked with an asterisk. We first examined difference d; since it was significant, differences c and g were examined. Since c was significant, b and f were examined. As b was not significant, a was not tested, but since f was significant, e and h were examined. We could not examine i and j since g was not significant.

The reason for this is to avoid anomalies. Suppose that i were just more than the critical value, while g was just less than the critical value. This is possible since the critical value for i is less than that for g. Concluding that difference g was not significant is equivalent to saying that the difference between II and V (as populations) is zero, while if i were significant, the difference between III and V would be more than zero, yet III is between II and V. To avoid such a contradiction, the above procedure must be followed.

Continuing with the data of example 1, we refer to the table of differences which is reproduced below.

	S	M	B	I
S	—			
M	7.71	—		
B	17.00*	9.29	—	
I	24.25*	16.54*	7.25	—

Significant differences are marked with an asterisk. We have $24.25 > 18.18$, 17.00 and 16.54 are both greater than 16.43; no other differences are significant, since all three of the others are less than 13.54.

EXAMPLE 2   Use the Newman–Keuls multiple range test to evaluate differences between means for the data of example 1, section 9.2.

SOLUTION   Means were 67, 63, 47 for groups 3, 2, 1 respectively. Arranging in a table, we obtain the values of r.

	3	2	1
3	1		
2	2	1	
1	3	2	1

The values for computing CV_r are $n = 10$, $MSE = 244$, so $CV_r = q_r \sqrt{244/10} \doteq 4.94 q_r$. We have df for $MSE = 27$, so the following table can be constructed:

r	q_r	CV_r
3	3.51	17.34
2	2.91	14.38

The table of differences is as follows:

	3	2	1
3	—		
2	4	—	
1	20*	16*	—

*Significant at the 0.05 level.

EXAMPLE 3   A researcher wishes to test the mileage of five leading brands of gasoline. She obtains 40 different automobiles of the same make and year and divides them randomly into five groups. Each of the groups uses one and only one brand of gasoline and keeps careful records for one month while driving at random over different types of terrain and conditions, but roughly comparable. Using the results below, perform a complete analysis of variance, including *post hoc* tests, as indicated, to determine whether there are differences among the various brands of gasoline and, if so, precisely where these differences exist. Use the 0.05 level of significance. One automobile was wrecked, and the records were unavailable.

| | | **Miles Per Gallon** | | |
| | | *Brand* | | |
E	G	P	S	T
17.6	13.4	15.8	15.1	19.3
16.9	14.6	15.8	16.2	14.8
17.1	15.6	12.9	13.7	17.3
12.9	17.5	14.2	16.8	18.1
15.9	14.8	13.7	17.3	17.7
16.6	15.8	14.1	14.8	17.3
17.4	15.4	13.8	16.1	14.8
14.9	13.2	13.0		16.5

SOLUTION   Although there are many variables which may be uncontrolled, such as drivers, miles driven, etc., we assume that these have been satisfactorily handled and examine only the numbers presented. We summarize the data as follows:

	E	G	P	S	T	Total
Σx	129.3	120.3	113.3	110.0	135.8	608.7
Σx^2	2107.33	1822.41	1613.27	1737.92	2322.30	9603.33
n	8	8	8	7	8	39
$\bar{x}$	16.16	15.04	14.16	15.71	16.98	
s^2	2.50	1.91	1.24	1.56	2.44	

$F_{max} = 2.50/1.24 \doteq 2.02 \ngtr 8.12$ ($F_{max_{.05}}(5,8)=8.12$), and the normality assumption appears reasonable, so analysis of variance appears to be appropriate.
    Since

$$\frac{(129.3)^2}{8} + \frac{(120.3)^2}{8} + \frac{(113.3)^2}{8} + \frac{(110.0)^2}{7} + \frac{(135.8)^2}{8} \doteq 9537.21,$$

$$SST = 9537.21 - (608.7)^2/39 \doteq 36.81$$

$$SSE = 9603.23 - 9537.21 = 66.02$$

$$TSS = 9603.23 - (608.7)^2/39 \doteq 102.83$$

The results of the analysis can be summed up as follows.

Source of Variation	df	SS	MS	F
Treatments	4	36.81	9.20	4.74*
Error	34	66.02	1.95	
Total	38	102.83		

$F_{.05}(4,34) = 2.63$
*Significant at the 0.05 level

Thus *post hoc* tests are appropriate. To use the Scheffé test, note that $CV_d = \sqrt{2(5-1)(1.95)(2.63)/7.78} \doteq 2.30$. Only T vs. P gives a difference as great (see table of differences, below). To use the more powerful Newman–Keuls test, arrange the means from highest to lowest, then calculate CV_r in each case, as follows:

	T	E	S	G	P
T	1				
E	2	1			
S	3	2	1		
G	4	3	2	1	
P	5	4	3	2	1

We then have $CV_r = q_r \sqrt{(1.95)/7.78} \doteq 0.50q_r$.

r	q_r	CV_r
5	4.08	2.04
4	3.82	1.91
3	3.47	1.74
2	2.88	1.44

The table of differences, with significant differences asterisked, is given below.

	T	E	S	G	P
T	—				
E	0.82	—			
S	1.27	0.45	—		
G	1.94*	1.12	0.67	—	
P	2.82*	2.00*	1.55	0.88	—

Thus group T was significantly better than groups G and P, and group E was significantly better than group P. No other conclusions may be reached.

•Problems

In problems 1–4 perform analysis of variance, if appropriate, and *post hoc* tests if necessary.

1. An attitude test is given to 40 participants, 10 in each of 4 educational groups, to determine intensity of commitment toward a hot social issue. Unfortunately, 1 participant failed to complete the test and 1 made a mistake about educational status, so that results are only available for 39 subjects, as given here.

Attitude Score			
Educational Attainment (Grades)			
Less than 8	8–11	12–15	16 or More
12	12	14	9
9	11	8	13
13	13	11	9
11	7	15	16
8	16	12	17
7	10	11	15
14	9	13	8
9	12	16	15
11	10	14	17
8		15	
6			

Test, at the 0.05 level, the hypothesis that differences among the groups are attributable to chance.

2. A comparison of recovery rates of patients suffering from a disease and given three different treatments is given below.

	Treatment		
	A	B	C
Days to	3	7	4
Recovery	8	6	3
	6	9	5
	9	5	2
	7	5	6
	4	6	3
	9	5	2

Use the 0.05 level to test the hypothesis that there is a difference in recovery rates which may be attributable to a difference in the treatments.

3. A researcher wishes to test the mileage of three different types of gasoline. She uses each gasoline in each of six different cars, varying the orders so that all possible orders are used. Although the results are matched, they can also be tested as independent samples, although this method is less sensitive. Use the data here to determine if there is any difference in the mileages obtained for the gasolines. Each car was driven each time over the same course. Use $\alpha = 0.05$.

Gasoline		
A	B	C
17.6	10.8	11.9
13.4	9.7	12.6
19.2	11.3	16.7
15.7	10.6	10.2
13.8	10.1	9.8
18.8	12.2	13.4

4. A researcher wishes to compare the effectiveness of three different types of mathematics instruction. Thirty tenth grade students of equal ability and background are selected and divided randomly into three groups, ten in each group. Each group is taught by the same teacher, but by a different teaching method. After one semester of instruction, a final examination was administered with the following results.

Group A	Group B	Group C
71	73	91
74	59	82
83	84	88
64	91	68
95	75	76
74	68	98
88	75	85
96	83	81
57	94	79
66	87	87

Does this evidence support a contention that the three methods do not yield equal results? Use a 0.05 level of significance.

•Additional problems

Perform *post hoc* analysis on those problems in sections 9.2 and 9.3 for which a significant F was obtained.

9.5   THE RANDOMIZED COMPLETE BLOCK

In problem 3 of the preceding section, a researcher used three different types of gasoline in each of six different cars. In such a case it would be reasonable to expect some differences due to differences in cars as well as differences in gasolines. The variable to be tested, namely differences among the various gasolines was affected by a variable which was not controlled, the differences between cars. A method of measuring such effects is called the **randomized complete block**. A variable which cannot be controlled, but has some influence on the results is called a **block**. To control the effect of this variable and to enable us to analyze this effect, each treatment is assigned in random order to a block. The terminology arose from agricultural usage in which the effects of various methods, such as fertilizer, had to be tested on different plots of ground in which soil conditions might vary from plot to plot so that it was difficult to tell what differences were due to differences in fertilizer and differences in soil condition. If each of the fertilizers to be tested were used on each plot of ground, each plot, or block received each treatment so that each block was *complete*. To be able to analyze the results, it was necessary that the treatments be assigned to the blocks at random, hence the term *randomized complete block*. The method may be considered an extension of matched pairs. Two examples will be given here.

Suppose that we have four different brands of gasoline, all of the same grade, and we use each one in each of five cars, in random order, and obtain the mileage for each gasoline in each car.

Car	Gasoline				
	A	*B*	*C*	*D*	
1	11.8	12.4	10.6	13.1	
2	14.6	14.9	15.6	16.4	
3	21.3	24.2	20.6	23.7	
4	14.1	15.3	12.4	16.8	
5	13.1	17.3	16.1	18.6	
Σx	74.9	84.1	75.3	88.6	322.9
Σx^2	1176.51	1494.79	1193.05	1630.46	5,494.81
$\bar{x}$	15.0	16.8	15.1	17.7	
s^2	13.6	20.1	14.8	15.1	

Means and variances are given to one decimal place. Proceeding as in one-way analysis of variance, we have $F_{max} \doteq 1.48$, which is satisfactory; then

$$\frac{(74.9)^2}{5} + \frac{(84.1)^2}{5} + \frac{(75.3)^2}{5} + \frac{(88.6)^2}{5} = 5,240.574$$

so we have

$$SST = 5,240.574 - (322.9)^2/20 \doteq 27.35$$

$$SSE = 5,494.81 - 5,240.574 \doteq 254.24$$

$$TSS = 5,494.81 - (322.9)^2/20 \doteq 281.59$$

For a one-way analysis of variance on the effect of the gasolines, four samples with five cars each, the following table summarizes the results.

Source of Variation	df	SS	MS	F
Treatments	3	27.35	9.12	0.57
Error	16	254.24	15.89	
Total	19	281.59		
$F_{.05}(3, 16) = 3.24.$				

Thus there is no significant difference.

It is obvious from examining the data, however, that there are differences due to cars. Car 3 is clearly getting better mileage than all the others, while car 1 gets poorer mileage than all the others. The total sum of squares is 281.59, of which 27.35 is attributable to differences in treatments. The remainder, 254.24 is attributable to differences in cars and to experimental error. In the usual one-way analysis of variance situation, the amount attributable to differences in cars cannot be assessed; in the randomized complete block, however, it can be determined in exactly the same way as the treatments, by looking at each block as a sample. We reproduce the table below. The symbolism is as follows: T_i = the sum of the x's for treatment i, B_j = the sum of the x's for block j, Σx_i^2 is the sum of the x^2's for treatment i, Σx_j^2 is the sum of the x^2's for block j.

			Miles Per Gallon			
			Gasoline			
Car	A	B	C	D	B_j	Σx_j^2
1	11.8	12.4	10.6	13.1	47.9	576.97
2	14.6	14.9	15.6	16.4	61.5	947.49
3	21.3	24.2	20.6	23.7	89.8	2025.38
4	14.1	15.3	12.4	16.8	58.6	868.90
5	13.1	17.3	16.1	18.6	65.1	1076.07
T_i	74.9	84.1	75.3	88.6	322.9	
Σx_i^2	1176.51	1494.79	1193.05	1630.46		5,494.81

Now

$$\frac{(47.9)^2}{4} + \frac{(61.5)^2}{4} + \frac{(89.8)^2}{4} + \frac{(58.6)^2}{4} + \frac{(65.1)^2}{4} \doteq 5,453.17$$

so the sum of squares attributable to the blocks is given by

$$SSB = 5{,}453.17 - (322.9)^2/20 \doteq 239.95$$

and the sum of squares attributable to experimental error is

$$SSE \doteq 281.59 - 239.95 = 14.29$$

The degrees of freedom for the blocks (five blocks) is 4, so the degrees of freedom for error is reduced to 12. Then MSE is $14.29/12 \doteq 1.19$ and F for treatments is $9.12/1.19 \doteq 7.66$ which is considerably higher than before. Further, the critical value of F is now $F_{.05}(3, 12)$, or 3.49, which is a little higher, but the obtained F is significant. In addition, $F_{.01}(3, 12) = 5.95$, so the F for treatments is significant at the 0.01 level. An F for blocks can also be computed; for 4 and 12 degrees of freedom, $F_{.05} = 3.26$ and $F_{.01} = 5.41$. The data can be summarized as shown below.

Source of Variation	df	SS	MS	F
Treatments	3	27.35	9.12	7.66*
Blocks	4	239.95	59.99	50.41*
Error	12	14.29	1.19	
Total	16	281.59		

*Significant for $\alpha = 0.01$

Post hoc analysis is appropriate. To use the Newman–Keuls method, we would have $n = 5$ (number in each sample), $MSE = 1.19$, so $CV_r = q_r \sqrt{1.19/5} \doteq 0.488 q_r$. Means are 15.0, 16.8, 15.1, 17.7 for A, B, C, D, respectively, so the following table lists r.

	D	B	C	A
D	1			
B	2	1		
C	3	2	1	
A	4	3	2	1

Since F was significant at the 0.01 level, we can use both 0.05 and 0.01 critical values for q_r for comparisons, df (for MSE) = 12.

	$\alpha = 0.05$			$\alpha = 0.01$	
.r	q_r	CV_r	r	q_r	CV_r
4	4.20	2.05	4	5.50	2.68
3	3.77	1.84	3	5.04	2.46
2	3.08	1.50	2	4.32	2.11

We then set up the table of differences.

	D	B	C	A
D	–			
B	0.9	–		
C	2.6**	1.7*	–	
A	2.7**	1.8	0.1	–

**Significant at the 0.01 level.
*Significant at the 0.05 level.

Thus we conclude that gasoline D gives significantly greater mileage (at the 0.01 level) than gasoline C and gasoline A, and that gasoline B gives significantly greater mileage (at the 0.05 level) than gasoline C. The difference between B and A is nearly, but not quite, significant. A less conservative test, such as Duncan's, would probably conclude that there is significance there as well.

The entire procedure for a randomized complete block analysis of variance is summarized below. Each x_{ij} is the entry for treatment i, block j; T_i is the sum of the x's for treatment i; B_j is the sum of the x's for block j.

	Treatments					
Blocks	t_1	t_2	t_3	$\cdots$	t_k	B_j
b_1	x_{11}	x_{21}	x_{31}	$\cdots$	x_{k1}	B_1
b_2	x_{12}	x_{22}	x_{32}	$\cdots$	x_{k2}	B_2
b_3	x_{13}	x_{23}	x_{33}	$\cdots$	x_{k3}	B_3
$\vdots$	$\vdots$	$\vdots$	$\vdots$		$\vdots$	$\vdots$
b_n	x_{1n}	x_{2n}	x_{3n}	$\cdots$	x_{kn}	B_n
T_i	T_1	T_2	T_3	$\cdots$	T_k	Total

The computational formulas involve the following:

(1) $(\Sigma x)^2 / nk$

(2) $\dfrac{T_1^2 + T_2^2 + T_3^2 + \cdots + T_k^2}{n} = (\Sigma T^2)/n$

(3) $\dfrac{B_1^2 + B_2^2 + B_3^2 + \cdots + B_n^2}{k} = (\Sigma B^2)/k$

(4) Σx^2

Then

$$SST = (2) - (1)$$

$$SSB = (3) - (1)$$

$$SSE = (4) + (1) - (2) - (3)$$

$$TSS = (4) - (1)$$

The summary of the analysis of variance is as follows:

Source of Variation	df	SS	MS	F
Treatments	$k-1$	SST	$SST/(k-1)$	MST/MSE
Blocks	$n-1$	SSB	$SSB/(n-1)$	MSB/MSE
Error	$(k-1)\cdot(n-1)$	SSE	$SSE/(k-1)(n-1)$	
Total	$kn-1$	TSS		

Critical values of F are $F_\alpha(k-1,(k-1)\cdot(n-1))$ for treatments and $F_\alpha(n-1, (k-1)\cdot(n-1))$ for blocks.

EXAMPLE 1   An office manager wishes to assess the extent to which experience reduces errors in the handling of paper work. Four clerks are selected at random in each of three departments and classified for longevity —I, 0–3 mos., II, 3–12 mos., III, 1–3 yrs., IV, over 3 years. Each clerk within a department has about the same number and complexity of forms to process, but the number and complexity differ from department to department. The clerks are monitored for six weeks and the total number of errors recorded. This information is given below. Use analysis of variance and a 0.05 level of significance to determine if and where differences exist.

Department	Total Number of Errors			
	Experience category			
	I	II	III	IV
A	21	12	8	7
B	38	24	11	12
C	16	12	7	4

SOLUTION   In this problem there are no real treatments, since nothing is being manipulated, but the variable of interest is experience, so that can be considered to be treatments. Differences between departments would be expected, and, since each experience category occurs in each department, we can consider the departments to be blocks. Peripheral totals are determined and the analysis performed as follows.

	I	II	III	IV	
A	21	12	8	7	48
B	38	24	11	12	85
C	16	12	7	4	39
	75	48	26	23	172

(1) $(\Sigma x)^2/nk = (172)^2/12 \doteq 2{,}465.333$

(2) $(\Sigma T^2)/n = (75^2 + 48^2 + 26^2 + 23^2)/3 \doteq 3{,}044.667$

(3) $(\Sigma B^2)/k = (48^2 + 85^2 + 39^2)/4 = 2{,}762.5$

(4) $\Sigma x^2 = 21^2 + 12^2 + 8^2 + \cdots + 4^2 = 3{,}448$

Then

$$SST \doteq 3{,}044.667 - 2{,}465.333 \doteq 579.333$$

$$SSB \doteq 2{,}762.5 - 2{,}465.333 = 297.167$$

$$SSE \doteq 3{,}448 + 2{,}465.333 - 3{,}044.667 - 2{,}762.5 \doteq 106.167$$

$$TSS \doteq 3{,}448 - 2{,}465.333 \doteq 982.667$$

The analysis is summarized as follows:

Source of Variation	df	SS	MS	F
Experience	3	579.333	193.111	10.91**
Departments	2	297.167	148.583	8.40*
Error	6	106.167	17.694	
Total	11	982.667		

$F_{.05}(3,6) = 4.76;$ $F_{.01}(3,6) = 9.78;$
$F_{.05}(2,6) = 5.14;$ $F_{.01}(2,6) = 10.9.$

**Significant at the 0.01 level.
*Significant at the 0.05 level.

The above results show differences both among experience categories and among departments. *Post hoc* tests are in order. To check the differences between experience groups using the Newman–Keuls multiple range test, the critical value $CV_r = q_r \sqrt{(17.694)/3} \doteq 2.4286 q_r$. The means for the four samples are I:25.0, II:16.0, III:8.67, IV:7.67. Values of r can be obtained from the following table:

	I	II	III	IV
I	1			
II	2	1		
III	3	2	1	
IV	4	3	2	1

Since the difference was significant at the 0.01 level, we can use both 0.01 and 0.05 levels for q_r; $df = 6$.

$\alpha = 0.01$			$\alpha = 0.05$		
r	q_r	CV_r	r	q_r	CV_r
4	7.03	17.07	4	4.90	11.90
3	6.33	15.37	3	4.34	10.54
2	5.24	12.73	2	3.46	8.40

These values are then checked against a table of differences.

	I	II	III	IV
I	–			
II	9.00*	–		
III	16.33**	7.33	–	
IV	17.33**	8.33	1.00	–

**Significant at the 0.01 level.
*Significant at the 0.05 level.

We thus found that there is a significant difference in errors between clerks employed less than 3 months and those employed over 3 months. Differences between other pairs of groups were not found to be significant.

In the randomized complete block design, it is usual to have one entry in each treatment for each block. It is possible to have more than one entry, but in such a case there is a chance that a two-factor design will yield more information. Two-factor designs are presented in the next section.

•Problems

1. A controversy developed among several instructors as to whether the hour of the class had an effect on the performance of students. Each instructor who had class at 8:00, 10:00, 1:00, and 2:00 (there were three of them) gave a quiz to these classes and selected one paper at random for comparison. The results are given below. Test whether or not there is a difference among the classes which may be attributable to the hour taken. Use the 0.05 level of significance.

	Quiz Score			
	Hour of class			
Instructor	8:00	10:00	1:00	3:00
Jones	17	20	13	16
Smith	14	15	15	17
White	16	18	11	14

2. Several different advertising displays were developed to market a product. In order to see if it could be determined which was most effective, each of five different displays was used in four different stores, the order determined randomly, and the number of unit sales in one month of thirty days recorded. Using the data given below, determine whether any of the displays seemed to yield more sales. Use the 0.05 level of significance.

| Sales in One Month | | | | | |
Store	A	B	C	D	E
I	325	417	229	356	319
II	154	231	181	203	167
III	567	819	488	592	578
IV	144	207	113	216	149

Display

3. In problem 2, section 9.3, five companies submitted samples of paint for purchase consideration. Six samples of each paint are tested for drying time. Suppose that each paint is tested on each of six different surfaces, such as masonry, smooth dry wall, plaster, etc. Determine whether there are differences among the different paints insofar as drying time is concerned.

| Drying Time (Minutes) | | | | | | |
Company	A	B	C	D	E	F
I	34	36	29	38	35	32
II	30	32	28	34	31	30
III	30	32	27	34	31	30
IV	29	33	29	37	35	28
V	36	37	31	38	40	34

Surface

4. Four different candidates for a position were interviewed by seven top executives and rated for each of several traits on a scale of 1 to 5, and the ratings added to get a rating for each individual by each executive. The candidates were interviewed in random order. Using the information given below, test whether or not there are differences among the candidates according to the ratings. Use the 0.05 level of significance.

| Total Rating | | | | |
Raters	Lee	Jacobs	Wilkes	DeLap
Moore	42	25	29	33
Gaston	28	31	24	29
Heinrich	44	38	40	39
Seldon	33	30	31	28
TerHand	48	44	46	47
Waters	26	28	22	25
Pierce	42	41	37	45

Candidates

9.6   TWO WAY ANALYSIS OF VARIANCE (OPTIONAL)

In the preceding section two variables were considered; that is, the data was classified in two ways. If one of the ways of classifying the data is considered a block, so that we have an extension of matched pairs, we usually are interested only in one of the variables. If both variables are either being manipulated or are of interest, this is considered to be a two-way analysis or two-factor analysis. If each factor has only one observation for each level, the methods of the preceding section apply. If there are more than one observation in each level of a factor, somewhat more sensitive methods are useful. In this section we will examine a two-factor analysis with n observations per cell. Procedures to use when there are an unequal number in each cell can be found in various sources, such as Winer, *op cit.*, 445–449. In addition, we assume that each observation is made on a *different* subject. Specific cases for repetitions on the same subject require different approaches. Winer also has various methods of analyzing experiments in which the same subjects are subjected to repeated observations.

One of the advantages to having more than one observation per cell is that we may observe the interaction, if any, between the factors. It may be, for example, that factor A affects different levels of factor B differently. The sums of squares for the two factors are computed as SST and SSB in the preceding section, but the remainder of TSS includes that due to interaction as well as experimental error. An example will show the procedure.

Suppose we have three brands of gasoline, P, S, and T, and we use each brand in each of four makes and models of cars. The cars of each make and model are matched as to body type, engine, equipment, etc., so as to be comparable. There are six of each type of car (24 all together) so that we have two observations in each cell; a cell is one type of gasoline with one type of car, a total of 12 cells, two observations per cell. Suppose we have the following data.

	Mileage			
		Automobile		
Gasoline	J	G	H	E
P	11.8	19.5	15.4	23.8
	13.4	17.8	15.9	25.9
S	10.9	18.6	14.2	28.1
	10.2	18.1	17.3	29.7
T	15.6	18.3	13.3	22.5
	17.1	18.9	12.9	25.6

It is customary to denote one of the factors as treatment A, the other as treatment B. Here we will consider automobiles to be A and gasoline B. We prepare a summary table, listing the totals in each cell and for each level of each treatment as follows.

		AB Summary Table			
	J	G	H	E	A_i
P	25.2	37.3	31.3	49.7	143.5
S	21.1	36.7	31.5	57.8	147.1
T	32.7	37.2	26.2	48.1	144.2
B_j	79.0	111.2	89.0	155.6	434.8

The sums of squares for the treatments are obtained as usual, except that the divisors reflect the total number in each level. Since each A_i is the sum of eight numbers, divide by 8; since each B_j is the sum of six numbers, divide by 6. Then

$$(\Sigma A^2)/8 = (143.5^2 + 147.1^2 + 144.2^2)/8$$

$$= 7,878.0375$$

$$(\Sigma B^2)/6 = (79.0^2 + 111.2^2 + 89.0^2 + 155.6^2)/6$$

$$\doteq 8,456.46667$$

$$(\Sigma x)^2/24 = (434.8)^2/24$$

$$\doteq 7,877.12667$$

$$\Sigma x^2 = 11.8^2 + 13.4^2 + 19.5^2 + \cdots + 22.5^2 + 25.6^2$$

$$= 8,544.94$$

so that

$$SSA = 7,878.0375 - 7,877.12667 = 0.9108$$

$$SSB = 8,456.46667 - 7,877.12667 = 579.34$$

$$TSS = 8,544.94 - 7,877.12667 = 667.8133$$

Since there are more than one observation per cell, the remainder of the sum of squares is not all necessarily attributable to experimental error. The within-cell variation can be found by taking the sum of the squares of each cell total and dividing by the number in each cell. The cell totals are usually denoted by $A_i B_j$, being the total in the ith level of treatment A and the jth level of treatment B. The sum of their squares is (ΣAB^2); here we have

$$(\Sigma AB^2)/2 = (25.2^2 + 37.3^2 + 31.3^2 + \cdots + 26.2^2 + 48.1^2)/2$$

$$\doteq 8,527.24$$

We then have a new term, the sum of squares within cells, SSW, defined by

$SSW = \Sigma x^2 - (\Sigma AB^2)/n$; here $SSW = 8{,}544.94 - 8{,}527.24 = 17.7$. The remainder of the sum of squares is due to interaction between the two factors and is symbolized $SSAB$; here $SSAB = 667.8133 - 0.9108 - 579.34 - 17.7 = 69.8625$. Mean squares are computed by dividing sums of squares by the appropriate degrees of freedom. For treatment A, there are three kinds of gasoline, so $df = 2$; for treatment B, there are four kinds of cars, so $df = 3$. Interaction degrees of freedom are the product of the degrees of freedom for the treatments, here $df = 2 \cdot 3 = 6$. Degrees of freedom within the cells are given by the total number of degrees of freedom within the cells; here there are two observations per cell, so one degree of freedom per cell. There are 12 cells, so $12 \cdot 1$ or 12 degrees of freedom within cells. The total number of degrees of freedom is $N - 1$, where N is the total number of observations. Here $N = 24$, so there are 23 degrees of freedom. F values are found initially by dividing each mean square by MSW. If the F for interaction is significant, SSW and MSW become SSE and MSE; the source of variation due to experimental error is variation within the cells. *Post hoc* analysis is fairly tricky, but a number of procedures can be used. An analytic procedure is found in Winer, *op cit.*, 436–443. Graphical analysis is also useful. If the F for interaction is not significant, then interaction effects are part of the experimental error, and $SSAB + SSW = SSE$, degrees of freedom are combined and used to determine MSE, and F values for the treatments refigured using the new MSE. *Post hoc* analysis, if appropriate can be accomplished using the Newman–Keuls procedure.

The analysis for the present example is summarized below.

Source of Variation	df	SS	MS	F
Gasoline	2	0.9108	0.4554	0.309
Automobiles	3	579.34	193.1133	130.924**
Interaction	6	69.8625	11.644	7.894**
Within (Error)	12	17.7	1.475	
Total	23	667.8133		

$F_{.01}(2, 12) = 6.93$, $\qquad F_{.01}(3, 12) = 5.95$

**Significant at the 0.01 level

Since F for interaction is significant, the within-cells variation is the experimental error. This also indicates that different gasolines perform differently in different automobiles. A look at the data will confirm this. Gasoline T performed best in automobile J of the three gasolines, while S was clearly best in automobile E. P and S were best in automobile G, while S and T were best in automobile H. The nonsignificance of the F for gasoline shows that no one gasoline was best for all cars. The significant F for cars shows that there were indeed differences in mileage among the various types of cars. The significant F for interaction shows that different gasolines perform best for different cars.

Graphical analysis of interaction effects can be carried out by focussing on either treatment and plotting the results of the other treatments, connecting those for the same treatment. The hypothesis of no significance for interaction effects is equivalent to the hypothesis that these lines will be piecewise parallel. Graphs of the interaction effects for the gasoline–car experiment are given below. Means for each cell are plotted and connected as shown.

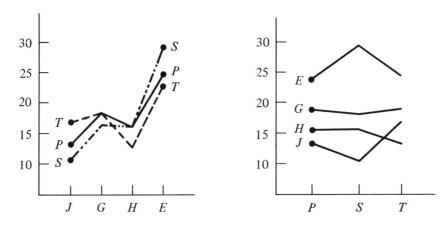

The interactions show most clearly on the chart to the right above. This is probably natural inasmuch as the difference due to cars was significant, so we would expect the lines to be more widely separated when they represent gasolines than when they represent cars, as at the left.

The procedures for a two-way analysis of variance are summarized below. The $A_i B_j$ are the sum totals for n entries in treatment A, level i, treatment B, level j. A_i is the sum of the x's for treatment A, level i; B_j is the sum of the x's for treatment B, level j. The individual x's are not shown. There are considered to be p levels of treatment A, q levels of treatment B, n observations in a cell. N is the total number of observations; $N = pqn$.

AB Summary Table

Treatment B	a_1	a_2	a_3	$\cdots$	a_p	B_j
			Treatment A			
b_1	A_1B_1	A_2B_1	A_3B_1	$\cdots$	A_pB_1	B_1
b_2	A_1B_2	A_2B_2	A_3B_2	$\cdots$	A_pB_2	B_2
b_3	A_1B_3	A_2B_3	A_3B_3	$\cdots$	A_pB_3	B_3
$\vdots$	$\vdots$	$\vdots$	$\vdots$		$\vdots$	$\vdots$
b_q	A_1B_q	A_2B_q	A_3B_q	$\cdots$	A_pB_q	B_q
A_i	A_1	A_2	A_3	$\cdots$	A_p	Total

The computational formulas involve the following:

(1) $(\Sigma x)^2 / N$

(2) $\dfrac{A_1^2 + A_2^2 + A_3^2 + \cdots + A_p^2}{qn} = (\Sigma A^2)/qn$

(3) $\dfrac{B_1^2 + B_2^2 + B_3^2 + \cdots + B_q^2}{pn} = (\Sigma B^2)/pn$

(4) $\dfrac{(A_1 B_1)^2 + (A_1 B_2)^2 + \cdots + (A_p B_q)^2}{n} = (\Sigma AB^2)/n$

(5) Σx^2

Then

$$SSA = (2) - (1)$$

$$SSB = (3) - (1)$$

$$SSAB = (4) + (1) - (2) - (3)$$

$$SSW = (5) - (4)$$

$$TSS = (5) - (1)$$

The summary of the initial analysis of variance is as follows:

Source of Variation	df	SS	MS	F
Treatment A	$p-1$	SSA	$SSA/(p-1)$	MSA/MSW
Treatment B	$q-1$	SSB	$SSB/(q-1)$	MSB/MSW
Interaction	$(p-1)(q-1)$	SSAB	$SSAB/(p-1)(q-1)$	$MSAB/MSW$
Within Cells	$N-pq$	SSW	$SSW/(N-pq)$	
Total	$N-1$	TSS		

If the interaction effect is significant, the differences among individual cells for each level of each treatment should be examined. If the interaction effect is not significant, $SSAB$ and SSW should be combined to form SSE. The revised analysis which should be used if interaction is not significant is given here.

Source of Variation	df	SS	MS	F
Treatment A	$p-1$	SSA	$SSA/(p-1)$	MSA/MSE
Treatment B	$q-1$	SSB	$SSB/(q-1)$	MSB/MSE
Error	$N-p-q+1$	SSE	$SSE/(N-p-q+1)$	
Total	$N-1$	TSS		

EXAMPLE 1   An experiment was conducted to determine the effect of background noise level in a factory upon the number of errors. Since task complexity was also considered a factor, a variety of levels of task complexity was also introduced. Each of the sixty employees was randomly assigned one of four different tasks and subjected to one of five different noise levels, three to each level of both treatments. The number of errors in a two-hour test period was recorded and is given below. Analyze the results to determine what effect noise level and task complexity have on errors and whether or not there is any interaction between the factors.

Task Complexity	\multicolumn{5}{Errors — Noise level (in ascending order)}				
	1	2	3	4	5
A	0	1	3	4	3
	2	0	1	2	5
	0	3	2	3	4
B	1	1	2	4	6
	1	3	3	3	7
	2	2	3	5	2
C	2	3	1	5	6
	1	2	4	6	8
	3	3	3	4	7
D	4	5	6	8	11
	5	8	7	10	9
	3	6	9	9	12

SOLUTION   The analysis is summarized as follows:

AB Summary Table

	1	2	3	4	5	B_j
A	2	4	6	9	12	33
B	4	6	8	12	15	45
C	6	8	8	15	21	58
D	12	19	22	27	32	112
A_i	24	37	44	63	80	248

(1) $(\Sigma x^2)/N = (248)^2/60 \doteq 1,025.0667$

(2) $(\Sigma A^2)/qn = (24^2 + 37^2 + 44^2 + 63^2 + 80^2)/12 = 1,187.5$

(3) $(\Sigma B^2)/pn = (33^2 + 45^2 + 58^2 + 112^2)/15 \doteq 1,268.1333$

(4) $(\Sigma AB^2)/n = (2^2 + 4^2 + 6^2 + \cdots + 22^2 + 27^2 + 32^2)/3 = 1,446$

(5) $\Sigma x^2 = 0^2 + 2^2 + 0^2 + 1^2 + 0^2 + 3^2 + \cdots + 11^2 + 9^2 + 12^2 = 1,508$

We have the following, then

Noise level: $SSA = (2)-(1) = 162.4333$
Task complexity: $SSB = (3)-(1) = 243.0667$
Interaction: $SSAB = (4)+(1)-(2)-(3) = 15.4333$
Within cells: $SSW = (5)-(4) = 62.0000$
Total: $TSS = (5)-(1) = 482.9333$

The analysis can be summarized as follows:

Source of variation	df	SS	MS	F
Noise level	4	162.4333	40.6083	26.199
Task complexity	3	243.0667	81.0222	52.272
Interaction	12	15.4333	1.2861	0.830
Within cells	40	62.0000	1.5500	
Total	59	482.9333		

Since the interaction is not significant, the interaction and within cells variation are combined to obtain experimental error. The revised analysis is given as follows:

Source of variation	df	SS	MS	F
Noise level	4	162.4333	40.6083	27.270**
Task complexity	3	243.0667	81.0222	54.410**
Error	52	77.4333	1.4891	
Total	59	482.9333		

$F_{.01}(4,52) = 3.71; \quad F_{.01}(3,52) = 5.04$
**Significant at the 0.01 level

Post hoc analysis using the Newman–Keuls multiple range test yields the following results:

Noise level

Means are A: 2.20; B: 3.00; C: 3.87; D: 7.47. Values of r are

	D	C	B	A
D	1			
C	2	1		
B	3	2	1	
A	4	3	2	1

$CV_r = q_r \sqrt{1.4891/12} = 0.3523 q_r$, so we have the following:

	$\alpha = 0.05$			$\alpha = 0.01$	
r	q_r	CV_r	r	q_r	CV_r
4	3.76	1.32	4	4.64	1.62
3	3.42	1.20	3	4.32	1.51
2	2.84	0.99	2	3.78	1.32

Differences between the means are given in the table below.

	D	C	B	A
D	—			
C	3.60**	—		
B	4.47**	0.87	—	
A	5.27**	1.67**	0.80	

**Significant at the 0.01 level

Thus level *D* produced significantly more errors than the other levels, level *C* produced significantly more errors than level *B*, all at the 0.01 level of significance.

Task complexity

Means are 1:2.0; 2:3.08; 3:3.67; 4:5.25; 5:6.67.
Values of *r* are

	5	4	3	2	1
5	1				
4	2	1			
3	3	2	1		
2	4	3	2	1	
1	5	4	3	2	1

$CV_r = q_r \sqrt{1.4891/15} = 0.3151q_r$, so we have the following:

	$\alpha = 0.05$			$\alpha = 0.01$	
r	q_r	CV_r	r	q_r	CV_r
5	4.00	1.26	5	4.86	1.53
4	3.76	1.18	4	4.64	1.46
3	3.42	1.08	3	4.32	1.36
2	2.84	0.89	2	3.78	1.19

Differences between the means are given in the table below.

	5	4	3	2	1
5	—				
4	1.42**	—			
3	3.00**	1.58**	—		
2	3.59**	2.17**	0.59	—	
1	4.67**	3.25**	1.67**	1.08*	—

**Significant at the 0.01 level.
*Significant at the 0.05 level.

Here level 5 produced significantly more errors than any of the other levels, level 4 produced significantly more errors than any other level except level 5, and level 3 had significantly more errors than level 1, all at the 0.01 level of significance. Level 2 had more errors than level 1 at the 0.05 level of significance.

EXAMPLE 2   A large firm has many stores, and it wished to see if it could determine whether education or experience was a better indication of potential success in a store manager. From its large number of stores, eight managers were selected at random from each of the categories H—completed high school or less, C—attended college, but did not graduate, B—received a bachelor's degree. Within each category the managers were further divided according to total experience in sales. It was found that equal cell sizes were obtained by having categories as follows: I—less than 5 years sales experience; II—5, but less than 10 years; III—10, but less than 15 years; IV—15 or more years sales experience. To assess degree of success, a formula based on such factors as stock, location, number of personnel, etc. (a regression equation) was developed to predict what sales should have been at that store during the preceding year. For each store manager the ratio of actual sales to predicted sales was determined. That data is given in the table below. Use analysis of variance to determine what, if any, relationship exists between education, experience, and success as a store manager using this criterion.

	Success Ratio		
	Education level		
Expreience	*H*	*C*	*B*
I	0.84	0.92	1.08
	0.89	0.86	1.12
II	0.94	0.96	1.12
	0.97	0.97	1.08
III	1.02	1.08	1.03
	0.99	1.03	1.06
IV	1.13	1.00	1.04
	1.01	1.04	0.98

SOLUTION   The summary table is presented below, together with all intermediate steps.

	AB Summary Table			
	H	*C*	*B*	B_j
I	1.73	1.78	2.20	5.71
II	1.91	1.93	2.20	6.04
III	2.01	2.11	2.09	6.21
IV	2.14	2.04	2.02	6.20
A_i	7.79	7.86	8.51	24.16

(1) $(\Sigma x)^2/N = (24.16)^2/24 \doteq 24.3211$

(2) $(\Sigma A^2)/nq = (7.79^2 + 7.86^2 + 8.51^2)/8 \doteq 24.3605$

(3) $(\Sigma B^2)/np = (5.71^2 + 6.04^2 + 6.21^2 + 6.20^2)/6 \doteq 24.3483$

(4) $(\Sigma AB^2)/n = (1.73^2 + 1.78^2 + \cdots + 2.04^2 + 2.02^2)/2 = 24.4481$

(5) $\Sigma x^2 = 0.84^2 + 0.89^2 + 0.92^2 + \cdots + 1.04^2 + 1.04^2 + 0.98^2 = 24.4652$

$$SSA = (2) - (1) = 0.0394$$

$$SSB = (3) - (1) = 0.0272$$

$$SSAB = (4) + (1) - (3) - (2) = 0.0604$$

$$SSW = (5) - (4) = 0.0171$$

$$TSS = (5) - (1) = 0.1441$$

Source of variation	df	SS	MS	F
Education	2	0.0394	0.0197	13.827**
Experience	3	0.0272	0.0091	6.370**
Interaction	6	0.0604	0.0101	7.063**
Within (Error)	12	0.0171	0.0014	

$F_{.01}(2, 12) = 6.93;$ $F_{.01}(3, 12) = 5.95;$ $F_{.01}(6, 12) = 4.82$
**Significant at the 0.01 level

According to these results, both education and experience have an effect on success ratio; even more importantly, interaction was significant. The interaction graphs are shown below.

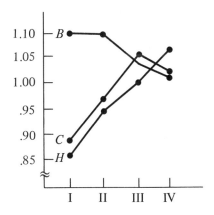
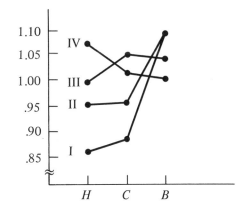

On the left above, high school graduates (groups *H* and *C*) seem to profit from experience, while college graduates (group *B*) do not. On the right, experience groups I and II appear to profit from college, while experience groups III and IV do not. One interpretation may be that a college degree can be a substitute initially for experience. A word of caution in a study such as this is appropriate, however. This is not a *longitudinal* study; that is, a study of the same people over a period of time. Rather it is a *cross-sectional* study; a study of different people at different points in their lives and careers, but at the same point in time. As such there are many other factors which may account for some of the differences. Those with recent college experience may well have studied different subjects than those with more remote college days. Also, those with more experience may have entered their careers from other fields. More specific analysis may be performed; they will not be discussed here, but can be found in other sources, such as Winer, *Op cit.*, 436–443.

NOTE   In order to test for homogeneity of variance, Hartley's F_{max} can still be used, if desired, but the usual small size of cell samples usually works against obtaining a meaningful result.

•Problems

1. Draw the interaction diagrams for the results of example 1.
2. A company is attempting to increase sales by using an incentive program. There are three different incentive programs which have been proposed, and they are to be tested in the field. The company has four different branches, and nine salesmen in each branch are randomly selected and divided randomly into three groups of three each. Group *A* is offered bonuses for sales increasing beyond a certain amount. No competition is involved; each salesman whose sales increase by that amount will receive a $500 bonus. In group *B*, a $1,000 bonus will be paid to the salesman of the three whose sales increase by the greatest amount. Group *C* is a combination of the two. A $500 bonus will be given to the salesmen who exceed the same increase as in group *A*, and a further $500 bonus will be given to the salesman of the three whose sales increase the most. Midway in the campaign, the increase in sales for each of the salesmen is given below. Use analysis of variance to determine if there appears to be any difference in the results which may be due to differences in incentive. Use the 0.05 level of significance.

		Sales Increases					
		Bonus Incentive Plan					
Branch Office	*A*	*B*	*C*	**Branch Office**	*A*	*B*	*C*
I	16	18	17	III	44	31	28
	22	27	34		27	33	54
	9	15	13		22	19	39
II	8	13	14	IV	17	19	24
	7	5	12		17	23	28
	6	11	10		14	17	31

3. A study being done by an interior decorating firm was designed to test the effect of color and intensity on working ability of individuals. Fifteen identical offices were painted. In each case the ceiling was white. Five different colors were used: blue, green, brown, orange, and yellow. In each case, three different intensities were selected, ranging from pastel, through primary, to highly intense. The cooperating companies placed four employees in the offices for one week's time, and at the end of the time the employees' work output effectiveness was rated on a scale from 1—distinctly below average, through 4—average (the employee's average), to 7—distinctly above average. Use the data given below to assess the effect of color and intensity on the work output effectiveness of the employees. All employees usually worked in offices painted white.

	Work Output Effectiveness		
	Intensity of color		
Color	**Pastel**	**Primary**	**Intense**
Blue	6	4	3
	5	5	4
	5	4	4
Green	7	6	4
	5	4	5
	5	5	4
Brown	3	4	4
	3	5	4
	4	4	5
Orange	5	6	4
	4	5	3
	5	6	3
Yellow	7	6	4
	4	6	4
	5	6	5

9.7 SUMMARY

To test for the differences between means of several groups, a method called analysis of variance is employed. Variance estimates for the populations from which the samples are drawn are obtained and a ratio obtained which is compared to the F distribution. If the obtained value of F is greater than the critical value, the hypothesis of equality is rejected and further analyses are indicated.

Assumptions for analysis of variance include normality of the populations from which the samples are drawn, homogeneity of the sample variances (which can be tested by means of Hartley's F_{max} test), and random selection of the samples.

If the samples are independent, and if there are k different samples subjected to k different treatments (possibly including a control group), the procedure is called one-way analysis of variance. We obtain sums of squares for treatments, for error, and total, divide the sum of squares for treatments (SST) by the degrees of freedom, $k-1$, to obtain the mean square for treatments (MST), divide the sum of squares for error (SSE) by the degrees of freedom, $N-k$, to obtain the mean square for error, MSE. Then $F = MST/MSE$ and it is compared to critical values for $k-1$ and $N-k$ degrees of freedom, with level of significance α, $F(k-1, N-k)$, from Table 7 or 8. If the value of F is significant, further tests are appropriate, such as Scheffé's test for significance between sample means or the Newman–Keuls multiple range test.

If the samples are matched, as an extension of the matched-pair t-test of Chapter 7, each matching is called a block, and the design is called the randomized complete block. Analysis of the complete block consists of obtaining SST and MST, as before, but, if there are n observations or subjects per sample, we obtain a sum of squares for blocks, SSB, and divide by $n-1$ degrees of freedom to obtain MSB. SSE consists of the remainder of TSS, and is divided by $(k-1)(n-1)$ degrees of freedom to obtain MSE. F-ratios are obtained from MST/MSE and MSB/MSE, as above. Subsequent tests are usually confined to the treatments, although blocks can also be tested.

If there are two different treatments, p of A and q of B, with n observations per cell (a cell is one level of A and one level of B), where $n > 1$, a two-way analysis of variance is appropriate. We obtain sums of squares for each treatment, SSA and SSB, a sum of squares for interaction between treatments, $SSAB$, and a sum of squares within the cells, SSW. Dividing by appropriate degrees of freedom, $MSA = SSA/(p-1)$, $MSB = SSB/(q-1)$, $MSAB = SSAB/(p-1)(q-1)$, $MSW = SSW/(N-pq)$. We first determine the F for interaction, $F = MSAB/MSW$. If this exceeds the critical value, interaction is significant, and we can obtain F values from MSA/MSW and MSB/MSW. Subsequent analysis is difficult, but much can be learned from interaction charts. If F for interaction is not significant, we combine $SSAB$ and SSW to obtain SSE; $MSE = SSE/(N-p-q+1)$, and F values for the treatments are MSA/MSE

and MSB/MSE. If either of these is significant, further analysis can be carried out by using the Scheffé or Newman–Keuls procedure as before.

•Problems

1. A paint manufacturer is trying to determine which of three pigments will give the brightest color in his paint. He uses five sample quarts of each of the three pigments to paint test surfaces, and compares their brightness using a light meter and identical lighting conditions. His results follow. Test the hypothesis of no difference in brightness among the three pigments at the 0.05 level of significance.

Light-Meter Readings		
Pigment		
A	B	C
54	63	58
61	72	67
63	55	73
52	66	78
74	64	57

2. A corrosion preventive coating was developed to compete with the leading brand. A comparison between the leading brand (A), the second brand (B), and the newly developed coating (C) was carried out by coating metals with the coating, exposing them to the usual conditions, then measuring the extent of corrosion by determining the depth of pitting in millimeters. Six different metals were used. Analyze the results at the 0.05 level.

	Depth of Pitting (mm)		
	Coating		
Metal	A	B	C
Iron	1.8	1.6	1.9
Brass	1.2	1.3	1.2
Copper	2.4	2.5	2.0
Steel	1.4	1.4	1.3
Magnesium alloy	2.6	2.5	2.1
Aluminum	1.7	1.6	1.7

3. A traffic checkpoint was established for the purpose of checking the speed deterring effect of various measures. The speed limit in the vicinity was 55 mph. For four different days, the following measures were employed: I—a

speed limit sign; II—a sign "speed limits strictly enforced"; III—a sign "speed radar controlled"; IV—a highway patrol car sitting by the side of the road with the speed limit sign. Speeds of cars going past were checked by radar. Only out-of-state cars were included in the results in order to eliminate bias due to local drivers noticing the differences. The speeds of out-of-state cars were recorded for the four days and are given below. Test the hypothesis that there is no difference between the methods of deterring speeding, using the 0.05 level.

		Speeds of Cars		
		Method		
	I	II	III	IV
	72	61	73	55
	55	60	60	57
	63	54	55	52
	61	55	62	62
	74	69	53	54
	52	58	49	55
	56	66	66	50
	67	73	62	58
	55	68	55	55
	68	53	53	62
	78	61	59	67
	71		61	
	66			

4. The paint manufacturer in problem 1 decided to test the various pigments on different types of wall surfaces in order to determine whether there might be a difference due to that variable. He painted each of four different types of surfaces with two samples of each pigment, then tested the resulting surfaces with a light meter. The readings are given below. Analyze the results.

	Light-Meter Readings		
		Pigment	
Surface	A	B	C
Smooth	78	74	68
	88	80	63
Rough	37	38	51
	42	37	48
Grainy	68	62	58
	70	61	64
Very rough	27	28	35
	23	29	40

CHAPTER 9

Glossary of Terms

analysis of variance
block
critical value for differences
  between samples
Hartley's F_{max}
homogeneous variances
interaction

mean square
Newman–Keuls test
post hoc tests
randomized complete block
Scheffé test
sum of squares
treatment

Glossary of Symbols

CV_d	critical value for differences between samples, in the Scheffé test
CV_r	critical value for differences between samples in the Newman–Keuls test
F_a	value of F for which a is the proportion of the area under the curve to its right
F_{max}	ratio of largest to smallest sample variance
MS	mean square
MSA	mean square due to treatment A
$MSAB$	mean square due to interaction between treatments A and B
MSB	mean square due to blocks, mean square due to treatment B
MSE	mean square due to error
MST	mean square due to treatments
MSW	mean square within cells
n	harmonic mean of sample sizes
q_r	statistic used in the Newman–Keuls test
SS	sum of squares
SSA	sum of squares due to treatment A
$SSAB$	sum of squares due to interaction between treatments A and B
SSB	sum of squares due to blocks, sum of squares due to treatment B
SSE	sum of squares due to error
SSW	sum of squares within cells
TSS	total sum of squares

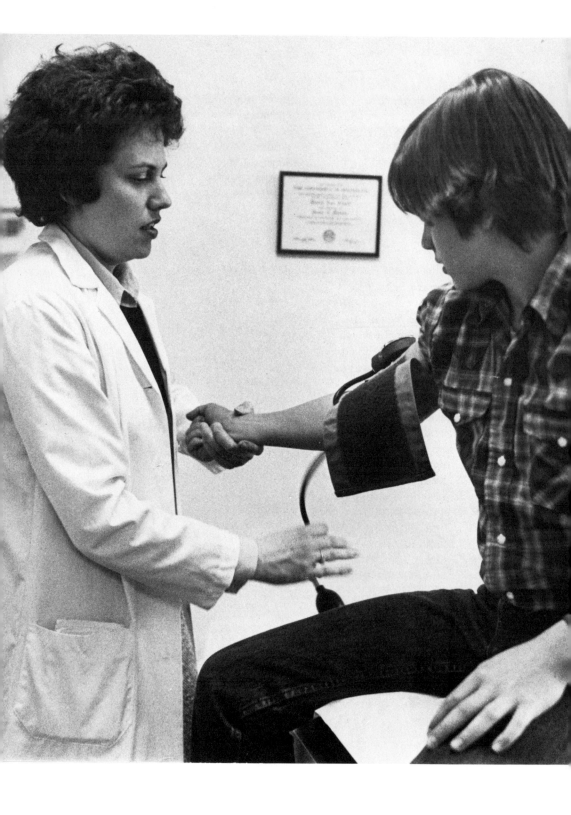

Regression and Correlation

10.1 LINEAR REGRESSION

With a few exceptions, such as contingency tables and two-way analysis of variance, we have been dealing with data confined to one variable. In this chapter we will consider two variables on one set of subjects; that is, related pairs of observations, each pair consisting of two observations on the same member of a sample. Athletes may be classified by height and weight; we may wish to investigate the relationship between amount of money spent on a research program and return from this investment. Two procedures often used for this are *regression analysis* and *correlation analysis*. These two procedures are related, but differ slightly in the emphasis and quite radically in their application. We shall first take up **regression analysis**; this technique is most useful when we feel that one variable influences or causes changes in a second one. An example is the supposition that weight of individuals influences blood pressure. This is an incomplete situation inasmuch as height certainly influences weight, and it is probably more reasonable to say that *extra* unneeded weight has an influence on blood pressure. Nonetheless, we shall begin with this rather simple example.

Suppose that we have the following set of data (weights and systolic blood pressures) on a group of ten men.

Subject	Weight	Systolic Blood Pressure
1	188	140
2	231	160
3	176	130
4	194	130
5	244	180
6	207	160
7	198	140
8	217	150
9	181	140
10	194	150

If we plot these on a graph, we notice a general upward trend.

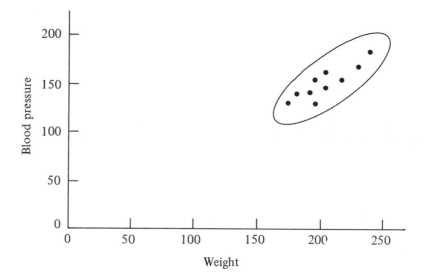

Concentrating on the circled area of the graph, and labelling each point, the upward trend becomes even more apparent and it is evident that there is a tendency for higher weights and higher blood pressures to go together. This does not indicate any *casual* relationship between them; it only indicates an association.

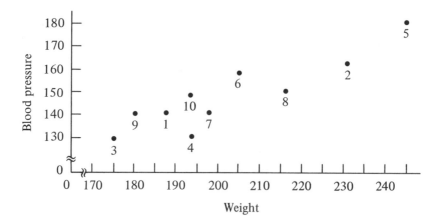

The above graphical approach is called a **scatterplot** or **scattergram**. It is quite useful in assessing whether there is a relationship between two variables, and, if so, what type of relationship.

Some examples of scattergrams are given below.

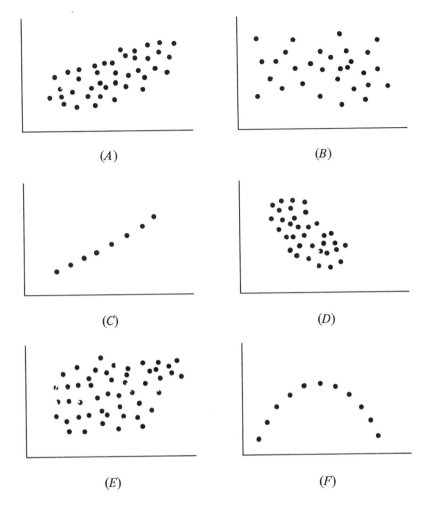

(A)

(B)

(C)

(D)

(E)

(F)

The weight-blood-pressure graph, and graphs (A), (C), and (D) above are good examples of a **linear trend**. In graph (B), there is no relationship between the variables, while in (E) there is a slight linear trend. Graph (F) represents an example of a *curvilinear trend*. The purpose of regression analysis is to be able to express one variable as a function of the other. That is, to determine a formula such that the substitution of one value of the independent variable will yield the best prediction for the value of the dependent variable most closely associated with it. Possible candidates for such prediction include simple linear regression, multiple linear regression, and nonlinear regression. For the rest of this section we will examine simple linear regression.

The general equation of a straight line is given by $y = A + Bx$, where B is the slope of the line and A is the y intercept, the y coordinate of the point $(0, A)$ at which the line crosses the y axis. An excellent example of a linear relationship, most likely expressable as a straight line function, would be usage of electricity (y) as a function of daily temperature (x) in hot weather, or usage of gas (y) as a function of daily temperature (x) in cold weather. In each case, energy usage depends on the temperature. In the first case the relationship is direct; as temperature goes up, electricity usage goes up. In the second case the relationship is inverse; as temperature decreases, energy usage increases. Both of these relationships are probably generally linear within limits. In each case it would probably be possible to obtain an expression of the form $y = A + Bx$ which would predict energy usage (y) for a specific daily temperature (x).

The model for simple linear regression assumes that there is a linear relationship between two variables which can be expressed in the form $y = A + Bx + e$. The symbol e (for error) represents deviations from the line which would be found if all population data were known. We would not expect, for instance, precisely the same gas usage on any two days with the same temperature. If the line given by $y = A + Bx$ is the line which best fits the data, the mean or expected value of the error variable is zero for any value of x. Then if we denote the expected value of y for a given x by $E(y|x)$, we have $E(y|x) = A + Bx$ as the ideal regression equation for estimating the mean of the y values for a particular value of x. Inasmuch as we generally have only sample information, we obtain estimates for the population parameters A and B from the samples. The estimates are denoted a and b and the sample estimate for y thus obtained is denoted $\hat{y}$ (y hat). The equation $\hat{y} = a + bx$ is called the sample regression line.

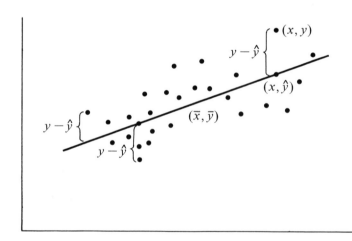

To obtain the values for a and b from the sample data, we use what is known as the *principle of least squares*. Note that the regression line (shown) will have the point $(x, \hat{y})$ on it for each value of x. The difference between the estimated value $\hat{y}$ and the actual observed value y is $(y - \hat{y})$. We assume that the best line will be one which minimizes these differences. Since some of the differences are positive and some are negative, we again employ the same strategem used in computation of the variance; we use the *squares* of the differences and look at their sum $\Sigma(y-\hat{y})^2$ for each value of x and y. The principle used is the **principle of least squares**; that the best fitting function or formula for a set of data is the function $\hat{y}=f(x)$ for which $\Sigma(y-\hat{y})^2$ is the least. Although use of the principle itself requires calculus, the results can be utilized without calculus; all that is required is to determine the nature of the function to be used and selection of the formulas which fit. A few such formulas will be given in section 10.5. In this section we confine ourselves to linear functions.

The least squares principle has several characteristics which render its use very desirable. As mentioned above, the sum of the squared deviations, Σ $(y-\hat{y})^2$ is a minimum; the deviations above the line equal those below the line so that $\Sigma(y-\hat{y})=0$; the function passes through the mean point $(\bar{x},\bar{y})$; if a set of data is a random sample of a larger population, the function obtained by the least squares technique provides coefficients (a and b for a linear function) which are unbiased estimates of the population parameters (such as A and B).

The technique consists of replacing $\hat{y}$ by the functional form of x in the expression $\Sigma(y-\hat{y})^2$, taking the partial derivative of the expression with respect to each of the coefficients, and setting these equal to zero. These result in the **normal equations**. The normal equations can then be solved for the coefficients. In the case of the linear regression line, we assume that the best fit will be a line of the form $\hat{y}=a+bx$. Then we must have $\Sigma(y-a-bx)^2$ to be a minimum. Taking the partial derivatives and setting them equal to zero results in the following normal equations:

$$\Sigma y = na + b\Sigma x$$

$$\Sigma xy = a\Sigma x + b\Sigma x^2$$

For more complicated expressions, it is often wise to use the normal equations and solve for the coefficients in each case. For the simple linear equation, we can eliminate a and solve for b to obtain the following expression:

$$b = \frac{\Sigma xy - (\Sigma x)(\Sigma y)/n}{\Sigma x^2 - (\Sigma x)^2/n}$$

One can multiply the top and bottom by n to obtain the raw data form of the equation

$$b = \frac{n\Sigma xy - (\Sigma x)(\Sigma y)}{n\Sigma x^2 - (\Sigma x)^2}$$

or observe from Chapter 9 that the expression $\Sigma x^2 - (\Sigma x)^2/n$ is the value of the sum of squares for x, *SSX*. If we denote the term $\Sigma xy - (\Sigma x)(\Sigma y)/n$ by

SSXY, we then have

$$b = \frac{SSXY}{SSX}.$$

Use of the latter form has some advantages in that the adjusted sums, *SSX*, *SSY*, and *SSXY* will be used in other applications. In either case, we can solve for *a* to obtain

$$a = \frac{\sum y - b \sum x}{n} = \bar{y} - b\bar{x}$$

since $\bar{x} = \sum x / n$ and $\bar{y} = \sum y / n$.

We thus have the following for a regression line $\hat{y} = a + bx$, where $\hat{y}$ is the value predicted from a particular value of *x*, and *a* and *b* are the

Regression Coefficients

$$b = \frac{n \sum xy - \left(\sum x\right)\left(\sum y\right)}{n \sum x^2 - \left(\sum x\right)^2} = \frac{SSXY}{SSX}$$

$$a = \frac{\sum y - b \sum x}{n} = \bar{y} - b\bar{x}$$

EXAMPLE 1   Determine a regression line for the weight-blood pressure data given previously and plot it on the graph.

SOLUTION   If we wish to predict blood pressure from weight, we let *x* represent weight, the independent variable, and *y* represent blood pressure, the dependent variable. Then we have

Subject	x	y	x^2	y^2	xy
1	188	140	35,344	19,600	26,320
2	231	160	53,361	25,600	36,960
3	176	130	30,976	16,900	22,880
4	194	130	37,636	16,900	25,220
5	244	180	59,536	32,400	43,920
6	207	160	42,849	25,600	33,120
7	198	140	39,204	19,600	27,720
8	217	150	47,089	22,500	32,550
9	181	140	32,761	19,600	25,340
10	194	150	37,636	22,500	29,100
$\sum =$	2,030	1,480	416,392	221,200	303,130

We do not need $\sum y^2$ now, but we will later. The adjusted sums are $SSXY = 303,130 - (1,480)(2,030)/10 = 2,690$ and $SSX = 416,392 - (2,030)^2/10 = 4,302$.

Then

$$b = 2,690/4,302 \doteq 0.625$$

and

$$a = \frac{1,480 - 0.625(2,030)}{10} = 21.125$$

Thus the regression equation is $\hat{y} = 21.125 + 0.625x$. The *predicted* blood pressure for a 160 pound man, then, is $21.125 + 0.625(160) \doteq 121$; for a 200 pound man it is $21.125 + 0.625(200) \doteq 146$.

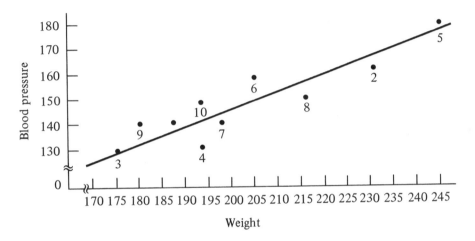

The line is plotted below.

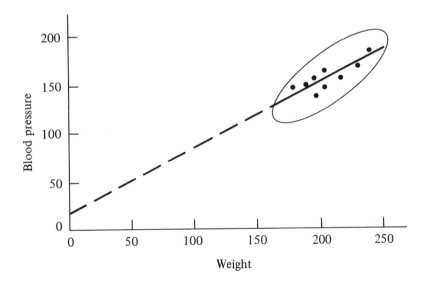

On the larger-area graph, the line is dotted outside the region containing the sample data points to indicate that it is not reliable there.

In a business setting, a demand function or similar function may be obtained for a regression line. Suppose that $\hat{y} = a + bx$ has x as units manufactured and y as total cost. Then one interpretation for the function would be as a representing fixed cost and b representing variable cost. In terms of a regression equation, however, this is not strictly true since we are confining both the range of x and the range of y to those values in the sample. Outside this range, the equation may be somewhat different.

•Problems

1. The duration of a particular illness is apparently related to the bacterial count of the infecting organism. Ten patients with the illness have a bacterial count taken and the duration of symptoms is observed. Derive a regression equation based on the data which will predict the duration of the illness based on the bacterial count.

Patient	Count (1,000s)	Duration (Days)
A	8	11
B	7	10
C	4	9
D	6	8
E	9	12
F	7	9
G	8	13
H	3	7
I	8	10
J	7	11

2. In a reforestation project, all the trees were planted at the same time and were watered by means of irrigation ditches. After ten years a random sample of the trees was examined to find their height and distance from the nearest irrigation ditch. Using these data, derive a regression equation to predict the probable height of a tree, given its distance from the nearest irrigation ditch.

Ht. (ft)	Distance (ft)	Ht. (ft)	Dist. (ft)	Ht. (ft)	Dist. (ft)
23	80	21	100	27	72
18	113	17	120	23	88
22	108	20	110	19	84
24	92	22	94	18	108
21	87	23	103	24	92
19	110	26	76	23	84
23	90	24	82	21	93

3. A corporation uses a screening test to aid in the discovery of potential sales ability of applicants for jobs as salesmen. Since situations vary, the regression equation is refigured monthly, based upon the latest available data for salesmen who have taken the test and been hired within the last six months. Using the data given here, figure out a suitable regression equation and use it to predict the probable adjusted gross sales of today's applicants who have scores of 83.97, 112, 124, and 146.

Scores	Adjusted Gross Sales (thousands of dollars)
97	141
132	113
88	94
154	157
143	118
119	131
157	148
89	107
134	158
135	136
162	159
155	146
113	122
124	131
108	113
136	94
117	124
182	237
130	118
122	145

10.2   INFERENCES IN THE LINEAR REGRESSION MODEL

A linear regression equation can be obtained for any set of data on two variables. The *value* of such an equation depends primarily on whether or not the data points are close to the line or are widely dispersed about it. In addition, we assume that the scatter of points about the regression line is uniform; that is, that the data points do not cluster more closely about the line in some portions of the line than others. We also assume that the scatter is random.

The least squares approach is designed to minimize the value of $\sum (y-\hat{y})^2$. This sum measures the actual variation of the data points around the line. Dividing the sum by $n-2$, the number of degrees of freedom (since there are two parameters estimated, A and B), yields a statistic similar to the variance. The square root of this is comparable to the standard deviation of a set of data and is called the standard error of estimate. For a sample this is denoted by s_e, and is given by

Standard Error of Estimate

$$s_e = \sqrt{\frac{\sum (y-\hat{y})^2}{n-2}}$$

The standard error of estimate can be treated in much the same way as the standard deviation of any sample. If we can assume that the parent population (in this case, the set of all deviations of y from $E(y|x)$ for all values of y) is normally distributed, or that the sample is sufficiently large so that the Central Limit Theorem applies, then approximately 2/3 of all data points will fall within one s_e of the sample regression line and 95% within two s_e of the line. Two forms for the standard error of estimate are more useful computationally, the first for raw data, the second for adjusted sums of squares. These can be verified easily by direct substitution.

Formulas for the Standard Error of Estimate

$$s_e = \sqrt{\frac{\sum y^2 - a \sum y - b \sum xy}{n-2}}$$

$$s_e = \sqrt{\frac{SSY - bSSXY}{n-2}}$$

EXAMPLE 1 Determine the standard error of estimate for the weight-blood pressure data of the previous section. Plot a 95% confidence interval for the scatter of the data using the assumption that the deviations for the population are normally distributed.

SOLUTION Recall from the data that $n = 10$, $\sum x = 2{,}030$, $\sum y = 1{,}480$, $\sum x^2 = 416{,}392$, $\sum y^2 = 221{,}200$, and $\sum xy = 303{,}130$. The adjusted sums are $SSX = 4{,}302$, $SSY = 2{,}160$, $SSXY = 2{,}690$, and the regression equation was $y = 21.125 + 0.625x$. Using the raw data formula,

$$s_e = \sqrt{(221{,}200 - 21.1(1{,}480) - (0.625)(303{,}130))/8} \doteq 7.74;$$

using the formula with adjusted sums of squares, $s_e = \sqrt{(2{,}160 - (0.625)(2{,}690))/8} \doteq 7.74$.

To plot a 95% confidence interval, we use an analogue of the Central Limit Theorem. The standard error of estimate, s_e, is used as a standard deviation for values of $y - \hat{y}$. If the population of points can be assumed to be normally distributed about the true regression line, so that the distribution of all values of $y - E(y|x)$ is normal with mean zero, then for a sample of n observations, the values of $(y - \hat{y})$ are distributed as Student's t with mean zero, with $n - 2$ degrees of freedom.

In this case, then, we use $s_e = 7.74$, $t_{.05} = 1.860$ for eight degrees of freedom, so $(7.74)(1.86) \doteq 14.40$, so that 95% of the sample points should lie within 14.40 units of the regression line. The 95% confidence interval for the scatter is plotted as the dotted line below.

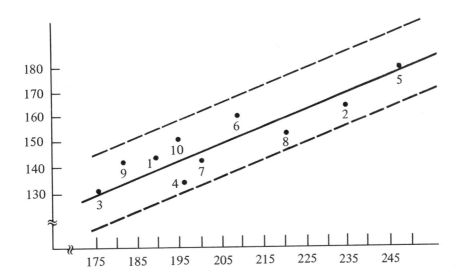

EXAMPLE 2   In a certain part of a southern town, data was collected for the consumption of electricity (in thousands of kilowatt hours, on a daily basis) and average mean temperature for the day. The following data was collected over a period of 52 days during the latter part of July, all of August, and the early part of September for last year. We use temperature as the independent (x) variable and KWH consumption as the dependent (y) variable since it is temperature which influences KWH consumption rather than the other way around.

$$n = 52 \qquad \sum x = 4,188.2 \qquad \sum x^2 = 338,972.14$$

$$\sum xy = 177,334.864 \qquad \sum y = 2,174.64 \qquad \sum y^2 = 94,352.8452$$

Determine a regression line for the data. One particular day the mean temperature was 86.3° and electricity consumption was 43.82 thousand KWH. Was this day out of line with the rest of the data?

SOLUTION   To determine the regression line and standard error, we obtain $SSX = 338,972.14 - (4,188.2)^2/52 \doteq 1,644.85$, $SSY = 94,352.8452 - (2,174.64)^2/52 \doteq 3,409.40$, $SSXY = 117,334.864 - (4,188.2)(2,174.64)/52 = 2,184.34$. Then

$$b = 2,184.34/1,644.85 \doteq 1.328$$

$$a = \frac{2,174.64 - (1.328)(4,188.2)}{52}$$

$$\doteq -65.140$$

so that the regression line is

$$\hat{y} = -65.140 + 1.328x$$

One interpretation would be that for each degree increase in temperature in this range (which would be about 70 to 90 degrees or so) each degree rise in temperature results in an increase of 1,328 KWH consumption of electricity for the day. The intercept, -65.140, has no real meaning in this case, except as a correction factor. Literally, a temperature of 0° would result in a negative electricity consumption, which is impossible.

For this set of data we have

$$s_e = \sqrt{\frac{3,409.40 - (1,328)(2,184.34)}{50}}$$

$$\doteq 3.189$$

Since $n = 52$, 95% of all sample points will lie within $(2.01)(3.189)$ or about 6.410 units of the line; that is, 95% of all values of $(y - \hat{y})$ will lie between -6.410 and 6.410. For a day on which the temperature averaged 86.3°, the expected KWH usage was $y = -65.140 + (1.328)(86.3) \doteq 49.466$ thousands. If actually 43.820 thousand were used, the difference is 5.646 thousand, which is within 95% confidence limits. Another way to look at it is to calculate a t value; here $t = (43.820 - 49.466)/3.189 \doteq -1.77$. Since -1.77 is not less than -2.01, we cannot reject a hypothesis that the difference is due to chance; however, the probability of deviating that far from the line by chance is less than 0.10, so that particular day might merit investigation.

Whether the regression equation has much merit, of course, depends upon whether or not there really is some nonhorizontal linear trend and whether the sample regression equation is a good approximation to the true population regression equation. If there really is a linear trend, then the value of B in the population regression equation is different from zero; for if there were no linear trend, the best approximation of y for any value of x would be $\bar{y}$, and we would have $A = \bar{y}$, $B = 0$. Above, in using s_e to determine confidence intervals for the scatter, we assumed that the scatter of the data for the population regression line was normal. Some additional assumptions are needed if inferences are to be made about b.

We assume that the scatter of points about the regression line is uniform; that is, that the data points do not cluster more closely about the line in some portions of the line than others. An example of nonuniform scatter occurs when larger values of y tend to produce wider scatter, such as when the scatter is approximately a constant percentage of x. In such a case, a log transformation replacing y by $\log y$ or $\ln y$ will make the scatter uniform. Another assumption is that the $(y - \hat{y})$ deviations are independent of each other. This is not true in *time series* data, when the independent variable is time. In this case, adjoining values are closely related, usually occurring in cycles. These two assumptions, in addition to the basic assumption of linearity and the assumption that the deviations in the population are normally distributed (for small samples) allow us to make additional inferences concerning the regression line.

To determine the significance of the regression equation is equivalent to testing the hypothesis that $B = 0$. If $B = 0$, the sample values of b/s_b will be distributed as t, where

Standard Error of the Regression Coefficient

$$s_b = \frac{s_e}{\sqrt{SSX}}$$

A $(1-\alpha)$ confidence interval for B has confidence limits $b+t_{\alpha/2}s_b$ and $b-t_{\alpha/2}s_b$ with $n-2$ degrees of freedom.

The regression constant, A, may also be estimated. The standard error, s_a, is given by

***Standard Error of
the Regression Constant***
$$s_a = s_e\sqrt{\frac{1}{n} + \frac{\bar{x}^2}{SSX}}$$

where n is the size of the sample from which the sample regression equation was obtained, $\bar{x}$ is the mean of the independent variable for that sample, and SSX is the sum of squares (adjusted) for the independent variable for that sample.

The uses of s_a are somewhat more limited, particularly since the value of a in the regression equation may have a questionable interpretation. It can, however, be used to estimate A; a $(1-\alpha)$ confidence interval for A has limits $a+t_{\alpha/2}s_a$ and $a-t_{\alpha/2}s_a$ with $n-2$ degrees of freedom.

EXAMPLE 3   Determine the significance of the regression coefficient and obtain 95% confidence intervals for A and B for the data of the preceding two examples.

SOLUTION   For the weight-blood pressure data of example 1, we have $\hat{y} = 21.125 + 0.625x$. Since $s_e \doteq 7.74$, $s_b \doteq 7.74/\sqrt{4,302} \doteq 0.118$. Then $t = 0.625/0.118 \doteq 5.297$. With eight degrees of freedom, $t_{.025} = 2.306$, so we may conclude that the hypothesis $B = 0$ can be rejected. A confidence interval for B is given by $0.625 \pm (2.306)(0.118)$; that is, 0.353 to 0.897. We can also calculate s_a; $s_a = 7.74\sqrt{(1/10) + (203)^2/4,302} \doteq 24.080$. Thus a 95% confidence interval for A is $21.125 \pm (2.306)(24.080)$; that is, -34.403 to 76.653. The small sample provides the reason that the intervals are so wide.

For the electricity consumption data of example 2, the regression equation was $\hat{y} = -65.140 + 1.328x$ and $s_e \doteq 3.189$. Then $s_b \doteq 3.189/\sqrt{1,644.85} \doteq 0.079$. To test the significance of b, we obtain $z = 1.328/0.079 \doteq 16.81$ so that we can conclude that B is different from zero. A 95% confidence interval for B has limits $1.328 \pm (2.01)(0.079)$; that is, 1.169 to 1.487. Similarly, $s_a = 3.189\sqrt{(1/52) + (80.54)^2/1,644.85} \doteq 6.348$, so the confidence limits for A are $-65.140 \pm (2.01)(6.348)$. A 95% confidence interval for A, then, is -77.899 to -52.381.

•Problems

1. Determine the standard error of estimate and significance of the regression coefficient for the data of problem 1, section 10.1.

2. Using the data of problem 2, section 10.1, obtain s_e and plot a 95% confidence interval for the scatter of the data. Use s_b to determine the significance of b and obtain 95% confidence intervals for A and B. Interpret these results. Two of the trees appear to be exceptions; one 84 feet from the ditch grew only to a height of 19 feet, while one 108 feet from the ditch grew to 22 feet. Can these be explained by sampling error or chance scatter, or should they be investigated more closely for other possibilities?

3. In problem 3, section 10.1, scores on a screening test were used to predict potential sales ability. Use s_e to investigate which, if any, of the salesmen in the sample are out of line with the rest of the sample with a 90% probability that such a difference is due to chance.

10.3   CORRELATION

In the preceding sections, we have examined methods of deriving a predictive model for one variable, given a second variable. Actual prediction techniques will be given in the next section. If both the variables are random samples drawn from normal populations, some additional facts may be obtained from the data.

The variation of the dependent variable consists of deviations of a single observation of y from the mean, $\bar{y}$. If the regression equation yields a reliable estimate for y, then the deviation of that estimate, $\hat{y}$, from the mean, is the variation of y which is explained by the independent variable, x. The remainder of the variation of y is said to be the unexplained variation. We thus have, for each value of y

$$(y-\bar{y})=(\hat{y}-\bar{y})+(y-\hat{y})$$

that is, the total variation of a value of y is equal to the explained variation plus the unexplained variation. Since the two parts are independent, a little arithmetic and a few assumptions gives us

$$\sum (y-\bar{y})^2 = \sum (\hat{y}-\bar{y})^2 + \sum (y-\hat{y})^2$$

which says that the total variation of the y values (SSY) is equal to the explained variation plus the unexplained variation. The ratio of explained variation to total variation is called the **coefficient of determination**. For a sample, this is symbolized as r^2, and we have

$$r^2 = \frac{\Sum (\hat{y} - \bar{y})^2}{\Sum (y - \bar{y})^2}$$

The coefficient of determination expresses the fraction of total variation of y which is explained by x. For the total population, the coefficient of determination is given by ρ^2 (ρ is the Greek letter "rho") and would be defined by

$$\rho^2 = \frac{E(\hat{y} - \bar{y})^2}{E(y - \bar{y})^2}$$

Since $E(y - \bar{y})^2 = E(\hat{y} - \bar{y})^2 + E(y - \hat{y})^2$, then $E(\hat{y} - \bar{y})^2 = E(y - \bar{y})^2 - E(y - \hat{y})^2$ so that

$$\rho^2 = \frac{E(y - \bar{y})^2 - E(y - \hat{y})^2}{E(y - \bar{y})^2}$$

$$= 1 - \frac{E(y - \hat{y})^2}{E(y - \bar{y})^2}$$

$$= 1 - \frac{\sigma_e^2}{\sigma_y^2}$$

that is, the coefficient of determination is equal to one minus the ratio of unexplained variation (the standard error of estimate, squared) to total variation (the variance of y).

We cannot say, however, that the sample coefficient of determination is equal to $1 - s_e^2/s_y^2$, since the degrees of freedom associated with the terms are different; $n-2$ for s_e and $n-1$ for s_y. Since $s_e^2 = (SSY - bSSXY)/(n-2)$, and $s_y^2 = SSY/(n-1)$, we can say that the sample coefficient of determination is given by

$$r^2 = 1 - \frac{SSY - bSSXY}{SSY}$$

$$= \frac{SSY - SSY + bSSXY}{SSY}$$

$$= \frac{bSSXY}{SSY} = b\frac{SSXY}{SSY}$$

$$= \frac{SSXY}{SSX} \cdot \frac{SSXY}{SSY} = \frac{(SSXY)^2}{SSX \cdot SSY}$$

The coefficient of determination (sometimes called the coefficient of linear determination) is a measure of the tendency of the data points to lie on a straight line. The values of r^2 range from 0 to 1; values close to 0 indicate little, if any, association between the two variables, while values near one indicate a great deal of association between the variables. Since the values of r^2 are always positive, they do not indicate whether the relationship, if any, is direct or inverse. The square root of the coefficient of determination is called the **coefficient of correlation**. It always takes the sign of b in the regression equation. This is automatic if one of the formulas given below is used.

Coefficient of Correlation

$$r = \frac{SSXY}{\sqrt{SSX \cdot SSY}}$$

$$r = \frac{n \sum xy - \sum x \sum y}{\sqrt{\left[n \sum x^2 - \left(\sum x \right)^2 \right]\left[n \sum y^2 - \left(\sum y \right)^2 \right]}}$$

The two formulas are equivalent, the second being more useful if raw data only are involved. Although it looks formidable, it is easy to apply, particularly with desk calculators.

The coefficient of correlation is one of the most widely used—and misused —statistics. Although it does, indeed, measure the association between two variables measured on the same data points, it does not necessarily imply any true causal relationship between the two variables; it may simply be a reflection of one or more variables affecting both the variables. Because it is the square root of r^2, it takes on values from $+1$ to -1. If $r=0$, there is little or no association between the variables; if r is close to $+1$ or -1, however, there is a great degree of association or correlation between the variables. A word of caution is in order, however. If $r=0.4, r^2=0.16$, so that, with $r=0.4$, only 16% of the total variation is explained by the relationship. If $r=-0.8$, however, $r^2=0.64$, and 64% of the total variation is explained. Thus if we have two correlation coefficients, r_1 and r_2, the relative degree of association is more accurately reflected by the *square* of their ratio, $(r_1/r_2)^2$. The scattergrams of section 10.1 are reproduced here, together with the correlations between the variables.

We emphasize again that to use correlation analysis, both variables must have distributions. If the x variable is restricted to certain fixed values, only regression techniques are applicable.

The relationship between a sample correlation coefficient and the true population coefficient is the same as that between any sample statistic and the

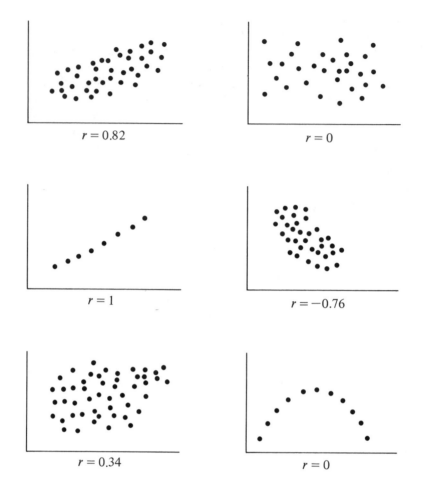

corresponding population parameter. Thus r can be considered as an estimate for ρ. The distribution of sample r from a population with true correlation ρ is not at all simple unless $\rho=0$. For large samples, $n>50$, sample r's for samples of size n drawn from a population for which $\rho=0$ are normally distributed with mean 0 and standard error $s_r=1/\sqrt{n}$. For large samples, then, the test statistic $z=r/(1/\sqrt{n})=r\sqrt{n}$ is normally distributed. For small samples, the statistic

$$t=r\cdot\sqrt{\frac{n-2}{1-r^2}}$$

follows a Student's t-distribution with $n-2$ degrees of freedom. To test the hypothesis $\rho=\rho_0$ (where $\rho_0\neq0$) as well as determination of confidence intervals for ρ requires a transformation known as **Fisher's z-statistic**, z_r. (See for example

D. V. Huntsberger and P. Billingsley, *Elements of Statistical Inference*, Third Edition (Allyn & Bacon, Inc., 1973), section 11.7.)

The use of the formula relating r to t above is equivalent to the formula $t = b/s_b$ from the preceding section. A little algebra, using adjusted sums of squares, is all that is necessary to derive one formula from the other.

EXAMPLE 1 Calculate the coefficient of correlation for the weight-blood pressure data of example 1, section 10.1, and determine whether or not the hypothesis $\rho = 0$ can be rejected.

SOLUTION The data are reproduced here.

Subject	x	y	x^2	y^2	xy
1	188	140	35,344	19,600	26,320
2	231	160	53,361	25,600	36,960
3	176	130	30,796	16,900	22,880
4	194	130	37,636	16,900	25,220
5	244	180	59,536	32,400	43,920
6	207	160	42,849	25,600	33,120
7	198	140	39,204	19,600	27,720
8	217	150	47,089	22,500	32,550
9	181	140	32,761	19,600	25,340
10	194	150	37,636	22,500	29,100
$\sum =$	2,030	1,480	416,392	221,200	303,130

Then

$$r = \frac{(10)(303,130) - (2,030)(1,480)}{\sqrt{[(10)(416,392) - (2,030)^2][(10)(221,200) - (1,480)^2]}}$$

$$= \frac{26,900}{\sqrt{929,232,000}}$$

$$\doteq 0.88$$

If sums of squares have already been calculated, or will be needed for regression analysis, they can be used instead. Here $SSXY = 303,130 - (1,480)(2,030)/10 = 2,690$, $SSX = 416,392 - (2,030)^2/10 = 4,302$, and $SSY = 221,200 - (1,480)^2/10 = 2,160$, so $r = 2,690/\sqrt{(4,302)(2,160)} \doteq 0.88$. To test the hypothesis $\rho = 0$, we obtain $t = 0.88\sqrt{8/(1 - 0.88^2)} \doteq 5.240$. If we had a one-sided alternative, claiming $\rho > 0$ (likely in this case), $t_{.05} = 1.860$ and $t_{.01} = 2.896$ for eight degrees of freedom, so that we may reject the hypothesis that there is no correlation between the two variables, and conclude that there is a positive association between the two; that is, increased weight is associated with increased blood pressure.

EXAMPLE 2   A graduate student in psychology hypothesizes that success in graduate school as measured by grade-point average is correlated positively with scores on the Graduate Record Examination; that high GRE scores and success in graduate school are associated. To test his hypothesis he takes a random sample of 75 graduate students' records and finds that the correlation between the two variables is 0.307. Does this support his hypothesis at a 0.01 level of significance?

SOLUTION   Since the sample is large we may use the test statistic $z = r\sqrt{n}$. The procedure warrants the hypothesis testing format. The research hypothesis is directional since he claims that $\rho > 0$; this means that high GRE scores and high GPA's go together and that low GRE scores and low GPA's go together. Hence we have the following.

1. H_0: $\rho = 0$
   H_1: $\rho > 0$
2. $\alpha = 0.01$
3. Criteria: Reject H_0 if $z > 2.33$.
4. Results: $n = 75, r = 0.307, z = 0.307\sqrt{75} \doteq 2.66$.
5. Conclusions: Reject H_0, there is some positive correlation.

NOTE   This shows only that there is some positive correlation between the two variables, not how big it is. A sample r of 0.307 means only that about 9.4% of the variance in GPA's is explained by factors in the GRE. In addition, there is certainly no *causation* to be imputed here, as both variables are certainly functions of another variable. Using Fisher's procedure, a 99% confidence interval of 0.014 to 0.552 is obtained.

•Problems

1. Several farmers in the same county employed varying amounts of fertilizer and obtained varying yields of corn. Use the data given here to find a regression equation to predict yield from amount of fertilizer employed. Then calculate the correlation coefficient between the 2 variables, and determine if it is significant at a 0.05 level of significance. Data are given in hundred-weight for fertilizer and tons for corn.

Fertilizer	8.3	9.2	7.7	8.4	8.8	9.6	10.3	8.7	9.1	9.4
Yield	13.6	15.4	12.8	13.4	14.6	15.8	15.5	14.1	14.9	15.6

2. The data that follows were obtained from student records. Calculate the correlation coefficient for the data and test its significance.

Subject	Grade-Point Average	Graduate Record Exam Score
1	2.34	910
2	3.61	1,340
3	3.08	1,160
4	2.77	1,420
5	3.13	960
6	2.54	830
7	2.47	940
8	2.38	1,060
9	2.91	1,230
10	3.17	1,080
11	3.28	940
12	2.08	760
13	3.14	1,110
14	3.03	880
15	2.86	1,040
16	2.89	1,320
17	3.13	940
18	2.07	1,020
19	2.71	780
20	2.64	970

3. A medical researcher measures the blood sugar level of cross country runners immediately before and after the race. He wishes to discover whether there is any correlation between the differences (before and after) and success in the race. The race has eighteen entrants. All runners had a net decrease in blood sugar levels after the race. Estimate if there is any correlation (at a 0.01 level of significance) if the following are the net decreases of the eighteen entrants in the order of finish, first to last: 10.8; 11.7; 9.7; 9.4; 10.3; 11.2; 8.8; 10.2; 7.4; 8.1; 7.7; 9.2; 6.4; 8.3; 9.4; 7.3; 6.1; 8.3.

4. A statistician noted that he threw a pair of dice, one red, one green, five times and received the following pairs: 5-4, 3-3, 6-4, 5-5, 2-4. Calculate the correlation coefficient relating the two dice if they are listed red first. Is this result surprising? Is it significant?

5. The top and bottom numbers which may appear on a die are as follows:

Top	1	2	3	4	5	6
Bottom	6	5	4	3	2	1

Calculate r for these values. Are the results surprising?

6. A horse owner is investigating the relationship between weight carried and the finish position of several horses in his stable. Calculate r and determine if it is significant.

Weight Carried	Position Finished
110	2
113	6
120	3
115	4
110	6
115	5
117	4
123	2
106	1
108	4
110	1
110	3
120	5
105	7
115	1
110	2
115	4
103	1
118	3
115	2
110	7
115	6
105	2
110	3

10.4 FORECASTING AND ANALYSIS OF VARIANCE IN LINEAR REGRESSION

A primary purpose for using regression is in predicting a value of the dependent variable from the independent variable. An attempt to predict values of y from values of x is called **forecasting**. Two types of forecasting are widely used: predicting a mean value of y for all future values of a given x, and predicting an individual value of y from an individual value of x. The former case is most useful when values of x are restricted to specific sets. As an example of this, suppose that a study is to be conducted to study the effectiveness of training in sales techniques. A total of eighteen new salesmen are given a training program ranging from five to thirty hours, in increments of five hours (three to a group) and the number of sales during their first month after the training program is recorded. Results were as follows.

Salesman	Hours of Training	First Month Sales
1	5	8
2	5	11
3	5	6
4	10	12
5	10	9
6	10	7
7	15	15
8	15	13
9	15	18
10	20	23
11	20	27
12	20	19
13	25	28
14	25	21
15	25	23
16	30	28
17	30	31
18	30	30

We proceed with the analysis by obtaining the regression equation $\hat{y} = 2.444 + 0.905x$. The correlation between the two variables is $r \doteq 0.939$. The standard error of estimate is $s_e \doteq 2.992$, the standard error of the regression coefficient is $s_b \doteq 0.083$. An interpretation of the equation could be that, on the average, a salesman with no training would sell 2.444 units, and each additional hour of training would be expected to produce an additional 0.905 units. This is a loose interpretation, of course, but we can make some prediction with it. For example, 10 hours of training would be expected to produce about 11.49 sales units. This is a point estimate for $E(y|x)$ where $x = 10$. An interval estimate for $E(y|x)$ would probably be more useful. Since sample regression equations will differ depending upon the precise makeup of the sample, point estimates for $E(y|x)$ will also vary, but will have a mean equal to $E(y|x)$, for a particular x, and will be normally distributed with a standard deviation symbolized by $\sigma_{E(y|x)}$. Since this would be dependent upon knowing the population parameters, a $(1 - \alpha)$ confidence interval for $E(y|x)$ is found by using $s_{E(y|x)}$ as an estimate for $\sigma_{E(y|x)}$ and the t-distribution where the value of $s_{E(y|x)}$ is given by the following.

Standard Error of Estimated Mean

$$s_{E(y|x)} = s_e \sqrt{\frac{1}{n} + \frac{(x - \bar{x})^2}{SSX}}$$

where s_e is the standard error of estimate for the sample, $\bar{x}$ is the mean of the x variable for the sample, n is the number in the sample, SSX is the adjusted sum of squares for x for the sample, and x is the particular value of x for which prediction of y is to be made. A $(1-\alpha)$ confidence interval for the value of $E(y|x)$, then, has confidence limits $\hat{y}\pm t_{\alpha/2}s_{E(y|x)}$ where both $\hat{y}$ and $s_{E(y|x)}$ are computed for a particular value of x. Thus for $n=18$, in the above example, $s_{E(y|x)}=2.992\sqrt{(1/18)+(x-17.5)^2/1312.5}$ for any given value of x. In particular, to determine a 95% confidence interval for the mean sales of all salesmen with ten hours of training, we find that $\hat{y}=11.49$ is the point estimate, with $t=2.120$ for 16 degrees of freedom, and, substituting in 10 for x, we obtain $s_{E(y|x)}\doteq0.939$, so that $11.49-(2.120)(0.939)$ and $11.49+(2.120)(0.939)$, or 9.50 and 13.48, are 95% confidence limits for the expected number (or mean number) of sales for salesmen with ten hours of training; that is, 9.50 to 13.48 is a 95% confidence interval for $E(y|x)$ if $x=10$.

A forecast interval for an *individual* value of x must also take into account the scatter of terms about the regression line. The standard error of forecast for an individual x is approximated by s_f, where s_f is given by the following formula.

Standard Error of Forecast	$$s_f=s_e\sqrt{1+\frac{1}{n}+\frac{(x-\bar{x})^2}{SSX}}$$

The symbols on the right side mean the same as in the preceding formula. Note that both standard errors increase as the values of x get further away from the mean of x. This is so because the sample regression equation is more reliable in the vicinity of $(\bar{x},\bar{y})$ than anywhere else. A 95% confidence interval for the mean sales of an *individual* salesman with ten hours of training would have the same values of $\hat{y}$ and t as above, 11.49 and 2.120, but we would have $s_f\doteq3.136$ so that the confidence limits are $11.49-(2.120)(3.136)$ and $11.49+(2.120)(3.136)$, and a 95% confidence interval for sales of a salesman with ten hours of training is 6.65 to 18.14. A representative graph of forecast intervals is shown below.

The dotted lines represent a confidence interval for sample scatter obtained from s_e. An additional standard error term can also be obtained and used. When predicting future values of y from a particular value of x, $s_{E(y|x)}$ is the standard error for the mean value of y, while s_f is the standard error for one value. If we wish to obtain a confidence interval for the mean of the next m values of y for a particular value of x, such a confidence interval will be centered at $\hat{y}$ (for that value of x), and have a standard error given by $s_e\sqrt{1/m+1/n+(x-\bar{x})^2/SSX}$. We again use $t_{\alpha/2}$ with $n-2$ degrees of freedom. Note that this is totally consistent with the others since if $m=1$ we obtain s_f and if m is infinitely large (*all* future values of y), $1/m$ is zero and we obtain $s_{E(y|x)}$.

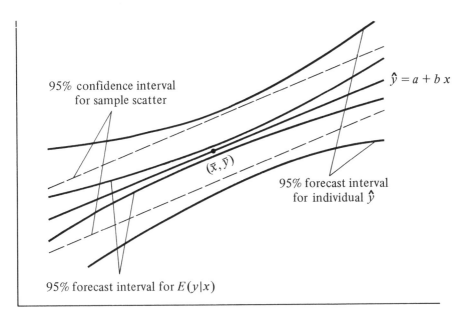

95% confidence interval
for sample scatter

$\hat{y} = a + bx$

$(\bar{x}, \bar{y})$

95% forecast interval
for individual $\hat{y}$

95% forecast interval for $E(y|x)$

EXAMPLE 1   Determine 95% forecast intervals for the mean first month's sales of all salesmen receiving 5, 15, and 30 hours instruction; determine a 95% forecast interval for the mean first month's sales for the next five salesmen receiving 10 hours of instruction; and determine a 95% forecast interval for the first month's sales of Fred Jones, who has just completed 20 hours of instruction.

SOLUTION   Important values needed here are $s_e \doteq 2.992$, $\bar{x} = 17.5$, $SSX = 1,312.5$, $n = 18$, $t_{.025} = 2.120$ (with 16 df), and $s_{E(y|x)} \doteq 2.992\sqrt{1/18 + (x - 17.5)^2/1,312.5}$. For $x = 5$, $\hat{y} \doteq 6.97$, $s_{E(y|x)} \doteq 1.250$, $t_{.025} \cdot s_{E(y|x)} = (2.120)(1.250) \doteq 2.65$, so a 95% forecast interval for $E(y|5)$ is 4.32 to 9.62 sales. For $x = 15$, $\hat{y} \doteq 16.02$, $s_{E(y|x)} \doteq 0.735$, $t_{.025} \cdot s_{E(y|x)} \doteq 1.56$, so a 95% forecast interval for $E(y|15)$ is 14.46 to 17.58. For $x = 30$, $\hat{y} \doteq 29.59$, $s_{E(y|x)} \doteq 1.250$, $t_{.025} \cdot s_{E(y|x)} \doteq 2.65$, so a 95% forecast interval for $E(y|30)$ is 26.94 to 32.24.

To obtain a forecast interval for the mean first month's sales of the next five salesmen receiving ten hours of instruction, we have $\hat{y} = 11.49$, the standard error is $2.992\sqrt{1/5 + 1/18 + (-7.5)^2/1,312.5}$ or about 1.634. Then $(2.120)(1.634) \doteq 3.47$, so a 95% forecast interval is 8.02 to 14.96 for those five salesmen.

For Fred Jones, $\hat{y} \doteq 20.54$, $s_f \doteq 2.992\sqrt{1 + 1/18 + (2.5)^2/1,312.5}$ or about 3.081; $(2.120)(3.081) \doteq 6.53$. Thus a 95% forecast interval for Fred Jones' first month sales is 14.01 to 27.07.

An additional bonus is possible if each value of x in the sample corresponds to at least two data points. Analysis of variance can be performed on the data to test the hypothesis of linearity. Each of the different values of x will correspond to a treatment, and TSS and SSE can be calculated as in one-way analysis of variance. The SST, however, consists of two parts; the sum of squares due to linearity, and the sum of squares due to nonlinearity. These latter two are symbolized SSR and SSD for sums of squares due to, respectively, regression, and deviation from linearity. SSR is the sum of the squared deviations $(\hat{y}-\bar{y})^2$, while SSD is the sum of the squared deviations of treatment means from the values on the regression line. Fortunately, an easy way exists to find both of these; $SSR = r^2 TSS$, and $SSD = SST - SSR$, or $SSD = TSS - SSR - SSE$. Degrees of freedom are equal to one for regression, $k-2$ for deviation from linearity, $n-k$ for error, and $n-1$ overall. An analysis of variance table, then, is the following.

Source of Variation	df	SS	MS	F
Linear Regression	1	SSR	SSR	MSR/MSE
Deviation from Linearity	$k-2$	SSD	$SSD/(k-2)$	MSD/MSE
Error	$n-k$	SSE	$SSE/(n-k)$	
Total	$n-1$	TSS		

The F-ratios obtained are checks for linearity, if greater than $F_\alpha(1, n-k)$, or nonlinearity, if greater than $F_\alpha(k-2, n-k)$. If the F for deviation is not significant, SSD and SSE can be combined, as well as the degrees of freedom, to form a new mean square, $(SSD + SSE)/(n-2)$. The F obtained by dividing SSR by this mean square will be the square of the t-values obtained by $t = b/s_b$ and $t = r\sqrt{(n-2)/(1-r^2)}$. Thus, if there is no evidence of deviation from linearity, all three tests are equivalent.

EXAMPLE 2   Perform analysis of variance on the data of example 1 to determine whether there is evidence of nonlinearity.

SOLUTION   The sums for the various treatments are 25, 28, 46, 69, 72, and 89. The sum of the squares of individual values is 7,231, and the total of all the values is 329. Then $TSS = 7,231 - (329)^2/18 \doteq 1,217.611$. $SSE = 7,231 - (25^2 + 28^2 + 46^2 + 69^2 + 72^2 + 89^2)/3 \doteq 100.667$. Then $SSR = (0.946)^2(1,217.611) \doteq 1,089.660$ and $SSD \doteq 27.284$.

The analysis is summarized below.

Source of Variation	df	SS	MS	F
Linear Regression	1	1,089.660	1,089.660	129.89[a]
Deviation from linearity	4	27.284	6.821	0.81
Error	12	100.667	8.389	
Total	17	1,217.611		
$F_{.01}(1, 12) = 9.33$			[a]Significant beyond the 0.01 level.	
$F_{.05}(4, 12) = 3.26$				

Since there is no evidence of nonlinearity, and there is evidence of linearity, we conclude that a straight line is a good fit for the data. Combining the two sums of squares, we have $(27.284 + 100.667)/16 \doteq 7.997$ and $1,089.660/7.997 \doteq 136.26$, which, with 1 and 16 degrees of freedom, is highly significant. Note that $\sqrt{136.26} \doteq 11.67$. In this regression analysis, $b \doteq 0.94$, $s_b \doteq 0.08$, and $0.94/0.08 \doteq 11.75$. The minor difference between the two is due to rounding. (Actually, $b \doteq 0.9355$, $s_b \doteq 0.0798$, etc.)

> **EXAMPLE 3** Using the data of example 2, section 10.2, construct a 90% forecast interval for electricity usage on a day when the mean temperature was 85°.

SOLUTION   Here $n = 52$, $s_e \doteq 3.189$, $SSX = 1,644.85$, $\bar{x} \doteq 80.54°$. Then $\hat{y}(85) = -65.140 + 1.328(85) = 47.74$ thousand KWH; $s_{\hat{y}(85)} = 3.189\sqrt{1 + 1/52 + (85 - 80.54)^2/1,644.85} \doteq 3.239$; $z_{.05} = 1.645$, so $(3.239)(1.645) \doteq 5.33$. The confidence limits, then, are $47.74 - 5.33$ and $47.74 + 5.33$, or 42.41 to 53.07. We thus have a 90% degree of confidence that, on a day when the temperature averages 85°, electricity usage will range between 42,410 and 53,070 KWH.

•Problems

1. Use the weight-blood pressure data of section 10.1, revisited in example 1 of section 10.2. Obtain a 95% forecast interval for the blood pressure of men weighing 180 pounds. Find a 99% forecast interval for the blood pressure of a man who weighs 200 pounds.

2. Use the data of problem 2, section 10.1 and 10.2 to obtain 95% forecast intervals for the height of all trees planted 100 feet from the ditch; for ten trees planted 100 feet from the ditch; and for one tree planted 100 feet from the ditch.

3. Use the data of problem 2, section 10.3, to obtain a 95% forecast interval for the Graduate Record Examination score of a single student with a GPA of 2.00, 2.50, 3.00, 3.50, and 4.00. Minimum and maximum possible values for GRE scores are, respectively, 200 and 1800.

4. The management of a large corporation decided to try reducing the price of its leading product in order to increase sales and therefore profits. Careful records were kept regarding sales and profits for six months preceding the experiment. Fifty widely separated retail outlets were selected to try the experiment. Reductions were randomly assigned from $2.00 to $10.00 per unit in increments of $2.00, and sales observed over three months, and the amount of change in net proceeds observed as a percentage increase or

decrease compared with the average of the preceding six months. Changes were adjusted to reflect differences in time periods. Obtain a regression equation for the data and analyze completely. Perform an analysis of variance on the regression model and obtain 95% forecast intervals for the mean expected percent of net proceeds in all outlets for each value of the independent variable.

Outlet	Reduction ($)	Percent Change in net
1	2	+5.1
2	2	−1.3
3	2	+4.4
4	2	+0.6
5	2	−0.4
6	2	+4.7
7	2	+3.2
8	2	+0.6
9	2	+1.9
10	2	+6.3
11	4	−1.4
12	4	+8.6
13	4	+1.8
14	4	+2.1
15	4	−1.7
16	4	+7.7
17	4	+3.6
18	4	−2.5
19	4	+5.6
20	4	+3.8
21	6	−11.2
22	6	+3.1
23	6	−2.4
24	6	+5.8
25	6	+0.3
26	6	−3.2
27	6	+1.3
28	6	+2.1
29	6	−3.2
30	6	−0.4
31	8	−7.2
32	8	+0.1
33	8	−1.6
34	8	−2.1

Outlet	Reduction ($)	Percent Change in net
35	8	−6.8
36	8	−7.2
37	8	−2.2
38	8	+4.2
39	8	−3.6
40	8	−1.5
41	10	−3.9
42	10	−8.6
43	10	−5.3
44	10	−9.3
45	10	−1.5
46	10	−3.2
47	10	−4.1
48	10	−0.9
49	10	+12.3
50	10	−3.1

10.5 CURVILINEAR REGRESSION (OPTIONAL)

The preceding portion of this chapter has been devoted to sets of data in which there is a linear trend. Quite often, if the data are plotted in a scattergram, some nonlinear trends are noticeable. In addition, analysis of variance on the regression model which yields a significant F for deviation from linearity (even if the F for linearity is significant) indicates that there is some curvilinear trend.

One of the types of curves most frequently encountered may be termed a curve with a point of diminishing return. Such a curve would be one which increases to a point, then decreases.

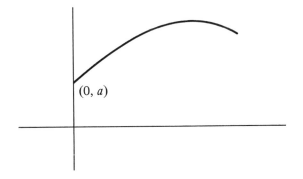

Such a curve is called a *parabola*, and has a regression equation $y = a + b_1 x + b_2 x^2$. For data which follows such a curve, the set of normal equations is as follows.

$$\sum y = na + b_1 \sum x + b_2 \sum x^2$$

$$\sum xy = a \sum x + b_1 \sum x^2 + b_2 \sum x^3$$

$$\sum x^2 y = a \sum x^2 + b_1 \sum x^3 + b_2 \sum x^4$$

These equations can be simplified somewhat by using deviation form data. We then have

$$SSXY = b_1 SSX + b_2 \left(\sum x^3 - \sum x \sum x^2 / n \right)$$

$$\left(\sum x^2 y - \sum x^2 \sum y / n \right) = b_1 \left(\sum x^3 - \sum x \sum x^2 / n \right) + b_2 \left(\sum x^4 - \left\{ \sum x^2 \right\}^2 / n \right)$$

and

$$a = \left(\sum y - b_1 \sum x - b_2 \sum x^2 \right) / n$$

If the curve opens downward, as in the figure above, b_2 is negative; if it opens upward, b_2 is positive.

Two other curves widely encountered are the exponential and logarithmic. Exponential curves are called growth and decay functions. A growth function is one which starts out slowly and increases rapidly after a point, and has the equation $y = b^x$ or $y = a(b^x)$ with b positive, and greater than one.

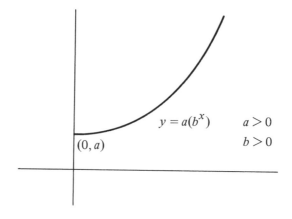

$$y = a(b^x) \qquad a > 0$$
$$b > 0$$

$(0, a)$

A decay function is one which decreases rapidly at first, and then more slowly. It also has the form $y = b^x$ or $y = a(b^x)$, but b is positive and less than one.

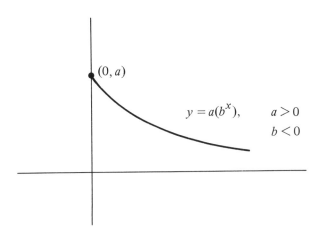

$(0, a)$

$$y = a(b^x), \qquad a > 0$$
$$b < 0$$

The equation $y = a(b^x)$ is equivalent to $\log y = \log a + x \log b$. An exponential equation can be found by using the linear regression formulas, replacing y by $\log y$ in every case. The values obtained for the constants will be $\log b$ and $\log a$, so they must be transformed by the formulas $a = 10^{\log a}, y = 10^{\log b}$. If a calculator with ln and e^x keys is available, use $\ln y = \ln a + x \ln b$, replacing y by $\ln y$ in every case and using $a = e^{\ln a}, b = e^{\ln b}$.

A curve which grows rapidly, then levels off, is a logarithmic function, $y = a + b \log x$, with b positive. If b is negative, the curve drops rapidly.

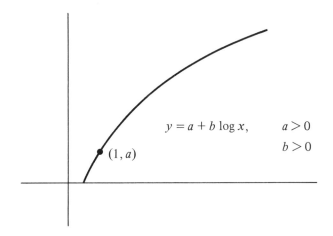

$$y = a + b \log x, \qquad a > 0$$
$$b > 0$$

$(1, a)$

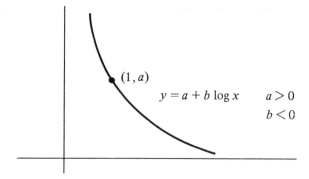

$$y = a + b \log x \qquad a > 0$$
$$b < 0$$

(1, a)

The plotting of such curves as the exponential and logarithmic can be facilitated by the use of semilogarithmic graph paper in which one axis is logarithmic, the other is the usual set of numbers. If the graph plotted on such paper appears to be a straight line, the best fit is either exponential or logarithmic. If the x axis is the usual one and the y axis is logarithmic, then the function is exponential; if the x axis is logarithmic and the y axis is the usual one, the function is logarithmic. Many other functions are possible and they are more properly the province of a calculus-based course.

If more than one curve appears possible as the best-fitting for a set of data, each possible curve should be obtained. In each case, calculate the standard error of estimate, $s_e = \sqrt{\sum (y - \hat{y})^2 / (n - k)}$, where k is the number of coefficients in the regression equation. The equation for which s_e is the smallest is the best fit.

This section will conclude with a rather lengthy example. Suppose that a manufacturer wishes to determine the optimum lot size for manufacturing a product and determine a regression equation for predicting unit cost from lot size. He produces four lots each of 500, 1,000, 1,500, 2,000, 2,500, and 3,000, obtaining the following per unit cost for each lot.

Lot size	Unit cost (cents)			
500	5.2,	4.9,	5.4,	5.2
1000	3.8,	4.1,	4.3,	4.0
1500	3.5,	3.3,	3.2,	3.4
2000	2.7,	2.3,	3.1,	2.8,
2500	1.9,	2.0,	2.2,	2.1
3000	2.6,	2.5,	2.7,	2.6

Analysis of variance could be performed on the data, of course, to determine exactly where and what differences exist. Since lot size is given in numbers, however, regression analysis is also appropriate. We rewrite the data as follows. The lot size, the independent variable, is called x, and the unit cost, the dependent variable, is y. We consider lot size in hundreds, to minimize the arithmetic, and have the following.

x (Lot size, hundreds)	y (unit cost, cents)
5	5.2
5	4.9
5	5.4
5	5.2
10	3.8
10	4.1
10	4.3
10	4.0
15	3.5
15	3.3
15	3.2
15	3.4
20	2.7
20	2.3
20	3.1
20	2.8
25	1.9
25	2.0
25	2.2
25	2.1
30	2.6
30	2.5
30	2.7
30	2.6

$n = 24$, $\sum x = 420$, $\sum x^2 = 9,100$, $\sum y = 79.8$, $\sum y^2 = 291.88$, $\sum xy = 1,201.5$,

$SSX = 1,750$, $SSY = 26.545$, $SSXY = -195$

Then $b = -195/1,750 \doteq -0.11143$, $a = 5.275$, so the regression equation is $\hat{y} = 5.275 - 0.111x$. The correlation coefficient is $r = -195/\sqrt{(1.750)(26.545)} \doteq -0.9047$. Then $s_e = \sqrt{26.545 - b(-195)/22} \doteq 0.468$. Since $s_b \doteq 0.468/\sqrt{1,750} \doteq 0.0112$, $b/s_b \doteq 9.963$ which is highly significant. If a scattergram is plotted, however, we see that not all is quite as simple; analysis of variance on the regression model also leads to a similar conclusion. The sums of the values of y in the six groups are, respectively, 20.7, 16.2, 13.2, 10.9, 8.2, and 10.4. $TSS = 26.545$, so $SSR = (-0.9047)^2(26.545) \doteq 21.727$. $SSE = 291.88 - (20.7^2 + 16.2^2 + 13.2^2 + \cdots + 10.4^2)/4 = 2.035$. Then $SSD = 26.545 - 21.727 - 2.035 = 2.783$. The analysis can be summarized as follows:

Source of variation	df	SS	MS	F
Linear Regression	1	21.727	21.727	192.274[a]
Deviation from linearity	4	2.783	0.696	6.159[a]
Error	18	2.035	0.113	
Total	23	16.545		

$F_{.01}(1,18) = 8.29$; $F_{.01}(4,18) = 4.58$
[a]Significant beyond the 0.01 level.

The analysis shows the presence of both linear and nonlinear trends. This probably means that there is considerable linearity in part of the data, but nonlinearity in the remainder. A scattergram will help to show the trend.

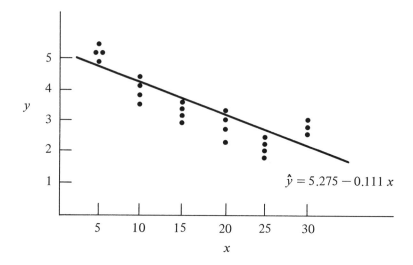

$\hat{y} = 5.275 - 0.111\,x$

To help sharpen the graphical analysis, we look at the mean of each group. In data in which the groups are not so sharply separated, we can group the data, then take the mean of the groups at the class mark to help draw the graph.

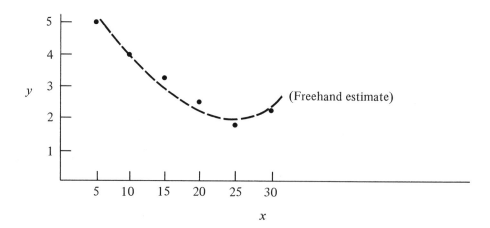

(Freehand estimate)

Since the data show a curve with one bend in it (called a relative minimum), we may have a parabola. This would be an equation of the form $\hat{y} = a + b_1 x + b_2 x^2$. In order to solve the normal equations, we also need $\sum x^3$, $\sum x^4$, and $\sum x^2y$. Now $\sum x^3 = 4(5^3 + 10^3 + \cdots + 30^3) = 220,500$, and $\sum x^4 = 4(5^4 + 10^4 + \cdots + 30^4) = 5,687,500$, and $\sum x^2y = 5^2(5.2) + 5^2(4.9) + \cdots + 30^2(2.6) = 23,997.5$. The normal equations, then, are

$$79.8 = 24a + 420b_1 + 9,100b_2$$

$$1,201.5 = 420a + 9,100b_1 + 220,500b_2$$

$$23,997.5 = 9,100a + 220,500b_1 + 5,687,500b_2$$

The modified equations (student please check) are

$$-195 = 1,750b_1 + 61,250b_2$$

$$-6,260 = 61,250b_1 + 2,237,083.333b_2$$

Multiplying the first equation by 35 ($61,250/1,750 = 35$), we have

$$-6,825 = 61,250b_1 + 2,143,750b_2$$

or $\qquad\qquad 6,825 = -61,250b_1 - 2,143,750b_2.$

Adding $\qquad -6,260 = 61,250b_1 + 2,237,083.333b_2$ we have

$$565 = \qquad\qquad 93,333.333b_2 \text{ so that}$$

$$b_2 \doteq 0.00605.$$

Substituting in either equation and solving, we have

$$b_1 \doteq -0.3232$$

and then

$$a = (79.8 + (0.3232)(420) - (0.00605)(9,100))/24$$

$$\doteq 6.687.$$

The regression equation, then, is $\hat{y} = 6.687 - 0.3232x + 0.00605x^2$. For a parabola, the standard error of estimate is

$$s_e = \sqrt{\frac{\sum y^2 - a\sum y - b_1\sum xy - b_2\sum x^2y}{n-3}}$$

$$= \sqrt{\frac{SSY - b_1 SSXY - b_2(\sum x^2y - \sum x^2 \sum y/n)}{n-3}}$$

where $SSX^2Y = \sum x^2y - \sum x^2 \sum y / n$. In this case we have

$$s_e = \sqrt{\frac{291.88 - (6.687)(79.8) - (-0.3232)(1,201.5) - (0.00605)(23,997.5)}{21}}$$

or

$$s_e = \sqrt{\frac{26.545 - (-0.3232)(-195) - (0.00605)(-6,260)}{21}}$$

$$\doteq 0.258$$

depending upon which formula is used. In either case, $s_e \doteq 0.258$, which is about half the size of the standard error obtained by using the regression line. From the data and the results, then, it would appear that the optimum lot size is 2,500 and the best regression equation is probably $\hat{y} = 6.687 - 0.3232x + 0.00605x^2$.

•Problems

1. In the salesman-training example of the preceding section, analysis showed that the evidence of a nonlinear trend was negligible. Nevertheless, find the equation of a parabola which fits the data and compare the s_e for the parabola with the s_e for the line. Which is the better fit?

2. Use the data of problem 1, section 10.1, to determine a parabola which fits the data. Compare with the regression line and calculate s_e for both regression equations to determine the better fit.

3. Use the data of problem 1, section 10.3, to plot a scattergram and draw a line which seems to fit. Derive a regression equation and test its significance. Calculate s_e. Sketch a curve through the same points. Derive a parabolic regression equation and test the significance of its coefficients if $s_{b_1} = s_e / \sqrt{SSX}$ and $s_{b_2} = s_e / \sqrt{\sum x^4 - (\sum x^2)^2 / n}$. Use the values of s_e to determine which is the better fit.

10.6 MULTIPLE REGRESSION (OPTIONAL)

Quite often more than one independent variable may have an influence, or may appear to have an influence upon a dependent variable. Regression analysis in such a situation may also be helpful.

If $x_1, x_2, x_3, \ldots, x_r$ are r independent variables, and y is a variable dependent upon these, a regression equation may be obtained in a manner analogous to the preceding sections. The simplest such equation is a linear equation,

$$\hat{y} = a + b_1 x_1 + b_2 x_2 + b_3 x_3 + \ldots + b_r x_r$$

Least squares analysis will yield the following normal equations:

$$\sum y = na + b_1 \sum x_1 + b_2 \sum x_2 + \ldots + b_r \sum x_r$$

$$\sum x_1 y = a \sum x_1 + b_1 \sum x_1^2 + b_2 \sum x_1 x_2 + \ldots + b_r \sum x_1 x_r$$

$$\sum x_2 y = a \sum x_2 + b_1 \sum x_1 x_2 + b_2 \sum x_2^2 + \ldots + b_r \sum x_2 x_r$$

$$\vdots \qquad \vdots \qquad \vdots$$

$$\sum x_r y = a \sum x_r + b_1 \sum x_1 x_r + b_2 \sum x_2 x_r + \ldots + b_r \sum x_r^2$$

These equations can be simplified if we use the adjusted sums of squares. Let $SSX_i = \sum x_i^2 - \left(\sum x_i\right)^2 / n,$

$SSX_i Y = \sum x_i y - \left(\sum x_i\right)\left(\sum y\right)/n$, and $SSX_i X_j = \sum x_i x_j - \left(\sum x_i\right)\left(\sum x_j\right)/n.$

Then

$$SSX_1 Y = b_1 SSX_1 + b_2 SSX_1 X_2 + \ldots + b_r SSX_1 X_r$$

$$SSX_2 Y = b_1 SSX_1 X_2 + b_2 SSX_2 + \ldots + b_r SSX_2 X_r$$

$$\vdots \qquad \vdots \qquad \vdots$$

$$SSX_r Y = b_1 SSX_1 X_r + b_2 SSX_2 X_r + \ldots + b_r SSX_r$$

and

$$a = \left(\sum y - b_1 \sum x_1 - b_2 \sum x_2 - \cdots - b_r \sum x_r\right)/n.$$

The standard error of estimate is given by

$$s_e = \sqrt{\frac{SSY - b_1 SSX_1 Y - b_2 SSX_2 Y - \cdots - b_r SSX_r Y}{n - r - 1}}$$

or

$$= \sqrt{\frac{\sum y^2 - a \sum y - b_1 \sum x_1 y - b_2 \sum x_2 y - \cdots - b_r \sum x_r y}{n - r - 1}}$$

A coefficient of multiple determination and one of multiple correlation can also be calculated to estimate the proportion of variance of y explained by the various factors. For a sample, if R is the coefficient of multiple correlation,

$$R = \sqrt{1 - \frac{(n-r-1)s_e^2}{SSY}} \; = \sqrt{\frac{b_1 SSX_1 Y + b_2 SSX_2 Y + \cdots + b_r SSX_r Y}{SSY}}$$

Of more interest are the correlations between pairs of variables, the *intercorrelations*. Let r_{0i} represent the correlation between y and the variable x_i, and r_{ij} represent the correlation between x_i and x_j. As usual, $r_{0i} = SSX_i Y / \sqrt{(SSX_i)(SSY)}$, $r_{ij} = SSX_i X_j / \sqrt{(SSX_i)(SSX_j)}$. A high value of r_{0i} indicates that that variable has influence on y, while a low value indicates that the variable does not. Of even more consequence are the values of r_{ij}. One of the assumptions of the linear model is that pairs of variables are uncorrelated. High correlation between two variables means that one of the variables is probably a function of the other and can be replaced by that function; that is, one of the variables can be eliminated, the one of the two which has a lower correlation with y.

Computer programs are available for multiple linear regression models which print out the intercorrelations as well as the multiple regression equation. See for example Spurr and Bonini, *Statistical Analysis for Business Decisions* (Irwin, 1973), Chapter 17. This section will conclude with an example with two independent variables.

EXAMPLE 1   The following data were obtained on usage of power at a manufacturing plant. Y represents number of thousands of KWH of electricity used in a particular day, x_1 represents average temperature during the 16-hour working day, and x_2 represents output of the plant in thousands of units. Develop a regression equation for usage of electricity and analyze the results.

Day	MKWH (y)	Av. Temp. (x_1)	Output (x_2)
1	11.76	81.8	117.7
2	10.84	80.6	118.2
3	12.74	84.4	123.4
4	9.88	79.7	102.7
5	13.66	85.9	106.2
6	10.39	81.5	105.7
7	12.44	85.8	107.6
8	10.89	78.9	108.1
9	12.16	83.7	110.6
10	11.43	85.2	117.9

SOLUTION   We have the following sums.

$\sum x_1 = 827.5$ $\sum x_1^2 = 68,535.69$ $\sum x_2 = 1,118.1$ $\sum x_2^2 = 125,446.45$

$\sum y = 116.19$ $\sum y^2 = 1{,}362.1291$ $\sum x_1 x_2 = 92{,}555.53$ $\sum x_1 y = 9{,}636.744$

$\sum x_2 y = 13{,}009.393$ and $n = 10$

Adjusted sums of squares are as follows;

$SSX_1 = 60.06$, $SSX_2 = 431.689$, $SSY = 12.11749$, $SSX_1 X_2 = 32.755$,

$SSX_1 Y = 22.0215$ $SSX_2 Y = 18.1891$

The normal equations are

$$116.19 = 10a + 827.5 b_1 + 1{,}118.1 b_2$$

$$9{,}636.744 = 827.5a + 68{,}535.69 b_1 + 92{,}555.53 b_2$$

$$13{,}009.393 = 1{,}118.1a + 92{,}555.53 b_1 + 125{,}446.45 b_2$$

Adjusted equations are

$$22.0215 = 60.06 b_1 + 32.755 b_2$$

$$18.1891 = 32.755 b_1 + 431.689 b_2$$

Multiplying the first equation by 32.755 and the second by 60.06,

$$721.3142325 = 1{,}967.2653 b_1 + 1{,}072.890025 b_2$$

$$1{,}092.437346 = 1{,}967.2653 b_1 + 25{,}927.24134 b_2$$

Subtracting the first equation from the second we get

$$371.1231135 = 24{,}854.35132 b_2$$

so that $b_2 = 371.1231135/24{,}854.35132 \doteq 0.014931917 \doteq 0.01493$. We carry all calculations through using all available decimal places, then round the answers at the end. Substituting in the first equation we have

$$22.0215 = 60.06 b_1 + 32.755(0.014931917)$$

$$22.0215 = 60.06 b_1 + 0.489094945$$

$$21.53240506 = 60.06 b_1$$

$$b_1 = 21.53240506/60.06 \doteq 0.358514903 \doteq 0.3585$$

We check this in the second equation. Using the rounded values it checks satisfactorily; using more decimal places, it checks almost exactly.

$$\text{Then } a = \frac{116.19 - 0.3585(827.5) - 0.01493(1,118.1)}{10}$$

$$\doteq -19.7176 \text{ (using calculator values)}$$

The regression equation, then, is

$$y = -19.7176 + 0.3585x_1 + 0.01493x_2$$

It should be noted that the relative magnitude of the b coefficients does not indicate their relative importance in influencing y. A method of assessing the relative importance is to use the ratio $b_1\sqrt{SSX_1}\,/b_2\sqrt{SSX_2}$. Each coefficient is then adjusted in terms of its own units. Here the ratio is equal to $0.3585(\sqrt{60.06}\,)/0.01493(\sqrt{431.689}\,) \doteq 8.95557$; this indicates that x_1 has nearly nine times the influence of x_2. Using standard errors of the coefficients as in previous sections would bear this out. The correlations are $r_{01} = 22.0215/\sqrt{(60.06)(12.11749)} \doteq 0.816$, $r_{02} = 18.1891/\sqrt{(431.689)(12.11749)} \doteq 0.251$; the first is significant, the second is not. The intercorrelation is $r_{12} \doteq 0.203$, which is not significant. Thus the assumption that the independent variables are not correlated seems valid. However, the amount of production is seen to have little influence on power consumption, so we might well use a linear regression equation with just x_1 as the independent variable. This can be found to be $\hat{y} = -18.650 + 0.3667x_1$. For this equation the standard error of estimate is $s_e = \sqrt{(12.11749 - 0.3667(22.0215))/8} \doteq 0.711$. For the multiple regression equation, the standard error is

$$s_e = \sqrt{(12.11749 - 0.3585(22.0215) - 0.01493(18.1891))/7} \doteq 0.751.$$

Since the standard error is less for the line than for the multiple equation, we conclude that the line is a better fit. This does not rule out the possibility, however, that a curvilinear equation might be an even better fit.

•Problems

1. It had been hypothesized that two drugs were both helpful in the treatment of a disease. The correct amount of each drug to give had not been determined, and it was also considered likely that a combination of the

drugs would be most helpful. Injections were started as soon as possible after admission and continued until the patient was out of danger; that is, until the patient had reached satisfactory condition in the judgment of the attending physician. In order to minimize problems of other variables, all conditions were kept as similar as possible; same physician, same nursing staff, etc. The time of day, of year, etc., was impossible to control, of course. Given the following results, construct a multiple regression equation for predicting time to recovery, calculate s_e, R, and all correlations. What conclusions can you draw?

Patient Number	Drug 1 (ml) x_1	Drug 2 (ml) x_2	Hours to satisfactory condition
1	0	5	46
2	0	10	40
3	0	15	38
4	0	20	35
5	5	5	41
6	5	10	36
7	5	15	35
8	5	20	33
9	10	5	39
10	10	10	34
11	10	15	30
12	10	20	33
13	15	5	42
14	15	10	33
15	15	15	34
16	15	20	35

2. The data of the preceding problem can also be treated as a randomized complete block, although it is not actually a block design, really two-factors. Analyze using analysis of variance. What is the superiority of regression over analysis of variance in this case?

3. A multiple regression equation was obtained as follows:

$$\hat{y} = 21.4 + 0.32x_1 - 0.044x_2 + 113.2x_3 + 81.44x_4 - 13.1x_5$$

The intercorrelation matrix is given below. The correlation between pairs of variables is given by the intersection of the row and column so numbered; y is variable 0. For example, $r_{24} = -0.1320$.

Variable Number	0	1	2	3	4	5
0	1.0000	0.4123	−0.7143	0.6731	0.0234	−0.5628
1		1.0000	−0.0143	0.8230	0.0451	−0.0387
2			1.0000	−0.3013	−0.1320	0.1349
3				1.0000	0.2041	−0.5011
4					1.0000	−0.0043
5						1.0000

(a) Which variable seems to have the most effect on y?

(b) Which variable could most likely be eliminated simply by dropping it from consideration?

(c) Which variable could probably be eliminated by combining it with another variable? Which other variable?

10.7 SUMMARY

Regression analysis and correlation analysis can be performed on data classified in two or more categories. A regression equation is a function of one or more independent variables which is used to predict values of some dependent variable. If both the dependent and independent variables can be considered as random samples, a coefficient of correlation between the variables can be obtained to assess the degree of association between the variables. If the independent variable or variables are fixed or predetermined (as is often the case with controlled experiments) correlation coefficients are not generally valid.

The first step in determining the relationships between two variables is often the use of a scattergram in which the data are laid out visually for whatever information can be determined from them. Once it has been decided what form the regression equation is most likely to take, normal equations can be obtained and solved to obtain the regression coefficient(s) and constant. For the linear regression equation, $\hat{y} = a + bx$, the coefficients are given as follows:

Regression Coefficients

$$b = \frac{n \sum xy - \left(\sum x \right)\left(\sum y \right)}{n \sum x^2 - \left(\sum x \right)^2} = \frac{SSXY}{SSX}$$

$$a = \frac{\sum y - b \sum x}{n} = \bar{y} - b\bar{x}$$

The value of the regression equation depends primarily upon the way the data points are scattered about the line. A measure of the scatter is given by the standard error of estimate.

Formulas for the Standard Error of Estimate

$$s_e = \sqrt{\frac{\sum y^2 - a\sum y - b\sum xy}{n-2}}$$

$$s_e = \sqrt{\frac{SSY - bSSXY}{n-2}}$$

Under certain assumptions, $1-\alpha$ of the sample points will lie within $t_{\alpha/2}s_e$ of the regression line.

Whether the regression equation is better than simply using $\bar{y}$ as an estimate for any value of x depends upon whether the regression coefficient b is significantly different from zero. If it is, valid confidence intervals for both A and B (the population parameters) can be obtained. Significance for b depends on the value of b/s_b, and confidence intervals have limits $b \pm t_{\alpha/2}s_b$ and $a \pm t_{\alpha/2}s_a$ where the standard errors are given below.

Standard Error of the Regression Coefficient

$$s_b = \frac{s_e}{\sqrt{SSX}}$$

Standard Error of the Regression Constant

$$s_a = s_e\sqrt{\frac{1}{n} + \frac{\bar{x}^2}{SSX}}$$

Predicting future values of the dependent variable from particular values of the independent variable is called forecasting. A $(1-\alpha)$ forecast interval for $E(y|x)$, the mean of all future values of y for a particular value of x, has limits

$\hat{y} \pm t_{\alpha/2} s_{E(y|x)}$ where $\hat{y}$ is the predicted value of y for that x as obtained from the sample regression equation, and the standard error is given by

Standard Error of Estimated Mean

$$s_{E(y|x)} = s_e \sqrt{\frac{1}{n} + \frac{(x - \bar{x})^2}{SSX}}$$

A forecast interval for one individual instance of y predicted from a particular value of x has limits $\hat{y} \pm t_{\alpha/2} s_f$. Again, $\hat{y}$ is the predicted y value for that x; the standard error is equal to

Standard Error of Forecast

$$s_f = s_e \sqrt{1 + \frac{1}{n} + \frac{(x - \bar{x})^2}{SSX}}$$

The correlation coefficient between two variables is given by the following formulas.

Coefficient of Correlation

$$r = \frac{SSXY}{\sqrt{SSX \cdot SSY}}$$

$$r = \frac{n \sum xy - \sum x \sum y}{\sqrt{\left[n \sum x^2 - \left(\sum x \right)^2 \right]\left[n \sum y^2 - \left(\sum y \right)^2 \right]}}$$

The significance of r, the likelihood that the true population correlation, ρ, is different from zero, is investigated by means of the formula $t = r\sqrt{(n-2)/(1-r^2)}$ (for small samples) or $z = r\sqrt{n}$ for large samples. All calculations involving t have $n-2$ degrees of freedom in the two variable situation.

The chapter also covered, briefly, analysis of variance in the regression model, curvilinear and multiple regression.

•Problems

1. The following data was obtained about the incidence of absenteeism among city employees during the year and their relative "job-pride" as measured by an index developed by a sociologist. Calculate r and determine its significance.

Days Absent	8	1	3	11	6	7	3	8	10	24	6	2
"Job-pride" index	63	82	59	73	84	67	81	73	63	94	81	90

2. In problem 1, the employee with the highest "job-pride" index was absent the most. Assume that this was due to unavoidable factors and refigure r. How does this affect its significance?

3. Use the data of problem 1 with the employee with highest absences omitted. If a regression equation is to be calculated, which variable should be the independent variable and which the dependent variable? Why? Determine a regression equation and plot a graph. Indicate the points to show how well the line agrees with the scattergram. Does a curvilinear trend appear? Determine s_e and sketch a 95% confidence interval for the scatter on the graph. Put the previously omitted point back on the graph and compare it with the line and the other points.

4. A stock market analyst claims there is some relationship between the price of lettuce and the Dow–Jones Stock Average. He investigates five random days during the past few months and obtains the following data. Obtain r and test whether or not his hypothesis seems to be supported.

Cost of Lettuce (cents)	57	61	49	53	39
Dow-Jones Average	768.5	796.25	759.5	756.75	748.5

5. Scores made by students in a statistics class on the mid-term and final examinations are given here. Develop a regression equation which may be used to predict final examination scores from the mid-term score.

Student	Mid-Term	Final
1	98	90
2	68	82
3	100	97
4	74	78
5	88	77
6	98	93
7	45	82
8	85	77
9	64	80
10	87	99
11	91	98
12	94	77
13	96	95
14	80	95
15	89	92
16	70	80
17	64	75
18	75	65
19	99	88
20	67	78
21	75	63
22	96	93
23	49	53
24	100	90
25	76	53
26	71	88
27	77	84
28	73	58
29	55	88
30	65	63

(a) Determine 95% confidence intervals for the regression coefficient and the regression constant.

(b) Calculate r and investigate its significance.

(c) Investigate the significance of the regression coefficient. Compare the obtained value of t with the value obtained in (b).

(d) Obtain a 99% forecast interval for the mean score on the final examination for students in the future scoring 80 on the mid-term.

(e) Suppose that 5 students score 80 on the mid-term next quarter. Obtain a 99% forecast interval for the mean of these students on the final examination.

(f) Forecast the final examination score next quarter of a student who scores 80 on the mid-term. Use 99% confidence.

CHAPTER 10

Glossary of Terms

coefficient of correlation
coefficient of determination
coefficient of multiple
   correlation
curvilinear trend
deviation from linearity
forecasting
intercorrelation
least squares, principle of
linear trend

logarithmic function
multiple regression
normal equations
parabola
regression line
scattergram
scatterplot
standard error of estimate
standard error of estimated mean
standard error of forecast

Glossary of Symbols

A, B	population regression coefficients
a, b	sample regression coefficients
e	error; deviations from the population regression line
$E(y\|x)$	expected value of y for a given value of x
ρ	population coefficient of correlation
ρ^2	population coefficient of determination
R	coefficient of multiple correlation
MSD	mean square for deviation from linearity
MSR	mean square for linear regression
r	sample coefficient of correlation
r^2	sample coefficient of determination
SSD	sum of squares for deviation from linearity
SSR	sum of squares for linear regression
SSX	sum of squares for x
$SSXY$	sum of squares for xy (cross product)
SSY	sum of squares for y
s_a	standard error of the regression constant (A)
s_b	standard error of the regression coefficient (B)
s_e	standard error of estimate for the sample regression line
$s_{E(y\|x)}$	standard error of estimated mean
s_f	standard error of forecast
$\hat{y}$	estimated value of y from sample regression equation

Time Series and Index Numbers

11.1 TIME SERIES ANALYSIS

A **time series** is defined as a series of observations on a variable over a period of time. In general, such a series has regular intervals between observations. This simplifies the analysis. A time series differs from the type of data studied in the preceding chapter in that there is only one observation of the dependent variable per value of the independent variable (time), and successive values of the dependent variable are related to each other. The latter difference is one of the reasons that regression analysis is not appropriate; one of the assumptions underlying regression analysis is that the scatter about the regression line (or curve) is uniform and random. This assumption is not met in time series data.

An example of a time series is the following unemployment data.[†]

Year	Unemployed (1,000)	Percent of Work Force
1948	2,276	3.8
1949	3,637	5.9
1950	3,288	5.3
1951	2,055	3.3
1952	1,883	3.0
1953	1,834	2.9
1954	3,532	5.5
1955	2,852	4.4
1956	2,750	4.1
1957	2,859	4.3
1958	4,602	6.8
1959	3,740	5.5
1960	3,852	5.5
1961	4,714	6.7
1962	3,911	5.5
1963	4,070	5.7
1964	3,786	5.2
1965	3,365	4.5

Year	Unemployed (1,000)	Percent of Work Force
1966	2,875	3.8
1967	2,975	3.8
1968	2,817	3.6
1969	2,832	3.5
1970	4,088	4.9
1971	4,993	5.9
1972	4,840	5.6
1973	4,304	4.9
1974	5,076	5.6
1975	7,830	8.5
1976	7,132	7.6

A graph of the total number unemployed during this period is given below.

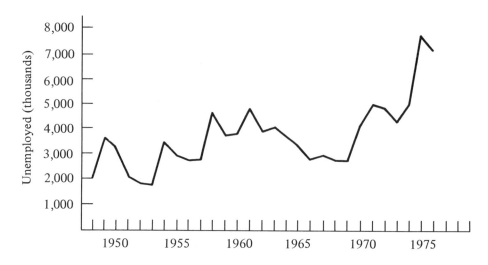

Note that the graph shows a general upward trend. The overall long-term tendency of the data is called the **trend**, or **secular trend**. The long-term up and down movements around the trend are called **cyclical variation** (sometimes cycles). If the time intervals between observations are three months or less, we sometimes observe regular variations within the year which are **seasonal variations**. Any movements of the series not accounted for by the above are called **irregular** or **residual variation**, and may be attributed to chance events. These components are generally given the letters T, C, S, and I. If the observed variable is denoted by Y, then Y is a function of T, C, I, and, if the data is for small enough time periods, S. Many different models can be derived, just as in regression analysis. If these components have no influence or interaction with each other, then the components simply add together to form Y; $Y = T + C + S + I$. If they all interact with each other, then $Y = T \cdot C \cdot S \cdot I$. These two models are

†U.S. Bureau of the Census, Pocket Data Book USA, 1976

the most frequently used, but others are possible. If cyclical and seasonal variation interact with each other, but not with the trend, we might have $Y = T + C \cdot S \cdot I$; or seasonal variation may be independent of the other two, which interact with each other, and $Y = T \cdot C \cdot I + S$. Based on the assumptions which are made, these components can be isolated by using the techniques of time-series analysis. A graphical analysis of the total number unemployed is presented below. A trend line or curve is fitted using the method of least-squares.

In the analyses which follow, the capital letters, X, Y, T, C, S, I, are employed to indicate general variables. Small letters, x, y, indicate particular values of the variable, and estimated values of the dependent variable are indicated by $\hat{y}$.

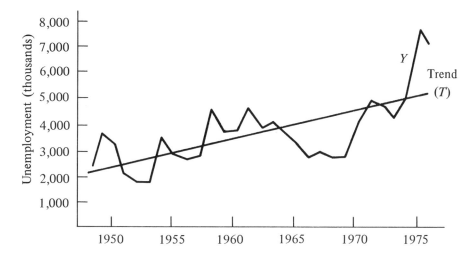

The usual model for decomposition is the multiplicative model, $Y = T \cdot C \cdot I$. Successive decomposition yields the graphs shown below.

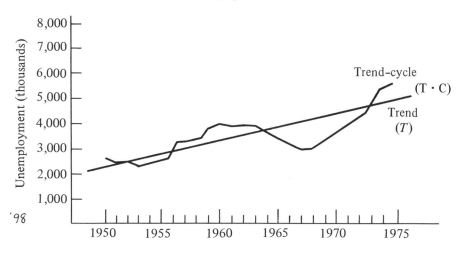

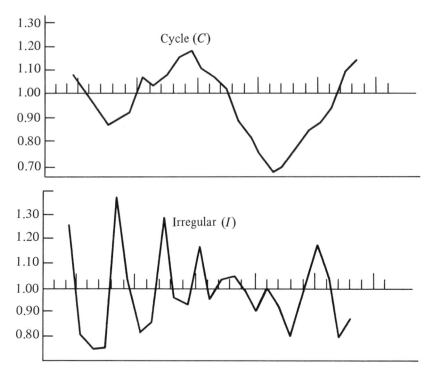

Prior to the widespread use of calculators, it was usual to employ some transformations to simplify calculation of the trend line. (See, for example, Summers and Peters, *Basic Statistics in Business and Economics* (Wadsworth, 1973).) Since computation with fairly large and irregular numbers is no longer a problem, this is no longer necessary, as the transformation—particularly from half-years to years—requires more actual arithmetic than straight calculations. For our initial example, we will use the following data on annual sales of a local dry-goods store from 1963 through 1977.

Year	Sales (Thousands of dollars)
1963	30.8
1964	38.8
1965	42.5
1966	58.0
1967	52.6
1968	49.9
1969	57.1
1970	57.8
1971	56.8
1972	61.0
1973	80.0
1974	85.0
1975	74.4
1976	72.6
1977	75.5

The first step in the analysis is to obtain the trend line. Data can be simplified by renumbering the years from 1 on. Computations are as follows.

Year	Renumbered Year (x)	Sales (y)	x^2	xy
1963	1	30.8	1	30.8
1964	2	38.8	4	77.6
1965	3	42.5	9	127.5
1966	4	58.0	16	232.0
1967	5	52.6	25	263.0
1968	6	49.9	36	299.4
1969	7	57.1	49	399.7
1970	8	57.8	64	462.4
1971	9	56.8	81	511.2
1972	10	61.0	100	610.0
1973	11	80.0	121	880.0
1974	12	85.0	144	1,020.0
1975	13	74.4	169	967.2
1976	14	72.6	196	1,016.4
1977	15	75.5	225	1,132.5
Totals	120	892.8	1,240	8,029.7

Then $b = \dfrac{15(8,029.7) - (120)(892.8)}{15(1,240) - (120)^2} \doteq 3.17,$

and $a = \dfrac{892.8 - (3.17)(120)}{15} \doteq 34.17$

The trend line, then, is given by $\hat{y} = 34.17 + 3.17x$, where x is the number of years after 1962. A graph of the data is given below.

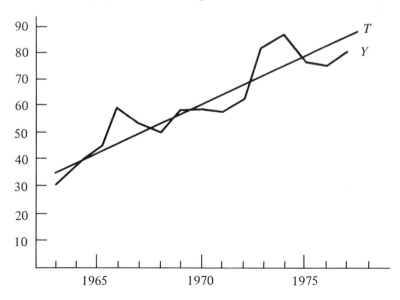

To isolate the cyclical component, it is usual to employ a method known as the *moving average*. The purpose of this method is to smooth out irregularities caused by chance occurrences and to be able to observe the cyclical movements. The examples given will use the multiplicative model, but a similar analysis can be performed using the additive model, merely subtracting rather than dividing.

A **moving average** consists of the average of several consecutive time periods, changed from time to time by replacing the earliest time period by the next one. It is simpler to use an odd number of periods for the average, since an even number of periods would be centered midway between the two middle time periods. One rule to follow is that the moving average should be for as short a period as possible, but enough to smooth out irregularities. Thus, if a moving average for three years still displays irregularities, a moving average should be recalculated for five year periods. One disadvantage of using larger periods, as will be seen, is a loss of a time period both at the beginning and the end of the series for each pair of time periods after the first used for the average. A five-year moving average would lose two time periods at the beginning of the series, and two at the end.

For the data here, we calculate a three-year moving average as follows. The average for 1963–1964–1965 would be $30.8+38.8+42.5$ divided by 3; that is, about 37.4. This would be centered at 1964. The average for 1964–1965–1966 would be $38.8+42.5+58.0$ divided by 3; that is, about 46.4. Computations for all the years are given below.

Year	Y	Three-Year Sum	Moving Average
1963	30.8		
1964	38.8	112.1	37.4
1965	42.5	139.3	46.4
1966	58.0	153.1	51.0
1967	52.6	160.5	53.5
1968	49.9	159.6	53.2
1969	57.1	164.8	54.9
1970	57.8	171.7	57.2
1971	56.8	175.6	58.5
1972	61.0	197.8	65.9
1973	80.0	226.0	75.3
1974	85.0	239.4	79.8
1975	74.4	232.0	77.3
1976	72.6	222.5	74.2
1977	75.5		

The graph of the original data is shown below with the moving average superimposed upon it.

When the moving average is graphed on the trend line, the cyclical pattern is clearly established. For this reason, the moving average is also called the **trend-cycle** line.

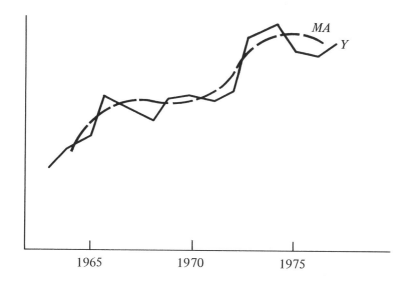

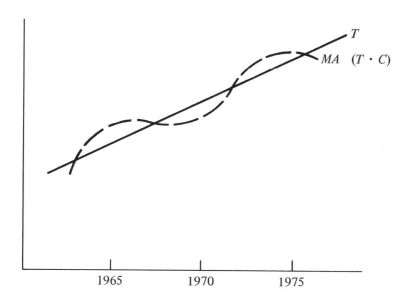

The final step in analyzing the cycle is to remove it from the trend line. In the multiplicative model, we divide MA by T to obtain $C = MA/T$. This expresses the moving average as a proportion of the trend value at this point. Since $Y = T \cdot C \cdot I$, then $Y = T(MA/T)I = MA \cdot I$, so that $I = Y/MA$. We can then use the regression equation (trend line) to find T, then determine the values of C and I for each year, as follows.

Year	Y	T	3-yr MA	C (MA/T)	I (Y/MA)
1963	30.8	37.3			
1964	38.8	40.5	37.4	0.92	1.04
1965	42.5	43.7	46.4	1.06	0.92
1966	58.0	46.8	51.0	1.09	1.14
1967	52.6	50.0	53.5	1.07	0.98
1968	49.9	53.2	53.2	1.00	0.94
1969	57.1	56.4	54.9	0.97	1.04
1970	57.8	59.5	57.2	0.96	1.01
1971	56.8	62.7	58.5	0.93	0.97
1972	61.0	65.9	65.9	1.00	0.93
1973	80.0	69.0	75.3	1.09	1.06
1974	85.0	72.2	79.8	1.09	1.07
1975	74.4	75.4	77.3	1.03	0.96
1976	72.6	78.5	74.2	0.94	0.98
1977	75.5	81.7			

The graphs for the cycle (C) and irregular variation (I) are given below.

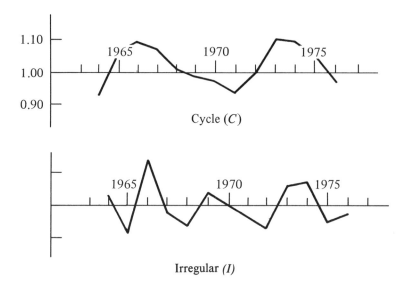

Cycle (C)

Irregular (I)

We may summarize the computations for our analysis as follows. If $Y = T \cdot C \cdot I$, then $C = MA/T$, and $I = Y/MA$, where T is the trend, MA is the moving average, C is the cycle, I is the irregular variation, and Y is the observed value of the series.

EXAMPLE 1   Use the method given above to verify the graphs given earlier for the 1948–1976 unemployment data. Use a five-year moving average.

SOLUTION We begin numbering the years starting with 1948 as 1 through 1976 as 29. The sum of the first n positive integers is always $\frac{1}{2}n(n+1)$, so here $\Sigma x = \frac{1}{2}(29)(30) = 435$. The sum of the first n squares is always $n(n+1)(2n+1)/6$, so here $\Sigma x^2 = (29)(30)(59)/6 = 8,555$. $\Sigma y = 2,276 + 3,637 + \cdots + 7,132 = 108,768$. It only remains to find Σxy. This is $1(2,276) + 2(3,637) + \cdots + 29(7,132) = 1,854,690$. Then

$$b = \frac{29(1,854,690) - (435)(108,768)}{29(8,555) - (435)^2} \doteq 109.94$$

and

$$a = \frac{108,768 - (109.94)(435)}{29} \doteq 2,101.58.$$

The trend line is then given by T: $\hat{y} = 2,101.58 + 109.94x$. The graph of this line is shown in figure 2 and figure 3. To obtain C and I, we employ a five-year moving average, centered at 1950, 1951, etc., through 1974. The computations are shown in the table below. The moving average for year 3 is given by $(2,276 + 3,637 + 3,288 + 2,055 + 1,883)/5$; for year 4, it is given by $(3,637 + 3,288 + 2,055 + 1,883 + 1,834)/5$. We can simplify computations by adding a column for **moving total**. Each moving total can be obtained from the previous one by dropping the "oldest" value of Y and adding the "next" value.

Year X	Y	5-yr Moving Total	5-yr MA	T	C (MA/T)	I (Y/MA)
1	2,276	—	—	2,211.5	—	—
2	3,637	—	—	2,321.5	—	—
3	3,288	13,139	2,627.8	2,431.4	1.08	1.25
4	2,055	12,697	2,539.4	2,541.3	1.00	0.81
5	1,883	12,592	2,518.4	2,651.3	0.95	0.75
6	1,834	12,156	2,431.2	2,761.2	0.88	0.75
7	3,532	12,851	2,570.2	2,871.1	0.90	1.37
8	2,852	13,827	2,765.4	2,981.1	0.93	1.03
9	2,750	16,595	3,319.0	3,091.0	1.07	0.83
10	2,859	16,803	3,360.6	3,200.9	1.05	0.85
11	4,602	17,803	3,560.6	3,310.9	1.08	1.29
12	3,740	19,767	3,953.4	3,420.8	1.16	0.95
13	3,852	20,819	4,163.8	3,530.7	1.18	0.93
14	4,714	20,287	4,057.4	3,640.7	1.11	1.16
15	3,911	20,333	4,066.6	3,750.6	1.08	0.96
16	4,070	19,846	3,969.2	3,860.6	1.03	1.03
17	3,786	18,007	3,601.4	3,970.5	0.91	1.05
18	3,365	17,071	3,414.2	4,080.4	0.84	0.99
19	2,875	15,818	3,163.6	4,190.4	0.75	0.91
20	2,975	14,864	2,972.8	4,300.3	0.69	1.00
21	2,817	15,587	3,117.4	4,410.2	0.71	0.90

Year X	Y	5-yr Moving Total	5-yr MA	T	C (MA/T)	I (Y/MA)
22	2,832	17,705	3,541.0	4,520.2	0.78	0.80
23	4,088	19,570	3,914.0	4,630.1	0.85	1.04
24	4,993	21,057	4,211.4	4,740.0	0.89	1.19
25	4,840	23,301	4,660.2	4,850.0	0.96	1.04
26	4,304	27,043	5,408.6	4,959.9	1.09	0.80
27	5,076	29,182	5,836.4	5,069.9	1.15	0.87
28	7,830	—	—	5,179.8	—	—
29	7,132	—	—	5,289.7	—	—

These values can be verified, if needed, by noting that the basic decomposition formula is $Y = T \cdot C \cdot I$. This formula must hold true for each value of X. Thus, for year 3, it must be true that $3,288 = (2,431.4)(1.08)(1.25)$, allowing for rounding error, of course. For year 20, we must have $2,975 = (4,300.3)(0.69)(1.00)$. For year 3, the product is 3,282, and for year 20, the product is 2,967. Since both C and I have been rounded to two decimal places, the agreement is close enough. The graphs of C and I are given in figures 4 and 5.

TECHNICAL NOTE   One rule to follow is that the MA should be for as few years as possible, but as many as needed to produce the desired smoothing effect. It sometimes will be desirable to use an even number of years. A four-year MA will be obtained by using half of the first and last years; that is, half of year 1, all of years 2, 3, 4, and half of year 5 will produce a four year moving total which, if divided by 4, will be centered at year 3. For a four-year MA for the data of example 1, we would take $\frac{1}{2}(2,276) + 3,637 + 3,288 + 2,055 + \frac{1}{2}(1,883)$ for a moving total of 11,059.5 and a moving average of 2,764.9 centered at year 4. For the MA centered at year 20, we would have $(\frac{1}{2}(3,365) + 2,875 + 2,975 + 2,817 + \frac{1}{2}(2,832))/4 = 2,941.4$.

•Problems

1. Consider the following time series data.

Year	Y	Year	Y
1	9	9	24
2	12	10	24
3	15	11	21
4	18	12	18
5	15	13	18
6	15	14	21
7	18	15	24
8	21		

a. Plot the data on a graph. Does there appear to be a cyclical component?
b. Use least-squares to plot a trend line.
c. Construct a three-year moving average for the data; plot this on a graph with the trend line.
d. Use the methods of this section to construct the cyclical component and irregular component and plot on separate graphs.

2. Repeat the decomposition of the dry-goods store sales, using a four-year moving average and compare the two results.

3. Refer to the unemployment data given at the beginning of this section. Perform a complete time-series analysis on the *percent* unemployed and compare the results with those of example 1. Use a five-year moving average and graph T, $T \cdot C(MA)$, C, and I.

4. Annual sales of the Great Bend Hardware company and associates for 1952 through 1977 are given below. Use time series analysis and a five-year moving average to determine trend, cycle, and irregular components. How many years does the cycle appear to last?

Year	Sales ($1,000's)	Year	Sales ($1,000's)
1952	153	1965	394
1953	163	1966	516
1954	191	1967	519
1955	259	1968	551
1956	297	1969	527
1957	315	1970	658
1958	236	1971	720
1959	277	1972	631
1960	309	1973	635
1961	380	1974	632
1962	361	1975	747
1963	409	1976	835
1964	501	1977	796

11.2 SEASONAL VARIATION

A time series in which the period between observations is less than a year may exhibit periodical regular variations called **seasonal variations**. For the purposes of most time series analysis, these seasonal variations occur on a regular yearly basis, although in some cases they may have a different period. In the multiplicative model as presented in the previous section, the actual observations, represented by Y, are the product of a trend component, T, a cyclical component (period usually of several years), C, a seasonal component, S, and irregular variation, I. The preceding section demonstrated a method of decomposing an annual time series into components T, C, and I. The method will work with any time period as long as an additional seasonal component is not present. If such a component is present, Y must be decomposed into $T \cdot C \cdot S \cdot I$. Various methods exist, depending upon which component is isolated first. In this text, we will show how to isolate S; dividing Y by S then yields $T \cdot C \cdot I$, which may be decomposed by the methods of the preceding section.

Briefly, the method is as follows. Write the time series in such a way that the seasonal periods (quarters, months, weeks) can be summed for the entire series. The grand totals are averaged and each season's total divided by the average to obtain the seasonal component. Dividing the observed values of Y results in the *seasonally adjusted* (or deseasonalized) total for that time period. These are equal to Y/S or $T \cdot C \cdot I$ and can be further analyzed to obtain T, C, and I. In the example shown, quarterly data are used. The same method, however, can be used for monthly, weekly, or even daily data.

EXAMPLE 1   The following data represents the number of new starts in each quarter for Acme Builders. Analyze the data to see whether a seasonal component appears to exist and, if so, adjust the data seasonally and determine trend, cycle, and irregular variation components. Graph the results. In data which show seasonal variation, the moving average is usually computed on a moving total equal to a one year period, in this case four quarters.

Year	Quarter	Number of Starts	Year	Quarter	Number of Starts
1972	1	32	1975	1	47
	2	25		2	36
	3	21		3	36
	4	21		4	35
1973	1	33	1976	1	46
	2	27		2	37
	3	28		3	41
	4	35		4	48
1974	1	54	1977	1	66
	2	51		2	56
	3	46		3	51
	4	38		4	49

SOLUTION   We arrange the data and add up the quarterly data as follows.

Year	Quarter			
	1	2	3	4
1972	32	25	21	21
1973	33	27	28	35
1974	54	51	46	38
1975	47	36	36	35
1976	46	37	41	48
1977	66	56	51	49
TOTALS	278	232	223	226	959 Avg. $= 239.75$
Ratio to avg.	1.160	0.968	0.930	0.943	

Our seasonal component, then consists of the ratios given in the last line of the above table. That is, first quarter totals average about 115% of a "typical" quarter, and so forth. The "seasonally adjusted" totals are given in the table below in the column marked Y/S.

TIME (X)	Year	Quarter	Starts (Y)	Seasonal Index (S)	Seasonally adjusted Starts (Y/S)
1	1972	1	32	1.160	27.6
2		2	25	0.968	25.8
3		3	21	0.930	22.6
4		4	21	0.943	22.3
5	1973	1	33	1.160	28.4
6		2	27	0.968	27.9
7		3	28	0.930	30.1
8		4	35	0.943	37.1
9	1974	1	54	1.160	46.6
10		2	51	0.968	52.7
11		3	46	0.930	49.5
12		4	38	0.943	40.3
13	1975	1	47	1.160	40.5
14		2	36	0.968	37.2
15		3	36	0.930	38.7
16		4	35	0.943	37.1
17	1976	1	46	1.160	39.7
18		2	37	0.968	38.2
19		3	41	0.930	44.1
20		4	48	0.943	50.9
21	1977	1	66	1.160	56.9
22		2	56	0.968	57.9
23		3	51	0.930	54.8
24		4	49	0.943	52.0

The next step is to compute the trend line from the deseasonalized data, using the values of X and Y/S above. We have $\Sigma X = \frac{1}{2}(24)(25) = 300$, $\Sigma X^2 = (24)(25)(49)/6 = 4{,}900$, $\Sigma Y = 27.6 + 25.8 + \cdots + 52.0 = 958.9$, and $\Sigma XY = (1)(27.6) + (2)(25.8) + \cdots + (24)(52.0) = 13{,}444.5$. We then have

$$b = \frac{24(13{,}444.5) - (300)(958.9)}{24(4{,}900) - (300)^2} \doteq 1.268$$

and

$$a = \frac{958.9 - (1.268)(300)}{24} \doteq 24.104$$

Thus the trend line is given by $\hat{y} = 24.104 + 1.268x$ where x represents the number of quarters after 1971.

We now obtain a four-quarter moving average of the deseasonalized data, and calculate C and I as well. Recall that a four-term moving total uses half of the first and fifth observation, and centers the average at the third observation. Our first moving total here, then, is $\frac{1}{2}(27.6) + 25.8 + 22.6 + 22.3 + \frac{1}{2}(28.4) = 98.7$.

The computations are summarized in the table below.

X	Y/S	4 quarter moving total	4 qtr MA	T	C (MA/T)	I ((Y/S)/MA)
1	27.6			25.4		
2	25.8			26.6		
3	22.6	98.7	24.7	27.9	0.89	0.91
4	22.3	100.15	25.0	29.2	0.86	0.89
5	28.4	104.95	26.2	30.4	0.86	1.08
6	27.9	116.1	29.0	31.7	0.91	0.96
7	30.1	132.6	33.2	33.0	1.01	0.91
8	37.1	154.1	38.5	34.2	1.13	0.96
9	46.6	176.2	44.0	35.5	1.24	1.06
10	52.7	187.5	46.9	36.8	1.27	1.12
11	49.5	186.05	46.5	38.1	1.22	1.06
12	40.3	175.25	43.8	39.3	1.11	0.92
13	40.5	162.1	40.5	40.6	1.00	1.00
14	37.2	155.1	38.8	41.9	0.93	0.96
15	38.7	153.1	38.3	43.1	0.91	1.01
16	37.1	153.2	38.3	44.4	0.86	0.97
17	39.7	156.4	39.1	45.7	0.86	1.02
18	38.2	166.0	41.5	46.9	0.88	0.92
19	44.1	181.5	45.4	48.2	0.94	0.97
20	50.9	199.95	50.0	49.5	1.01	1.02
21	56.9	215.15	53.8	50.7	1.06	1.06
22	57.9	221.05	55.3	52.0	1.06	1.05
23	54.8			53.3		
24	52.0			54.5		

The graphs of each of the components are the following.

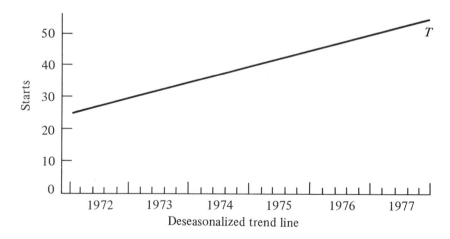

Deseasonalized trend line

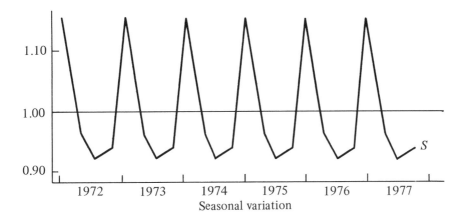

Seasonal variation

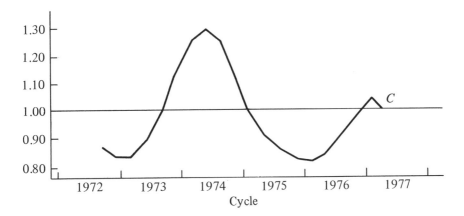

Cycle

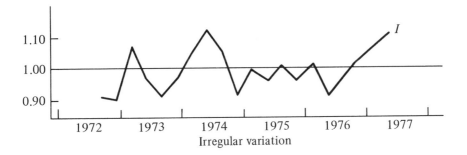

Irregular variation

We summarize the results and show that each value of the housing-starts variable is a product of a trend component, a cyclical component, a seasonal component, and an irregular residual component. In symbols, $Y = T \cdot C \cdot S \cdot I$.

Quarter	Y	=	T	·	C	·	S	·	I
1	32								
2	25								
3	21	=	27.9	·	0.89	·	0.930	·	0.91
4	21	=	29.2	·	0.86	·	0.943	·	0.89
5	33	=	30.4	·	0.86	·	1.160	·	1.08
6	27	=	31.7	·	0.91	·	0.968	·	0.96
7	28	=	33.0	·	1.01	·	0.930	·	0.91
8	35	=	34.2	·	1.13	·	0.943	·	0.96
9	54	=	35.5	·	1.24	·	1.160	·	1.06
10	51	=	36.8	·	1.27	·	0.968	·	1.12
11	46	=	38.1	·	1.22	·	0.930	·	1.06
12	38	=	39.3	·	1.11	·	0.943	·	0.92
13	47	=	40.6	·	1.00	·	1.160	·	1.00
14	36	=	41.9	·	0.93	·	0.968	·	0.96
15	36	=	43.1	·	0.91	·	0.930	·	1.01
16	35	=	44.4	·	0.86	·	0.943	·	0.97
17	46	=	45.7	·	0.86	·	1.160	·	1.02
18	37	=	46.9	·	0.88	·	0.968	·	0.92
19	41	=	48.2	·	0.94	·	0.930	·	0.97
20	48	=	49.5	·	1.01	·	0.943	·	1.02
21	66	=	50.7	·	1.06	·	1.160	·	1.06
22	56	=	52.0	·	1.06	·	0.968	·	1.05
23	51								
24	49								

The original data is graphed below.

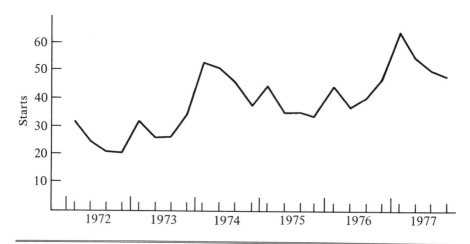

Forecasting with time series data does not have the advantage of the known variation characteristics that forecasting with regression analysis data does. The best that we can do is use the known trend equation, the known seasonal variation components, and, in some cases, an educated guess at the cyclical data, to forecast future time series values. If we symbolize estimated values of Y, T, S, and C by $\hat{Y}$, $\hat{T}$, $\hat{S}$, and $\hat{C}$, we have $\hat{Y} = \hat{T} \cdot \hat{S} \cdot \hat{C}$. If we can estimate C pretty closely, usually by examination of the charted data, we may be justified in using a range for C; if not, then it is best to use $\hat{C} = 1.00$, perhaps with an observation that, at this period of time, it appears likely that the cycle will be up (or down) so that actual values may be expected to be slightly (or somewhat) above (or below) those estimated.

> **EXAMPLE 2** Forecast number of starts for the four quarters of 1978 using the results of example 1. Forecast number of starts for the third quarter of 1980.

SOLUTION   For the four quarters of 1978, using the trend equation $y = 24.104 + 1.268x$, the deseasonalized values for quarters numbered 25, 26, 27, 28 are, respectively, 55.8, 57.1, 58.3, and 59.6. Multiplying each by the seasonal components, we obtain the results 64.7, 55.3, 54.2, and 56.2. Without detailed adjustments for cycle, preferably using longer term data, these are our best estimates. We can observe, however, what appears to be about a three-year cycle here, which would put 1978 about at or below the trend line.

For 1980, the third quarter would be numbered 35 in our numbering system (8 years and 3 quarters after 1971), so the trend equation would give us $24.104 + 1.268(35) \doteq 68.5$. Multiplying by the third-seasonal component, 0.930, we obtain 63.7 as our estimate of the number of starts for the third quarter of 1980.

•Problems

1. A stereo equipment manufacturing company has kept careful records of the quarterly sales (in dollars) of its main line of components. The sales for the last five years are given below. Plot the data in a frequency polygon. Does there appear to be any trend? Does there appear to be seasonal variation? Does there appear to be a cycle? Use the methods of this section to obtain the values of T, S, C, and I, and graph the data. Sales are given in thousands of dollars.

Year	Quarter			
	1	2	3	4
1973	63.5	90.2	77.7	112.8
1974	92.5	101.7	105.2	105.4
1975	98.0	90.6	88.0	105.8
1976	67.8	111.2	117.1	120.3
1977	113.8	128.4	128.3	151.6

2. The last quarter of 1977 was the best sales year in the history of the company discussed in problem 1. Do you think that this can be explained in terms of trend cycle, and seasonal variation, or do some other factors (irregular, residual) enter into it in a big way?

3. Using the data of problem 1, predict sales of stereo equipment for the next three quarters; make conjectures as to whether actual sales will be above or below these predictions, due to cyclical variation.

4. The number of patients treated in the emergency room of a hospital varies by month. The monthly seasonal indexes are as follows:

January	1.18
February	1.12
March	1.08
April	1.04
May	0.98
June	0.91
July	0.90
August	0.86
September	0.93
October	0.88
November	1.00
December	1.12

During the month of March, 1978, the emergency room handled 11,814 patients. What is the seasonally adjusted figure for March? Assuming the trend to be approximately constant, about how many patients should they expect to handle in August? In January, 1979?

5. Suppose that the hospital discussed in problem 4 has a trend line which shows a seasonally adjusted increase of about 107 patients per month. If we let x represent the number of months after December, 1977, determine T, the trend equation. Use this equation to determine the expected number of patients in August, 1978 and in January, 1979.

6. The number of auto loan applications at a bank for the past four years is given below. Determine the seasonal variation, the trend line, cycle, and irregular variation.

Month	Year			
	1974	1975	1976	1977
January	1,916	1,407	2,128	2,340
February	2,220	1,890	2,701	3,182
March	2,909	2,431	3,690	3,471
April	3,145	2,534	3,996	4,847
May	3,028	2,602	3,923	4,818
June	2,725	2,760	3,881	5,027
July	2,501	2,695	3,988	5,475
August	2,542	2,596	3,783	5,024
September	2,527	2,718	3,533	4,543
October	2,180	2,678	3,519	4,858
November	1,787	2,483	3,218	4,599
December	1,505	2,720	2,693	3,931

7. Use the results of problem 6 to determine the expected number of auto loan applications during the months of June, 1978 and March, 1979.

11.3 INDEX NUMBERS

In the previous sections we encountered cyclical, seasonal, and irregular variations expressed as a proportion of some hypothetical norm. If these numbers had been multiplied by one hundred, they would have met with a more common definition of **index numbers**. Simply stated, index numbers measure the relative change in a variable over a period of time as compared with some base period. The most commonly used index number is the *consumer price index*, which measures the relative change in a fixed set of consumer goods. It is not an index of the cost of living, although related, since it does not, and cannot, take into account all factors pertaining to the cost of living.

The most common types of indexes are price, quantity, and value indexes. Price indexes regularly used include the Consumer Price Index, Wholesale Price Index, and Spot Market Price Index, all published monthly by the U.S. Bureau of Labor, and Stock Price Averages, published nearly continuously by Dow–Jones, and by Standard and Poor. Quantity indexes include the index of Industrial Production, prepared by the Federal Reserve Board monthly, and such weekly indexes as Business Week Index and the Steel Production Index. The U.S. Bureau of Labor also publishes Manufacturing Production-Worker

Payrolls, a value index, each month. In this section we shall discuss the construction of simple and composite indexes of each type, changing the base period, and splicing together two or more indexes.

Index numbers can be constructed from any set of related items, and for any period of time. For illustrative purposes we will use the following data (hypothetical) for the output of a meat packing plant. Prices given for each year are the average prices received per pound of packed meat, and quantities given are in total tons packed for the year.

	Data for Packem & Co.					
	Beef		*Pork*		*Veal*	
	Price	Tons	Price	Tons	Price	Tons
1973	$0.78	1,374	$0.54	684	$1.02	72
1974	0.82	1,482	0.71	816	1.34	67
1975	0.97	1,676	0.82	654	1.27	88
1976	1.18	1,384	0.74	786	1.33	79
1977	1.09	1,446	0.81	844	1.42	78

In the construction of index numbers, we must first select a base year. Base years should be those in which the level of data is "normal," or "average." This would be one in which a cyclical component would be about 1.00. This is to avoid undue influences of a recessionary or inflationary nature. The data obtained for use should be valid; it should accurately reflect the facts we wish to index. If possible, it should coincide with other base periods used in order to be comparable with those index numbers. The U.S. Office of Management and Budget has tried to standardize government indexes. Base years for governmental business have been 1947–49, 1957–59, and 1967 in successive decades. Finally, a good base year should have the advantage of as much information as possible; the 1967 base year was selected to coincide with censuses taken of transportation, business, manufactures, construction industries, etc., which were conducted that year.

A simple index is obtained by dividing the value, price, quantity, etc., in each year by the similar measure in the base year and multiplying by 100. If we select 1973 as the base year, we obtain a price index for beef as follows:

Year	Price	Price ÷ 1973 price	Index
1973	$0.78	0.78 ÷ 0.78 = 1.00	100
1974	0.82	0.82 ÷ 0.78 ≐ 1.05	105
1975	0.97	0.97 ÷ 0.78 ≐ 1.24	124
1976	1.18	1.18 ÷ 0.78 ≐ 1.51	151
1977	1.09	1.09 ÷ 0.78 ≐ 1.40	140

This indicates that prices rose 51% from 1973 to 1976. Quantity indexes are similarly constructed. A beef quantity index is as follows:

Year	Quantity	Quantity ÷ 1973 quantity	Index
1973	1,374	1,374 ÷ 1,374 = 1.00	100
1974	1,482	1,482 ÷ 1,374 ≐ 1.08	108
1975	1,676	1,676 ÷ 1,374 ≐ 1.22	122
1976	1,384	1,384 ÷ 1,374 ≐ 1.01	101
1977	1,446	1,446 ÷ 1,374 ≐ 1.05	105

Construction of a value index requires determining the value of the data to be indexed and constructing the index in the same manner. In this case, we have price per pound and tons and would need to multiply tons by 2,000 to obtain pounds in order to get the value. In 1973, for example, beef would have had a value of $0.78 \cdot 1,374 \cdot 2,000 = \$2,143,440$. In 1974, the value would be $0.82 \cdot 1,482 \cdot 2,000 = \$2,430,480$. (Actually, since the tonnage is given to the nearest ton, we cannot assume accuracy beyond, probably, the nearest thousand dollars.) The index for 1974, then, would be $(2,430,480)/(2,143,440)$ times 100, or 113. Since we are interested in the *relative* change in the value, note that the 2,000 in the numerator and the 2,000 in the denominator would divide out, so that—as long as prices are in the same units from year to year and quantities are in the same units from year to year—we can obtain a value index by dividing the product of price and quantity for each year by the product of price and quantity for the base year, then multiplying by 100. Using this technique we obtain the value index for beef as follows.

Year	Price	·	Quantity	=	Product	Value Index
1973	0.78	·	1,374	=	1,072	100
1974	0.82	·	1,482	=	1,215	113
1975	0.97	·	1,676	=	1,625	152
1976	1.18	·	1,384	=	1,633	152
1977	1.09	·	1,446	=	1,576	147

Thus the value of the beef packed by the plant has increased by 47% from 1973 to 1977.

Of more interest, usually, are the composite indexes which are so often used. The Consumer Price Index, for example, is a composite of the cost of a fixed set of goods and services purchased by lower income workers in cities. It assumes that the same goods and services are purchased each year in the same quantity and determines the cost of these goods. The cost relative to that of the base year is the index. It does not measure the cost of living generally, although it is, of course, one measure thereof. The method used is called the aggregative method, and is useful when we know the prices and quantities in the base year and the prices in each subsequent year. We assume that all quantities remain fixed as of the base year, and calculate cost (or prices) of that particular set of goods or services. In this example we calculate the cost, at current year prices, of 1,374 tons of beef, 684 tons of pork, and 72 tons of veal. The ratio of this value to the 1973 value (times 100) gives us the price index for the price of meat for the Packem & Co. data. The method is given below.

	Prices			Prices times Base year weights				
Year	Beef	Pork	Veal	Beef 1,374	Pork 684	Veal 72	Total	Index
1973	0.78	0.54	1.02	1,072	369	73	1,514	100
1974	0.82	0.71	1.34	1,127	486	96	1,709	113
1975	0.97	0.82	1.27	1,333	561	91	1,985	131
1976	1.18	0.74	1.33	1,621	506	96	2,223	147
1977	1.09	0.81	1.42	1,498	554	102	2,154	142

A similar method may be employed to find quantity indexes, the quantity each year being multiplied by the base year prices (or costs) as weights, the total then being divided by the base year total (and multiplied by 100) to obtain the index.

If only index numbers for price or quantity are available, and if base year weights for values may be obtained, an alternate method may be used, called the method of relatives. In 1973, value weights are 1,072, 369, and 73 for beef, pork, and veal, respectively. These constitute, respectively, 0.71, 0.24, and 0.05 of the total. If we have price or quantity indexes, we can use these weights to compile a composite index, weighing each individual simple index by its weight as given below, to obtain the same price index.

	Price Indexes			Price Indexes times relative weights			
Year	Beef	Pork	Veal	Beef 0.71	Pork 0.24	Veal 0.05	Total (index)
1973	100	100	100	71	24	5	100
1974	105	131	131	75	31	7	112
1975	124	152	125	88	36	6	130
1976	151	137	130	107	33	7	147
1977	140	150	139	99	36	7	142

The two methods will yield identical results if intermediate calculations are carried out to several decimal places. The differences between the two methods here are the results of intermediate rounding. The aggregative method will always yield slightly more precise results.

A value index is computed from raw data by calculating value in the current year as a fraction of value in the base year, times 100. The value index for the packing company data is computed below.

Year	Beef Pr.	Beef Qty.	Beef Val.	Pork Pr.	Pork Qty.	Pork Val.	Veal Pr.	Veal Qty.	Veal Val.	Total	Index
1973	0.78	1,374	1,072	0.54	684	369	1.02	72	73	1,514	100
1974	0.82	1,482	1,215	0.71	816	579	1.34	67	90	1,884	124
1975	0.97	1,676	1,626	0.82	654	536	1.27	88	112	2,274	150
1976	1.18	1,384	1,633	0.74	786	582	1.33	79	105	2,320	153
1977	1.09	1,446	1,576	0.81	844	684	1.42	78	111	2,371	157

The three indexes, price, quantity, and value, are summarized for the packing company data.

Year	Price	Quantity	Value
1973	100	100	100
1974	113	110	124
1975	131	116	150
1976	147	105	153
1977	142	110	157

It is occasionally necessary to change base years, either to enable comparisons to be made between index numbers based on different years, or to compare subsequent changes with a specific reference year, such as 1978. Too, it may be psychologically desirable to keep index numbers from getting too big. A Consumer Price Index of 160, based on 1967, sounds somewhat better than an index of 323, based on 1947, although the information contained therein is the same. The term "better," here is not defined.

Changing index numbers based on one base period to another base period is a matter of a simple ratio. Each index number is simply multiplied by the ratio of the index number in the old base year (always 100) to that of the new base year. To shift the index numbers above to 1975 as a base year, we simply multiply each number by the proper ratio. In the case of shifting the price indexes to 1975 as a base year, we would simply multiply each of the indexes by 100/131, or about 0.76. The results are these.

Year	Index
1973	81
1974	85
1975	100
1976	122
1977	113

Splicing index numbers together is done when two or more indexes purport to measure the same thing, but include years that are different. For instance, we may have an index for meat prices for the year 1965 to 1975, and wish to combine the two indexes. Suppose we have the prices for 1965 to 1975 as follows, with the base year 1967.

Year	Index
1965	91
1966	98
1967	100
1968	104
1969	98
1970	112
1971	116
1972	122
1973	131
1974	138
1975	144

In order to splice together the two series, we first decide which year is more accurate for our purposes. Common years are given the index number of the more reliable series. The extreme year of each series is used to splice the two together by converting one to the other, then using the ratio to convert all other numbers in the series converted. Suppose we wish to use the Packem & Co. data, and use the earlier series as an estimate for the Packem data since earlier data is scarce. Since we have data for 1973 to 1977, we discard the data for 1974 and 1975 from the older series. Let us use the Packem index with 1975 as a base, as shown above. The common year is 1973; the index for the Packem series is 81, for the older series it is 131. If each number of the older series 1973 and before is multiplied by 81/131 (about 0.62), we will have achieved the splice.

Year	Old Series	Multiplier	Packem Series	Spliced Series
1965	91	0.62		56
1966	98	0.62		61
1967	100	0.62		62
1968	104	0.62		64
1969	98	0.62		61
1970	112	0.62		69
1971	116	0.62		72
1972	122	0.62		76
1973	131	0.62	81	81
1974	138	Discard	85	85
1975	144	Discard	100	100
1976			122	122
1977			113	113

If a different base year is desired, this can be accomplished using the method shown before.

•Problems

1. Use the data above to obtain simple price indexes for pork and veal.
2. Use the data above to obtain simple quantity indexes for pork and veal.
3. Use the data above to obtain simple value indexes for pork and veal.
4. Obtain a quantity index for the meat data by use of the method of relatives.
5. Obtain a quantity index for the meat data by use of the aggregative method.
6. Obtain a value index for the Packem Co. data with the addition of chicken. The data for chicken are as follows: 1973, 132 tons at $0.38; 1974, 155 tons at $0.42; 1975, 182 tons at $0.40; 1976, 151 tons at $0.51; and 1977, 168 tons at $0.47.
7. Change the value index obtained in problem 6 to a base of 1975.
8. Use the unemployment data of the first section of this chapter to obtain an index of unemployment (total numbers) using a base of 1967. Calculate an index of unemployment (percentage) using a base of 1967, and compare the two.
9. A mercantile index of retail sales of mercantile goods has been compiled for the year 1971 through 1977 as follows:

1971	100
1972	107
1973	111
1974	115
1975	109
1976	117
1977	122

A previous index, used before the present index was compiled, had the following index of sales of mercantile goods, using 1967 as a base year.

1959	73	1967	100
1960	82	1968	99
1961	84	1969	101
1962	88	1970	104
1963	94	1971	107
1964	98	1972	115
1965	101	1973	123
1966	96		

Assuming that the current index is more reliable, splice the two indexes together using 1971 as a base. Now shift the base to 1967. Go back to the original data and splice the indexes together using 1967 as a base, and compare the two methods.

11.4 SUMMARY

This chapter was concerned with changes that take place over a period of time. An analysis of long term changes with observations taken at regular intervals is called a time series. A set of such observations is generally broken down into the overall trend (or secular trend), cycle, seasonal variation, and irregular (or residual) variation. Symbolically, this is given as $Y = T \cdot C \cdot S \cdot I$, where we assume that the effects are multiplicative. Additive effects, and combinations of additive and multiplicative effects are possible, and analysis is done in much the same way as shown for the multiplicative model.

If the intervals between observations are less than a year, usually three months, or less, we must first deseasonalize the data (or seasonally adjust the data) by obtaining the seasonal component, S. We can then divide each value of Y by its seasonal component to obtain the seasonally adjusted values, $Y/S = T \cdot C \cdot I$. For data in which the time period is one year or longer, there is no seasonal component, and all the data is deseasonalized to begin with.

We then use the methods of least squares analysis to obtain the overall trend, T. This is quite often a linear regression equation, $\hat{y} = a + bx$. The individual values of $\hat{y}$ constitute the values of T. A moving average, MA, is then constructed, with as few as three or as many values as needed to "smooth" the data and discern a trend. Each value of the moving average for a given time is divided by the corresponding value of T, the result being the cyclical component. In symbols, $C = MA/T$. It follows that $I = Y/MA$ (or $(Y/S)/MA$, in the case of deseasonalized data) will give the irregular component.

Forecasting from time series data is obtained by forecasting a value of $\hat{y}$ from the trend equation and multiplying by the appropriate seasonal component (if any). There is no exact way to determine the cyclical component, although a rough approximation can often be obtained from a detailed examination of the cycle.

Index numbers are a strictly descriptive measure of the change in a variable over a period of time. Simple index numbers are obtained by dividing the value of the variable in any year by the value of the variable in the base year, then multiplying by 100. Index numbers are generally employed to measure price, quantity, or value. Composite index numbers for price or quantity may be obtained by using the method of relatives or the aggregative method. Value indexes can be obtained only by the aggregative method.

The chapter also gave methods for changing the base year and for splicing together different sets of index numbers.

•Problems

1. The following table gives the demand, in thousands of units, of a part manufactured by the Arjay Electronic Mfg. Co. for the past two years. Obtain seasonal (monthly) components for the data.

Month	Year			
	1974	1975	1976	1977
January	112.3	140.4	115.9	93.3
February	116.0	141.2	109.6	93.5
March	126.0	135.3	113.6	96.0
April	123.6	139.7	109.6	103.6
May	127.8	136.8	107.4	102.2
June	133.5	135.8	104.8	103.0
July	141.1	138.2	109.9	112.6
August	139.6	134.6	108.4	114.2
September	147.7	133.5	104.7	117.6
October	144.4	130.1	103.2	121.4
November	150.7	135.6	103.1	124.1
December	149.7	134.2	111.0	127.2

2. Use the results of problem 1 to forecast the probable demand for March, 1979, if the trend equation gives $\hat{y} = 118.6$. The prediction for October, 1980, using the trend equation, is 134.1. What would be the forecast if seasonal fluctuations are taken into account?

3. Oil production for the Rodberry Oil Company, in millions of barrels, for the past 25 years, is given below. Determine the trend line, cycle, and irregular variation for the years 1953 to 1972. Check the trend line by plotting the expected values for 1973 through 1977 against the actual values. How might the discrepancy be explained?

Year	Production	Year	Production	Year	Production
1953	5.12	1961	10.94	1970	19.68
1954	5.66	1962	12.02	1971	21.10
1955	5.82	1963	12.64	1972	22.88
1956	6.58	1964	12.90	1973	24.28
1957	7.42	1965	14.20	1974	26.58
1958	7.98	1966	15.06	1975	28.84
1959	8.86	1967	15.84	1976	30.60
1960	9.44	1968	17.04	1977	32.28
		1969	18.28		

4. The following table shows production of lumber in thousands of board feet by the North Woods Pine Tree Log Company for a five year period. Determine seasonal indexes, trend, cycle, and irregularity. Forecast production for the next two subsequent years, by quarter.

Quarter	Year				
	100 1973	*110* 1974	*116* 1975	*105* 1976	*108* 1977
First	200.6	223.3	285.5	302.0	294.6
Second	297.0	325.8	342.4	349.6	337.6
Third	295.2	329.2	341.6	335.2	335.4
Fourth	257.4	294.3	325.6	311.1	307.2

The following data are used for problems 5–8. Three related commodities have prices and quantities (prices are averages) for the years given.

Year	Commodity					
	A		B		C	
	Price	Quantity	Price	Quantity	Price	Quantity
1967	$1.08	10.7	$0.65	77.1	$0.17	194.7
1968	1.13	12.5	0.63	81.6	0.19	196.1
1969	1.22	15.1	0.70	88.1	0.22	204.7
1970	1.09	17.2	0.72	90.5	0.24	211.7
1971	1.17	16.9	0.66	94.5	0.31	176.7
1972	1.33	14.4	0.78	80.9	0.26	196.8
1973	1.28	15.1	0.81	81.7	0.29	202.4
1974	1.34	15.4	0.89	89.1	0.31	198.7
1975	1.41	14.8	0.94	85.4	0.33	203.7
1976	1.43	15.2	0.98	86.2	0.39	201.9
1977	1.39	15.8	1.04	85.7	0.44	209.6

5. Construct simple price indexes for each of the commodities, using 1967 as a base year.

6. Construct a composite price index for these commodities, using the results of problem 5, and the method of relatives, with 1967 as the base year.

7. Use the aggregative method to construct a composite quantity index for these commodities, using 1967 as base year.

8. Construct a composite value index for these commodities, using 1967 as base year.

9. Using the results of problem 8, shift the base year to 1977 and construct the resulting value index.

10. Use the methods of time series analysis to examine the price index constructed in problem 6 for evidence of cycle and trend. Decompose the index numbers into trend, cycle, and residual. What are your conclusions?

CHAPTER 11

Glossary of Terms

base year	quantity index
change of base year	residual variation
cycle	seasonal variation
cyclical variation	seasonally adjusted
decomposition of time series	secular trend
deseasonalized	splicing series
index numbers	time series
irregular variation	trend
moving average	trend line
moving total	value index
price index	

Glossary of Symbols

C	cyclical time series component
I	irregular time series component
MA	moving average
S	seasonal variation
T	trend

Chapter 12

Nonparametric Tests

12.1 INTRODUCTION

Most of the statistical tests described in this text require an important assumption to be met if they are to be correctly applied. This assumption is that the population of data from which a sample or samples are drawn is normally distributed. These statistical tests allow considerable latitude, and deviations from normality are permissible. The Central Limit Theorem, for instance, allows the normality assumption to be bypassed for samples sufficiently large. If the distribution from which a sample is drawn is badly skewed or is otherwise grossly nonnormal, however, for smaller samples these statistical tests will not yield meaningful results.

A second assumption upon which most of the tests rest is that meaningful sample statistics, such as the mean and standard deviation, can be derived from the sample(s) and used to estimate the corresponding population parameters. Data which are nominal in nature (such as "increase, decrease, no change"), or ordinal (ranked) do not yield such meaningful results.

Statisticians have devised alternate procedures which can be used to test hypotheses about data which are nonnormal or for which meaningful sample statistics cannot be calculated. Since these tests do not depend on the shape of the distribution, they are called **distribution-free tests**. Since they do not depend upon population parameters, such as the mean and the variance, they are also called **nonparametric tests**. We have already discussed one of the most important nonparametric techniques, the Chi-Square test.

Most experimental situations yield data which can be tested in the usual way. If the data comes from a distribution which is bounded on one end, however, there is a good chance the distribution will not be normal. For example, income distributions are bounded at their lower end, at zero, while they are practically unlimited at their upper end. Distributions of incomes tend to bunch up around the lower, limited end. If you are working with data which comes from a bounded distribution such as this, it is a good idea to construct a histogram from the sample before conducting any statistical tests. If the histogram shows that the data is nonnormal, nonparametric tests may be called for. It may also be useful to use Pearson's index of skewness to check for the degree of skewing. For samples of less than 50 for which the population standard deviation is not known, parametric tests are not appropriate for nonnormal data. Ranked data also require nonparametric tests.

Many nonparametric tests have been devised. Articles and books have been written about them.[†] Five convenient and widely used alternatives will be used here. These tests are not as sensitive as their parametric counterparts, however, and will fail to reject H_0 as often in cases where either test is applicable.

12.2   THE SIGNS TEST

A common research problem involves the testing of two paired samples, either before-and-after observations, or matched pairs. The t- or z-test can be used only if the assumptions are met. A convenient alternative is the **signs test** which is derived from the binomial distribution.

To use the signs test, calculate the difference between the values of each pair and record the sign of each difference. If there is no change, we would expect approximately equal numbers of plus and minus signs. This would correspond to a null hypothesis that $\pi = 0.50$, where π is the probability that a particular difference is positive. If there is no difference in a pair, it is dropped from the calculations since it yields no information. If there is really no difference, and if $\pi = 0.50$ is reasonable, there will still be some chance variation, and we can observe which sign is more frequently occurring, and refer to Table 2 to determine the probability of this occurring by chance if $\pi = 0.50$. Thus, if we have a sample of 20 pairs, and if there are, say 5 plus and 15 minus signs, we refer to Table 9 with $n = 20, r = 15$, and observe that that probability of 15 or more of one sign is 0.021. If our alternate hypothesis is one-sided, this is the probability we will compare with α. If the alternate hypothesis is two-sided, we must compare it with $\alpha/2$, since half the rejection region will be in each tail.

EXAMPLE 1   Forty retail outlets belonging to a department store chain are compared with each other with respect to certain characteristics. On the basis of this comparison, the forty outlets are divided into twenty matched pairs. Then the forty outlets are randomly assigned to one of two groups with one member of each matched pair in each group. The groups are called A and B. The managers of group A stores are given an intensive course in improved sales techniques. The managers of group B stores are promised bonuses for increased sales. At the end of six months, sales

[†]See for instance Sidney Siegel, *Non-parametric Statistics for the Behavioral Sciences* (McGraw-Hill, 1956).

increases for the stores are compared in order to assess the most effective means of increasing sales. Use the signs test on the following data to determine if either method is more effective. Use the 0.05 level of significance.

Pair	A	B	Difference
		Increased Sales (Thousands Of Dollars)	
1	13	7	+6
2	2	4	−2
3	−1	3	−4
4	4	12	−8
5	11	14	−3
6	7	9	−2
7	12	6	+6
8	−3	2	−5
9	−4	−1	−3
10	7	3	+4
11	5	6	−1
12	2	5	−3
13	1	−1	+2
14	0	7	−7
15	5	8	−3
16	2	1	+1
17	3	9	−6
18	4	5	−1
19	−2	1	−3
20	3	5	−2

SOLUTION   Using the experimental procedure, we have the following results:

1. H_0: There is no difference between the techniques in increasing sales.
   H_1: There is a difference between the techniques in increasing sales.
2. $\alpha = 0.05$
3. Criteria: Since the alternate hypothesis is two-sided, we obtain the probability of our result from Table 2; if this probability is less than 0.025, we reject H_0.
4. Results: There are 15 minus signs; from Table 2, the probability of 15 or more of the same sign is 0.021.
5. Conclusions: Since 0.021 is less than 0.025, we reject H_0 and conclude that a system of bonuses is more effective in increasing sales than an intensive training course.

The signs test may also be used as a quick test for a hypothesis that a median of a population is a particular value. If we take a sample and wish to test the hypothesis that the median of the population is a certain value, say Md_0, we examine our sample and see how many of the values are above this hypothetical median $(+)$, and how many are below the median $(-)$. Values at Md_0 are not used. The larger of these numbers is used as r in Table 2 (for n equal to the sum of $+$ and $-$ numbers) to obtain the probability to compare to α, as before.

EXAMPLE 2   A typing school claims that in a six-week intensive course, it can train students to type, on the average, at least 60 words per minute. A random sample of 12 graduates is given a typing test and the median number of words per minute typed by each of these students is given below. Test the hypothesis that the median typing speed of graduates is at least 60 words per minute.

Student	Words per minute	WPM-60
A	81	$+21$
B	76	$+16$
C	53	-7
D	71	$+11$
E	66	$+6$
F	59	-1
G	88	$+28$
H	73	$+13$
I	80	$+20$
J	66	$+6$
K	58	-2
L	70	$+10$

SOLUTION   Using the experimental procedure, we have:

1. H_0: $Md=60$
   H_1: $Md>60$
2. $\alpha=0.05$ is a good choice.
3. Criteria: Since the alternate hypothesis is one-sided, we obtain the probability of our result from Table 2 and compare with 0.05. If the probability is less than 0.05, we reject H_0.
4. Results: Since $n=12, r=9$, we obtain the probability of 9 or more sign changes as 0.073, which is not less than 0.05.
5. Conclusions: Fail to reject H_0. Since the signs test is not very powerful, we may wish to use a stronger test, such as the Wilcoxon T-test, discussed in the next section. We note that if 10 of the 12 had had a result of more than 60 words per minute, the result would have been significant since $P\ (r=10)=0.019$ which is less than 0.05. If the result *had* been significant, the conclusions would have been all the stronger because the signs test is not very powerful.

For large samples, generally considered $n>25$ for the signs test, the normal approximation to the binomial may be used, correcting for continuity. Since $p=0.50$ for this, we have the mean equal to $\frac{1}{2}n$ and the standard deviation equal to $\frac{1}{2}\sqrt{n}$. The actual value of z can be computed using the formula

$$z = \frac{\left(x - \frac{1}{2}\right) - \frac{1}{2}n}{\frac{1}{2}\sqrt{n}}$$

where x is the larger number of sign changes and the subtraction of $\frac{1}{2}$ is to correct for continuity. The value obtained can then be compared to the critical value of z which is appropriate for the direction of the test and the value of α. NOTE   As mentioned before, in the event of ties, or of values at the median, all sign changes of 0 are dropped before evaluating the results.

•Problems

1. Fifteen beginning salespeople at a large store were carefully matched by age, sex, race, educational level, and department, and randomly divided into two groups, 1 of each pair in each group. One group was given a short course in sales techniques, the other group was not. At the end of six months, sales during the sixth month were compared. Units differed from department to department, so that sales are not comparable between pairs. Use the signs test to determine if the course was effective in increasing sales. Use the 0.05 level of significance.

| | Sales | |
Pair Number	Instructed	Not Instructed
1	13	10
2	39	39
3	6	4
4	77	79
5	10	8
6	32	27
7	16	12
8	87	74
9	15	11
10	33	37
11	18	11
12	51	43
13	15	15
14	30	17
15	22	25

2. In the past, the number of defectives produced by a machine per lot of 1,000 has had a median of 8. To test whether the machine is still producing the same number of defectives, the output of the machine for the past week is randomly sampled, and 30 lots of 1,000 are examined for defectives. The number of defectives in each lot is given below. Use the signs test, with the 0.05 level of significance, to determine if the machine is maintaining its quality, or if, as the quality control expert suspects, the number of defectives per lot is increasing. The number of defectives in the 30 lots is as follows: 3, 11, 6, 22, 9, 12, 11, 12, 7, 12, 8, 14, 10, 7, 6, 8, 16, 10, 9, 10, 13, 8, 4, 10, 12, 9, 13, 11, 9, 10.

3. An employee for a food processing plant noticed a marked reduction in deterioration in unrefrigerated food which had been exposed to certain radiation. She matched 10 food samples by type, quantity, degree of freshness, and source, and exposed 1 of each pair to the radiation. She then determined the deterioration rate of the food over the period of one week by an analysis of various factors, including nutritive value, remaining moisture, and so forth. Test, at the 0.05 level, whether the radiation reduced deterioration rate, using the signs test. Higher values indicate a higher deterioration rate.

	Deterioration Rate	
Pair Number	Not Exposed	Exposed
1	0.32	0.19
2	0.18	0.21
3	0.28	0.21
4	0.34	0.17
5	0.22	0.24
6	0.17	0.12
7	0.41	0.24
8	0.23	0.28
9	0.30	0.18
10	0.26	0.17

4. To test the effectiveness of an antilitter campaign, a group of 50 people at a convention was asked to listen to a ten-minute demonstration on the effects of littering. Afterward, they were asked whether they were more, or less, opposed to littering than before the demonstration. Of the 46 who responded, 22 said that they were more opposed, 12 said that they were less opposed, and 12 said they had not changed their feelings. Ignoring the

problems involved in the analysis of such data (nonrandomness, degree of feeling before, etc.), use the signs test to determine whether the demonstration had the desired effect. Use the 0.05 level of significance.

12.3   THE WILCOXON T-TEST

In the event that the signs test is inconclusive and if the differences can be ranked, we can use the **Wilcoxon T-test**. Somewhat more powerful than the signs test, the Wilcoxon T-test makes use of the magnitude of the differences. To perform this test, rank the absolute differences (without regard to sign) from smallest to largest. Observe which sign, $+$ or $-$, occurs less frequently. The sum of the absolute values of the differences of the less frequently occurring signs is designated T. This value is then compared with Table 11. If the obtained value of T is *less* than the critical value, the probability is less than α (for a one-sided alternative) that a type I error would be made in rejecting H_0. For a two-sided alternative, the value of α is double that given in the table.

EXAMPLE 1   Use the Wilcoxon T-test to test the typing school data of example 2 of the previous section.

SOLUTION   The table is reproduced below.

Student	Words per minute	WPM $-$ 60
A	81	$+21$
B	76	$+16$
C	53	$- 7$
D	71	$+11$
E	66	$+ 6$
F	59	$- 1$
G	88	$+28$
H	73	$+13$
I	80	$+20$
J	66	$+ 6$
K	58	$- 2$
L	70	$+10$

Differences are ranked from lowest to highest without regard to sign. Ties are given the mean rank of all the ranks occupied by the number. In this example, a difference of 6 occupies ranks 3 and 4, so each is assigned rank 3.5. Differences of zero are ignored. There are fewer negative than positive differences, so the sum of the ranks of negative differences is computed. This is $1+2+5$ or 8. This is the value of T.

Difference	Rank	Common rank (if different)
−1	1	
−2	2	
+6, +6	3, 4	3.5
−7	5	
+10	6	
+11	7	
+13	8	
+16	9	
+20	10	
+21	11	
+28	12	

Using the experimental procedure we have:

1. H_0: $Md = 60$ H_1: $Md > 60$
2. $\alpha = 0.05$
3. Criteria: The alternate hypothesis is one-sided, so this is a one-tailed test. From Table 11, reject H_0 if $T < 17$.
4. Results: $T = 8$
5. Conclusions: Since $8 < 17$, we reject H_0 and conclude that the claim is valid.

If the assumptions of normality and interval data are valid, which they may be in this case, we could use a t-test. Here we would have $t = 3.377$, which is significant at the 0.01 level. Note that $T = 8$ is also significant at the 0.01 level.

For samples greater than 25 a transformation may be used to link T with the normal distribution so that the obtained value of z may be compared with the usual critical values of z. This transformation is

$$z = \frac{T - n(n+1)/4}{\sqrt{\dfrac{n(n+1)(2n+1)}{24}}}$$

where T is the sum of the less frequent ranks and n is the sample size ($n > 25$).

•Problems

1. Use the Wilcoxon T-test with the data of problem 2 of the preceding section.

2. Use the Wilcoxon T-test with the data of problem 3 of the preceding section.

3. Explain why the Wilcoxon T-test cannot be used with the data of problem 4 of the preceding section.

4. Explain why the Wilcoxon *T*-test should not be used with the data of problem 1 of the preceding section.

5. A large chain of grocery stores wishes to test the effectiveness of an advertising display on the sales of a certain product. Sixty of their retail stores were paired on pertinent characteristics such as size, weekly volume, usual stock of the product, type of community, etc. By flipping a coin, one store in each of the thirty pairs was selected to display the product, while the other store was to carry it as usual. Given the following data, use the Wilcoxon *T*-test to determine whether or not the display has the effect of increasing sales. Use the 0.05 level of significance.

	Weekly Sales	
	Without	With
Pair	Display	Display
1	68	74
2	91	90
3	66	69
4	56	64
5	79	84
6	63	60
7	91	84
8	64	72
9	91	99
10	67	73
11	40	46
12	84	93
13	111	95
14	78	83
15	97	109
16	65	73
17	93	96
18	74	69
19	80	73
20	95	108
21	112	114
22	76	73
23	31	47
24	72	81
25	98	100
26	44	43
27	81	79
28	98	114
29	54	61
30	72	90

12.4 THE MANN–WHITNEY U-TEST

For independent samples, a nonparametric technique can be used if the assumptions for parametric tests are not met. This alternative, the **Mann–Whitney U-test**, is a convenient alternative to the t- and z-tests for independent samples, and also makes use of ranks. In this test the two samples are ranked in order from lowest to highest as if they were one sample, and the sum of the ranks in each sample is calculated. Then the U statistic is the smaller of the numbers calculated from the formula

$$U = n_1 n_2 + \frac{n_1(n_1+1)}{2} - R_1$$

or

$$U = n_1 n_2 + \frac{n_2(n_2+1)}{2} - R_2$$

where n_1 and n_2 are the sizes of the samples and R_1 and R_2 are the rank sums of the corresponding samples. For small samples, if both n_1 and n_2 are less than 10 (some statisticians say 8), special tables must be used,[†] and if U is smaller than the critical value, H_0 can be rejected. For samples of at least 10 each, the distribution of U can be related to the standard normal curve by the statistic

$$z = \frac{U - n_1 n_2/2}{\sqrt{n_1 n_2(n_1 + n_2 + 1)/12}}$$

In using this statistic, it is unimportant whether the larger or smaller value obtained from the formulas is used. The values for z will be numerically equal, but opposite in sign. Note that tied observations are again given the mean of the common ranks.

EXAMPLE 1 Twenty-three applicants for a position are interviewed by three administrators and rated on a scale of 5 as to suitability for the position. Each applicant is given a "suitability" score which is the sum of the three numbers. Although college education is not a requirement for the position, a personnel director felt that it might have some bearing on suitability for the position. Raters made their ratings on the basis of individual interviews and were not told the educational background of the applicants. Twelve of the applicants had completed at least two years of college. Use the Mann–Whitney U-test to determine whether there was a

[†]See for instance Sidney Siegel, *op cit.*, pp. 274 ff.

difference in the scores of the two groups. Use a 0.05 level of significance. Group A had an educational background of less than two years of college, while group B had completed at least two years of college.

"Suitability" Scores	
Group A	Group B
7	8
11	9
9	13
4	14
8	11
6	10
12	12
11	14
9	13
10	9
11	10
	8

SOLUTION   To rank the data, it is frequently helpful to have a worksheet, particularly when there is a large mass of data. Such a worksheet could list the values from low to high for each group (perhaps using a tally system), then list all ranks, computing the common ranks. Finally, the ranks for the scores in each sample can be listed. The completed sheet might resemble the following.

Scores			Common Rank	Ranks	
A	B	Ranks		A	B
4		1	1	1	
6		2	2	2	
7		3	3	3	
8	8, 8	4,5,6	5	5	10
9, 9	9, 9	7,8,9,10	8.5	17	17
10	10, 10	11,12,13	12	12	24
11,11,11	11	14,15,16,17	15.5	46.5	15.5
12	12	18,19	18.5	18.5	18.5
	13, 13	20,21	20.5		41
	14, 14	22,23	22.5		45
			Totals	105	171

A useful check is to observe that the sum of the two rank sums must be equal to $\frac{1}{2}N(N+1)$, where N is the total number of observations. Here $N=23$, $\frac{1}{2}(23)(24)=276=105+171$, which checks. This serves as a check for internal consistency.

Then, since $n_1 = 11, n_2 = 12, R_1 = 105, R_2 = 171$, we have $U = (11 \cdot 12) + \frac{1}{2}(11)(11+1) - 105 = 198 - 105 = 93$, or $U = (11 \cdot 12) + \frac{1}{2}(12)(12+1) - 171 = 210 - 171 = 39$. Since the smaller value is 39, we have $U = 39$. If a table with critical values of U for $n_1 = 11, n_2 = 12$ is available, we may use it. If not, we perform the transformation to z, obtaining

$$z = \frac{39 - 11 \cdot 12/2}{\sqrt{\dfrac{(11)(12)(11+12+1)}{12}}} = \frac{-27}{\sqrt{264}} \doteq -1.66$$

Since our alternate hypothesis, from the statement of the problem, would be simply that there is some difference between the two groups, the critical value for z would be 1.96 (or -1.96). We cannot reject the hypothesis of equality on the basis of this test. It might be best, however, to reserve judgement and take another sample.

•Problems

1. A biologist investigating the toxicity of a certain substance is also concerned with finding a chemical which will retard the substance's toxic properties. He puts equal amounts of the substance into two tanks filled with goldfish and then puts a predetermined amount of a chemical into tank A. He observes how many hours pass before the goldfish succumb to the effects of the toxic substance. The following gives the number of hours of survival of each goldfish in the two tanks after the tanks have been infected.

Tank A	55, 57, 61, 63, 65, 66, 66, 67, 68, 68, 69, 70, 70, 72, 76
Tank B	48, 52, 54, 55, 57, 60, 63, 65, 68, 69, 70, 70, 71, 73, 75

   Can he assert, at $\alpha = 0.05$, that the chemical retards the toxic properties of the substance? Use the U-test.

2. A business manager wants to place an order for carbon paper and wishes to test two different brands, which cost the same, to determine if there is a difference in the number of copies each brand will make. She has a secretary randomly use twenty of each brand and record the number of copies made by each carbon before it becomes unusable. Using the data below, use the U-test and a 0.05 level of significance to determine whether it is reasonable to maintain that there is no difference in the number of copies for each brand.

   Brand A: 16, 14, 11, 7, 13, 14, 18, 12, 14, 16, 14, 11, 12, 16, 14, 13, 11, 13, 16, 17

   Brand B: 14, 17, 12, 14, 15, 18, 12, 11, 13, 8, 15, 19, 14, 17, 15, 16, 12, 17, 11, 13

12.5 THE KRUSKAL–WALLIS H-TEST

If several independent samples are involved, analysis of variance is the usual procedure. Failure to meet the assumptions needed for analysis of variance makes its value doubtful, so an alternative technique was developed called the **Kruskal–Wallis One-Way Analysis of Variance**, or the **H-test**.

As is done in the Mann–Whitney U-test, all data are ranked as if they were in one sample, from lowest to highest, then the rank sums of each sample are calculated. The H-statistic is calculated from the formula

$$H = \frac{12}{N(N+1)}\left(\frac{R_1^2}{n_1} + \frac{R_2^2}{n_2} + \cdots + \frac{R_k^2}{n_k}\right) - 3(N+1)$$

where $n_1, n_2, \ldots, n_k$ are the number in each of k samples, $N = n_1 + n_2 + \cdots + n_k$, and $R_1, R_2, \ldots, R_k$ are the rank sums of each sample. If there are ties, the usual procedure is followed, but H is fairly sensitive to ties, so if there are very many of them a correction should be made.[†] The effect of the correction is to increase slightly the value of H, so its use is not imperative. For small samples, H must be compared to critical values in a table,[††] but if there are at least five in each sample, H is approximately distributed as Chi-Square with $k-1$ degrees of freedom, and Table 6 can be used.

> **EXAMPLE 1** Consider the data of example 1 of the previous section. Suppose that the groups of applicants were regrouped into three groups, group X, with no college, group Y, with some college, but no college degree, and group Z, with a college degree. Analyze the results using the H-test and a 0.05 level of significance.

SOLUTION   The groups and the rankings are given below.

Background X		Background Y		Background Z	
Score	Rank	Score	Rank	Score	Rank
7	3	11	15.5	8	5.
9	8.5	12	18.5	13	20.5
4	1	9	8.5	14	22.5
8	5	9	8.5	11	15.5
6	2	10	12	12	18.5
11	15.5	10	12	14	22.5
10	12	8	5	13	20.5
11	15.5			9	8.5
	$R_1 = 62.5$		$R_2 = 80.0$		$R_3 = 133.5$

[†]Siegel, *op cit.*, p. 188.
[††]Siegel, *op cit.*, pp. 282–283.

The value of H is computed as follows:

$$H = \frac{12}{23(24)} \frac{(62.5)^2}{8} + \frac{(80.0)^2}{8} + \frac{(133.5)^2}{7} - 3(24)$$

$$\doteq (1/46)(3{,}630.3482) - 72$$

$$\doteq 6.921$$

Since there are at least five in each sample, we can compare H with Chi-Square. From Table 6, the critical value for $\chi^2_{.05}$ with two degrees of freedom is 5.991. Since $6.921 > 5.991$, we conclude that there are nonchance differences among the groups. *Post hoc* analysis with the H-test is not nearly as accurate as with analysis of variance. Further information about the H-test may be found in Siegel, *op cit.*, or in other sources, such as W. J. Conover, *Practical Nonparametric Statistics* (John Wiley & Sons, Inc., 1971).

•Problems

1. Residual levels of DDT, in parts per billion, were measured in the blood of fish, for samples taken from four estuaries of a certain bay. Use the H-test to determine, at the 0.05 level of significance, whether we can conclude that there is no difference among the groups in DDT blood level.

<table>
<tr><th colspan="4">DDT Levels, PPB In The Blood</th></tr>
<tr><th colspan="4">Estuary</th></tr>
<tr><th>A</th><th>B</th><th>C</th><th>D</th></tr>
<tr><td>15</td><td>6</td><td>26</td><td>16</td></tr>
<tr><td>11</td><td>21</td><td>11</td><td>28</td></tr>
<tr><td>27</td><td>9</td><td>9</td><td>41</td></tr>
<tr><td>9</td><td>13</td><td>17</td><td>27</td></tr>
<tr><td>33</td><td>11</td><td>7</td><td>16</td></tr>
<tr><td>16</td><td>10</td><td>24</td><td>22</td></tr>
<tr><td>22</td><td>15</td><td>18</td><td>18</td></tr>
<tr><td>28</td><td>13</td><td>14</td><td>37</td></tr>
<tr><td>11</td><td>17</td><td>13</td><td>26</td></tr>
<tr><td>21</td><td>12</td><td>17</td><td>19</td></tr>
<tr><td>17</td><td>8</td><td>15</td><td>32</td></tr>
<tr><td>22</td><td>13</td><td>19</td><td>27</td></tr>
</table>

2. A businessman wishes to use the best sales technique to display and sell a certain product. He displays the product in 3 different displays in each of 3 comparable stores, changing the display weekly. He obtains 6 weekly sales reports on each display (2 at each store, staggering the weeks). Use the *H*-test to determine if there are differences among the groups at a 0.05 level of significance.

Sales, Total Units		
Display		
1	*2*	*3*
86	77	81
79	80	75
83	69	73
81	74	84
75	71	76
79	72	85

12.6 THE SPEARMAN RANK-DIFFERENCE CORRELATION COEFFICIENT

If we have a set of data classified in two ways, both variables at least in an ordinal classification, an alternative to the Pearson correlation coefficient is the **Spearman rank-difference correlation coefficient, R** (sometimes symbolized r_s). In order to calculate *R*, we arrange the data in ranks, either lowest to highest or highest to lowest. The order is not important as long as both variables are ranked in the same way. We then compute the difference in rank, *d*, for each pair. We use the data of the weight-blood pressure example of section 10.1 and again in section 10.3 to illustrate the method.

Subject	Weight *x*	Blood-Pressure *y*	Rank of *x*	Rank of *y*	*d*	d^2
1	188	140	8	7	1	1
2	231	160	2	2.5	−.5	.25
3	176	130	10	9.5	.5	.25
4	194	130	6.5	9.5	−3	9
5	244	180	1	1	0	0
6	207	160	4	2.5	1.5	2.25
7	198	140	5	7	−2	4
8	217	150	3	4.5	−1.5	2.25
9	181	140	9	7	2	4
10	194	150	6.5	4.5	2	4
						27

If there are ties, the rank of *each* tied value is the mean of all positions the tied values occupy. In *y*, for instance, 160 occupies ranks 2 and 3, so each of these values has rank $(2+3)/2=2.5$; 140 occupies ranks 6, 7, and 8, so each of these values has rank $(6+7+8)/3=7$.

Then we apply the Spearman formula*

$$R=1-\frac{6\left(\sum d^2\right)}{n(n^2-1)}$$

Here $\sum d^2=27, n=10$, so

$$R=1-\frac{6(27)}{10(99)}\doteq0.84.$$

This value is slightly different than $r=0.88$. The Spearman formula is not as sensitive to differences of degree; the difference between 244 and 217 is 27, while the difference between 188 and 176 is 12, but each pair differs in rank by 2.

There is, incidentally, a correction factor which can be applied if the number of ties is large, but it is rarely used unless the number of ties is extremely large.

The significance of R is calculated by using the transformation $t=R\sqrt{(n-2)/(1-R^2)}$ for small samples, less than 30, and the transformation $z=R\sqrt{n-1}$ for large samples. These are compared with appropriate critical values. For small samples, there are $n-2$ degrees of freedom. The significance of $R=0.84$ is tested using the transformation $t=(0.84)\sqrt{8/(1-0.84^2)}=4.379$, which is highly significant.

EXAMPLE 1 A husband and wife are each asked, independently, to rank eleven well-known public figures 1 through 11 in order of degree to which they admire them. Using the data given here, test the hypothesis that husband and wife tend to rate these figures in the same way. Use $\alpha=0.05$.

Public Figure	A	B	C	D	E	F	G	H	I	J	K
Husband	6	11	4	5	1	7	2	9	8	3	10
Wife	4	10	3	2	1	8	6	5	11	7	9

*The same results will be obtained if the Pearson formula is used. The Spearman formula is the Pearson formula applied to a set of data given in ranks.

SOLUTION   Since the data are already in ranks, the Spearman R must be used and converted to a t-score. The hypothesis being tested is that the population correlation is zero; the alternate is that the population correlation is positive, since rating in the same way would yield a positive correlation. Then

$$R = 1 - \frac{6(74)}{11(120)} = 1 - \frac{444}{1,320}$$

$$= 1 - 0.336 = 0.664$$

Then

$$t = 0.664\sqrt{(11-2)/(1-0.664^2)}$$

$$\doteq 2.663$$

With nine degrees of freedom, the value of $t_{.05}$ is 1.833. Since $2.663 > 1.833$, we conclude that the population correlation is positive and that husbands and wives do tend to rate these figures in the same way.

•Problems

1. Two professors rated eleven students in terms of ability. Use the data given here to estimate if the correlation between the ratings is significant.

Student	Professor X	Professor Y
A	1	4
B	7	8
C	8	10
D	3	1
E	6	5
F	10	9
G	9	11
H	2	3
I	11	7
J	4	2
K	5	6

2. A medical researcher measures the blood sugar level of cross country runners immediately before and after the race. He wishes to discover whether there is any correlation between the differences (before and after)

and success in the race. The race has eighteen entrants. All runners had a net decrease in blood sugar levels after the race. Estimate if there is any correlation (at a 0.01 level of significance) if the following are the net decreases of the eighteen entrants in the order of finish, first to last: 10.8; 11.7; 9.7; 9.4; 10.3; 11.2; 8.8; 10.2; 7.4; 8.1; 7.7; 9.2; 6.4; 8.3: 9.4; 7.3; 6.1; 8.3.

12.7 SUMMARY

In the event that data are given in ranks, or that the assumptions underlying the usual tests cannot be met, it is possible to use tests which do not make the assumption that the data are normally distributed, and do not depend on calculation of means or standard deviations. These are called **distribution-free** or **nonparametric** tests. Five alternative nonparametric tests were discussed in this chapter. Instead of the *t*- or *z*-test on the mean of one sample, or the paired or correlated *t*- or *z*-test for related samples, one may use the **signs test** or the **Wilcoxon T-test**. If two samples are independent, the **Mann–Whitney U-test** may be used instead of the *t*- or *z*-test. The **Kruskal–Wallis H-test** may be used in place of one-way analysis of variance. Finally, the **Spearman rank-difference correlation coefficient** may be used as an alternative to the Pearson correlation coefficient.

One of the advantages of these nonparametric tests is that they are relatively easy to use. Calculations may be done quickly, and, if significant results are obtained, no further work is necessary. It should be noted, however, that these tests are less powerful than their counterparts which depend on the assumptions. Using these tests you are more likely to make a type II error, so it is usually wise to use the standard tests whenever possible, reserving the nonparametric tests for those cases in which the assumptions are not valid.

•Problems

1. Use the signs test and the *T*-test for the data of example 1, section 7.4.
2. Use the *U*-test for the data of example 3, section 7.4. The critical value of *U* for $n_1 = 4$, $n_2 = 5$, is 4. That is, the obtained value of *U* must be less than 4.
3. Use the signs test and the *T*-test for the data of problem 2, section 7.4.
4. Use the signs test and the *T*-test for the data of problem 7, section 7.4.
5. Use the signs test and the *T*-test to test the hypothesis that $Md = 16$ for the data of problem 4, section 7.2. Repeat with the data of problem 10, section 7.2, assuming the same characteristics for the second sample as the first.

6. Test the hypothesis that $Md = 10.0$ for the data of problem 7, section 7.2.

7. Use the appropriate nonparametric tests for the data of problems 9 and 10 of section 7.4. For two samples of five each, U must be less than five in order to be significant at the 0.05 level.

8. Use the H-test for the data of example 2, section 9.2.

9. Use the H-test for the data of problem 3, section 9.2.

10. Use the H-test for the data of example 1, section 9.1 (example 1, section 9.3).

11. Use the H-test for the data of problem 1, section 9.3.

12. Use the H-test for the data of problem 2, section 9.3.

13. Calculate R and test its significance for the data of problem 1, section 10.1.

14. Calculate R and test its significance for the data of problem 3, section 10.3.

15. Calculate R and test its significance for the data of problem 6, section 10.3.

CHAPTER 12

Glossary of Terms

distribution-free tests

Kruskal–Wallis H-test

Mann–Whitney U-test

nonparametric tests

signs test

Spearman rank-difference correlation coefficient

Wilcoxon T-test

Glossary of Symbols

H	statistic for Kruskal–Wallis H-test
Md_0	hypothetical population median
R	Spearman correlation coefficient
T	statistic for Wilcoxon T-test
U	statistic for Mann–Whitney U-test

Decision Theory

13.1   DECISION CRITERIA

Many, if not most, business decisions are made in an atmosphere of uncertainty. Decisions to go ahead with a new product are made with the knowledge that there is the possibility of being wrong. Some feel that the decision of the Ford Motor Company, in 1956, to introduce a new automobile, the Edsel, failed to take into account the recession of 1957–1959, which made the decision a financial disaster. The decision of CBS to introduce their method of sending and receiving color television, rather than converting to the RCA system (which is now in wide use) was another error. An investor's decision to put his money into buggy whip stock, instead of the new-fangled automobile, is another example of an error. Stocking up on straight razors, in anticipation of the passing of the "fad" for safety razors is a mistake a general store owner might have made. In each case, the decision was made with certain criteria in mind. According to these criteria, and the probabilities assigned to possible outcomes, the decisions were correct; in retrospect, either the criteria, or the probabilities were wrong.

Suppose that an investor decides to buy either stock A or stock B. In the event of a recession, he would lose $100 on stock A, and would lose $1,000 on stock B. If the economy remains about the same, he would make $200 on stock A, but lose $500 on stock B. In the event of a surging economy, however, he would make $2,000 on stock A, and $5,000 on stock B. These facts can be summarized in a **payoff table**, as shown.

Event:	Decision: Purchase	
	Stock A	Stock B
Economy surges	+2,000	+5,000
Economy same	+ 200	− 500
Recession	− 100	−1,000

The decision to be made is whether to purchase stock *A* or stock *B*. Clearly, if the investor knew which event would occur, there would be no problem. One possible criterion is called the *maximax* decision criterion; it is also sometimes called the *optimist's choice*. All the decisions are examined, the maximum gain for each decision is noted, and the maximum of those is the desired choice. Thus we are maximizing the maximum gain for each decision. This criterion assumes that the best possible outcome will occur. In this case, the maximum gain for stock *A* is $2,000, the maximum gain for stock *B* is $5,000, and the maximum of these is $5,000, so stock *B* should be purchased. A second possible criterion is called the *minimax* decision criterion (sometimes the *maximin*) and is obtained by determining the minimum gain for each decision, then selecting the maximum of these. In this case the minimum gain for stock *A* is a loss of $100, the minimum gain for stock *B* is a loss of $1,000, and the maximum of these is the loss of $100 (since -100 is greater than $-1,000$). Under this criterion stock *A* should be purchased. This criterion assumes that, whatever decision is made, the worst possible outcome will occur (so that this is often called the *pessimist's choice*) and the best of these should be selected to minimize loss. Both of these criteria ignore probabilities. Suppose, for example, that there is a very small chance of recession, and an even smaller chance that the economy will surge. In this case, stock *A* would be the better choice. If one were inclined to the opinion that there would be a recession, it would be a better decision to bury the money in the basement. Most intelligent decisions make some use of probabilities, either known or assumed. Consider the case of the Typer's Clerical Services, Incorporated. Typer's employs clerks, secretaries, etc., paying a wage of $15 per day, then hiring them out to businesses on a daily basis, collecting a fee of $20 for each one. Typer's used to hire only on a daily basis, but found that it can get better quality employees, hence more repeat business, if the employees are hired on a permanent basis. Demand for their service fluctuates from 15 to 35 per day. For the sake of simplicity in this example, we will deal only in multiples of five. Over the past 250 days, the distribution of demand has been as follows:

Demand	Frequency	Relative frequency
15	30	0.12
20	50	0.20
25	80	0.32
30	70	0.28
35	20	0.08

Making use of these probabilities, we find that the *expected value* of this distribution is 25.0. Maximum profit occurs, of course, if 35 are hired and 35 demanded. If fewer than 35 are demanded, however, less profit is made, and, if only 15 are demanded, income is $300 (15·$20) while expenses are $525 (35·$15), for a net loss of $225. If 15 are hired, daily net profit of $75 is assured, no matter if more than 15 are demanded, but Typer's has lost the opportunity to make more profit in the latter case. It is easy to see that the maximax decision would be to hire 35 and the minimax decision to hire 15. Common sense dictates neither extreme, and hiring 25 (the expected demand) would be a reasonable decision. This decision, however, ignores economic factors; hiring one person more than needed results in $15 less profit, while hiring one less than needed results in $5 lost potential profit. For example, if 30 are hired, the cost is $450. Each person demanded brings in $20, so the payoff table for the decision "hire 30 persons" is as follows:

Event Demand is	Payoff
15	-150
20	-50
25	50
30	150
35	150

Since the probability for each event is assumed to be known, the **expected monetary value** EMV) for the decision "hire 30 persons" is given by $EMV(30) = (-150)(0.12) + (-50)(0.20) + (50)(0.32) + (150)(0.28) + (150)(0.08)$
$= 42.00$.
Similar EMV's can be determined for each decision and the optimal decision dictated by the maximum EMV, denoted EMV^*.

EXAMPLE 1 Determine the optimal decision for Typer's by computing the payoff table and calculating the EMV for each decision.

SOLUTION The payoff table is given below. The reader should verify each entry. The EMV for each event is determined in the usual way, as above.

Event : Demand is	Prob.	Decision: Hire 15	20	25	30	35
15	0.12	75	0	-75	-150	-225
20	0.20	75	100	25	-50	-125
25	0.32	75	100	125	50	-25
30	0.28	75	100	125	150	75
35	0.08	75	100	125	150	175
	EMV	75	88	81	42	-25

Since the expected monetary value for the decision "hire 20 people" is greatest, this should be Typer's decision.

Another way of approaching the problem is through **opportunity loss** (or regret). Opportunity loss is the difference between a perfect decision for each event and the decision actually made. For example, if the decision is made to hire 20 people, and the demand is actually 25, the opportunity loss is $25 ($125 - 100$), which is the difference between the value of the decision made ($100) and the value of the correct, or optimal decision ($125). If the demand were actually 15, the opportunity loss would be $75, which is equal to $75 - 0$. An opportunity loss table may be constructed for the same data as given below. Expected opportunity loss for each decision is given as well.

Event:				Decision: Hire		
Demand is	Prob.	15	20	25	30	35
15	0.12	0	75	150	225	300
20	0.20	25	0	75	150	225
25	0.32	50	25	0	75	150
30	0.28	75	50	25	0	75
35	0.08	100	75	50	25	0
	EOL	51	38	45	84	151

The optimal expected opportunity loss (denoted EOL^*) is 38, which is associated with the optimal act, "hire 20 persons." Not too surprisingly, this is the same decision arrived at by consideration of monetary values. The distinct advantage of using opportunity loss, however, is that it may often be used with less complete information than required for EMV, and yield the same results. The value of EOL^* is often referred to as the "cost of uncertainty." If it were possible to know in advance how many persons would be needed each day, and that many were hired, Typer's would have "perfect information." If 20 were needed, they could have 20 come that day, etc. If perfect information were available, Typer's would make $75 12% of the time, $100 20% of the time, $125 32% of the time, $150 28% of the time, and $175 8% of the time, so that the expected monetary value under certainty (EVC) is $126. The reader may verify that, for each decision, $EMV = EVC - EOL$. In particular, $EMV^* = EVC - EOL^*$. The difference between EMV^* and EVC is often called the **expected value of perfect information** ($EVPI$) since this is the expected additional value of certainty over uncertainty. Obviously, $EVPI = EOL^*$; the usefulness of the $EVPI$ is that it puts an upper bound on the amount one would be willing to pay for additional information, which would enable a more accurate decision to be made. If, for example, a fortune teller were to offer to predict the number of people each day for $40, and guarantee the result, it would not be worth it since the EOL^* is only $38.

EXAMPLE 2 A manufacturer assembles calculators. Crucial to the assembly process is the wiring in of the memory chip. If defective, it renders the calculator nonfunctional and the calculator must be dismantled and the chip replaced. If this is done, the cost is $1.15 per calculator. An alternative is to test each chip, discarding if defective. The cost of this process is 15 cents per chip. Approximately 90% of the chips are good, and the remainder are defective. Construct a payoff table and determine the optimal act by consideration of the *EMV*'s. Construct an opportunity loss table and determine the optimal act by consideration of the *EOL*'s. Determine the cost of uncertainty in two ways.

SOLUTION The payoff table in this case is a table of costs so that we wish to minimize cost.

Event :		Decision :	
Chip is	Probability	Test each one	Assemble without testing
Good	0.90	0.15	. 0
Bad	0.10	0.15	1.15
	EMV	0.15	0.115

Since we are dealing with *costs*, we wish to take the lowest *EMV*, so *EMV** = 0.115 and the optimal act is to assemble without testing. Perfect information would allow us to test the bad ones (10% of the time) at a cost of 15¢ each, and assemble the good ones without testing 90% of the time, so *EVC* is $0.015 and the cost of uncertainty is 0.115 − 0.015 or 10¢ per chip. It is rather awkward to have to distinguish between gain and loss, and since opportunity loss is *always* positive, it is probably better to use opportunity loss tables as a general principle. The opportunity loss table is given below.

Event :		Decision:	
Chip is	Probability	Test each one	Assemble without testing
Good	0.90	0.15	.0
Bad	0.10	.0	1.00
	EOL	0.135	0.10

Thus *EOL** = 0.10 or 10¢. This is also the cost of uncertainty and the *EVPI*. The optimal act or decision is to assemble without testing.

A further analysis of the situation of example 2 (sometimes called **sensitivity analysis**) can be performed to determine the probabilities associated with each of the decisions, and what probability is a so-called "break-even" point. Let *p* represent the probability that a chip is good. Then 1-*p* is the probability that the chip is bad. The break-even point is reached when *EOL* for one decision is equal to *EOL* for the other. The *EOL* for "test each one" is $0.15p$ and the *EOL* for "assemble without testing" is $1.00(1-p)$. If these are equal, $0.15p = 1.00(1-p)$; $0.15p = 1-p$; $1.15p = 1$; $p = 1/1.15 = 20/23$ or about 0.87. If p is greater than $20/23$, we would assemble without testing; if p is less than $20/23$, we would test each chip. If $p = 20/23$, either act is acceptable.

> **EXAMPLE 3**   Returning to the example of the stock which opened this section, decide which stock should be purchased if the probability that the economy surges is subjectively estimated at about 0.25, that it remains the same is subjectively estimated at about 0.65, and the probability of a recession is then about 0.10.

SOLUTION   The payoff table can be used to determine that the *EMV* of purchasing stock *A* is $(2,000)(0.25) + (200)(0.65) + (-100)(0.10) = 620$, while the *EMV* for stock *B* is $(5,000)(0.25) + (-500)(0.65) + (-1,000)(0.10) = 825$. Using the *EMV** criterion, stock *B* should be purchased.

Several points of difference should be noted between example 3 and the earlier examples. The first is that the probabilities being used are subjective rather than historical. Although the latter requires a subjective decision to treat the historical probabilities as accurate representations of future events, on this assumption they are surely more likely to be accurate than subjective evaluations alone. A second is that the stock decision is a one-time-only decision rather than a recurring process. One of the advantages of using *EMV** (or *EOL**) as a criteria is that, with expected value, we have an overall long-term average. With a single decision, although the expected value may be highest, there is no compensating second chance to make up for an incorrect decision. Finally, there is the **utility** value of money. An investor who cannot afford a loss of $1,000, perhaps not even $500, has no business buying a stock which might become a disaster. As an illustration, suppose that you are selling your used Jaguar *XKE* for $7,500. The buyer offers you a sporting proposition. He will give you $7,500 for the car, or he will flip a coin and let you call it. If you call it right, he will give you $20,000 for the car; if you are wrong, he gets the car for nothing. The *EMV* for the coin flip is $10,000 compared to $7,500 for the straight sale. Using the *EMV** criteria, you should flip the coin because you have the higher expected return. However can you afford to lose the $7,500? This is a decision that must be made. How much is the loss going to affect you? What utility does the first $7,500 have to you? The reader might wish to verify that *EMV** = 10,000, *EOL** = 3,750, *EVC* = 13,750, and *EVPI* = 3,750, all of which are academic exercises compared to the real issue of the utility value of the money. A good discussion of utility may be found in *An Introduction to Quantitative Methods for Decision Making*, Second Edition, by Richard E. Trueman (Holt, Rinehart & Winston, 1977), pages 159–174.

•Problems

1. The Prudent Investors Corporation is required to have an annual audit. Due to a change in personnel, there is more work than usual this year, and Prudent is considering the hiring of an outside consultant to do the job rather than the firm usually employed, Jiggs & Stone. J & G will do the job for a flat fee of $1,500, while the consultant charges $75 per hour. A preliminary estimate of the time required to do the job by Prudent's chief accountant yields his estimate as follows:

Hours required	0–15	16–20	21–25	26–30	over 30
Probability	0	0.60	0.30	0.10	0

   (a) Construct the payoff table in terms of cost and find *EMV**.
   (b) Construct an opportunity loss table and determine *EOL**.
   (c) Use the results of (a) or (b) to determine the optimal act and the *EVPI*.
   (d) What would be the decision using the maximax criterion?
   (e) What would be the decision using the minimax criterion?
   (Hint: Use the class mark of each class to determine your answers.)

2. A manufacturer of piston rings has three machines which produce the rings. Recently quite a few rings have been returned as defective, indicating that one of the machines is producing a high percentage of defectives. To identify and repair the machine would cost $1,500 if done immediately, but if it could be postponed until the beginning of the next fiscal year, $500 could be written off, so that the cost would only be $1,000. Between now and then, the machine will produce approximately 10,000 rings, each defective one costing the company 50 cents to replace. An immediate determination of the proportion of defectives produced by the machine will be made. For what proportion of defectives will the two decisions be economically equal? For what proportions will it be better to repair the machine now? For what proportions will it be better to repair the machine later?

3. A bakery manufactures its products each morning. One particularly perishable item, a whipped cream butter cake, must be sold on the day of manufacture or discarded. The item costs $2.00 to make, and sells for $4.25. If the probability distribution for demand is given below, determine, using an opportunity loss table, the number that should be baked each day.

Number demanded	0	1	2	3	4	5	6
Probability	0.1	0.3	0.2	0.15	0.1	0.1	0.05

4. Repeat problem 3 if the distribution is Poisson with a mean of 2.5.

5. Best Aluminum Company has discovered that one of its extruders has been producing extrusions of less than first-rate quality. Extrusions are processed and packed without inspection, so that approximately 1/5 of all extrusions

ready for shipment are seconds. Inspection before shipping would require unpacking and repacking, and would cost approximately $5 per piece. One alternative would be to sell all the extrusions as seconds, at a discount of $10 apiece; another alternative would be to fill all the orders as usual, guaranteeing to replace any seconds with first-rate quality. This would result in a loss of ten dollars in packing and shipping, plus a good-will loss estimated at $10 per defective item. Make up an opportunity loss table and determine the optimal act. What is the cost of uncertainty?

6. An investor has $100,000 to invest. He is trying to decide whether to invest in high grade municipal bonds which have a guaranteed rate of interest of 6% per year for five years, to invest in an appliance business, or to buy a piece of land. The appliance business offers him 15% of the business profits as interest, with the principal to be returned in five years. On the basis of past performance, he feels that the business will have a yearly profit of $30,000 to $80,000 with the following probabilities:

profit (thousands)	30	35	40	50	60	70	80
probability	0.15	0.20	0.30	0.15	0.10	0.05	0.05

The land is presently zoned for apartments, but there are several groups trying to have the zoning changed. One group is trying to have it rezoned residential R-1 (there are no apartments in the neighborhood), while a second group is trying to have it rezoned commercial in order to build a shopping center. If the first group is successful, the value of the land will drop to about $50,000 and remain the same for the next five years. If the second group is successful, the land will increase in value, probably to about $250,000 in five years. If the zoning remains as it is presently, the land will probably be worth about $120,000 in five years. The probability that the first group is successful is estimated to be about 0.25, while the probability that the second group is successful is estimated to be about 0.10.

(a) Which decision would be made using the maximax criterion?

(b) Which decision would be made using the minimax criterion?

(c) Draw up a payoff table for each decision and determine the optimal decision by determining the expected profit for each action. (Ignore any differences due to taxation.)

13.2   DECISION TREES

The methods of the preceding section are most useful when there is only one decision to be made, particularly if the number of possible choices is numerous. For cases in which there are two or more decisions to be made in sequence, or where there are sequential probabilities involved, a **decision tree** may be useful.

A decision tree is similar to the probability tree diagram discussed earlier, except that it usually incorporates both probability branches and decision branches. For example, suppose that Spilco Oil Company has to decide whether to sell a certain tract of land, now, for a profit of $100,000, keep the land for possible future use, or drill for oil. If they keep the land, they may sell it in the future, drill for oil, or continue to hold it. Because of the uncertain future, the management feels that such a course of action has a present value of either $200,000, or $75,000, or $25,000, depending on a variety of conditions; probabilities for these values are estimated at 0.2, 0.7, and 0.1, respectively. If they drill for oil now, they will either strike oil, which they feel has a probability of 0.6, or they will not. If they do strike oil, the land will have a value of $200,000; if not, the land will have a value of only $25,000. In either case, the cost of drilling the well will be $15,000. The decision tree can be diagrammed as below; it is conventional to use a box representing a decision point, and a circle representing a probability or event point. Figures at the extreme right represent payoffs for each course of action. If there are various costs or payoffs at an intermediate point, it is a good idea to include these on the branches, as well as probabilities, where necessary. All values are in thousands of dollars.

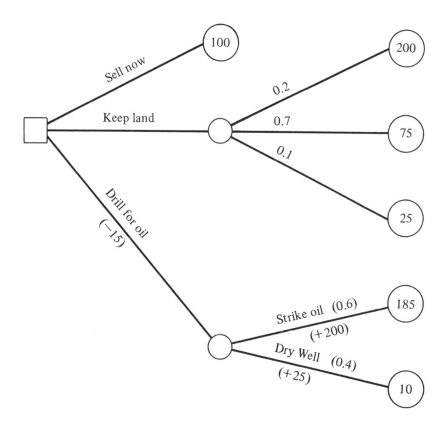

Evaluation of the decision tree is accomplished by determining the expected value of each course of action representing a probability point, then choosing the course of action representing the greatest expected value at each decision point. In this way, the optimum path for greatest expected value will be obtained automatically. In the above tree, the *EMV* for the action "drill for oil" is $(0.6)(185) + (0.4)(10) = 115$; the *EMV* for the action "keep the land" is $(0.2)(200) + (0.7)(75) + (0.1)(25) = 95$; the *EMV* for the action "sell now" is, of course, 100. Courses of action which are discarded are usually indicated by striking a double line through the branch. *EMV*'s for each probability point or decision point are usually written in the box or circle, if large enough, otherwise above the box or circle. The reduced decision tree for the above problem is shown below.

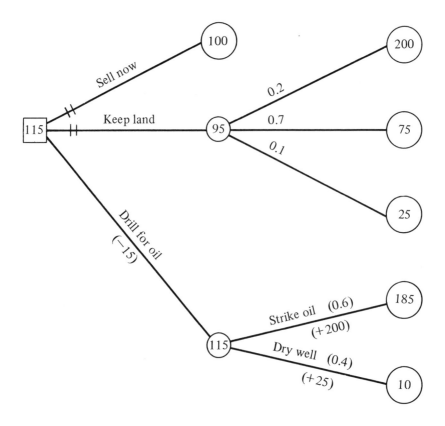

The optimal action is to drill for oil. Note that the maximax decision (optimist's) would be to keep the land for a possible profit of $200,000, while the minimax decision (pessimist's) would be to sell now for a sure profit of $100,000.

> EXAMPLE 1 The Macon Proffitts Company is trying to decide whether or not to market a new product, a CB radio. They feel that if they can market the radio within 90 days, they will receive a large share of the market, and they value this share at $500,000. They concede that there is about a 0.2 chance that they will receive less than a large share, but will still receive a share worth $400,000 in this case. If they take 120 days to enter the market, they feel that the probability of receiving a large share of the market, worth $500,000, drops to 0.5, the probability of receiving a moderate share, worth $400,000, becomes 0.3, and the probability of receiving a small share, worth $250,000 is 0.2. If they take 150 days to enter the market, there is virtually no likelihood that they will receive a large share of the market, a 0.4 probability of receiving a moderate share of the market, a 0.5 probability of receiving a small share, and a 0.1 probability that the venture will be a disaster, returning only about $100,000. The entry into the market is governed by the time it will take to "tool up" for the job and the profits are somewhat mitigated by "tooling up" costs. The equipment necessary will cost (against profits) $50,000. If Macon decided to use their own personnel, it will probably take 150 days to complete the process, with only a 0.2 chance of taking 120 days. On the other hand, it would cost only $10,000 because of using company personnel. Hiring a specialist, Ace Tooling Up Corp., would cost a flat fee of $30,000, no matter how long it took, and Ace estimates it would probably take 120 days, with a probability of 0.2 of taking 90 days, and 0.1 of taking 150 days. The Wheeler Dealers, Inc., will guarantee that it will be done in 120 days, or forfeit their fee of $25,000, but asks for a $15,000 bonus if it is done in 90 days. The estimate is 0.3 that it can be done in 90 days, 0.6 in 120 days, and 0.1 in 150 days. What course of action should the Macon Proffitts Company take?

SOLUTION The decision tree is shown on page 418. Note that the numbers to the extreme right give *net* payoff to Macon Proffitts. Verify these. Numbers above each circle give expected payoff, given the listed probabilities. Final returns give the expected payoff for the action "hire Wheeler Dealers" as highest among the several possibilities.

> EXAMPLE 2 Tri-State Products, Inc., is considering extending their market area to include some territory not previously included. If they do enter the market, they can do so with a large advertising campaign or a small one. If the venture is a failure, they will lose the costs of entry, about $50,000, regardless of the type of campaign. If the venture is a success, a small advertising campaign would yield profits of about $400,000 above costs of entry, while a large advertising campaign would increase profits

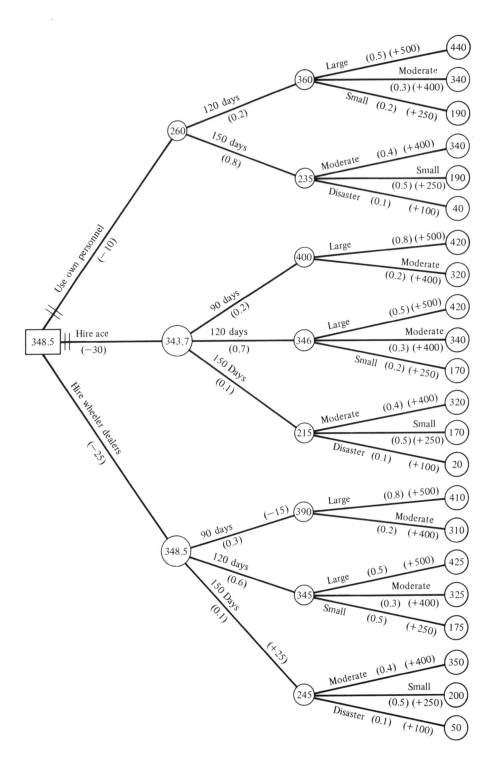

about 20%. The cost of a large advertising campaign would be $100,000, while a small campaign would cost $40,000. Tri-State has been successful about 40% of the time in such ventures, and they are willing to estimate the probability of success from past experience. Opinjon Research Company has offered, at a cost of $30,000, to make a survey of the area and make a prediction of success or failure to help make the decision as to whether or not to enter the market. ORC is not infallible, but they offer research and statistics which indicates that they have correctly predicted success in 90% of the cases in which such a venture has been successful, and correctly predicted failure in 70% of cases of failure. Draw a decision tree and determine the optimal approach Tri-State should use.

SOLUTION   A decision tree is shown on page 420. Note that the probabilities of success and failure vary according to what has gone before. If ORC predicts success, the probability of success is high; if they predict failure, the probability of success is low; if no information is given, the probability of success is 0.4, based on historical data.

Computation of expected payoffs can be calculated as before, as far as possible, as shown on page 421, but a problem develops when it comes to determining the expected payoffs for the survey data, because none of the probabilities needed for the computations are known directly. The decision "do not enter market" is a valid alternative at any decision point. It has been omitted after the outcome "predicts success" because it obviously would not be a reasonable alternative.

The computations proceeded from left to right. If no survey is taken, and if a large advertising campaign is undertaken, there is a 0.4 probability of netting $380,000, and a 0.6 probability of losing $150,000, for an expected value of $(380)(0.4) + (-150)(0.6) = 62$ thousand dollars. Similarly, if a small advertising campaign is undertaken, the expected payoff is 90 thousand dollars. Since the box indicates a decision point, we choose the alternative with the largest expected payoff, so that, if no survey is made, Tri-State should use a small advertising campaign. If a survey is taken, then a decision must be made as to whether to mount a large or small advertising campaign *after* the results of the survey. Thus the probabilities of success and failure in these cases alter with the results of the survey. If the survey predicts success, we expect the probability of success to be substantially greater than 0.4; if it predicts failure, we would predict the probability of success to be *less* than 0.4. What we need in these cases is the probability of success *if* ORC predicts success, the probability of failure *if* ORC predicts success, and the probabilities of success and failure *if* ORC predicts failure. These are known as **conditional probabilities**, with the condition given by the "if" clause. We also need the probability that ORC will predict success and the probability that ORC will predict failure. One method of obtaining all this information is the use of a **joint probability** table. Such a table can be constructed from the given information as will be shown below.

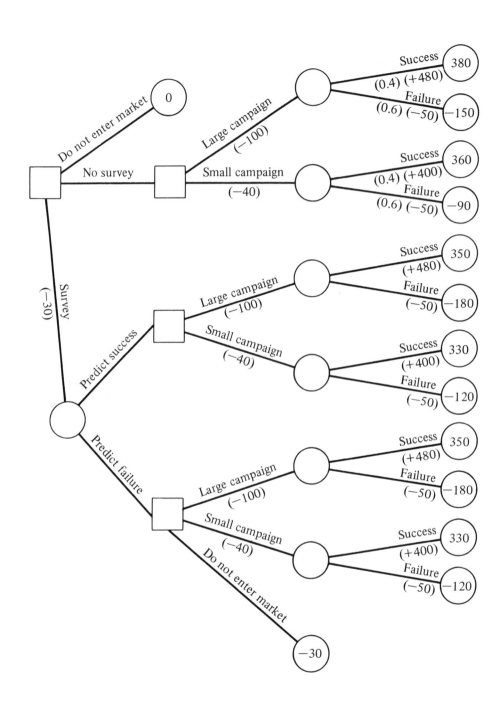

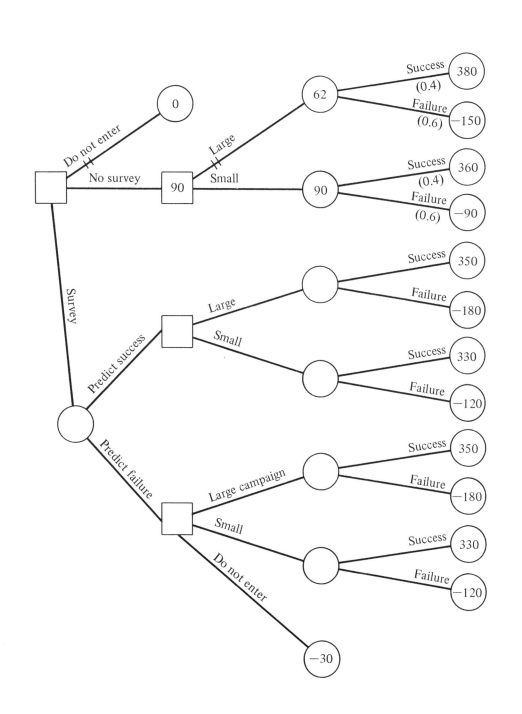

	ORC predicts		
Outcome	Success	Failure	
Success	(0.9)	(0.1)	0.40
Failure	(0.3)	(0.7)	0.60

The entries in the body of the table are in parentheses because they are only temporary. The 0.9 refers to the probability that ORC predicts success *if* the outcome is a success. The entry that should be in that space is the joint probability of the two events; that is, the probability that ORC predicts success *and* the outcome is a success. Since we assume that the probability of success is 0.40, and that ORC will predict success 90% of those times, the probability of both events is (0.90)(0.40) or 0.36. Similarly, the probability that ORC predicts success and the outcome is a failure is (0.1)(0.40)=0.04. The probability that ORC predicts failure and the outcome is a success is (0.3)(0.60)=0.18, while the probability that ORC correctly predicts failure is (0.7)(0.60)=0.42. The information in the joint probability table may be summed up as follows:

	ORC predicts		
Outcome	Success	Failure	
Success	0.36	0.04	0.40
Failure	0.18	0.42	0.60
	0.54	0.46	1.00

In this table, the entries in the body of the table represent joint probabilities while the entries on the margin of the table represent simple or total probabilities for the individual events. In this case, 0.54 is the probability that ORC will predict success (if all the assumptions made are correct) and the probability that they will predict failure is 0.46. (These are sometimes called, confusingly, marginal probabilities, since they are on the margin of the table. Since the term "marginal" has a totally different meaning in much work in economics, we will not use this term here.) To determine the probability that the outcome will be success if ORC predicts success, simply take 0.36/0.54. Thus 36/54, or 2/3 of the time success is predicted, the outcome will be a success; thus 1/3 of the time success is predicted, the outcome will be a failure (18/54). If failure is predicted, the probability of success is 0.04/0.46 (or 2/23) and the probability of failure is 0.42/0.46 or 21/23. We can now complete the decision tree by filling in the probabilities where needed.

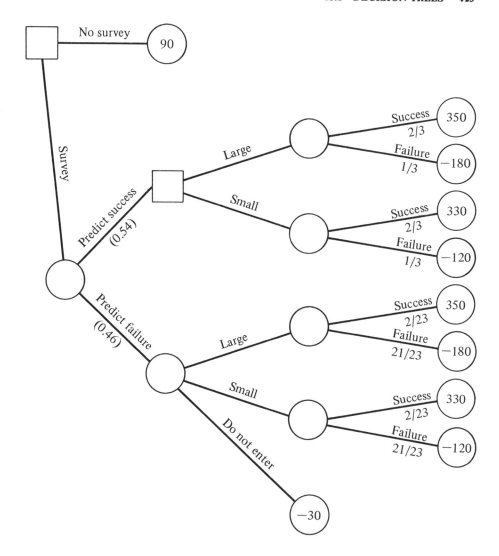

Computation of expected values in each case allows successive decisions to be made, in reverse order.

The final decision, as shown on the next page, is to enter the market without a survey, and to have a small advertising campaign. The final decision tree, as it would appear after all entries had been made, all computations completed, and all decisions made, is given on page 425.

Note that the cost of the survey is the deciding factor. If a survey is taken, the expected net payoff is 83.4, which is 113.4 less the cost of the survey. The value of the survey, then, is 113.4−90 or 23.4 thousand dollars. If a survey could

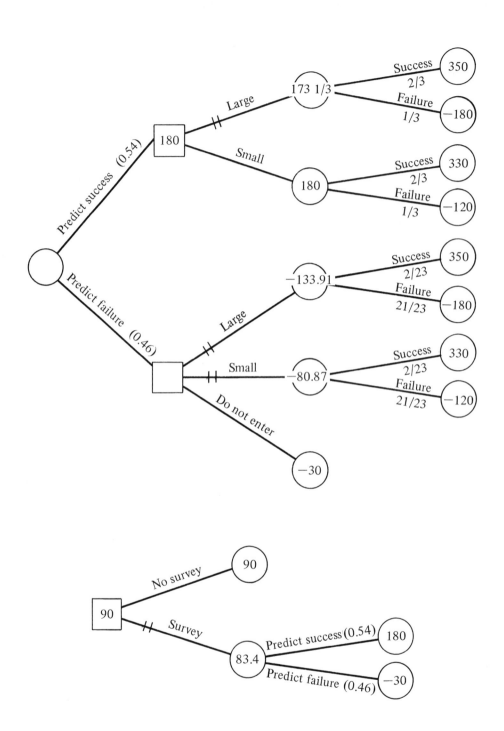

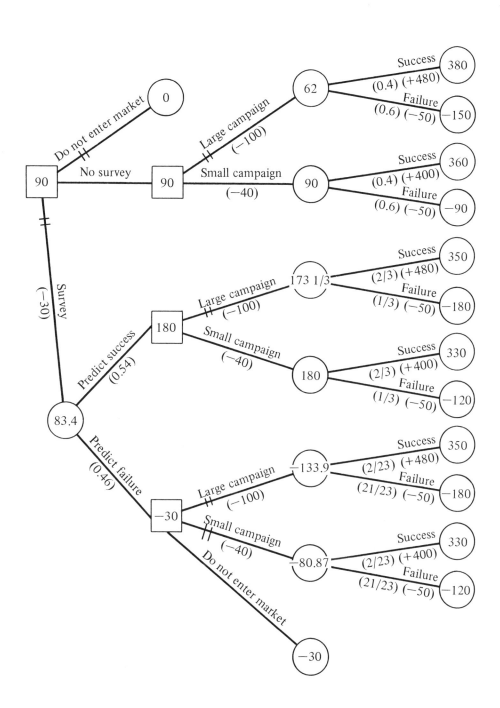

be had for less than $23,400, it would be worth doing; if it cost more, it would not. One other observation is in order. In the case of prediction of failure, it might have been possible for the expected value of entering the market to exceed that of not entering the market. Using the *EMV** criterion, Tri-State would have entered the market. At this point, however, the utility of money enters in, so that other decision criteria might be employed here.

•Problems

1. Dynamic Electric Corporation has accepted a government contract to develop a new transistorized component for a tracking device. Three approaches are considered to be possible by the Dynamic research team. Approach *A* would be certain to develop the component, but would cost approximately $75,000. Approach *B* is somewhat more risky, but costs only $40,000. The research team estimates that approach *B* has a probability of success of about 0.6. Approach *C* is even more risky, having a probability of only 0.3 of success, but has the virtue of costing only $15,000. If either approach *B* or *C* is used, and fails, approach *A* must be used because of time constraints. What should be Dynamic's approach?

2. Suppose p_1 is the probability of approach *B* being successful and p_2 is the probability of approach *C* being successful. Determine the values of p_1 and p_2 such that all three possible approaches are equally valid.

3. Suppose that the time constraints were removed from problem 1 and that all three approaches could be tried, if desired. Which approaches should be tried, and in what order?

4. An executive is considering changing the major thrust of his company's advertising from newspapers to television. An estimate of the cost increase is given at $6,000 per week. Depending upon the market reached, increases in revenue above production costs (not adjusting for advertising costs) are estimated at $15,000, with a probability of 0.2, $10,000 with a probability of 0.3, $5,000 with a probability of 0.4, or no change with a probability of 0.1. Because such a switch involves quite a commitment and changing back to newspaper would involve a large changeover cost, he is considering hiring a firm to develop a more refined assessment of the market. The firm will charge $100,000, which will be charged to the advertising budget at a rate of $2,500 per week until it is paid off. The firm guarantees to predict the revenue correctly (to the nearest $5,000 per week, as above) and concedes the probabilities given above are accurate; that is, the firm promises perfect information. What course of action should the executive follow?

5. Zero Manufacturing Company has developed a new product and is considering whether or not it should be marketed immediately, or test marketed first. Success will mean a profit of about $500,000, failure a loss of $150,000

in production and marketing costs. Probability of success has been estimated at 0.5. If they test market, one of two market areas can be used. These two areas have been used and tested extensively in the past. Records indicate that products which have been generally successful were successful in area *A* 90% of the time, successful in area *B* 70% of the time. Products which were failures were failures in area *A* 80% of the time, and in *B* 70% of the time. The greater success rate of area *A* can be partially explained by the greater size of the area, partially by the slightly different marketing techniques which may be used there. In any case, it is more expensive to test market products in area *A* than in *B*, and it is estimated that test marketing the new product in *A* would cost $100,000 as against $50,000 in *B*. If the choice is between marketing immediately, test marketing in one of the test areas, or withdrawing the product entirely, draw up a decision tree and determine which action should be taken. Perfect information would yield a profit of $500,000 without test marketing. What is the cost of uncertainty (i.e., the *EVPI*)?

6. In problem 5, a junior executive suggests using test market *B*, and marketing the product if it is successful there, and then using test market *A* if the product is unsuccessful in *B*. Is this alternative better than the one chosen in problem 5? Is any other alternative possible? What are the relative merits of other alternatives? What is the best course of action?

13.3 REVISING PROBABILITIES

In the previous section we used a joint probability table to obtain probabilities after a survey was taken. Such methods can be extended to all kinds of sampling, using what is known as *Bayes' Rule*. To use this method requires that we have a **prior probability distribution**, the probability that we know or think each possible outcome has, a sample result of some kind, and a **posterior probability distribution**, the probability we think each outcome has as a result of our sample result.

As an example, suppose that ten cartons sit on the shipping dock. Each was labelled clearly, but a rain washed off the labels. The cartons were placed there at random, after they were packed, and there is no way of telling which is which. These cartons were all packed for customer orders, but for different customers. Four of the cartons contain 200 phonograph cartridges type M91, and 600 cartridges, type M95; six of the cartons contain 800 cartridges, type M91, and 200 cartridges, M95. There is no way to be sure which is which except by removing enough of the cartridges to *know* that there are over 200 of one type or the other. We can, however, get some information by sampling.

Suppose we select a carton at random. The probability that it is of type I (200 M91, 600 M95) is 0.40, and the probability that it is of type II is 0.60. We open it and remove one cartridge. It will be either type M91 or type M95.

Suppose that it is type M91. We wish to determine the probability that the carton is of either type I or type II given that we obtained a type M91 cartridge. According to Bayes' Rule, P(Type I, given M91) = P(Type I *and* M91) divided by P(M91 given Type I) plus P(M91 given Type II). We can summarize the calculations necessary in a table.

(1) Event: Carton Selected is	(2) Prior Probability of Event	(3) Conditional Probability of M91, Given Event	(4) Joint Probability of M91 and Event (2)×(3)	(5) Posterior Probability of Event (4)÷Sum
Type I	0.4	0.25	0.10	0.17
Type II	0.6	0.80	0.48	0.83
			0.58	

Column 2 gives the prior probability distribution, the known probability of each kind of carton. Column 3 gives the probability of drawing an M91 cartridge *if* the carton selected is of the type in the first column. Column 4 gives the probability of *both* events occurring, their joint probability. The sum of all the probabilities in column 4 is the total probability of getting a type M91 cartridge. Column 5 is obtained by dividing each of the probabilities in column 4 by the sum of all the probabilities in column 4. The result is the posterior probability distribution, the probabilities of each type of carton based on the results of the sample. Thus if the cartridge drawn is a type M91, the probability that the carton from which it was drawn is type I is 0.10/0.58, or about 0.17, while the probability that it is type II is 0.48/0.58, or about 0.83. A similar distribution can be calculated for drawing of an M95 cartridge. The table for the calculations in this case is given below.

(1) Event: Carton Selected is	(2) Prior Probability of Event	(3) Conditional Probability of M95, Given Event	(4) Joint Probability of M95 and Event (2)×(3)	(5) Posterior Probability of Event (4)÷Sum
Type I	0.4	0.75	0.30	0.71
Type II	0.6	0.20	0.12	0.29
			0.42	

Thus if a truck pulls in to pick up one of the cartons, we may draw one cartridge from a carton. If the cartridge is an M91, the probability is about 0.83 that it is a type II carton and 0.17 that it is a type I carton; if the cartridge is an M95, the probability is about 0.71 that it is a type I carton and 0.29 that it is a type II carton.

We may extend the method by drawing samples of more than one. If we draw a sample of two, for instance, we may use the binomial (since the probabilities do not change appreciably) to calculate the conditional probabilities. Suppose we draw two M91 cartridges from a carton. We may obtain the probability from Table 2 (by interpolation, since $p = 0.25$), or simply calculate that $P(2) = (0.25)^2 = 0.0625$ if they were drawn from a type I carton. If they were drawn from a type II carton, $P(2) = (0.8)^2 = 0.64$. We may perform all of the calculations as before.

(1) **Event:** Carton Selected is	(2) Prior Probability of Event	(3) Conditional Probability of 2 M91, Given Event	(4) Joint Probability of 2 M91 & Event (2)×(3)	(5) Posterior Probability of Event (4)÷Sum
Type I	0.4	0.0625	0.025	0.06
Type II	0.6	0.64	0.384	0.94
			0.409	

Thus, for a sample of 2 cartridges drawn from a carton picked at random, the probability is 0.409 that both will be M91, and, if they are, the probability is very high (about 0.94) that the carton selected is type II. Similar calculations can be made for the other two outcomes, namely, one of each type, and two M95. If both are type M95 (a 0.249 probability), the probability is about 0.90 that the carton is type I. For the other possibility, one of each type (probability 0.342), the results are inconclusive, (0.44 for type I, 0.56 for type II), and an additional cartridge might be drawn for additional information.

The foregoing examples give a justification for *sequential sampling*, sampling not of a given size, but until a preset confidence level has been reached. We may decide to sample until we are 95% or 90% sure of our result, then draw a conclusion. If we had wanted to be 90% sure of correctly labelling a carton, we could draw two cartridges and draw a conclusion if they are both of the same type. If not, draw one more, calculate the distribution based on this sample and see if we can be 90% certain (we can't), then draw another one, and so on. This procedure is quite useful when testing procedures are costly or involve destruction of the sample.

•Problems

1. A calculator repairman going out on the job has three boxes of chips. His partner needs one of them, he needs the other two. The boxes have somehow been mixed up. One of them contains 50 M3003, 30 J2162, 20 Q1007; the second has 10 M3003, 20 J2162, 50 Q1007, and 20 S113Z; the

third has 60 M3003, 10 J2162, and 30 S113Z. To determine which is which, they take a sample from each box.

(a) Determine the posterior distribution if a sample of one chip is of type M3003.
(b) Repeat (a) for each of the other possibilities.
(c) Use a sample of size 2 to obtain the posterior distribution.
(d) What is your analysis of the decisions to be made in each of the foregoing events if the repairmen wish to be 80% certain they are taking the right boxes?

2. Verify the probabilities given for the example in this section for the other outcomes of the sample of two cartridges.

3. Use the data of the cartridge example to determine the probabilities for a sample of size 3. Determine the probability of each of the four possible outcomes and the posterior distribution associated with each.

4. A machine turning out parts has been erratic in the proportion of defectives it turns out. The proportion of defectives could range from 1% to 20%. If the proportion of defectives is 10% or less, no problems are encountered, but if it is more than 10% the entire lot should be inspected. For convenience, we consider only the possibilities 1%, 5%, 10%, 20%. Of the last 100 lots turned out by the machine, the proportion of defectives had the following distribution.

% defective	1	5	10	20
Proportion	.20	.30	.30	.20

We select a random sample of size n and look at the number of defectives in the sample. The methods of this section are used to determine the posterior probability distribution for the proportion of defectives in the day's production. Determine the posterior probability distribution for each possible outcome for a sample of size

(a) one.
(b) two.
(c) three.
(d) four.

13.4 SUMMARY

When several alternatives are faced in an atmosphere of uncertainty, criteria for making a decision must be employed. All possible alternatives and outcomes must be investigated, and the possibilities should be displayed either in a payoff table or a decision tree. A payoff table is most useful in the event that there is only one decision to be made. If there are several decisions, a decision tree is probably more useful. Payoffs can be determined in terms of monetary value, profits, costs, or opportunity loss. Opportunity loss is the difference between the profit, cost, or other monetary value associated with a particular decision in a given situation, and the profit, etc., associated with the best decision in a given situation. Each particular decision has associated with it an expected monetary value (EMV) and the greatest EMV (EMV^*) is usually the optimal decision. In the case of costs, costs usually represent opportunity losses and, like opportunity loss, the smallest expected cost would be the optimal decision. Each decision has an expected opportunity loss (EOL), and the decision with the minimum EOL (EOL^*) is the optimal decision. If we knew which outcome was going to happen, we would be able to choose the best alternative. If we chose the best alternative for each possible outcome, the expected value associated with this would be the expected value under certainty (EVC). For any decision, $EMV + EOL = EVC$, so that $EMV^* + EOL^* = EVC$. The cost of uncertainty is EOL^* since this is the difference between the expected monetary value and the expected return if the right decision were made in each case. This is also called the expected value of perfect information ($EVPI$) since this is the additional value that perfect information would yield.

An additional method of gaining information is by sampling and revising prior probabilities in the light of sample information. Bayes' Rule is used to obtain posterior distributions which can then be used for making decisions or for additional revision.

•Problems

1. A supply of souvenir buttons has been printed up by a sports supplier in anticipation of the Weehawken Wolves winning the Continental League Pennant and playing in the world wide series. The cost of printing up 10,000 buttons was $2,800, and the buttons are designed to sell for $1 apiece. Unfortunately, the Wolves have been having problems lately, and the supplier has doubts about them winning the pennant. If they do not, he estimates that only about 1,000 of the buttons could be sold anyway, and for only 50 cents apiece. This would cause a loss which they are not prepared to cover. If the Wolves do win the pennant however, the supplier estimates that various amounts are likely to be sold for $1 apiece, according to the following probability table:

Demand (thousands)	5	6	7	8	9	10
Probability	0.1	0.2	0.3	0.2	0.1	0.1

   At the rate they are going, however, he estimates that the Wolves have only about a 40% chance of winning the pennant. Two vendors, however, appear to have a little more faith in the wolves. Ducky Sales has offered him $3,500 for the entire supply, while Dandee Distributors has offered him $2,500 plus half of any profits they might make. Which course of action should the company take? What is the *EVPI*?

2. In the preceding problem, suppose that a sports analysis firm is willing to undertake, for a fee of $1,000, a detailed analysis of the Wolves' chances of winning the pennant. Historically, the Wolves have won 20% of the league's pennants. The firm has predicted this correctly 80% of those times, but has also predicted that the Wolves would win the pennant 30% of the times when they did not. Assume that the history of the Wolves may be used to assess the probability of their winning the pennant for the purpose of deriving relevant probabilities. Should he hire the firm or stick to the decision he made in problem 1? If he hires the firm, what would be his decision in the event that they predicted the Wolves would win the pennant? What if they predicted the Wolves would not win it?

3. The Delta Construction Company has been given a construction job in Argentina. One of the machines they will use for the job contains a part which is constantly under stress. The part breaks randomly on the average of once in five days of normal use and has to be replaced. Amount of use has no effect on the breakage and a newly installed part is just as likely to break as one which has been in use for ten days or more. Delta orders the parts from Trico Casting Co. The job is expected to take ten days, and all plans are made accordingly. The important decision to be made now is how many parts should be taken with them. Each part they take with them now will cost $250, plus $25 for shipping. If they do not take enough parts with them, they will have to order the additional needed parts from Trico. Each needed additional part will have to be airlifted at a cost of $250 in addition to the cost of the part. This is the last use the company will have for these parts, so that any which are not used for the job will be left at the site and have no salvage value. How many parts should Delta take with them?

4. Warren Stamping and Diecast Company is considering the purchase of a replacement for one of their machines which is wearing out. Both the replacement machines cost the same, so cost is not a factor. Machine *A* produces the parts it is designed to produce at a cost of $1.25 apiece, while machine *B* produces the machines at a cost of $1.10 apiece. On the other hand, machine *B* costs $130 per day to operate while machine *A* only costs $100 per day to operate. Demand for the part varies, ranging from 50 to 300 parts per day, and both machines are capable of producing 300 parts per day. If demand for any one day falls below 100 parts, the machines are not operated that day and the demand put over to the following day. For what average demand would the decision as to which machine to purchase make no difference? For what average demand should machine *A* be purchased? Machine *B*?

5.. A shipping clerk is afraid that he has made a mistake by mixing up several orders. Company A ordered 300 red buttons and 700 blue ones, while company B ordered 200 red buttons and 300 blue ones and company C ordered 300 red and 200 blue buttons. They were packed in cartons of 500 each, company A's order in two cartons, each with the same proportion of each kind of button. He has just addressed one of the cartons to company B. To be sure, he opens it and looks at a sea of red and blue buttons. He reaches in and takes a handful of buttons randomly from somewhere in the middle and finds that he has 5 red buttons and 9 blue buttons in his sample. Calculate the posterior probability distribution for the type of the carton, assuming they were completely mixed up to begin with. Should he go ahead and send the carton to company B?

6. At an auction, a company is informed that there are 200 lots of merchandise available for auction of which 60 contain 10% irregulars, 40 contain 20% irregulars, 80 contain 30% irregulars, and the remainder contain 40% irregulars. The lots are not labelled, but a random sample of five from each lot has been selected and the samples are available for inspection. Calculate a posterior distribution for the percent defective based on the number of irregulars in each sample. Suppose the company is willing to accept 10% or 20% defectives, but no more. How many irregulars, at the maximum, in a sample of five will they allow in a lot on which they are willing to bid?

CHAPTER 13

Glossary of Terms

Bayes' rule	joint probability
conditional probability	maximax criteria
cost of uncertainty	minimax criteria
decision	opportunity loss
decision tree	payoff table
event	perfect information
expected monetary value	posterior probability distribution
expected opportunity loss	prior probability distribution
expected value of perfect information	regret
	sequential sampling
expected value under certainty	utility value of money

Glossary of Symbols

EMV	expected monetary value
EMV*	optimal expected monetary value
EOL	expected opportunity loss
EOL*	minimum expected opportunity loss
EVC	expected value under certainty
EVPI	expected value of perfect information
□	decision point
O	probability point

Appendix A

Mathematics Review

A certain amount of mathematical knowledge is required of students taking a course in elementary statistics. Although many students do not need this review, it is included because some areas seem to cause more difficulty than others.

DECIMALS

To add or subtract decimals, you should have the same number of digits following the decimal point in each decimal. Then it is best to write them vertically, aligning the decimal point.

EXAMPLES

612.312 + 83.4 Write as

$$\begin{array}{r} 612.312 \\ 83.400 \\ \hline 695.712 \end{array}$$

48.27 − 11.304. Write as

$$\begin{array}{r} 48.270 \\ -11.304 \\ \hline 36.966 \end{array}$$

To multiply two decimals, multiply in the normal manner, ignoring the decimals. Then count the total number of digits following the decimal point in the two decimals. The product will contain that many integers following the decimal point (begin counting from the right).

EXAMPLE 4.316×11.2 will have $3+1$ or 4 digits following the decimal point in the product, thus:

$$\begin{array}{r} 4.316 \\ \underline{11.2} \\ 8632 \\ 4316 \\ \underline{4316} \\ 48.3392 \end{array}$$

To divide two decimals, arrange in usual fashion.

EXAMPLE   To divide 11.3143 by 2.46 arrange as

$$2.46 / \overline{11.3143}$$

Count the number of digits in the divisor (two, in this example). Point off that many digits to the right of the decimal point in the dividend, indicating the position with a caret, as follows:

$$2.46 / \overline{11.31\hat{4}3}$$

The decimal point in the quotient goes above the caret, as shown:

$$\begin{array}{r} 4.5993 \\ 2.46 / \overline{11.31\hat{4}3} \\ \underline{984} \\ 1474 \\ \underline{1230} \\ 2443 \\ \underline{2214} \\ 2290 \\ \underline{2214} \\ 760 \end{array}$$

Zeros may be added when needed, as in this example.

FRACTIONS

Addition and subtraction of fractions is accomplished by finding a common denominator. For instance, the fractions 2/3 and 3/5 have a common denominator 15, that is, 15 is a multiple of both 3 and 5. Since $2/3 = 10/15$ and $3/5 = 9/15$.

$$2/3 + 3/5 = 10/15 + 9/15 = 19/15 \quad \text{or} \quad 1\frac{4}{15}$$

Another way to obtain the sum is to note that

$$\frac{2}{3} + \frac{3}{5} = \frac{(2\cdot5)+(3\cdot3)}{15} = \frac{10+9}{15} = \frac{19}{15}$$

In fact, $(a/b + (c/d) = (ad+bc)/bd$ regardless of the fractions. It is not absolutely necessary to find the *least* (or smallest) common denominator. For instance, $5/6$ and $3/4$ have 12 as the least common denominator, but 24 is also a common denominator (as are 36, 48, etc.). We can change $5/6$ to $10/12$, $3/4$ to $9/12$, to obtain

$$5/6 + 3/4 = 10/12 + 9/12 = 19/12 = 1\frac{7}{12}$$

but we can also use the rule stated as follows:

$$\frac{5}{6} + \frac{3}{4} = \frac{(5\cdot4)+(6\cdot3)}{24} = \frac{20+18}{24} = \frac{38}{24} = 1\frac{14}{24}$$

Since $14/24 = 7/12$, the results are the same.

Reducing fractions is accomplished by factoring common terms from both numerator and denominator, then dividing them out (or noting that the fraction a/a equals one).

EXAMPLE

$$\frac{120}{165} = \frac{5\cdot24}{5\cdot33} = \frac{5}{5}\cdot\frac{24}{33} = 1\cdot\frac{24}{33} = \frac{24}{33}$$

$$\frac{24}{33} = \frac{3\cdot8}{3\cdot11} = \frac{3}{3}\cdot\frac{8}{11} = 1\cdot\frac{8}{11} = \frac{8}{11}$$

Thus,

$$\frac{120}{165} = \frac{3\cdot5\cdot8}{3\cdot5\cdot11} = \frac{8}{11}$$

This is especially useful in evaluating expressions such as

$$\frac{8\cdot7\cdot6\cdot5\cdot4}{5\cdot4\cdot3\cdot2\cdot1}$$

Since $5 \cdot 4$ appears in both numerator and denominator and since $3 \cdot 2 = 6$, we can cancel *like factors* and obtain

$$\frac{8 \cdot 7 \cdot \cancel{6} \cdot \cancel{5} \cdot \cancel{4}}{\cancel{5} \cdot \cancel{4} \cdot \cancel{3} \cdot \cancel{2} \cdot 1} = 56$$

In order to cancel numbers in a fraction in which the numerator or denominator consists of a sum, such as $(18 + 15)/12$, it is necessary to write the sum in factored form, and then bring out the common factor using the distributive principle. For example

$$\frac{18 + 15}{12} = \frac{(3 \cdot 6) + (3 \cdot 5)}{12} = \frac{3(6 + 5)}{12} = \frac{\cancel{3}(6 + 5)}{\cancel{3} \cdot 4} = \frac{6 + 5}{4}$$

Multiplying fractions is done by multiplying numerators and multiplying denominators, so that

$$\frac{3}{5} \cdot \frac{8}{11} = \frac{3 \cdot 8}{5 \cdot 11} = \frac{24}{55}$$

If common factors occur, you should cancel them before obtaining the answer,

$$\frac{5}{18} \cdot \frac{3}{10} = \frac{5 \cdot 3}{18 \cdot 10} = \frac{5 \cdot 3}{3 \cdot 6 \cdot 2 \cdot 5} = \frac{1}{6 \cdot 2} = \frac{1}{12}$$

Dividing fractions is best done simply by writing them as a complex fraction,

$$\frac{11}{18} \div \frac{13}{15} = \frac{\dfrac{11}{18}}{\dfrac{13}{15}}$$

then multiplying numerator and denominator of the complex fraction by both denominators of the two simple fractions, and simplifying

$$\frac{11}{18} \div \frac{13}{15} = \frac{\dfrac{11}{18}}{\dfrac{13}{15}} = \frac{\dfrac{11}{18} \cdot 18 \cdot 15}{\dfrac{13}{15} \cdot 18 \cdot 15} = \frac{\dfrac{11}{\cancel{18}} \cdot \cancel{18} \cdot 15}{\dfrac{13}{\cancel{15}} \cdot 18 \cdot \cancel{15}} = \frac{11 \cdot 15}{13 \cdot 18} = \frac{11 \cdot 5 \cdot 3}{13 \cdot 6 \cdot 3} = \frac{11 \cdot 5}{13 \cdot 6} = \frac{55}{78}$$

EXPONENTS

Exponents are those little numbers or symbols above and to the right of another number or symbol. The exponent tells how many times the other number, called the base, should be multiplied by itself. For instance, $2^3 = 2 \cdot 2 \cdot 2 = 8$. A symbol such as P^r indicates that P (whatever it represents) is used as a factor r times.

To combine numbers with exponents, it is generally necessary to perform the indicated operations. That is,

$$3^2 + 3^3 = (3 \cdot 3) + (3 \cdot 3 \cdot 3) = 9 + 27 = 36$$

and

$$3^2 \cdot 4^4 = 3 \cdot 3 \cdot 4 \cdot 4 \cdot 4 \cdot 4 = 576$$

If, however, two numbers with the same base are to be multiplied, the product is the base number with an exponent which is the sum of the exponents. Thus

$$3^2 \cdot 3^5 = 3^{2+5} = 3^7$$

and

$$P^a \cdot P^b = P^{a+b}$$

Similarly, division of two such numbers is accomplished by subtracting exponents

$$\frac{3^8}{3^5} = 3^{8-5} = 3^3 = 27$$

and

$$\frac{P^a}{P^b} = P^{a-b}$$

If $a = b$, we have $P^a / P^a = P^{a-a} = P^0$. Since $P^a / P^a = 1$, it follows that $P^0 = 1$. In addition, since $P^{-3} = P^{0-3} = P^0 / P^3 = 1/P^3$, it follows that a negative exponent is a reciprocal fraction. For instance, $2^{-4} = 1/2^4 = \frac{1}{16}$.

SIGNED NUMBERS

Combining signed numbers is quite important. To do so, you should remember that if two numbers of different signs are added, the sum is their difference, with the sign of the numerically larger retained. Thus,

$$-3 + \quad 5 = +2$$

$$-3 + (-5) = -8$$

$$3 + (-5) = -2$$

Subtraction of signed numbers is equivalent to the addition of signed numbers with the sign of the number subtracted changed, as in

$$-3-\quad 5=-3+(-5)=-8$$

$$-3-(-5)=-3+\quad 5=+2$$

$$3-\quad 5=\quad 3+(-5)=-2$$

$$3-(-5)=\quad 3+\quad 5=+8$$

Multiplication or division of signed numbers is done by multiplying or dividing in the ordinary way, and affixing a positive sign if the numbers are *both* positive or both negative, and a negative sign if there is one of each. Thus,

$$(-2)(-4)=+8 \quad \text{or} \quad (-2)(+4)=-8$$

$$\frac{-4}{-2}=+2 \quad \text{or} \quad \frac{-4}{+2}=-2$$

ORDER RELATIONS

If two numbers are not equal, one is greater than the other. This is indicated by use of the sign $>$ or $<$. Since 5 is greater than 3, we have $5>3$ or $3<5$. The latter is usually read "3 is less than 5." A double use of the signs can be used, for instance, to show that x is between a and b, as follows:

$$a<x<b$$

Technically, this says "a is less than x and x is less than b," but this is identical to saying that x is between a and b. To show the cases in which the end points may be included, the symbols $\geq$ and $\leq$ are employed. They are read "greater than or equal to" and "less than or equal to," respectively. Thus, if z can take a value of 1.96, or greater, this is indicated by $z \geq 1.96$. The relation $z > 1.96$ would rule out the possibility of z being equal to 1.96.

SQUARE ROOTS

Table 1 is provided to help you take square roots. Numbers from 1.00 to 9.9. are listed in the first column in each page of the table. The second column gives the square root of the number listed, and the third column gives the square root of ten times the number listed. For instance, the square root of 1.62 is listed in the second column opposite 1.62 in the first column, and we have $\sqrt{1.62}=1.273$. The square root of 14 is listed in the third column opposite 1.40, since $14=10\times1.40$. Thus $\sqrt{14}=3.742$. To find the square root of any other number than those from 1.00 to 99.9, a few simple techniques may be used. First, if the number has more than three signficant figures, you can estimate the square root by taking the numbers above and below it, or use another table, or desk calculator, or one of the techniques which are taught in the lower grades.

To calculate the square root of a number above 99.9, pair digits to the left of the decimal point, starting at the decimal point, thus

$$\sqrt{3\ \overparen{8\ 2}\ \overparen{0\ 0}} \quad \text{or} \quad \sqrt{\overparen{4\ 6}\ \overparen{0\ 0}\ \overparen{0\ 0}}$$

The numbers of pairs, or pairs plus a single digit, gives the number of digits to the left of the decimal point, in the square root. In the first example, there will be three; in the second, four. If all digits are paired, the root will be found in the $\sqrt{10n}$ column; if there is a single digit, it will be found in the $\sqrt{n}$ column. For $\sqrt{382,000}$, we note that there will be three digits left of the decimal point and that $\sqrt{38.2} = 6.181$. Then $\sqrt{382,000} = 618.1$. For $\sqrt{4,600,000}$, there will be four digits to the left of the decimal point and $\sqrt{4.60} = 2.145$. Then $\sqrt{4,600,000} = 2,145$.

To calculate the square root of a number less than 1.00, a similar technique applies. The pairing begins at the decimal point and stops when a pair contains a digit other than zero, thus,

$$\sqrt{0.\overparen{00}\overparen{04}32} \quad \text{or} \quad \sqrt{0.\overparen{00}\overparen{00}\overparen{00}743}$$

Each *pair* of zeros places a zero to the right of the decimal point in the square root. If the first pair with a non-zero digit has the first digit zero, the appropriate root is found in the $\sqrt{n}$ column; if the first digit is not zero, the root is found in the $\sqrt{10n}$ column. In the examples here, $\sqrt{4.32} = 2.078$, so $\sqrt{.000432} = .02078$; $\sqrt{74.3} = 8.620$, so $\sqrt{0.000000743} = 0.000862$. This can be displayed easily by using the following format.

$$\overset{\textstyle 0.0\ 0\ 0\ 6\ 017}{\sqrt{0.\overparen{00}\overparen{00}\overparen{00}\overparen{03}62}}$$

LINEAR EQUATIONS

A linear equation is an equation containing one variable, usually x, y, or z, in which no expression containing the variable is of higher order than first degree. That is, the variable does not have exponents. Linear equations in two variables or more are not needed for this text and will not be discussed here. Usually a linear equation can be simplified by combining like terms on each side to obtain a form like

$$ax + b = cx + d$$

where the a, b, c, d represent some known constants. In combining terms, remember that multiplication and division should be performed before addition and subtraction. Terms within parentheses should be combined as far as possible before removing the parentheses. A negative sign on the outside of parentheses applies to all terms within the parentheses and removal of the parentheses necessitates changing the sign of all terms within the parentheses (see example that follows). Then proceed to get the x terms all on one side, usually the left, and all other terms on the right side (or other side) by adding the negative of the term you wish to transfer to both sides. Thus

$$ax + b + (-b) = cx + d + (-b)$$

$$ax = cx + (d - b)$$

$$ax + (-cx) = cx + (-cx) + (d - b)$$

$$(a - c)x = d - b$$

Finally, divide both sides by the coefficient of x, and

$$x = \frac{d - b}{a - c}$$

EXAMPLE   Solve the equation:

$$8x + (4 - 2x) + 3 = 3x - 2(7 + 4x) + 11$$

for x, we combine terms as follows:

$$8x + 4 - 2x + 3 = 3x - (14 + 8x) + 11$$

$$6x + 7 = 3x - 14 - 8x + 11$$

$$6x + 7 = -5x - 3$$

Then we combine the terms so that the x terms are on the left side and the other terms are on the right side. Recall that the negative of $-5x$ is $+5x$.

$$6x + 7 + (-7) = -5x - 3 + (-7)$$

$$6x = -5x - 10$$

$$5x + 6x = -5x + 5x - 10$$

$$11x = -10.$$

Finally, divide both sides by 11 to obtain

$$x = -\frac{10}{11}$$

If desired we can check our solution by substituting the values of x into the original equation.

$$8\left(-\frac{10}{11}\right) + 4 - 2\left(-\frac{10}{11}\right) + 3 = -\frac{80}{11} + \frac{44}{11} + \frac{20}{11} + \frac{33}{11}$$

$$= -\frac{80}{11} + \frac{97}{11}$$

$$= \frac{17}{11}$$

$$3\left(-\frac{10}{11}\right) - 2\left[7 + 4\left(-\frac{10}{11}\right)\right] + 11 = -\frac{30}{11} - 2\left(\frac{77}{11} - \frac{40}{11}\right) + \frac{121}{11}$$

$$= -\frac{30}{11} - 2\left(\frac{37}{11}\right) + \frac{121}{11}$$

$$= -\frac{30}{11} - \frac{74}{11} + \frac{121}{11}$$

$$= -\frac{104}{11} + \frac{121}{11}$$

$$= \frac{17}{11}$$

Since substitution of $-\frac{10}{11}$ for x yields the same value for each side, we conclude that this is the solution of the equation.

If the equation involves fractions two methods work equally well. Either the fractions can be carried along, combining where needed, or both sides of the equation can be multiplied by a common multiple of all the denominators (preferably the least common multiple). The resulting equation can be solved as before.

The following example wil be solved both ways. The check is left to the student.

EXAMPLE Solve the equation:

$$\frac{2}{3}x - \frac{1}{3} = \frac{1}{2}x - \frac{1}{4} - \frac{1}{6}x$$

Solving by the first method, we have

$$\frac{2}{3}x - \frac{1}{3} = \frac{1}{2}x - \frac{1}{6}x - \frac{1}{4}$$

$$\frac{2}{3}x - \frac{1}{3} = \frac{3}{6}x - \frac{1}{6}x - \frac{1}{4}$$

$$\frac{2}{3}x - \frac{1}{3} = \frac{1}{3}x - \frac{1}{4} \quad \left(\text{since} \quad \frac{2}{6} = \frac{1}{3}\right)$$

$$\frac{2}{3}x - \frac{1}{3} + \frac{1}{3} = \frac{1}{3}x - \frac{1}{4} + \frac{1}{3}$$

$$\frac{2}{3}x = \frac{1}{3}x + \left(\frac{1}{3} - \frac{1}{4}\right)$$

$$\frac{2}{3}x = \frac{1}{3}x + \left(\frac{4}{12} - \frac{3}{12}\right)$$

$$\frac{2}{3}x = \frac{1}{3}x + \frac{1}{12}$$

$$\frac{2}{3}x - \frac{1}{3}x = \frac{1}{12}$$

$$\frac{1}{3}x = \frac{1}{12}$$

Then we multiply both sides by whatever is necessary to make the left side equal to x.

$$3 \cdot \frac{1}{3}x = 3 \cdot \frac{1}{12}$$

$$x = \frac{1}{4}$$

Now if we had had, say $\frac{3}{5}x=\frac{9}{2}$, we would have multiplied both sides by $\frac{5}{3}$ and had $\frac{5}{3}\cdot\frac{3}{5}x=\frac{5}{3}\cdot\frac{9}{2}$ or $x=\frac{15}{2}$.

Solving the equation in the second way, we multiply both sides by some common multiple of the denominators 3, 2, 4, 6. Obviously their product, 144, will work, but a little thought will reveal that 12 is the least common multiple so we have

$$12\left(\frac{2}{3}x-\frac{1}{3}\right)=12\left(\frac{1}{2}x-\frac{1}{4}-\frac{1}{6}x\right)$$

$$8x-4=6x-3-2x$$

$$8x-4=4x-3$$

$$8x-4+4=4x-3+4$$

$$8x=4x+1$$

$$8x-4x=4x-4x+1$$

$$4x=1$$

$$x=\frac{1}{4}$$

Appendix B

Probability

RULES OF PROBABILITY

If an experiment is performed, the set consisting of all possible outcomes is called the **sample space** for the experiment. The sample space is usually denoted by S. Each outcome is called a **point** of the sample space or a **sample point**. A sample space can best be obtained by listing every possible outcome in its simplest form. If a coin is to be tossed three times, for example, the sample space of possible outcomes of heads and tails is given by

$$S = \{(H,H,H),(H,H,T),(H,T,H),(H,T,T),$$

$$(T,H,H),(T,H,T),(T,T,H),(T,T,T)\}$$

Each of the eight possible outcomes thus becomes a point of the sample space.

> **EXAMPLE 1** An experiment consists of tossing a coin and rolling a die. Give the sample space for the experiment.

SOLUTION   The sample space consists of twelve outcomes since there are two possible outcomes for the coin and six for the die. Applying the multiplication rule, $2 \cdot 6 = 12$. These outcomes are as follows:

$$S = \{(H,1),(H,2),(H,3),(H,4),(H,5),(H,6),$$

$$(T,1),(T,2),(T,3),(T,4),(T,5),(T,6)\}$$

An alternate representation is given below in which each dot represents the point of the sample space corresponding to the outcome on the coin (to the left) and on the die (above).

447

die coin	1	2	3	4	5	6
H	.	.	.	.	.	.
T	.	.	.	.	.	.

Any collection of points in the sample space is called an **event** or **simple event**. The set of no points is the **empty set**, denoted by $\varnothing$, and is included for completeness. In the experiment in which a coin is tossed three times, the event "heads appear twice" consists of the points $(H, H, T), (H, T, H)$, and (T, H, H).

EXAMPLE 2   Three dice are rolled. List the points of the sample space corresponding to the event "a total of six is obtained on the upper faces."

SOLUTION   It may help if we imagine the dice to be of three different colors, say red, yellow, green. We let the ordered triple $(1, 2, 3)$ represent the numbers on, respectively, the red, yellow, and green die. There are six such orders (by Permutation Rule A). Other possibilities are $(1, 1, 4)$ and its permutations, three in all, and $(2, 2, 2)$. No other possible outcomes add up to six. The ten points which correspond to the event: "a total of six on the three dice" are as follows:

$$"6" = \{(1, 2, 3), (2, 1, 3), (1, 3, 2), (3, 1, 2), (3, 2, 1),$$
$$= (2, 3, 1), (1, 1, 4), (1, 4, 1), (4, 1, 1), (2, 2, 2)\}$$

NOTE   A listing of all sample points for the experiment and extraction of those which correspond to "6" is possible, but cumbersome since there are $6 \cdot 6 \cdot 6$ or 216 points in the sample space for the experiment.

The classical definition of probability can be used to determine the probability of an event, if each of the sample points is equally likely. In this case the probability of an event is equal to the number of sample points in the event divided by the number of points in the sample space. In example 2, the probability of obtaining a six on one roll of three dice is 10/216 (or 5/108 or about 0.046) since the points are equally likely. There are ten points in the event and 216 in the sample space. We symbolize this by writing

$$P(6) = 10/216$$

The symbol **P(6)** is read "P of 6" or "probability of 6." It does not refer to multiplication, but is a way of symbolizing a probability even if we do not know its value.

EXAMPLE 3   Suppose that a drawing of one marble is to be made from a box containing three white marbles, four red marbles, and one clear marble. Determine the following probabilities: P(the marble is red), P(the marble is white), P(the marble is not red).

SOLUTION   The sample space may be illustrated schematically by using a **Venn diagram** as illustrated below.

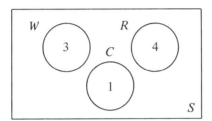

In this diagram, W represents the set of white marbles, R represents the set of red marbles, C represents the set of clear marbles, and S represents the sample space. The number of marbles in each set is marked within the set. If there were marbles which did not belong to any of the sets, that number would appear outside the circles, but in S. There are 4 red marbles, of the total of 8, so $P(R)=4/8$, or 0.5. Similarly there are three white marbles, so $P(W)=3/8$. Five marbles are not white, so this probability is $5/8$. To symbolize this event, not white, we write **W'**, read W-prime, so that $P(W')=5/8$. An event of this type, consisting of sample points not in another event, is called a *complement*. The **complement** of any event A, denoted A', consists of all sample points not in A.

In the preceding example, the events did not have any points in common. Such events are said to be **mutually exclusive**. If two events are mutually exclusive, they cannot both occur at the same time. The three events, R, W, C, accounted for all points of the sample space. Such events are said to be **exhaustive**. (Exhaustive events need not be mutually exclusive.) Complementary events are any two events which are *both* mutually exclusive and exhaustive.

EXAMPLE 4   A die is tossed once. Determine the probability of obtaining (a) at least a 3; (b) at most a 4; (c) more than 4; (d) 5 or less; (e) 2 or more; and (f) less than 5.

SOLUTION   The sample space is $\{1,2,3,4,5,6\}$, each point with probability

1/6. The set corresponding to each event with its probability follows:

	Set	Symbol	Value
(a)	$\{3,4,5,6\}$	$P(x \geq 3)$	4/6 or 2/3
(b)	$\{1,2,3,4\}$	$P(x \leq 4)$	4/6 or 2/3
(c)	$\{5,6\}$	$P(x > 4)$	2/6 or 1/3
(d)	$\{1,2,3,4,5\}$	$P(x \leq 5)$	5/6
(e)	$\{2,3,4,5,6\}$	$P(x \geq 2)$	5/6
(f)	$\{1,2,3,4\}$	$P(x < 5)$	4/6 or 2/3

DISCUSSION   Many students have difficulty with the concepts "greater than," "less than," "at least," and "at most." Note that "at least k" means either "k" or "greater than k," while "greater than k" excludes k. Note also that there is a basic difference in cases where integers only are involved. In the case of integers, the events "$x > 4$" and $x \leq 5$ are identical. Both cases include all integers from 5 on. Where real or rational numbers are involved, however, these events are different since, for instance, 4.3 is greater than 4 and hence satisfies $x > 4$, but it is less than 5 and hence does not satisfy $x \leq 5$.

In the preceding examples, some of the rules by which probability is calculated are seen. First, we observe that we are working only with one sample space for each of the probability models we have examined. Then it is obvious that the probability of a particular event occurring must be positive or zero, that is, $P(A) \geq 0$ for any event A. The probability of any event, however, cannot exceed one, so $P(A) \leq 1$. Combining these two statements, we obtain the **first probability rule**: The probability of an event is expressed as a real number from zero to one, inclusive, or $0 \leq P(A) \leq 1$. Further, the sum of the probabilities of the sample points which make up the sample space is one. Thus the probability of *some* event in the sample space occurring is one, and the probability of no event in the sample space occurring is zero; that is, if S represents the whole sample space, $P(S) = 1$, and if $\varnothing$ represents the empty set, $P(\varnothing) = 0$.

In example 4, note that the events given in (b) and (c) are complementary and the sum of their probabilities is equal to one. This is true for any complementary events, so we here summarize the probability rules for simple events.

Probability	1.	For any event $A, 0 \leq P(A) \leq 1$
Rules for	2.	For any sample space $S, P(S) = 1: P(\varnothing) = 0$
Simple Events	3.	For any event $A, P(A') = 1 - P(A)$

Probabilities can also be calculated for combinations of simple events. Such combinations are called **compound events**. There are two types of compound events. The probability that *either* event *A* or event *B* (or both) will occur is symbolized by *P*(*A or B*); the probability that *both* event *A* and event *B* will occur is symbolized by *P*(*A and B*). Rules governing compound events can best be illustrated by an example.

Suppose that one marble is to be drawn from a box containing three solid white marbles, four solid red marbles, two with red and white stripes, and one clear marble. We let *W* represent the event "white marble" and *R* represent "red marble." A marble with red and white stripes is considered to belong to *both W* and *R*. A Venn diagram for the sample space is given here.

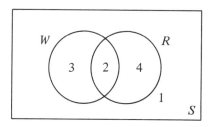

For the simple events, *W* and *R*, we note that *P*(*W*)=0.5 since 5 of the ten marbles have white markings, and *P*(*R*)=0.6, since 6 of the ten marbles have red markings. There are a total of 9 marbles which have either red or white markings (or both), so we have *P*(*W or R*)=0.9. Similarly, exactly two of the marbels have *both* red *and* white markings, so *P*(*W and R*)=0.2. Now note that *P*(*W*)+ *P*(*R*)=0.5+0.6=1.1. This is not equal to *P*(*W or R*) since the overlapping portion is counted twice, so *P*(*W and R*) must be subtracted from 1.1 to obtain the correct value for *P*(*W or R*). This leads to the **general rule of addition**: If *A* and *B* are events in the same sample space, the probability that at least one will occur is the sum of the individual probabilities minus the probability that both will happen.

Addition Rule ***for Probability***	For any events, *A* and *B*, in a sample space $P(A \text{ or } B) = P(A) + P(B) - P(A \text{ and } B)$

In the marble case we observe that *P*(*A or R*)=0.9 and *P*(*W*)+ *P*(*R*)− *P*(*W and R*)=0.5+0.6−0.2=0.9. A little arithmetic gives us a useful consequence of the addition rule, namely *P*(*A and B*)= *P*(*A*)+ *P*(*B*)− *P*(*A or B*).

Now if two events, A and B, are mutually exclusive, they cannot both occur, so $P(A \text{ and } B) = 0$. We then have the special case of the addition rule, for mutually exclusive events. If A and B are mutually exclusive events, the probability that one (or both) of them will occur is the sum of their probabilities.

Addition Rule for Probability (*Special Case*)	If A and B are mutually exclusive events, $$P(A \text{ or } B) = P(A) + P(B)$$

Applications of the probability rules for simple and compound events will enable us to determine probabilities for many different events. In the example with ten marbles, some of the events are given here, together with their probabilities. The student should take the time to verify each one before going on.

Event The marble drawn has markings which are	Probability Symbol	Value
White	$P(W)$	0.5
Red	$P(R)$	0.6
White and Red	$P(W \text{ and } R)$	0.2
White or Red	$P(W \text{ or } R)$	0.9
Not White	$P(W')$	0.5
Not Red	$P(R')$	0.4
Neither white nor red	$P(W' \text{ and } R')$	0.1
Not white and not red	$P(W' \text{ and } R')$	0.1
Not both white and red	$P(W \text{ and } R)'$	0.8
Not white or not red	$P(W' \text{ or } R')$	0.8
White but not red	$P(W \text{ and } R')$	0.3
Red but not white	$P(W' \text{ and } R)$	0.4

Note that the events "white and red" and "white but not red" are mutually exclusive, and their union is simply the event "white." In terms of probability, $P(W) = P(W \text{ and } R) + P(W \text{ and } R')$. This special rule has many applications and can be written as follows: If A and B are any events, $P(A) = P(A \text{ and } B) + P(A \text{ and } B')$.

A summary of the **probability rules** presented in this section is now appropriate:

1. For any event, $A, 0 \le P(A) \le 1$
2. For any sample space $S, P(S) = 1; P(\emptyset) = 0$
3. For any event $A, P(A') = 1 - P(A)$
4. If A and B are any events,
$$P(A \text{ or } B) = P(A) + P(B) - P(A \text{ and } B)$$
5. If A and B are mutually exclusive,
$$P(A \text{ or } B) = P(A) + P(B)$$
6. If A and B are any events,
$$P(A) = P(A \text{ and } B) + P(A \text{ and } B')$$

•Problems

1. If $P(A) = 0.6$ and $P(B) = 0.7$, under what conditions may A and B be mutually exclusive?
2. If A and B are mutually exclusive and $P(A) = 0.4$ and $P(B) = 0.5$, what is $P(A \text{ or } B)$?
3. A psychologist states that if a rat enters a maze, the probability that he will emerge at point A is 0.44, at point B is 0.29, at neither is 0.17. Do you agree or disagree with his assertion? Why?
4. An enthusiastic football fan claims that there are only 2 chances in 15 that his team will lose while the probability that it will win is 0.9. A second fan, more conservative, agrees that there are only 2 chances in 15 of losing, but that the probability of winning is only 0.8. Comment on these two claims.
5. A family is considering buying a dog. If the probability that they will buy a small dog is 0.1, that they will buy a medium-sized dog is 0.3, that they will buy a large dog is 0.2, and that they will buy a very large dog is 0.1, what is the probability that the family will buy a dog?
6. An urn contains 3 white, 2 red, 1 blue, and 4 black balls. If one ball is drawn at random, what is the probability that it is
   (a) black?
   (b) either black or white?

(c) not white?

(d) both red and blue?

7. Of 10 students, 3 are mathematics majors, one of whom is from New York. Of the 10 students, 4 are from New York. If a student is chosen at random from among these 10, what is the probability that he is

(a) a math major from New York?

(b) a New Yorker who is not a math major?

(c) either from New York or a math major?

(d) neither a math major nor from New York?

(e) not from New York?

(f) either not a math major or not from New York?

(g) not a math major?

(h) either a math major or else not from New York?

8. From experience, the toll taker feels that the probability that an automobile paying a toll on the Sunshine Skyway is a Chevrolet is 0.21, that it is a Ford is 0.17, that it is a Pontiac is 0.11. Assuming he is correct, if an automobile pulls up to pay a toll, what is the probability that it is

(a) a Chevrolet or a Ford?

(b) a Ford or a Pontiac?

(c) neither a Chevrolet nor a Pontiac?

(d) none of these three makes?

INDEPENDENT EVENTS AND CONDITIONAL PROBABILITY

If a coin is tossed twice in succession, the probability that the first toss comes up a head is $1/2$. If the first toss is a head, the probability that the second toss is a head is $1/2$. If the first toss is a tail, the probability that the second toss is a head is still $1/2$. In other words, the probability of a head on the second toss does not depend upon the outcome of the first toss. The results of the first toss have absolutely no bearing on the outcome of the second toss. The two outcomes are *independent*. Two events are said to be **independent** if neither outcome affects the probability of occurrence of the other. The probability of two heads in succession on two successive tosses of a coin can be determined with reference to the sample space. There are four equally likely points since $S = \{(H,H), (H,T), (T,H), (T,T)\}$ and exactly one of them is the event "two heads," so the probability is $1/4$. We can also reason that $1/2$ of the tosses will be heads the first time, and $1/2$ of those will be heads the second time, so $1/4$ will be heads both times. The reasoning is correct and leads to the special case of the **multiplication rule for probability**.

Multiplication Rule ***for Probability*** (*Special Case*)	*If A and B are independent events, then* $P(A \ and \ B) = P(A) \cdot P(B)$

The concept of independence is central to probability and needs more foundation than the intuitive approach given above. A sounder understanding of this concept can be obtained by examining **conditional probability**.

Consider two sets of playing cards—set X consisting of two aces and three kings, and set Y consisting of three aces and one king. If an experiment consists of tossing a coin to decide which set to pick (heads, X, tails, Y), and then we shuffle the set and look at the top card, it is apparent that the probability of getting a king is much greater if set X is selected than if set Y is selected. Three-fifths of the cards in set X are kings while only $1/4$ of those in set Y are kings. Now, if the event K means that a king is on top, while X means that set X is selected, $P(K|X)$ (read "probability of K, given X") is the probability that if set X is selected, a king will be on top. Similarly, $P(K|Y)$ is the probability that if Y is selected, a king will be on top. Then $P(A|X)$ and $P(A|Y)$ are the probabilities that an ace is on top if X and Y are selected, respectively. From the information given previously,

$$P(K|X) = 3/5, P(K|Y) = 1/4, P(A|X) = 2/5, P(A|Y) = 3/4$$

The sum of these probabilities is greater than one, so that these events cannot be considered all a part of the same sample space.

Now the sample space corresponding to this experiment has four points whose probabilities can be determined intuitively as follows: X will be selected half of the time; $3/5$ of those times a king will be selected, so that X will be selected *and* a king will turn up about $(3/5) \cdot (1/2)$ or $3/10$ of the time. Hence $P(K \ and \ X) = 3/10$. Similarly $P(A \ and \ X) = (2/5) \cdot (1/2) = 2/10$, $P(K \ and \ Y) = (1/4) \cdot (1/2) = 1/8$. $P(A \ and \ Y) = (3/4) \cdot (1/2) = 3/8$. We note that in each case $P(A \ and \ B) = P(A|B) \cdot P(B)$ so that

$$\frac{P(A \ and \ B)}{P(B)} = P(A|B)$$

This gives us the formal definition of conditional probability.

Conditional Probability

If an event B is given $(P(B)\neq0)$, the conditional probability of A is defined by

$$P(A|B)=\frac{P(A \text{ and } B)}{P(B)}$$

The event B is called a restricted sample space.

The definition of conditional probability gives us the general form of the multiplication rule for probability since if $P(A|B)=P(A \text{ and } B)/P(B)$, then $P(A \text{ and } B)=P(A|B)\cdot P(B)$ and we have

Multiplication Rule for Probability

For any events A and B,

$$P(A \text{ and } B)=P(A|B)\cdot P(B)$$

EXAMPLE 1 Consider a group of 40 students, 20 of whom take an English course and 16 take a business course. Of these two groups, 12 are taking both. Determine $P(B|E)$ *and* $P(E|B)$.

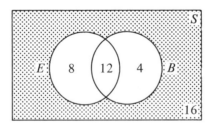

SOLUTION $P(E)=20/40=0.50$, $P(B=16/40=0.40$, $P(E \text{ and } B)=12/40=0.30$ where E and B constitute the obvious events. If one student is selected and it is known that he is taking an English course, then he is one of 20 students in set E. Since 12 of the students taking English also take business, the probability that our English-taking student takes business is $12/20$ or 0.60. By the rule for conditional probability,

$$P(B|E) = \frac{P(B \text{ and } E)}{P(E)} = \frac{0.30}{0.50} = 0.60$$

Thus, the probability of B for the restricted sample space E is, as expected, the conditional probability of B given E. Similarly, 12 of the 16 students taking business also take English. By the rule,

$$P(E|B) = \frac{P(E \text{ and } B)}{P(B)} = \frac{0.30}{0.40} = 0.75$$

Since $12/16 = 0.75$, we have affirmed the rule once again.

Returning to the example which opened the section, suppose we wish to know the probability before tossing the coin that the card we turn up will be a king. There are only two possibilities: we select set X by obtaining a head and draw a king, or we select set Y and draw a king. Since X and Y are complementary we know that

$$P(K) = P(K \text{ and } X) + P(K \text{ and } Y) = 3/10 + 1/8 = 34/80 = 17/40$$

Naturally, since K and A are complementary, $P(A) = 1 - 17/40 = 23/40$. Another way to state $P(K) = P(K \text{ and } X) + P(K \text{ and } Y)$ is

$$P(K) = P(K|X) \cdot P(X) + P(K|Y) \cdot P(Y)$$

Applying the same reasoning to the addition rule, we have the **rule of total probability**.

Rule of Total Probability

If $B_1, B_2, \ldots, B_n$ are mutually exclusive events which make up the sample space, then
$$P(A) = P(A|B_1) \cdot P(B_1) + P(A|B_2) \cdot P(B_2) + \cdots + P(A|B_n) \cdot P(B_n).$$

EXAMPLE 2   A golfer has a probability of getting a good shot equal to 9/10 if he uses the correct club. If he uses an incorrect club, the probability drops to 7/10. If only one club is correct for a particular shot and he has 14 clubs in his bag, determine the probability that he gets a good shot in the unlikely event that he chooses one of the clubs at random.

SOLUTION   Let G represent the event "he gets a good shot" and C represent the event "he uses the right club." Then $P(G|C)=9/10$, $P(G|C')=7/10$, $P(C)=1/14$, and $P(C')=13/14$. By the rule of total probability, then,

$$P(G)=P(G|C)\cdot P(C)+P(G|C')\cdot P(C')$$

$$=(9/10)(1/14)+(7/10)(13/14)$$

$$=9/140+91/140$$

$$=100/140$$

$$=5/7$$

A tree diagram approach to this problem may prove helpful. Let the first step represent selection of club, the second step represent the actual shot. Probabilities are multiplied on each branch by virtue of the multiplication rule.

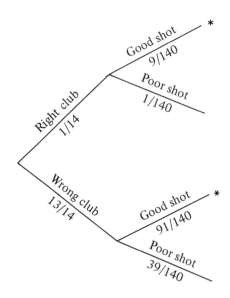

We find the outcomes which correspond to the good shot (marked above) and the probabilites of each. Then we simply add up the probabilities to obtain $P(G)$.

The similarities between the general and special multiplication rules for probability lead us to ask how independence and conditional probability are related, since this is the only difference between the events. To answer that question let us examine the group of 40 students of example 1. Of these, 20 take an English course, 16 take a business course. Twelve students take both. Suppose we bet, with a friend, that we can guess whether or not a particular student takes an English course. We can ask him one question and one question only, and it may not pertain to whether he takes English or not. Since $P(E|B)=0.75$ and $P(E|B')=0.33$, we can considerably improve our chances of winning by asking whether the student is taking a business course. If so, we should guess that he is taking an English course since 0.75 of the students taking a business course take an English course. That is, $P(E|B)$ and $P(E)$ are different so that occurrence or nonoccurrence of event B has an effect on the probability of event E.

Now the game has changed. Our friend has another group of 40 students. Twenty of these take accounting, 16 take math, but now only 8 of those take both. The rules remain the same, only now we must guess whether or not a student takes accounting. We confidently sit down to determine how to guess after we find out whether or not he takes math. We have $P(A)=0.50$, $P(M)=0.40$, $P(A \text{ and } B)=0.20$. Then $P(A|M)=0.20/0.40=0.50$. But then $P(A|M)=P(A)$; that is, the proportion of math students taking accounting is equal to the proportion of students taking accounting in the whole sample space. Further,

$$P(A|M') = \frac{P(A \text{ and } M')}{M'} = \frac{0.30}{0.60} = 0.50 = P(A)$$

again. Thus, whether a student takes math or not has no effect whatsoever on the probabilty of the student's taking accounting. The two events are truly **independent**.

Independent Events	Two events, A and B, are independent if and only if $P(A|B) = P(A)$.

Note that if both A and B are independent, then

$$P(A|B) = \frac{P(A \text{ and } B)}{P(B)} = P(A), \quad \text{so} \quad P(A \text{ and } B) = P(A) \cdot P(B),$$

which is the special case of the multiplication rule for probability. That is, the probability that both will occur is then the product of their individual probabilities (but only if the events are independent).

Moreover, if the events are independent,

$$P(B|A) = \frac{P(B \text{ and } A)}{P(A)} = \frac{P(A \text{ and } B)}{P(A)} = \frac{P(A) \cdot P(B)}{P(A)} = P(B)$$

Thus, if the probability that the home team will win any particular game of the World Series is 0.6, the probability of a clean sweep (winning the first four games) by one team is (0.6) (0.6) (0.4) (0.4) or 0.0576. This is assuming independence of outcomes which is not very likely. Recall that the first two games are played on one field, the next two games on the other team's field.

EXAMPLE 3   An urn contains 3 red balls and 2 white balls. A ball is drawn, then replaced. What is the probability that a white ball will be drawn three times in a row?

SOLUTION   The probability of drawing a white ball on any particular drawing is 2/5. Successive drawings are independent, since the ball drawn is replaced. Therefore, the probability, $P(WWW)$, is $(2/5) \cdot (2/5) \cdot (2/5)$ or $(2/5)^3$ which is 8/125 or 0.064.

EXAMPLE 4   Two dice are thrown and the total number of dots observed. List a sample space for the experiment, together with associated probabilities.

SOLUTION   We must consider the dice separately to arrive at an accurate space—for example, we could have one red, and one green. The probability of obtaining a "1" on each die, hence a total of two, is $(1/6) \cdot (1/6)$ or 1/36. Thus $P(2) = 1/36$. There are two ways to obtain three—"2" on the red die, "1" on the green, or vice versa. Again each has a probability of 1/36. These two outcomes are mutually exclusive, so $P(3) = 2/36$ or 1/18. Continuing, we have the following table:

x	$P(x)$
2	1/36
3	2/36
4	3/36
5	4/36
6	5/36
7	6/36
8	5/36
9	4/36
10	3/36
11	2/36
12	1/36

CAUTION   Many students confuse the terms "independent" and "mutually exclusive." These terms are different, and apply to different things. This can be shown easily by observing that if A and B are events with nonzero probabilities, if they are mutually exclusive, $P(A \text{ and } B) = 0$, while if they are independent, $P(A \text{ and } B) \neq 0$. Mutually exclusive events are events which cannot both occur at the same time, while independent events are events which do not influence each other.

A striking example of this can be given by football games. If Florida and Alabama play football games on a given day, the events "Florida wins" and "Alabama wins" are independent unless they play each other. In that case, the events are mutually exclusive.

•Problems

1. Find $P(A \text{ and } B)$ if $P(A) = 2/3$, $P(B) = 1/5$ and
   (a) $P(A|B) = 1/10$ (c) $P(A|B) = P(A)$
   (b) $P(B|A) = 1/10$ (d) $P(B|A) = P(B)$
2. In a group of 100 students, it is found that 80 take an English course, 60 take a mathematics course, and 10 take neither. Are the two events independent? Why?
3. If $P(A) = 0.30$, $P(B) = 0.50$, and A and B are mutually exclusive events, find
   (a) $P(A|B)$ (b) $P(B|A)$
4. If a coin is tossed five times, what is the probability of getting a head on the first and last tosses, and tails on the middle three?
5. Fifteen white marbles and 6 red marbles are placed in a box. What is the probability of drawing 3 white marbles
   (a) if the marbles are replaced after each drawing?
   (b) if the marbles are not replaced?
6. In a set of 60 teachers, 20 teach history, 6 are coaches. It is found that coaching and teaching history are independent events. How many of the coaches teach history?
7. The owner of a department store is giving away a door prize by randomly selecting one of 1,000 slips filled out by the customers (only one to a customer). The breakdown into those who are regular customers and those who are not and also into those who purchased a special sale item is as follows:

	Regular Customers	Not Regular Customers	Totals
Sale Item Purchasers	350	130	480
Nonpurchasers	210	310	520
Totals	560	440	1000

If R represents the event "prize is won by a regular customer," P the event "prize is won by a sale item purchaser," find each of the following probabilities:

(a) $P(R)$	(e) $P(R\|P')$	(i) $P(R'\|P)$
(b) $P(R\|P)$	(f) $P(P\|R')$	(j) $P(P'\|R)$
(c) $P(P)$	(g) $P(R'\|P')$	
(d) $P(P\|R)$	(h) $P(P'\|R')$	

8. A die is cast three times. What is the probability
   (a) of obtaining three 6's?
   (b) of not obtaining three 3's?
   (c) of obtaining the same uppermost face on all three tosses?
   (d) of obtaining three different faces?
   (e) of obtaining a total of 15 for the three throws?

9. A beginning bowler has a probability of $1/5$ of getting a strike if he uses the proper weight ball. If he uses the improper weight, the probability drops to $1/8$. There are 6 balls in the rack, only 2 of which are the proper weight for him. If he chooses a ball at random, what is the probability that he will get a strike?

10. A machine produces parts and they are stored in a large bin. The parts are then boxed for shipment. On the average 1 box in 50 contains one or more defective parts. If a company orders 4 boxes of parts, what is the probability that all 4 boxes contain at least one defective part? What is the probability that no defective parts will be in any of the boxes? Assume independence of the outcomes.

Tables

TABLE 1

TABLE 1

Square Roots

n	$\sqrt{n}$	$\sqrt{10n}$	n	$\sqrt{n}$	$\sqrt{10n}$	n	$\sqrt{n}$	$\sqrt{10n}$
1.00	1.000	3.162	1.13	1.063	3.362	1.26	1.122	3.550
1.01	1.005	3.178	1.14	1.068	3.376	1.27	1.127	3.564
1.02	1.010	3.194	1.15	1.072	3.391	1.28	1.131	3.578
1.03	1.015	3.209	1.16	1.077	3.406	1.29	1.136	3.592
1.04	1.020	3.225	1.17	1.082	3.421	1.30	1.140	3.606
1.05	1.025	3.240	1.18	1.086	3.435	1.31	1.145	3.619
1.06	1.030	3.256	1.19	1.091	3.450	1.32	1.149	3.633
1.07	1.034	3.271	1.20	1.095	3.464	1.33	1.153	3.647
1.08	1.039	3.286	1.21	1.100	3.479	1.34	1.158	3.661
1.09	1.044	3.302	1.22	1.105	3.493	1.35	1.162	3.674
1.10	1.049	3.317	1.23	1.109	3.507	1.36	1.166	3.688
1.11	1.054	3.332	1.24	1.114	3.521	1.37	1.170	3.701
1.12	1.058	3.347	1.25	1.118	3.536	1.38	1.175	3.715

TABLE 1—Square Roots (continued)

n	$\sqrt{n}$	$\sqrt{10n}$	n	$\sqrt{n}$	$\sqrt{10n}$	n	$\sqrt{n}$	$\sqrt{10n}$
1.39	1.179	3.728	1.80	1.342	4.243	2.21	1.487	4.701
1.40	1.183	3.742	1.81	1.345	4.254	2.22	1.490	4.712
1.41	1.187	3.755	1.82	1.349	4.266	2.23	1.493	4.722
1.42	1.192	3.768	1.83	1.353	4.278	2.24	1.497	4.733
1.43	1.196	3.782	1.84	1.356	4.290	2.25	1.500	4.743
1.44	1.200	3.795	1.85	1.360	4.301	2.26	1.503	4.754
1.45	1.204	3.808	1.86	1.364	4.313	2.27	1.507	4.764
1.46	1.208	3.821	1.87	1.367	4.324	2.28	1.510	4.775
1.47	1.212	3.834	1.88	1.371	4.336	2.29	1.513	4.785
1.48	1.217	3.847	1.89	1.375	4.347	2.30	1.517	4.796
1.49	1.221	3.860	1.90	1.378	4.359	2.31	1.520	4.806
1.50	1.225	3.873	1.91	1.382	4.370	2.32	1.523	4.817
1.51	1.229	3.886	1.92	1.386	4.382	2.33	1.526	4.827
1.52	1.233	3.899	1.93	1.389	4.393	2.34	1.530	4.837
1.53	1.237	3.912	1.94	1.393	4.405	2.35	1.533	4.848
1.54	1.241	3.924	1.95	1.396	4.416	2.36	1.536	4.858
1.55	1.245	3.937	1.96	1.400	4.427	2.37	1.539	4.868
1.56	1.249	3.950	1.97	1.404	4.438	2.38	1.543	4.879
1.57	1.253	3.962	1.98	1.407	4.450	2.39	1.546	4.889
1.58	1.257	3.975	1.99	1.411	4.461	2.40	1.549	4.899
1.59	1.261	3.987	2.00	1.414	4.472	2.41	1.552	4.909
1.60	1.265	4.000	2.01	1.418	4.483	2.42	1.556	4.919
1.61	1.269	4.012	2.02	1.421	4.494	2.43	1.559	4.930
1.62	1.273	4.025	2.03	1.425	4.506	2.44	1.562	4.940
1.63	1.277	4.037	2.04	1.428	4.517	2.45	1.565	4.950
1.64	1.281	4.050	2.05	1.432	4.528	2.46	1.568	4.960
1.65	1.285	4.062	2.06	1.435	4.539	2.47	1.572	4.970
1.66	1.288	4.074	2.07	1.439	4.550	2.48	1.575	4.980
1.67	1.292	4.087	2.08	1.442	4.561	2.49	1.578	4.990
1.68	1.296	4.099	2.09	1.446	4.572	2.50	1.581	5.000
1.69	1.300	4.111	2.10	1.449	4.583	2.51	1.584	5.010
1.70	1.304	4.123	2.11	1.453	4.593	2.52	1.587	5.020
1.71	1.308	4.135	2.12	1.456	4.604	2.53	1.591	5.030
1.72	1.311	4.147	2.13	1.459	4.615	2.54	1.594	5.040
1.73	1.315	4.159	2.14	1.463	4.626	2.55	1.597	5.050
1.74	1.319	4.171	2.15	1.466	4.637	2.56	1.600	5.060
1.75	1.323	4.183	2.16	1.470	4.648	2.57	1.603	5.070
1.76	1.327	4.195	2.17	1.473	4.658	2.58	1.606	5.079
1.77	1.330	4.207	2.18	1.476	4.669	2.59	1.609	5.089
1.78	1.334	4.219	2.19	1.480	4.680	2.60	1.612	5.099
1.79	1.338	4.231	2.20	1.483	4.690	2.61	1.616	5.109

n	$\sqrt{n}$	$\sqrt{10n}$	n	$\sqrt{n}$	$\sqrt{10n}$	n	$\sqrt{n}$	$\sqrt{10n}$
2.62	1.619	5.119	3.03	1.741	5.505	3.44	1.855	5.865
2.63	1.622	5.128	3.04	1.744	5.514	3.45	1.857	5.874
2.64	1.625	5.138	3.05	1.746	5.523	3.46	1.860	5.882
2.65	1.628	5.148	3.06	1.749	5.532	3.47	1.863	5.891
2.66	1.631	5.158	3.07	1.752	5.541	3.48	1.865	5.899
2.67	1.634	5.167	3.08	1.755	5.550	3.49	1.868	5.908
2.68	1.637	5.177	3.09	1.758	5.559	3.50	1.871	5.916
2.69	1.640	5.187	3.10	1.761	5.568	3.51	1.873	5.925
2.70	1.643	5.196	3.11	1.764	5.577	3.52	1.876	5.933
2.71	1.646	5.206	3.12	1.766	5.586	3.53	1.879	5.941
2.72	1.649	5.215	3.13	1.769	5.595	3.54	1.882	5.950
2.73	1.652	5.225	3.14	1.772	5.604	3.55	1.884	5.958
2.74	1.655	5.235	3.15	1.775	5.612	3.56	1.887	5.967
2.75	1.658	5.244	3.16	1.778	5.621	3.57	1.889	5.975
2.76	1.661	5.254	3.17	1.780	5.630	3.58	1.892	5.983
2.77	1.664	5.263	3.18	1.783	5.639	3.59	1.894	5.992
2.78	1.667	5.273	3.19	1.786	5.648	3.60	1.897	6.000
2.79	1.670	5.282	3.20	1.789	5.657	3.61	1.900	6.008
2.80	1.673	5.292	3.21	1.792	5.666	3.62	1.903	6.017
2.81	1.676	5.301	3.22	1.794	5.675	3.63	1.905	6.025
2.82	1.679	5.310	3.23	1.797	5.683	3.64	1.908	6.033
2.83	1.682	5.320	3.24	1.800	5.692	3.65	1.910	6.042
2.84	1.685	5.329	3.25	1.803	5.701	3.66	1.913	6.050
2.85	1.688	5.339	3.26	1.806	5.710	3.67	1.916	6.058
2.86	1.691	5.348	3.27	1.808	5.718	3.68	1.918	6.066
2.87	1.694	5.357	3.28	1.811	5.727	3.69	1.921	6.075
2.88	1.697	5.367	3.29	1.814	5.736	3.70	1.924	6.083
2.89	1.700	5.376	3.30	1.817	5.745	3.71	1.926	6.091
2.90	1.703	5.385	3.31	1.819	5.753	3.72	1.929	6.099
2.91	1.706	5.394	3.32	1.822	5.762	3.73	1.931	6.107
2.92	1.709	5.404	3.33	1.825	5.771	3.74	1.934	6.116
2.93	1.712	5.413	3.34	1.828	5.779	3.75	1.936	6.124
2.94	1.715	5.422	3.35	1.830	5.788	3.76	1.939	6.132
2.95	1.718	5.431	3.36	1.833	5.797	3.77	1.942	6.140
2.96	1.720	5.441	3.37	1.836	5.805	3.78	1.944	6.148
2.97	1.723	5.450	3.38	1.838	5.814	3.79	1.947	6.156
2.98	1.726	5.459	3.39	1.841	5.822	3.80	1.949	6.164
2.99	1.729	5.468	3.40	1.844	5.831	3.81	1.952	6.173
3.00	1.732	5.477	3.41	1.847	5.840	3.82	1.954	6.181
3.01	1.735	5.486	3.42	1.849	5.848	3.83	1.957	6.189
3.02	1.738	5.495	3.43	1.852	5.857	3.84	1.960	6.197

TABLE 1—Square Roots (*continued*)

n	$\sqrt{n}$	$\sqrt{10n}$	n	$\sqrt{n}$	$\sqrt{10n}$	n	$\sqrt{n}$	$\sqrt{10n}$
3.85	1.962	6.205	4.26	2.064	6.527	4.67	2.161	6.834
3.86	1.965	6.213	4.27	2.066	6.535	4.68	2.163	6.841
3.87	1.967	6.221	4.28	2.069	6.542	4.69	2.166	6.848
3.88	1.970	6.229	4.29	2.072	6.550	4.70	2.168	6.856
3.89	1.972	6.237	4.30	2.074	6.557	4.71	2.170	6.863
3.90	1.975	6.245	4.31	2.076	6.565	4.72	2.173	6.870
3.91	1.977	6.253	4.32	2.078	6.573	4.73	2.175	6.878
3.92	1.980	6.261	4.33	2.081	6.580	4.74	2.177	6.885
3.93	1.982	6.269	4.34	2.083	6.588	4.75	2.180	6.892
3.94	1.985	6.277	4.35	2.086	6.595	4.76	2.182	6.899
3.95	1.987	6.285	4.36	2.088	6.603	4.77	2.184	6.907
3.96	1.990	6.293	4.37	2.090	6.611	4.78	2.186	6.914
3.97	1.992	6.301	4.38	2.093	6.618	4.79	2.189	6.921
3.98	1.995	6.309	4.39	2.096	6.626	4.80	2.191	6.928
3.99	1.997	6.317	4.40	2.098	6.633	4.81	2.193	6.935
4.00	2.000	6.325	4.41	2.100	6.641	4.82	2.195	6.943
4.01	2.002	6.332	4.42	2.102	6.648	4.83	2.198	6.950
4.02	2.005	6.340	4.43	2.105	6.656	4.84	2.200	6.957
4.03	2.008	6.348	4.44	2.107	6.663	4.85	2.202	6.964
4.04	2.010	6.356	4.45	2.110	6.671	4.86	2.205	6.971
4.05	2.012	6.364	4.46	2.112	6.678	4.87	2.207	6.979
4.06	2.015	6.372	4.47	2.114	6.686	4.88	2.209	6.986
4.07	2.017	6.380	4.48	2.117	6.693	4.89	2.211	6.993
4.08	2.020	6.387	4.49	2.119	6.701	4.90	2.214	7.000
4.09	2.022	6.395	4.50	2.121	6.708	4.91	2.216	7.007
4.10	2.025	6.403	4.51	2.124	6.716	4.92	2.218	7.014
4.11	2.027	6.411	4.52	2.126	6.723	4.93	2.220	7.021
4.12	2.030	6.419	4.53	2.128	6.731	4.94	2.223	7.029
4.13	2.032	6.427	4.54	2.131	6.738	4.95	2.225	7.036
4.14	2.035	6.434	4.55	2.133	6.745	4.96	2.227	7.043
4.15	2.037	6.442	4.56	2.135	6.753	4.97	2.229	7.050
4.16	2.040	6.450	4.57	2.138	6.760	4.98	2.232	7.057
4.17	2.042	6.458	4.58	2.140	6.768	4.99	2.234	7.064
4.18	2.045	6.465	4.59	2.142	6.775	5.00	2.236	7.071
4.19	2.047	6.473	4.60	2.145	6.782	5.01	2.238	7.078
4.20	2.049	6.481	4.61	2.147	6.790	5.02	2.241	7.085
4.21	2.052	6.488	4.62	2.149	6.797	5.03	2.243	7.092
4.22	2.054	6.496	4.63	2.152	6.804	5.04	2.245	7.099
4.23	2.057	6.504	4.64	2.154	6.812	5.05	2.247	7.106
4.24	2.059	6.512	4.65	2.156	6.819	5.06	2.249	7.113
4.25	2.062	6.519	4.66	2.159	6.826	5.07	2.252	7.120

n	$\sqrt{n}$	$\sqrt{10n}$	n	$\sqrt{n}$	$\sqrt{10n}$	n	$\sqrt{n}$	$\sqrt{10n}$
5.08	2.254	7.127	5.49	2.343	7.409	5.90	2.429	7.681
5.09	2.256	7.134	5.50	2.345	7.416	5.91	2.431	7.688
5.10	2.258	7.141	5.51	2.347	7.423	5.92	2.433	7.694
5.11	2.261	7.148	5.52	2.349	7.430	5.93	2.435	7.701
5.12	2.263	7.155	5.53	2.352	7.436	5.94	2.437	7.707
5.13	2.265	7.162	5.54	2.354	7.443	5.95	2.439	7.714
5.14	2.267	7.169	5.55	2.356	7.450	5.96	2.441	7.720
5.15	2.269	7.176	5.56	2.358	7.457	5.97	2.443	7.727
5.16	2.272	7.183	5.57	2.360	7.463	5.98	2.445	7.733
5.17	2.274	7.190	5.58	2.362	7.470	5.99	2.447	7.740
5.18	2.276	7.197	5.59	2.364	7.477	6.00	2.449	7.746
5.19	2.278	7.204	5.60	2.366	7.483	6.01	2.452	7.752
5.20	2.280	7.211	5.61	2.369	7.490	6.02	2.454	7.759
5.21	2.283	7.218	5.62	2.371	7.496	6.03	2.456	7.765
5.22	2.285	7.225	5.63	2.373	7.503	6.04	2.458	7.772
5.23	2.287	7.232	5.64	2.375	7.510	6.05	2.460	7.778
5.24	2.289	7.239	5.65	2.377	7.517	6.06	2.462	7.785
5.25	2.291	7.246	5.66	2.379	7.523	6.07	2.464	7.791
5.26	2.293	7.253	5.67	2.381	7.530	6.08	2.466	7.797
5.27	2.296	7.259	5.68	2.383	7.537	6.09	2.468	7.804
5.28	2.298	7.266	5.69	2.385	7.543	6.10	2.470	7.810
5.29	2.300	7.273	5.70	2.387	7.550	6.11	2.472	7.817
5.30	2.302	7.280	5.71	2.390	7.556	6.12	2.474	7.823
5.31	2.304	7.287	5.72	2.392	7.563	6.13	2.476	7.829
5.32	2.307	7.294	5.73	2.394	7.570	6.14	2.478	7.836
5.33	2.309	7.301	5.74	2.396	7.576	6.15	2.480	7.842
5.34	2.311	7.308	5.75	2.398	7.583	6.16	2.482	7.849
5.35	2.313	7.314	5.76	2.400	7.589	6.17	2.484	7.855
5.36	2.315	7.321	5.77	2.402	7.596	6.18	2.486	7.861
5.37	2.317	7.328	5.78	2.404	7.603	6.19	2.488	7.868
5.38	2.319	7.335	5.79	2.406	7.609	6.20	2.490	7.874
5.39	2.322	7.342	5.80	2.408	7.616	6.21	2.492	7.880
5.40	2.324	7.348	5.81	2.410	7.622	6.22	2.494	7.887
5.41	2.326	7.355	5.82	2.412	7.629	6.23	2.496	7.893
5.42	2.328	7.362	5.83	2.415	7.635	6.24	2.498	7.899
5.43	2.330	7.369	5.84	2.417	7.642	6.25	2.500	7.906
5.44	2.332	7.376	5.85	2.419	7.649	6.26	2.502	7.912
5.45	2.335	7.382	5.86	2.421	7.655	6.27	2.504	7.918
5.46	2.337	7.389	5.87	2.423	7.662	6.28	2.506	7.925
5.47	2.339	7.396	5.88	2.425	7.668	6.29	2.508	7.931
5.48	2.341	7.403	5.89	2.427	7.675	6.30	2.510	7.937

TABLE 1—Square Roots (*continued*)

n	$\sqrt{n}$	$\sqrt{10n}$	n	$\sqrt{n}$	$\sqrt{10n}$	n	$\sqrt{n}$	$\sqrt{10n}$
6.31	2.512	7.943	6.72	2.592	8.198	7.13	2.670	8.444
6.32	2.514	7.950	6.73	2.594	8.204	7.14	2.672	8.450
6.33	2.516	7.956	6.74	2.596	8.210	7.15	2.674	8.456
6.34	2.518	7.962	6.75	2.598	8.216	7.16	2.676	8.462
6.35	2.520	7.969	6.76	2.600	8.222	7.17	2.678	8.468
6.36	2.522	7.975	6.77	2.602	8.228	7.18	2.680	8.473
6.37	2.524	7.981	6.78	2.604	8.234	7.19	2.681	8.479
6.38	2.526	7.987	6.79	2.606	8.240	7.20	2.683	8.485
6.39	2.528	7.994	6.80	2.608	8.246	7.21	2.685	8.491
6.40	2.530	8.000	6.81	2.610	8.252	7.22	2.687	8.497
6.41	2.532	8.006	6.82	2.612	8.258	7.23	2.689	8.503
6.42	2.534	8.012	6.83	2.613	8.264	7.24	2.691	8.509
6.43	2.536	8.019	6.84	2.615	8.270	7.25	2.693	8.515
6.44	2.538	8.025	6.85	2.617	8.276	7.26	2.694	8.521
6.45	2.540	8.031	6.86	2.619	8.283	7.27	2.696	8.526
6.46	2.542	8.037	6.87	2.621	8.289	7.28	2.698	8.532
6.47	2.544	8.044	6.88	2.623	8.295	7.29	2.700	8.538
6.48	2.546	8.050	6.89	2.625	8.301	7.30	2.702	8.544
6.49	2.548	8.056	6.90	2.627	8.307	7.31	2.704	8.550
6.50	2.550	8.062	6.91	2.629	8.313	7.32	2.706	8.556
6.51	2.551	8.068	6.92	2.631	8.319	7.33	2.707	8.562
6.52	2.553	8.075	6.93	2.632	8.325	7.34	2.709	8.567
6.53	2.555	8.081	6.94	2.634	8.331	7.35	2.711	8.573
6.54	2.557	8.087	6.95	2.636	8.337	7.36	2.713	8.579
6.55	2.559	8.093	6.96	2.638	8.343	7.37	2.715	8.585
6.56	2.561	8.099	6.97	2.640	8.349	7.38	2.717	8.591
6.57	2.563	8.106	6.98	2.642	8.355	7.39	2.718	8.597
6.58	2.565	8.112	6.99	2.644	8.361	7.40	2.720	8.602
6.59	2.567	8.118	7.00	2.646	8.367	7.41	2.722	8.608
6.60	2.569	8.124	7.01	2.648	8.373	7.42	2.724	8.614
6.61	2.571	8.130	7.02	2.650	8.379	7.43	2.726	8.620
6.62	2.573	8.136	7.03	2.651	8.385	7.44	2.728	8.626
6.63	2.575	8.142	7.04	2.653	8.390	7.45	2.729	8.631
6.64	2.577	8.149	7.05	2.655	8.396	7.46	2.731	8.637
6.65	2.579	8.155	7.06	2.657	8.402	7.47	2.733	8.643
6.66	2.581	8.161	7.07	2.659	8.408	7.48	2.735	8.649
6.67	2.583	8.167	7.08	2.661	8.414	7.49	2.737	8.654
6.68	2.585	8.173	7.09	2.663	8.420	7.50	2.739	8.660
6.69	2.587	8.179	7.10	2.665	8.426	7.51	2.740	8.666
6.70	2.588	8.185	7.11	2.666	8.432	7.52	2.742	8.672
6.71	2.590	8.191	7.12	2.668	8.438	7.53	2.744	8.678

n	$\sqrt{n}$	$\sqrt{10n}$	n	$\sqrt{n}$	$\sqrt{10n}$	n	$\sqrt{n}$	$\sqrt{10n}$
7.54	2.746	8.683	7.95	2.820	8.916	8.36	2.891	9.143
7.55	2.748	8.689	7.96	2.821	8.922	8.37	2.893	9.149
7.56	2.750	8.695	7.97	2.823	8.927	8.38	2.895	9.154
7.57	2.751	8.701	7.98	2.825	8.933	8.39	2.897	9.160
7.58	2.753	8.706	7.99	2.827	8.939	8.40	2.898	9.165
7.59	2.755	8.712	8.00	2.828	8.944	8.41	2.900	9.171
7.60	2.757	8.718	8.01	2.830	8.950	8.42	2.902	9.176
7.61	2.759	8.724	8.02	2.832	8.955	8.43	2.903	9.182
7.62	2.760	8.729	8.03	2.834	8.961	8.44	2.905	9.187
7.63	2.762	8.735	8.04	2.835	8.967	8.45	2.907	9.192
7.64	2.764	8.741	8.05	2.837	8.972	8.46	2.909	9.198
7.65	2.766	8.746	8.06	2.839	8.978	8.47	2.910	9.203
7.66	2.768	8.752	8.07	2.841	8.983	8.48	2.912	9.209
7.67	2.769	8.758	8.08	2.843	8.989	8.49	2.914	9.214
7.68	2.771	8.764	8.09	2.844	8.994	8.50	2.915	9.220
7.69	2.773	8.769	8.10	2.846	9.000	8.51	2.917	9.225
7.70	2.775	8.775	8.11	2.848	9.006	8.52	2.919	9.230
7.71	2.777	8.781	8.12	2.850	9.011	8.53	2.921	9.236
7.72	2.778	8.786	8.13	2.851	9.017	8.54	2.922	9.241
7.73	2.780	8.792	8.14	2.853	9.022	8.55	2.924	9.247
7.74	2.782	8.798	8.15	2.855	9.028	8.56	2.926	9.252
7.75	2.784	8.803	8.16	2.857	9.033	8.57	2.927	9.257
7.76	2.786	8.809	8.17	2.858	9.039	8.58	2.929	9.263
7.77	2.787	8.815	8.18	2.860	9.044	8.59	2.931	9.268
7.78	2.789	8.820	8.19	2.862	9.050	8.60	2.933	9.274
7.79	2.791	8.826	8.20	2.864	9.055	8.61	2.934	9.279
7.80	2.793	8.832	8.21	2.865	9.061	8.62	2.936	9.284
7.81	2.795	8.837	8.22	2.867	9.066	8.63	2.938	9.290
7.82	2.796	8.843	8.23	2.869	9.072	8.64	2.939	9.295
7.83	2.798	8.849	8.24	2.871	9.077	8.65	2.941	9.301
7.84	2.800	8.854	8.25	2.872	9.083	8.66	2.943	9.306
7.85	2.802	8.860	8.26	2.874	9.088	8.67	2.944	9.311
7.86	2.804	8.866	8.27	2.876	9.094	8.68	2.946	9.317
7.87	2.805	8.871	8.28	2.877	9.099	8.69	2.948	9.322
7.88	2.807	8.877	8.29	2.879	9.105	8.70	2.950	9.327
7.89	2.809	8.883	8.30	2.881	9.110	8.71	2.951	9.333
7.90	2.811	8.888	8.31	2.883	9.116	8.72	2.953	9.338
7.91	2.812	8.894	8.32	2.884	9.121	8.73	2.955	9.343
7.92	2.814	8.899	8.33	2.886	9.127	8.74	2.956	9.349
7.93	2.816	8.905	8.34	2.888	9.132	8.75	2.958	9.354
7.94	2.818	8.911	8.35	2.890	9.138	8.76	2.960	9.359

TABLE 1—Square Roots (*continued*)

n	$\sqrt{n}$	$\sqrt{10n}$	n	$\sqrt{n}$	$\sqrt{10n}$	n	$\sqrt{n}$	$\sqrt{10n}$
8.77	2.961	9.365	9.18	3.030	9.581	9.59	3.097	9.793
8.78	2.963	9.370	9.19	3.032	9.586	9.60	3.099	9.798
8.79	2.965	9.376	9.20	3.033	9.592	9.61	3.100	9.803
8.80	2.966	9.381	9.21	3.035	9.597	9.62	3.102	9.808
8.81	2.968	9.386	9.22	3.036	9.602	9.63	3.103	9.813
8.82	2.970	9.391	9.23	3.038	9.607	9.64	3.105	9.818
8.83	2.972	9.397	9.24	3.040	9.612	9.65	3.106	9.823
8.84	2.973	9.402	9.25	3.041	9.618	9.66	3.108	9.829
8.85	2.975	9.407	9.26	3.043	9.623	9.67	3.110	9.834
8.86	2.977	9.413	9.27	3.045	9.628	9.68	3.111	9.839
8.87	2.978	9.418	9.28	3.046	9.633	9.69	3.113	9.844
8.88	2.980	9.423	9.29	3.048	9.638	9.70	3.114	9.849
8.89	2.982	9.429	9.30	3.050	9.644	9.71	3.116	9.854
8.90	2.983	9.434	9.31	3.051	9.649	9.72	3.118	9.859
8.91	2.985	9.439	9.32	3.053	9.654	9.73	3.119	9.864
8.92	2.987	9.445	9.33	3.055	9.659	9.74	3.121	9.869
8.93	2.988	9.450	9.34	3.056	9.664	9.75	3.122	9.874
8.94	2.990	9.455	9.35	3.058	9.670	9.76	3.124	9.879
8.95	2.992	9.460	9.36	3.059	9.675	9.77	3.126	9.884
8.96	2.993	9.466	9.37	3.061	9.680	9.78	3.127	9.889
8.97	2.995	9.471	9.38	3.063	9.685	9.79	3.129	9.894
8.98	2.997	9.476	9.39	3.064	9.690	9.80	3.130	9.899
8.99	2.998	9.482	9.40	3.066	9.695	9.81	3.132	9.905
9.00	3.000	9.487	9.41	3.068	9.701	9.82	3.134	9.910
9.01	3.002	9.492	9.42	3.069	9.706	9.83	3.135	9.915
9.02	3.003	9.497	9.43	3.071	9.711	9.84	3.137	9.920
9.03	3.005	9.503	9.44	3.072	9.716	9.85	3.138	9.925
9.04	3.007	9.508	9.45	3.074	9.721	9.86	3.140	9.930
9.05	3.008	9.513	9.46	3.076	9.726	9.87	3.142	9.935
9.06	3.010	9.518	9.47	3.077	9.731	9.88	3.143	9.940
9.07	3.012	9.524	9.48	3.079	9.737	9.89	3.145	9.945
9.08	3.013	9.529	9.49	3.081	9.742	9.90	3.146	9.950
9.09	3.015	9.534	9.50	3.082	9.747	9.91	3.148	9.955
9.10	3.017	9.539	9.51	3.084	9.752	9.92	3.150	9.960
9.11	3.018	9.545	9.52	3.085	9.757	9.93	3.151	9.965
9.12	3.020	9.550	9.53	3.087	9.762	9.94	3.153	9.970
9.13	3.022	9.555	9.54	3.089	9.767	9.95	3.154	9.975
9.14	3.023	9.560	9.55	3.090	9.772	9.96	3.156	9.980
9.15	3.025	9.566	9.56	3.092	9.778	9.97	3.157	9.985
9.16	3.027	9.571	9.57	3.094	9.783	9.98	3.159	9.990
9.17	32028	9.576	9.58	3.095	9.788	9.99	3.161	9.995

TABLE 2
Cumulative Binomial Probabilities

n	r	.01	.05	.10	.20	.30	.40	.50	.60	.70	.80	.90	.95	.99	r
2	0	1	1	1	1	1	1	1	1	1	1	1	1	1	0
	1	020	098	190	360	510	640	750	840	910	960	990	998	1−	1
	2	0+	002	010	040	090	160	250	360	490	640	810	902	980	2
3	0	1	1	1	1	1	1	1	1	1	1	1	1	1	0
	1	030	143	271	488	657	784	875	936	973	992	999	1−	1−	1
	2	0+	007	028	104	216	352	500	648	784	896	972	993	1−	2
	3	0+	0+	001	008	027	064	125	216	343	512	729	857	970	3
4	0	1	1	1	1	1	1	1	1	1	1	1	1	1	0
	1	039	185	344	590	760	870	938	974	992	998	1−	1−	1−	1
	2	001	014	052	181	348	525	688	821	916	973	996	1−	1−	2
	3	0+	0+	004	027	084	179	312	475	652	819	948	986	999	3
	4	0+	0+	0+	002	008	026	062	130	240	410	656	815	961	4
5	0	1	1	1	1	1	1	1	1	1	1	1	1	1	0
	1	049	226	410	672	832	922	969	990	998	1−	1−	1−	1−	1
	2	001	023	081	263	472	663	812	913	969	993	1−	1−	1−	2
	3	0+	001	009	058	163	317	500	683	837	942	991	999	1−	3
	4	0+	0+	0+	007	031	087	188	337	528	737	919	977	999	4
	5	0+	0+	0+	0+	002	010	031	078	168	328	590	774	951	5
6	0	1	1	1	1	1	1	1	1	1	1	1	1	1	0
	1	059	265	469	738	882	953	984	996	999	1−	1−	1−	1−	1
	2	001	033	114	345	580	767	891	959	989	998	1−	1−	1−	2
	3	0+	002	016	099	256	456	656	821	930	983	999	1−	1−	3
	4	0+	0+	001	017	070	179	344	544	744	901	984	998	1−	4
	5	0+	0+	0+	002	011	041	109	233	420	655	886	967	999	5
	6	0+	0+	0+	0+	001	004	016	047	118	262	531	735	941	6
7	0	1	1	1	1	1	1	1	1	1	1	1	1	1	0
	1	068	302	522	790	918	972	992	998	1−	1−	1−	1−	1−	1
	2	002	044	150	423	671	841	938	981	996	1−	1−	1−	1−	2
	3	0+	004	026	148	353	580	773	904	971	995	1−	1−	1−	3
	4	0+	0+	003	033	126	290	500	710	874	967	997	1−	1−	4
	5	0+	0+	0+	005	029	096	227	420	647	852	974	996	1−	5
	6	0+	0+	0+	0+	004	019	062	159	329	577	850	956	998	6
	7	0+	0+	0+	0+	0+	002	008	028	082	210	478	698	932	7
8	0	1	1	1	1	1	1	1	1	1	1	1	1	1	0
	1	077	337	570	832	942	983	996	999	1−	1−	1−	1−	1−	1
	2	003	057	187	497	745	894	965	991	999	1−	1−	1−	1−	2
	3	0+	006	038	203	448	685	855	950	989	999	1−	1−	1−	3
	4	0+	0+	005	056	194	406	637	826	942	990	1−	1−	1−	4
	5	0+	0+	0+	010	058	174	363	594	806	944	995	1−	1−	5
	6	0+	0+	0+	001	011	050	145	315	552	797	962	994	1−	6
	7	0+	0+	0+	0+	001	009	035	106	255	503	813	943	997	7
	8	0+	0+	0+	0+	0+	001	004	019	058	168	430	663	923	8

TABLE 2—Cumulative Binomial Probabilities (*continued*)

n	r	.01	.05	.10	.20	.30	.40	.50	.60	.70	.80	.90	.95	.99	r
9	0	1	1	1	1	1	1	1	1	1	1	1	1	1	0
	1	086	370	613	866	960	990	998	1−	1−	1−	1−	1−	1−	1
	2	003	071	225	564	804	929	980	996	1−	1−	1−	1−	1−	2
	3	0+	008	053	262	537	768	910	975	996	1−	1−	1−	1−	3
	4	0+	001	008	086	270	517	746	901	975	997	1−	1−	1−	4
	5	0+	0+	001	020	099	267	500	733	901	980	999	1−	1−	5
	6	0+	0+	0+	003	025	099	254	483	730	914	992	999	1−	6
	7	0+	0+	0+	0+	004	025	090	232	463	738	947	992	1−	7
	8	0+	0+	0+	0+	0+	004	020	071	196	436	775	929	997	8
	9	0+	0+	0+	0+	0+	0+	002	010	040	134	387	630	914	9
10	0	1	1	1	1	1	1	1	1	1	1	1	1	1	0
	1	096	401	651	893	972	994	999	1−	1−	1−	1−	1−	1−	1
	2	004	086	264	624	851	954	989	998	1−	1−	1−	1−	1−	2
	3	0+	012	070	322	617	833	945	988	998	1−	1−	1−	1−	3
	4	0+	001	013	121	350	618	828	945	989	999	1−	1−	1−	4
	5	0+	0+	002	033	150	367	623	834	953	994	1−	1−	1−	5
	6	0+	0+	0+	006	047	166	377	633	850	967	998	1−	1−	6
	7	0+	0+	0+	001	011	055	172	382	650	879	987	999	1−	7
	8	0+	0+	0+	0+	002	012	055	167	383	678	930	988	1−	8
	9	0+	0+	0+	0+	0+	002	011	046	149	376	736	914	996	9
	10	0+	0+	0+	0+	0+	0+	001	006	028	107	349	599	904	10
11	0	1	1	1	1	1	1	1	1	1	1	1	1	1	0
	1	105	431	686	914	980	996	1−	1−	1−	1−	1−	1−	1−	1
	2	005	102	303	678	887	970	994	999	1−	1−	1−	1−	1−	2
	3	0+	015	090	383	687	881	967	994	999	1−	1−	1−	1−	3
	4	0+	002	019	161	430	704	887	971	996	1−	1−	1−	1−	4
	5	0+	0+	003	050	210	467	726	901	978	998	1−	1−	1−	5
	6	0+	0+	0+	012	078	247	500	753	922	988	1−	1−	1−	6
	7	0+	0+	0+	002	022	099	274	533	790	950	997	1−	1−	7
	8	0+	0+	0+	0+	004	029	113	296	570	839	981	998	1−	8
	9	0+	0+	0+	0+	001	006	033	119	313	617	910	985	1−	9
	10	0+	0+	0+	0+	0+	001	006	030	113	322	697	898	995	10
	11	0+	0+	0+	0+	0+	0+	0+	004	020	086	314	569	895	11
12	0	1	1	1	1	1	1	1	1	1	1	1	1	1	0
	1	114	460	718	931	986	998	1−	1−	1−	1−	1−	1−	1−	1
	2	006	118	341	725	915	980	997	1−	1−	1−	1−	1−	1−	2
	3	0+	020	111	442	747	917	981	997	1−	1−	1−	1−	1−	3
	4	0+	002	026	205	507	775	927	985	998	1−	1−	1−	1−	4
	5	0+	0+	004	073	276	562	806	943	991	999	1−	1−	1−	5
	6	0+	0+	001	019	118	335	613	842	961	996	1−	1−	1−	6
	7	0+	0+	0+	004	039	158	387	665	882	981	999	1−	1−	7
	8	0+	0+	0+	001	009	057	194	438	724	927	996	1−	1−	8
	9	0+	0+	0+	0+	002	015	073	225	493	795	974	998	1−	9

							p								
n	r	.01	.05	.10	.20	.30	.40	.50	.60	.70	.80	.90	.95	.99	r
	10	0+	0+	0+	0+	0+	003	019	083	253	558	889	980	1−	10
	11	0+	0+	0+	0+	0+	0+	003	020	085	275	659	882	994	11
	12	0+	0+	0+	0+	0+	0+	0+	002	014	069	282	540	886	12
13	0	1	1	1	1	1	1	1	1	1	1	1	1	1	0
	1	122	487	746	945	990	999	1−	1−	1−	1−	1−	1−	1−	1
	2	007	135	379	766	936	987	998	1−	1−	1−	1−	1−	1−	2
	3	0+	025	134	498	798	942	989	999	1−	1−	1−	1−	1−	3
	4	0+	003	034	253	579	831	954	992	999	1−	1−	1−	1−	4
	5	0+	0+	006	099	346	647	867	968	996	1−	1−	1−	1−	5
	6	0+	0+	001	030	165	426	709	902	982	999	1−	1−	1−	6
	7	0+	0+	0+	007	062	229	500	771	938	993	1−	1−	1−	7
	8	0+	0+	0+	001	018	098	291	574	835	970	999	1−	1−	8
	9	0+	0+	0+	0+	004	032	133	353	654	901	994	1−	1−	9
	10	0+	0+	0+	0+	001	008	046	169	421	747	966	997	1−	10
	11	0+	0+	0+	0+	0+	001	011	058	202	502	866	975	1−	11
	12	0+	0+	0+	0+	0+	0+	002	013	064	234	621	865	993	12
	13	0+	0+	0+	0+	0+	0+	0+	001	010	055	254	513	878	13
14	0	1	1	1	1	1	1	1	1	1	1	1	1	1	0
	1	131	512	771	956	993	999	1−	1−	1−	1−	1−	1−	1−	1
	2	008	153	415	802	953	960	994	999	1−	1−	1−	1−	1−	2
	3	0+	030	158	552	839	960	994	999	1−	1−	1−	1−	1−	3
	4	0+	004	044	302	645	876	971	996	1−	1−	1−	1−	1−	4
	5	0+	0+	009	130	416	721	910	982	998	1−	1−	1−	1−	5
	6	0+	0+	001	044	219	514	788	942	992	1−	1−	1−	1−	6
	7	0+	0+	0+	012	093	308	605	850	969	998	1−	1−	1−	7
	8	0+	0+	0+	002	031	150	395	692	907	988	1−	1−	1−	8
	9	0+	0+	0+	0+	008	058	212	486	781	956	999	1−	1−	9
	10	0+	0+	0+	0+	002	018	090	279	584	870	991	1−	1−	10
	11	0+	0+	0+	0+	0+	004	029	124	355	698	956	996	1−	11
	12	0+	0+	0+	0+	0+	001	006	040	161	448	842	970	1−	12
	13	0+	0+	0+	0+	0+	0+	001	008	047	198	585	847	992	13
	14	0+	0+	0+	0+	0+	0+	0+	001	007	044	229	488	869	14
15	0	1	1	1	1	1	1	1	1	1	1	1	1	1	0
	1	140	537	794	965	995	1−	1−	1−	1−	1−	1−	1−	1−	1
	2	010	171	451	833	965	995	1−	1−	1−	1−	1−	1−	1−	2
	3	0+	036	184	602	873	973	996	1−	1−	1−	1−	1−	1−	3
	4	0+	005	056	352	703	909	982	998	1−	1−	1−	1−	1−	4
	5	0+	001	013	164	485	783	941	991	999	1−	1−	1−	1−	5
	6	0+	0+	002	061	278	597	849	966	996	1−	1−	1−	1−	6
	7	0+	0+	0+	018	131	390	696	905	985	999	1−	1−	1−	7
	8	0+	0+	0+	004	050	213	500	787	950	996	1−	1−	1−	8
	9	0+	0+	0+	001	015	095	304	610	869	982	1−	1−	1−	9
	10	0+	0+	0+	0+	004	034	151	403	722	939	998	1−	1−	10
	11	0+	0+	0+	0+	001	009	059	217	515	836	987	999	1−	11
	12	0+	0+	0+	0+	0+	002	018	091	297	648	944	995	1−	12

TABLE 2—Cumulative Binomial Probabilities (*continued*)

n	r	.01	.05	.10	.20	.30	.40	.50	.60	.70	.80	.90	.95	.99	r
	13	0+	0+	0+	0+	0+	0+	004	027	127	398	816	964	1−	13
	14	0+	0+	0+	0+	0+	0+	0+	005	035	167	549	829	990	14
	15	0+	0+	0+	0+	0+	0+	0+	0+	005	035	206	463	860	15
16	0	1	1	1	1	1	1	1	1	1	1	1	1	1	0
	1	149	560	815	972	997	1−	1−	1−	1−	1−	1−	1−	1−	1
	2	011	189	485	859	974	997	1−	1−	1−	1−	1−	1−	1−	2
	3	001	043	211	648	901	982	998	1−	1−	1−	1−	1−	1−	3
	4	0+	007	068	402	754	935	989	999	1−	1−	1−	1−	1−	4
	5	0+	001	017	202	550	833	962	995	1−	1−	1−	1−	1−	5
	6	0+	0+	003	082	340	671	895	981	998	1−	1−	1−	1−	6
	7	0+	0+	001	027	175	473	773	942	993	1−	1−	1−	1−	7
	8	0+	0+	0+	007	074	284	598	858	974	999	1−	1−	1−	8
	9	0+	0+	0+	001	026	142	402	716	926	993	1−	1−	1−	9
	10	0+	0+	0+	0+	007	058	227	527	825	973	999	1−	1−	10
	11	0+	0+	0+	0+	002	019	105	329	660	918	997	1−	1−	11
	12	0+	0+	0+	0+	0+	005	038	167	450	798	983	999	1−	12
	13	0+	0+	0+	0+	0+	001	011	065	246	598	932	993	1−	13
	14	0+	0+	0+	0+	0+	0+	002	018	099	352	789	957	999	14
	15	0+	0+	0+	0+	0+	0+	0+	003	026	141	515	811	989	15
	16	0+	0+	0+	0+	0+	0+	0+	0+	003	028	185	440	851	16
17	0	1	1	1	1	1	1	1	1	1	1	1	1	1	0
	1	157	582	833	977	998	1−	1−	1−	1−	1−	1−	1−	1−	1
	2	012	208	518	882	981	998	1−	1−	1−	1−	1−	1−	1−	2
	3	001	050	238	690	923	988	999	1−	1−	1−	1−	1−	1−	3
	4	0+	009	083	451	798	954	994	1−	1−	1−	1−	1−	1−	4
	5	0+	001	022	242	611	874	975	997	1−	1−	1−	1−	1−	5
	6	0+	0+	005	106	403	736	928	989	999	1−	1−	1−	1−	6
	7	0+	0+	001	038	225	552	834	965	997	1−	1−	1−	1−	7
	8	0+	0+	0+	011	105	359	685	908	987	1−	1−	1−	1−	8
	9	0+	0+	0+	003	040	199	500	801	960	997	1−	1−	1−	9
	10	0+	0+	0+	0+	013	092	315	641	895	989	1−	1−	1−	10
	11	0+	0+	0+	0+	003	035	166	448	775	962	999	1−	1−	11
	12	0+	0+	0+	0+	001	011	072	264	597	894	995	1−	1−	12
	13	0+	0+	0+	0+	0+	003	025	126	389	758	978	999	1−	13
	14	0+	0+	0+	0+	0+	0+	006	046	202	549	917	991	1−	14
	15	0+	0+	0+	0+	0+	0+	001	012	077	310	762	950	999	15
	16	0+	0+	0+	0+	0+	0+	0+	002	019	118	482	792	988	16
	17	0+	0+	0+	0+	0+	0+	0+	0+	002	023	167	418	843	17
18	0	1	1	1	1	1	1	1	1	1	1	1	1	1	0
	1	165	603	850	982	998	1−	1−	1−	1−	1−	1−	1−	1−	1
	2	014	226	550	901	986	999	1−	1−	1−	1−	1−	1−	1−	2
	3	001	058	266	729	940	992	999	1−	1−	1−	1−	1−	1−	3
	4	0+	011	098	499	835	967	996	1−	1−	1−	1−	1−	1−	4

							p								
n	r	.01	.05	.10	.20	.30	.40	.50	.60	.70	.80	.90	.95	.99	r
	5	0+	002	028	284	667	906	985	999	1−	1−	1−	1−	1−	5
	6	0+	0+	006	133	466	791	952	994	1−	1−	1−	1−	1−	6
	7	0+	0+	001	051	278	626	881	980	999	1−	1−	1−	1−	7
	8	0+	0+	0+	016	141	437	760	942	994	1−	1−	1−	1−	8
	9	0+	0+	0+	004	060	263	593	865	979	999	1−	1−	1−	9
	10	0+	0+	0+	001	021	135	407	737	940	996	1−	1−	1−	10
	11	0+	0+	0+	0+	006	058	240	563	859	984	1−	1−	1−	11
	12	0+	0+	0+	0+	001	020	119	374	722	949	999	1−	1−	12
	13	0+	0+	0+	0+	0+	006	048	209	534	867	994	1−	1−	13
	14	0+	0+	0+	0+	0+	001	015	094	333	716	972	998	1−	14
	15	0+	0+	0+	0+	0+	0+	004	033	165	501	902	989	1−	15
	16	0+	0+	0+	0+	0+	0+	001	008	060	271	734	942	999	16
	17	0+	0+	0+	0+	0+	0+	0+	001	014	099	450	774	986	17
	18	0+	0+	0+	0+	0+	0+	0+	0+	002	018	150	397	835	18
19	0	1	1	1	1	1	1	1	1	1	1	1	1	1	0
	1	174	623	865	986	999	1−	1−	1−	1−	1−	1−	1−	1−	1
	2	015	245	580	917	990	999	1−	1−	1−	1−	1−	1−	1−	2
	3	001	067	295	763	954	995	1−	1−	1−	1−	1−	1−	1−	3
	4	0+	013	115	545	867	977	998	1−	1−	1−	1−	1−	1−	4
	5	0+	002	035	327	718	930	990	999	1−	1−	1−	1−	1−	5
	6	0+	0+	009	163	526	837	968	997	1−	1−	1−	1−	1−	6
	7	0+	0+	002	068	334	692	916	988	999	1−	1−	1−	1−	7
	8	0+	0+	0+	023	182	512	820	965	997	1−	1−	1−	1−	8
	9	0+	0+	0+	007	084	333	676	912	989	1−	1−	1−	1−	9
	10	0+	0+	0+	002	033	186	500	814	967	998	1−	1−	1−	10
	11	0+	0+	0+	0+	011	088	324	667	916	993	1−	1−	1−	11
	12	0+	0+	0+	0+	003	035	180	488	818	977	1−	1−	1−	12
	13	0+	0+	0+	0+	001	012	084	308	666	932	998	1−	1−	13
	14	0+	0+	0+	0+	0+	003	032	163	474	837	991	1−	1−	14
	15	0+	0+	0+	0+	0+	001	010	070	282	673	965	998	1−	15
	16	0+	0+	0+	0+	0+	0+	002	023	133	455	885	987	1−	16
	17	0+	0+	0+	0+	0+	0+	0+	005	046	237	705	933	999	17
	18	0+	0+	0+	0+	0+	0+	0+	001	010	083	420	755	985	18
	19	0+	0+	0+	0+	0+	0+	0+	0+	001	014	135	377	826	19
20	0	1	1	1	1	1	1	1	1	1	1	1	1	1	0
	1	182	642	878	988	999	1−	1−	1−	1−	1−	1−	1−	1−	1
	2	017	264	608	931	992	999	1−	1−	1−	1−	1−	1−	1−	2
	3	001	075	323	794	965	996	1−	1−	1−	1−	1−	1−	1−	3
	4	0+	016	133	589	893	984	999	1−	1−	1−	1−	1−	1−	4
	5	0+	003	043	370	762	949	994	1−	1−	1−	1−	1−	1−	5
	6	0+	0+	011	196	584	874	979	998	1−	1−	1−	1−	1−	6
	7	0+	0+	002	087	392	750	942	994	1−	1−	1−	1−	1−	7
	8	0+	0+	0+	032	228	584	868	979	999	1−	1−	1−	1−	8
	9	0+	0+	0+	010	113	404	748	943	995	1−	1−	1−	1−	9

TABLE 2—Cumulative Binomial Probabilities (*continued*)

n	r	.01	.05	.10	.20	.30	.40	.50	.60	.70	.80	.90	.95	.99	r
	10	0+	0+	0+	003	048	245	588	872	983	999	1−	1−	1−	10
	11	0+	0+	0+	001	017	128	412	755	952	997	1−	1−	1−	11
	12	0+	0+	0+	0+	005	057	252	596	887	990	1−	1−	1−	12
	13	0+	0+	0+	0+	001	021	132	416	772	968	1−	1−	1−	13
	14	0+	0+	0+	0+	0+	006	058	250	608	913	998	1−	1−	14
	15	0+	0+	0+	0+	0+	002	021	126	416	804	989	1−	1−	15
	16	0+	0+	0+	0+	0+	0+	006	051	238	630	957	997	1−	16
	17	0+	0+	0+	0+	0+	0+	001	016	107	411	867	984	1−	17
	18	0+	0+	0+	0+	0+	0+	0+	004	035	206	677	925	999	18
	19	0+	0+	0+	0+	0+	0+	0+	001	008	069	392	736	983	19
	20	0+	0+	0+	0+	0+	0+	0+	0+	001	012	122	358	818	20
21	0	1	1	1	1	1	1	1	1	1	1	1	1	1	0
	1	190	659	891	991	999	1−	1−	1−	1−	1−	1−	1−	1−	1
	2	019	283	635	942	994	1−	1−	1−	1−	1−	1−	1−	1−	2
	3	001	085	352	821	973	998	1−	1−	1−	1−	1−	1−	1−	3
	4	0+	019	152	630	914	989	999	1−	1−	1−	1−	1−	1−	4
	5	0+	003	052	414	802	963	996	1−	1−	1−	1−	1−	1−	5
	6	0+	0+	014	231	637	904	987	999	1−	1−	1−	1−	1−	6
	7	0+	0+	003	109	449	800	961	996	1−	1−	1−	1−	1−	7
	8	0+	0+	001	043	277	650	905	988	999	1−	1−	1−	1−	8
	9	0+	0+	0+	014	148	476	808	965	998	1−	1−	1−	1−	9
	10	0+	0+	0+	004	068	309	668	915	991	1−	1−	1−	1−	10
	11	0+	0+	0+	001	026	174	500	826	974	999	1−	1−	1−	11
	12	0+	0+	0+	0+	009	085	332	691	932	996	1−	1−	1−	12
	13	0+	0+	0+	0+	002	035	192	524	852	986	1−	1−	1−	13
	14	0+	0+	0+	0+	001	012	095	350	723	957	999	1−	1−	14
	15	0+	0+	0+	0+	0+	004	039	200	551	891	997	1−	1−	15
	16	0+	0+	0+	0+	0+	001	013	096	363	769	986	1−	1−	16
	17	0+	0+	0+	0+	0+	0+	004	037	198	586	948	997	1−	17
	18	0+	0+	0+	0+	0+	0+	001	011	086	370	848	981	1−	18
	19	0+	0+	0+	0+	0+	0+	0+	002	027	179	648	915	999	19
	20	0+	0+	0+	0+	0+	0+	0+	0+	006	058	365	717	981	20
	21	0+	0+	0+	0+	0+	0+	0+	0+	001	009	109	341	810	21
22	0	1	1	1	1	1	1	1	1	1	1	1	1	1	0
	1	198	676	902	993	1−	1−	1−	1−	1−	1−	1−	1−	1−	1
	2	020	302	661	952	996	1−	1−	1−	1−	1−	1−	1−	1−	2
	3	001	095	380	846	979	998	1−	1−	1−	1−	1−	1−	1−	3
	4	0+	022	172	668	932	992	1−	1−	1−	1−	1−	1−	1−	4
	5	0+	004	062	457	835	973	998	1−	1−	1−	1−	1−	1−	5
	6	0+	001	018	267	687	928	992	1−	1−	1−	1−	1−	1−	6
	7	0+	0+	004	133	506	842	974	998	1−	1−	1−	1−	1−	7
	8	0+	0+	001	056	329	710	933	993	1−	1−	1−	1−	1−	8
	9	0+	0+	0+	020	186	546	857	979	999	1−	1−	1−	1−	9
	10	0+	0+	0+	006	092	376	738	945	996	1−	1−	1−	1−	10

								p							
n	r	.01	.05	.10	.20	.30	.40	.50	.60	.70	.80	.90	.95	.99	r
	11	0+	0+	0+	002	039	228	584	879	986	1–	1–	1–	1–	11
	12	0+	0+	0+	0+	014	121	416	772	961	998	1–	1–	1–	12
	13	0+	0+	0+	0+	004	055	262	624	908	994	1–	1–	1–	13
	14	0+	0+	0+	0+	001	021	143	454	814	980	1–	1–	1–	14
	15	0+	0+	0+	0+	0+	007	067	290	671	944	999	1–	1–	15
	16	0+	0+	0+	0+	0+	002	026	158	494	867	996	1–	1–	16
	17	0+	0+	0+	0+	0+	0+	008	072	313	733	982	999	1–	17
	18	0+	0+	0+	0+	0+	0+	002	027	165	543	938	996	1–	18
	19	0+	0+	0+	0+	0+	0+	0+	008	068	332	828	978	1–	19
	20	0+	0+	0+	0+	0+	0+	0+	002	021	154	620	905	999	20
	21	0+	0+	0+	0+	0+	0+	0+	0+	004	048	339	698	980	21
	22	0+	0+	0+	0+	0+	0+	0+	0+	0+	007	098	324	802	22
23	0	1	1	1	1	1	1	1	1	1	1	1	1	1	0
	1	206	693	911	994	1–	1–	1–	1–	1–	1–	1–	1–	1–	1
	2	022	321	685	960	997	1–	1–	1–	1–	1–	1–	1–	1–	2
	3	002	105	408	867	984	999	1–	1–	1–	1–	1–	1–	1–	3
	4	0+	026	193	703	946	995	1–	1–	1–	1–	1–	1–	1–	4
	5	0+	005	073	499	864	981	999	1–	1–	1–	1–	1–	1–	5
	6	0+	001	023	305	731	946	995	1–	1–	1–	1–	1–	1–	6
	7	0+	0+	006	160	560	876	983	999	1–	1–	1–	1–	1–	7
	8	0+	0+	001	072	382	763	953	996	1–	1–	1–	1–	1–	8
	9	0+	0+	0+	027	229	612	895	987	999	1–	1–	1–	1–	9
	10	0+	0+	0+	009	120	444	798	965	998	1–	1–	1–	1–	10
	11	0+	0+	0+	003	055	287	661	919	993	1–	1–	1–	1–	11
	12	0+	0+	0+	001	021	164	500	836	979	999	1–	1–	1–	12
	13	0+	0+	0+	0+	007	081	339	713	945	997	1–	1–	1–	13
	14	0+	0+	0+	0+	002	035	202	556	880	991	1–	1–	1–	14
	15	0+	0+	0+	0+	001	013	105	388	771	973	1–	1–	1–	15
	16	0+	0+	0+	0+	0+	004	047	237	618	928	999	1–	1–	16
	17	0+	0+	0+	0+	0+	001	017	124	440	840	994	1–	1–	17
	18	0+	0+	0+	0+	0+	0+	005	054	269	695	977	999	1–	18
	19	0+	0+	0+	0+	0+	0+	001	019	136	501	927	995	1–	19
	20	0+	0+	0+	0+	0+	0+	0+	005	054	297	807	974	1–	20
	21	0+	0+	0+	0+	0+	0+	0+	001	016	133	592	895	998	21
	22	0+	0+	0+	0+	0+	0+	0+	0+	003	040	315	679	978	22
	23	0+	0+	0+	0+	0+	0+	0+	0+	0+	006	089	307	794	23
24	0	1	1	1	1	1	1	1	1	1	1	1	1	1	0
	1	214	708	920	995	1–	1–	1–	1–	1–	1–	1–	1–	1–	1
	2	024	339	708	967	998	1–	1–	1–	1–	1–	1–	1–	1–	2
	3	002	116	436	885	988	999	1–	1–	1–	1–	1–	1–	1–	3
	4	0+	030	214	736	958	996	1–	1–	1–	1–	1–	1–	1–	4
	5	0+	006	085	540	889	987	999	1–	1–	1–	1–	1–	1–	5
	6	0+	001	028	344	771	960	997	1–	1–	1–	1–	1–	1–	6
	7	0+	0+	007	189	611	904	989	999	1–	1–	1–	1–	1–	7
	8	0+	0+	002	089	435	808	968	998	1–	1–	1–	1–	1–	8

TABLE 2—Cumulative Binomial Probabilities (*continued*)

n	r	.01	.05	.10	.20	.30	.40	.50	.60	.70	.80	.90	.95	.99	r
	9	0+	0+	0+	036	275	672	924	992	1−	1−	1−	1−	1−	9
	10	0+	0+	0+	013	153	511	846	978	999	1−	1−	1−	1−	10
	11	0+	0+	0+	004	074	350	729	947	996	1−	1−	1−	1−	11
	12	0+	0+	0+	001	031	213	581	886	988	1−	1−	1−	1−	12
	13	0+	0+	0+	0+	012	114	419	787	969	999	1−	1−	1−	13
	14	0+	0+	0+	0+	004	053	271	650	926	996	1−	1−	1−	14
	15	0+	0+	0+	0+	001	022	154	489	847	987	1−	1−	1−	15
	16	0+	0+	0+	0+	0+	008	076	328	725	964	1−	1−	1−	16
	17	0+	0+	0+	0+	0+	002	032	192	565	911	998	1−	1−	17
	18	0+	0+	0+	0+	0+	001	011	096	389	811	993	1−	1−	18
	19	0+	0+	0+	0+	0+	0+	003	040	229	656	972	999	1−	19
	20	0+	0+	0+	0+	0+	0+	001	013	111	460	915	994	1−	20
	21	0+	0+	0+	0+	0+	0+	0+	004	042	264	786	970	1−	21
	22	0+	0+	0+	0+	0+	0+	0+	001	012	115	564	884	998	22
	23	0+	0+	0+	0+	0+	0+	0+	0+	002	033	292	661	976	23
	24	0+	0+	0+	0+	0+	0+	0+	0+	0+	005	080	292	786	24
25	0	1	1	1	1	1	1	1	1	1	1	1	1	1	0
	1	222	723	928	996	1−	1−	1−	1−	1−	1−	1−	1−	1−	1
	2	026	358	729	973	998	1−	1−	1−	1−	1−	1−	1−	1−	2
	3	002	127	463	902	991	1−	1−	1−	1−	1−	1−	1−	1−	3
	4	0+	034	236	766	967	998	1−	1−	1−	1−	1−	1−	1−	4
	5	0+	007	098	579	910	991	1−	1−	1−	1−	1−	1−	1−	5
	6	0+	001	033	383	807	971	998	1−	1−	1−	1−	1−	1−	6
	7	0+	0+	009	220	659	926	993	1−	1−	1−	1−	1−	1−	7
	8	0+	0+	002	109	488	846	978	999	1−	1−	1−	1−	1−	8
	9	0+	0+	0+	047	323	726	946	996	1−	1−	1−	1−	1−	9
	10	0+	0+	0+	017	189	575	885	987	1−	1−	1−	1−	1−	10
	11	0+	0+	0+	006	098	414	788	966	998	1−	1−	1−	1−	11
	12	0+	0+	0+	002	044	268	655	922	994	1−	1−	1−	1−	12
	13	0+	0+	0+	0+	017	154	500	846	983	1−	1−	1−	1−	13
	14	0+	0+	0+	0+	006	078	345	732	956	998	1−	1−	1−	14
	15	0+	0+	0+	0+	002	034	212	586	902	994	1−	1−	1−	15
	16	0+	0+	0+	0+	0+	013	115	425	811	983	1−	1−	1−	16
	17	0+	0+	0+	0+	0+	004	054	274	677	953	1−	1−	1−	17
	18	0+	0+	0+	0+	0+	001	022	154	512	891	998	1−	1−	18
	19	0+	0+	0+	0+	0+	0+	007	074	341	780	991	1−	1−	19
	20	0+	0+	0+	0+	0+	0+	002	029	193	617	967	999	1−	20
	21	0+	0+	0+	0+	0+	0+	0+	009	090	421	902	993	1−	21
	22	0+	0+	0+	0+	0+	0+	0+	002	033	234	764	966	1−	22
	23	0+	0+	0+	0+	0+	0+	0+	0+	009	098	537	873	998	23
	24	0+	0+	0+	0+	0+	0+	0+	0+	002	027	271	642	974	24
	25	0+	0+	0+	0+	0+	0+	0+	0+	0+	004	072	277	778	25

Table 2 is taken from Table IV, Part B, of *Probability: A First Course*, Second Edition, 1970, by Mosteller, Rourke, and Thomas, Addison-Wesley.

TABLE 3
Cumulative Poisson Probabilities

m

x	.001	.002	.003	.004	.005	.006	.007	.008	.009	.01	.02	.03	.04	.05	.06	.07	.08	.09	.10	.15	x
0	1	1	1	1	1	1	1	1	1	1	1	1	1	1	1	1	1	1	1	1	0
1	001	002	003	004	005	006	007	008	009	010	020	030	039	049	058	068	077	086	095	139	1
2													001	001	002	002	003	004	005	010	2
3																				001	3

m

x	.20	.25	.30	.40	.50	.60	.70	.80	.90	1.0	1.1	1.2	1.3	1.4	1.5	1.6	1.7	1.8	1.9	2.0	x
0	1	1	1	1	1	1	1	1	1	1	1	1	1	1	1	1	1	1	1	1	0
1	181	221	259	330	393	451	503	551	593	632	667	699	727	753	777	798	817	835	850	865	1
2	018	026	037	062	090	122	156	191	228	264	301	337	373	408	442	475	507	537	566	594	2
3	001	002	004	008	014	023	034	047	063	080	100	121	143	167	191	217	243	269	296	323	3
4				001	002	003	006	009	013	019	026	034	043	054	066	079	093	109	125	143	4
5							001	001	002	004	005	008	011	014	019	024	030	036	044	053	5
6										001	001	002	002	003	004	006	008	010	013	017	6
7														001	001	001	002	003	003	005	7
8																			001	001	8

m

x	2.1	2.2	2.3	2.4	2.5	2.6	2.7	2.8	2.9	3.0	3.1	3.2	3.3	3.4	3.5	3.6	3.7	3.8	3.9	4.0	x
0	1	1	1	1	1	1	1	1	1	1	1	1	1	1	1	1	1	1	1	1	0
1	878	889	900	909	918	926	933	939	945	950	955	959	963	967	970	973	975	978	980	982	1
2	620	645	669	692	713	733	751	769	785	801	815	829	841	853	864	874	884	893	901	908	2
3	350	377	404	430	456	482	506	531	554	577	599	620	641	660	679	697	715	731	747	762	3
4	161	181	201	221	242	264	286	308	330	353	375	397	420	442	463	485	506	527	547	567	4

TABLE 3 Cumulative Poisson Probabilities (continued)

m

x	2.1	2.2	2.3	2.4	2.5	2.6	2.7	2.8	2.9	3.0	3.1	3.2	3.3	3.4	3.5	3.6	3.7	3.8	3.9	4.0	x
5	062	072	084	096	109	123	137	152	168	185	202	219	237	256	275	294	313	332	352	371	5
6	020	025	030	036	042	049	057	065	074	084	094	105	117	129	142	156	170	184	199	215	6
7	006	007	009	012	014	017	021	024	029	034	039	045	051	058	065	073	082	091	101	111	7
8	001	002	003	003	004	005	007	008	010	012	014	017	020	023	027	031	035	040	045	051	8
9			001	001	001	001	002	002	003	004	005	006	007	008	010	012	014	016	019	021	9
10								001	001	001	001	002	002	003	003	004	005	006	007	008	10
11													001	001	001	001	002	002	002	003	11
12																		001	001	001	12

m

x	4.1	4.2	4.3	4.4	4.5	4.6	4.7	4.8	4.9	5.0	5.1	5.2	5.3	5.4	5.5	5.6	5.7	5.8	5.9	6.0	x
0	1	1	1	1	1	1	1	1	1	1	1	1	1	1	1	1	1	1	1	1	0
1	983	985	986	988	989	990	991	992	993	993	994	994	995	995	996	997	997	997	997	998	1
2	915	922	928	934	939	944	948	952	956	960	963	966	969	971	973	976	978	979	981	983	2
3	776	790	803	815	826	837	848	857	867	875	884	891	898	905	912	918	923	928	933	938	3
4	586	605	623	641	658	674	690	706	721	735	749	762	775	787	798	809	820	830	840	849	4
5	391	410	430	449	468	487	505	524	542	560	577	594	610	627	642	658	673	687	701	715	5
6	231	247	263	280	297	314	332	349	366	384	402	419	437	454	471	488	505	522	538	554	6
7	121	133	144	156	169	182	195	209	223	238	253	268	283	298	314	330	346	362	378	394	7
8	057	064	071	079	087	095	104	113	123	133	144	155	167	178	191	203	216	229	242	256	8
9	024	028	032	036	040	045	050	056	062	068	075	082	089	097	106	114	123	133	143	153	9
10	010	011	013	015	017	020	022	025	028	032	036	040	044	049	054	059	065	071	077	084	10
11	003	004	005	006	007	008	009	010	012	014	016	018	020	023	025	028	031	035	039	042	11
12	001	001	002	002	002	003	003	004	005	005	006	007	008	010	011	012	014	016	018	020	12
13			001	001	001	001	001	001	002	002	002	003	003	004	004	005	006	007	008	009	13
14									001	001	001	001	001	001	002	002	002	003	003	004	14
15																001	001	001	001	001	15
16																				001	16

TABLE 3   Cumulative Poisson Probabilities (continued)

m

x	6.1	6.2	6.3	6.4	6.5	6.6	6.7	6.8	6.9	7.0	7.1	7.2	7.3	7.4	7.5	8.0	8.5	9.0	9.5	10.0	x
0	1	1	1	1	1	1	1	1	1	1	1	1	1	1	1	1-	1-	1-	1-	1-	0
1	998	998	998	998	998	999	999	999	999	999	999	999	999	999	999	1-	1-	1-	1-	1-	1
2	984	985	987	988	989	990	991	991	992	993	993	994	994	995	995	997	998	999	999	1-	2
3	942	946	950	954	957	960	963	966	968	970	973	975	976	978	980	986	991	994	996	997	3
4	857	866	874	881	888	895	901	907	913	918	923	928	933	937	941	958	970	979	985	990	4
5	728	741	753	765	776	787	798	808	818	827	836	844	853	860	868	900	926	945	960	971	5
6	570	586	601	616	631	645	659	673	686	699	712	724	736	747	759	809	850	884	911	933	6
7	410	426	442	458	473	489	505	520	535	550	565	580	594	608	622	687	744	793	835	870	7
8	270	284	298	313	327	342	357	372	386	401	416	431	446	461	475	547	614	676	731	780	8
9	163	174	185	197	208	220	233	245	258	271	284	297	311	324	338	407	477	544	608	667	9
10	091	098	106	114	123	131	140	150	151	170	180	190	201	212	224	283	347	413	478	542	10
11	047	051	056	061	067	073	079	085	092	099	106	113	121	129	138	184	237	294	355	417	11
12	022	025	028	031	034	037	041	045	049	053	058	063	068	074	079	112	151	197	248	303	12
13	010	011	013	014	016	018	020	022	024	027	030	033	036	039	043	064	091	124	164	208	13
14	004	005	005	006	007	008	009	010	011	013	014	016	018	020	022	034	051	074	102	130	14
15	002	002	002	003	003	003	004	004	005	006	006	007	008	009	010	017	027	041	060	083	15
16	001	001	001	001	001	001	002	002	002	002	003	003	004	004	005	008	014	022	033	049	16
17							001	001	001	001	001	001	001	002	002	004	007	011	018	027	17
18												001	001	001	001	002	003	005	009	014	18
19															001	001	002	003	005	007	19
20																		001	002	003	20
21																			001	002	21
22																				001	22

TABLE 4

Areas Under the Normal Curve

z	.00	.01	.02	.03	.04	.05	.06	.07	.08	.09
0.0	.0000	.0040	.0080	.0120	.0160	.0199	.0239	.0279	.0319	.0359
0.1	.0398	.0438	.0478	.0517	.0557	.0596	.0636	.0675	.0714	.0753
0.2	.0793	.0832	.0871	.0910	.0948	.0987	.1026	.1064	.1103	.1141
0.3	.1179	.1217	.1255	.1293	.1331	.1368	.1406	.1443	.1480	.1517
0.4	.1554	.1591	.1628	.1664	.1700	.1736	.1772	.1808	.1844	.1879
0.5	.1915	.1950	.1985	.2019	.2054	.2088	.2123	.2157	.2190	.2224
0.6	.2257	.2291	.2324	.2357	.2389	.2422	.2454	.2486	.2517	.2549
0.7	.2580	.2611	.2642	.2673	.2704	.2734	.2764	.2794	.2823	.2852
0.8	.2881	.2910	.2939	.2967	.2995	.3023	.3051	.3078	.3106	.3133
0.9	.3159	.3186	.3212	.3238	.3264	.3289	.3315	.3340	.3365	.3389
1.0	.3413	.3438	.3461	.3485	.3508	.3531	.3554	.3577	.3599	.3621
1.1	.3643	.3665	.3686	.3708	.3729	.3749	.3770	.3790	.3810	.3830
1.2	.3849	.3869	.3888	.3907	.3925	.3944	.3962	.3980	.3997	.4015
1.3	.4032	.4049	.4066	.4082	.4099	.4115	.4131	.4147	.4162	.4177
1.4	.4192	.4207	.4222	.4236	.4251	.4265	.4279	.4292	.4306	.4319
1.5	.4332	.4345	.4357	.4370	.4382	.4394	.4406	.4418	.4429	.4441
1.6	.4452	.4463	.4474	.4484	.4495	.4505	.4515	.4525	.4535	.4545
1.7	.4554	.4564	.4573	.4582	.4591	.4599	.4608	.4616	.4625	.4633
1.8	.4641	.4649	.4656	.4664	.4671	.4678	.4686	.4693	.4699	.4706
1.9	.4713	.4719	.4726	.4732	.4738	.4744	.4750	.4756	.4761	.4767
2.0	.4772	.4778	.4783	.4788	.4793	.4798	.4803	.4808	.4812	.4817
2.1	.4821	.4826	.4830	.4834	.4838	.4842	.4846	.4850	.4854	.4857
2.2	.4861	.4864	.4868	.4871	.4875	.4878	.4881	.4884	.4887	.4890
2.3	.4893	.4896	.4898	.4901	.4904	.4906	.4909	.4911	.4913	.4916
2.4	.4918	.4920	.4922	.4925	.4927	.4929	.4931	.4932	.4934	.4936
2.5	.4938	.4940	.4941	.4943	.4945	.4946	.4948	.4949	.4951	.4952
2.6	.4953	.4955	.4956	.4957	.4959	.4960	.4961	.4962	.4963	.4964
2.7	.4965	.4966	.4967	.4968	.4969	.4970	.4971	.4972	.4973	.4974
2.8	.4974	.4975	.4976	.4977	.4977	.4978	.4979	.4979	.4980	.4981
2.9	.4981	.4982	.4982	.4983	.4984	.4984	.4985	.4985	.4986	.4987
3.0	.4987	.4987	.4987	.4988	.4988	.4989	.4989	.4989	.4990	.4990
3.1	.4990	.4991	.4991	.4991	.4992	.4992	.4992	.4992	.4993	.4993
3.2	.4993	.4993	.4994	.4994	.4994	.4994	.4994	.4995	.4995	.4995
3.3	.4995	.4995	.4996	.4996	.4996	.4996	.4996	.4996	.4996	.4997
3.4	.4997	.4997	.4997	.4997	.4997	.4997	.4997	.4997	.4998	.4998
3.5	.4998	.4998	.4998	.4998	.4998	.4998	.4998	.4998	.4998	.4998

Table 4 is taken from Table B.2 of *Introduction to Statistical Inference* by E. S. Keeping, Van Nostrand Reinhold.

TABLE 5

Critical Values of *t*

Degrees of Freedom	Proportion in the Tail			
	0.050	0.025	0.010	0.005
1	6.314	12.706	31.821	63.657
2	2.920	4.303	6.945	9.925
3	2.353	3.182	4.541	5.841
4	2.132	2.776	3.747	4.604
5	2.015	2.571	3.365	4.032
6	1.943	2.447	3.143	3.707
7	1.895	2.365	2.998	3.499
8	1.860	2.306	2.896	3.355
9	1.833	2.262	2.821	3.250
10	1.812	2.228	2.764	3.169
11	1.796	2.201	2.718	3.106
12	1.782	2.179	2.681	3.055
13	1.771	2.160	2.650	3.012
14	1.761	2.145	2.624	2.977
15	1.753	2.131	2.602	2.947
16	1.746	2.120	2.583	2.921
17	1.740	2.110	2.567	2.898
18	1.734	2.101	2.552	2.878
19	1.729	2.093	2.539	2.861
20	1.725	2.086	2.528	2.845
21	1.721	2.080	2.518	2.831
22	1.717	2.074	2.508	2.819
23	1.714	2.069	2.500	2.807
24	1.711	2.064	2.492	2.797
25	1.708	2.060	2.485	2.787
26	1.706	2.056	2.479	2.779
27	1.703	2.052	2.473	2.771
28	1.701	2.048	2.467	2.763
29	1.699	2.045	2.462	2.756
∞	1.645	1.960	2.326	2.576

Table 5 is taken from Table 12 of the *Biometrika Tables for Statisticians*, Volume 1, Third Edition, by Pearson and Hartley.

TABLE 6
Critical Values of Chi-Square

Degrees of Freedom	Proportion to the right							
	0.990	0.975	0.950	0.900	0.100	0.050	0.025	0.010
1	0.000157	0.000982	0.00393	0.0158	2.706	3.841	5.024	6.635
2	0.0201	0.0506	0.1026	0.2107	4.605	5.991	7.378	9.210
3	0.1148	0.2158	0.3518	0.5844	6.251	7.815	9.348	11.34
4	0.2971	0.4844	0.7107	1.065	7.779	9.488	11.14	13.28
5	0.5543	0.8312	1.145	1.161	9.236	11.07	12.83	15.09
6	0.8721	1.237	1.635	2.204	10.64	12.59	14.45	16.81
7	1.239	1.690	2.167	2.833	12.02	14.07	16.01	18.48
8	1.646	2.180	2.733	3.490	13.36	15.51	17.53	20.09
9	2.088	2.700	3.325	4.168	14.68	16.92	19.02	21.67
10	2.558	3.247	3.940	4.865	15.99	18.31	20.48	23.21
11	3.053	3.816	4.575	5.578	17.28	19.68	21.92	24.72
12	3.571	4.404	5.226	6.304	18.55	21.03	23.34	26.22
13	4.107	5.009	5.892	7.042	19.81	22.36	24.74	27.69
14	4.660	5.629	6.571	7.790	21.06	23.68	26.12	29.14
15	5.229	6.262	7.261	8.547	22.31	25.00	27.49	30.58
16	5.812	6.910	7.962	9.312	23.54	26.30	28.84	32.00
17	6.408	7.564	8.672	10.08	24.77	27.59	30.19	33.41
18	7.015	8.231	9.390	10.86	25.99	28.87	31.53	34.80
19	7.633	8.906	10.12	11.65	27.20	30.14	32.85	36.19
20	8.260	9.591	10.85	12.44	28.41	31.41	34.17	37.57
21	8.897	10.28	11.59	13.24	29.62	32.67	35.48	38.93
22	9.542	10.98	12.34	14.04	30.81	33.92	36.78	40.29
23	10.20	11.69	13.03	14.85	32.01	35.17	38.08	41.64
24	10.86	12.40	13.85	15.66	33.20	36.42	39.36	42.98
25	11.52	13.12	14.61	16.47	34.38	37.65	40.65	44.31
26	12.20	13.84	15.38	17.29	35.56	38.88	41.92	45.64
27	12.88	14.57	16.15	18.11	36.74	40.11	43.19	46.96
28	13.56	15.31	16.93	18.94	37.92	41.34	44.46	48.28
29	14.26	16.05	17.71	19.77	39.09	42.56	45.72	49.59
30	14.95	16.79	18.49	20.60	40.26	43.77	46.98	50.89
40	22.16	24.43	26.51	29.05	51.80	55.76	59.34	63.69
60	37.48	40.48	43.19	46.46	74.40	79.08	83.30	88.38
80	53.54	57.15	60.39	64.28	96.58	101.9	106.6	112.3
100	70.06	74.22	77.93	82.36	118.5	124.3	129.6	135.8
120	96.92	91.57	95.70	100.6	140.2	146.6	152.2	159.0
	0.010	0.025	0.050	0.100	0.100	0.050	0.025	0.010
	Area in left tail				Area in right tail			

Table 6 is taken from Table 8 of the *Biometrika Tables for Statisticians*, Volume 1, Third Edition, by Pearson and Hartley.

TABLE 7
Critical Values of $F_{.05}$

Degrees of freedom for numerator

	1	2	3	4	5	6	7	8	9	10	12	15	20	24	30	40	60	120	∞
1	161	200	216	225	230	234	237	239	241	242	244	246	248	249	250	251	252	253	254
1	161	200	216	225	230	234	237	239	241	242	244	246	248	249	250	251	252	253	254
2	18.5	19.0	19.2	19.2	19.3	19.3	19.4	19.4	19.4	19.4	19.4	19.4	19.4	19.5	19.5	19.5	19.5	19.5	19.5
3	10.1	9.55	9.28	9.12	9.01	8.94	8.89	8.85	8.81	8.79	8.74	8.70	8.66	8.64	8.62	8.59	8.57	8.55	8.53
4	7.71	6.94	6.59	6.39	6.26	6.16	6.09	6.04	6.00	5.96	5.91	5.86	5.80	5.77	5.75	5.72	5.69	5.66	5.63
5	6.61	5.79	5.41	5.19	5.05	4.95	4.88	4.82	4.77	4.74	4.68	4.62	4.56	4.53	4.50	4.46	4.43	4.40	4.37
6	5.99	5.14	4.76	4.53	4.39	4.28	4.21	4.15	4.10	4.06	4.00	3.94	3.87	3.84	3.81	3.77	3.74	3.70	3.67
7	5.59	4.74	4.35	4.12	3.97	3.87	3.79	3.73	3.68	3.64	3.57	3.51	3.44	3.41	3.38	3.34	3.30	3.27	3.23
8	5.32	4.46	4.07	3.84	3.69	3.58	3.50	3.44	3.39	3.35	3.28	3.22	3.15	3.12	3.08	3.04	3.01	2.97	2.93
9	5.12	4.26	3.86	3.63	3.48	3.37	3.29	3.23	3.18	3.14	3.07	3.01	2.94	2.90	2.86	2.83	2.79	2.75	2.71
10	4.96	4.10	3.71	3.48	3.33	3.22	3.14	3.07	3.02	2.98	2.91	2.85	2.77	2.74	2.70	2.66	2.62	2.58	2.54
11	4.84	3.98	3.59	3.36	3.20	3.09	3.01	2.95	2.90	2.85	2.79	2.72	2.65	2.61	2.57	2.53	2.49	2.45	2.40
12	4.75	3.89	3.49	3.26	3.11	3.00	2.91	2.85	2.80	2.75	2.69	2.62	2.54	2.51	2.47	2.43	2.38	2.34	2.30
13	4.67	3.81	3.41	3.18	3.03	2.92	2.83	2.77	2.71	2.67	2.60	2.53	2.46	2.42	2.38	2.34	2.30	2.25	2.21
14	4.60	3.74	3.34	3.11	2.96	2.85	2.76	2.70	2.65	2.60	2.53	2.46	2.39	2.35	2.31	2.27	2.22	2.18	2.13
15	4.54	3.68	3.29	3.06	2.90	2.79	2.71	2.64	2.59	2.54	2.48	2.40	2.33	2.29	2.25	2.20	2.16	2.11	2.07
16	4.49	3.63	3.24	3.01	2.85	2.74	2.66	2.59	2.54	2.49	2.42	2.35	2.28	2.24	2.19	2.15	2.11	2.06	2.01
17	4.45	3.59	3.20	2.96	2.81	2.70	2.61	2.55	2.49	2.45	2.38	2.31	2.23	2.19	2.15	2.10	2.06	2.01	1.96
18	4.41	3.55	3.16	2.93	2.77	2.66	2.58	2.51	2.46	2.41	2.34	2.27	2.19	2.15	2.11	2.06	2.02	1.97	1.92
19	4.38	3.52	3.13	2.90	2.74	2.63	2.54	2.48	2.42	2.38	2.31	2.23	2.16	2.11	2.07	2.03	1.98	1.93	1.88
20	4.35	3.49	3.10	2.87	2.71	2.60	2.51	2.45	2.39	2.35	2.28	2.20	2.12	2.08	2.04	1.99	1.95	1.90	1.84
21	4.32	3.47	3.07	2.84	2.68	2.57	2.49	2.42	2.37	2.32	2.25	2.18	2.10	2.05	2.01	1.96	1.92	1.87	1.81
22	4.30	3.44	3.05	2.82	2.66	2.55	2.46	2.40	2.34	2.30	2.23	2.15	2.07	2.03	1.98	1.94	1.89	1.84	1.78
23	4.28	3.42	3.03	2.80	2.64	2.53	2.44	2.37	2.32	2.27	2.20	2.13	2.05	2.01	1.96	1.91	1.86	1.81	1.76
24	4.26	3.40	3.01	2.78	2.62	2.51	2.42	2.36	2.30	2.25	2.18	2.11	2.03	1.98	1.94	1.89	1.84	1.79	1.73
25	4.24	3.39	2.99	2.76	2.60	2.49	2.40	2.34	2.28	2.24	2.16	2.09	2.01	1.96	1.92	1.87	1.82	1.77	1.71
30	4.17	3.32	2.92	2.69	2.53	2.42	2.33	2.27	2.21	2.16	2.09	2.01	1.93	1.89	1.84	1.79	1.74	1.68	1.62
40	4.08	3.23	2.84	2.61	2.45	2.34	2.25	2.18	2.12	2.08	2.00	1.92	1.84	1.79	1.74	1.69	1.64	1.58	1.51
60	4.00	3.15	2.76	2.53	2.37	2.25	2.17	2.10	2.04	1.99	1.92	1.84	1.75	1.70	1.65	1.59	1.53	1.47	1.39
120	3.92	3.07	2.68	2.45	2.29	2.18	2.09	2.02	1.96	1.91	1.83	1.75	1.66	1.61	1.55	1.50	1.43	1.35	1.25
∞	3.84	3.00	2.60	2.37	2.21	2.10	2.01	1.94	1.88	1.83	1.75	1.67	1.57	1.52	1.46	1.39	1.32	1.22	1.00

Degrees of freedom for denominator

Table 7 is taken from Table 18 of the *Biometrika Tables for Statisticians*, Volume 1, Third Edition, by Pearson and Hartley.

TABLE 8
Critical Values of $F_{.01}$

	Degrees of freedom for numerator																		
	1	2	3	4	5	6	7	8	9	10	12	15	20	24	30	40	60	120	∞
1	4,052	5,000	5,403	5,625	5,764	5,859	5,928	5,982	6,023	6,056	6,106	6,157	6,209	6,235	6,261	6,287	6,313	6,339	6,366
2	98.5	99.0	99.2	99.2	99.3	99.3	99.4	99.4	99.4	99.4	99.4	99.4	99.4	99.5	99.5	99.5	99.5	99.5	99.5
3	34.1	30.8	29.5	28.7	28.2	27.9	27.7	27.5	27.3	27.2	27.1	26.9	26.7	26.6	26.5	26.4	26.3	26.2	26.1
4	21.2	18.0	16.7	16.0	15.5	15.2	15.0	14.8	14.7	14.5	14.4	14.2	14.0	13.9	13.8	13.7	13.7	13.6	13.5
5	16.3	13.3	12.1	11.4	11.0	10.7	10.5	10.3	10.2	10.1	9.89	9.72	9.55	9.47	9.38	9.29	9.20	9.11	9.02
6	13.7	10.9	9.78	9.15	8.75	8.47	8.26	8.10	7.98	7.87	7.72	7.56	7.40	7.31	7.23	7.14	7.06	6.97	6.88
7	12.2	9.55	8.45	7.85	7.46	7.19	6.99	6.84	6.72	6.62	6.47	6.31	6.16	6.07	5.99	5.91	5.82	5.74	5.65
8	11.3	8.65	7.59	7.01	6.63	6.37	6.18	6.03	5.91	5.81	5.67	5.52	5.36	5.28	5.20	5.12	5.03	4.95	4.86
9	10.6	8.02	6.99	6.42	6.06	5.80	5.61	5.47	5.35	5.26	5.11	4.96	4.81	4.73	4.65	4.57	4.48	4.40	4.31
10	10.0	7.56	6.55	5.99	5.64	5.39	5.20	5.06	4.94	4.85	4.71	4.56	4.41	4.33	4.25	4.17	4.08	4.00	3.91
11	9.65	7.21	6.22	5.67	5.32	5.07	4.89	4.74	4.63	4.54	4.40	4.25	4.10	4.02	3.94	3.86	3.78	3.69	3.60
12	9.33	6.93	5.95	5.41	5.06	4.82	4.64	4.50	4.39	4.30	4.16	4.01	3.86	3.78	3.70	3.62	3.54	3.45	3.36
13	9.07	6.70	5.74	5.21	4.86	4.62	4.44	4.30	4.19	4.10	3.96	3.82	3.66	3.59	3.51	3.43	3.34	3.25	3.17
14	8.86	6.51	5.56	5.04	4.70	4.46	4.28	4.14	4.03	3.94	3.80	3.66	3.51	3.43	3.35	3.27	3.18	3.09	3.00
15	8.68	6.36	5.42	4.89	4.56	4.32	4.14	4.00	3.89	3.80	3.67	3.52	3.37	3.29	3.21	3.13	3.05	2.96	2.87
16	8.53	6.23	5.29	4.77	4.44	4.20	4.03	3.89	3.78	3.69	3.55	3.41	3.26	3.18	3.10	3.02	2.93	2.84	2.75
17	8.40	6.11	5.19	4.67	4.34	4.10	3.93	3.79	3.68	3.59	3.46	3.31	3.16	3.08	3.00	2.92	2.83	2.75	2.65
18	8.29	6.01	5.09	4.58	4.25	4.01	3.84	3.71	3.60	3.51	3.37	3.23	3.08	3.00	2.92	2.84	2.75	2.66	2.57
19	8.19	5.93	5.01	4.50	4.17	3.94	3.77	3.63	3.52	3.43	3.30	3.15	3.00	2.92	2.84	2.76	2.67	2.58	2.49
20	8.10	5.85	4.94	4.43	4.10	3.87	3.70	3.56	3.46	3.37	3.23	3.09	2.94	2.86	2.78	2.69	2.61	2.52	2.42
21	8.02	5.78	4.87	4.37	4.04	3.81	3.64	3.51	3.40	3.31	3.17	3.03	2.88	2.80	2.72	2.64	2.55	2.46	2.36
22	7.95	5.72	4.82	4.31	3.99	3.76	3.59	3.45	3.35	3.26	3.12	2.98	2.83	2.75	2.67	2.58	2.50	2.40	2.31
23	7.88	5.66	4.76	4.26	3.94	3.71	3.54	3.41	3.30	3.21	3.07	2.93	2.78	2.70	2.62	2.54	2.45	2.35	2.26
24	7.82	5.61	4.72	4.22	3.90	3.67	3.50	3.36	3.26	3.17	3.03	2.89	2.74	2.66	2.58	2.49	2.40	2.31	2.21
25	7.77	5.57	4.68	4.18	3.86	3.63	3.46	3.32	3.22	3.13	2.99	2.85	2.70	2.62	2.53	2.45	2.36	2.27	2.17
30	7.56	5.39	4.51	4.02	3.70	3.47	3.30	3.17	3.07	2.98	2.84	2.70	2.55	2.47	2.39	2.30	2.21	2.11	2.01
40	7.31	5.18	4.31	3.83	3.51	3.29	3.12	2.99	2.89	2.80	2.66	2.52	2.37	2.29	2.20	2.11	2.02	1.92	1.80
60	7.08	4.98	4.13	3.65	3.34	3.12	2.95	2.82	2.72	2.63	2.50	2.35	2.20	2.12	2.03	1.94	1.84	1.73	1.60
120	6.85	4.79	3.95	3.48	3.17	2.96	2.79	2.66	2.56	2.47	2.34	2.19	2.03	1.95	1.86	1.76	1.66	1.53	1.38
∞	6.63	4.61	3.78	3.32	3.02	2.80	2.64	2.51	2.41	2.32	2.18	2.04	1.88	1.79	1.70	1.59	1.47	1.32	1.00

Degrees of freedom for denominator

TABLE 9
Critical Values of F_{max}

df	α	\multicolumn{9}{c}{k = number of variances}
		2	3	4	5	6	7	8	9	10
4	.05	9.60	15.5	20.6	25.2	29.5	33.6	37.5	41.4	44.6
	.01	23.2	37.	49.	59.	69.	79.	89.	97.	106.
5	.05	7.15	10.8	13.7	16.3	18.7	20.8	22.9	24.7	26.5
	.01	14.9	22.	28.	33.	38.	42.	46.	50.	54.
6	.05	5.82	8.38	10.4	12.1	13.7	15.0	16.3	17.5	18.6
	.01	11.1	15.5	19.1	22.	25.	27.	30.	32.	34.
7	.05	4.99	6.94	8.44	9.70	10.8	11.8	12.7	13.5	14.3
	.01	8.89	12.1	14.5	46.5	18.4	20.	22.	23.	24.
8	.05	4.43	6.00	7.18	8.12	9.03	9.78	10.5	11.1	11.7
	.01	7.50	9.9	11.7	13.2	14.5	15.8	16.9	17.9	18.9
9	.05	4.03	5.34	6.31	7.11	7.80	8.41	8.95	9.45	9.91
	.01	6.54	8.5	9.9	11.1	12.1	13.1	13.9	14.7	15.3
10	.05	3.72	4.85	5.67	6.34	6.92	7.42	7.87	8.28	8.66
	.01	5.85	7.4	8.6	9.6	10.4	11.1	11.8	12.4	12.9
12	.05	3.28	4.16	4.79	5.30	5.72	6.09	6.42	6.72	7.00
	.01	4.91	6.1	6.9	7.6	8.2	8.7	9.1	9.5	9.9
15	.05	2.86	3.54	4.01	4.37	4.68	4.95	5.19	5.40	5.59
	.01	4.07	4.9	5.5	6.0	6.4	6.7	7.1	7.3	7.5
20	.05	2.46	2.95	3.29	3.54	3.76	3.94	4.10	4.24	4.37
	.01	3.32	3.8	4.3	4.6	4.9	5.1	5.3	5.5	5.6
30	.05	2.07	2.40	2.61	2.78	2.91	3.02	3.12	3.21	3.29
	.01	2.63	3.0	3.3	3.4	3.6	3.7	3.8	3.9	4.0
60	.05	1.67	1.85	1.96	2.04	2.11	2.17	2.22	2.26	2.30
	.01	1.96	2.2	2.3	2.4	2.4	2.5	2.5	2.6	2.6
∞	.05	1.00	1.00	1.00	1.00	1.00	1.00	1.00	1.00	1.00
	.01	1.00	1.00	1.00	1.00	1.00	1.00	1.00	1.00	1.00

Table 9 is taken from Table 31 of the *Biometrika Tables for Statisticians*, Volume 1, Third Edition, by Pearson and Hartley.

TABLE 10
Critical Values of q_r

r = number of steps between ordered means

df for MSE	α	2	3	4	5	6	7	8	9	10	11	12	13	14	15
1	.05	18.0	27.0	32.8	37.1	40.4	43.1	45.4	47.4	49.1	50.6	52.0	53.2	54.3	55.4
	.01	90.0	135	164	186	202	216	227	237	246	253	260	266	272	277
2	.05	6.09	8.3	9.8	10.9	11.7	12.4	13.0	13.5	14.0	14.4	14.7	15.1	15.4	15.7
	.01	14.0	19.0	22.3	24.7	26.6	28.2	29.5	30.7	31.7	32.6	33.4	34.1	34.8	35.4
3	.05	4.50	5.91	6.82	7.50	8.04	8.48	8.85	9.18	9.46	9.72	9.95	10.2	10.4	10.5
	.01	8.26	10.6	12.2	13.3	14.2	15.0	15.6	16.2	16.7	17.1	17.5	17.9	18.2	18.5
4	.05	3.93	5.04	5.76	6.29	6.71	7.05	7.35	7.60	7.83	8.03	8.21	8.37	8.52	8.66
	.01	6.51	8.12	9.17	9.96	10.6	11.1	11.5	11.9	12.3	12.6	12.8	13.1	13.3	13.5
5	.05	3.64	4.60	5.22	5.67	6.03	6.33	6.58	6.80	6.99	7.17	7.32	7.47	7.60	7.72
	.01	5.70	6.97	7.80	8.42	8.91	9.32	9.67	9.97	10.2	10.5	10.7	10.9	11.1	11.2
6	.05	3.46	4.34	4.90	5.31	5.63	5.89	6.12	6.32	6.49	6.65	6.79	6.92	7.03	7.14
	.01	5.24	6.33	7.03	7.56	7.97	8.32	8.61	8.87	9.10	9.30	9.49	9.65	9.81	9.95
7	.05	3.34	4.16	4.69	5.06	5.36	5.61	5.82	6.00	6.16	6.30	6.43	6.55	6.66	6.76
	.01	4.95	5.92	6.54	7.01	7.37	7.68	7.94	8.17	8.37	8.55	8.71	8.86	9.00	9.12
8	.05	3.26	4.04	4.53	4.89	5.17	5.40	5.60	5.77	5.92	6.05	6.18	6.29	6.39	6.48
	.01	4.74	5.63	6.20	6.63	6.96	7.24	7.47	7.68	7.87	8.03	8.18	8.31	8.44	8.55
9	.05	3.20	3.95	4.42	4.76	5.02	5.24	5.43	5.60	5.74	5.87	5.98	6.09	6.19	6.28
	.01	4.60	5.43	5.96	6.35	6.66	6.91	7.13	7.32	7.49	7.65	7.78	7.91	8.03	8.13
10	.05	3.15	3.88	4.33	4.65	4.91	5.12	5.30	5.46	5.60	5.72	5.83	5.93	6.03	6.11
	.01	4.48	5.27	5.77	6.14	6.43	6.67	6.87	7.05	7.21	7.36	7.48	7.60	7.71	7.81
11	.05	3.11	3.82	4.26	4.57	4.82	5.03	5.20	5.35	5.49	5.61	5.71	5.81	5.90	5.99
	.01	4.39	5.14	5.62	5.97	6.25	6.48	6.67	6.84	6.99	7.13	7.26	7.36	7.46	7.56
12	.05	3.08	3.77	4.20	4.51	4.75	4.95	5.12	5.27	5.40	5.51	5.62	5.71	5.80	5.88
	.01	4.32	5.04	5.50	5.84	6.10	6.32	6.51	6.67	6.81	6.94	7.06	7.17	7.26	7.36
13	.05	3.06	3.73	4.15	4.45	4.69	4.88	5.05	5.19	5.32	5.43	5.53	5.63	5.71	5.79
	.01	4.26	4.96	5.40	5.73	5.98	6.19	6.37	6.53	6.67	6.79	6.90	7.01	7.10	7.19
14	.05	3.03	3.70	4.11	4.41	4.64	4.83	4.99	5.13	5.25	5.36	5.46	5.55	5.64	5.72
	.01	4.21	4.89	5.32	5.63	5.88	6.08	6.26	6.41	6.54	6.66	6.77	6.87	6.96	7.05
16	.05	3.00	3.65	4.05	4.33	4.56	4.74	4.90	5.03	5.15	5.26	5.35	5.44	5.52	5.59
	.01	4.13	4.78	5.19	5.49	5.72	5.92	6.08	6.22	6.35	6.46	6.56	6.66	6.74	6.82
18	.05	2.97	3.61	4.00	4.28	4.49	4.67	4.82	4.96	5.07	5.17	5.27	5.35	5.43	5.50
	.01	4.07	4.70	5.09	5.38	5.60	5.79	5.94	6.08	6.20	6.31	6.41	6.50	6.58	6.65
20	.05	2.95	3.58	3.96	4.23	4.45	4.62	4.77	4.90	5.01	5.11	5.20	5.28	5.36	5.43
	.01	4.02	4.64	5.02	5.29	5.51	5.69	5.84	5.97	6.09	6.19	6.29	6.37	6.45	6.52
24	.05	2.92	3.53	3.90	4.17	4.37	4.54	4.68	4.81	4.92	5.01	5.10	5.18	5.25	5.32
	.01	3.96	4.54	4.91	5.17	5.37	5.54	5.69	5.81	5.92	6.02	6.11	6.19	6.26	6.33
30	.05	2.89	3.49	3.84	4.10	4.30	4.46	4.60	4.72	4.83	4.92	5.00	5.08	5.15	5.21
	.01	3.89	4.45	4.80	5.05	5.24	5.40	5.54	5.56	5.76	5.85	5.93	6.01	6.08	6.14
40	.05	2.86	3.44	3.79	4.04	4.23	4.39	4.52	4.63	4.74	4.82	4.91	4.98	5.05	5.11
	.01	3.82	4.37	4.70	4.93	5.11	5.27	5.39	5.50	5.60	5.69	5.77	5.84	5.90	5.96
60	.05	2.83	3.40	3.74	3.98	4.16	4.31	4.44	4.55	4.65	4.73	4.81	4.88	4.94	5.00
	.01	3.76	4.28	4.60	4.82	4.99	5.13	5.25	5.36	5.45	5.53	5.60	5.67	5.73	5.79
120	.05	2.80	3.36	3.69	3.92	4.10	4.24	4.36	4.48	4.56	4.64	4.72	4.78	4.84	4.90
	.01	3.70	4.20	4.50	4.71	4.87	5.01	5.12	5.21	5.30	5.38	5.44	5.51	5.56	5.61
∞	.05	2.77	3.31	3.63	3.86	4.03	4.17	4.29	4.39	4.47	4.55	4.62	4.68	4.74	4.80
	.01	3.64	4.12	4.40	4.60	4.76	4.88	4.99	5.08	5.16	5.23	5.29	5.35	5.40	5.45

Table 10 is taken from Henry Scheffe: *The Analysis of Variance* (New York: John Wiley & Sons, Inc., 1959), pp. 434–436.

TABLE 11

Critical Values of *T*

Sample Size *n*	Probability that T is less than the Critical Value			
	0.050	0.025	0.010	0.005
5	1			
6	2	1		
7	4	2		
8	6	4	2	
9	8	6	3	2
10	11	8	5	3
11	14	11	7	5
12	17	14	10	7
13	21	17	13	10
14	26	21	16	13
15	30	25	20	16
16	36	30	24	19
17	41	35	28	23
18	47	40	33	28
19	54	46	38	32
20	60	52	43	37
21	68	59	49	43
22	75	66	56	49
23	83	73	62	55
24	92	81	69	61
25	101	90	77	68

Table 11 is taken from *Some Rapid Approximate Statistical Procedures* (1964) p. 28 by F. Wilcoxon and R. A. Wilcox. It is reproduced with the kind permission of Lederle Laboratories.

TABLE 12

Random Numbers

	1	2	3	4	5	6	7	8	9	10	
1	48461	14952	72619	73689	52059	37086	60050	86192	67049	64739	1
2	76534	38149	49692	31366	52093	15422	20498	33901	10319	43397	2
3	70437	25861	38504	14752	23757	59660	67844	78815	23758	86814	3
4	59584	03370	42806	11393	71722	93804	09095	07856	55589	46020	4
5	04285	58554	16085	51555	27501	73883	33427	33343	45507	50063	5
6	77340	10412	69189	85171	29082	44785	83638	02583	96483	76553	6
7	59183	62687	91778	80354	23512	97219	65921	02035	59847	91403	7
8	91800	04281	39979	03927	82564	28777	59049	97532	54540	79472	8
9	12066	24817	81099	48940	69554	55925	48379	12866	51232	21580	9
10	69907	91751	53512	23748	65906	91385	84983	27915	48491	91068	10
11	80467	04873	54053	25955	48518	13815	37707	68687	15570	08890	11
12	78057	67835	28302	45048	56761	97725	58438	91528	24645	18544	12
13	05648	39387	78191	88415	60269	94880	58812	42931	71898	61534	13
14	22304	39246	01350	99451	61862	78688	30339	60222	74052	25740	14
15	61346	50269	67005	40442	33100	16742	61640	21046	31909	72641	15
16	66793	37696	27965	30459	91011	51426	31006	77468	61029	57108	16
17	86411	48809	36698	42453	83061	43769	39948	87031	30767	13953	17
18	62098	12825	81744	28882	27369	88183	65846	92545	09065	22655	18
19	68775	06261	54265	16203	23340	84750	16317	88686	86842	00879	19
20	52679	19595	13687	74872	89181	01939	18447	10787	76246	80072	20
21	84096	87152	20719	25215	04349	54434	72344	93008	83282	31670	21
22	63964	55937	21417	49944	38356	98404	14850	17994	17161	98981	22
23	31191	75131	72386	11689	95727	05414	88727	45583	22568	77700	23
24	30545	68523	29850	67833	05622	89975	79042	27142	99257	32349	24
25	52573	91001	52315	26430	54175	30122	31796	98842	37600	26025	25
26	16586	81842	01076	99414	31574	94719	34656	80018	86988	79234	26
27	81841	88481	61191	25013	30272	23388	22463	65774	10029	58376	27
28	43563	66829	72838	08074	57080	15446	11034	98143	74989	26885	28
29	19945	84193	57581	77252	85604	45412	43556	27518	90572	00563	29
30	79374	23796	16919	99691	80276	32818	62953	78831	54395	30705	30
31	48503	26615	43980	09810	38289	66679	73799	48418	12647	40044	31
32	32049	65541	37937	41105	70106	89706	40829	40789	59547	00783	32
33	18547	71562	95493	34112	76895	46766	96395	31718	48302	45893	33
34	03180	96742	61486	43305	34183	99605	67803	13491	09243	29557	34
35	94822	24738	67749	83748	59799	25210	31093	62925	72061	69991	35
36	34330	60599	85828	19152	68499	27977	35611	96240	62747	89529	36
37	43770	81537	59527	95674	76692	86420	69930	10020	72881	12532	37
38	56908	77192	50623	41215	14311	42834	80651	93750	59957	31211	38
39	32787	07189	80539	75927	75475	73965	11796	72140	48944	74156	39
40	52441	78392	11733	57703	29133	71164	55355	31006	25526	55790	40
41	22377	54723	18227	28449	04570	18882	00023	67101	06895	08915	41
42	18376	73460	88841	39602	34049	20589	05701	08249	74213	25220	42
43	53201	28610	87957	21497	64729	64983	71551	99016	87903	63875	43
44	34919	78901	59710	27396	02593	05665	11964	44134	00273	76358	44
45	33617	92159	21971	16901	57383	34262	41744	60891	57624	06962	45
46	70010	40964	98780	72418	52571	18415	64352	90636	38034	04909	46
47	19282	68447	35665	31530	59832	49181	21914	65742	89815	39231	47
48	91429	73328	13266	54898	68795	40948	80808	63887	89939	47938	48
49	97637	78393	33021	05867	86520	45363	43066	00988	64040	09803	49
50	95150	07625	05255	83254	93943	52325	93230	62668	79529	65964	50

Table 12 is taken from STATISTICAL TABLES by F. James Rohlf and Robert R. Sokal. W. H. Freeman and Company. Copyright © 1969.

Answers to Selected Problems

CHAPTER 1

SECTION 1.1

1. (a) $168 - 72 = 96$
   (b) $96 \div 12 = 8$
   (c)

161–168	161–170
153–160	151–160
145–152	141–150
137–144	131–140
129–136	121–130
121–128	111–120
113–120	101–110
105–112	91–100
97–104	81–90
89–96	71–80
81–88	73–80
65–72	

2. (a) 19.5, 26.5, 33.5, 40.5, 47.5, 54.5   (c) 6

3. (a) 10   (d) 100–109

4.

Sales (in Dollars)	No. of Outlets	Rel. Freq.	Cum. Freq.
10–20	15	0.19	15
21–31	20	0.25	35
32–42	14	0.18	49
43–53	6	0.08	55
54–64	10	0.12	65
65–75	8	0.10	73
76–86	5	0.06	78
87–97	2	0.02	80

6.

Pollution Indices	No. of Days	Rel. Freq.	Cum. Freq.
26–30	2	0.017	2
31–35	3	0.025	5
36–40	5	0.042	10
41–45	16	0.133	26
46–50	15	0.125	41
51–55	15	0.125	56
56–60	20	0.167	76
61–65	13	0.108	89
66–70	15	0.125	104
71–75	7	0.058	111
76–80	2	0.017	113
81–85	4	0.033	117
86–90	3	0.025	120

7. (e)

47.0–48.9	2
49.0–50.9	4
51.0–52.9	6
53.0–54.9	6
55.0–56.9	5
57.0–58.9	4
59.0–60.9	2
61.0–62.9	1

SECTION 1.2

2.

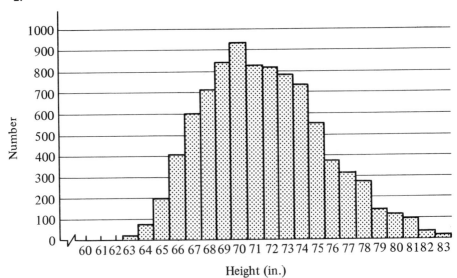

3.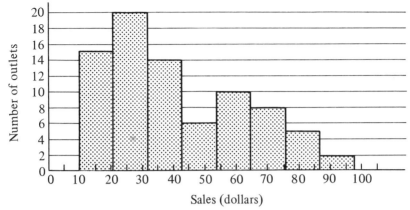

Sales (dollars)

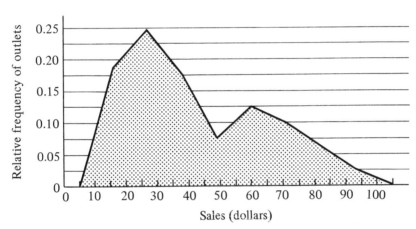

Sales (dollars)

5.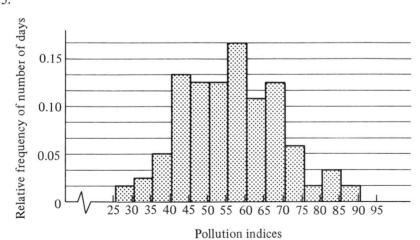

Pollution indices

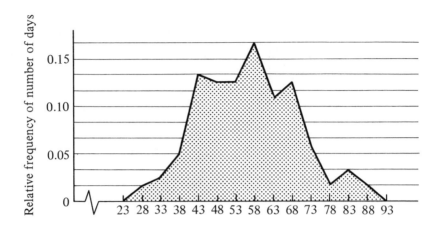

6.

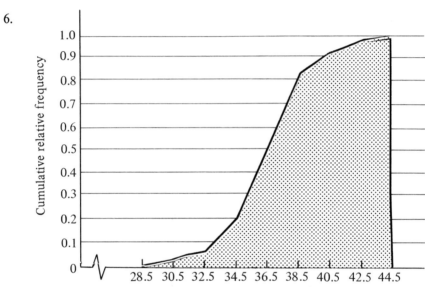

7.

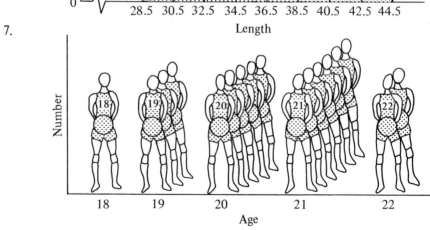

9. (a)

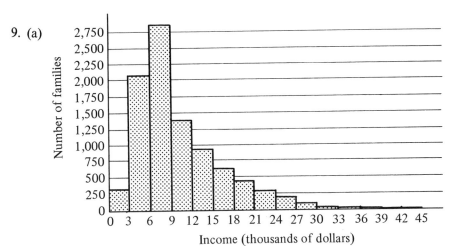

(b)

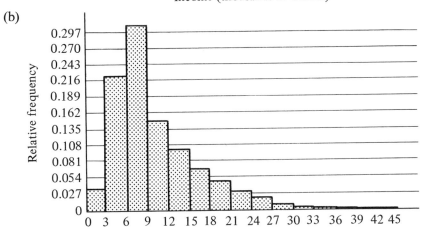

(c)

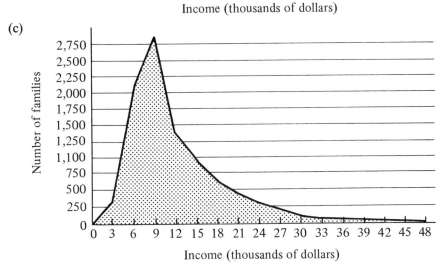

(d)

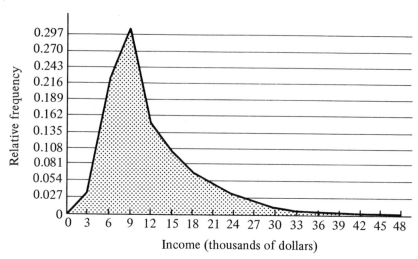

(e)

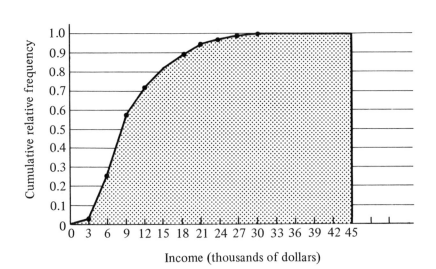

SECTION 1.3

1. $363 - 107 = 256$; $256 \div 11 \doteq 23$; $25 \times 11 = 275$, so we can conveniently begin at, say, 100.5 and go to 375.5. Thus we might have the following (other

answers are possible):

| | | The class may also |
Class	Class mark	be written as
100.5–125.5	113	101–125
125.5–150.5	138	126–150
150.5–175.5	163	151–175
175.5–200.5	188	176–200
200.5–225.5	213	201–225
225.5–250.5	238	226–250
250.5–275.5	263	251–275
275.5–300.5	288	276–300
300.5–325.5	313	301–325
325.5–350.5	338	326–350
350.5–375.5	363	351–375

3. The class interval is 50, so each class extends 25 units above and below the class mark, so the class limits are 101–150, 151–200, 201–250, 251–300, 301–350, 351–400, 451–500, 501–550, and 551–600. The class boundaries are 100.5, 150.5, 200.5, 250.5, 300.5, 350.5, 400.5, 450.5, 500.5, 550.5, and 600.5.

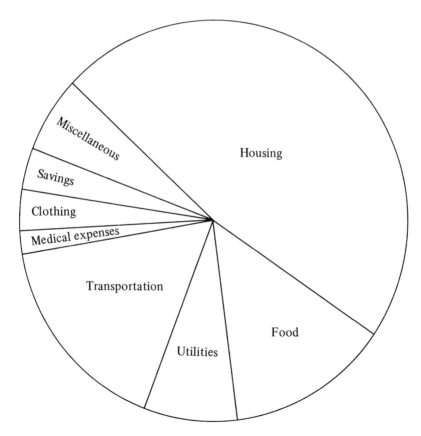

4. (a) 140 (b) 180–199, 200–219, 220–239, 240–259, 260–279, 280–299, 300–319, 320–339. (c) 14 or 15

6. (a) 16.995, 18.995 (b) 0.01 (hundredths) (c) 13.995
   (d) 2.00 (e) 10.94

10. The total expenses are $800, so each expenditure must be represented as a fraction of $800. If we wish, we may calculate the number of degrees for each one as well. Thus housing is 0.475 (171°), food is 0.1375 (49.5°), utilities, 0.075 (27°), transportation, 0.16875 (60.75°), medical expenses, 0.01875 (6.75°), clothing, 0.03125 (11.25°), savings, 0.03125 (11.25°) and miscellaneous, 0.0625 (22.5°). The chart below is one representation.

CHAPTER 2

SECTION 2.1

1. $\bar{x}=25$; md$=(23+26)/2=24.5$; there is no mode.

3. $\bar{x}=4.31$; md$=3.02$; no mode.

4. $\bar{x}=172.51$; md$=171$; mode$=170$ and 174, or no mode.

6. $\bar{x}\doteq17.54$; md$\doteq17.7$; modal class 17.00–18.99.

7. $\bar{x}\doteq71.6$; md$=71$ (from raw scores), md$=71.3$ (from the table); mode$=70$, modal class is 69–71.

10. $\bar{x}=56.7$; md$=57$; mode$=54$.

11. $\bar{x}\doteq33.3$; md$=33$; mode$=34$.

13. $\bar{x}\doteq\$10,055$; md$\doteq\$8,361$; modal class is $6,000 to $8,999.

SECTION 2.2

1. $s^2=16$; $s=4$.

3. $s^2\doteq9.86$; $s\doteq3.14$.

4. md$\doteq98.3$, $Q=15.2$.

6. $s\doteq3.87$.

9. $s\doteq22.47$.

11. $s \doteq 13.05$.

14. $s \doteq \$6,028$; $Q \doteq \$3,540$; Index $\doteq 0.84$.

SECTION 2.3

1. -2.5; -1.92; -1.17; -0.25; 0.5; 1.67; 2.83.

3. 100.58; 141.04; 181.84; 236.92 (or 101; 141; 182; 237).

6. $p_5 \doteq \$3,242$; $p_{27} \doteq \$6,102$; $p_{44} \doteq \$7,771$; $p_{63} \doteq \$10,278$; $p_{82} \doteq \$15,024$; $p_{94} \doteq \$21,591$.

SECTION 2.4

2. (a) $\bar{x} = 48.5$; md $= 47.5$.
   (b) $s = 15.70$; rule of thumb, about 19.
   (c) 1.61; -1.67.
   (d) $Q = 9$.

4. (a) $\bar{x} = 45.5$; md $= 44.5$; mode $= 44$.
   (b) $s \doteq 5.79$.
   (c) $Q = 6$.
   (d) $p_{15} = 37$; $p_{44} = 44$; $p_{58} = 47$; $p_{83} = 54$.

5. (a) about 5% (empirical rule).
   (b) as much as 25% (Chebyshev's rule).

7. For Mr. Jones, $z = 1.2$; for Mr. Adams, $z = 1.0$. Thus Mr. Jones' blood pressure is higher, compared to his group, than Mr. Adams'.

CHAPTER 3

SECTION 3.1

3. Theoretically the 13 hearts divide the 39 remaining cards into 14 parts which, on the average, will be equal. Therefore each part will contain 39/14 or about 2.79 cards, on the average. The part before the first heart will average this many and, adding the first heart, we obtain 3.79.

4. 75.

6. 2/3; 1/12.

8. (a) 0.4   (c) 0.7

SECTION 3.2

2. (a)

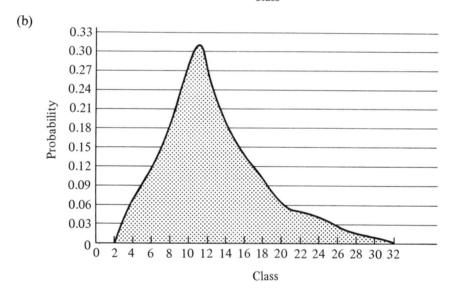

(b)

(c) $\mu = 12.8$, $s^2 = 176.4 - (12.8)^2 = 12.56$, so $x \doteq 3.54$.

3. $\mu = 5.9$; $\sigma^2 = 0.89$; $\sigma \doteq 0.94$.

5. $7,100.

7. 5.50; 1.79.

8. 1 7/8; 15/16.

10. −1/19 dollars.

SECTION 3.3

1. (a) 0.38   (b) 0.28   (c) 0.68   (d) 0.51

2. (a) A (b) A (c) B

4. $n = 50$

6. (a)

x	$P(x)$
2	3/28
3	5/28
4	3/14
5	3/14
6	5/28
7	3/28

(b) $\mu = 4.5$; $\sigma = 1.5$.

CHAPTER 4

SECTION 4.1

2. $P(2) = 2/5$; $P(3) = 2/5$; $P(4) = 1/5$; $\mu = 14/5$; $\sigma^2 = 14/25$.

4.

x	0	1	2	3
$P(x)$	0.09	0.33	0.41	0.17

5. $P(7) = 6/36$, $P(11) = 2/36$, $P(7 \text{ or } 11) = 8/36$, or $p = 2/9$; $n = 4$, $1 - p = 7/9$, so we have, for x successes,

x	$P(x)$
0	$\binom{4}{0}(2/9)^0(7/9)^4 = 2{,}401/6{,}561 \doteq 0.366$
1	$\binom{4}{1}(2/9)^1(7/9)^3 = 2{,}744/6{,}561 \doteq 0.418$
2	$\binom{4}{2}(2/9)^2(7/9)^2 = 1{,}176/6{,}561 \doteq 0.179$
3	$\binom{4}{3}(2/9)^3(7/9)^1 = 224/6{,}561 \doteq 0.034$
4	$\binom{4}{4}(2/9)^4(7/9)^0 = 16/6{,}561 \doteq 0.002$

Then $\mu = 4(2/9) = 8/9$; $\sigma^2 = 4(2/9)(7/9) = 56/81$.

7. $P(3) \doteq 0.320$;
   $P(2) \doteq 0.305$;
   $P(1) \doteq 0.145$;
   $\mu \doteq 2.56$.

9.

Hypergeometric			Binomial	
x	$P(x)$		x	$P(x)$
0	0.1295		0	0.1317
1	0.3303		1	0.3292
2	0.3320		2	0.3292
3	0.1643		3	0.1646
4	0.0400		4	0.0412
5	0.0038		5	0.0041

11.

Hypergeometric			Binomial	
x	$P(x)$		x	$P(x)$
0	0.3275		0	0.3277
1	0.4098		1	0.4096
2	0.2049		2	0.2048
3	0.0511		3	0.0512
4	0.0064		4	0.0064
5	0.0003		5	0.0003

SECTION 4.2

1. $P(x \geq 11) = 0.952$; $P(x \geq 12) = 0.887$, so $P(11) = 0.065$.

2. $P(x \leq 5) = 1 - P(x \geq 6) = 1 - 0.019 = 0.981$; $P(5) = 0.054$.

3. $P(x > 18) = P(x \geq 19) = 0.332$; $P(20) = 0.106$.

4. $P(x > 14) = 0.034$; $P(x < 14) = 0.922$.

5. $P(x \geq 7) \doteq 0.543$; $P(x \geq 8) \doteq 0.356$, so $P(7) \doteq 0.187$.

6. $P(x < 12) = 1 - P(x \geq 12) \doteq 0.003$; $P(12) \doteq 0.005$.

7. $p = 0.60$.   8. $r = 13$.

9. $r = 14$.   10. $r = 11$.

11. 0.655.   13. 0.156.

14. 0.030.   15. 0.633; 0.656.

18. 0.103; 0.170.   19. 0.087; 0.114.

SECTION 4.3

1. 0.064.

2. 0.109; 16.35.

5. (a) 0.263   (b) 0.264   (c) 0.264.

7. (a) 0.264   (b) 0.264   (c) 0.264.

8. (a) 0.011   (b) 0.011   (c) 0.015.

10. $70.

SECTION 4.4

1. No; probability is about 0.075.

4. (a) 3 or fewer   (b) 4 or fewer   (c) 2 or fewer   (d) It cannot be concluded that the drug is effective. $\beta = 0.766$.

5. $x \geq 3$; $x < 3$.

SECTION 4.5

1. 6

2. If $p = 0.6$, $P(x \geq 9) \doteq 0.046$; investigate.

3. (c) Fit is reasonably close. For example, $P(3) = 0.24$ and $P(4) = 0.15$; corresponding Poisson probabilities are 0.214 and 0.134.

4. $P(9 \leq x \leq 12) \doteq 0.693$.

5. $P(9 \leq x \leq 12) \doteq 0.663$.

7. 0.522; 0.150; probability of calling three or more by chance is only 0.026.

8. 0.002; yes.

9. 0.323.

11. Marked degree of ESP on mind reading; some clairvoyant ability.

CHAPTER 5

SECTION 5.2

1. (a) -1.60 (b) 1.30   (c) -1.74 (d) -0.29 (e) 0.63   (f) 2.50.

2. (a) 29.75   (b) 34.83   (c) -15.09 (d) 16.30   (e) 8.87   (f) 23.85.

3. (a) 0.4854 (b) 0.3508+0.4382=0.7890 (c) 0.4983−0.4406=0.0577
  (d) 0.1879−0.0478=0.1401 (e) 0.4988+0.4484=0.9472
  (f) 0.1664+0.4817=0.8481.

4. (a) 0.5000−0.4236=0.0764 (b) 0.5000−0.3485=0.1515
  (c) 0.5000+0.2794=0.7794 (d) 0.5000+0.4778=0.9778.

5. (a) 0.6826 (b) 0.9544 (c) 0.9974 (d) 0.7994 (e) 0.8990 (f) 0.9500
  (g) 0.9802 (h) 0.9902.

6. If 0.1230 of the area under the normal curve is to the right of z, 0.8770 is to
  the left of z, and 0.3370 is between 0 and z. Therefore $z=1.16$.

7. (a) 0.1075 (b) 0.3085 (c) 0.8389 (d) 0.6844 (e) 0.2435 (f) 0.8321
  (g) 0.2025
  (h) for $z=0.48$, 0.1884 lies between 193.4 and 200, so 0.5000−0.1884 or
  0.3156 lies above 200; for $z=-0.98$, 0.3365 lies between 180 and 193.4
  so 0.1635 lies below 180; therefore 0.3156+0.1635 or 0.4791 lies above
  200 or below 180 (and 0.5209 lies between 180 and 200).

8. If 0.1446 of the area of a normal distribution lies above a score, then 0.3554
  lies between the score and the mean. Thus $z=1.06$. Since $1.06=(121-100)/\sigma$, then $\sigma=21/1.06\doteq19.8$.

9. $=971.5$.

10. 27.

11. (a) 2.33 (b) 2.58 (c) 1.96 (d) 1.645 (e) 1.28
  (f) −2.33 (g) −2.58 (h) −1.96 (i) −1.645 (j) −1.28

SECTION 5.3

1. (a) 6,680 (b) 72.55 oz.

2. 0.0044

4. 0.9569; 0.1210; 1,210.

6. 0.8790.

7. Company A; cost is 4.90 cents vs. 5.08 cents for company B.

9. 0.0034.

11. 0.0359.

12. $\mu=152$, $\sigma=18$.

SECTION 5.4

2. 59, 61

3. $x \geq 177$; at least 40% are watching the show.

SECTION 5.5

1. (a) 0.6268 (b) 0.0301 (c) 0.1736 (d) 110.8 (e) 117.9
 (f) 86.1 (g) 0.3944 (h) 0.7324.

3. 76.27.

6. 0.0062

7. (a) 0.0108 (b) 0.0179 (c) 0.9515.

8. 0.0049; 0.0571; 0.0170.

11. 0.5714; solution involves a quadratic equation, 93.

CHAPTER 6

SECTION 6.1

1. (a) 10 (b) 3.16 (c) 1 (d) 16.67 (e) 8.33 (f) 12.5
 (g) 8.84 (h) 3.125.

3. (a) 0.0853 (b) 0.0749.

4. $n = 16$.

6. Approximately 0.4648 to 0.4681, depending on rounding.

7. 0.0038.

10. $\bar{x} = 21.4$; $s_{\bar{x}} \doteq 0.24$.

SECTION 6.2

1. 2.074 to 2.086; 2.072 to 2.088.

4. No.

5. 10.53 to 11.31; 10.40 to 11.44.

7. The probability is 0.98 that the error will be less than 0.42.

9. 0.9936.

10. $10,706 to $12,180; $10,855 to $12,031.

11. (a) 0.9356 (b) 0.9250 (c) 0.8858 (d) 0.9342.

SECTION 6.3

1. 2,305; (use $P=0.60$ as a reasonable estimate.)

3. 0.32 to 0.48; 0.30 to 0.50.

4. 122 (Note: correction factor must be used.)

7. About 0.78; about 0.73.

8. about 530.

SECTION 6.4

1. 0.07 to 0.11; 0.06 to 0.12 (or 0.067 to 0.113; 0.063 to 0.117).

3. $1,168 to $3,972.

4. −0.038 to 0.166.

5. 0.07 to 0.21.

8. −0.028 to 0.118.

SECTION 6.5

1. 0.568 to 0.692; 0.539 to 0.721.

2. −0.005 to 0.121.

4. 0.10 to 0.13.

5. 4.58 to 5.74; 2.63 to 5.63; −0.31 to 2.37.

SECTION 6.6

2. 0.015 to 0.020; 0.014 to 0.021; 0.014 to 0.022; 0.014 to 0.023.

3. $F \doteq 1.19$, appropriate; $F \doteq 2.90$, not appropriate.

SECTION 6.7

2. (a) 500 (b) 666.

3. 28,128 to 29,156; 27,945 to 29,339.

4. $F \doteq 1.41$; 0.1 to 1.3.

6. 97.

7. 15.65 to 16.39; 15.58 to 16.46.

9. 0.60 to 0.80; 0.57 to 0.83.

10. The probability is 0.95 that the error will be less than 0.048.

11. 0.02 to 0.24.

13. 0.075 to 0.165; 0.06 to 0.18.

14. 148.1 to 159.9; 145.7 to 162.3.

15. -0.005 to 0.065 (or -0.01 to 0.07)

CHAPTER 7

SECTION 7.1

1. The researcher's conclusion is that the implements are not less than 24,000 years old, which is false. A type I error is made by rejecting a true hypothesis, so his hypothesis must have been that the implements were less than 24,000 years old—which he rejected. If he made a type II error he must have accepted the hypothesis which is identical with his conclusion.

2. H_0: $\mu = 32$; H_1: $\mu < 32$. H_0: $\mu = 32$; H_1: $\mu > 32$.

6. (a) H_0: $\mu_A = \mu_B$; H_1: $\mu_A > \mu_B$ or H_1: $\mu_A \neq \mu_B$
   (b) No
   (c) Reserve judgment.

SECTION 7.2

2. $z = 2.62$; yes.

3. $z = 1.43$; accept.

6. $z = 2.07$; claim is substantiated.

7. $t = -2.418$; the lot is acceptable with the given level of significance.

9. $t = 1.50$; no.

10. $t = -2.20$; weight is less than 16 oz.

12. Below 227.6 or above 232.4 oz.

SECTION 7.3

1. $z = 3.05$; stock only brand B.

3. $z = 0.83$; accept shipment.

4. $z = -2.74$; reject the claim.

6. $z = 5.56$; the contention that the dice are loaded is substantiated.

8. $z = 6.18$; at least one-third of students favor co-ed dorms.

SECTION 7.4

1. $z = 0.62$; the difference is not significant.

3. $z = 1.13$; no significant difference.

4. $t = -2.61$; deny.

6. $t = 1.96$; fail to reject H_0.

9. $t = 5.252$; procedure is effective.

10. $t = 1.418$; procedure is not effective.

SECTION 7.5

1. $z = 0.91$; firm B will get the contract.

2. $z = -2.14$; company B.

4. $z = 0.67$; no.

5. $z = 2.79$; differences probably real; should not be pooled.

SECTION 7.6

1. $z = 2.54$; yes.

4. $t = 1.507$; the difference is not significant.

7. $z = 1.11$; the jockey's hypothesis is not supported.

9. Yes; $z = 2.16$; company A.

10. $p_A \doteq 0.69$, $p_B \doteq 0.80$, $z = -3.14$; company B.

12. $t = -2.236$; no.

13. $t = 1.62$; no.

16. $z = -4.24$; attitudes do differ.

17. Variances are homogeneous; $t = -0.54$; no significant difference.

CHAPTER 8

SECTION 8.1

1. $\chi^2 = 2.558$; difference is attributable to chance.

2. $\chi^2 = 9.551$; observed differences are significant and there is some relationship between party preference and issue.

4. $\chi^2 = 39.216$; proportions are different.

SECTION 8.2

2. $\chi^2 = 2.871$; they appear to be independent.

3. $\chi^2 = 9.489$; the data support a contention that income level and home-owning status are not independent. Examination of the data bear out the contention that low income families are more likely to rent than to own homes; however, the reasons he cites are not necessarily supported. All that is supported is that significantly fewer low income people than higher income people own homes.

5. $\chi^2 = 5.00$; not independent.

8. $\chi^2 = 17.558$; not independent.

9. $\chi^2 = 5.410$; no association.

SECTION 8.3

1. $\chi^2 = 2.2$; die is fair.

2. $\chi^2 = 26.886$; reject the hypothesis.

4. $\chi^2 = 15.864$; reject H_0. Examination of the data leads to the conclusion that those with a course in college algebra had better grades than those with a course in logic and, by inference, that a course in college algebra is better preparation for statistics than a course in logic.

5. $\chi^2 = 9.540$; conformance is satisfactory.

7. $\chi^2 = 14.667$; manufacturer's claim is refuted.

SECTION 8.4

2. $\chi^2 = 7.024$; the hypothesis is supported.

3. $\chi^2 = 4.533$; the coin does not appear to be biased.

5. Combining categories 5–8, $\chi^2 < 1$; excellent fit.

7. $\chi^2 = 641.347$; he can conclude that there is a relationship. The data would lead one to suspect that the B factor (it occurs in AB also) is related.

8. $\chi^2 = 4.476$; df $= 4$, substantiates hypothesis of no difference.

11. $\chi^2 = 21.636$; difference is significant.

CHAPTER 9

SECTION 9.2

2. $F = 17.95$; not representative.

3. $F = 21.33$; differences are significant.

SECTION 9.3

2. $F = 3.62$; differences are significant.

4. $F = 6.45$; there appears to be a relationship between amount of drug injected and stress level at which adrenalin is released.

SECTION 9.4

2. $F = 5.502$; differences are significant. Treatment C has significantly shorter recovery time than either A or B.

4. $F = 0.97$; not significant.

SECTION 9.5

2. B is significantly better than E, A, or C.

4. $F = 2.62$; not significant.

SECTION 9.6

2. $F = 4.49$; C significantly higher than A and B.

SECTION 9.7

2. $F = 1.367$; not significant.

4. Significant interaction; $F = 9.88$.

CHAPTER 10

SECTION 10.1

2. $\hat{y} = 36.54 - 0.156x$ $(r = -0.782)$

SECTION 10.2

2. $s_e = 1.687$; 95% confidence interval is $\hat{y} - 3.53$ to $\hat{y} + 3.53$. $s_b = 0.028$, $t = -5.47$; b is significantly different from zero. A 95% confidence interval for B is -0.215 to -0.096. A 95% confidence interval for A is 30.85 to 42.23. $\hat{y} - 19 = 4.45$, while $\bar{y} - 22 = -2.28$ for the respective $\hat{y}$. The first is outside the 95% confidence interval while the second is not. The height of the tree 108 feet from the ditch is probably due to chance, while the other may be, but bears closer investigation.

SECTION 10.3

1. $y = 2.94 + 1.3x$; $r = 0.91$; significant.

2. $r = 0.42$; $t = 1.96$; not significant.

4. $r = 0.43$; not significant.

6. $r = 0.08$; not significant.

SECTION 10.4

2. 20.1 to 21.8; 19.5 to 22.3; 17.3 to 24.6.

SECTION 10.5

2. $\hat{y} = 7.634 - 0.310x + 0.092x^2$

SECTION 10.6

1. $\hat{y} = 44.9 - 0.27x_1 - 0.51x_2$; $s_e = 2.682$; $R = 0.80$; $r_{01} = -0.374$; $r_{02} = -0.707$; $r_{12} = 0$.

3. (a) x_2 (b) x_4 (c) x_1; x_5.

SECTION 10.7

1. $r = 0.22$.

2. $r = -0.48$.

5. (a) 0.177 to 0.734; 22.69 to 67.50
   (b) $r \doteq 0.534$; $t = 3.346$ 2.048
   (c) $s_b = 0.136$; $t = 3.346$.
   (d) 75.7 to 87.3
   (e) 66.3 to 96.7
   (f) 49.5 to 100 (assuming 100 is maximum score; otherwise 49.5 to 113.5).

CHAPTER 11

SECTION 11.1

2.

Year	3	4	5	6	7	8	9	10	11	12	13
C	1.04	1.05	1.05	1.02	0.97	0.95	0.97	1.02	1.06	1.06	1.03
I	0.94	1.18	1.00	0.92	1.04	1.02	0.93	0.91	1.10	1.11	0.96

4. (selected years)

Year	3	4	6	9	12	15	17	20	21	24
C	1.11	1.13	1.03	0.90	0.97	0.99	1.00	1.01	1.00	0.99
I	0.90	1.06	1.14	0.99	1.00	1.04	0.99	1.14	0.96	1.02

Depending on interpretation, the cycle is either 7 or 14 years.

SECTION 11.2

1. Values of S are 0.842, 1.009, 0.998, 1.152. For seasonally adjusted values of y (Y/S), $\hat{y} = 80.19 + 2.220x$. Selected values of T, C, I, S are given below.

Quarter	Y/S	4Q MA	T	C	I	S
4	98.0	95.2	89.1	1.07	0.87	1.152
7	105.4	102.7	95.7	1.07	1.03	0.998
10	89.8	96.5	102.4	0.94	0.93	1.009
13	80.5	96.4	109.0	0.88	0.84	0.842
16	104.5	119.0	115.7	1.03	0.88	1.152

3.

Quarter	$T \cdot S$	C Prediction
21	106.8	above 1
22	130.2	about 1
23	131.0	below 1

Cycle appears to have about a 14 quarter period.

5. Assume March, 1978 is as expected. Then $Y/S \doteq 10,939$ for March. Working backward and subtracting 3×107 for January, February, March, we find the base for December, 1977, to be 10,618. Then the seasonally adjusted trend line is given by $\hat{y} = 10,618 + 107x$, where x is the number of months after December, 1977. For August we would expect $(0.86)(11,474)$ or about 9,868 patients. For January, $(1.18)(12,009)$ or about 14,171.

SECTION 11.3

2.

Year	Pork	Veal
1973	100	100
1974	119	93
1975	96	122
1976	115	110
1977	123	108

4.			7.		
	1973	100		1973	67
	1974	110		1974	83
	1975	116		1975	100
	1976	105		1976	102
	1977	109		1977	105

9.					
	1959	73	1969	101	
	1960	82	1970	104	
	1961	84	1971	107	
	1962	88	1972	114	
	1963	94	1973	119	
	1964	98	1974	123	
	1965	101	1975	117	
	1966	96	1976	125	
	1967	100	1977	131	
	1968	99			

SECTION 11.4

1. Selected values of S are as follows:
   Jan: 0.946; Apr: 0.976; Jul: 1.028; Sep: 1.031; Dec: 1.070.

4. Selected values of T, C, I, S are given below:

Quarter	T	C	I	S
3	277.2	0.95	1.04	1.075
8	295.4	1.06	0.96	0.982
13	313.7	1.05	1.07	0.858
18	331.9	0.97	0.97	1.085

Predicted values for quarters 21, 24, 27, respectively, are 294.1, 347.4, 392.1.

7.
1967	100
1968	105
1969	114
1970	120
1971	116
1972	107
1973	110
1974	114
1975	112
1976	113
1977	114

CHAPTER 12

SECTION 12.2

1. $p = 0.046$; course was effective.

3. $p = 0.172$; not significant.

SECTION 12.3

2. $T = 15$; course was effective.

5. $T = 83.5$; $z = -3.06$.

SECTION 12.4

2. $U = 176.5$; not significant.

SECTION 12.5

2. $H = 5.719$; reserve judgment.

SECTION 12.6

2. $R = 0.75$; $t = 4.536$.

SECTION 12.7

2. $U = 5$.

4. With the signs test $P(x \geq 4) = 0.188$, so $\alpha = 0.376$; not significant. $T = 1$ is also not significant.

6. $T = 6$; $6 < 8$, so the median is probably less than 10.

8. $H = 6.235$; reject H_0.

10. $H = 5.693$; not significant.

12. $H = 9.762$; reject H_0.

15. $R = -0.12$; not significant.

CHAPTER 13

SECTION 13.1

1. (a) EMV*=$1,500   (b) EOL*=$90   (c) EVPI=$90
   (d) use J&S   (e) use consultant (expect cost to be about $1,350).

3. Bake 2. EMV*=$2.375, EOL*=$2.9125.

5. EOL*=$4. Fill orders as usual.

SECTION 13.2

1. Try C.

2. $p_1=8/15$ $(p_2=1/5)$

5. Market without testing. EMV=$175,000 vs. $110,000 and $102,500. EVPI= $75,000.

SECTION 13.3

1. (a) 0.417, 0.083, 0.500
   (c) Ten possible samples. Example, if 1 M3003 and 1J2162 are drawn, the probabilities are 0.652, 0.087, 0.261.
   (d) Only "conclusive" outcomes are 1 M3003, 1 S113Z (third box), 1 Q1007, 1S113Z (second box), and 2 Q1007 (second box).

4. (a) With no defectives, probabilities are about 0.217, 0.312, 0.296, 0.176. With one defective, the probabilities are 0.023, 0.172, 0.345, 0.460.
   (c) With no defectives, 0.251, 0.333, 0.283, 0.133; with one defective, 0.030, 0.207, 0.372, 0.391; with two defectives, 0.010, 0.072, 0.272, 0.646; with three defectives, 0+, 0.019, 0.155, 0.826.

SECTION 13.4

1. Sell to Ducky; EVPI=$1,520.

4. 200; A for less than 200, B for more than 200.

6. Selected posterior distributions:
   for zero defective: 0.588, 0.206, 0.212, 0.024;
   for two defectives: 0.099, 0.185, 0.559, 0.156;
   for four defectives: 0.007, 0.063, 0.555, 0.376.
   for zero and one defective, expected values are, respectively, 0.17 and 0.23,

so, using that criterion, they should select only those with zero defective. On the other hand, if there is one defective $P(10\%$ or $20\%) \doteq 0.515$, while $P(30\%$ or $40\%) \doteq 0.486$, so they could accept a lot with one defective, using that criterion. For two or more defectives, both the expected values and $P(30\%$ or $40\%)$ are too high.

APPENDIX B

RULES OF PROBABILITY

1. None since $P(A) + P(B) > 1$ and the sum of the probabilities of all the mutually exclusive points in a sample space is exactly 1.

2. $P(A \text{ or } B) = P(A) + P(B) = 0.9$.

3. Since all the possible outcomes are stated and they are mutually exclusive, the sum must be 1. But $0.44 + 0.29 + 0.17 = 0.90$, which is not possible. He is mistaken.

4. $2/15 + 0.9 \doteq 1.033$ (or $31/30$) which is greater than 1. Since these are mutually exclusive, the statement is false. However, $2/15 + 0.8 = 14/15$. Since there are other possibilities (tie, cancellation), the second fan's statement is not inconsistent with the rules of probability. This does not, however, increase his likelihood of being correct.

5. 0.7.

6. (a) 0.4　(b) 0.7　(c) 0.7　(d) 0　(*not* ∅).

7. Four are neither, so
   (a) 0.1　(b) 0.3　(c) 0.6　(d) 0.4　(e) 0.6　(f) 0.9　(g) 0.7　(h) 0.7.

8. (a) 0.38　(b) 0.28　(c) $1 - (0.21 + 0.11) = 0.68$　(d) $1 - 0.49 = 0.51$.

INDEPENDENT EVENTS AND CONDITIONAL PROBABILITY

1. (a) $1/50$　(b) $1/15$　(c) $2/15$　(d) $2/15$.

2. Since 10 take neither, 90 take one or the other or both. Since $80 + 60 = 140$, and $140 - 90 = 50$, then 50 take both. Thus $P(E \text{ and } M) = 0.50$. Now $P(M) = 0.60$, but $P(M|E) = 0.50/0.80 = 0.625$. Since they are not equal, the events are not independent. Other approaches are possible.

3. If A and B are mutually exclusive, $P(A \text{ or } B) = 0$; if either event occurs, the other cannot, so $P(A|B) = P(B|A) = 0$.

4. $1/32$.

5. (a) 0.36 (b) 0.34.

6. 2.

7. (a) 0.56 (b) 0.73 (c) 0.48 (d) 0.62 (e) 0.40 (f) 0.30 (g) 0.60 (h) 0.70 (i) 0.27 (j) 0.38.

8. (a) $1/216$ (b) $215/216$ (c) $1/36$ (d) $5/9$ (e) $5/108$ or about 0.046.

9. $3/20$.

10. 0.00000016; about 0.92.

Index

Chapter Opening Picture Credits

1. Courtesy of Pan Am Airways/Monkmeyer Press Photo Service.
2. From Monkmeyer Press Photo Service.
3. Photo by Mimi Forsyth/Monkmeyer Press Photo Service.
4. Photo by Peter Mackay/Monkmeyer Press Photo Service.
5. Photo by Marion Faller/Monkmeyer Press Photo Service.
6. Photo by Hugh Rogers/Monkmeyer Press Photo Service.
7. Photo by Sybel Shelton/Monkmeyer Press Photo Service.
8. Photo by Bill Anderson/Monkmeyer Press Photo Service.
9. Photo by Winifred Luten/Monkmeyer Press Photo Service.
10. Photo by Mimi Forsyth/Monkmeyer Press Photo Service.
11. From Monkmeyer Press Photo Service.
12. Photo by Jim Cron/Monkmeyer Press Photo Service.
13. Photo by Mimi Forsyth/Monkmeyer Press Photo Service.